Books by David Nasaw

*Schooled to Order: A Social History of Public Schooling
in the United States*

Children of the City: At Work and At Play

Going Out: The Rise and Fall of Public Amusements

The Chief: The Life of William Randolph Hearst

Extraordinary Acclaim for *The Chief*

"A highly readable portrait of a fascinating individual."
— **Gray Brechin,** *San Francisco Chronicle* **(front page)**

"The best biography I read in 2000. With access to vast documentary material unexplored by previous biographers, Nasaw finds a real human being inside the overwhelming Hearst mythology, a poor little rich boy who never really grew up and never really got what he wanted."
— **Jonathan Yardley,** *Washington Post*

"Intriguing . . . a must-read." — **Dana Frank,** *The Nation*

"The definitive work . . . outstandingly researched, elegantly but not flamboyantly written, and fair in its conclusions about Hearst's astonishing career." — **Conrad Black,** *Wall Street Journal*

"Even to open *The Chief,* David Nasaw's wonderful new biography of William Randolph Hearst, is to be swept away by the narrative flowing through its pages . . . What distinguishes Mr. Nasaw's telling of it is the skill with which he has tapped a whole new watershed of sources . . . What further marks Mr. Nasaw's account is his evenhandedness, his refusal to trade on popular mythology about Hearst."
— **Orville Schell,** *New York Times*

"This magisterial new biography of Hearst . . . works on a large, even heroic, canvas." — **Kevin Starr,** *Los Angeles Times*

"It is impossible to start reading about William Randolph Hearst without imagining Orson Welles in the role, but by the time you finish David Nasaw's riveting and exhilarating biography (and it will be hard to put down), you'll have an altogether fresh picture of the complex, swashbuckling, larger-than-life 'Chief.'"
— **Jean Strouse, author of** *Morgan: American Financier*

"Scrupulous honesty distinguishes this biography."
— **Harold Evans,** *New York Times Book Review* **(front page)**

"Must be regarded as the definitive study . . . It's hard to imagine a more complete rendering of Hearst's life." — **Hardy Green,** *Business Week*

"A superb biography . . . far and away the best . . . Given access to Hearst's correspondence with his editors and his family, Nasaw has used the raw material brilliantly to paint a richly textured picture of the man who for decades did so much to shape political debate." — **John F. Stacks,** *Time*

"Every chapter of David Nasaw's biography is as rich in human insight as its subject was rich in material possessions."

— **Martin F. Nolan,** *Boston Sunday Globe*

"[An] absorbing and sympathetic portrait . . . Nasaw has used these new documents and interviews to make an enigmatic and elusive man almost knowable, puncturing some shopworn Hearstian myths along the way."

— **Susan E. Tiftt,** *Chicago Tribune* (front page)

"Utterly absorbing." — *Vanity Fair*

"A fascinating biography that does justice to all facets of a picturesque personality. David Nasaw has not only uncovered new material, but he sets Hearst in a broad political and cultural context and writes about him engagingly, lucidly, and fair-mindedly. It is a superb portrait and a superb book." — **Arthur M. Schlesinger, Jr.**

"Enjoyably filled with anecdotes and revealing incidents. Nasaw has written a colorful, yet careful biography of one of the century's most controversial media innovators." — **Rob Stout,** *Denver Post*

"The first full biography of William Randolph Hearst in forty years . . . is such a stunner that it demands reading right now."

— **Don DeNevi,** *Palo Alto Daily News*

"Nasaw . . . is an engaging writer who lets his fascinating subject take the lead . . . By returning skillfully and often to the details of Hearst's day-to-day life, Nasaw keeps his subject human and believable, no easy task when writing about such a colorful and forceful man."

— **Kimberly B. Marlowe,** *Seattle Times*

"The definitive study of a defining figure." — *GQ*

"Filled with fascinating details and surprising new facts, David Nasaw's splendid biography of the Chief reconfigures William Randolph Hearst's troubled and turbulent life and times." — **Blanche Wiesen Cook**

"*The Chief* deserves a prominent place on the American journalism bookshelf." — **Herbert Mitgang,** *American Scholar*

"David Nasaw's superb biography of William Randolph Hearst is both a portrait of a colorful, powerful, and controversial publisher and an important cultural history of the birth of modern mass media." — **Alan Brinkley**

"Nasaw's judicious and comprehensive biography sensibly seeks to understand its subject, not to judge him." — *The New Yorker*

THE CHIEF

The Life of William Randolph Hearst

━━━⟋⟍⟋⟍⟋⟍━━━

David Nasaw

A Mariner Book
HOUGHTON MIFFLIN COMPANY
BOSTON · NEW YORK

First Mariner Books edition 2001

Visit our Web site: www.houghtonmifflinbooks.com.

Library of Congress Cataloging-in-Publication Data
Nasaw, David.
The chief : the life of William Randolph Hearst / David Nasaw.
p. cm.
Includes bibliographical references and index.
ISBN 0-395-82759-0
ISBN 0-618-15446-9 (pbk.)
1. Hearst, William Randolph, 1863–1951.   2. Publishers and publishing
— United States — Biography.   3. Newspaper publishing — United
States — History — 19th century.   4. Newspaper publishing — United
States — History — 20th century.   I. Title.
Z473.H4 N37 2000
070.5'092 — dc21 [B] 99-462122

Printed in the United States of America

Book design by Robert Overholtzer

QUM 10 9 8 7 6 5 4 3 2 1

Frontispiece: William Randolph Hearst, May 1922
(Marc Wanamaker/*Bison Archives*)

Photographs follow pages 112, 272, and 464

ACKNOWLEDGMENTS

I wish to express my appreciation to Randolph A. Hearst, who took time to speak with me about his father, and to Frank A. Bennack, Jr., president and chief executive officer of the Hearst Corporation, who arranged for me to examine material, previously unavailable to researchers, in William Randolph Hearst's Bronx warehouse and in the bunkhouse at the San Simeon Ranch. Hearst's grandsons, John (Bunky) Hearst, Jr. and Austin Hearst, and Austin's wife Kathryn and John's wife Barbara also shared valuable information with me about the Chief.

Steve Fraser first suggested that I write a biography of Hearst and helped me conceive the project. Virginia Barber, my agent, provided me with encouragement and a thoughtful reading of an early draft. Patricia Strachan, my editor at Houghton Mifflin, has — with good humor and consummate skill — seen the project through to completion. Sarah Goodrum, also at Houghton Mifflin, has assisted me with photo research and permissions.

Arthur Schlesinger, Jr. and Amanda Smith gave me entrée to Joseph P. Kennedy's papers, which helped unlock the mystery of Hearst's finances. I have profited from my many conversations with Arthur Schlesinger, Jr. on Hearst, Franklin Roosevelt, and the New Deal.

I am enormously grateful to those who work at the Hearst San Simeon State Historical Monument for the kindness they have shown me on every occasion. John Horn, the historian at the Hearst Castle, has been of invaluable assistance through every stage of the research and writing, promptly answering every query sent his way. Hoyt Fields, chief curator, arranged for me to examine the oral history collection that is housed in the Tour Guides Library. Vicki Kastner guided me through the grounds and buildings on the hillside and has been a steady source of information on the Hearst collections. Horn and Kastner also read the final manuscript and offered their suggestions. John Blades and Sandra Barghini graciously assisted me during their tenures at the Castle. Sandra Heinemann read and generously commented on the San Simeon sections of my manuscript.

Nancy Loe was an early guide to the sources and a valued tutor on Julia Morgan and her papers. I am appreciative of the efforts of Mike Line in Special Collections at the California Polytechnic State University library which houses the Morgan papers. The librarians and archivists at the Bancroft Library at Berkeley have been uniformly helpful. I wish particularly to thank Bonnie Hardwick and Peter Hanff. Dace Taube at the Regional History Collection at the University of Southern California guided me through the *Los Angeles Herald-Examiner* archives. Ned Comstock helped me with material at the Warner Bros. Archives, also at the University of Southern California. I am also appreciative of the help provided me by the curators and archivists at the Huntington Library, the National Archives, the Hoover Institution Archives, the Sterling Memorial Library at Yale University, the Franklin D. Roosevelt Library, the Columbia University Rare Books and Manuscripts Library, the Harvard University Archives, the New York Times Company Archives, the Syracuse University Library Department of Special Collections, the Margaret Herrick Library at the Academy of Motion Pictures Arts and Sciences, the Manuscripts and Archives Division and the Billy Rose Theater Collection of the New York Public Library, and the Manuscripts Division of the Library of Congress.

I have been assisted throughout by a small army of research assistants led by my mother, Beatrice Nasaw, who has worked almost full-time on this project since its inception, and read and helped to copyedit the final manuscript. I was also fortunate in having the assistance of a number of wonderful graduate students from the History program at the City University of New York Graduate Center, among them Dorothy Browne, David Barber, Tracy Morgan, Hilary Hallett, Carol Quirke, Terence Kissack, Shawn Savage, and Steven Naftzger.

I am grateful to all my colleagues at the Graduate Center for their encouragement and assistance. Blanche Wiesen Cook shared her insights and research on the Roosevelts with me; Phil Cannistraro, his knowledge of Hearst's relationship with Mussolini. I benefited as well from discussions with Tom Kessner, George Custen, Jack Diggins, David Rosner, Richard Powers, Mike Wallace, James Oakes, Josh Freeman, and Abe Ascher. Dana Frank offered me her research on Hearst's Buy American campaign. I've had some wonderful discussions about biography with Jean Strouse, Patricia Bosworth, and with Alan Brinkley who was also kind enough to read and comment on my final draft. Arthur Goren helped me with information on Hearst's efforts to create a Jewish homeland. Nora Jaffee did invaluable research in Mexico. John Creelman introduced me to the Creelman papers at Ohio State. Bob Board met with me in Los Angeles and shared his remarkable collection of Marion Davies films and memorabilia. My dear friend Bob Edelman has been encouraging throughout.

I owe special thanks to Jon Wiener, Ann Fabian, Tom Leonard, and Beth Rashbaum for reading all 1,400 pages of my next-to-last draft and offering their suggestions for revision.

My greatest debt of gratitude is to Dinitia Smith, who has been my partner in this as in everything else I have done in the past two decades. With good humor and infinite patience, she has listened to my every Hearst story, carefully read every word of every draft — from proposal to bound galley — corrected my syntax and improved my prose. I thank her for her kindness, her love, and her unflagging support.

I wish to acknowledge the financial support of the City University of New York through the PSC-CUNY research award program.

CONTENTS

V. A MASTER BUILDER

VI. THE KING AND QUEEN OF HOLLYWOOD

VII. THE DEPRESSION

VIII. NEW DEALS AND RAW DEALS

IX. THE FALL

PREFACE

WILLIAM RANDOLPH HEARST was a huge man with a tiny voice; a shy man who was most comfortable in crowds; a war hawk in Cuba and Mexico but a pacifist in Europe; an autocratic boss who could not fire people; a devoted husband who lived with his mistress; a Californian who spent half his life in the East. The son of a Forty-Niner emigrant from Missouri who had made millions by digging in the earth, Hearst did not identify with those who had inherited wealth or social position. He considered himself a self-made man, because, like his father and his mother, he invented himself: as art collector, builder, journalist, publisher, and politician. His ambitions were limitless, but so too were his talents and resources. He was in all things defined by contradiction, larger than life.

When Hearst was in college, he wrote his father that he intended to do something in publishing and politics — and he did, becoming San Francisco's, then New York's, and finally the nation's most powerful publisher. He served two terms in Congress, came in second in the balloting for the Democratic presidential nomination in 1904, and was, for half a century, a major force in American politics — at the national, state, and local levels. He was also one of the twentieth century's greatest spenders. *Fortune* magazine, in 1935, reported that his art collections were worth at least $20 million (a quarter of a billion dollars in today's currency) and his ranches, mines, orchards, and packing plants, another $30 million. His real estate holdings in New York City were assessed at $41 million. He was, according to *Fortune*, the city's "number one realtor."

There has never been — nor, most likely, will there ever again be — a publisher like William Randolph Hearst. The Chief, as he was known by those who worked for him, built the nation's first media conglomerate by extending his newspaper empire horizontally into syndicated feature, photo, and wire services; magazines; newsreels; serial, feature, and animated films; and radio. With each triumph, his sense of omnipotence swelled. The opportunities were limitless for expanding his empire — and his audiences — and he capitalized on every one of them.

Decades before synergy became a corporate cliché, Hearst put the concept into practice. His magazine editors were directed to buy only stories which could be rewritten into screenplays to be produced by his film studio and serialized, reviewed, and publicized in his newspapers and magazines. He broadcast the news from his papers over the radio and pictured it in his newsreels. He was as dominant and pioneering a figure in the twentieth-century communications and entertainment industries as Andrew Carnegie had been in steel, J. Pierpont Morgan in banking, John D. Rockefeller in oil, and Thomas Alva Edison in electricity. At the peak of his power in the middle 1930s, *Time* magazine estimated his newspaper audience alone at 20 million of the 120 plus million men, women, and children in the nation. His daily and Sunday papers were so powerful as vehicles of public opinion in the United States that Adolf Hitler, Benito Mussolini, and Winston Churchill all wrote for him.

In the great tradition of nineteenth-century orator-editors like Horace Greeley, Charles Dana, William Cullen Bryant, and Joseph Pulitzer, Hearst took upon himself the role of tribune of the people. Through the first decades of the twentieth century, as older press lords died off and were replaced by a new breed of editors who, like Adolph S. Ochs of the *New York Times,* shunned publicity and made sure their names appeared only on their mastheads, Hearst employed the power of the media to set the national political agenda, first as a muckraking, progressive trustbuster, then, in his seventies, as an opponent of the New Deal and a stalwart anti-Communist. He set the topics, dictated the tone, and edited all the editorials in his papers — the major ones he wrote himself and displayed prominently on his front pages; he endorsed candidates for office and condemned them when they betrayed their promises; he emblazoned his name on his magazines, his newsreels, and his radio outlets; he proudly proclaimed that while other newspapers merely reported the news, his newspapers "made" it.

I did not set out to write a biography of William Randolph Hearst, but to use him as a focal point from which to discuss the interpenetration of culture and politics in the twentieth century. Only as I began my research did I come to realize that the story of William Randolph Hearst was yet to be told. There were some fine biographies dating from the 1950s and 1960s, but none had been able to call upon the vast archival resources that have become available since then. I was able to start fresh, to detour around the anecdotal information that my predecessors had had to rely on, and to base my study on hundreds of thousands of letters, telegrams, memoranda, transcripts of phone messages, articles, and editorials that Hearst had written or that had been written to or about him.

I began at the Bancroft Library in Berkeley, California, which held collections of Hearst correspondence dating back to the 1860s, when Hearst's mother Phoebe arrived in San Francisco from Missouri with her husband, the millionaire miner and future United States senator George Hearst. I moved on from there to dozens of manuscript collections scattered across the country: the papers of every president from William McKinley to Franklin Delano Roosevelt; those of Hearst's editors, friends, political advisers and adversaries, and of his architect at San Simeon, Julia Morgan. At the Hearst San Simeon Historical Monument, I was given access to an extensive unpublished oral history collection that contained dozens of interviews with friends, family, servants, and business associates. At the end of my research, I was able to fill in some of the missing pieces by consulting private and business papers that had been stored in a warehouse in the Bronx since the early 1920s and at a bunkhouse at one of the Hearst Corporation ranches in San Simeon.

The Hearst I discovered was infinitely more fascinating than the one I had expected to find. This was also Winston Churchill's experience during his visit with Hearst at San Simeon and Los Angeles in 1929. "Hearst was most interesting to meet," Churchill wrote his wife Clementine, who had remained in England. "I got to like him — a grave simple child — with no doubt a nasty temper — playing with the most costly toys. A vast income always overspent: ceaseless building and collecting . . . two magnificent establishments, two charming wives; complete indifference to public opinion, a strong liberal and democratic outlook, a 15 million daily circulation, oriental hospitalities, extreme personal courtesy (to us at any rate) and the appearance of a Quaker elder — or perhaps better Mormon elder." After a long weekend at San Simeon, Churchill was driven to Los Angeles where he stayed "at the Biltmore Hotel — which is the last word in hotels. . . . I met all the leading people. . . . These Californian swells do not of course know Hearst," Churchill wrote his wife. "He dwells apart. . . . They regard him as the Devil."[1]

I

Great Expectations

❧ 1 ❧

A Son of the West

WILLIAM RANDOLPH HEARST did not speak often of his father. He preferred to think of himself as sui generis and self-created, which in many ways he was. Only in his late seventies, when he began writing a daily column in his newspapers, did he remind his readers — and himself — that he was the son of a pioneer. In a column about the song "Oh Susannah," which he claimed his father had sung to him, Hearst recounted the hardships George Hearst had endured on his thousand-mile trek from Missouri to California in 1850. There was a pride in the telling and in the story. His father had been one of the lucky ones, one of the stronger ones. While others had "died of cholera or were drowned by the floods or were killed by the Indians [or] tarried by the wayside under crude crosses and little hasty heaps of stone," his father had stayed the course, braved "the difficulties and dangers" and "at length . . . reached California in safety."[1]

The moral of the story was a simple one. Nothing had been given the Hearsts. There were no "silver spoons" in this family. They had scrapped and fought and suffered and, in the end, won what was rightfully theirs.

William Randolph Hearst grew to manhood in the city of great expectations on the edge of the continent. He was a son of the West, or, more particularly, of Gold Rush San Francisco. The child and the city grew up together in the second half of the nineteenth century. San Francisco's population in 1870 was nearly three times what it had been in 1860. By 1880, San Francisco had a quarter of a million residents, was the ninth largest city in the nation and the premier metropolis of the West. The city's riches expanded even faster than its population. California's gold boom of the late 1840s and early 1850s had been followed by Nevada's silver boom in the early 1860s, and wherever riches were mined west of the Mississippi, they found their way into San Francisco. Money from the mines went into San

Francisco's stock markets or real estate; it was deposited in its banks, and spent in its brothels, hotels, theaters, saloons, and gambling halls.[2]

With the constant influx of new people and capital, the city on the hills never had a chance to grow old. The Gold Rush mentality, permanently fixed in narrative form by storytellers, historians, and mythmaking adventurers, would dominate the culture and sensibility of San Franciscans for generations to come. There was gold in the hills — and silver and the richest agricultural land the world had ever seen — but that wealth did not sit on the surface ready for picking. It took sweat and savvy and years of labor to pull it up out of the earth.

George Hearst was one of the tens of thousands of adventurers lured to California by the promise of gold. He had been born in 1820 or 1821 — he wasn't quite sure when — to a relatively prosperous Scotch-Irish family with American roots reaching back to the seventeenth century. George grew to manhood the only healthy son (he had a crippled brother and a younger sister) of the richest farmer in Meramec Township, Franklin County, Missouri. He was virtually unschooled, having acquired no more than a bit of arithmetic and the rudiments of literacy in classrooms.

Franklin County, Missouri, was rich in copper and lead deposits. George's father, William Hearst, owned at least one mine and was friendly with a nearby group of French miners and smelters. On his trips to their camp, which he supplied with pork, Hearst was often accompanied by his son George. "I used to stay about there a good deal," George recalled later in life. "I naturally saw that they had a good deal of money. I think that that was what induced me to go into mining. Farming was such a slow way to make money. You could make a living at it and that was about all."[3]

William Hearst died when George was about twenty-two years of age. George took over the family farm, did some mining, for a time even ran a little store out on the public road, and then, as he recalls, "this fever broke out in California." Rumors of gold strikes near San Francisco had begun to drift east in the winter of 1848. In his December 1848 message to Congress, President James Polk confirmed that the stories, though "of such extraordinary character as would scarcely command belief, [had been] corroborated by authentic reports of officers in the public service." By January of 1849, every newspaper in the country was carrying front-page stories about the gold rush. "Poets, philosophers, lawyers, brokers, bankers, merchants, farmers, clergymen," reported the *New York Herald* on January 11, 1849, "all are feeling the impulse and are preparing to go and dig for gold and swell the number of adventurers to the new El Dorado."[4]

George Hearst read the newspapers and dissected the rumors. He almost went West in 1849, but was deterred — temporarily — by mining colleagues who warned him that there was nothing new in stories of Western gold. "Next year, however, I made up my mind sure to go. . . . I recollect talking over California with my mother. She did not like it at all, but when I told her they were making $40 and $50 a day there and that it seemed to me it was by far the best thing to do, as it was pretty hard pulling here, she said that if they were doing that, she had no doubts I would make something, too, and she agreed for me to go."

In the spring of 1850, George Hearst left Missouri for California with a party of fifteen, including several of his cousins. His mother and sister rode with him for the first few days, said their final farewells, and turned back. He would be gone for ten years.

Like many who traveled to the gold fields, George caught a case of cholera. He recovered with the help of "a little bit of brandy which I gave $16 a gallon for in St. Louis . . . and some pills which a man in St. Louis gave me." He was still shaking with fever when, in October, he crossed over the Sierra Nevada mountains through Carson Pass south of Lake Tahoe.[5]

By the time he reached California, the earliest strikes had been played out, the richest claims bought and registered. George Hearst and his companions spent their first California winter within miles of John Sutter's original strike on the American River. After months of shoveling wet gravel, living in leaky cabins, eating salt pork and beans, and finding little or no gold, they moved north to Grass Valley and Nevada City where a new lode had been discovered.[6]

There are two different ways to mine for gold. Placer miners look for it in riverbeds or streams, collect it in pans or sluices, wash away the sand, and sell the gold dust left behind. Quartz miners dig shafts into the ground in search of rock formations that have gold embedded in them. George Hearst arrived in the digging fields too late to cash in on the early placer mining bonanza. He had, however, invaluable experience in quartz mining. In Missouri, he had taught himself to read rock formations and, more importantly, to estimate the cost of bringing ore to the surface and refining it. Within a year of his arrival in the Grass Valley/Nevada City region, he was locating, buying, and selling claims in quartz mines.

For the better part of the decade, George Hearst would remain in and around Nevada City. Although one of California's largest — and most prosperous — mining towns, Nevada City was little more than an extended miners' camp, with a primitive residential section, a few storefronts and churches, and dozens of saloons, brothels, and gambling halls. The vast majority of the town's residents were male, most of them newly arrived. Hearst prospered in this environment. He was at home at the poker table, the saloon, and probably the brothel as well. He was not among the town's merchant, mining, or professional elites, but after years of prospecting, buying, selling, and trading claims — and for a time, running a general store — he was making a decent living and building a reputation as a good judge of rock formations and a relatively honest businessman.[7]

In 1859, word reached Nevada City of a new strike in the Washoe district on the eastern ledge of the Sierra Nevada mountains, about 100 miles away. It was rumored that a group of placer miners had found an extraordinarily rich vein of gold mixed with heavy blue-black "stuff" on property owned by a crazy old miner named Henry Comstock. The first sample, secretly shipped across the mountains to Nevada City, had been found to be rich in silver as well as gold. A second sample was transported by mule over the mountains and assayed by Melville Atwood, a close friend and sometime partner of Hearst. It proved to be so rich in gold and silver that Atwood doubted the veracity of his tests. Though the Washoe district was a mule trip of four or five days, across the Sierra Nevada mountains, Atwood and Hearst with two other partners rode across the mountains to inspect the lode for themselves.[8]

By the time they arrived in the mining camp that would later be known as Virginia City, Nevada, the original claims had changed hands several times. The new owners, like the old ones, still had no idea of the value of their holdings. Hearst did. He contracted to buy as large a portion of the available claims as he could and then rode back across the mountains to raise funds to pay for them.

Proceeding at a feverish pace, Hearst and his hired hands dug forty-five tons of ore out of the ground that spring of 1859, loaded it on pack mules, and trekked across the mountains to smelt and sell it in San Francisco. The ore appeared so worthless that it took days to find a smelter. But it was, as Hearst had believed, the "find" that every miner dreams of.[9]

While most of his colleagues in Virginia City had, in the first flush of excitement, sold their claims outright, Hearst not only held on to his, but poured every penny he earned back into his mines. He invested in new hoisting and pumping equipment, in underground timbering, and in a small private army of toughs to protect his property from claim bandits. By the spring of 1860, when the last obstacle to fortune was removed with the arrival of the U.S. Army and the defeat and removal of the local Paiute Indians, George Hearst was on his way to becoming a millionaire.

After ten years in the digging fields, George Hearst returned to Missouri in the fall of 1860 to comfort his sick mother and display his newfound fortune. His mother died soon after his return, but George remained in Missouri for two more years, taking care of family business and looking for a wife.

It was not uncommon for miners to marry late in life after they had made their fortunes. Hearst had already proposed to a woman in Virginia City, but been turned down by her family who considered him a poor match. He was forty years old — much older than the women he courted, but he was in perfect health, which was rare for a miner, stood tall and straight, with a muscular build and a full blond beard.

The woman he chose to court in Missouri was Phoebe Apperson, a schoolteacher twenty years his junior. Like George, she came from a Scotch-Irish family of small farmers with American roots stretching back over a hundred years. It is quite possible that Phoebe and George had known each other earlier — though she had been only eight when he left Missouri for California. They were both from the same township and were in fact distantly related. Still, these similarities notwithstanding, they made a rather odd couple. Phoebe was small and delicate, with grayish blue eyes, fair skin, an oval face. She was a plain-looking woman but not unattractive, a Southern lady in bearing, and a church-going Presbyterian. George stood a foot taller and weighed twice what she did. He was uncouth, loud, and semiliterate, seldom changed his shirtfront, wore his beard long, bushy, and ragged at the edges, spit tobacco juice, liked nothing better for dinner than what he called hog and hominy, and had not seen the inside of a church in decades.

Though, like her beau, Phoebe Hearst had begun her formal education in a one-room schoolhouse, she had actually graduated and gone on to a seminary in the next county. She had worked as a primary school teacher of factory children at the Meramec Ironworks in nearby Phelps County and as a tutor and governess in the home of a successful miner and smelter.

The marriage took place in June 1862, in the midst of the Civil War. The couple had planned to leave at once for California, but because Missouri was a Union state, and George was not only not in the army but so outspoken a supporter of the Confederacy that he had already been jailed once for uttering seditious remarks about secession, it took him almost three months to get the "passport" he needed to cross the Union lines. Finally, in late September he and his now pregnant bride boarded a train for New York City, where they met a steamer bound for Panama. In early November

1862 they arrived in San Francisco and moved into a suite at the Lick House, the newest and most luxurious hotel in the city.[10]

In his absence, George's mines had been incorporated and stock offered on the San Francisco exchange established to handle the Comstock claims. Although a frenzy of silver speculation had driven share prices to astronomical heights and made Hearst a millionaire, the legal challenges to his claims had multiplied as rapidly as the price of his stocks. Mining law gave the owners of a claim property rights to the entire ledge of ore that branched out from it. But because only the courts could determine if bodies of ore at a distance from the original claim were pieces of it or separate lodes, Hearst, like every other mine owner in the Comstock, found himself embroiled in one suit after another.[11]

George Hearst could have remained with his wife in San Francisco while his associates ran his mines, his lawyers fought his legal battles, and the exchanges traded his mining stocks. But he chose not to. Within weeks of arriving in San Francisco, he sent and paid for Phoebe's parents to come west to be nearer their daughter, moved his bride of six months into new quarters in the Stevenson House, a hotel with accommodations for permanent guests, and left San Francisco for his mining camp across the mountains.[12]

Six months later, on April 29, 1863 — with George still away — Phoebe gave birth to William Randolph Hearst, a robust baby boy named for his deceased grandfathers. Sonny, as his absentee father referred to him, was doted on by his mother, his grandmother, and Eliza Pike, his Irish-Catholic wet nurse, who, according to Hearst's first biographer, worried so much about his immortal soul that she took him to be baptized.

"'But Eliza,' protested the mother, 'I am a Presbyterian.'

"'No matter, madam, the baby is a Christian.'"[13]

Soon after the birth, Phoebe, the baby, and Eliza Pike moved into a solid brick home on Rincon Hill. George remained hundreds of miles away, in a region of the West still not connected with San Francisco by railroad. Husband and wife communicated with letters hand-delivered across the mountains by George's business associates.

For the next twenty years, George and Phoebe Hearst would be apart far more than they would be together. Both, if we can believe their letters, suffered from the arrangement, but Phoebe had the more difficult time, at least at first. George was at home in the West and had become accustomed to the predominantly male world of the mining camps. Phoebe was new to the West, new to city life, and a young mother — she had been eight months shy of her twenty-first birthday when her son was born.

Perhaps to compensate his wife for his absence, in the spring of 1864, as their son celebrated his first birthday, George bought Phoebe an elegant new home on Chestnut Street, north of Russian Hill, overlooking San Francisco Bay. With her husband hundreds of miles away and her parents preparing to depart for the new farm in Santa Clara which George had bought for them, Phoebe was left to make the move on her own. In early June, she sent Willie away with Eliza Pike to the baths at Santa Cruz so that she could devote her attention to the move.

"It seems a month since you left," she wrote Eliza in mid-June. "I am *terribly* lonely, I miss Baby every minute. I think and dream about him. We all feel lost. . . . I have had another letter from Mr. Hearst . . . he expects to be home soon, but don't say what he means by soon, a week, or a month . . . Kiss Willie for me and write me how he is. I hope you will wean him. . . . I am going to telegraph Mr. Hearst to know what to do about moving up on the hill, we have only two weeks more. I don't think I can come down to see you I will be so very busy. Write often. I feel anxious to hear from you. Oh dear what am I going to do."[14]

Left on her own by her husband and by her parents who had moved south to their new farm, Phoebe adjusted to life as a single mother. She learned to make decisions by herself, run the household, and raise Willie. She was assisted of course by her husband's wealth, which provided her with a household filled with servants and the incentive and leisure to educate herself — and her boy. She visited San Francisco's art museums, studied French, prepared herself for her first grand tour of Europe, and made the acquaintance of Bay Area artists and writers, inviting many of them to tea.

Her major project was her son. As he grew up, she taught him to read and write and ride a horse. He became her escort and her cultural partner. Together they learned French, visited the museums, attended the operetta, and traveled up and down the California coast. All of this was communicated over the years in long, carefully handwritten letters to Eliza Pike, who by now had left the Hearst household but for years remained Phoebe's close friend.

In the summer of 1865, Phoebe took her two-year-old son for an extended trip to visit her parents at Santa Clara, then to resort hotels in Santa Cruz and San Jose. Phoebe wrote Eliza Pike a long letter from San Jose:

I have been out of town four weeks. We are having our house made much larger, it will be yet a month before it is finished. You know me well enough, to know that I will be glad to get home again, although I have been having a very nice time. The first week I was at Ma's . . . I enjoyed the drive over the mountains to Santa Cruz. The scenery is beautiful. I think it is a lovely place. I only stayed two days. The fare at the hotel was so wretched that I could not stand it, baby ate little or nothing, if we had not taken some chicken and crackers with us I don't know what the child would have done. I felt so uneasy about him for they have colera-morbus so badly in San Francisco and in fact everywhere that we hear of. I was so afraid he would take it, I thought it best for me to leave. I went to stay there three or four weeks, the place is *crowded* with people from the City . . . You will wonder where Mr. Hearst is all this time. He has been on several little trips and the rest of the time in the City. He did not go to Santa Cruz but comes to see us once a week when he is in the City. I am very well this summer. Willie keeps well and fat though he grows tall. He is as brown as a berry and so active and mischievous, he is a very good boy — you have no idea how much he talks. You would be astonished. He seems to understand everything. He often talks of you. He likes his books so much. Can tell you about Cocky Locky and Henny Penny, knows more of Mother Goose than ever . . . Before I came away we had been going out a great deal, there was a splendid operetta troupe at the Academy of Music. We went six or eight nights (not in succession), saw the best operas. I enjoyed it very much. . . . I think we will go to the Sandwich Islands [Hawaii] sometime. It must be a delightful climate, but you know how foolish I am about leaving Mr. Hearst. . . . I have been doing splendidly in French, am sorry to lose all this time being away, but I read some every day so as to not forget. I have just finished a French novel which was very interesting. Willie knows several words in French. He is so cunning . . . Accept my love and wishes for your success and happiness and a great many kisses from Willie, if he could see you, he would have marvelous things to tell you. He is such a chatterbox.[15]

With the departure of Eliza Pike, the only person besides her parents whom Phoebe trusted entirely with her son, Phoebe assumed full-time care of the boy. Willie responded to his mother's attention as children often do: by being absolutely charming, like a puppy wagging his tail. He learned his letters, showered his mother with kisses, and grew jealous of the time she spent with her brother Elbert, who had joined the rest of the family in California. Willie — or Billy Buster, as his father had taken to calling him now — was a handsome boy, tall for his age, with light brown, almost blond hair, and clear blue eyes. Though he seldom saw his father, he quickly adjusted to life in a household filled with women — family, friends, and servants — all of whom participated in superintending his childhood. Their new home on Chestnut Street was located on top of an embankment that looked down on the Bay. Willie grew up in the sunshine, surrounded by lots of land, pets, and a beautiful hanging garden. From a distance, it seemed to be an idyllic childhood and as an adult William Randolph Hearst would describe it as such to his chosen biographer, Cora Older. But there were tensions, most of

Tune in to 1077 The End Saturday nights at midnight for Gabba Gabba Hey, The End's Punk Rock Show. For two hours, host Rob Femur fills the airwaves with punk tunes from the late 70's to now.

LAST WEEK GABBA GABBA HEY FEATURED SONGS FROM

Social Distortion, Against Me, Fugazi, NOFX, Operation Ivy, Ramones, Black Flag, X, Methadones, Bouncing Souls, Dead Milkmen, Decedents, Alkaline Trio and more..

Email Rob and let him know what you want to hear this Saturday
thefemurs@hotmail.com

THEend
SEATTLE'S ALTERNATIVE 107.7

them having to do with George's extended absences and his enveloping financial problems.[16]

Like most miners, even the most successful, George Hearst's fortunes fluctuated wildly. Since it was virtually impossible to determine accurately where one claim ended and another began, mining entrepreneurs could spend half their lives — and hundreds of thousands of dollars in the courts — protecting their claims, bribing judges, hiring experts, and keeping armies of lawyers on retainer. Claim dispute cases took years to come to judgment — and until they did, it was difficult, if not impossible, to raise money by selling stock.

As a mining entrepreneur, George made his money not from getting ore out of the ground, but from buying and selling stock in mines. This all took capital — and connections to capital. When silver prices were high, he had no difficulty raising money to finance new ventures and pay off his old debts. But when prices fell, as they inevitably did, opportunities vanished and debts accumulated. George was a gambler, firmly convinced that in the long run everything would come out all right. He refused to plan with any other outcome in mind.

In the middle 1860s, he extended his investments — and his debts — from mines and mining stock to real estate. He bought commercial real estate in San Francisco in anticipation of the completion of the transcontinental railroad and purchased, for $30,000, forty thousand acres of ranch land two hundred miles to the south, near San Simeon Bay in the Santa Lucia Mountains. The land was in a coastal region rich with mineral deposits. It was also valuable for agriculture.

In 1865, George Hearst was in his mid-forties, past the age when most successful miners return to civilization to enjoy the fruits of their labor. In the fall, he returned to San Francisco to accept the Democratic nomination for the state assembly. He had a young wife, a young son, sufficient business dealings and court cases in San Francisco to keep him busy, and close ties to the local Democratic party clubs which he had been supporting for several years. It is unlikely that he had intended to retire from mining entirely. The state legislature was in session only a few months a year, which left him with long stretches of time to return to the digging fields.

The Democratic party in 1865 was in the midst of a revival brought about by the arrival of large numbers of German and Irish immigrants and Southerners from border states like Missouri who, like Hearst, were Democrats and opposed the Civil War. It was their votes that elected George Hearst in November.

Though Sacramento, the state capital, was closer to San Francisco than the digging fields of Nevada and Idaho, Phoebe and George still lived apart most of the time. "Mr. Hearst is at home now," Phoebe confided to her diary on New Year's Day, 1866, but "he will return to Sacramento on Wednesday. I will be lonely again. He is absent so much. . . . Times are hard. My husband has lost a *great* deal of money lately. He is feeling low spirited and I feel like encouraging all I possibly can. This is the beginning of a new year. May God help me to do my duty in all things."[17]

When George was unable to come home to San Francisco for the weekend — which was most of the time — Phoebe and Willie were left with no choice but to take the overnight steamer to Sacramento. They stayed with George at the Brannan House on Front and J Streets. "He misses his big playroom and many toys," Phoebe wrote in her diary on January 9. She was every bit as miserable as Willie in Sacramento. She felt out of place among the politicians' wives and lost in the whirl of social events. She was also worried about her "perfect" son's increasingly imperfect behavior.

On January 4, Willie, almost three years old now, had put castor oil on her handsome moiré antique dress "so I had to dress twice." On January 10, when Governor Stanford's wife and her sister came calling, he misbehaved again. On February 11, he was "very full of mischief and I always feel anxious for fear he will act badly and disturb someone." On February 15, he misbehaved so badly that she had to remove him from the table. On February 16, back home again, she confided to her diary that she was no longer "comfortable anywhere else. When Willie is with more children he is so much harder to control."[18]

Many years later, Phoebe would confess to her grandson, Bill Hearst, Jr. that his father hadn't been "easy to discipline" as a child. "His forte was an irrepressible imagination."[19]

In adulthood, Hearst would take pride in his boyish misbehavior. In 1941, at the age of 78, he devoted several of his "In the News" columns to stories of childhood pranks — setting his room on fire, hurling a cobblestone through his dancing instructor's window, tying a string tight around the tail of a neighbor's cat, shooting at pigeons out of a hotel window with a toy cannon loaded with real gunpowder. Though he wrote these articles to recapture a lost childhood and to show his readers that he was much more of a "regular" guy than the tyrant and tycoon he had been portrayed as for half a century, what is most striking is that each of these vignettes tells the same tale of a small boy trying desperately to call attention to himself.

In one of the stories, little Willie sets off fireworks in his bedroom after the grownups have gone to bed. "Then he opened the door and shrieked down the silent halls of the sleeping house: 'Fire! Fire! Fire!' Then he shut the door, locked it and awaited events." As smoke filled the hallway, his parents tried to break down the door to his room, while the cook called firemen who pried open his window and "turned the hose on Willie and his fireworks." The story ends with Willie being "warmed" good-naturedly by his father. "But, with all his pretense of severity, Willie's pap never did warm Willie as he deserved. If he had done so Willie might have grown up to be a better — columnist." What comes across is the story of a little boy trying to establish some connection with his parents. The joke at the end covers the child's astonishment — and perhaps disappointment — at not being severely reprimanded and thereby taken seriously.

In another column on youth and child-rearing, Hearst cited a Professor Shaler who "once told his class at Harvard that he did not mind boys being bad as long as they were not wicked." Hearst concluded with a veiled retroactive explanation of his childhood misbehavior. "Sometimes boys are bad just because they do not want to be considered sissies."

Did Willie worry, as a child, that he was a sissy? Probably. It must not have been easy living up to the image of his tobacco-chewing, millionaire miner father. Though Willie was big and, despite Phoebe's constant worries, healthy, he was neither athletic nor particularly rugged. When Willie's father questioned whether the small private school he attended was doing him any good and suggested that he might instead go to the public schools, Phoebe asked if the public schools were not "rather rough-and-tumble for a delicate child like Willie?"

"'I do not see anything particularly delicate about Willie,' replied Willie's father . . . 'If the public schools are rough-and-tumble they will do him good. So is the world rough-and-tumble. Willie might as well learn to face it.'"

Before ending this particular story, Hearst paused to correct his mother's characterization. "Willie was not delicate at all, but he was something of a 'mother's boy' — and has always been mighty glad of it."

What are we to make of these stories? They are a strange amalgam of apology and pride, a plea for understanding combined with an arrogant self-defense. They are, as well, an attempt by an old man to make sense of his history by mythologizing his less than idyllic childhood.[20]

Phoebe Apperson had married a rich man and had expected to live as a rich man's wife, but by early 1866, only three and a half years into her marriage, she was forced to retrench. The Ophir mine in the Comstock region had played itself out sooner than expected, George had suffered a disastrous loss in the courts, and, as he later told an interviewer, "lost all the loose money I had" in San Francisco real estate ventures. Nothing was hidden from Phoebe. Though his investments would eventually pay out, he did not know when. Nor could he predict when friends and partners like William Lent — whose son Gene was Willie Hearst's best friend — would pay back the money they owed him.

"I feel that we must live more quietly and be economical," Phoebe wrote in the diary she kept in early 1866. "I have sent the horses to Pa's. . . . We have sold the Rockaway [carriage] for two hundred dollars. The coachman goes away tomorrow. By doing this we will save $100 every month." That Sunday, she was forced to miss church. "Have no carriage and the mud is terrible." Two weeks later, after waiting nearly an hour for her hired carriage to arrive, she complained in her diary that she missed her "own team very much, but I must not complain for we must live according to our means."[21]

Had financial woes been the only family problems in the Hearst household, young Willie might have been less affected by them. But Phoebe and George were in the midst of what appeared to be an extended argument. Though George was now far from the mining camps, he continued to live as though he were a single man. He may have been seeing other women. He drank and smoked too much, paid little attention to dress and deportment, did not even keep his boots clean. He refused, for one reason or another, sickness or weariness or simple stubbornness, to accompany her to church. "My husband is not a member of any church, and comes so near to being an infidel it makes me *shudder*," she had written on February 4. "It is hard for me to contend against this influence on my boy. He will soon be large enough to notice these things."[22]

There were other difficulties as well. George wanted to stay out late at social occasions, but Phoebe worried too much about Willie to have a good time. After the Legislative Ball in Sacramento in 1866, she wrote, "Instead of enjoying myself I cried until I was almost sick. I felt uneasy about Baby and wanted to go home before Geo. was really ready. He was angry etc., etc. . . . Oh! I wish I never had to go to another party."[23]

In the spring of 1866, after the assembly session had recessed, Phoebe took a vacation from her troubles — and her three-year-old child. She sailed away to the Hawaiian Islands for a month with her brother Elbert, who was sixteen. George spent the spring and summer in Idaho investigating new mining properties. Willie was shipped off to his grandparents' farm in Santa Clara.

In June, Phoebe returned to California, but then left Willie again in September to visit George in Idaho. This time, she was gone for over a month. She wrote a letter to Eliza Pike after she got back to San Francisco:

I went on up the country to Walla Walla and from there took the stage and went to a valley on the Lewiston road. There I waited three days until Geo. came. He was so glad to see me. It repaid me fully for the long trip. He had been sick and looked worse than I ever saw him, he was not ready to come home, was obliged to return to the mountains away out on the clear water above the Columbia River. So after staying there about twelve days I left for home. I could not go with him to the mines or be near him, but I was glad I went to see him. I enjoyed the trip very much, saw some of finest scenery in the world. . . . I was gone just a month . . . I was glad to get home again to see Willie. He was well and fat. He has grown tall too. . . . Willie is sound asleep. I wish you could see him — he is a great comfort to me. He talks to me sometimes when we are alone like an old man, he understands so much. He does not want to go to his grandma's again, seems to be afraid all the time that I will go away and leave him again. He says he likes this home best, and loves me as big as the house and sky and *everything*.[24]

Phoebe accepted the burden of being a miner's wife and went out of her way to visit and spend time with her husband in the mining camps, but he never quite reciprocated. His visits to San Francisco were always abbreviated, often unannounced, usually stopovers on longer journeys from one mining camp to another. She learned to live without him and to concentrate her attention and affection on her son. George arrived in San Francisco in November 1866, then left for a new mining camp almost as soon as he had arrived. "He was absent from the City a long while, his trip was by no means profitable," Phoebe wrote Eliza, and went on:

I don't think of going there this year with him — you know he can't stay at home long — I have made up my mind to not fret about it. I cannot help feeling lonely but may as well take things quietly. I am so well and fleshy you would be quite surprised. I was obliged to alter two or three of my closest fitting dresses, isn't that funny? But no signs of a little sister yet . . . Willie is not so fond of [Elbert] as he used to be. I scarcely ever leave Willie with anyone now — he can't bear to stay when I go down town and he is very good usually when he goes visiting with me. I don't think Alice [the new nanny] is cross to him, but she is very careless and I dislike for him to learn any of her habits. He being with me so constantly has made him perfectly devoted to me. He is a real little calf about me, he never wants anyone else to do anything for him, as I think I love him better than ever before, some days I do very little but amuse him. He knows several of his letters and will soon learn them all. He is very wise and sweet. I have wanted to have his picture taken, but he has had a small ringworm on his face and I have been waiting for that to disappear entirely which will soon be the case.[25]

Phoebe's disappearances (two of them, each a month long, in a four-month period), coupled with George's extended absences, may have taken a toll on their son. Phoebe confided to Eliza that Willie had been "very much put out when his father came home because he could not sleep with me. I talked to him and told him when his Papa went away again, he could sleep with me. He said, well, he wished he would go."[26]

Willie took sick early in 1867 — he was a few months shy of his fourth birthday — and Phoebe put aside everything to nurse him back to health. "Being with me so constantly, he became very babyish, and wanted his Mama on all occasions, when he was sick," she wrote Eliza. "He would say so often day and nights 'Mama I want to tell you something.' I would say — 'What Willie.' His answer would be, '*I love you.*' His Papa laughed at me a great deal about it, saying Willie waked me up in the night to tell me he loved me, bless his little heart. I delighted to have him well again. . . . Willie talks a great deal and in that manly way. He asks reasons for everything and when he tells anything he gives his reasons. He has improved very much. Has fine ideas. Thinks a great deal. I have taught him most of his letters. He loves books and play both. . . . I have taken him with me when I go out, so that he thinks I can't go without him and it is almost the case. . . . He is a great comfort to me, and I hope he will be a good man, they are scarce. . . . Mr. Hearst has been home all this winter. Has been very well. We begin to feel more like married people than before, we have been very quiet, have not attended a single party and only been to the theatre once and to see the Japanese jugglers once. Took Willie both times those jugglers are splendid. . . . Willie tried to turn summersetts, climb poles."

George's continuing financial problems had brought an end to their social life. "The finest party ever given in California will be at the Lick House . . . the dining room so surpasses anything I have ever seen . . . We have an invitation," Phoebe wrote Eliza, "but are not going. I would have to get a handsome dress. It would be both troublesome and expensive and often after all would not pay. I don't care about all the furbelows and vanity. . . . We have a good home and enough to live on. That is much to be thankful for. If our little man is spared to us we will try to give him a fine education if nothing more. . . . I am still studying French, one lesson per week. Will soon be through. I can speak very well now . . . A great many are going to the world's fair [in Paris]. I wish I could go, but I can't, and it does no good to think about it."[27]

In 1867, after one two-year term, George retired from the state assembly. His financial problems were more serious than ever. While they were able to hold on to their home in San Francisco, their land at San Simeon, and some of their stocks, there was very little left over. George returned to the digging fields, this time as adviser or partner in mines up and down the West Coast, from Idaho to Mexico. He and Phoebe renewed their separate lives. There was no talk of his returning home to stay now. He was a full-time consultant and entrepreneur, on the road twelve months a year.

Phoebe's and George's correspondence was marked by a strange competition as each tried to convince the other that he or she led the more difficult life, Phoebe particularly, because George's extended absences made it difficult for her to have the second child she so fervently wished for. In her letters to Eliza, she reported regularly that there were "no signs" yet of a little sister for Willie, but that she kept hoping next month might be different.[28] George's letters were filled with worries about his health, his homesickness, and the trustworthiness of his companions. Each insisted that the other did not visit often enough or, having visited, did not stay long enough.

In the spring of 1867, with George in Idaho — and money still very much an issue — Phoebe decided to rent out her San Francisco house and move south to her parents' farm for the summer. Everything was so uncertain, she wrote Eliza. She didn't see a bright future. The following summer, she rented her house again, but this time for six months, and with Willie, who was now five, traveled East on free railroad passes which George had secured during his tenure in the state assembly. Worried that during her absence George would abandon all the "civilizing" she had brought to the marriage, she wrote him constantly with reminders to change his clothing regularly.

"I do hope you will have respect enough for yourself and me to keep yourself *well* dressed and *clean*," she wrote him in mid-July. "Nothing can make me feel worse than to think you are going about shabby and dirty . . . Please write me if you have any new clothes and if you have your washing done and be sure not to forget to pay for it. I know how care[less] and forgetful you are, though you don't intend to be so."[29]

It was not easy for anyone to travel across the country in the middle 1860s, especially a young woman and a five-year-old boy without family or servants to assist them. Phoebe was undaunted. After visiting her relatives in Missouri, she traveled to Reading, Pennsylvania, where she deposited Willie with Eliza Pike, then set off with family friends to tour the East Coast. Phoebe and Willie's great adventure did not go entirely as planned. In her letters, Phoebe complained about Willie's wildness when they were together and about missing him when they were apart. Their first extended separation was so painful that she wrote Eliza an urgent letter from Baltimore where she was visiting, begging her to bring Willie on the next train south for a short visit.[30]

In September, while she was enjoying one of her side trips without her son, he came down with a serious case of food poisoning and she had to return to Reading to be with him. Willie begged to be taken home. Phoebe instead took him back to Missouri for another visit with his cousins. Unwilling to ride the railways again without a male escort, Phoebe asked George to come and fetch them. When he refused, citing the demands of his Idaho mines, she booked passage on steamers from New York to California via Panama.

On the second steamer leg of their long journey home, just outside Acapulco, Willie fell ill again, this time with typhoid fever. George met their ship in San Francisco and stayed with Phoebe and Willie at the Lick House until the boy was healthy. When he had recovered from his illness, Phoebe, worried not only about his health but about her own, took him to Santa Clara for the rest of the winter. Though she had been vaccinated more than thirteen times, she was particularly fearful of contracting smallpox in the city. Willie did not return home to Chestnut Street until March 1, 1869. He was nearly six years old now and had been away for almost a year.[31]

Willie should have begun school in the fall of 1868 when he was five and a half, but Phoebe had instead taken him with her on their Eastern tour. The following September, she kept him at home again. Finally, when he was seven and a half, she enrolled him in a small private school on Vallejo Street, only to withdraw him two months later to accompany her on an extended visit to her parents' ranch in Santa Clara. "I did not like to have him out of school even for such a short time," she wrote to Eliza Pike, "but the weather is or has been so lovely I thought it best to come down here before the rain commenced. I have heard Willie's lessons every day so he will be able to go on with his class." Early in the new year, Phoebe let Willie return to school to complete the grade.[32]

When Willie switched to a public school the following year, Phoebe instructed the servants to keep steady watch on the boy's whereabouts and companions. According to Cora Older, who was later chosen by Hearst to write his biography and given access to family papers, Phoebe was so worried about the "toughs" in his class that she sent her coachman to fetch him after school. Only after Willie pleaded with her for permission to walk home like the other boys did she relent.[33]

"I take great pleasure in amusing and interesting him at home," Phoebe informed Eliza Pike in May of 1871, just after Willie's eighth birthday, "so that he may be kept as much as possible from bad children. Of course, I must allow him to have company often but I manage to watch them closely. So far he is a very innocent child and I mean to keep him so just as long as I can. . . . He is a great comfort to us. Mr. Hearst is so proud of him and too indulgent to try to keep from spoiling him. . . . Mr. Hearst often says he would not like to have Willie on a jury if his Mama was concerned, for whether it was justice or not, he would decide in my favor. . . . I am so sorry we have no other children. We love babies so dearly, why we are not blessed I cannot understand . . . I have had the dressing room adjoining my bedroom all fixed up for Willie, a nice bed put up. It is a pretty little room and so near me, he is very much pleased."[34]

At age nine, after he had had only two years of classes, Phoebe removed Willie from school once more, probably so that he could spend all his time with her. The following spring, she rented out the Chestnut Street house for a year, secured from George a ten-thousand-dollar bill of credit, and deputized her ten-year-old son to take her on the grand tour of Europe she had dreamed of since her marriage.

For the next eighteen months, mother and son visited every important museum, gallery, palace, and church in Ireland, Scotland, England, France, Italy, Switzerland, Holland, Belgium, Austria, and Germany, most of them more than once; they perfected their French and Willie learned German; they met the pope in Rome and had dinner with the American consul; they read Shakespeare in the evening and travel books all day long; and together they acquired an education in European art, culture, and history.

Phoebe had originally planned to return to California in the fall of 1873, but soon after arriving began talking about extending her stay. "If you are fully decided you cannot come, I shall not feel contented to remain away many months longer," Phoebe wrote to George in August of 1873, still early in their tour, "though as we are here, and never likely to come again, we ought to see all that it is possible to see and try not to be homesick. I want you to write me what you think. I am sure you are lonely and need us to cheer you. I feel conscience stricken about having so much enjoyment with you at home worrying and working. Does my love and my society when with you compensate for all? I hope we will yet have many happy years together. Willie certainly will have great benefit by this trip. It is in many respects better than school."[35]

Phoebe had long planned for this trip, though she had envisioned traveling with her husband George at her side, not ten-year-old Willie. Left to her own devices, she booked trains, hired carriages, located and negotiated the fee for room and boarding in appropriately priced *and* respectable hotels, found interesting people to travel with, arranged for Willie to have drawing, French, German, arithmetic, and English lessons, organized guided tours and day trips, and found time every evening to write several dense but legible twenty-page letters without errors, ink smudges, or spelling mistakes — and all this on relatively modest resources.

Their trip unfolded into a journey of epic proportions. While George complained of being "ill" and "blue" and missing his wife "and the Boy" more than ever, he never hesitated to send Phoebe the letters of credit she requested with permission to extend her stay. Unlike most American tourists who traveled straight to Florence or Rome, Phoebe began her trip in Scotland, Ireland, and England, toured Germany and the low countries, wintered in Italy, and then traveled north to Paris where Willie temporarily attended school with Eugene Lent, his friend from San Francisco.[36]

Willie, Phoebe reported, had been a bit homesick early on, but he was as energetic and enthusiastic a tourist as she was. From Florence, where they spent much of November and December, Phoebe wrote Eliza with a description of their daily activities. Willie had three hours of lessons in the morning and then went out with his mother "to the galleries, palaces, churches, etc." In the evenings, while Willie prepared the next day's lessons and read books on Italy, Phoebe wrote her letters or studied. She had, in mid-December, "just finished reading 'Notes on Italy' by Hawthorne." On the weekends, mother and son went on "excursions to the various places a little in the suburbs or on the surrounding hills where we have grand views of the city and surroundings. Sundays we go to church, in the afternoon, take a delightful drive around the city or in the beautiful park. So we are *always* busy. . . . I wish we could stay another year."[37]

The financial news from home continued to be bad. The bankruptcy of the Northern Pacific Railroad and the failure of Jay Cooke and Company, one of the nation's largest investment houses, had turned the American economy upside down. Businessmen like George Hearst, already heavily in debt, were squeezed even tighter in the Panic of 1873 as 1800 American banks folded and those still solvent scrambled to call in outstanding loans. Though George managed to hold on to his real estate, he was forced to dispose of most of his remaining assets.[38]

Phoebe suggested that they sell their Chestnut Street house. "We can board in Oakland and live much cheaper," she wrote her husband from Paris in April of 1874. "Let the money for the place be invested or put at interest for Willie and I. It may be all we will have to educate him."[39]

When Willie Hearst returned to San Francisco in October of 1874, he found that his childhood home and all that was in it had been sold to pay his father's debts, as Phoebe had suggested. Willie and his mother were forced to board with family friends and then move into rented quarters.

Willie Hearst would spend the rest of his boyhood moving from school to school and from rented quarters to rented quarters. He had, however, already begun to find an antidote to the continued disruptions in his daily life. While in Europe, Phoebe had written George that their son was becoming a collector. He was intent on surrounding himself with objects that belonged to him and could not be taken away. "He wants all sorts of things," she wrote on July 28, and then, a week later, added that he had developed "a mania for antiquities, poor old boy" and enjoyed, above all else, talking about all the wonderful things he and his mother were going to bring back home. In London, he tried to convince his mother to buy him the four specially bred white horses that pulled the English royal carriages. In Germany, he collected the colorful comic books the Germans called *Bilderbücher*, and coins, stamps, beer steins, pictures of actors and actresses, and porcelains. In Venice, he bought glass objects. Phoebe tried to persuade him that they could not buy everything they saw, but, as she confessed to George, the boy "gets so fascinated, his reason and judgement forsake him."[40]

Werner Muensterberger, the author of *Collecting: An Unruly Passion*, has observed that many great collectors suffer as children from the sudden and unexplained absence of their parents. To alleviate feelings of vulnerability, "aloneness and anxiety," he says, they invest their favorite objects with magical qualities; those objects, in turn, provide them with the sense of permanence, affirmation, and security that is missing from their lives. Young Willie Hearst at age ten had already begun to invest an inordinate amount of energy in accumulating and possessing "objects," in some part, we might suspect, because, in Muensterberger's words, they could "be relied upon to satisfy a demand instantly. Their essential function [was] to be there always."[41]

Hearst's childhood was defined by impermanence. He had, by the time he was ten years old, lived many different lives: the rich boy in the mansion at the top of the hill, the new kid forced to attend public school because his father had run out of money, the pampered child who toured Europe, the boy who boarded with his mother. There was no center, no place that he could call his own. His parents and grandparents were transplants from Missouri. He himself had been born and raised in San Francisco, but had lived almost as much of his life on the road. School had provided no continuity, not even from grade to grade. He was shifted and shunted, withdrawn and newly enrolled in school after school, without rhyme or reason. It was hard to keep friends or feel that you belonged to a place — or it to you — when you were always being pulled away.

His father he seldom saw and never knew. The one fixed point in his life was his mother, to whom he was devoted. But she too had disappointed him, disappearing too often and too early. And it was she who was always uprooting him from Chestnut Street, the only home he had ever known: to Sacramento and Santa Clara, to the East for six months, and Europe for eighteen.

❧ 2 ❧

To Europe Again
and on to Harvard

FROM 1874 TO 1880, between ages eleven and seventeen, Willie Hearst continued to live a nomadic existence. He was a clever boy, rather well-read, able to speak and read German and French, and quite knowledgeable about history and art. Still, he had yet to distinguish himself academically, perhaps because he was continually changing schools. In 1876, when he was thirteen and should have been preparing for high school, Phoebe pulled him out of the classroom again to accompany her on an extended visit East. They attended the Philadelphia Exposition, then traveled to Boston and New York where they called on Samuel Tilden, who was running for president on the Democratic ticket.

These were critical years for the Hearst family. After selling his Comstock stock in the middle 1860s, George Hearst had become a partner in a number of mining ventures, some successful, some less so, before he and his partners at last struck it rich in the Eureka and Pioche silver mines in eastern Nevada and the Ontario thirty-five miles outside of Salt Lake City, Utah. The Ontario, which had been bought for $30,000, would in George Hearst's lifetime yield the partners, net, about $14 million.

In the spring of 1877, Hearst visited the Black Hills in the Dakota territory to investigate rumors of a lode of gold ore which, though low-grade, was so huge it might never run out. After seeing the property for himself, he contacted his partners in San Francisco to urge them to buy as much land as they could, as quickly as they could. The Homestake Mining Company was incorporated almost immediately, as Hearst and his partners continued to buy up land and water rights in the area and build their own railroad. Homestake alone would make the Hearst family wealthy beyond imagination. But it was only one of the several major finds which would begin to pay off for the Hearst family in the late 70s and early 80s. After

Homestake came Anaconda in Butte, Montana. Local miners had known that the region held valuable silver and copper deposits, but they had not had the capital to find out how valuable. Hearst and his partners did. They dug and timbered hundreds of feet under the ground, constructed an enormous smelter to reduce the ore, bought up all the water rights in the region, built a railroad link to get their ore to market, and erected their own town where they housed, provisioned, and entertained their workers.[1]

Hearst's share of the Ontario, Homestake, and Anaconda mines, as well as a number of smaller but profitable mines elsewhere in the West and in Mexico propelled him and his family into the front rank of the fabulously wealthy. Never again would they have to worry about recessions, depressions, panics, or selloffs. They could live like royalty — if they chose — with more money than they could spend in their lifetimes. But they did not.

While Phoebe harbored dreams of climbing higher in San Francisco society — and pulling her son along with her — George Hearst was content to remain on the outer fringes. Though returned from the mining camps — for good — he indulged himself in an almost visceral disdain for the amenities of upper-class life: clean shirtfronts, sculpted whiskers, shined boots. His wife ignored him as best she could, when she wasn't trying to reform him. She concentrated her attention on their son. Though Will Hearst, unlike his father, dressed and had the manners of a young gentleman, he too existed on the margins of San Francisco society. He did not regularly attend any school in San Francisco, much less any elite one, nor was he a member of any youth or church groups. His friends were the children of his father's business associates or his mother's social acquaintances.

Phoebe had done little about her son's formal education, but now, in the late 1870s, the family's fortunes secured, she made up her mind to send the boy to Harvard, the Eastern college that wealthy San Franciscans had adopted as their own. To prepare him for college, Phoebe enrolled Will in St. Paul's Episcopal School near Concord, New Hampshire, where Will Tevis, the son of one of George's mining partners, was already a student.

Distressed at the thought that Will would be leaving home without her, Phoebe arranged for a farewell tour of Europe, and brought along Philip Barry, a tutor from Berkeley, to prepare Will for St. Paul's. Will's friend, Eugene Lent, and his mother made up the rest of the party. They arrived in Paris in the spring of 1879 and remained there through August. The boys spent part of every day sightseeing and acquainting themselves with the city's finer restaurants and theaters. In the mornings and before and after dinner, Will worked with Mr. Barry on geography, Greek, Latin, history, algebra, and arithmetic, all subjects he would need at St. Paul's and Harvard.[2]

Phoebe was not nearly as energetic on this tour as she had been on their first one. In July, she left Paris to take a "rest cure" at the Capterets, an exclusive resort in the Pyrenees known for its treatment of infertile women. She remained there for the rest of the summer. Barry accompanied the boy back to New York. In late August or early September, Will was taken to St. Paul's, either by Barry or family friends, and then left on his own, at sixteen years of age, three thousand miles from home and an ocean away from his mother. Seventy years later, Hearst reminisced in his newspaper column that he had been sent away to New Hampshire because it was "thought desirable to untie him from his mother's apron strings." He was, at the time, much less sanguine about the separation.[3]

Will was miserable from the moment he arrived in New Hampshire, and he let his parents know exactly how he felt. He had never before been away from home or from his mother for an extended period of time, nor in the company of young men who were destined for "society." He did not fit in — and did not want to. "This is the best place to get homesick that I ever saw," he wrote his mother. "Everything is so dull, I am just homesick all the time."[4]

With Phoebe away in Europe, George Hearst tried his best to take up the role of parent and console his son by mail. Unfortunately, he had little to offer except barely literate homilies: "I hope you will stand in like a man and take it as it comes good and bad until I see you and we will talk it over and we may be able to lift out some of objectionable parts."[5]

Though Will may have been cheered to get mail from his father, it was his mother he missed. In letter after letter he reminded her how much he suffered from her absence:

"I want to see you so bad. If I could only talk how much more I could say than I can write in a letter."[6]

"I have settled into a state of perpetual homesickness, which although not quite so bad as when I first came, is pretty bad and I think it will continue until I see you again. I never knew how much time there was in two months before and how long it could be strung out."[7]

"I feel very despondent and lonely all the time and wish for you to come awful bad. It has been over a week since I received a letter, and I feel very anxious for fear you are sick. If you are I would rather know. It is the next thing to speaking with you to write and receive a letter. It is all I can do to keep from crying sometimes when how much alone I am and how far away you are. I often think of the last morning at Carterets and the only thing that comforts me is that the time is getting shorter every day till you will be here."[8]

Will hated everything about St. Paul's — the food, the fasting on Friday, the lessons, the daily regimen and rituals, and the cold. What bothered him most was the loss of the unstructured, almost carefree life he had enjoyed in San Francisco. He was incensed that the school authorities allowed the boys to "only go into town once a month, and only have four dollars a month to spend and out of that have to come bats and balls and all such things."[9]

Seventy years later, in his newspaper column, he still remembered how "thoroughly unhappy" he had been at St. Paul's where they tried so hard to make him into a gentleman, where, instead of playing "baseball on a vacant lot," as he had in San Francisco, he was supposed to play cricket on a "spic-and-span and much-mowed lawn."[10]

Like his father, Will Hearst was deeply uncomfortable with the rituals of upper-class life, with cricket and unsmiling headmasters, with Latin and Greek, and compulsory chapel led by pompous preachers who reminded him of the African-American vaudevillian Gus Williams. "It is almost like a catholic church," he wrote his mother of school chapel. "We have to bow whenever we come to Jesus Christ in the creed, and Dr. spoke the other day of the holy virgin. I think he is an old hypocrite and I know you will think so when you see him."

Will was the new boy in a school where his classmates had been together for several years. While he was able to room with "little Tevis," his friend from San Francisco, he complained to his mother that his roommate "always wants to go to bed at about nine o'clock while I have to stay up and study."[11]

In November, when Phoebe finally returned from her rest cure to visit her boy at St. Paul's, he begged her to take him with her back to San Francisco. She refused. He finished out the year at St. Paul's, but did not return the following September. "His retirement was voluntary," a classmate remembered. "He was not happy there."[12]

Formal photographs taken at around this time picture Will as a young aristocrat of the West, a handsome lad, tall, thin, his sandy hair cut short and parted to the left. What the formal portraits can't show is the shy smile and the awkward stance of a young man a bit unsure of himself in social situations.[13]

We don't know much about the two years Will spent in San Francisco after leaving St. Paul's. No doubt bowing to her son's wishes, Phoebe did not enroll him in another secondary school, but instead hired tutors to prepare him for his Harvard entrance examinations. He lived with his parents in a mansion on "millionaires' row" on Van Ness Street and spent more time than ever with his father, who had now permanently retired from the mines to devote himself to politics.

Young Will's major preoccupation appears to have been the theater. It was here, he tells us, that he fell in love for the first time, with the teenage actress Lillian Russell, who was performing "in a light comedy called 'Fun in a Photograph Gallery.' Your columnist was about sixteen or seventeen too, and after having become such a frequent visitor to the theater that the ushers began to call him by his first name, decided that the tense, dramatic and ecstatic situation could only be solved by an honorable and impassioned proposal offered the young lady." At the last minute, his nerve failed him.[14]

In December of 1881, Will traveled East again with his mother, who had decided to tour Europe with a young protégé, Eleanor Calhoun, an aspiring actress who claimed to be the great-niece of the renowned South Carolina senator John C. Calhoun. Eleanor visited the Hearsts at the Hotel Buckingham in New York and traveled with them to Boston and Cambridge where Phoebe, in anticipation of Will's passing his entrance examinations, shopped for furniture her son might need for his suite of rooms at Harvard. Eleanor and Will spent a few evenings at the theater before returning, with Phoebe, to New York.

On January 18, Will saw his mother and Eleanor off to Europe. "What a hard day this has been leaving my dear boy," Phoebe wrote in her diary. "Going so far away. We sailed at 3 P.M. Dear Will was brave and kept trying to make us laugh." "How I miss my dear Will," she added the following day. "He is indeed a part of my life." She had nothing to say about her husband whom she was also leaving behind.[15]

Will returned to San Francisco to prepare for his Harvard entrance examinations. There is no evidence that he gave any further thought to Eleanor Calhoun. A few years older and much more mature than he, she was, in any event, out of reach for the gangly young man who, while she was traveling in Europe, would be studying for his college entrance examinations. Prospective students were examined over a three-day period in Latin, Greek, Ancient History and Geography, Mathematics, Physics, English Composition, French or German, and two electives. As tutors were given advance notice of the texts their charges would be tested on, 90 percent of those who took the entrance examinations were admitted for the fall 1882 term, Will Hearst among them.[16]

Nineteen-year-old Will Hearst spent his last summer in California — as he had the previous two years — at leisure. With other wealthy San Franciscans, he joined the seasonal exodus to Monterey — the Newport of northern California — where he resided in the luxurious Hotel Del Monte. It was here, according to his chosen biographer, Cora Older, that he met and was "enthralled" by Sybil Sanderson, the daughter of a San Francisco judge. Sybil was also spending her last summer on the West Coast before moving to Paris to continue her operatic studies. A soprano with enormous range, she was already at age seventeen being compared to Adelina Patti, the most famous opera singer in the world.[17]

According to Cora Older, who learned much of what she included in her book from Hearst himself, young Will fell head over heels in love with Sybil — and she with him: "It was a time when the beauty of Monterey, the old Spanish Capital of California, was most glamorous. . . . Will Hearst and Sybil Sanderson strolled up and down these streets of romance. They boated, they swam, they rode, they wandered on the white sands by day, and under the pale moon they were betrothed."[18]

Their romance lasted only as long as the season. At summer's end, Sybil's mother and sister, with her consent, whisked her away to Paris. Though according to Cora Older, Will thought seriously about following Sybil to Paris, in the end he decided instead to board the train to Cambridge with his mother and begin his freshman year at Harvard College.

Will could well have afforded to live in the luxurious, centrally heated private dormitories that had been built for Harvard's young millionaires on the "Gold Coast" — a quarter mile away from campus so that residents would not be subject to compulsory chapel regulations — but he did not, probably because he had not been invited to. He moved instead into 46 Matthews Hall, a suite of rooms in a monstrously large, ten-year-old Gothic building in Harvard Yard. Phoebe redecorated his rooms in Harvard crimson, equipped him with a library, and hired a maid and valet to look after her boy.[19]

While Harvard was less parochial than it had been, fully two thirds of the class came from within a hundred-mile radius of Cambridge. Only eight members of Hearst's class were from California.[20] Fortunately for Will, Gene Lent, his childhood friend, and Jack Follansbee, also from San Francisco, had preceded him to Cambridge. Both were well-connected sophomores, eager to show him around campus. Follansbee, tall, stylishly dressed, with dark black hair and a red mustache, assumed the role of prime mentor and friend. "He is in the class above me but has been very kind — giving me good advice and the benefit of his experience," Will wrote his parents. "In fact, he has been the best friend I have had in College so far, and I shall be sadder to see him go than I would have been at the departure of any number of fellow freshmen." Jack had, according to Will, done quite well in his first year — his "college course has been very successful and his habits and deportment have been such as to make him a favorite not only with the fellows but with the professors as well" — but he and Will overlapped for less than a year in Cambridge. Jack had to leave in the spring of his sophomore year, while Will was still a freshman. According to Will, Jack had to "go into business" when his uncle, who had been paying his way, ran into financial difficulties.

Will implored his father to find a position for Jack Follansbee, not simply to repay him for his kindness, but because "he is a splendid fellow, Papa, and in aiding him you will be aiding yourself, for I don't know where you can find a young man with the brightness, the sound sense and the pluck that Jack Follansbee has. He is a tall, strong fellow with an honest, attractive countenance and he is highly honorable and proud. . . . Now, what I want you to do is to get him a *good* position and one where he will have a chance to rise — as he surely will if the opportunity offers." He expected, he wrote his mother, that Jack would, in future, become "to me what Chambers and McMasters [George Hearst's chief advisers] have been to papa. Men who have grown up in the business and have a knowledge and an interest in it as well as a friendship for me; for I know I have few better friends than Jack and there is no one that I am fonder of." His prediction was only partially borne out. Though Jack may have done odd jobs for George, he was not given a full-time position in George's real estate or mining businesses. Jack Follansbee had spent a pampered childhood, drank far too much, and, though intensely loyal to Will, was not prepared to become anyone's full-time assistant or adviser. He would, nonetheless, become a permanent fixture in the Hearst family. In the years to come, he would correspond regularly with Phoebe, keeping her up to date on her son's activities and reassuring her when she was most worried about her boy. Jack remained Will's loyal friend as well, always willing to drop what he was doing to help out in an emergency. Will repaid that loyalty by providing for him for the rest of his life.[21]

There were several ways of making one's mark at Harvard. Hearst chose the most difficult: election to the top social clubs. Each spring, the sophomore class surveyed the new class of freshmen and divided them by social criteria — they had no other available — into hierarchically ranked groups of ten. The social clubs, also in hierarchical order, chose their members from the top "tens." D.K.E., or "Dickey," took the highest ranking "ten."

As a Californian whose parents had neither the social skills nor the connections necessary to open doors in Cambridge or Boston, Hearst was at something of a disadvantage. What he did have on his side was the handsome set of rooms Phoebe had furnished for him, a winning though slightly diffident personality, perhaps the largest allowance on campus — $150 a month, equal to $2,500 a month in 1990s currency — and an enormous capacity to mobilize others on his behalf. In a long letter to his mother in which he itemized all the money he had spent on doctor bills and dinners and the photographs of his room which she had requested, he added "a few lines of explanation to Papa," who he feared might misunderstand when he asked for more money "to get on": "When I said 'get on,' I meant — as I supposed you knew — get on the D.K.E. and, although I am conceited enough to suppose that I am fully capable of advancing myself as far as studies go, I recognize that it is impossible to be a successful college politician and to reach the highest point without having members of your own class to push you up and upper classmen to pull."[22]

Will scheduled a full round of dinners, punches, beer parties, and receptions in his Matthews Hall suite and in restaurants in Cambridge and Boston, with the implicit promise that he would continue such royal entertainments for his fellow club members. He was elected to D.K.E. in the spring of his freshman year.[23]

Harvard under President Charles W. Eliot had removed many of the regulations and restrictions that had made life so miserable for Will at St. Paul's. Aside from chapel, which was compulsory for those who lived on campus — though Will refused to attend — students had a rather remarkable degree of freedom at Harvard to "elect" their courses and attend if and when they chose. Grades were determined by end-of-the-term examinations on which 50 percent was considered passing. "To prepare these you spend as much time as you consider necessary," Hearst wrote his father, "so, you see, a fellow can study or loaf just as he pleases and if he manages to skim through his examinations all right, nothing is said. . . . I think a fellow ought to get an average of 70% and that is what I shall try for."[24]

Aside from the most promising students, who were early taken under the wing of their instructors, faculty had little to do with students besides giving three hours' worth of lectures a week and conducting examinations at the end of the semester. According to George Santayana, also a member of the class of 1886, "Teachers and pupils seemed animals of different species, useful and well disposed towards each other, like a cow and a milkmaid; periodic contributions could pass between them, but not conversation."[25]

In December, as Will finished his first semester, Phoebe came East to entertain him for the holidays. George had promised to join them, but, as
usual, he backed out at the last minute. "I was pleasantly surprised by a letter from you," Will wrote him from Phoebe's hotel suite in New York. "I
suppose it was for me although you signed yourself 'Your loving husband.'
. . . I have been spending a week's vacation in New York with Mama and
have had a splendid time. . . . Don't you remember that you said you were
coming to New York to spend Xmas with your Billy Buster? Well, I did not
much believe it then, but I wish you would come on and see the College."[26]

With some help from tutors, Will got through his first year at Harvard
with some surprisingly high grades, 93% in Chemistry, 80% in Greek, 78%
in Latin, 74% in Classical Lectures, 77% in German, and a barely passing
55% in Physics. Though he had done well in Analytic Geometry, for some
reason he never took the final. For his second year, Will chose to take Political Economy, Mathematics, and Philosophy; he quickly dropped Philosophy because, as he wrote his mother, it was "too dry and learned and full of
big words and generally incomprehensible for me." He also registered for
Fine Arts with Professor Charles Eliot Norton.[27]

Professor Norton, already a legend in Boston and at Harvard, was precisely the kind of educated gentleman Phoebe had hoped would teach her
son. Norton had corresponded with Ruskin, translated Dante, and wrote
regularly for the best literary magazines. He had taken on himself the task
of cultivating the taste of Harvard gentlemen, steering them away from the
vulgarity of the American present to the treasures of the distant European
past. Fine art, Norton taught, civilized men and made them moral. To live
among beautiful things was, he believed, to open oneself up to their restor-
ative powers. A well-ordered, well-decorated, and artfully furnished residence was an antidote to the disorder in the world outside. It soothed the
soul, mended the spirit, and improved the character.[28]

Though Hearst enjoyed Norton's lectures, it is clear from his letters
home that the high point of his second year was his election as business
manager of the *Harvard Lampoon*, replacing Eugene Lent who had not
been able to raise the funds necessary to keep the magazine afloat. Business
managers were traditionally chosen for the size of their allowances, but
Hearst, instead of subsidizing the *Lampoon* out of his own or his parents'
pockets, engaged in a full-scale advertising and marketing campaign to
make the journal self-sufficient. He solicited local merchants to buy ads,
wrote to advertisers in other Ivy League publications, and enlisted his
mother to sell subscriptions to members of the San Francisco Harvard

Club: "The Lampoon is peculiarly Harvard, beginning with its red cover, and all the way through and it ought to be supported by Harvard men with contributions and subscriptions."[29]

In an effort to bring a modicum of order to the magazine which, according to George Santayana, was "always late and not always funny," Hearst rented a room for the writers in Brattle Street, "with a carpet and a genuinely American stove," and bought subscriptions to all the French comic papers. The writers, for their part, "turned a cold shoulder on Hearst's munificence" and continued to meet in their dormitory rooms and dining hall instead.[30]

Hearst didn't much care, as he had accomplished his purpose. In his first experience in publishing, he had expanded the *Lampoon*'s circulation by 50 percent, increased advertising revenue by 300 percent, and converted the bottom line from a deficit of $200 to a surplus of $650. Though he wrote his mother that he intended "as soon as the rush of business is over [to] attempt to write a few serious chronic articles," he was at present, he informed her, "wholly business" and enormously successful at it.[31]

In the spring of his sophomore year, Will was elected to Porcellian, a rather patrician club that had numbered both Oliver Wendell Holmeses and Theodore Roosevelt among its members, and Med. Facs., the most secret, most esteemed, and apparently, most criminal, of all the secret societies, its only major activity being the theft and defacement of prominent Harvard statues, plaques, and markers. Though its membership included the most prominent of Harvard students and admission bestowed great honor, the society's misdeeds were so notorious that when, in 1905, initiates were discovered stealing yet another statue and local papers ran stories about it, the society's alumni voted to disband it and seal its papers until 1976.[32]

Though Will never ceased complaining about the unforgiving New England climate and the colds, sore throats, and tonsillitis it inflicted on him, he was clearly having the time of his life. In less than two years, he had accomplished a small miracle. He had gotten himself elected to the top clubs on campus, earned a reputation as a first-class dandy, grown an impressive mustache, found a splendid tailor, and acquired a pet alligator named Charlie, who lived with him in his suite. He had also been invited to join the Hasty Pudding Club and was cast in a featured role in one of its infamous blackface burlesques. He would, he wrote his mother, have been cast in the next had the fellows not discovered "in the last play a certain tendency of mine to cut rehearsals and make myself generally scarce at a time when I was most needed."[33]

Part of the secret to his social success was his adept use of an ever-expanding allowance. His rooms at Matthews Hall had become a social center of sorts and free pub for his California friends, *Lampoon* associates, and influential players and backers of the Harvard baseball club. As was expected of campus politicians and men of wealth, he backed all the Harvard teams, donating over $100 a year in dues to the crew, baseball, and football associations. When, in his sophomore year, the Harvard baseball team did well enough to advance to the intercollegiate championship, Will wrote his mother for extra money to host a dinner for the players, "first, because they have done so well and deserve it, and secondly, because I should like to be Vice President of the Inter-Collegiate Base Ball Association and I don't see why I shouldn't. Do you?"[34]

Though he had reached the pinnacle of Harvard society, Hearst did not take the next step forward from the college's clubhouses into Boston's drawing rooms. From the 1880s on, the better Harvard social clubs — such as those Hearst had joined — had served as recruiting grounds for Boston society, providing a well-stocked reservoir of eligible young men for coming-out balls, sociables, and weekend house parties. But Hearst, though his election to the better clubs should have certified him as eligible, was never invited to spend his summers at Newport or Bar Harbor or to escort anyone's sister to a coming-out dance on the South Shore.

There hung about him the aura of the outsider, of the arriviste who spent too freely and too openly to buy himself a position in society he was not entitled to by birth. As Santayana would later put it rather bluntly, "He was little esteemed in the college."[35]

Hearst didn't appear to care. Instead of attempting to ingratiate himself with Boston society, for which he had no use whatsoever, he gravitated toward the demimonde, spending more and more time at Boston's and New York's musical comedy theaters and after-hours clubs and restaurants. In his freshman year, Jack Follansbee had introduced Will to Tessie Powers, a waitress from Cambridge, whom Jack was "keeping." Most of what we know about Tessie comes from Anne Apperson Flint, Will's cousin. Anne, who was raised by Phoebe and became her confidante, was interviewed by W. A. Swanberg in 1960. Unfortunately, much of her recollection appears to have been colored by personal animus against her cousin, who, she implied, had robbed her of Phoebe's estate.

In her interview, Apperson claimed that Jack's uncle, who paid his way at Harvard, "clamped down on him [in his second year there]; Jack wasn't able to continue keeping her. So he asked W. R. [as Will Hearst would be called in adult life] to take her over. She was said to be a very nice girl, well behaved, quiet, everyone said that about her, very ladylike. She had trouble in her background — small-town country girl who became a waitress. She was very devoted to W. R."

There was nothing peculiar in a Harvard boy keeping a Cambridge girl. Will was not the first or last of his class to have a mistress in town. The problem was not that he was enjoying a sexual liaison with a Cambridge working girl, but that he was consorting with her in public. Where other Harvard men had casual relationships with a variety of pick-ups and kept women, Tessie quickly became Will's steady companion. They spent time together in Cambridge and Boston and he took her with him when he traveled to New York on vacations and to New Haven to cheer on Harvard teams against Yale.

"He didn't care what the world thought," Anne Apperson recalled. As he was doing nothing wrong, he had nothing to hide, even from his mother. "He evidently talked perfectly frankly with his mother — shocked her to death. She was very stiff-laced, very proper, very disapproving of anything that wasn't perfectly straight and above board. But he evidently told her, from Harvard right on, or else someone else told her, and she would speak to him about it, and he would say yes — he never denied any of it."

Though Phoebe had tried her best to make her boy into a gentleman, he was his father's son as well as hers and preferred, like George Hearst, to do as he pleased when it came to women. At age twenty, he already carried about him the sense of invulnerability that would remain with him for the rest of his life. He was charming, gifted, wealthy, and, though thin, handsome, tall, and quite good-looking. With the exception of the one horrid year at prep school in New Hampshire, he had led a charmed life and always had his way. He could not imagine that any harm might come from a relationship with a Cambridge girl he cared for. He was devoted to Tessie from the very beginning, and had no desire — nor, he thought, any need — to hide her away. He "took her everywhere — and that was a constant fight with his mother, who simply could not stand it."[36]

Phoebe, beside herself with fear that her boy was going to do himself irreparable harm, corresponded directly with Will's friends. She was worried more about Will's indiscretions than the fact that he was having an affair. Though, according to Anne Apperson, she knew that Jack Follansbee had introduced Will to Tessie, she did not hold this against him. It was not Jack's fault that Will did not know how to behave. Her major concern in early 1884, as Will entered the second semester of his sophomore year, was the anonymous letters she had been receiving. The letters themselves have not survived, but the accusations made in them were so offensive that

Phoebe asked Jack to burn the correspondence in which she referred to them. She was, she told Jack, mortally afraid that copies of these letters had also been forwarded to officials at Harvard.[37]

She also shared her fears in letters to Orrin Peck who was, with Gene Lent, Will's oldest friend. Phoebe had, in 1862, met two-year-old Orrin and his parents on the Panama steamer that took her and her husband to San Francisco. She had remained close to the Pecks ever since. She provided Mrs. Peck with a monthly allowance, Janet, Orrin's sister, with music lessons in Europe, and Orrin with an allowance large enough to support him in Munich where he studied painting. In return for her friendship — and patronage — Phoebe expected Orrin and Janet, as she did Jack Follansbee, to report back to her on Will.

Orrin, as he would all his life, tried his best to reassure Phoebe that she "had no reason to cry over what dear Will does. He will *never* do anything to disgrace himself or his friends. . . . Nastiness is not born in him and I would hate him if he didn't possess a mixture of boyishness and devilishness — neatly spiced with a college wittiness surging here and there on to wickedness."[38]

"Nastiness," the word Peck used in his letters defending his friend, had a particular connotation one hundred years ago, "denoting something disgusting in point of smell, taste, or even moral character." It was "not considered a proper word to be used in the presence of ladies."[39] Peck used it no doubt because Phoebe had already raised the issue of Will's immorality. She was frightened that despite her best precautions her son was following in the footsteps of his rough-hewn, Forty-Niner father. While his Harvard classmates had learned from their fathers how to behave in society, she feared that all Will had learned from his was a healthy contempt for society and its rules of deportment.

Though he was never much of a drinker, Will's behavior in Cambridge, like his father's in San Francisco, remained on the outer edge of respectability. He kept his shirtfronts clean and his boots polished, but his entertainments in his rooms were too frequent and too boisterous, his cigars too large, and his spending habits excessive even by Harvard standards. When, in the fall of his junior year, he was elected vice president of the Intercollegiate Base Ball Association, he attributed his victory entirely to his having hosted a steady succession of drinking parties in his rooms. As he wrote his mother, "My long swiping [slang for drinking] has at last received its reward."[40] Gene Lent had had to take a leave of absence from the college to gain control of his own drinking. Ostensibly to help his friend, but perhaps because he too was drinking too much, Will told his mother that he too had "signed the pledge — total abstinence . . . I think it will be the saving of Gene if he sticks it out and I think he will. Ginger ale is good enough for me nowadays, and I'm not too high for plain cold water."[41]

To stop drinking in college — or even to learn to drink moderately — was a rare accomplishment for a man of Hearst's social position and one he was proud of. His father was a heavy drinker and had been all his life, as were most of his friends at Harvard. Will's decision, made in college and adhered to the rest of his life, to give up drinking himself but host social gatherings at which liquor was abundant, put him at an enormous advantage. Sober, he was able to control events while those around him lost their bearings.

Will and his mother corresponded regularly during his years at Harvard. Will complained about the weather, gossiped about his friends, and asked for money. Phoebe grumbled about his profligate ways and sent him exactly what he had asked for.

Will's letters were carefully crafted, filled with irony bordering on sarcasm, and lengthy descriptions of the New England landscape and the weather he heartily despised. "I am beginning to get awfully tired of this place," he wrote early in his first year, "and I long to get out West somewhere where I can stretch myself without coming in contact with the narrow walls with which the prejudice of the beaneaters has surrounded us. I long to get out in the woods and breathe the fresh mountain air and listen to the moaning of the pines. It makes me almost crazy with homesickness when I think of it and I hate this weak, pretty New England scenery with its gentle rolling hills, its pea green foliage, its vistas, tame enough to begin with but totally disfigured by houses and parts which could not be told apart save for the respective inhabitants. I hate it as I do a weak, pretty face without force or character. I long to see our own woods, the jagged rocks and towering mountains, the majestic pines, the grand impressive scenery of the 'far west.' I shall never live anywhere but in California and I like to be away for a while only to appreciate the more when I return."

All this complaining was, as it usually was in his letters to his mother, prelude to complaints about the state of his finances. He regularly confessed to managing his allowance poorly and as regularly pledged to do better next time. "I think I shall take a Political Economy course in hopes that it will teach me to regulate my money affairs better. I have a good deal of money lent, without any interest, and I fear with very little thanks." There proceeded a long explanation of what had happened to the extra $50 that Phoebe had sent him, the gist of which was that he had nothing left. "Oh my," he concluded, "Harvard is no place for a poor boy."[42]

William Randolph Hearst was not a poor boy, but he felt strapped nonetheless because his expenses were so extraordinary. In response to another letter from his mother asking him to account for the $150 monthly allowance and the $500 extra she had sent him, he explained that he had paid $200 for room and board and over $100 on "dues" for Harvard's crew, baseball, and football clubs. He had also taken a trip to New York to order some clothes, paid $30 to subscribe to "a German, a French and two English papers," probably for the *Lampoon* reading room. His D.K.E. fee was $50; he and Eugene had given "a punch down in his room, which cost us about $20 a piece"; he had spent $15 for "provisions for my room," $14 for "a loving cup," and "had two or three dinners in town and several things which I can't remember now but will write about when I come across."[43]

There was a lightness of tone in these letters; Will's pleas were insistent, yet gentle. He did not demand money as his due, nor, if his letters are to be trusted, did he regard unlimited funding as his birthright. Each letter painstakingly offers an elaborate accounting of prior spending before establishing the need for new funds. The arguments are presented clearly and forcibly, but with reluctance. As he told his mother in the spring of his sophomore year, he "hated to talk about money in my letters. You think I'm so mercenary," but then proceeded to explain how his allowance had been eaten up by doctor's bills for the chronic sore throat that had been bothering him since he got to Cambridge: "My doctor's bills! oh! those doctor's bills! Oliver [his Boston doctor] I owe $50. The Springfield doctor $30. And the Cambridge doctor marks at present $18, but is steadily rising. Every sneeze costs somewhere between fifty cents and one dollar."[44]

Will was never without a sense of humor in this correspondence, in stark contrast to his mother who displayed no levity at all. Though her son was now a Harvard man — and a rather successful one at that — Phoebe refused to let go. The more buoyantly self-confident and independent he became, the more she complained about his callous disregard for those who loved him. Her boy had been her best friend, her confidant, her traveling companion. She was not prepared to let too much distance get between them. She worried most of all that her son would not be able to cope without his mother watching over him. He had a tendency, she feared, to let things slide. He was forever putting off important tasks. In one particularly revealing letter, she chastised him for not writing his father to remind him of his upcoming twenty-first birthday. Had he written that letter, she suggested, he would have gotten a better present than the $200 he received. (He had received another $100 from Phoebe for a total of $300, a huge sum of money for a college sophomore's birthday in 1884, when a year's tuition at

Harvard cost $150 and full board in Memorial Hall, where the freshmen dined, $200.)

Will's failure to write his father was the least of his sins. He had failed to visit her dear old friends in Cambridge, Mr. and Mrs. Anthony, whom he had promised to call on. He was not writing home often enough, and when he did, forgot to answer the questions his mother had asked. "It grieves me deeply that you *never* regard any promises made to your mother. If you ever realize how I feel about it, I cannot understand how it is possible for you to be so utterly indifferent to my wishes. I am mortified and grieved beyond your comprehension." Her letter continues, growing shriller and shriller. "I wish you to let me know when you will start home. I *insist* that Rachel [his maid at Harvard] is to do your packing, for she knows my wishes about things you are to bring. When will you start and what route do you intend coming? *Answer.* There is so much I am anxious to know about you but would only be wasting time and strength to ask. I hope you will remember about not needing *thin summer* clothing here. You know last year you could not wear your very light suits. Did you find your overcoat? Of course I know you will never answer this question, but it *may* remind you that you need it and *must* find it. I shall be happy when we hear from you."[45]

She did hear from him soon — in a conciliatory apologetic letter he mailed two days before his twenty-first birthday: "You must know that my intentions are good and that I mean to write regularly. But if, as it is said, the road to a certain place is paved with good intentions, I think I must have contributed largely to the improvement of the paths in that region.

"The days slip by so easily. When the recitations are over the base ball begins and so between work and play the good intentions are neglected and never bear fruit. . . .

"I have the dumps today and I feel rather homesick and I wish I could enjoy my birthday at home and with you and father instead of with a lot of fellows who don't care whether I am twenty one or thirty so long as the dinner is good and the wine plenty. . . .

"I won't write any further or I will relapse into a funereal strain inconsistent with the rejoicing and hilarity which is supposed to accompany ones twenty first birthday.

"I for my part don't see why anyone should rejoice on entering the duties and responsibilities which are supposed to attend the age of manhood? I should prefer to be nineteen again and be twenty one only when it is necessary to leave College and begin the work of life in earnest.

"Well goodbye and expect to hear from your reformed child almost constantly."[46]

§3§

"Something Where I Could Make a Name"

WILL ENTERED HARVARD with only the vaguest idea of why he was there or what he would do after graduation. College had been his mother's idea and he and his father had gone along in large part because they had nothing better to offer as an alternative. George was not enamored of the idea of higher education, but in this as in so many other matters concerning their boy, he deferred to his wife. Having attended only a few years of common school in Missouri, he had little advice to offer Will in Cambridge, other than to warn him against taking philosophy and to instead study something practical like Spanish or engineering. Harvard was, he feared, preparing his son only for a life of leisure. Will tried to reassure his father that this was not the case. "I hope Papa will understand that I know that I may have to work my way in the world and that I do not feel terrified at the prospect," he wrote his mother during his first year, "although, of course, I should prefer to have enough money to be able to turn my time to politics or science or something where I could make a name."[1]

What Will wanted was an allowance large enough to allow him to live like a gentleman. He had no intention of remaining idle forever, but neither did he plan on having to work for a living. His father had already accumulated more money than he or Phoebe or Will could ever spend. In signaling to his father that he might be interested in turning his time to politics, Will was making a safe bet for the future. Following a not uncommon career trajectory in the West, George Hearst had two years earlier returned from the digging fields to devote his fortune and remaining years to politics. It was not unreasonable to believe that he would welcome and support his son should he decide to follow in his footsteps.

Although he had been away from politics for almost a decade and a half,

George Hearst had forgotten nothing. To curry the favor of Democratic leaders whose support he needed to win the party's nomination for governor or senator, George Hearst in October of 1880 bought the failing *Evening Examiner,* the only Democratic paper in San Francisco, and converted it into a morning paper. In San Francisco, as in almost every other American city in the late nineteenth century, the key to winning elections was getting out the vote. Most voters knew well before the election whom they were going to vote for — if, that is, they were going to vote. It was the task of the machines — from the boss on top to the local precinct and ward captains — to get them to the polls. To accomplish this, they needed the assistance of a daily newspaper to keep the party's faithful informed of the candidate's comings and goings, of upcoming rallies, of the issues, such as they were, and to remind them of the paramount importance of casting their votes.

With a newspaper of his own — and plenty of money to throw around to the local Democratic clubs — George Hearst became a major political power. Had he been better educated or more literate, he might have taken charge of the *Examiner* himself, turning it into a twelve-month-a-year campaign organ for himself and his party. Instead he appointed his trusted associate and private attorney Clarence Greathouse as editor.

The *Examiner* had been losing money for some time. Though Greathouse was able to build its circulation, he could not rescue it financially. When Phoebe complained that the money could be better spent elsewhere, George assured her that the paper would, in time, turn a profit: "I think the *Examiner* will be good property after this [and we] will get all of the patranige, [sic] so you see we have some good luck. Some people are very jelous [sic] and some talk of starting another democratic paper. I say go ahead, they will soon go. It can't be done by talk, as we know, and but few will put up the coin. I hope the Boy will be able, as I think he will, to take charge of the paper soon after he leaves college, as it will give him more [power] than anything else."[2]

While it is clear from this letter — and from several others — that George Hearst intended or rather hoped that his son would take over the *Examiner,* Will Hearst would, in the years to come, insist that his decision to become a publisher had been met by adamant opposition from his father. Will declined to give his father or anyone else credit for his entrance into newspaper publishing because doing so would have diminished his portrait of himself as a self-made man. Like other children of great men, Hearst both fed off and disowned his inheritance.[3]

* * *

Phoebe tried to dissuade her husband from running for office again. He would, she feared, not only make a fool of himself on the campaign stump, but impoverish the family by spending money to buy votes. As usual, Will sided with his mother and joined her in ridiculing George's political ambitions. He agreed that George Hearst had no business wasting the family fortune on futile attempts to buy himself a senate seat. While Will admitted that he too had extravagant tastes, they were not, he wrote his mother, "half as costly nor yet as exasperating as Senatorial aspirations. A terrible disease this, and I'm told it runs in the family. Every man, in this world, has his specialty, and when a man is fortunate enough to have found it, he is foolish beyond measure to leave it for something else. . . . Why my father should abandon the nag which has carried him faithfully for so many years to mount the fickle animal that has thrown him once is more than I can understand. It is more than folly. It is tempting providence. If Thackeray had attempted politics his name would have been buried beneath his ashes. If Jay Gould had fostered a mania for literature, the acme of his success would probably have been a serial story in the Boys and Girls weekly."[4]

Though Will did as his mother asked and tried to talk George out of running for office, he was not entirely displeased when his father overrode his and Phoebe's opposition. Father and son had in common a love of politics, unswerving loyalty to the Democratic party, and undying hostility to the unholy alliance of the Republicans and the railroad magnates. They were probably never closer than in the fall of 1884, when, at opposite ends of the continent, they campaigned for Grover Cleveland for the presidency.

Just as George Hearst, with his own newspaper boosting his candidacy, was the most visible Democrat in San Francisco in the fall of 1884, so was his son, with an all but unlimited budget and a flair for the spectacular, the most recognizable Democrat at Harvard. As only 28 of the more than 200 members of Hearst's Harvard class identified themselves as Democrats, it was almost inevitable that Will would assume a leadership role on campus. "I am campaigning very hard, and hope to carry Massachusetts for Cleveland," he reported gleefully to his mother. "We have organized a club of forty members which includes all the democratic dudes in college and, for a fact, most of the swells are for Cleveland. . . . Tell pa that a few hundred to push the campaign would come in very handy."[5]

His efforts — and his father's money — resulted in his first political triumph: a mammoth flag raising, bonfire, and parade in the center of Harvard Yard. "At eight o'clock, in response to the murmurs of the mob," he wrote to his parents, the day after the rally, "the orator of the evening was introduced and made a few remarks on Mr. Cleveland's honesty and ability, holding him up in contrast to Mr. Blaine [the Republican nominee]. He finished his speech by proposing three cheers for Grover and as the crowd howled in response, the band played, rockets shot up into the night and the glorious flag unfurled and waved acknowledgment. . . . Finally as the evening was drawing to a close a gentleman in the crowd mounted the rostrum and said that it gave him great pleasure to note the interest taken in Cleveland's election by the young men as well as the old. That here was an example where Papa Hearst in one end of the continent and Sonny Hearst at the other were both working in the same great cause. He then proposed three cheers for Father and Son and I was quite overcome and ran away and hid so that I wouldn't have to make a speech and this ended the flag raising."[6]

These were heady and expensive times for young Will. He had not only been taken into yet another new club, for which, he hinted, he might need a raise in his allowance "for the better enjoyment of its privileges," but had spent a great deal of money on the Cleveland campaign and bet even more on its outcome. "If Cleveland is elected," he wrote his mother, "I shall be a millionaire, if not I shall be a pauper."[7]

Cleveland was elected in November of 1884, but unfortunately for George Hearst California had gone Republican, which meant that a Republican would be returned to Washington. (The state legislatures, not the voters, elected their state's senators in 1884.) Will was disappointed for his father and for himself. Directly contradicting the information he had earlier given his mother, he now instructed her to "tell papa that his political information isn't reliable and that I have lost almost as much money on the California election as I won on the general result. And now with my customary plea. Give me one penny for bread. This is to say send me a few dollars to defray the expenses of a club life and a political campaign."[8]

Despite the jocular tone of his correspondence, Will's interest in politics was serious. A sophomore theme written after the election displayed a grasp of national politics remarkable for a college student. Having grown up in California politics where the Republican party was owned by the Southern Pacific Railroad and the Democrats were for sale to his own father, Hearst had no illusions about the way political parties worked. In his sophomore theme, which was not turned in until late in the first semester of his junior year, he argued that the 1884 presidential election in which Republican Mugwumps had deserted the party rather than support James G. Blaine, a candidate they believed hopelessly corrupt, demonstrated that Independents now held "the balance of power [because] they represent the unselfish politicians of the country and are the party averse to corruption and fraud. As a consequence both parties will have to cater to the wishes of the Independents, that is to say to the wishes of the educated unprejudiced nonpartisan element of politics." At age twenty-one, young Will was already laying out the political route he would travel twenty years later, when he ran for office on an Independent line.[9]

In later years, Hearst explained in a signed article in his newspapers that he had not been asked to leave Harvard "because he was a dumb cluck . . . That was only part of the reason. The rest of the reason was politics." The Cleveland rally he had organized in the Yard had, he claimed, been so loud, so boisterous, so exuberant, and so conspicuous an occasion that "everyone saw it and heard it — and everybody complained about it. We had a great banner stretched across the street in front of Mrs. Buckman's boarding house, where your college editor lived . . . We had fireworks. The house was fired — just a little, not much; and your columnist was fired — much. There was no apparent appreciation of patriots in Harvard."

Cora Older, Hearst's handpicked biographer, offered a parallel but slightly more believable version of the events leading up to his expulsion. According to Older, Will was not expelled after the Cleveland rally, but "rusticated," or temporarily suspended. When his suspension ended, however, "he returned to Harvard the same rollicking youth. Again he majored in jokes, pranks and sociability. He was the leader of a group bent on converting Harvard into a play world. He himself seldom drank even beer, but his friends were Harvard's merriest roysterers. More and more were their misdemeanors held to be a violation of discipline and order." One of those pranks, which Older didn't mention but others did, involved the delivery of customized chamber pots to his professors, each of them elaborately embossed on the inside bottom with the name of the recipient.[10]

Though the stories of Hearst's pranks at Harvard were widely reported and may, indeed, have had some truth to them, there is no evidence that Will was expelled from Harvard because of his practical jokes. On the contrary, the Harvard records indicate that he was placed on academic probation in November of his sophomore year, a full twelve months before the Cleveland rally. His problem at Harvard was not his pranks, but his failure to pay attention to his course work. His grades fell off badly in his second year. His highest mark was a 70% in Chemistry 2. He received a 61% in Rhetoric, a 66% in Political Economy 1, a mid-year grade of 57% in History, and a 60% in Professor Charles Eliot Norton's Fine Arts course. In July, his transcript noted that he had been placed on probation for failing to "satisfactorily . . . perform his work in Themes" and being absent from his Political Economy 4 examination.[11]

With the headstrong confidence that would see him through future crises, Hearst returned to Harvard in the fall of 1884. Instead of lightening his course load or cutting back on his extracurricular activities, he enrolled in six courses and organized a "club" to campaign for the Democrats in the November elections. "I am so busy and am working so hard," he wrote his mother, "that my hair is all falling out and my head is becoming as bumpy as an old potato."[12]

Phoebe knew better. In reply to Will's letter about "working so hard," she informed him that she had had a visit from Harold Wheeler, a family friend and president of the Harvard Club of San Francisco: "He *kindly* remarked that you had what was called an *incentive* to study this year. Of course I knew he meant that you *must* work or be suspended and I am very much afraid it will be the latter. You cannot realize my extreme anxiety about you. It would almost kill me if you should not go through college in a creditable manner."[13]

While Will showed no concern about his future at Harvard, Phoebe was panicked. She put the family mansion on the market and hired a suite of rooms at the Brunswick Hotel in Madison Square in New York City. Although she believed she could better supervise Will's activities from the East Coast, her move to New York backfired. Instead of spending his weekends and vacations making up the course work he owed, Will now had a built-in excuse to leave Cambridge to visit his mother in New York.[14] Either he believed that Harvard would never ask him to leave or he had decided it wasn't worth his trouble to stay. He had, it appears, made up his mind to move to San Francisco and take over the *Examiner* for his father. Earlier that spring, he had asked his mother to show "Papa" the letter he had written about his success at the *Lampoon* "and tell him just to wait till Gene [Lent] and I get hold of the old *Examiner* and we'll boom her in the same way — she needs it."[15]

Though George was not about to let his son give up on Harvard — he abhorred quitters — he was more anxious than ever to secure Will's help on the *Examiner*. In a particularly self-pitying letter to Phoebe, he complained that with his boy away at college and his wife in New York, he was "quite lonsam at all times. . . . What is a home without a wife and baby? . . . At all events I want to see the Boy very much. So anxious for him to get through. The *Examiner* is about the hardest thing of all to no [sic] what to do with or how to do it. . . . Can you find out about the newspaper men?" The *Examiner* was in need of "a man that understands the printing business from the bottom up and all the way through, so as to be able to take full charge of the paper. . . . We know such a man is hard to get. . . . Perhaps Will can attend to it?"[16]

With his father's encouragement, Will became unpaid consultant and editor-in-waiting for the *Examiner*. In November of 1884, he wrote his mother that he had "made the preliminary arrangements with E. L. Thayer, President of, and chief contributor to, the *Harvard Lampoon* to send the *Examiner* a weekly letter during a year's trip to Europe beginning next summer. Thayer, although very young, is already noted for his letters, some of which have appeared in the *New York Times*. He is willing to write for us at the rate of $10 a column. He is very witty in a quiet way and makes his letters very entertaining."[17] Will was already a good judge of talent. When, only a few years later, he took over the *Examiner*, one of his first hires was his friend "Phinny" Thayer. Though ill health forced Thayer to resign from his staff position at the *Examiner*, he continued to send in a weekly humor column. He is remembered today for his poem "Casey at the Bat," which was first published in the *San Francisco Examiner*.

Though Will should have been studying for his upcoming examinations and making up his incompletes, he spent the Christmas holidays of his junior year in New York, interviewing potential editors for the *Examiner*. Phoebe was so delighted by the interest and the "anxiety" her boy exhibited in his new task that she let him stay an extra three days instead of returning to Cambridge to catch up on his course work. "He says," Phoebe reported to George, "it seems dreadful to stay another year in college when he might be at work doing something to help you along with all the business you have."[18]

From New York, Will wrote a long letter to his father urging him to hire Ballard Smith, who had been the assistant managing editor at the *New York Herald* before moving to Joseph Pulitzer's *New York World,* where he was managing editor. "The most striking objection to Mr. Ballard Smith is that he is very high priced. But I am convinced and I think you are that the paper must be built up and that cheap labor has been entirely ineffectual. The paper requires a head that has ability, enterprise and experience — that has all three. Let one of these factors be absent and the thing will score another failure. Naturally such a man commands a high salary and you must reconcile yourself, either to paying it or giving up the paper. . . . You could not even sell the paper at present so I think this is the only thing to be done. I will give you the benefit of my large head and great experience on this subject — and not charge you a cent. Mr. Ballard Smith will state his terms and I would say, 'Mr. Smith, I guarantee you this amount and promise you a certain interest in the paper in case you make it a glittering success. You are to have entire control of the paper, Mr. Smith, with the privilege of employing whomever you please.'"

As if he were the self-made millionaire and George the twenty-year-old who had never worked a day in his life, Will guaranteed his father that if his advice were followed, the newspaper would "in one year . . . be paying expenses. By that time I will be out of college and if I have succeeded in developing any talent for writing, I will take a minor position in the office and endeavor to learn the business." Will closed his letter by requesting that his father keep him informed on the future of the *Examiner.* "I shall expect an answer to all these questions for I feel that I ought to know a little of your business by the time I get out of college which is not now far off."[19]

When three and a half weeks had passed without any response to his long list of suggestions for improving the *Examiner,* Will wrote again. Though his tone was softened a bit by the self-deprecating style he had begun to cultivate, it is difficult not to discern his bitterness at being ignored by his father. "I wrote you not long ago and inserted in my letter a mild request for an answer, but the answer never came. I stated a few business points that I thought might be of interest and gave you some ideas on the way to conduct your private affairs and yet you did not respond. Will you kindly take some slight notice of your only son? Will you be so good as to answer his letters and let him know that you at least appreciate his kindness in allowing you to draw upon his large experience and gigantic intellect?" Will closed his letter by asking again that he be given at once, as part of his inheritance, an income-producing property: "I shall probably graduate from college a mild inoffensive creature with a large hole in my pocket and it would be a great relief to me to know that I was possessed of something that will not slip through and leave me alone in a cold cold world. Please commit the following to memory and take one every night before going to bed. . . . Procure some kind of a ranch, mine, line of steam ships or something that Jack [Follansbee] and I can go into."[20]

There was no answer from his father.

In February of 1885, the Harvard faculty, noting that Will had still not made up the deficiencies in his course work, voted to keep him on probation until the end of the year. Will responded, not by doing any more schoolwork, but by taking on a major role as Pretzel, the German valet in the Hasty Pudding's spring production of "Joan of Arc, or the Old Maid of New Orleans."[21]

In mid-March, still having heard nothing from his father, he sent him a telegram, in care of Alfred A. Wheeler, George Hearst's chief assistant, asking for permission to leave Harvard a year early — as his mother had earlier suggested — to help out at the *Examiner*. Will did not write his father directly because he had learned, from bitter experience, that such requests disappeared unanswered. Wheeler, as Will had expected, got an immediate answer: "Gave your father yesterday the . . . telegram you had sent expressing a desire to come here and 'go to work.' I asked him what he replied and he said 'Tell him to stand in like a man and stick to his studies to the end.'" Wheeler could not help but add that he agreed with George entirely. He too urged Will to stay at Harvard "for your own sake, if not to gratify the hopes and wishes which you know are dearest to your mother's heart. . . . I am perfectly aware how entirely within your powers the attainment of that degree is. If there had been any fair division of your time between amusement and study, I am certain nobody at Harvard would have found the taking of his degree an easier matter than yourself."[22]

On March 31, the Harvard faculty voted that "Hearst, Junior . . . be informed that probation will be closed at the end of the year, unless the Faculty expressly vote otherwise."[23] The next day, Will left Cambridge with sixty members of the Hasty Pudding Club to spend his Easter break in New York City performing "Joan of Arc" at the University Club. Phoebe was concerned with the way he looked and wrote him so from her New York hotel the day after he returned to Cambridge. There was no longer any anger in her voice. She was transformed back into the doting mother worrying herself sick about her boy:

"My darling boy, I am so very lonely since you went away and my thoughts are constantly with you. I hope you can write to me tomorrow if only a few lines. . . . I hope you had a comfortable journey and began work in earnest and on time the following morning." She had sent his cutaway coat to the tailors to have a button put on and would forward it with his laundry as soon as it was ready. "If you come down again soon have your clothes packed in time to get in night dress, etc., that you really need. Be sure to send 'Charley' [his pet alligator, who had died] to be embalmed. He will decay and cause illness if left in the house. *Don't fail* to see Dr. Oliver [Will's physician and a prominent member of the Cambridge community] and tell him the whole history of our troubles. Let me know about your bills and if you come down in two weeks you shall have the money, or if not it shall be sent. I keep feeling anxious about how badly you were looking. You were out every night and nearly all night too, before you came here and then up late while here. Do take care of your health. Life is not worth living if one has ill health and there is time enough to 'have fun' and it will be more fun if you take it gradually. This is not a lecture dear, only a loving reminder that I am anxious for you to have all that is best in life, in the best way."[24]

Although her letter to Will was without recrimination, Phoebe was becoming increasingly vexed by the men in her life. As she wrote Janet Peck, Orrin Peck's sister and one of her confidantes, she wanted desperately "to pack up and go over to Munich and stay at least one year, though there does not seem to be much prospect of my being able to go. . . . After Will finishes college in June '86, it may be that we can take a trip. This will depend upon circumstances." To protect herself from the realization that her boy was now beyond her control, she emphasized his devotion to his mother: "Will comes down every two weeks and stays from Saturday morning until Monday morning. The Dean of the College gives him permission to do this. He spent his Easter vacation here and enjoyed it very much and it was a comfort to have him with me for he is more thoughtful than ever before in his life."[25]

What Phoebe refused to admit to her friend was her fear that her son, like his father before him, had been swallowed up by a male culture defined by deceit, bad habits, and poor manners. George had promised but failed to join her in New York. Will, after agreeing to celebrate his birthday with her in New York, had not only failed to show up, but had not even had the decency to telegram her not to expect him. Chastised for his lack of consideration of the woman who loved him most in this world, he jokingly spun out a convoluted story about closed telegraph offices and a thesis of 150 pages and reassured her that she had no cause to worry about his missing his birthday celebration: "The boys who are thoroughly alive to the importance of this occasion are going to give me a small dinner at the club and I assure you that I will not get 'full' nor will I in any other way injure my constitution, damage my reputation, or stain my immaculate record."[26]

His junior year ended almost as it had begun. While he passed Forensics with a 74%, Natural History 8 with a 64%, and made up his sophomore themes, he failed Natural History 18 with a 40% and did not sit for his final examinations in Political Economy 3, History 13, or Chemistry 1.[27]

At term's end, Will left Cambridge to spend the summer in San Francisco. In late August, he received a letter from J. Rathbone, a classmate, who had heard a rumor that he had been expelled and wanted him to know that "little tears" had been shed on his behalf. Tongue in cheek, Rathbone wrote of his dismay "that the college has failed to appreciate your ability to guide the youths in the college to a higher standard — morally and otherwise. If any such action has been taken it is a dear shame and I should be most proud and happy to say as much to that August body of blockheads."[28]

Will returned to Cambridge in the fall, though he knew that he would not be permitted to register. In early October, he reported tersely to his parents in San Francisco that he had been "requested not to return. Saw the President, said if I went to a good climate and studied with a competent instructor, I should probably be allowed to pass my examinations in June. Shall I engage instructor? What salary are you willing to pay?"[29]

Phoebe responded by return telegram. "Have the Faculty met and made final decision?" She already knew the answer, as the rest of her telegram made clear. "Can you study in New York or where best to go? Willing to pay salary that is right for best instruction. Shall I go east?"[30]

Phoebe and George did what they could to get their son back in Harvard's good graces. George packed and shipped — at great expense — a four-hundred-pound gift box of mining specimens for Harvard's chemistry laboratory. Phoebe contacted Dr. Oliver, who on the Hearsts' behalf met with the Dean. "The Faculty wish to get William away from this class as they think his influence is bad," Oliver reported after his meeting. "The Dean says he was repeatedly warned and told he must do differently but the warning was without effect. He did not consider William a 'mauvais sujih,' [a bad lot] but a young man who was heedless, thoughtless in certain ways and thoroughly indifferent to his college studies and consequently a bad example to his class-mates." Dr. Oliver reassured Phoebe, as best he could, that the Dean thought Will to be "morally all right." He was being expelled for academic failures exacerbated by "heedlessness." The Dean suggested that Will take a leave of absence and, if the president and the faculty agreed, return to Harvard a year later and graduate in 1887.[31]

Phoebe, who had returned to a rented house in San Francisco for the summer and early fall, packed her bags immediately and departed for New York City. Her initial interview with Will confirmed her suspicions that he had been unfairly picked on. She was outraged, she wrote George, to find out that when their boy "went to see the Dean, he was obliged to wait until that stern individual was ready to look up and speak to him. The Dean then said, 'You here again . . .' He would not give Will any encouragement and evidently wanted to get rid of him." Fortunately, President Eliot was "very kind" and suggested to Will that he leave Cambridge for "New York, Philadelphia, or Baltimore and secure a competent Tutor and prepare for the final examinations next June."

Phoebe was prepared to let Will stay in Cambridge to work with a tutor, but warned George that he must cooperate by cutting off the boy's magnificent allowance:

> If he continues to spend too much money and neglect study it will not be my fault and you can take the blame upon yourself. I will not be held responsible when you go on giving him the means to do just as he pleases. . . . If he is to have $250 per month, I can tell you that he will *not* study much. . . . It is only throwing temptation in his way, for he will come to New York and meet the fellows and have dinners and go on in a way that will surely bring us sorrow. He informed me today that he should come here for the short vacation at Thanksgiving and the long one during the holidays. I remarked that he had been enjoying one long vacation all of his life. . . . I am willing to do anything that may be best for Will but it is discouraging to have him utterly indifferent and thinking only of his own pleasures.[32]

Phoebe could not quite make up her mind whether her boy was an innocent led astray by his Harvard companions or a ringleader in their escapades. Whatever the case, she determined to separate him from the "boys" who kept him from his studies. "The fellows will not let him alone," she complained to George in late October. She decided that the only way to get him to study was to remove him from Cambridge to New York because "there are no college men here and not likely to be for some time."

Will agreed to do as she requested and moved into Phoebe's suite at the Brunswick:

> The last three days he has done splendidly. At ten o'clock goes to bed, gets up promptly at eight, exercises with dumb bells for half an hour, breakfasts at nine, goes out to walk, comes in and commences to study at ten. We lunch alone, he goes out and walks for another hour, then studies until six. In the evening we both go out for a short walk or "drive." Then read or write until ten . . . We have agreed to go to the theatre only on Saturday evenings . . . If I can possibly induce him to continue in this way, he will do twice the work that would be done at College and he will improve in health.[33]

In November, Phoebe traveled to Cambridge to see President Charles Eliot who was "extremely kind and agreeable, asked numerous questions and made some suggestions." Even with his dismal academic performance, Harvard was still not ready to send Will Hearst away. She returned to New York, filled with hope once again, only to have it dashed when Will, after insisting that he be allowed to bring three of his Harvard friends to New York City for the horse show, spent five full days carousing with them instead of studying. "During that time," she wrote George in San Francisco, "he spent two hundred dollars and the bills for their rooms and restaurant charges were sent to me . . . It was simply outrageous . . . For a day or two after they left Will could not settle down to do much and he looked badly. Late hours and dissipation affect him. Of course I don't know how much he drank, but I do know he was not intoxicated at all, nor even funny as they call it, but even the amount he must have drank did him no good. Theatres, horse show, late suppers and women, consumed the two hundred dollars quickly."[34]

Persuaded that Will would never be able to get past the distractions of New York nightlife, Phoebe took him to Baltimore to look for lodgings, then to Washington, D.C., where they rented a house and waited for George to join them. Senator John Miller, who had been elected to the Senate in 1884 by the Republican majority in the California state senate, was dying. Since vacant seats were filled by the governor, who was a Democrat, it was widely believed that George Hearst would be named to replace him. Will wrote his father at some length, forgetting for the moment that he had just been expelled from Harvard:

> We have decided to spend the winter in Washington, not only because the climate there is delightful and very conducive to mental exertion, but because I will have there opportunities of hearing the debates in Congress, familiarizing myself with legislative methods of procedure, and thus at once assisting my present college studies and preparing the way for a brilliant entree into the political arena, some time in the future. My three ambitions, as you know, are law, politics and journalism, and under favorable circumstances it might be possible to combine all three. And so while you are serving your country from the Senator's bench, the pride and support of your declining years will be expanding himself so as to be able to wear gracefully the mantle that will one day fall upon him, and not be completely hidden by its ample folds. In fact, we may one day read in the papers that "The Honorable Geo. Hearst, having served twelve years as Senator of the United States is about to retire from public life. The loss of such an ardent advocate of their rights will be greatly deplored by the people throughout the Union, but they will be partially compensated by the knowledge that his son has just been elected to Congress and has devoted himself to the cause which the elder Hearst has so nobly upheld."

To prepare for this eventuality, Will had been "on the lookout for a suitable residence for the Senator and Congressman that are to be." The house he had chosen was especially desirable because it was both imposing and unassuming:

> Imposing, that it may seem to appreciate the importance of its position in sheltering two such immortals, and unassuming as if it were at the same [time] sensible of the views of the occupants towards the people. . . . More-

over, it possesses still another attraction. It is surrounded on all sides by land belonging to us and this gives the impression that we might have built a larger house had we so desired but that with true democratic humility we had limited ourselves to the existing modest structure.[35]

Though he was ostensibly prepping to take final examinations at Harvard, Will was in fact spending his days — his evenings were devoted to the theater — studying the newspaper industry, in preparation for his return to San Francisco to take over his father's newspaper. His text was Joseph Pulitzer's *New York World*.

Pulitzer, a Hungarian immigrant, had come to the United States during the Civil War, volunteered for the Union Army, served for a year, then gone to St. Louis, where he became a reporter for Carl Schurz's German-language daily, the *Westliche Post*. He bought the *St. Louis Evening Post* at a bankruptcy auction in 1878 and merged it with the *Dispatch*. By 1881, the paper was the leading evening paper in St. Louis and was turning a healthy profit. But Pulitzer, still only in his middle thirties, was restless. His child, Ralph, suffered from bad asthma; his wife was regularly snubbed by the city's elite because her husband's newspaper was too vulgar and too radical; and Pulitzer himself suffered from nervous exhaustion and failing eyesight. When, in 1882, his brilliant managing editor and chief editorial writer, John Cockerill, shot and killed Alonzo Slayback, a local attorney with whom the paper had been trading insults, Pulitzer had had enough. Though Cockerill was never indicted for murder — he claimed that he had shot Slayback in self-defense — the scandal had a disastrous effect on the newspaper, which lost not only its editor, but a good number of subscribers.[36]

Pulitzer had long dreamed of leaving St. Louis and moving to New York where he could "speak to a nation" instead of a Midwest city. In 1883, while Hearst was in his freshman year at Harvard, Pulitzer bought the *New York World* from financier Jay Gould for $346,000, hardly a bargain for a paper with a circulation of about 11,000. Pulitzer knew what he was doing. New York City had a huge and growing working-class and immigrant population which was virtually ignored by the city's other dailies. Pulitzer intended to put out a morning newspaper for them.

As a successful immigrant entrepreneur who had worked his way up the social ladder, Pulitzer understood, as perhaps no other publisher of daily papers, that working people wanted to be educated and entertained, not condescended to or uplifted. With more and more men and women born into the working classes now moving into white-collar positions, class boundaries were less distinct than they had ever been, especially in cities like New York (and San Francisco) where most wage earners did not work in large factories.

To draw readers from both sides of the line that separated white and blue collar work, to appeal to working people who identified with their class and those who aspired to climb out of it, Pulitzer adopted the same strategies as other cultural entrepreneurs. He established an urban institution which, like the department store, the vaudeville theater, and the amusement park, transcended traditional categories of class, ethnicity, occupation, and neighborhood to appeal to an inclusive, rather than an exclusive urban population. His newspaper had no obvious class markings; it was meant to be read by urban residents on both sides of the middle-class divide.

There was at the time no such paper in the city. The *Sun* had become much too respectable and long-winded, even dull; the *Daily News,* a Tammany penny paper not to be confused with the 1920s tabloid was too plebeian; the *Tribune* was too conservative and too closely associated with the Republican party; the *Herald,* at three cents, was priced too high for daily consumption; the *Times* and *Evening Post* were impossibly dull.

The *World* would be different. Pulitzer succeeded not only in drawing readers from all of the competing papers, but in enticing those who were not yet in the habit of reading a daily paper. Though Pulitzer charged only two cents for the *World,* there was nothing cheap about it. Like the new entertainment moguls, he wrapped his product in the most lavish packaging possible. He upgraded his plant and printing equipment — and advertised the fact as often as he could.[37]

More important than the new machinery were the crusading Democratic politics and the look, the feel, the overall appearance of his newspaper, particularly its front page. On taking over the *World,* Pulitzer immediately reduced the wording of the masthead from *The New York World* to simply *The World,* separating the words with an illustration of two globes and a printing press from which rays of light emanated. On either side of the masthead, he added "ears," small boxes with promotional matter about the paper. He further opened up the front page by employing woodcuts as illustrations just under the masthead, breaking up what had been a solemn, unrelieved six-column wall of text.

Pulitzer's triumph in New York was aided enormously by the fact that his was a Democratic paper and, almost alone among New York's dailies, strongly supported Cleveland in 1884. According to Pulitzer's biographer George Juergens, the *World*'s readership had at the end of one year increased fourfold and "at the end of two years by tenfold. Nothing like it had ever been seen before." With the increase in circulation came a rise in advertising revenues and profitability. In the first year of operation, according to the *Journalist,* the *World* earned $150,000. Each succeeding year saw increased earnings.[38]

None of this was lost on Hearst, who had begun reading the *World* in Cambridge during his tenure as business manager of the *Lampoon* and continued, with almost obsessive interest, during his year in exile in New York and Washington. It would not have been difficult for him or for any astute observer of the daily press to see why certain newspapers, like Pulitzer's *World,* sold so much better than their competitors. Nor was it any secret how much money Pulitzer was making. He did not hide his financial succcss, but displayed it proudly for all to see in his mansions, his art collection, his dinners at Delmonico's, and his yachts.[39]

In later years, Hearst would claim in one of his daily columns that after leaving Harvard, he had gone to New York "to join the staff of the *New York World* and give Mr. Pulitzer a few pointers about how to conduct a newspaper." Though some commentators, unfamiliar with the humorous tone he used to warn readers not to take him seriously — or literally — have asserted that he did indeed apprentice himself to the *World,* there is no evidence of this. On the contrary, it would have been impossible for him to do so during the year's hiatus he took between Harvard and his return to San Francisco to edit the *Examiner.*[40]

Though he did not work at the *World,* his correspondence with his father suggests that he was reading it daily, studying every element in its makeup, and comparing it daily with the *Examiner.* In one of his lectures, written in late 1885, Will wrote:

I have just finished and dispatched a letter to the Editor of the *Examiner,* in which I recommended Eugene Lent to his favorable notice, and commented on the illustrations, if you may call them such, which have lately disfigured the paper. . . . In case my remarks should have no effect and he should continue in his career of desolation let me beg of you to remonstrate with him and thus prevent him from giving the finishing stroke to our miserable little sheet. I have begun to have a strange fondness for our little paper — a tenderness like unto that which a mother feels for a puny or deformed offspring, and I should hate to see it die now after it had battled so long and so nobly for existence; in fact, to tell the truth, I am possessed of the weakness which at some time or other of their lives pervades most men; I am convinced that I could run a newspaper successfully. Now if you should make over to me the *Examiner* — with enough money to carry out my schemes — I'll tell you what I would do. . . . It would be well to make the paper as far as possible original, to clip only some such leading journal as the *New York World* which is undoubtedly the best paper of that class to which the *Examiner* belongs — that class which appeals to the people and which depends for its success upon enterprise, energy and a certain startling originality . . . And to accomplish this we must have — as the *World* has — active, intelligent and energetic young men; we must have men who come out west in the hopeful buoyancy of youth for the purpose of making their fortunes. . . . And now to close with a suggestion of great consequence, namely, that all these changes be made not by degrees but at once so that the improvement will be very marked and noticeable and will attract universal attention and comment.

He ended his letter with a few words about his preparation for his upcoming Harvard examinations: "I am getting on . . . well enough to spend considerable time in outside reading and in journalistic investigation." And then, in an almost self-mocking note of exasperation, closed it, "Well goodbye. I have given up all hope of having you write to me, so I suppose I must just scratch along and trust to hearing of you through the newspapers."[41]

Though George Hearst, as he had predicted, did not answer his letter, Will continued to bombard him with suggestions for improving the *Examiner*. In January of 1886, he sent him another letter, with copies of the *New York Evening Post*, the *New York Tribune*, and illustrations from the *World* to prove his point that the *Examiner* was putting out a newspaper inferior in paper quality, type, typesetting, layout, and illustrations. "It is a positive insult to our readers to set before them such pictures of repulsive deformity as these and yet such abortions are not entirely out of place in an article that comes to a climax with a piece of imbecility so detestable that it would render the death of the writer justifiable homicide." He closed this letter, as he did most of his others on the subject, by asking when his father was coming East and plaintively begging for a response of some kind: "I want to talk with you. Do you receive any of my letters? Please answer when you get this and tell me if you want me to look around and try to find some capable people for the dad gasted old paper."[42]

Though it should have been apparent from his continual references to the *Examiner* and his avoidance of much discussion of his studies that Will had given up on Harvard, his mother and father refused to face facts. In early February 1886, they dispatched Dr. Oliver, their surrogate in Cambridge, to meet again with President Eliot to plead Will's case. President Eliot agreed that Will would be allowed to take his final examinations and graduate with his class if he petitioned the faculty *at once* to allow him to return, included a recommendation from his tutor, and declared "that he means to work and that he will work and that there will be no more 'punches' or suppers in his rooms [and] that he will not leave Cambridge during the term."

"Mr. Eliot," Oliver wrote George, "agreed with me that it was Will's associates rather than Will himself who did wrong and I came away with the idea that the President was very favorably inclined towards Master Will and would do his part if the young man will agree to do his."[43]

Will had no intention of adhering to such a Spartan regimen, especially after March 1886, when his father was appointed to fill the unexpired term of Senator Miller after Miller's death. Unfortunately, the Democratic governor who had named George to the Senate seat made the mistake of calling a special session of the state legislature. Once in session, the Republican-dominated state senate was empowered to override the governor and elect its own candidate to serve out Senator Miller's term. After only a few weeks in Washington, George Hearst was sent back to California for what he hoped would be a relatively short stay. If, as he expected, the Democrats won a majority in the state senate in the November 1886 elections, they, not the Republicans, would elect the next senator. George Hearst began at once to do everything he could — and spend all he could — to win a state senate majority for his party and a six-year term in the U.S. Senate for himself.

Phoebe stayed behind to look after their son, who instead of working with his tutor had been commuting between Washington and New York. He had been elected early in 1886 to the Lotos Club, which offered its members meals and lodging and was conveniently located on 21st Street within walking distance of the city's theater and entertainment district, where Will spent a good deal of his time.[44]

Will was distracted that spring not only by his father's politicking, but by the return of Eleanor Calhoun, his mother's protégé, whom he had first met in New York in December of 1881. Eleanor had stopped over in Washington to visit Phoebe on her way to London, where she intended to study Shakespearean acting. Like Sybil Sanderson, Will's first love, Eleanor Calhoun was gorgeous, artistically inclined, and a bit eccentric. Two or three years older than Will, she had, in her middle twenties, already cultivated a theatrical presence that was welcome at the social and cultural events which Phoebe, in preparation for her own career as a senator's wife, had begun to offer at her Washington home.

"Whatever she saw in me, I don't know," Hearst confided to Cora Older, who wrote rapturously of his and Eleanor's courtship. "He wooed her with flowers, gifts and ardent devotion, but no wooing was necessary," Older continued. "Eleanor Calhoun was as rapturously devoted to him as he was to her. They had like tastes, a romantic love of the theater and literature. Both were young and handsome. They became engaged."[45]

In May of 1886, Will forwarded his petition to the Harvard faculty requesting that he be permitted to sit for his examinations. The petition was refused. Will was not surprised and, it appeared, was quite happy to have the matter settled at last. He wrote his mother:

> I have gone to New Haven to see the Harvard-Yale baseball game, but will be back in Boston Saturday night. I write this note to prevent you from allowing Miss Calhoun to attempt the disagreeable and impossible task of conciliating the faculty. Nor do you attempt it either. You will only succeed in increasing the faculty's already exaggerated idea of their own importance without accomplishing a thing. I don't propose to eat any more crow myself nor to serve any to the rest of the family so if you please we will proceed with the next course. Moreover, for fear that you would be bad form and would insist upon being helped twice, I have just practically upset the pepper in the plate. I assured the gentlemen of the Faculty of Harvard College that I didn't regret so much having lost my degree as having given them an opportunity to refuse it to me, and "an abject grovel in the characteristic Japanese style" would hardly be consistent with the above statement.
>
> Don't [show] this letter to Miss Calhoun. Only tell her that the decision of the Faculty was final and that there is no appeal from it.[46]

He was now on his own — or was he? He had no training, no money of his own, and no word from his father as to his future prospects. For the time being, none of this mattered. He was in love with Eleanor Calhoun and intended to marry her. He did not apologize to his mother or father for his expulsion — indeed, he appears not to have mentioned it again in his letters. It was summertime and he intended to spend his vacation in California, the only place on earth he felt truly at home.

His summer headquarters was the Hotel Del Monte in Monterey, the resort of choice for San Francisco's elites. In mid-July, he wrote his mother in Washington, in the charming style that had so often in the past won her over to his side: "Though I have always been known as William the Wise and renowned for the brilliancy and appropriateness of my ideas, I have never been more worthy of my soubriquet or more deserving of my fame than at the present moment. An idea has come upon me. An idea so large, so magnificent in its proportions that it all but fills the spacious chambers of my mighty mind." And so he continued for another full paragraph before at last getting to the point, obviously fearful that once he did, his mother would say no. He wanted his mother to bring Eleanor Calhoun and her mother to Monterey for a brief holiday at the Hotel Del Monte. "There is tennis, bowling and the baths; there is a little whirl of gayety in the evening — a very small eddy indeed — there are a number of very pleasant people, more than I thought San Francisco could boast and I am positive that we could spend three days or so in a very delightful manner here." The letter fairly overflows with frantic good cheer and closes with a postscript, "Did you get the delirious letters [no doubt about his love for Eleanor]? Keep 'em."[47]

This time, Will sadly misjudged his mother's intentions. Though she had sponsored Eleanor in San Francisco and introduced her to Will, Phoebe had no intention of permitting her only son to marry an aspiring actress. Miss Calhoun, she wrote in a letter to Orrin Peck, was "wonderfully bright and even brilliant," but she was also "erratic, visionary, indolent and utterly wanting in order and neatness with extravagant tastes and no appreciation of values." Worse yet, Phoebe was convinced that the young woman she had introduced to Will years before was a fortune hunter who had hatched a plot with her mother to snare her young and innocent son. While Eleanor was only a few years older than Will, "in worldly experience and craft," Phoebe wrote Orrin Peck, "she is twenty years his senior."[48]

In an attempt to separate Will from Eleanor and "give love a chance to cool," Phoebe and George sent him to Mexico to inspect the 670,000-acre Babicora ranch in Chihuahua, about 250 miles southwest of El Paso, which George had acquired in 1884. Though Will had no desire to work in Mexico — in any capacity other than as absentee landlord — he agreed to go. Without any means of support outside his allowance, he had no choice but to obey his parents' wishes, though as he wrote Phoebe while en route, he was "certain" that he would "get very tired of this business before three months are over." His one hope was that having done as they asked, he would be rewarded with a piece of property large enough to support him in the future, whatever he decided to do.[49]

Will was not enthusiastic at first about being exiled from Monterey to Mexico. He wired his mother to send him his macintosh, his waterproof boots, his blue trousers, and "different kinds of preserves and some crackers." He also wanted the *Examiner* to be delivered to him by Wells Fargo. While he caustically joked that he "wouldn't think of leaving [Mexico] for theatricals," he offered to return to help his father and the Democrats prepare for the November elections.[50]

Though Will had no intention of remaining in Mexico to oversee the family properties, he understood that, having left Harvard under a cloud, he had now to convince his father that he had a head for business. When George Hearst, as usual, declined to answer his son's letters, Will communicated with him through Phoebe. The government of President Porfirio Díaz, which had privatized Indian communal lands in four Mexican states, was prepared to hire George Hearst to survey those lands and would, in return, give him one-third of the land surveyed with the right to buy another third "with government scrip at its face value."[51]

It was a propitious time to buy Mexican land. President Díaz was hungry for foreign capital but, because of repeated failures to repay past debts, was unable to raise much in Europe. To attract American investors, he had repealed the legislation that had set aside the subsoil as a national reserve, thereby giving foreign investors like George Hearst carte blanche to expropriate Mexico's mineral wealth.[52]

The possibilities for profit in Mexico were endless, and Will described every one of them to his father. The land was rich in gold, perfect for grazing cattle, and there were limitless opportunities for building "lastingly profitable" railroads. Whatever George decided to do, Will urged him not to let the moment pass. "I really don't see what is to prevent us from owning all Mexico and running it to suit ourselves."

Here was the opportunity Will had been looking for to acquire property of his own and do so in such a way as to make his father proud. He was not asking for a handout — or not exactly. He instructed his mother to let George know that he wished only "the money necessary for the survey and the benefit of his advice and then with that push let me go it alone." If George didn't want to cover the costs of the land survey, Will would try to raise the money elsewhere. Or if, as Will hoped, his father wanted to fund the venture, he could pay for it by selling some of the Hearst property in New Mexico or stock in their lesser mines.

Will was determined to escape the fate of a rich man's son born a generation too late. The myth of the settled frontier, which would be articulated by Frederick Jackson Turner in 1893, was a living reality for Will Hearst in 1886. He was the dandified, Harvard-educated son of a California Forty-Niner. His father's generation had settled the West, cleared the land, built the railroads, discovered and mined the precious metals, and made their oversized fortunes. If there were no more internal frontiers to settle, there remained foreign ones — and Mexico was the most promising. "We are pioneers in Mexico," he wrote to his father. "We have all the opportunities open to us, that ever pioneers in California had and we should improve them."

Father and son together would conquer a new world as father had conquered the old one, but only if George were smart enough to follow William's advice. "You have experience now and matured judgment. You have also great influence with the government here and then you have Verger [Hearst's manager in Mexico] and Follansbee and me all overflowing with youthful energy." George's "connections" and "reputation," already considerable, would be enhanced by election to the Senate which, his son informed him, "will be worth a million dollars to you at the very least here in Mexico. It will give you so much power, it will so impress these fellows. Now work your advantages; use your experience and your judgment, exert your influence; work Verger and Follansbee and me and there is no reason why we should not soon be as rich as Crocker or anybody . . . Stir yourself daddy pop. First get elected by all means and then between December and the time you take your seat we can raise enough money to work all our remaining things in a way that will allow us to sit back and watch the coffers swell."

For a youth of twenty-three, with no experience in the business world, this was a remarkable proposal of partnership, displaying a rare combination of vision, pragmatism, and cold ambition. Never before, with the possible exception of his fundraising for the *Lampoon*, had Will displayed anything approaching the determination he now exhibited to his father. He deployed humor, flattery, and what on the surface looked like real business acumen to convince the senator to front him the $40–$50,000 he needed, recognizing full well that a good deal of the money to be made would be generated by depriving Mexicans of their own lands and selling it at a premium to American "nincompoops." But that was not his or his father's concern. All that mattered was the end product.

His father did not enter into the partnership his son had proposed. But he was impressed enough by Will's newfound business sense to reward him and Jack Follansbee with 100,000 acres of land adjoining the family ranch in Chihuahua. When Will returned to California, Follansbee remained behind to manage their new ranch.

Will ended his letter to his father with a reminder that he still intended to marry Eleanor. "If, as you say, in a few years I could pick the girl of all the girls I wanted in the world, I would not change my mind. Nay, my Pop. There has been time to give my love a chance to cool were it so inclined but it obstinately refuses so to do. If I were serious before, I am desperately in earnest now." He closed with advice for his father on the upcoming election campaign. "Have you arranged it so you are sure to get elected? Have you got that Map and have you marked out the . . . Republican districts . . . that may be persuaded [to vote Democratic]? Have you decided how many of these doubtful ones are essential and have you dispensed the lubricator where it will do the most *good?*"[53]

As expected, the Democrats won a majority of the seats in the California state senate in the November 1886 elections and in January would elect George Hearst to the United States Senate, though not without being severely attacked in the press for choosing a semiliterate miner, who, critics charged, had paid for the votes that sent him to Washington. Will, of course, was delighted at this turn of events. The new senator would need someone to manage his political affairs — and his newspaper — in San Francisco. Who better than his Harvard-educated son? Will had proved to his father that he had a head for business and demonstrated, at the same time, that he had no desire to manage his real estate or mining properties. As there was no question any longer of his returning to Harvard and he had no preparation, training, or inclination for any other line of work, the only option remaining was for George to let him take over the *Examiner*.

Will returned from Mexico in time to celebrate the Christmas holidays — and his father's election to the Senate. It should have been a time for rejoicing as both father and son were only weeks away from assuming the positions they had coveted for some time: George in the U.S. Senate, Will at the *Examiner*. But the Eleanor Calhoun problem would not go away. Will was determined on marriage; Phoebe was every bit as determined to prevent him from ruining his life by marrying the actress she considered a fortune hunter. She was, she wrote Orrin Peck three days before Christmas, literally sick with worry about her boy:

> You well know all that I have been to him, the devotion lavished upon him. You also know he is selfish, indifferent and undemonstrative as his father. Both have their good qualities, but the other sides of their natures are most trying. Will is a brilliant fellow, has improved wonderfully in many respects, has not bad habits, given up the foolishness and carelessness of a great part of his college life, and is immensely interested in business. You would be greatly surprised to see how he works and how very capable he is. Mr. H. is very much pleased with Will's business abilities. You will wonder how it is with all this that I am so unhappy about my boy. You will understand when I tell you that he is *desperately* in love with Miss Calhoun, the *actress*. He has simply gone mad about her, and she is quite willing for she wants to marry a man who has money. . . . Oh! Dear! if I could tell you half of all I have gone through in connection with this affair, you would be astonished. We oppose the marriage but may not be able to prevent it. I feel that it will ruin my boy's life to marry such a designing woman. . . . All she cares for is to spend money, enjoy luxury, and receive admiration. Will would be disillusioned in a few years and when just

in his prime be burdened with an old invalid wife. . . . Now you know a little of my anxiety. Miss C. knows that we oppose their plans and has made Will so *ugly* and cruel to me, I can never forgive her. Don't on any account let Will know that I have told you a word of this he would only be more determined and disagreeable.[54]

Phoebe and George, who believed that Will was too young to marry (George, after all, had waited until he was in his forties), bided their time, hoping that Eleanor would in the end return to London to pursue her acting career. In January, Will took the train East to see her in Washington and stopped over briefly in St. Louis to interview a possible business manager for the *Examiner*. The tone of the letter he sent to his father suggests that he was putting together his own management team in preparation for taking over the *Examiner*. H. H. Small, the man he interviewed, was "a bright, clever man," but Will was not convinced he was the best possible man for the job and did not engage him. "The paper must start out under the new management with every advantage," he warned his father. "Another failure would be an end to the *Examiner* I think. It has made so many efforts to get on its feet and has failed so many times that people are beginning to despair of its ever amounting to anything, and now if with all the prestige that will accrue to it through the illustrations, names to be connected with it, it should hesitate, it would be lost."[55]

Will arrived in Washington in mid-January. Soon afterward, Eleanor Calhoun announced to the press that she and Will were engaged. Phoebe was furious, both with her son for not listening to reason — hers — and with Eleanor and her mother who had tried to force the issue by announcing the engagement. "I may just as well be frank with you," she wrote Janet Peck from Washington, "and admit that it is impossible for me to write a letter to anyone. I am so distressed about Will that I don't really know how I can live if he marries Eleanor Calhoun. She is determined to marry him and it seems as if he must be in the toils of the Devil fish. I cannot write more about it now. We are trying to delay matters. . . . I am so heartbroken I have no pleasure or pride in anything. Hope to feel better when I write again."[56]

Phoebe may have been "heartbroken," but not to the point where she was immobilized. By mid-February, she wrote George in San Francisco that she had accomplished her task with the help of Lloyd Tevis, the "cold, hard man" who had been George's business partner and now acted as her intermediary. She had let Miss Calhoun know that Will would be disinherited if he married without his parents' approval. If the engagement were broken off, however, Eleanor would be protected and placed "right before the world." Phoebe may also have offered Eleanor and her mother a cash settlement to move to London.

"Will and I had a talk tonight," she wrote George, "and he has regained his reason, and wants to do all that is right and best. . . . We both feel most positive that this marriage could result in nothing but misery. He has behaved well and is manly and honorable." The plan was for Will to leave Washington at once for California, ostensibly to see his father. From San Francisco, he would then, according to Phoebe, write Eleanor "a blue letter, telling her that . . . he would not be willing to marry her unless he could place her well" which he could not because his father had promised to cut him off if he married. "This would give her an opportunity to break the engagement, which I think she will do when she finds there is no *money* in it."

"We must be firm and kind and help him get out of this," Phoebe advised George. "He will talk freely with you but will feel sensitive about any comments from others." The boy was distressed, but he was also "so deeply interested in the paper that," she was convinced, "he will be all right. He worried a great deal for two or three days, but he eats and sleeps well, and has too much strength of character to be seriously affected by this."[57]

Phoebe understood her son well. There was no further discussion of Eleanor, except for a note from Will to his mother insisting that "Eleanor [be] treated with all the consideration possible." As he left Washington for San Francisco, Will assured his father that he was now "anxious to begin work on the *Examiner*. I have all my pipes laid, and it only remains to turn on the gas. One year from the day I take hold of the thing our circulation will have increased ten thousand. . . . We must be alarmingly enterprising, and we must be startlingly original. We must be honest and fearless. We must have greater variety than we have ever had. . . . There are some things that I intend to do new and striking which will constitute a revolution in the sleepy journalism of the Pacific slope and will focus the eyes of all that section on the *Examiner*. I am not going to write you what these are, for the letter might get lost, or you might leak. You would be telling people about the big things that Billy Buster was proposing to bring out in the paper, and the first thing I knew somebody else would have it."[58]

Will returned to San Francisco alone. He never did get a chance to talk to his father, who had already left for the East Coast. Their trains had crossed somewhere between San Francisco and Washington.

George Hearst took his oath of office as a United States senator in Washington on March 4, 1887. That same day, in San Francisco, the name "W. R. Hearst, Proprietor" appeared for the first time on the masthead of the *San Francisco Examiner*.

II

Proprietor and Editor

§ 4 §

At the *Examiner*

T HE *SAN FRANCISCO EXAMINER* had been losing money for so long that no one, including George Hearst, believed it possible that an inexperienced twenty-four-year-old Harvard dropout would be able to accomplish much with it. Will had won his prize — after two years of lobbying and the sacrifice of his fiancée. He was now the proud "proprietor" of the third largest daily in the nation's ninth largest city.

In early 1887, he moved back to California, after an absence of over four years. Instead of settling in San Francisco, however, he relocated across the Bay in Sausalito where he leased what a Chicago newspaper referred to in 1894 as "one of the finest villas that can be found fronting the San Francisco Bay." He did not live alone.[1]

According to his son Bill Hearst, Jr., Will was accompanied to California by Tessie Powers, the waitress he had met in Cambridge: "She had been his mistress at Harvard, and apparently in Washington and New York. . . . By all accounts, Tessie was pretty and fun, and adored Willie. Pop never hid his living with Tessie."[2]

Though Tessie would remain a fixture in Will's life for more than a decade, we know very little about her. There are no surviving photographs or descriptions; no biographical information; we don't know where she was born or where she died. Bill, Jr. believed that his father and Tessie saw each other in New York and Washington, but we do not know whether Will visited her during his courtship of Eleanor Calhoun or resumed their relationship only after Eleanor returned to London.

To call Tessie Powers a "mistress" is to misrepresent the nature of her relationship with Hearst. She was his primary companion during his years in San Francisco. They lived together in his home in Sausalito, traveled together, and entertained his friends and associates from the *Examiner*. Like other men of his class, Hearst could have lived in two worlds, following a night with Tessie with one at a society cotillion. But he chose not to. Like his father, he avoided polite San Francisco society and his mother's friends and acquaintances. He neither courted nor appeared in public with respectable, eligible women; he did not join any men's clubs or lodges or associations.

His mother and father, of course, knew everything that was going on, but they were powerless, it seemed, to do much about it. They may also have believed that Tessie Powers was no more than a youthful indiscretion that Will would grow out of.

Though twenty-four years of age, Will Hearst looked and some would say behaved even younger. Florence Finch Kelly, who met him for the first time in the summer of 1887 when she moved to San Francisco with her husband, who had been appointed city editor of the *Examiner*, remembered him as "tall, slender, good-looking, very blond, with a pink and white complexion and a little golden mustache, boyish and slightly diffident in manner and still a bit under the influence of the impish high spirits of youth."[3] Hearst spent most of his waking hours at the *Examiner* and commuted back and forth across the Bay in his fifty-foot speed boat, the *Aquila*, reportedly the fastest boat on the Pacific Coast, which he had persuaded his parents to build for him, perhaps as another consolation prize for breaking off his engagement to Eleanor Calhoun. Whatever free time he had — and there wasn't much of it — was spent with Tessie and a mixed and shifting assortment of *Examiner* reporters and editors.

As at Harvard, Will quickly made himself the center of his own party. He had brought with him not only Tessie but several *Lampoon* colleagues from Cambridge, including his boyhood friend Gene Lent, the cartoonist Fred Briggs, the humorist "Phinny" E. L. Thayer, and "Cosy" Noble, who would edit his Sunday paper. According to John Winkler, the author of a multipart *New Yorker* profile in 1927 and two biographies — the second under the supervision of Hearst's son — "He'd take some of the staff out to help him fly kites, set off firecrackers and balloons, sail boats and steam launches at Sausalito and over San Francisco Bay." Or they would go down to his father's ranch at San Simeon along the central coast, "to ride after cattle, catch trout or shoot at quail." With Tessie and his friends from the paper, he went out regularly to the theater and the vaudeville hall and hosted sailing parties up and down the Bay and, on one occasion at least, as far as Hawaii.[4]

For a man who didn't like society, as his mother had described him in a letter to Orrin Peck, the newsroom was a perfect work site. There was no trace of "society," no hint of gentility or deference of any sort. Will Hearst, though one of the youngest and most inexperienced men in the office, was the boss, and beloved, according to Ambrose Bierce, a future employee, for the generous salaries he gave his new hires, a full 50 percent more than most of them had been making elsewhere.[5]

Jimmy Swinnerton, who worked for Hearst as a cartoonist in San Francisco and then in New York, recalled that Will was as "common as an old shoe." He remained shy among strangers though quick to laugh, in a remarkably adolescent high-pitched voice. According to his cousin Anne Apperson Flint, he also had the "flabbiest handshake of anyone." She remembered being astonished "every time my hand touched his. He just took your hand and dropped it."[6]

While the *Examiner,* which Will took over in the spring of 1887, had improved under his father's ownership, its circulation of 15,000 was significantly less than that of the *San Francisco Call* and the *San Francisco Chronicle,* its major competitors. The *Call* had been losing circulation for some time, but the *Chronicle,* owned and managed by Michel De Young after the death of his brother Charles, had increased its sales by 50 percent, to 37,500, between 1880 and 1886.[7]

Both the *Call* and the *Chronicle* specialized in political news, most of it local, both were tied to the Republican party, and both were run by experienced editors. Hearst was not in the least bit awed. In an article in the *Overland Monthly,* a San Francisco magazine, he criticized the competition for never having caught up with the "change in the character of the people and in their needs." San Francisco, he argued, was no longer a backwater frontier town. It had in recent years "shown itself to possess all the characteristics of a cosmopolitan city," including a large and growing immigrant population hungry for commercial amusements, and it had become a thriving center of national and international commerce.[8]

Will Hearst had not returned to his hometown — after living in Boston, New York, and Washington and traveling extensively in Europe — to publish a provincial newspaper that filled its front pages, as the *Examiner* did, with stories of saloon fights and advertisements for "Winter Dress Goods" and "Sneezing Catarrh" patent medicines. He intended, as he had promised his father, to work a "revolution in the sleepy journalism of the Pacific slope" by importing the journalistic techniques, strategies, and innovations that Pulitzer had pioneered in New York City. His first step, taken even before he was officially in charge, was to make the *Examiner* a cosmopolitan newspaper by contracting with the *New York Herald* for the exclusive San Francisco franchise to publish its cabled articles, including those written in Paris by the paper's editor, James Gordon Bennett, Jr. As the *Journalist,* the newspaper publishers' chief trade journal, reported in February 1887, news of this "masterstroke of enterprise . . . falls like a bombshell on the other morning papers."[9]

With the cables from the *Herald*, the new *Examiner* carried so much national and international news that it was expanded from six to ten pages. In a flash, Will Hearst had changed the face of the *Examiner* and journalism on the West Coast. "The *Examiner*'s enterprise has awakened a sleepless activity in the *Call* and *Chronicle*," the *Journalist* reported in mid-March. "They have too much at stake to allow the *Examiner* to find them asleep in the future." The *Call*, limited in resources, dropped out of the competition, but De Young at the *Chronicle* trumped Hearst by signing an exclusive cable agreement with Joseph Pulitzer's *New York World*, the leading newspaper in New York and the nation.[10]

"We are having a hard fight with the *Examiner* against the other papers out here . . . Right now is a crisis in the history of our paper," Will wrote his father in Washington soon after taking over the *Examiner*. "If we hesitate a moment or fall back a step we are lost and we can never hope to make anything out of the *Examiner* while it remains in our hands. . . . Papa you must do your best for us and you must do it immediately. Delay would be as fatal as neglect." Will wanted his father to go immediately to New York to meet with the top editors of the *World* and "make friends with these powerful eastern newspaper men. They would appreciate a visit from a U.S. Senator, they would feel flattered. Make yourself agreeable to them. Tell them how you admire the newspaper business and how you determined your son should be a newspaper man — if you found he possessed talent enough. That you were determined that he should not be simply a newspaper proprietor, but should be an editor, a newspaper man, etc. etc. Tickle them a little. Say that I told you what a great paper the *World* was and you wanted to see it, etc, etc. Then the first thing you know they will do anything they can for us."

At age twenty-four, Hearst had developed a ruthless, scheming side to him which he now presented to his father. Though he pressed the senator to ingratiate himself with the editors of the *World*, he confessed that in the New York circulation wars, he stood for the *Herald*, the *World*'s chief competitor, with all his force: "It is an honest and brave paper and one can respect it. It is the kind of paper I should like the *Examiner* to be, while the *World* is, because of the Jew that owns it, a nasty, unscrupulous damned sheet that I despise but which is too powerful for us to insult." There was, regrettably, nothing unique in Will's anti-Semitic slurs on Pulitzer and his newspaper. While he had failed to get a degree at St. Paul's or at Harvard, he had been sufficiently socialized into upper-class Protestant society to re-gard Jews, in the words of Leonard Dinnerstein, as "dishonest businessmen always out for material gain . . . alien upstarts trying to wedge their way into restricted social circles." He differed from his publishing colleagues only in keeping such thoughts pretty much to himself.[11]

Hearst intended to use all the leverage he had as the son of a rich and powerful senator to boost the *Examiner*'s circulation and profits. When he had difficulty getting the company that sold papers on Central Pacific trains to carry the *Examiner,* he asked his father to request that California's senior senator Leland Stanford, the president of the railroad, intercede on the *Examiner*'s behalf.[12] When he discovered that George's friends and busi-ness associates were placing their advertisements in the *Chronicle* instead of the *Examiner,* he demanded that his father do something about it: "As these sons of bitches are principally indebted to you for whatever they have, I think this is the god-damndest low down business I ever heard of. I don't apologize for the swear words for I think the circumstances excuse them. Now if you will telegraph Stump [George's business manager in San Fran-cisco] a *hot* telegram to withdraw all your business from these firms . . . and not to give them any more until they advertise in the *Examiner* and *not* in the *Chronicle,* I think we can accomplish something."[13] When he learned that the *Examiner* was not getting its fair share of government contracts to print laws, notices, bulletins, advertisements, and other documents, he asked his father to do what he could to remove the director of the Port of San Francisco and the California surveyor general from office, because they were both "violent enemies of the paper and positively use their influence against it to prevent our getting advertisements."[14]

Will was having the time of his life, fighting the fight of his life. At the *Lampoon,* he had been only the business manager, scorned or ignored by the paper's editors and writers. Now, at the *Examiner,* he was in the center of things, the boss, the chief. He relished his role as virtuous underdog, fighting the entrenched power of the *Chronicle,* which was, he hinted in a letter to his father, stealing his ideas as fast as he introduced them in his own newspaper. "The *Chronicle* is fighting tremendously hard, and it does not hesitate to adopt any idea we bring out. . . . If they see anything good they grab it. This gives us a hard row to hoe, but we are hoeing it vigorously and hope to keep advancing. You must do all you can in the East to help us." The letter was signed, "Your hard working son."[15]

As editor and publisher, Will worked from ten in the morning to well past midnight, every night, prying into every corner, learning the business from the top down. "I don't suppose I will live more than two or three weeks if this strain keeps up," he wrote his mother, only half joking. "I don't get to bed until about two o'clock and I wake up at about seven in the morning and can't get to sleep again, for I must see the paper and compare it with the *Chronicle*. If we are the best, I can turn over and go to sleep with quiet satisfaction but if the *Chronicle* happens to scoop us, that lets me out of all sleep for the day. The newspaper business is no fun and I had no idea quite how hard a job I was undertaking when I entered upon the editorial management of the *Examiner*."[16]

As Will had warned his father a year earlier, he needed a loyal cadre of Harvard revolutionists to make his revolution in West Coast journalism.[17] To back up his recruits from the *Lampoon*, and to add the leaven of experience and a knowledge of San Francisco, he brought in the Scotch-born and brilliantly acerbic Arthur McEwen to write editorials, made Edward Townsend, his father's secretary, his business manager, and hired a new staff of illustrators, cartoonists, and city reporters.

Within weeks of arriving at the *Examiner*, he crossed the Bay to Oakland to offer Ambrose Bierce a position writing editorials and "a column of prattle for the Sunday edition." Bierce was, in 1887, in his early forties. After serving in the Union army in the Civil War, he had wandered west to San Francisco where he acquired a "considerable local reputation" writing bitterly caustic editorials and short comic pieces for San Francisco weeklies. He enjoyed what he was doing — especially the total freedom he had to write what he pleased — but he was short of money and had not yet achieved the wide audience or the fame he believed he deserved.

Bierce had no idea who the young man was who appeared unannounced at his door. "His appearance, his attitude, his manner, his entire personality suggested extreme diffidence. I did not ask him in, instate him in my better chair (I had two) and inquire how we could serve each other. If my memory is not at fault I merely said: 'Well,' and awaited the result.

"'I am from the San Francisco *Examiner*,' he explained in a voice like the fragrance of violets made audible, and backed a little away.

"'O,' I said, 'you come from Mr. Hearst.'

"Then that unearthly child lifted its blue eyes and cooed; 'I am Mr. Hearst.'"

Though he may have looked like a child, Hearst was smart enough to know what mattered to Bierce. His offer of journalistic freedom and more money than Bierce had ever earned — or imagined he would ever earn — was quickly accepted.[18]

For his managing editor, Will imported Sam Chamberlain from New York. Chamberlain, who had worked for James Gordon Bennett, Jr., the owner of the *New York Herald,* as an editor of Bennett's *New York Evening Telegram* and his English-language paper in Paris, had many qualities to recommend him. He was a remarkable-looking man and an extraordinarily fastidious dresser, with a monocle in one eye and a fresh gardenia in his lapel. He was also a master at the sort of "stunt" journalism that had won Pulitzer's *World* so many new readers. His only drawback was his drinking — which was more than considerable.

Winifred Black, one of the reporters hired by Chamberlain, remembered the *Examiner* as "a place full of geniuses. . . . Nowhere was there ever a more brilliant and more outrageous, incredible, ridiculous, glorious set of typical newspaper people than there was in that shabby old newspaper office."[19] Though her only work experience before joining the *Examiner* had been playing Henriette in a touring company of *The Two Orphans,* Black could write well, was fearless, and under the pen name Annie Laurie became one of the paper's leading "sob sisters," Hearst's feature writers known for their ability to bring tears to the eyes of their readers.

Black's first big assignment, one typical of the "stunt" journalism that was instrumental in raising the *Examiner*'s circulation and lowering its reputation among its colleagues, was to investigate "rumors of queer doings at the City Receiving Hospital." To get herself admitted, she dressed herself in old clothes, put a few drops of belladonna in her eyes, and "walked up and down Kearny Street three or four times before I could get my courage to the sticking point . . . finally I staggered, stumbled, and pretended to fall. . . . I was so frightened and excited that I was undoubtedly as white as a sheet; and the belladonna gave my eyes a sort of glazed stare." She was carted off to the Receiving Hospital where she "found that the stories we had heard about the gross cruelty and neglect were true. When my story came out in the *Examiner* the next day . . . the whole staff of the hospital was removed, and the Governor of the state telegraphed asking the authorities to clean up first and investigate afterwards. Everybody in all the public institutions started to watch for redheaded girls to be sure of what happened when they were around."[20]

As editor, Will was intent on remaking the editorial content of the *Examiner.* But he was publisher as well and in that capacity had to worry about production, distribution, and advertising. With the help of George Pancoast, a printer from Boston who became his first secretary, Hearst learned a great deal about modern printing technologies. He was convinced, as he would be for the rest of his publishing career, that for a paper to look good, it had to be printed with the finest equipment available, no matter what the cost. Soon after taking control of the *Examiner,* he asked his father to "see Mr. Hoe of Printing Press fame" and to make inquiries about purchasing a new "photographic instrument" and a "routing machine for fine plates." When his father was, as usual, too busy to respond to his son's request, Will directed Edward Townsend, George's secretary and the *Examiner*'s business manager, to buy the equipment and arrange for training for the pressmen and engravers.[21]

Because San Francisco, a city of no more than 350,000, had three strong morning papers, Hearst recognized that he would have to expand the *Examiner*'s circulation base by delivering papers by railway north to Sacramento and south to Santa Cruz and San Jose. To make sure everybody in the Bay Area knew what he was doing, he devoted half of his front page on May 23, 1887, to the story. The language was characteristically overblown and self-important, but it made the point Hearst wanted: that the *Examiner* was more than just another daily, that it intended to perform a public service for its readers. "To North! . . . To South! . . . The bond is welded which knits together in unity and brotherhood the great metropolis of the West with the country around it . . . Too long . . . have the people of the city and the people of the country held their aims and problems far apart. But now their elder sister, San Francisco, says to the younger boroughs and cities of the State: 'We are one in purpose; ours is the common cause of universal progress, of the grander education, of the moral and healthful improvement of this splendid heritage, this earthly paradise — California.'"[22]

Hearst's achievement, despite the quality of the prose which described it, was substantial. As the *Journalist* would announce in June and again in October, the *Examiner* had, under Hearst's management, become the state's first truly metropolitan daily.[23]

To attract the attention and circulation he needed to make his "revolution," it was necessary, Hearst knew, to change the form as well as the content and distribution of his newspaper. The *Examiner* that he inherited in March of 1887 was, even by San Francisco standards, a decidedly uninviting newspaper. The front page was made up of dozens of stories and advertisements laid out in a nine-column unbroken wall of text. Will reduced the number of columns and the number of stories, doubled the size of the headlines, and eliminated the advertisements that had crowded the lower right-hand side of the page. Above the masthead, he inserted black-bordered endorsements and reports on the *Examiner*'s circulation. The major change was the insertion of line drawings which extended across several columns of the page. Illustrations, he had lectured his father the year before, do not simply "embellish a page, [they] attract the eye and stimulate the imagination of the lower classes and materially aid the comprehension of an unaccustomed reader and thus are of particular importance to that class of people which the *Examiner* claims to address."[24]

In his first few months as editor, Will changed the makeup of the paper so often that the *Journalist* in New York City felt compelled to comment on it. The only constant was his generous use of drawings on page one to draw the attention of potential readers. The illustrations grew in size and number. On April 22, fully half the front page was devoted to illustrated "Impressions of Life and Nature by California Artists." Five days later, the paper printed twenty-two different line drawings to illustrate its front-page story about the wedding of Miss Hattie Crocker, Will's contemporary and the daughter of the banker and railroad magnate Charles Crocker.[25]

The front page was his billboard, his advertisement for the new *Examiner.* On April 3, 1887, he let San Franciscans know what was in store for them by devoting all of page one and, indeed, most of that morning's paper to the fire that had destroyed the Hotel Del Monte, the luxury resort in Monterey where Joseph Pulitzer had recently stayed and where Will had romanced Sybil Sanderson and Eleanor Calhoun. The *Examiner* had been scooped on the breaking story but quickly caught up with its rivals. Hearst hired a train to carry a carload of writers and artists to Monterey to report firsthand. Not only was the resulting Monterey fire edition of the *Examiner* — at fourteen pages — the largest yet published in San Francisco, but the size of the type, the width of the headlines, and the quality of the illustrations that took up the front page that day were truly sensational:

HUNGRY, FRANTIC FLAMES. They Leap Madly Upon the Splendid Pleasure Palace by the Bay of Monterey, Encircling Del Monte in Their Ravenous Embrace From Pinnacle to Foundation. Leaping Higher, Higher, Higher, With Desperate Desire. Running Madly Riotous Through Cornice, Archway and Facade. Rushing in Upon the Trembling Guests with Savage Fury. Appalled and Panic-Stricken the Breathless Fugitives Gaze Upon the Scene of Terror. The Magnificent Hotel and Its Rich Adornments Now a Smoldering Heap of Ashes. The "Examiner" Sends a Special Train to Monterey to Gather Full Details of the Terrible Disaster. Arrival of the Unfortunate Victims on the Morning's Train — A History of Hotel del Monte — The Plans for Rebuilding the Celebrated Hostelry — Particulars and Supposed Origin of the Fire.[26]

It was this kind of excess and excitement that Hearst intended to bring to his newspaper every day. In his *Overland Monthly* article, Hearst would reply to the "gentleman who had said the *Examiner* was a 'sensational paper' . . . that he hoped it was." Interviewed by the *Journalist* in December of

1888, he would say that while his long-term goal was to make the *Examiner* a "first-class newspaper entirely aside from its sensational features," his immediate aim was "to get the people to look at the paper" and to do this required that "he do many things out of the usual order."[27]

Will experimented by putting different kinds of stories on his front page. In mid-May of 1887, baseball scores began to appear on the bottom of page one; by June, sports stories on baseball, boxing, horse racing from Jerome Park in New York City, and yacht racing had become regular front-page features. His goal was to attract the widest possible circulation. Newspapers in smaller cities like San Francisco, he explained in his April 1888 *Overland Monthly* article, did not have the luxury of addressing particular classes and still making a profit: "To have a large circulation," a San Francisco daily "must address almost everybody . . . it must have articles to suit the different classes."[28]

Hearst wanted every resident of San Francisco — baseball cranks and horse-racing enthusiasts, yachting aficionados and Sarah Bernhardt fans, recent immigrants anxious for news from abroad, businessmen concerned with international commerce, readers with a literary bent, even those with interests on the salacious side — to find something to read in his newspaper. While sending his sob sisters out on "stunts," publishing international news cables from the *New York Herald,* beefing up his sports coverage, and giving Ambrose Bierce and Arthur McEwen, his chief editorial writer, forums to insult whomever they pleased, he added new higher-class literary features. In late May, he began serializing a Jules Verne story on the front page; the next month, he introduced H. Rider Haggard's novel *Allan Quatermain.* He had specifically directed Townsend to pay whatever he had to get the Quatermain story because, as he explained, Haggard was "enormously popular among all classes."[29]

To the dismay of his critics, and some of his own writers, including Arthur McEwen, Hearst also published more than his share of salacious front-page articles about naked ladies and adulterers. More titillating material was found on the inside pages where it could be accompanied by racy drawings of women in various states of undress, some of them rather bold, like the half-dozen illustrations of ballerinas in tights and tutus which accompanied "The Poetry of Motion. A History of the Ballet From the Earliest Times. The Goddesses of Dance," and the drawings of women frolicking in bathing suits which illustrated the article which asked, "Shall We Co-Bathe? An Englishman Says the Sexes Must Not Mingle in the Surf. Some Pastors Say So Too. Splashes On the Subject From a Number of Well-Known Clergymen."[30]

It did not take long for Hearst to find the formula he was looking for. Within weeks of taking over the paper, he began to run crime stories on his front pages, and he continued to add them. The pre-Hearst 1880 *Examiner* had devoted about 10 percent of its news space to crime stories; the Will Hearst version gave more space, 24 percent, to crime than to any other news topic. But it was not simply the quantity of the crime coverage that marked the new *Examiner;* it was the quality and narrative form of the reporting.[31]

In the grand tradition of James Gordon Bennett's *New York Herald,* which had exploited the 1836 murder of the prostitute Helen Jewett to the point where the future lawyer George Templeton Strong, then a Columbia University sophomore, would record in his diary that everyone was talking about the case, Hearst's reporters focused attention on selected incidents of violent crime by treating them as morality plays and examining them from every conceivable angle.[32]

The *Examiner*'s first major front-page crime story appeared on May 19, 1887, on the right-hand side of the front page under the headline, "THUGS! . . . A Band of Murderers Discovered in San Francisco. . . . Killing Men to Collect Their Insurance . . . Unnumbered Awful Crimes Laid at the Door of These Molochs." Though the story carried no byline, its first sentence referred to the role played by *Examiner* reporters in uncovering "the most frightful conspiracy in the modern criminal annals of the civilized world." Hearst not only inserted his reporters into his crime and scandal stories, but made them the heroes and heroines of a morality play within a play. *Examiner* crime stories uncovered two layers of criminality at once. They exposed the original crimes in all their bestiality and then analyzed at great length the blundering, sometimes criminal, incompetence of the officials investigating and prosecuting the case. Because the police and prosecutors were not doing their job, the *Examiner* reporters were forced to do it for them. Readers were reminded again and again that the city's foulest criminals would have gone unpunished save for "The Invincible Determination of the 'Examiner' to Bring Them to Justice."[33]

Through the first summer of Hearst's tenure at the *Examiner,* there were reports, editorials, and cartoons about the corrupt police and hack politicians who were depriving San Franciscans of the civic improvements they not only deserved, but had paid for with their taxes. The crimes of corruption were legion: there was jury tampering, murder, cover-up, bribery, kidnapping, all waiting to be exposed by the *Examiner* staff. No institution was safe from scrutiny. The newspaper found corruption in Folsom Prison, in the surveyor general's office, even in the privately managed but publicly funded Home for the Care of Inebriates.[34]

The lead editorial on October 30 reminded its readers — yet again — that *Examiner* reporters gave "Justice a lift when her chariot gets mired down":

> *Examiner* reporters are everywhere; they are the first to see everything, and the first to perceive the true meaning of what they see. Whether a child is to be found, an eloping girl to be brought home or a murder to be traced, one of our staff is sure to give the sleepy detectives their first pointers . . . The *Examiner* reporter is a feature of modern California civilization. His energy, astuteness and devotion make him the one thing needed to redeem the community from the corruption that seems to have selected this period as its peculiar prey.[35]

Having found a successful formula for his newspaper — one that created "buzz" and attracted readers — Hearst pushed it as far as he could. On March 1, 1888, to choose a day at random, the *Examiner*'s front-page headlines were:

> SAD SCENES. The Julia's [a capsized steamer] Victims Borne to the Cities of the Dead. A MOURNFUL HOLIDAY.
>
> TIGHTENING THE GRIP. Every Day Brings More Evidence Against the Opium Ring.
>
> MURDERED BY CHINESE. Thomas Gibbs, a Tramp, Fatally Stabbed by Supposed Garroters. A Cold-Blooded Deed. Knifed Without Pause, and Because He Wanted to Defend Himself.
>
> BUTCHERED AS THEY RAN. The Fearful Climax to a Land Dispute in Texas. Seven Negroes Killed. Five Shot Dead and Two Perish in a Burning Cabin.
>
> A TALE RETOLD. The Sudden Stoppage of a Train Between Stations. Cool-Headed Robbers. The Engineer and Fireman Compelled to Assist the Desperadoes.
>
> KILLED FOR HIS MONEY. The Horrible Crime to Which a Young Villain Has Confessed. A Man Decapitated. Insanity of the Victim's Widow — The Murderer's Mother Greatly Affected.

As Hearst remade the paper, the writing got better, more focused, and more detailed. Articles took on the pace and coloring of short stories. While the prose was at times hackneyed, it was often first-rate. In the finest tradition of newspaper journalism (like the O. Henry stories that would appear in the *New York World* in the early 1900s), it was never easy to tell where reporting ended and fiction began. As Michael Robertson, the author of *Stephen Crane, Journalism, and the Making of Modern American Literature,* observes, this mingling of genres was common to "journalistic discourse at the turn of the century. . . . Newspaper reporters and readers of the 1890s were much less concerned with distinguishing among fact-based reporting, opinion, and literature." The cult of objectivity which would define journalistic standards — if not always journalistic practices — later in the twentieth century was not yet in place. What readers expected of their newspapers was not literal, but figurative truth. They wanted a map of the city with the "feel" of events, the "sense" of being there, and this is what Hearst gave them every day.[36]

Following the examples of New York editors — Benjamin Day and Charles Dana of the *Sun,* James Gordon Bennett and his son at the *Herald,* Horace Greeley at the *Tribune,* and most recently and spectacularly, Joseph Pulitzer at the *World* — Hearst found in the daily life of the city and its humblest inhabitants some of his strongest source material. In the Sunday, May 29, 1887, paper, five full columns were devoted to an article entitled "NIGHT WATCHES. From Evening Till Morning in San Francisco Streets. Toilers in Darkness. Men and Women Who Toil Not, Neither Do They Sleep." The story was an account of a journey through the city, beginning on Market Street at 7:30 in the evening and ending at 5:30 the next morning. The prose is vivid, the line drawings beautifully crafted, the descriptions of the city and its denizens after dark haunting. Was this short fiction or firsthand reportage or a bit of both? Whatever the proportion of fact to fiction, it made for a fine story.[37]

If in the features he added to the paper Hearst was reaching out to a broader constituency than the one that had traditionally bought and read the *Examiner,* editorial policies remained much as they had been, with one exception. As he had earlier warned his father, the *Examiner* was not going to be a Democratic party organ. It reserved the right to criticize any and all politicians, when they deserved it.[38]

Under Will's stewardship, the *Examiner* was defiantly prolabor, anticapital, and antirailroad. It defended labor's right to unionize and strike and supported Samuel Gompers's call for the eight-hour day. This prolabor stance was tainted with virulent anti-Asian racism. As the historian Roger Daniels has written, from the 1870s onward California's workingmen tended to attribute all their ills to the presence of cheap "'Mongolian' labor, and, consequently, directed their protests against the Chinese and the men who employed them." Almost every labor leader, every labor newspaper, and every politician and publisher who courted the workingman's favor enlisted in the campaign to exclude Chinese, and later Japanese, immigrants from entering the nation. The *Examiner* was not the most virulent opponent of Asian immigration. Other California dailies, including the

Chronicle, were every bit as racist. Still, because Hearst's paper positioned itself as a Democratic newspaper dedicated to the cause of working people, his editorialists and reporters endlessly repeated organized labor's argument that Chinese gang-laborers, imported by the railroads and other large corporations, were robbing "white" workers of their livelihood and destroying San Francisco by promoting gambling, lotteries, and houses of ill fame in Chinatown, and crime and opium addiction everywhere else. The attacks were relentless and inevitably linked to demands for exclusion of the "Mongolian horde."[39]

While Hearst broke no new ground in his racist diatribes against Asian immigrants, unlike his competitors he took practical steps to demonstrate his commitment to "white labor." Because, as the *Examiner* alerted its readers in January 1889, the Chinese hordes were multiplying at "an alarming rate," the paper offered to sponsor a "labor train" to bring white laborers to California to replace the Asian. Though nothing came of this proposal, in February the *Examiner* opened a free employment service for white male and female applicants competing for work with Chinese laborers.[40]

This was but one of the many free services Hearst and the *Examiner* offered San Franciscans. Like the workingman's saloon and the political clubhouse, Hearst's newspaper served as an unofficial public agency, an honest broker, an unpaid intermediary between the people and their government. As a front-page advertisement on March 24, 1892, triumphantly claimed, San Franciscans could on any given day get help from the *Examiner* if they had "Indian Depredation claims to collect, a patent to secure, a pension to get, a land title to straighten out, or any business to do with the Government."[41]

It is difficult to put much faith in newspaper circulation figures before 1914, when the Audit Bureau of Circulations was established. Still, even discounting Hearst's own boasting on his front pages, there is no doubt that he succeeded in dramatically improving the circulation of the *Examiner.* In the first few weeks, circulation, as he wrote his father, had "increased at the rate of about 40 or 50 a week," but soon jumped to "50 a day." The *Examiner's* circulation doubled in its first year and, by 1890, it had drawn even with the *Chronicle's.*[42]

All of this cost money, which George Hearst reluctantly paid, not because he wished to indulge his son but because having lost money for years on the *Examiner,* he was now willing to invest whatever it took to turn the paper into a profit-making enterprise. Will was not given carte blanche, but had to persuade his father and Irwin Stump, the senator's chief financial adviser, that every expenditure made sense. Most of the time, he got his way. He convinced the senator to pay for an expanded staff of editors and writers, for two new web presses, nicknamed the "Monarch" and "Jumbo," built especially for the *Examiner* by Hoe and Company, and for the new Linotype machines manufactured by Ottmar Mergenthaler, which enabled compositors to set type much faster by operating the keyboard on a machine that cast type in metal strips, line by line.[43]

Though in the years to come critics like A. J. Liebling would complain that Hearst's only contribution to the newspaper industry had been the use "of money like a heavy club" to bludgeon his competitors into submission, the reality was that Hearst had, for the most part, spent his father's money wisely in San Francisco. There was an old adage in the mining business that it took a mine to dig a mine, meaning that only those with millions to invest stood any chance of making any money in the industry. Though Liebling might have bemoaned the fact, the truth was that by 1880 newspaper publishing had also become a big business which required "big money" to enter. Readers, able to choose between several competing papers, wanted their money's worth and more. Hearst succeeded in San Francisco — as he would soon succeed in New York — because he had the resources to give those readers what they wanted: a bigger, better looking, better written, better printed and illustrated paper than his competitors could offer.[44]

We have no idea how long it took before the *Examiner* began to pay off on the senator's investment. We do know that in 1890 when George Hearst's reminiscences were recorded for a possible autobiography, he claimed that the *Examiner* was already on a paying basis. "After I had lost about a quarter of a million by the paper," he told his interviewer, "my boy Will came out of school, and said he wanted to try his hand at the paper . . . He said . . . that the reason that the paper did not pay was because it was not the best paper in the country. He said that if he had it he would make it the best paper, and that then it would pay. I . . . agreed to stand by him for two years. Now, I don't think there is a better paper in the country. . . . I believe it is now worth upwards of a million."[45]

❧ 5 ❧

"I Can't Do San Francisco Alone"

WILL HEARST, still several years shy of thirty, had proved himself an extraordinarily capable newspaper editor and proprietor, but the strain had been enormous. In the newspaper business, you are only as good as today's issue, as this week's circulation figures, and though he had made steady progress, he was competing against Michel De Young of the *Chronicle,* a veteran publisher with an experienced staff and capital of his own to invest. De Young matched Hearst every step of the way and then, in November of 1888, went him one better by announcing that he was going to build a monumental new, fully electric office building for the *Chronicle.*

Though it would cost a few million dollars to erect a similar modern structure for the *Examiner,* Hearst insisted to his father that it be done — and immediately. The new *Chronicle* building, he wrote his father, was undoing all he had done to make the *Examiner* the city's leading newspaper. "That damned Chronicle building is a tremendous advertisement and helps them immensely. Everybody talks about it and everybody thinks it is pretty fine and there is great difficulty getting subscribers away from a paper that is doing a big thing like that. The effect upon the advertiser is even worse. . . . How long do you suppose it will be before we can put up a building — a stunner that will knock his endways and make him as sick as he is now making me. I hope it won't be long. I am getting pretty tired and worried."

The cost of buying a downtown site and constructing a building would be immense, but Will was certain that it could be done. He had been talking it over with Irwin Stump, George's treasurer and chief financial adviser, and had agreed to reduce his salary to a thousand a month (equivalent to around $20,000 today). "We'd like to cut you down a little if you don't mind," Will wrote his father. "Can't you sell that stable pretty soon. You promised faithfully you would sell it years ago."[1]

Only days later, Will took up his argument again: "I wish you could come out right away. I want to talk with you and arrange a plan of campaign. It is hard to write everything." De Young's plans for the new *Chronicle* building were, Will explained to the senator, proceeding apace: "He is going to put in his tower the largest clock face in the world. The *New York Sun* had a column about this clock . . . It had an effect on Grandpa even. He said, 'Dear me, that fellow must make an awful lot of money' . . . I tell you the whole country knows about that building and is impressed by it. . . . We are losing subscribers, we are losing advertisements, we are losing prestige. I tell you, governor, we have got to do something. We have either got to go in and win or we have got to go out of the business. I am doing the best I can. I have sent my girl away and I am working at the paper all the time. . . . I can't do any more."[2]

Will, in the end, got his way. On May 21, 1890, it was announced on the front page of the *San Francisco Examiner* that land had been purchased to erect a new building at the corner of Market and Third.

It had not taken long for William Randolph Hearst to make a success for himself as a newspaper publisher. But he was still, in his dealings with his father, a little boy begging for a handout. He had told his father he had sent Tessie away in the hope that this would convince his parents that he was in dead earnest about the *Examiner.* As long as he ran one of his father's businesses, his business and personal life would be inextricably linked.

Though Will was now, in his mid-twenties, a successful businessman, his mother did not leave him alone. She had only recently rescued him from what she was sure would have been a personal disaster by separating him from Eleanor Calhoun. But instead of settling down to marry a respectable woman, he had taken up again with his Cambridge waitress. Phoebe was not a prude. She was well aware that other men had mistresses, but they, unlike her son Will, had the good sense to entertain them in the backrooms of tenderloin saloons or in private dining rooms, privileged spaces where they could misbehave without their sins being bruited about. Will was placing his future at risk — or so Phoebe believed — not because he "kept" a woman, but because he was so open about it.

For the next five years, Phoebe and Will would engage in a marathon battle over Tessie, with George on the sidelines, unable or unwilling to fully take his wife's side. In early 1888, Phoebe won the first round and Tessie was sent away — at least for the time being. From Munich, Orrin Peck, who was

Will's oldest and dearest friend but owed allegiance to Phoebe, who supported his art studies, congratulated his patron. "How was it you got rid of that young lady?" he wrote Phoebe in Washington. "Mastered her in her own language? and left out the oaths? A masterpiece I assure you worthy of a [word illegible] lawyer."[3]

In the summer of 1888, Phoebe returned to San Francisco, where she had rented a home for herself at Taylor and Sacramento Street. She did not ask Will to meet her at the train station because, as she wrote George who remained in Washington, she wanted to spare herself the disappointment when he didn't show up. She made her own way to her hotel, had breakfast, and then telephoned the *Examiner,* only to be told that Will had gone to the baseball game. She met instead with Irwin Stump and got a full — and rather frightening — accounting of Will's spending. Will appeared at her hotel "just as dinner was served and remained until ten o'clock," Phoebe wrote her husband. "He really seems glad to see me and has shown me more kind feeling and affection during the last four hours than he has shown during as many years. We had a quiet, reasonable and thorough discussion of the subject that has caused anxiety [Tessie Powers]. Tomorrow we will spend most of the day and evening together and I will write you fully."

Though her meeting with Will had gone well, she was quite distressed by what she had learned from Irwin Stump earlier in the afternoon: "Will has been spending an enormous amount of money, more than you and me together. . . . However I will talk more with Will and see Townsend [George's former secretary and now the *Examiner*'s business manager] and get an idea of the needs and expenses of the paper and a more thorough understanding of personal affairs. Then you will be able to judge of the amount required, and act accordingly. Things have been going on in rather a bad way. I am anxious to save you any unhappy hours and think it best not to go into details now."[4]

Over the next few weeks, Phoebe learned, to her horror, that her son had in a year's time spent $184,513 on the *Examiner,* equivalent to about $3.7 million today, and another $47,939, or $950,000, on himself. She blamed George entirely for their son's carelessness and urged him to reduce the boy's allowance: "If you have any courage, it might be well to say a few words to Will."[5]

Unwilling to leave the matter to George — whom she had never trusted to rein in their boy — Phoebe met several times with Will and Townsend, and together they agreed on a plan to reduce spending, "but of course not to the extent of injuring the paper." Phoebe was enormously relieved that she had, in the end, been able to reason with her grown son. "It has been such a comfort to be with him so much and to have him *talk, not grunt* and be ugly," she wrote George in Washington. "He has been kind, thoughtful and considerate and has shown me so much affection that I scarcely know how to express my happiness. I feel ten years younger. Tenderness and love, is more to a mother than all else."[6]

The Hearsts had locked themselves into a cage with no way out. Phoebe and George treated their son like a wayward child who could not be trusted with money of his own; he fulfilled their every expectation by overspending whatever allowance they provided him. To make matters worse, while they scolded Will for his bad habits, George and Phoebe exercised no restraint over their own spending. George was expanding his West Coast horse-racing stable, trying in this as in other fields to outdo his colleague and rival, Senator Leland Stanford. Phoebe was spending a fortune to provide for needy friends and their children, including the Pecks. She also supported three free kindergartens for poor children in San Francisco, was an officer of the Mount Vernon Ladies Association of the Union which raised money to restore George Washington's home, and was a president and contributor to the Century Club of California, a San Francisco organization of wealthy, activist women, which, with her financial assistance, campaigned for the election of women to the San Francisco School Board.[7]

She was also, at enormous expense, becoming the premier hostess in Washington, D.C. She and George had bought the thirty-room mansion built in 1870 by President Cleveland's secretary of the treasury, Charles Fairchild, and remodeled it from top to bottom. The finished product, opened to Washington society with a colonial costume ball in February 1889, was in the words of Judith Robinson, Phoebe's biographer, "high Victorian in style . . . with exotic oriental touches that showed Phoebe's desire to stand out from the crowd. . . . There was a plethora of cupids, satin and romantic marble statues, including busts of Phoebe and Will by the Italian sculptor Ansiglioni. The rooms were in rose, blue, or ivory, and the fireplaces had black onyx Mexican mantelpieces. It was a house dominated by the tastes of a 'refined and cultivated' woman and always fragrant with the aroma of fresh flowers." There were separate living suites for Phoebe and George and sumptuously ornate public rooms, including a music room, salon, reception hall, library, dining room, supper room, and huge ballroom lined with tapestries that ran one-half the length of the ground floor.[8]

Like the miner and railroad baron families who had arrived on the East Coast before them, Phoebe and George Hearst spent prodigiously to erase all signs of their parvenu status. If the newspapers and local Washington society gave Phoebe relatively high marks for taste, her son who had studied with Charles Eliot Norton, the nation's foremost art historian, at Harvard, was not so sure. Just as he had taken it upon himself to advise his father on business in Mexico and at the *Examiner,* he appointed himself as art adviser to his mother. If he and his mother were at constant loggerheads on his relationships with other women, they thought alike when it came to the importance of filling their homes with decorative arts.

In early 1889, as Phoebe completed the remodeling of her Washington mansion, her son, exhausted by the strain of editing and publishing a daily paper, left California for his first trip to Europe without his mother. From Rome, he wrote that he had, as he put it, been struck by the "art fever terribly. Queer, isn't it? I never thought I would get it this way. I never miss a gallery now and I go and mosey about the pictures and statuary and admire them and wish they were mine. My artistic longings are not altogether distinct from avarice, I am afraid. . . . I want some of these fine things and I want you to have some of these fine things and do you know, my beloved mother, there is a way in which you might get them. If, instead of buying a half a dozen fairly nice things, you would wait and buy one fine thing, all would be well. As it is at present we have things scattered from New York to Washington to San Francisco, more than a house could hold and yet not among them a half a dozen things that are really superb."

It was, Will advised his mother, a great time to buy fine art in Italy because the people were heavily taxed and the government "nearly bankrupt. . . . Some wealthy American or Englishman will soon step in and . . . will have a collection almost equal to that of some of these national galleries. I wish I could be the rich American. I wish you could be. How nice it would be if we could exchange all our alleged pictures for two or three masterpieces. . . . In price, they are the same but in value how different. Well I for my small part am not going to buy any more trinkets. . . . Go thou and do likewise, mama, dear, if you don't you will be mad at yourself next time you come abroad. What's the good of more trinkets when we haven't room for those we have? Save your money, momey, and *wait.* All things come to him who waits (and saves his money) even Van Dykes."[9]

The jocular tone of Will's letter may well have been an attempt to win back the affections of his mother, who was furious with him once again. Phoebe had learned through her informants in San Francisco that Tessie had returned to Sausalito soon after she, Phoebe, had left the city for Washington in late fall 1888. The truth, which Phoebe could not accept, was that Tessie filled a void in Will's emotional life that he dared not leave empty. His attachment to her was more than that of rich man and mistress. Had it only been that he could have avoided his mother's censure by patronizing prostitutes like other men of his class.

Will did not attempt to lie to his mother about Tessie. When she questioned his excessive expenditures, he forwarded to her a list of the bills he had paid: "You have often asked of me what I *could* do with my money and that I must squander it on the girl. . . . Doubtless some of these things (but look over them yourself) I could have got along without, but a fellow does like to live a little and be interested in something. I don't like to beg and I wish more than anything in the world that I had paying property enough to cover all my reasonable expenses."[10]

What is most remarkable about this letter is that Will does not deny that he is living with or spending money on "the girl"; he says only that he is not squandering his allowance on her. As this letter to his mother demonstrates so vividly, Hearst's life, in all its aspects, remained an open book to his parents. He was always under surveillance, never left alone. Irwin Stump, George's treasurer, monitored his finances, Edward Townsend reported on his expenditures at the newspaper, and Phoebe, through her spies, watched over his personal life.

In June of 1889, Phoebe set off on her own tour of Europe with her friend and mentor in the kindergarten movement, Mary Kinkaid. Though the purpose of her trip was educational — she visited kindergartens and archeological museums across the continent — she also took time out to go to the Bayreuth Wagner festival and tour the Hermitage in St. Petersburg. Her letters to George were filled with news of her travels and her traveling companions and complaints about her ingrate of a son. She did not plan, she wrote from Moscow in August, to return to the States before October "unless there is some serious trouble that you feel I ought to be home. I cannot think of anything excepting about Will and he does not recognize the fact that I am in existence, therefore I fail to see how it matters to him." The following month, she wrote again, from Munich, to ask if George had induced "Will to change his manner of living. I suppose you hear from him occasionally. I never do. How is it possible for him to devote his time and attention to a *prostitute* and utterly ignore his *mother*? He will surely have his punishment." In October, from London, she criticized George again for his failure to do anything about his only son's increasingly outrageous behavior: "Do you intend to continue your indulgence? The paper *still* draws heavily upon *you* and it will *never* pay expenses while you supply funds. *You* will *purchase* the place at Sausalito and you will pay for it, thereby encouraging his present shameful manner of living. I *try* not to be utterly crushed by this sorrow, but it is hard to bear."[11]

Will's only response to his mother's complaints — when he was not attempting to change the subject by discussing art — was to complain about how hard he was working and how tired he was of living in San Francisco. After the first year at the *Examiner* in which he was rooted to the office, he had begun to spend more and more time away. In a letter to his mother, written from New York City during one of his frequent and lengthy stays there, he made it clear that he was not looking forward to returning to San Francisco:

> I am on my way now and what a fearfully stupid trip it is. I wish I had stayed in Washington and my paper would behave itself. The best thing would be to have our home in Washington and a paper in New York and then I wouldn't have to go three thousand miles every time I wanted to brace up the office.
>
> I wish I knew whether you were going to stay in Washington long and what you were going to do after your stay there is over. Between you and me I am getting so I do hate San Francisco. They say San Francisco is all right for men but I can't see how it is unless one wants to get full every night. There are plenty of saloons. I shall have some hard work and that will occupy me until things are running smoothly but after that you have got to come out or I have got to go East. I can't do San Francisco alone. Write me about it.

No doubt sensing that he had gone too far in expressing his melancholy, Will closed his letter with a warning about his father's drinking and a promise that he would, on returning to San Francisco, turn over a new leaf. "Tell the governor to go slow on that toddy business. It has knocked out many a good man. . . . Don't worry about me in San Francisco a bit. I'm not going to be giddy. I am going to be a highly respectable citizen and a credit to my family."[12]

Will was right to worry about his father. A lifetime of hard work and hard drinking was finally catching up with the senator. In December of 1890, he took ill, and traveled to New York to visit a specialist who diagnosed his problem as a "serious derangement of the bowel," but prescribed no treatment. A month later, Will was summoned to Washington, D.C., to sit at his father's deathbed. Jack Follansbee met him there. The senator remained alive far longer than the doctors had expected, but died on February 28. After a Washington funeral service, the body was shipped West, accompanied by family, friends, and eighteen congressmen, nine from each party — who, if we are to believe the front-page story published in the *New York Times,* enjoyed themselves immensely on the train ride West. In an article headlined, "No Water in Their Tanks. Nothing But Liquor On the Hearst Funeral Train," the paper reported that the train that carried the senator home to San Francisco was the site of a weeklong drinking party fueled by generous donations of California wine. "They were opening bottles every minute night and day, and at many stopping places invited people into the baggage car to drink," reported an outraged temperance leader whose own train was stuck behind the Hearst train for the five-day trip across the country.[13]

The *Examiner* covered the death and the San Francisco funeral (but not the funeral train) in enormous detail. The funeral was held at Grace Episcopal Church. In front of the casket was a floral arrangement in the shape of the *Examiner*'s front page with a portrait of the senator. George Hearst was eulogized as a humble but wise champion of the people, a self-made American hero, and a man beloved by thousands. The *Examiner*'s front page, bordered in black, recounted the story of the man who had "started mining with a pick and shovel on his shoulder" and ended up a millionaire and United States senator.

The assumption had been that the senator's only son and heir would inherit everything, but when the will was read, Will learned that his father had left him not one penny, not one acre of land, not one share of mining stock. The entire estate, all the land, all the stocks, and the *San Francisco Examiner* went to Phoebe, with a clause directing her to "make suitable provisions" for William Randolph Hearst. The *New York Times* estimated the value of the estate at between $15 and $20 million, the bulk of it in real estate and mining stocks. Phoebe was also left with the senator's extensive debts, mortgages, and outstanding loans and obligations. The year before his death, Irwin Stump had warned the senator against allowing his friends to lead him "into new adventures." He had apparently been investing or loaning money to business colleagues whom Stump, like Phoebe, regarded as less than reliable. "You are spending money at the rate of near one million dollars per year, more than your income," Stump had warned him. "You must go slow in your expenditures or you must commence selling property to keep up."[14]

The fact that George left less money and more debt than had been expected did not bother Will as much as the fact that he was given nothing. All his life he had tried to prove to his father that he was worthy of his respect. If he had failed at Harvard, he had succeeded magnificently at the *Examiner*, turning a moribund, bankrupt daily into a profitable enterprise. But it had been in vain. George's will clearly demonstrated that up until his dying day he regarded his son — or had been convinced by Phoebe — that

Will was so lacking in judgment that he could not be trusted with his own patrimony. Instead of attaining financial independence, Will Hearst was placed in an even more precarious situation. No longer able to petition both parents for help in the hope that one or the other would support his case, he would now have to go begging to his mother when he needed money.

Mother and son had a difficult time coming to terms with their new relationship. Will made matters worse, much worse, by continuing to hold on to Tessie. From Munich, Orrin Peck wrote to console Phoebe and support Will. "Poor Will. It has been a most hard blow for him — You have the courage of a General and can battle through anything. Still you must show signs of the great strain and if you are obliged to remain in San Francisco will be obliged to be burdened with ———. I wrote Will I wished you could get away from all of those painful scenes." The three dashes in Peck's letter stood for Tessie, whose very name Peck was afraid to mention.

Peck tried as best he could to lessen the tensions between mother and son. "I never heard of a man showing more confidence and respect — in a will — for his wife than did he. At the same time he knew what is yours is Will's — and this is right — Your only child and a pretty plagued good boy at that — Just think for a moment. Since Will's birth he has had more advantages than some Princes — and has never known the lack of money and I don't think should be made to feel it — when we consider how other boys with a quarter of his means carry on?"[15]

Five months after his father's death, in the summer of 1891, Will Hearst went shopping for a New York City newspaper. He had lived in Sausalito and worked in San Francisco for four years now. Though not yet thirty years of age, he had achieved everything he had hoped for as publisher of the *Examiner*. It was time to look beyond San Francisco to the larger world. For Hearst, just as it had been for Joseph Pulitzer a decade earlier, New York City was the logical next stop.

As he wrote his mother, he had "seen every newspaperman in New York — had a long talk with Cockerill," the St. Louis editor whom Pulitzer had brought to New York to edit the *World* after his acquittal on murder charges. Cockerill had done yeoman work at the *World* and was, in the view of many insiders, the man most responsible for its success. In 1890 after years of working with Pulitzer who, as his health deteriorated, became more tyrannical and less accessible, Cockerill had resigned and bought a share of a new penny morning paper, the *Morning Advertiser.* When he offered Hearst a share of his paper, Will considered it carefully but declined:

"I really don't care as much for a one-cent paper as for a two or three-cent paper [like the *World* and *Herald,* the premier papers in the city] so I am not crazy to go in with him. I think there is another way to get into New York perhaps even better than through Mr. Cockerill. I dined with Ballard Smith the other night and we talked newspaper till we were black in the face. He is now in full charge of the *World*. . . . He says Pulitzer is going to give him an interest in the paper."[16]

Will, it appears, was considering the possibility of buying into the *World*. Pulitzer, who had had a total breakdown and given up day-to-day management of his newspapers in 1888, had taken ill again during a world cruise in the summer of 1890, lost most of his remaining eyesight, and come close to death. Given these facts, it was not outlandish for Hearst to believe that Pulitzer would, in the near future, be prepared to entertain an offer for his New York newspaper. Still, he and Ballard Smith were mistaken if they believed there was any possibility of Pulitzer giving up control. He would hold on to the *World* until his death and pass it on, in his will, to his heirs.

Will Hearst turned thirty in 1893, no closer to financial independence than he had been six years earlier when he returned to San Francisco to take over the *Examiner*. He was spending more and more time away from San Francisco on extended tours of Europe and business trips to the East. His life was in a holding pattern. He had again, in 1892, tried to buy a second newspaper and dispatched his new business manager, Charles Palmer, to Chicago and New York. But nothing had come of it. Even had Palmer found a suitable property, it is not clear how Will could have paid for it. He had no money of his own and it was unlikely that Phoebe would give him any as long as he "kept" Tessie.

According to his cousin Anne Apperson Flint, Will was not only living with Tessie but had taken her with him on his 1892 tour of Europe. Since his mother was touring the same European cities that summer and was likely to stay in the same hotels, eat in the same restaurants, and visit the same museums and galleries, Will carefully planned his travels so as not to overlap with Phoebe's. The two met up only in Munich, where they visited Orrin Peck together. Tessie was left behind with George Pancoast, Hearst's friend, consultant on printing presses, and for the moment his private secretary.

The ostensible purpose of Will's visit to Munich was, as his mother wrote a friend, to get his portrait painted by Orrin Peck early in his trip "before he became *too brown* from his tramping life."[17]

The portrait, which hangs today in the Gothic Study at San Simeon, is the best likeness we have of the young Hearst. He sits back comfortably on a wooden chair or bench, one arm resting on the edge of the bench, the other on a side table. He is dressed formally in a dark vested suit, his immaculate white shirtfront topped by a red bow tie. Hearst's eyes are a steely blue-green; his hair a sandy brown, cut short and parted in the middle; his handlebar mustache perfectly curled at each end. The facial features are those of a youth; the gaze and pose that of an established businessman very much at home in the world. The portrait radiates self-confidence, power, control. His friend did him the singular honor of painting him as he wanted to be seen.

Like all portraits, it tells only a half-truth. Will Hearst was not, at age twenty-nine, in control of his life. With no property of his own, he remained entirely dependent on his mother for his position at the *Examiner* and his livelihood. He desperately wanted to leave San Francisco for New York, but could not do so without a sizable loan or gift from Phoebe, which, he knew, would not be forthcoming as long as he lived with Tessie.

In 1893, after a decade of living together, Will and Tessie parted, this time forever. As with every aspect of his life with Tessie, we know almost nothing about their final days together or why Tessie left San Francisco. Anne Apperson Flint told W. A. Swanberg in a 1960 interview that the final straw for Phoebe was her son's decision to take Tessie with him to Europe. All summer long, Phoebe worried that she and Tessie might run into one another in London or Paris. According to Flint, Phoebe returned from Europe determined to break up their relationship, threatened Tessie with criminal action if she did not leave San Francisco, and offered her money if she did. Tessie accepted the offer and left Will and San Francisco.

"That was when we all went to live at the Palace Hotel," his cousin recalled, "and he gave up Sausalito, and he lived at the Palace with his mother; and she sent for Orrin Peck. The four of us were there, going out every night to some French restaurant, doing something every night to keep him entertained, because he was so unhappy — and he was unhappy. He was furious at his mother. He was missing Tessie."

Still, in the end, instead of fighting to get Tessie back, Will took her departure as a fait accompli. As he had with Eleanor Calhoun, he accepted the implicit bargain that Phoebe offered him. He gave up his girl and expected something in return. His first request was for a change in the terms under which he received his allowance and salary from the *Examiner*. He was not, he made it clear, requesting "an *increase of my salary* so much as a *change of the manner of delivering it.* . . . I think I might properly have now what was doubtless too much for me three years ago." Instead of having to go to

Irwin Stump for money to pay his bills, Will wanted his mother to deposit to his "credit at any bank on the first of each month a definite sum of $2,500" which he could then spend or save as he saw fit. "As long as I come to ask him for an extra thousand dollars here and there, he will treat me as a child, asking 10 cents for soda water. 'Can't you get along with five cents! Soda water isn't very good for you anyhow. Well, come around next month and I will talk to you about it.' There is mixed with this parental patronage an air of business mistrustfulness such as you might meet at a bank where you were overdrawing your account. This is annoying but it is unavoidable I think under the present system."

There was something almost pathetic in thirty-year-old Will Hearst's asking his mother for a regular salary. He promised her that if she paid him one, he would not only "get into the habit of laying something away [but would] invest *one half* of all income from the paper, the ranch and all property that I may have or acquire." He would, he assured her, continue to report on his business dealings to Irwin Stump: "My books will be at his command so that he can see that I am faithfully carrying out my part of the plan." He also guaranteed her — in writing — that if she agreed to the new arrangement, he would cease demanding or desiring "*any* extra money. I will not be asking you for a thousand dollars on Christmas, a thousand on my birthday . . . a few thousand now and then for unforeseen expenses. I give you my word to this. . . . You have always been most kind and generous to me and given me extra money whenever I asked for it but don't you think it would be better for me if I didn't ask for it so often, if I were put now on a more independent and manly footing?"[18]

The "manly" was critical here. Real men didn't have to go begging to their mothers — or their mothers' accountants — for spending money. Nor did they allow themselves to be spied on. Will could not endure his mother's suspicions or her surveillance. Despite Will's remonstrances, Phoebe did nothing to remove the constraints on his independence. The tension between the two continued to grow, until it became almost unbearable. In 1894, Phoebe "caught" Will with a lease on a New York City apartment and accused him of renting it for Tessie. Will explained that he had indeed leased rooms in Manhattan, but only because he planned to spend more time there and wanted to save money on hotel bills. He was not, he emphasized, "fitting up any girl's rooms as might be inferred."[19]

With no money or property of his own and his mother watching over his every move in San Francisco, Will felt trapped. He considered buying property in Mendocino County for a home, but the land was too expensive and too far from San Francisco. "It takes three days to get to the redwoods and as many to get back so I would have to take a regular vacation every time I made the trip, and I can't afford the time when I am working on the paper. What I could get the most fun and rest out of would be a yacht. It would be right here in the bay ready whenever wanted and I could take a two hours' trip or a two days' trip as the opportunity offered." Although he had been spending more and more time away from San Francisco and his paper, he wrote his mother that he had "made up my mind to work very hard on the paper from now on. I must positively build myself papers in Chicago and New York and if I have the ability in London, too. I am beginning to get old and if this great plan is to be carried out I have no time to lose, and I am going to devote myself to business, first putting the *Examiner* on so satisfactory a basis that it will get along without much attention from me and will produce enough to enable me to buy my first paper elsewhere."[20]

With no vacation retreat of his own — and no money to buy or build one — Will was constrained to use his father's horse ranch in Pleasanton. Phoebe, ever vigilant, instructed her cousin Edward Clark to find out if he was "taking queer people" there. While the term "queer" did not in the 1890s have the sexual connotations it has today, it was a decidedly uncomplimentary and unfriendly way for a mother to refer to her son's weekend guests. Clark reassured Phoebe that while he could not "say positively" that Will was not inviting "queer people" to the Pleasanton ranch, "I can say truthfully that I do not believe it. He goes there quite often and has taken young men on several occasions but I have never heard of anything different and do not believe it to be the case." When Will tried to build a home for himself on the Pleasanton property, Phoebe forbade him to do so and hired his architect, A. C. Schweinfurth, to design a house for her instead.[21]

§ 6 §

Hearst in New York:
"Staging a Spectacle"

A T THIRTY-TWO YEARS OF AGE, Will felt he could no longer wait to start up a second paper in New York City. Nor was Phoebe, now that Tessie had gone, inclined to deny him his wish.

In the summer of 1895, while Will toured Europe, Phoebe instructed Edward Clark, her new financial adviser, to consult with a lawyer on the advisability of either giving Will half of the income from George's estate or making him her partner in the mines and real estate she had inherited. She had hired Clark, her second cousin from Missouri, to help her sort out her finances.

Clark responded cautiously to Phoebe's plan to transfer half of her estate to her son. "A full and complete partnership makes each partner liable for the acts of the other and should [Will] enter into obligations to enable him to publish a paper in New York it would add to your debt." Ten days later, Clark reported that Mr. Eels, the New York attorney whom he had contacted on Phoebe's behalf, was unalterably opposed to her dividing the senator's estate with her son or entering into any sort of partnership arrangement with him. "It would be unwise and dangerous to sign an agreement to give Mr. Hearst half of any part of your income for the reason that if in the course of time Mr. Hearst should die and any one make claim (lawfully or unlawfully) of relationship to him it would cause you much trouble . . . If such person could establish such claim you could be sued for an accounting for the period of such agreement and it would be possible to annoy you in many ways."

Clark had, on Phoebe's instructions, told the lawyer "only what was necessary . . . so he could give the legal advice you wish." But that "necessary" information had to have included Will's illicit relationship with Tessie and the possibility that he had had similar relationships with other women who might, after his death, make claims against his estate. The only way to protect the family's assets from such claims or from paternity suits should Will predecease his mother was to keep everything in Phoebe's name. "It would be much better," the lawyer advised, "to arrange with Mr. Hearst to give him a stated amount, each month, than to give him an agreement that he is to receive one half. . . . Regarding what you say about your right to use money during your life and to will it to whom you choose, Mr. Eels [says] you have the right, absolutely, to do as you wish in all things. That Mr. Hearst hasn't the slightest legal claim in any way."[1]

Given Mr. Eels's advice and her own suspicions about her son's trustworthiness with money, Phoebe refused to bestow on him a share of George's estate or enter into any sort of partnership with him. "Wm . . . will probably be unpleasant," she wrote Orrin Peck in late September, "but no partnership for me under existing state of things."[2]

When Will returned from Europe in August, he was informed by Clark that Phoebe had decided not to divide George's estate with him. Though we do not know the content of their conversations, it is probable that Clark, with whom Will would maintain a business relationship for the rest of his life, explained to him precisely why Eels had advised Phoebe not to make him her partner.

The issue of Will's inheritance had resurfaced both because he was in need of funds to buy a newspaper in New York and because Phoebe was entering into negotiations to sell a major share of her Anaconda stock. George had, at his death, owned 39 percent of the Anaconda shares. Since his death, his partner James Ben Ali Haggin (a Kentuckian whose maternal grandfather had been Turkish) had bought up much of the remaining stock. Phoebe had never trusted Haggin nor, for that matter, any of George's other partners. When the Rothschild interests made an offer for 25 percent of the Anaconda shares for $7.5 million, Phoebe agreed to sell. Her share of the proceeds amounted to $2,925,000.[3]

While Phoebe was negotiating to sell her Anaconda shares, Will was shopping for his newspaper. There were three for sale: the *New York Recorder*, which had been founded in early 1891 by James B. Duke, the tobacco millionaire, but had never made a dent in the crowded morning field; the *New York Times,* a once prosperous morning paper which, at an asking price of $300,000, was outrageously overpriced given its circulation of less than 10,000; and the *Morning Journal,* which had been founded by Joseph Pulitzer's brother Albert in 1882 as a one-cent morning paper. Though the *Morning Journal* was regarded as nothing more than a scandal sheet, it had done well until 1894 when in the midst of a severe depression, Albert Pulitzer doubled its price to two cents in an attempt to compete with his brother's *World*. Circulation plummeted and in early 1895, Albert Pulitzer sold the paper at an enormous profit to John McLean, the publisher of the *Cincinnati Enquirer*.

McLean, like Pulitzer and Hearst before him, and like Adolph Ochs, who would come to New York from Chattanooga the next year, was convinced that he would succeed in New York because he had succeeded elsewhere. He quickly discovered that to do so he had to find a niche for his paper in the overcrowded New York morning field. After little more than a year of losing money without gaining circulation or advertisers, McLean, in a last-ditch rescue effort, dropped the price of his daily back down to a penny, only to discover that potential readers were no more willing to buy it at that price than they had been at two cents. By the fall of 1895, he was ready to unload his newspaper for whatever he could get for it.

According to *The Fourth Estate*, a publishers' trade journal, the last week of September 1895 was "one of the wildest in the history of metropolitan newspaper gossip." Ever since Hearst had returned from Europe, the town had been buzzing with rumors that he had put bids on the *Journal*, the *Recorder*, the *Times*, and Pulitzer's *World*. The last rumor was effectively squelched in the October 3 issue of *The Fourth Estate*, which reported that "a gentleman in a position to speak authoritatively of Mr. Hearst's plans [no doubt Hearst himself speaking off the record] said yesterday that while it may be true that he wants a metropolitan property, and that it may not be long before he gets it, Mr. Hearst would not buy the *World* if it were for sale . . . because he is too young and ambitious a man to accept the fruit of another man's labors, and if he enters New York journalism will do so in a way to win his own spurs."[4]

Irwin Stump, whom Phoebe had sent to New York to watch over the prodigal son, reported to her that McLean had offered to sell Will a piece of the *Morning Journal* and run it in partnership with him. Will had turned down the proposal because he wanted full control of his New York daily. "He is acting with deliberation and caution on the newspaper proposition in New York, and does not feel disposed to jump until he sees where he is going to land."[5]

One of Will's problems in closing a deal was that he did not yet know how much money his mother was going to provide him for his New York paper. William, Stump wrote Phoebe, had agreed not "to do anything definite until the Anaconda business is settled, as the purchase of either journal means considerable ready money." In late September, Hearst imported Sam Chamberlain, the managing editor of his *San Francisco Examiner*, to join the final negotiations. He had narrowed his choices to the *Recorder*, which was for sale for $400,000, and the *Morning Journal*, which was priced at $200,000. After another round of negotiations in which he got McLean to lower his price, Will bought the *Morning Journal* and McLean's German-language daily, the *Morgen Journal*, for $150,000.[6]

While Hearst's biographers — with Cora Older the sole exception — have asserted that Phoebe gave Will the $7.5 million she received from the sale of Anaconda stock to spend on his newspaper, the truth, as we have seen, was that her share of the proceeds was less than $3 million and Will got no more than $150,000 of that to buy McLean's papers, along with an additional $250,000 that Stump estimated would be necessary to bring the paper "up to Will's standard."[7]

There was every expectation in New York's newspaper community that Hearst would fail as miserably as John McLean, his much more experienced predecessor. New York City already had eight other established morning newspapers. Joseph Pulitzer's *World*, a two-cent paper, reigned supreme with a circulation of around 250,000. Its major competitor was James Gordon Bennett, Jr.'s *Herald*, also priced at two cents, with a circulation of just under 200,000 and an absentee owner who lived full-time in Paris and was paying less and less attention to his paper. Charles Dana's venerable *Sun*, now at two cents, remained a lively, well-written paper, though its circulation languished at under 100,000. The *Sun*, the original "penny paper," had been a mainstay of metropolitan journalism until Dana in 1888 inexplicably refused to endorse the New Yorker Grover Cleveland for the presidency and lost a large part of his core Democratic readership. The remaining morning dailies drew on a more established, solidly Republican, middle- and upper-class audience. Whitelaw Reid's *Tribune*, still the most literary of New York's papers, had never regained the stature it had enjoyed under Horace Greeley; its circulation remained close to 75,000. The *New York Times*, as we have seen, continued to languish. While it looked for new owners, its circulation hovered around 10,000. The three other morning newspapers, the *Morning Advertiser*, *Press*, and *Recorder*, made up the rest of the morning market.[8]

Given the competition, Hearst's most difficult task would be getting New Yorkers just to look at his paper. He wasted no time letting them know what he had in store for them. Like a circus promoter, he knew how important it was to create an aura of excitement before the big show came to town. A genius at self-promotion, he allowed himself to be interviewed, off the record, by the editors of *The Fourth Estate,* who published their story on the front page under the headline, "W. R. Hearst Here. Has Come To Stay as Proprietor of the Journal . . . The Young Californian Has Both Money and Brains — The Combination May Mean a Metropolitan Revolution." Accompanying the article was a photograph of "William R. Hearst" as he wanted to be seen: unsmiling, solemn and mature beyond his years, with a full walrus mustache, well-starched collar, closely cropped hair still parted in the middle, and a fixed stare that made him look more like a Western bandit than a newspaper publisher.

"To intimate personal friends he has stated that he has entered a finish fight for metropolitan honors, and that he has no thought of a limited number of rounds," *The Fourth Estate* reported:

> He means to make the *Journal* a great journal with a big G and J. . . . New York is the field of his ambitions and with the resources of almost unlimited capital and absolutely exhausting courage he has entered the fight. . . . Mr. Hearst is not over thirty-four years old. He is a bachelor with twenty-five millions at his back and a big bold heart inside of him. He does not wear a sombrero or carry a pistol, but he has the courage that is usually associated with the two. He is shrewd without being cunning, rich and yet not riotous, kindly and without weakness, fair but far from foolish. He knows that he is hunting big game, but does not hesitate to tackle it. . . . He shows no suggestion of boastfulness when he speaks of spending millions as if they were mills.[9]

Will intended to get out his first issue before the talk had died down. Charles Palmer, his business manager in San Francisco who had come to New York to help him buy his newspaper, agreed to stay on; Sam Chamberlain also agreed to move to New York to become managing editor. Hearst telegrammed to San Francisco to order Winifred Black, who as "Annie Laurie" had become his most famous reporter, Homer Davenport, the *Examiner*'s chief illustrator and cartoonist, and Charlie Dryden, the lead sports writer, to take the next train East. They spent the first two days on the train speculating about why Hearst had sent for them, Black recalled in a later magazine article:

> It all seems so simple now. But at that time we had no more idea of a Hearst newspaper in New York than we had of one established at the top of the mountains of the moon. When we reached Omaha, Dryden came into the car, and his face was as white as a sheet.
>
> "I've got it!" he said. "The Chief's bought a New York paper. If I had known that, I wouldn't have stirred a step."
>
> "Neither would I," said Homer Davenport, who had left his young wife and a brand-new baby at home in San Francisco.

But of course that was all nonsense. We would have gone to the Fiji Islands or to Greenland's icy mountains if the Big Chief had wanted to send us to either of those probably delightful but rather remote places.

On arriving in New York, Black and her comrades discovered to their dismay that the daily Hearst had purchased was the *Morning Journal*, which, as Black remembered it, was "not much of a paper. 'The Chambermaids' Own,' they called it."[10]

The common opinion, according to the cartoonist Walt McDougall who worked at Pulitzer's *World*, was that Mr. Hearst would fail very quickly: "Ridiculed for his youth and assurance, condemned as a gross voluptuary, sneered at as a rich man's son rushing in where angels feared to tread . . . he was both pitied and jeered when it leaked out that he had bought the . . . *Journal*."[11]

Hearst was not only convinced that he would succeed, but expected to do so as extravagantly as he had in San Francisco. His strategy was simple, and given the competitive situation in New York, probably the only one possible. He decided to keep the price of the *Morning Journal* at a penny, but give readers as much news, entertainment, sports, and spectacle as Joseph Pulitzer's *World*, Bennett's *Herald*, and Dana's *Sun* provided for twice that price. At a penny a paper, it would be a long time before his revenues caught up with his costs, but he was convinced that if he gave New Yorkers a full-sized paper for a penny, they would flock to it.

Pulitzer had pursued the same course on entering New York in 1882. At that time, the city's only two-cent paper was Dana's *Sun*, but it offered its readers only four pages for that price. Pulitzer gave them eight and often twelve. His circulation doubled in four months. By the time the *Times* and the *Herald* reduced their price to two cents, Pulitzer had already attracted enough loyal readers to make his paper a success.

Hearst, like Pulitzer before him and like other mass marketers in the entertainment industry, expected that his low-priced strategy would pay off in a huge audience. He was prepared to sacrifice revenues while he built his circulation base by putting out the biggest and best paper available for half the price of the competition. Stump had put aside a quarter million dollars of Phoebe's money to upgrade the *Morning Journal*. Hearst spent it on new presses and a new staff.

On November 7, 1895, a month after buying the paper, Will Hearst published the first issue of his *New York Journal* with the "morning" dropped from the title to create a more striking logo. While the news printed that first week was rather pedestrian, the illustrations were spectacular — as they would continue to be for the life of the newspaper. On November 8, the front-page story on the marriage of magazine artist Charles Dana Gibson, the creator of the Gibson Girl, was illustrated with a beautifully rendered drawing of Gibson and his bride. The following Sunday, New Yorkers were greeted by their first front page of Hearstian proportions. Over an all but full-page drawing of two lugubrious criminals ran a large-type bold headline, with several layers of subheads beneath it:

LIGHT BREAKS THROUGH AT LAST. A Gang of Criminals Who Travel From Place to Place to Kill and Rob. Police are Now Prepared to Deal With a Most Startling Condition. The Morrisania Murder is Similar to Crimes Committed in Hoboken and Baltimore. Many Arrests Have Been Made. George Parker and Raymond Elroy, Lodging House Waifs, Locked Up at Police Headquarters for Further Identification in the Future.

In the middle of the page was a related article, again with an illustration: "The Man of the Hour, How Captain O'Brien, the Celebrated Detective Who Has Succeeded Inspector Byrnes, Regards the Two Men Under Arrest on Suspicion." At the bottom was an almost life-size drawing of a revolver and bullet. Two men had been arrested on suspicion of murder. That was all that had happened. We don't know what became of the two because the story was not covered by the other dailies and vanished from the *Journal* as miraculously as it had appeared. Still, for that one day New Yorkers were drawn to Hearst's paper, if for no other reason than to find out what these drawings of criminals, police detectives, and a revolver and bullet added up to.

To spread the word that a new paper had arrived in town, Hearst advertised the *Journal* with the flair of a vaudeville impresario. He hired bands and, week after week, papered the city with colored posters — on billboards, elevated trains, streetcars, and wagons — announcing the contents of next Sunday's *Journal*.[12]

Judging from some of the stories run on the front page, he had still not given up his dream of replicating the contents of the *Herald* and publishing a paper with sufficient news of "society" to attract the city's more prosperous residents. On November 12, 1895, he covered his entire front page with the "text" of a letter from Lord Dunraven who complained — at enormous length — of "fraud" in the America's Cup yacht race. For the rest of the week, there were front-page stories about scandals at the horse show. Then, on November 16, in the space on the important right-hand side of the front page that had been given over to horse-show news, he reverted to type and, following the pattern he had established in San Francisco, led with a spectacular crime story: "HELD AT BAY BY A MANIAC. Shot His Mother and a Housekeeper, and then Killed a Man. City of Montpellier, France Startled by an Extraordinary Crime."

The *Journal* had found the formula it would build on for the future. The front page would from now on be filled with stories about New York society set alongside articles about terrifying crimes against ordinary folk. On November 19, a slow day for news, the *Journal* carried page-one stories about striking construction workers, the rush of settlers into the Northwest, the America's Cup race controversy, and two innocent boys who had been "KILLED BY HYDROPHOBIA . . . Both Lads Barked and Snapped Like Dogs, Suffering Terrible Agonies. Little Ralph, in His Struggle Bit Through His Tongue and Lips Again and Again."

On November 24, Thanksgiving, the entire front page of the *New York Journal* was devoted to an exclusive report on the Harvard-Yale football game by Richard Harding Davis, perhaps the best known and most expensive journalist in the country. According to his biographer Arthur Lubow, Davis had no desire to write about a football game, but was unwilling to give Hearst a flat no and demanded "the preposterous sum of five hundred dollars. To his astonishment, the young publisher accepted his terms at once. The figure was generally said to be the highest sum ever paid to a reporter for an account of a single event. Hearst, however, got his money's worth . . . The edition sold out."[13]

Day after day, Hearst and his staff improved on their product. Their headlines were more provocative than anyone else's, their drawings more lifelike; the cartoons by Homer Davenport were sharply focused and brilliantly drawn, the writing throughout the paper outstanding, if, at times, a bit long-winded. Equally important in attracting new readers, the paper's layout was excellent, with text and drawings breaking through columns to create new full-page landscapes, and sensational bold headlines that seized the eye and quickened the imagination.

The measure of a commercially successful newspaper is not simply how well it reports the big events, but what it does when there are no dying statesmen, bloodthirsty desperadoes, or heinous crimes to write about. Hearst succeeded in New York not only because he knew how to report the big stories, but because he was a master at constructing news from nothing. News is not a phenomenon that exists in the real world, waiting to be discovered. Wars have been fought, tornadoes have raged, and hundreds of thousands of innocents have been slaughtered without ever becoming "news." An event becomes news only when journalists and editors decide to record it. More often than not, what determines whether an occurrence is newsworthy or not is the ease with which it can be plotted and narrated so that readers will want to read about it. If there are no discernible heroes or villains, no mysteries to uncover, no climaxes, denouements, triumphs or failures, if no one wins or loses in the end, then there is no story to tell.

Hearst's favorite news stories were front-page tragedies of conspiracy in which the public was the innocent victim, the police and city officials the corrupt villains, and the *Journal* reporters the brave heroes. It was with stories like these that he would make his mark. Like Pulitzer in the 1880s and James Gordon Bennett in the 1840s, he aimed to make his newspaper stories as engrossing and entertaining as they were informative. He did this by seeing to it that the stories were illustrated with dramatic line drawings, highlighted with bold, slashing headlines, and told in the style of mini-melodramas of daily life in the metropolis. On December 9, 1895, to take but one example, he converted what would ordinarily have been back-page filler about a young woman arrested for soliciting, and plotted, illustrated, and headlined the story into a place on the front page. Under a five-column-wide line drawing captioned "Lizzie Schauer and Some Types of the Professional Criminals With Whom She Has Been Forced to Associate," he presented the opening of his melodrama, in which poor, innocent Lizzie Schauer was forced to spend an evening in jail with a particularly sordid collection of miscreants. The happy resolution came the following day. Under a headline that read "The Liberation of Lizzie Schauer," the *Journal* reported how it had rescued Miss Schauer "from the workhouse where she had been committed by City Magistrate Mott on a charge of soliciting in the street."

Hearst was not content with challenging Pulitzer, Bennett, and Dana in the morning. He intended to compete with them on Sundays as well. The Sunday papers, packed with advertising and overstuffed with features, were the most profitable element in newspaper publishing. Here, as with his morning edition, Pulitzer was far ahead of his competitors with a Sunday circulation of 450,000. A key element in Pulitzer's success was his brilliant editor, Morrill Goddard, the pale, thin Dartmouth graduate who had virtually invented Sunday supplement journalism with spectacular pseudoscientific articles on "The Suicide of a Horse; Cutting a Hole in a Man's Chest to Look at His Intestines and Leaving a Flap That Works as if on a Hinge; Experimenting with an Electric Needle and an Ape's Brain; and Science Can Wash Your Heart," as well as fully illustrated stories of exotic murders and murderers, "Real American Monsters and Dragons," and scandals involving men of wealth in tuxedos and chorus girls in underwear.[14]

Instead of attempting to find a Sunday editor to compete with Goddard, Hearst made the man an offer he could not refuse. When Goddard hesitated because he was reluctant to desert the staff he had built at the *World,* Hearst hired them as well. Pulitzer, learning of Hearst's coup, authorized Solomon Solis Carvalho, his publisher, to bring Goddard back to the *World.* Carvalho contacted Goddard with a new offer, Goddard accepted it, and returned to the *World* for twenty-four hours, until he received Hearst's counter-counteroffer. Pulitzer was left with an empty office and one stenographer. Even the office cat, it was reported, had defected to Hearst.

Pulitzer, who was now almost completely blind, immediately left his home in Lakewood, New Jersey, for New York City, where he presided over an all-night meeting with S. S. Carvalho and John Norris, the *World's* business manager. After Arthur Brisbane, who had been working on special projects, was named to succeed Goddard, Pulitzer, with Carvalho and Norris in tow, departed for his vacation home on Jekyll Island, Georgia, to draw up war plans.

Though Hearst was still losing money, the circulation of the *Journal* was now approaching 150,000, less than the *World's* but rapidly gaining on it. By the time the three men reached Philadelphia, they had decided that the best way to destroy Hearst and the *Journal* was to drop the price of the *World* to a penny. No New Yorker in his right mind would buy Hearst's *Journal* when, for the same penny, he or she could have Pulitzer's *World.*[15]

The decision was made hastily and would turn out disastrously. In dropping the price of his paper, Pulitzer played directly into his young competitor's hands — as years before James Gordon Bennett, Jr. had played into Pulitzer's when he cut the price of the *Herald* to kill off Pulitzer's *World.* Hearst reacted brilliantly. In an editorial on February 10 entitled "An Unwilling Convert," the *Journal* welcomed the *World* to the ranks of the penny papers, the "true" journals of the people. Pulitzer's move to one cent had, as *The Fourth Estate* announced on its front page a few days later, energized Hearst, who was "not unaccustomed to fighting and rather enjoys the excitement of strife. . . . Both [Pulitzer and Hearst] are abundantly supplied with the sinews of war, and the struggle promises to be interestingly bitter."[16]

Smelling blood, Hearst moved in for the kill. He had convinced Phoebe and her cousin Edward Clark, now her chief financial adviser, that he knew what he was doing. Though he had long before spent the quarter of a million dollars that had been set aside to upgrade the *Journal,* his mother continued to grant him loans which she entered in her ledger books as notes to William R. Hearst. Either she expected him to repay the loans or, more likely, was keeping track so that she could cut him off when he had gone through the half-portion of the estate which was morally, though not legally, his.[17]

With the bravado of a marauding Western bandit, Hearst used the money he got from his mother to ruthlessly strip Pulitzer of his remaining talent. The week before Pulitzer's editor, Richard Farrelly, was to be honored at a birthday celebration to mark his elevation to managing editor at the *World*, he defected to Hearst. In April, S. S. Carvalho, the *World's* publisher, resigned to become Hearst's editor in chief. He would remain a Hearst editor and a member of his inner circle for the next thirty years, until he was in his eighties. Austere, unsmiling, with a goatee that made him look like an El Greco portrait, Carvalho provided the juvenile, flamboyant publisher with the ballast he needed. He became Hearst's right-hand man, just below him on the unwritten organizational chart.[18]

Town Topics, the society gossip sheet that was awash with anti-Semitic tirades against Pulitzer, took enormous pleasure in Hearst's victories. In early April 1896, it recounted the story of Richard Farrelly's defection in great detail: "How is Mr. Pulitzer to get unleavened bread when the young Egyptian from San Francisco is getting all the dough?" Two weeks later, *Town Topics* joked that Mr. Hearst would soon be attacked by labor organizations as a "monopolist of talent. Whenever he sees a brilliant intellect sparkle, he wishes to wear it on the bosom of the *Journal*. . . . He is perfectly willing to pay people for buying his paper, and he is still more willing to pay people for writing for his paper, and all the citizens of Great New York, or eventually all the citizens and aliens and Indians of full age in the United States, have either got to take the paper or write for it."[19]

While the accepted opinion was that Pulitzer's editors and reporters deserted to Hearst because he offered them outrageously high salaries and bonuses, insiders knew that there was more to the defections than mere money. Pulitzer had become an impossible man to work for, a nasty, vituperative, foul-mouthed martinet. Blind, and so sensitive to sound he had to eat alone lest he be disturbed by a dinner companion's biting on silverware, Pulitzer had abandoned New York but had been unable to settle down anywhere else. He wandered between his homes in Bar Harbor, Maine; Jekyll Island, Georgia; Lakeside, New Jersey; and Cape Martin on the French Riviera. Incapable of managing his papers at close hand, but unwilling to let go, he interfered at a distance, making it impossible for his chief editors and business managers to do their jobs. Because he believed he could get the best out of editors by putting them under battlefield conditions, Pulitzer continually moved people from job to job, hiring new editors to sit in judgment over old ones, changing or confusing the responsibilities of staff members so that there were no clear lines of authority and everyone had to look to him for instructions. The result was constant backbiting, feuds, and chaos.

Hearst had no doubt learned this much about Pulitzer from Ballard Smith and John Cockerill, two of the many *World* editors Pulitzer had victimized. As Will had told *The Fourth Estate* in October of 1895 when he arrived in New York City, he intended to do things differently at his newspaper. He would not pursue what he referred to as "the metropolitan idea of hire and fire," because he had "seen enough of the damage done to feel that . . . it is not well for a paper seeking good men to have them fear that they are taking big chances in leaving secure positions for shaky ones." To persuade experienced newspapermen to join a venture everyone was convinced would fail, Hearst had to offer more than big salaries. He had to guarantee security in the form of large multiyear contracts. This was, for the newspaper industry at least, almost unheard of. Until Hearst appeared on the scene, there had been no job protection for editors or reporters, no matter what their reputations.[20]

The competition with the *World*, a crusading Democratic paper, had sharpened Hearst's and the *Journal's* political focus. To compete with Pulitzer required that he establish himself, as Pulitzer had before him, as a champion of New York City's working people. Though he continued to dress like a dandy and live the life of a playboy, Will Hearst was, or believed himself to be, as authentic an advocate of the workingman as his rival. There was no blue blood in the Hearst family. While Will had been raised with a silver spoon in his mouth and gone to Harvard, he had never forgotten where his father came from. In New York, as in San Francisco, he ran a paper that was pro-labor, pro-immigrant, and anti-Republican. The *Journal* opposed the new Raines law, which harshly regulated saloons. It supported the "starving tailors" against the monstrous contractors, and demanded better treatment for arriving immigrants at Ellis Island.[21]

While there was no call to attack the Chinese and Japanese as in San Francisco, Hearst joined his competitors in denigrating African-Americans in "darky" cartoons and jokes. At the same time, however, he went out of his way to avoid offending the city's European ethnic groupings. While Joseph Pulitzer was regularly attacked in print with anti-Semitic slurs — the *Journalist* referred to him as "Jewseph" — Hearst's papers defended Jewish immigrants from anti-Semitic attacks. On June 14, 1896, the *Journal* published a full-page article headlined "Will the Jews Own New York? A New

York Minister Said So in His Sermon Last Sunday and the Journal Has Hunted Up the Real Facts." The *Journal* article listed "New York's Big Millionaires" and provided assorted charts, graphs, and illustrations to prove the minister wrong. The Jews did not own New York, the *Journal* informed its readers, no matter what the Reverend Isaac Haldeman had pronounced the Sunday before in his Baptist church at 71st Street and the Boulevard (i.e., Broadway).

"The ignorant, the debased and the downtrodden Jews are no more to be feared, as far as their influence upon or their power over the rest of the world is concerned, than the ignorant, the debased and the downtrodden of any other nation or people," the *Journal* explained. "The cultured Jew, who knows the history of his race and who has a decent pride in his ancestry, is a citizen of whom any community might well be proud. There is nothing to fear from him."

European immigrants were treated with respect in the *Journal*'s pages, though often with a heavy dose of sentimentality. The *Journal* regularly published quaint little vignettes about life on the Jewish and Italian East Sides and in German and Irish social clubs, as well as darker "naturalist" portraits of life "in the Tenderloin" by authors like Stephen Crane, at the time the best-selling author of *The Red Badge of Courage*.[22]

It was in his Sunday papers that Hearst, like Pulitzer, reached out most directly to the city's working and immigrant peoples. The Sunday papers reflected the vitality, prosperity, and optimism of the city's readers and the talent of its writers and artists. Even at a distance of one hundred years, there is something extraordinarily exhilarating about reading through a turn-of-the-century Sunday newspaper. Like continuous vaudeville in the 1890s, amusement parks in the 1900s, and the movie palaces in the 1920s, the Sundays were intentionally oversized, overstocked, and overwhelming. To attract customers who might not otherwise be ready to spend money on a commodity that was not absolutely necessary, the Sunday editors and publishers went out of their way to provide their readers with an incredible bargain — a newspaper of close to one hundred pages with enough in it to provide reading material for the rest of the week.

The Sundays were newspapers in name only. The first few pages looked much like the dailies, but from there on, the Sundays were a genre unto themselves, with separate staffs, printing and distribution schedules, and more than a few items that would have been out of place in any other sort of publication. On any given Sunday, readers of the Hearst papers were treated to lengthy illustrated stories on dinosaurs, extraterrestrials, or medical cures; several pages on Broadway personalities and shows; short stories and excerpts from the best or most popular current fiction; fully illustrated features on ballet dancers, chorus girls, actresses, and other scantily clad performers; and a variety of women's pages and family features. Included as well were three full-color supplements: the *American Humorist* with its comics, a sixteen-page *Sunday American Magazine,* and an eight-page *Women's Home Journal.*

The most visible, popular, and, over time, profitable of Hearst's Sunday features were his color comics. Pulitzer had published a Sunday humor page in 1889 and a color humor supplement in 1894. One of the more important contributors to this section was the artist Richard Outcault who in early 1896 had begun to draw a series of cartoons organized around a recurring group of characters, the most recognizable of whom was a bald-headed, jug-eared, buck-toothed urchin in a yellow nightshirt. Outcault's Yellow Kid became so popular a character that Pulitzer used him not just in his comic supplement but in the weekday advertisements for the Sunday paper.[23]

In the fall of 1896 when Hearst decided to match Pulitzer with a full-color Sunday humor magazine of his own, he custom-ordered specially designed color presses from the Hoe Company and stole Outcault and his Yellow Kid from the *World.* To make sure all of New York City knew what he was doing, he plastered the town with posters announcing the coming of the *American Humorist* and, in full-page announcements in his own papers, counted down the days to the arrival of the Yellow Kid, and "Eight Full Pages of Color That Make the Kaleidoscope Pale with Envy."[24]

On October 25, the *American Humorist* made its debut with a full front-page cartoon panel of the Yellow Kid leading a marching band of children into their new neighborhood. In the weeks to come, the stand-alone color supplement featured not only Yellow Kid cartoons, but gorgeous full-page theatrical drawings by Archie Gunn, sheet music, comic pages, jokes, and illustrations — all, as Hearst proclaimed, for the nickel it cost to buy the Sunday *Journal.*

Pulitzer tried to stay in the game by asking artist George Luks to draw his own cartoon using Outcault's characters, thereby giving New York two Yellow Kids every Sunday and providing a convenient nickname, "yellow journalism," for Hearst's and Pulitzer's newspapers in particular and their style of journalism in general. Unfortunately, on a limited budget and without the capital to install new color presses or the passion for the comics that Hearst had, Pulitzer could not keep pace.

In late 1897, a second comic strip with continuing characters, the *Katzenjammer Kids,* appeared in Hearst's Sunday *American Humorist.* In early 1900, *Happy Hooligan* made its debut. What all these strips had in common was not only artistic merit and imagination, but characters who were clearly immigrants. Happy Hooligan was an identifiable Irish-American tramp. The Katzenjammer Kids were German-Americans. The Yellow Kid looked Asiatic, was bald like the poor Eastern European kids whose heads were shaved to prevent lice, and had an Irish name, Mickey Duggan, and an Irish girlfriend. He lived in an Irish neighborhood, Hogan's Alley, bowled in Kelley's Alleys, and played outside Dempsey's Saloon. Among the Yellow Kid's friends were a wide variety of urban types, including an unnamed "darky" and the Ricodonna sisters, who appeared for one week as young prostitutes before being magically transformed into chorus girls.[25]

Over the years, as Hearst built a network of newspapers across the country and established his own features syndicate, he would add to the immigrants who were his first comic heroes a pantheon of American types, most of them recognizably urban. At one time or another, his comic pages included a quintessential middle-class boy in Outcault's *Buster Brown;* two working stiffs in Bud Fisher's *Mutt and Jeff;* an Irish bricklayer who has become a millionaire and his social-climbing wife in George McManus's *Maggie and Jiggs;* a rogue "sporting" man in Billy De Beck's *Barney Google;* a lower-middle-class Jewish businessman in Harry Hershfield's *Abie the Agent;* and a group of ethnically unidentifiable characters in Winsor McCay's *Little Nemo;* a middle-class "working girl" in Russ Westover's *Tillie the Toiler;* a sailor and his pals in E. C. Segar's *Popeye;* a middle-class married couple, Blondie and Dagwood Bumstead, in Chic Young's *Blondie* — and the cat and mouse in George Herriman's *Krazy Kat.* During the 1930s, these characters were joined by a new wave of action heroes: Flash Gordon, Secret Agent X-9, The Phantom, Mandrake the Magician, Prince Valiant, and young Hejji, drawn by Dr. Seuss.[26]

With his comics as with every other element of his newspapers, Hearst was a hands-on publisher, sometimes to the dismay and occasionally with the gratitude of his artists and editors. In the years to come, he would intervene to ban *A Piker Clerk* from the *Chicago American* because he thought it vulgar, suggest to Billy De Beck that he provide Barney Google with the "good-looking gal" that turned out to be the extraordinarily voluptuous Sweet Mama, and protect George Herriman's *Krazy Kat* from local editors who kept trying to remove it from their comic pages, claiming their readers just didn't "get it."[27]

While Pulitzer waited for his young rival to run out of money, Hearst continued to outspend him on equipment, advertising, and personnel. In editorials and advertisements, he teased Pulitzer and the *World* as representatives of an old, tired journalism being rapidly supplanted by the young, vibrant Hearst daily. Pulitzer fought back as best he could. When, in the spring of 1897, the United Press dissolved and the newspapers that had subscribed to it sought membership in the Associated Press, Pulitzer, a charter member of the A.P., approved the *Times, Herald,* and *Tribune* for membership but vetoed the Hearst papers. Had Hearst not acted quickly, the loss of a wire service franchise might have ended his newspaper career in New York City. Fortunately, he had the funds to buy himself a newspaper with an Associated Press franchise, the *New York Morning Advertiser,* and merge it and its wire service subscription with his *Morning Journal.*[28]

Hearst's raids on the *World* intensified in the fall of 1897 as he hired away Pulitzer's features editor Rudolph Block, city editor Charles Edward Russell, and then, astonishingly, Arthur Brisbane, who had replaced Goddard as the *World*'s Sunday editor. Brisbane, the son of Albert Brisbane, America's leading Fourierist and a founder of Brook Farm, was the perfect match for Hearst. He too was a "radical" of sorts, a supporter of Henry George and a champion of the workingman, but he was also a young editor on the make, who as his biographer put it, "craved power, popular success, and, above all, money." Brisbane and Hearst had been born just a year apart, were sons of larger-than-life fathers, and believed that they could do just about anything better than anyone else. Like Hearst, Brisbane was a dynamo and a brilliant newspaperman, with a flair for the spectacular and outrageous. Unlike his boss, however, he was nervous, thin, of medium height, a boor, a pedant, and rather humorless.[29]

Brisbane, according to his version of the events that led to his hiring, had rebuffed Hearst's first attempt to bring him to the *Journal.* Only as it became apparent that Hearst was as talented a publisher as he was a rich one and not about to disappear from the scene, did Brisbane contact him with a proposition. He wanted to take over the *Evening Journal,* which Hearst had started up in 1896 to compete with Dana's *Evening Sun,* Pulitzer's *Evening World,* and the *Evening Telegram,* James Gordon Bennett, Jr.'s evening paper. Hearst told Brisbane that he had made up his mind to close the evening paper, because it had a tiny circulation and he, William R. Hearst, was a "morning newspaper man." But he was willing, nonetheless, to give the *Evening Journal* one last chance, and agreed to let Brisbane share in whatever profits might accrue from increased circulation.[30]

Pulitzer had reined in Brisbane and forbidden him to expand headlines to fill the page. Hearst did not. He gave Brisbane the same marching orders for the evening paper he had given Goddard for the Sunday edition. He wanted increased circulation. Brisbane gave it to him. In creating a new evening edition and putting Brisbane in charge, Hearst was acknowledging that it was not going to be possible to create one newspaper that would reach all segments of the urban population. To do that, he needed an evening edition as well as the morning, Sunday, and German-language editions. While he had made the *Journal* as reader-friendly and accessible as any other morning paper in New York, many recently arrived immigrants and working people did not have the time, background, or inclination to wade through the longer, detailed, more literary articles it carried each day. Those who already read a morning paper wanted something different in the afternoon: less news, less analysis, less detail, more emphasis on sports and entertainment. Brisbane apparently gave his evening paper readers what they wanted. He condensed the news stories, added oversized boldface headlines to the front and inside pages, and illustrated his lead stories. Under Brisbane's leadership, the *Evening Journal* became Hearst's most profitable newspaper. Because it was so decidedly lowbrow, so clogged with advertisements, and so unliterary, it would never, however, be his favorite.

Arthur Brisbane would spend the next forty years working for Hearst in a variety of roles. Although not terribly well liked by his colleagues, he knew precisely what he had to do to remain in the Chief's good graces. He took whatever assignment was given him, followed Hearst's political line through its twists and turns over the next four decades, and was appropriately rewarded with a steadily escalating salary that made him the nation's highest-paid newspaperman.

Joseph Pulitzer did not sit idly by as the new kid in town stole away his most valuable editors, tens of thousands in circulation, and hundreds of thousands in revenues. Hearst, Pulitzer admitted to his managing editor, Don Seitz, posed an enormous threat to the *World* in the morning, the evening, and on Sundays, not only because he had money to spend, but because he had "brains and genius beyond any question, not only brains for news and features but genius for the self-advertising acts which have no parallel." Pulitzer urged his editors to stop looking at the *Journal* with "contempt" and acknowledge its genuine "strengths. . . . If we do not admit that the *Journal* is printed better and so far as pictures are concerned, is better, then we are blind." In coded messages sent to New York City — Pulitzer had devised a code name for every editor at the Hearst papers — Pulitzer directed his executives to gather information on the *Journal*'s efforts. He was convinced that Hearst had planted a spy in the *World* offices and intended to reciprocate: Hearst's paper, he said, "adopts our ideas without reserve;

adopt anything it may produce promptly if of value." He instructed Seitz in August to "find somebody in Geranium's [Pulitzer's code name for the *Journal*] office with whom you can connect, to discover exactly who furnishes their ideas, who is dissatisfied and obtainable or available even in the second class of executive rank." In December, after Brisbane's defection to the enemy, Pulitzer authorized Seitz to intensify his espionage into "the inner workings of the Geranium . . . with a view to ascertaining who is producing the good ideas. If it would be helpful, get some tactful and discreet man to assist you in getting information." Pulitzer approved the expenditure of "$25 a week, or more if required as a 'luncheon fund' to promote sociability! — a secret service, diplomatic fund, as it were."[31]

The competition for readers was costing both Hearst and Pulitzer a great deal of money. While their circulations and advertising were rising, their per-issue prices were too low to cover costs. Fearing perhaps that Phoebe and her cousin Edward Clark might be about to rein him in, Will contacted Pulitzer, in November of 1897, offering to raise the price of his paper to two cents, if Pulitzer would do the same. In return, he asked that Pulitzer drop his opposition to Hearst's application for an Associated Press franchise for his evening paper. Though delighted that Hearst had blinked first, Pulitzer was not prepared to give up anything. He sent his surrogates to meet with Hearst's, but the negotiations went nowhere.[32]

On arriving in New York City, Hearst had taken a suite of rooms at the Hoffman House on Fifth Avenue, off Madison Square, before moving to the nearby Worth House, where he leased, renovated, and refurnished the entire third floor with antique furniture and tapestries he had purchased in Europe. When the Worth House was put up for sale, he bought himself the four-story house, once owned by President Chester Arthur, at 123 Lexington Avenue on 28th Street, and installed George Thompson, whom he had stolen away from the Hoffman House, as his butler, major-domo, and gatekeeper. Rooms were set aside for Jack Follansbee, who stayed there on his frequent visits from Mexico, and Arthur Brisbane, who like Hearst and Follansbee was still a bachelor.[33]

Brisbane and Hearst got along well. "Your columnist and editor," Hearst would write many years later in a newspaper column, "took the night shift from 3 o'clock in the afternoon until 3 o'clock in the morning. His friend and associate, Arthur Brisbane, took the day shift for the afternoon paper from 6 o'clock in the morning until 6 o'clock at night — long hours and enjoyable ones for both. Oftentimes the writer would get home to his house on Lexington Ave. to have supper at 5 in the morning, and find Mr. Bris-

George Hearst circa
1860, when he returned
from California to
Missouri and married
Phoebe Apperson
(*Courtesy, Bancroft Library,
University of California,
Berkeley*)

Phoebe Hearst in her
wedding dress, 1862
(*Courtesy, Bancroft Library,
University of California,
Berkeley*)

George Hearst in the late
1880s, when he served as a
U.S. senator from California
(*Courtesy, Bancroft Library,
University of California, Berkeley*)

Phoebe Hearst at age
seventy-three, marching in the
San Francisco Preparedness
Parade, July 1916
(*Courtesy, Bancroft Library,
University of California, Berkeley*)

William Randolph
Hearst as a young boy
(*Courtesy, Bancroft Library,
University of California,
Berkeley*)

and as a teenager
(*Copyright © Hearst
Castle™/Hearst San Simeon
State Historical Monument™*)

With a friend (left)
at Harvard College
(*Courtesy, Bancroft
Library, University of
California, Berkeley*)

and in his middle twenties
(*San Francisco Examiner*)

Phoebe and Will at Phoebe's Hacienda, in Pleasanton, California
(*Special Collections, California Polytechnic State University*)

William Randolph Hearst and Millicent Hearst in the wedding picture published in the Hearst newspapers on April 29, 1903 (*Culver Pictures, Inc.*)

Millicent and Hearst with their sons George (standing), Bill, Jr. (seated), and John Randolph (in Millicent's arms), in late 1910 (*San Francisco Examiner*)

The Chief in his middle forties
(*Courtesy, Bancroft Library, University of California, Berkeley*)

On the reviewing stand with New York dignitaries to welcome American soldiers returning from Europe, March 26, 1919. From left to right: Governor Al Smith; Mayor John F. Hylan; Hearst; Alfred Johnson, a prominent local Democrat; and Assistant Secretary of the Navy Franklin Delano Roosevelt. (*Granger Collection, New York*)

With Bill, Jr., Millicent, and John, leaving New York for Europe on board the *Aquitania*, May 1922 (*Culver Pictures, Inc.*)

bane having 5 o'clock breakfast preliminary to keeping his 6 o'clock date on the *Journal*."

As in San Francisco, Hearst kept the hours of a morning-newspaper man: to bed at dawn, up at noon. On rising, he would take the short walk to the Hoffman House for his first appointments of the day, in the bar, under gorgeous Bouguereau murals of "nymphs in the nude." From the Hoffman House at Broadway and 25th Street, it was a short walk to Delmonico's at Fifth Avenue and 26th Street, where Hearst ate dinner, his main meal, at midday. After dinner, he traveled south to the *Journal* offices on Park Row and Spruce Street, usually arriving by three in the afternoon and staying through the early evening. Following his second meal of the day, a "late luncheon" at Shanley's or Rector's, it was time for the theater. Will's favorites were light musical comedies of the Weber and Fields variety, preferably with chorus girls, though he enjoyed vaudeville, straight comedy, and the circus as well.[34]

After the show, accompanied by that evening's handpicked company of newspapermen and chorus girls, Will would top off the day with a late-night supper at Jack's on Sixth Avenue, Jim's Chop House on Broadway, Martin's on University Place, or Delmonico's, and then return to the *Journal* office to put the next morning's paper to bed. He would, according to the *Journal* editor Willis Abbott, turn up "at about one thirty A.M. . . . full of scintillating ideas and therewith rip my editorial page to pieces. Other pages were apt to suffer equally, and it was always an interesting spectacle to me to watch this young millionaire, usually in irreproachable evening dress, working over the forms, changing a head here, shifting the position of an article there, clamoring always for more pictures and bigger type." While the composing room at this time of night was a nightmare of jagged nerves and competing egos, young William remained calm, polite, and well-mannered in the extreme. "Not once," according to Abbott, who worked with him for sixteen years, "did he ever show signs of irritation or lose his temper. . . . To those whom he knew and whose work he liked, he was in those days an ideal 'boss.' A good piece of work always brought a word of congratulation over the 'phone and not infrequently more substantial recognition."[35]

We know relatively little about Hearst's personal life. It is likely that his next steady companion after Tessie was Millicent Willson, the sixteen-year-old dancer from Brooklyn whom he met in 1896 or early 1897 while she was performing at the Herald Square Theatre alongside her eighteen-year-old sister, Anita, in *The Girl from Paris*. The Willson sisters were part of the chorus of "bicycle girls" who showed as much leg as possible without getting arrested. *The Girl from Paris* was a musical comedy review on the risqué side, with lots of singing and dancing and very little plot. Hearst saw the show several times with his old friend the printer George Pancoast, and may have been responsible for James Ford's tardy but spectacular review in the *Journal* on January 17.

When *The Girl from Paris* closed, the Willson sisters moved on to the Casino Theatre and an even naughtier musical comedy, *The Telephone Girl*, which the *New York Times* referred to as "coarse enough to be called nasty. Its subject is the everlasting contest of the sexes, and the treatment of it is from the point of view of barroom loafers and street girls." Millicent, who played "Toots," got a few good notices. Even the *Times* critic acknowledged, in an otherwise negative review, that her song and dance had shown "signs of vitality." *The Telephone Girl* may have been Millicent's last role on Broadway; there is no further record of her on stage.[36]

Phoebe's niece Anne Apperson Flint, who had moved to New York to attend the Spence School, lived at the Netherlands Hotel, where Phoebe's accountant and adviser Edward Clark had relocated with his wife to watch over Will. She recalled that there was quite a lot of "common talk" about Will Hearst's having taken up with two chorus girls half his age. Mrs. Clark, in particular, "was a little outraged" by it. Hearst had given Millicent "a hansom cab with a white horse . . . which she drove around in. This was well known. . . . We would all dodge when we'd see them because we didn't want to face them." Will not only escorted the girls to the theater and after-hours restaurants; he also, according to Henry Klein who worked at the *Journal* as a night telephone-story writer (he took dictation from reporters in the field), brought them along on his late-night trips to the composing room.[37]

Years later, Millicent would tell her friend, the Hearst reporter Adela Rogers St. Johns, that her mother had insisted that her sister Anita accompany her on her dates with Hearst. "When he asked me to go out with him . . . my mother was against it . . . I recall she said, 'Who *is* he? Some young fellow from out West somewhere, isn't he?' She insisted Anita had to come or I couldn't go. Well, he took us down to the *Journal* — the *New York Journal* — we'd hardly heard of it, and he showed us over it, *all over it*. I hadn't the foggiest notion what we were doing, walking miles on rough boards in thin, high-heeled evening slippers, and I thought my feet would kill me. Of course this wasn't our idea of a good time. We wanted to go to Sherry's or Bustanoby's. More than that, Anita kept whispering to me, 'We're going to get thrown out of here, Milly, the way he behaves you'd think he *owned* it.'"[38]

The sight of Will Hearst, with a young girl on either arm, promenading through the streets, snuggled together in a hansom cab, or touring the *Journal* offices was quite scandalous, even for New York. Will had chosen to live his life in New York on the margins of polite society, as he had in Cambridge and San Francisco. With a bit of effort, he might have taken the city by storm, but, as his cousin recalled, "he didn't care" what people thought of him and "despised" society. He did not attend society cotillions; he did not rent a box at the Metropolitan Opera; he did not join civic or reform associations; he did not attend society receptions or weddings; he did not court or escort eligible women to the theater; he lived downtown in Madison Square while fashionable New York moved northward; and he made no attempt whatsoever to marry well.[39]

Though he was not as closely watched as in San Francisco, the newspaper community in New York was too close-knit and too addicted to gossip, and his exploits too deliciously scandalous, to be ignored. In August of 1897, the *Journalist* informed its readers that "Billy Hearst is down the coast with a cottage, young friends and a yacht, sighing for the unattainable ... fully occupied with what he believes to be Pleasure — with a capital P." In October, "New Comer," the *Journalist*'s chief gossip columnist, who claimed that he had gotten to know the regulars fairly well by working at Hearst's morning paper, described it as "a sort of go-as-you-please place ... As near as I can get at it, Hearst is a very easy mark for girls, who like yachting, good feeding and jolly times in general; for men with schemes and odd suggestions; for men about town, who can post him in the ways of the world; for sharks and sharps, especially those who were educated in what the *Sun* is pleased to call, 'The Academy of Crime.' He is good-natured, kindly disposed, slow to suspicion, and very proud of his father's money."[40]

James L. Ford, Hearst's theater columnist at the *Journal*, recalled in his autobiography that he found it hard to take his employer "seriously, for he reminded me of a kindly child, thoroughly undisciplined and possessed of a destructive tendency that might lead him to set fire to a house in order to see the engines play water on the flames."[41]

As Upton Sinclair would write much later in his nonfiction book *The Industrial Republic,* Will Hearst had "turned traitor to his class ... instinctively, and without pangs. ... It seems to have pleased him to defy *all* their conventions. I was told, for example, that when he first came to New York, he made himself a scandal in the 'Tenderloin.' I was perplexed about that, for the members of our 'second generation' are generally well known in the Tenderloin, and nobody calls it a scandal. But one young society man who had known Hearst well gave me the reason — and he spoke with real gravity: 'It wasn't what he did — we all do it: but it was the way he did it. He didn't take the trouble to hide what he did.'"[42]

The veneer of invulnerability that Hearst so proudly wore was never pierced. But it was dented. The most serious attack, one whose effects would continue to wound him for the rest of his life, came in early 1897. The *San Francisco Examiner* had been engaged in an exceptionally bitter campaign against the Southern Pacific Railroad, which was trying to get the federal government to forgive its massive debts. In the course of this campaign, the paper had strenuously opposed the reelection of the Southern Pacific's major spokesman, the California congressman Grove Johnson. Johnson was defeated in November of 1896, but returned to Washington for the lame-duck session of early 1897 and took the floor of the House to accuse Hearst of having solicited and received bribes from the Southern Pacific. According to Johnson, Hearst had turned against the railroad only after it refused to continue paying his bribes. The story was on face value rather ridiculous. Hearst had sufficient resources of his own and did not need to take bribes from the railroad. More to the point was the fact that the *Examiner* had never stopped attacking the Southern Pacific, even after the date on which Hearst was supposed to have received his first payoff. What was most salient about Johnson's accusation was not his claim that Hearst had taken a bribe, which would fade in time, but his attack on Hearst's character, which did not. "At first, we Californians were suspicious of 'Our Willie,' as Hearst is called on the Pacific Coast," Johnson proclaimed from the floor of the House, and went on:

> We knew him to be a debauchee, a dude in dress, an Anglomaniac in language and manners, but we thought he was honest. We knew him to be licentious in his tastes, regal in his dissipations, unfit to associate with pure women or decent men, but we thought "Our Willie" was honest. We knew he was erotic in his tastes, erratic in his moods, of small understanding and smaller views of men and measures, but we thought "Our Willie," in his English plaids, his cockney accent, and his middle-parted hair, was honest. We knew he had sought on the banks of the Nile relief from loathsome disease contracted only by contagion in the haunts of vice, and had rivaled the Khedive in the gorgeousness of his harem in the joy of restored health, but we still believed him honest, though low and depraved. We knew he was debarred from society in San Francisco because of his delight in flaunting his wickedness, but we believed him honest, though tattooed with sin.[43]

Until Johnson's speech, such accusations had been conveyed only in anonymous letters — like the ones Phoebe had received from Cambridge — and published only in scandal sheets and weekly newspapers. Johnson's charges would be preserved forever in the *Congressional Record* and excerpted widely in the years to come — with added weight for having been delivered, in person, from the floor of the House.

Johnson's attack was political, of course, and as such unavoidable for Hearst, for whom there were no discernible boundaries between the vocations of publisher and politician. George Hearst had bought the *Examiner* for the sole purpose of boosting his political career. While Will, on taking it over, had made clear to his father that he did not intend to run the *Examiner* as a party organ, that did not mean that he was not going to take a political position on every local, state, and national issue of importance.

Hearst evinced no interest in running for electoral office in San Francisco or New York. He had been too young and had acted too scandalously to be elected in San Francisco, and he was a newcomer to New York. Still, as a loyal Democrat whose readers were for the large part Democrats as well, Will expected to play a role in New York politics in 1896, a presidential election year. Since 1868, every Democratic nominee for president had been a New Yorker, except for one Pennsylvanian, Winfield Hancock. The pattern was abruptly broken when William Jennings Bryan, an up-and-coming Nebraska journalist who had served one term in the House and then been defeated in a race for the Senate, was nominated. For New York Democrats, the choice of the man known as the great commoner was a nightmare. Bryan was not only too young and too inexperienced, he was an outspoken opponent of the trusts and monopoly and too committed to agrarian issues and constituencies to win votes in the cities. His pledge to increase the money supply, deflate the currency, and lower prices by coining silver was anathema to Eastern businessmen and bankers. In the days following Bryan's nomination, Eastern party leaders and newspaper publishers, aghast at the theft of their party by Western Populists and "free silver" radicals, withdrew all support from Bryan. In New York, he was abandoned not only by Tammany Hall, the state party organization, and the former New York governor, President Grover Cleveland, but also by Pulitzer, who had made his mark in New York as a Democrat.

Hearst's business advisers urged him to sit out the election as well. But his political advisers — including radicals like Arthur McEwen he had brought with him from San Francisco — counseled otherwise. Presidential election campaigns arrived only once every four years. Bryan was, like Hearst, young, a Westerner, and a radical. He was also the nominee of the Democratic party and, for this reason alone, deserved the support of Senator Hearst's only son. Hearst agreed.

As he recalled many years later, in its support of Bryan the *New York*

Journal was "like a solitary ship surrounded and hemmed in by a host of others, and from all sides shot and shell poured into our devoted hulk. Editorial guns raked us, business guns shattered us, popular guns battered us, and above the din and flame of battle rose the curses of the Wall Street crowd that hated us . . . Advertisers called on me and said they would take out every advertisement if I continued to support Bryan, and I told them to take out their advertisements, as I needed more space in which to support Bryan."[44] It was assumed that Hearst had backed Bryan because his family owned silver mines and stocks and would profit from the remonetization of silver. The truth was exactly the opposite. Though the Hearst family owned silver mines, it had larger investments in gold, which would depreciate significantly if Bryan were elected.

As a recent arrival in New York City, Hearst had no political base and no feel for local politics. But when Tammany Hall and the state Democratic party refrained from actively supporting Bryan, the *Journal* office became headquarters for the campaign. Hearst opened a subscription drive for funds to "educate" voters and promised to match every dollar received in the *Journal* offices. He printed a weekly "campaign extra" which Bryan supporters distributed free of charge. His reporters followed Bryan's every step along the campaign trail; interviews and articles were published daily. Easterners who wanted to read about Bryan or follow his campaign had no choice but to read the *Journal*. Circulation boomed for the morning *Journal* and the evening edition, which Hearst started up during the campaign.[45]

With unmatched energy and skill, Hearst concentrated his newspapers' resources on the task of winning voters to Bryan by ridiculing his Republican opponents. There were no ambiguities in Will Hearst's political universe: while individual Democrats might be corrupt, the party stood foursquare for the people. The Republicans, on the contrary, were the party of wealth, privilege, monopoly, and the railroads. William McKinley and Senator Mark Hanna, the Cleveland industrialist and financier who ran the party, represented it at its worst: smug, complacent, fat, and monied. Every day, the front page of the *Journal* was marked by Homer Davenport cartoons of a bloated "Boss Hanna" covered by dollar signs, and his puppet, a grossly overweight, buffoonish McKinley.

On Election Day, November 3, 1896, the *Journal* triumphantly displayed in the middle of its front page, in type as large as any Hearst had yet deployed, a telegram from Bryan thanking the editor of the *New York Journal* for the paper's "splendid fight in behalf of bimetallism and popular government." Beneath it was a second telegram, from Mark Hanna, McKinley's campaign manager, predicting, in much smaller type, that McKinley would win at least 311 votes in the Electoral College. On the left-hand side of the page, the *Journal* alerted its readers to:

WATCH THE JOURNAL'S STAR FOR THE ELECTION RETURNS

Colored Electric Lights from a Monster Balloon Will Flash the News to Greater New York and Jersey. If a Red Light Twinkles, Bryan is Leading; if Green, McKinley. Steady Red Glow Means Bryan Elected; Green, McKinley Wins. All Over the City Will Be the Journal's Bulletins, with Bands of Music, Stereopticons and Moving Pictures Showing Wonderful Views.

On the second page of the paper was the "Map Showing Locations of Journal Bulletins, Bands and Balloons" with the injunction to "Cut This Out and Carry It with You."

Though Bryan would lose the election — and every state north of Virginia and east of Kansas — Hearst would emerge as a winner in New York City. His brash and enthusiastic support of the Democratic candidate and his constant hammering away at Hanna and McKinley had resulted in increased circulation, a good deal of it from Pulitzer's papers which had, for the first time, declined to support a Democratic candidate for national office. On November 5, the *Journal* proudly declared that the Election Day circulation of its three editions, the morning, evening, and German-language, had reached 1.5 million, a journalistic record.

Hearst did not shy away from the power that came with the capacity to speak every day to hundreds of thousands of New Yorkers. Though he had not as yet decided to run for electoral office, he remained in the political arena after the election by taking on the "trusts," the generic term of disapproval used to describe the corporate monopolies that were growing stronger by the day.

The post–Civil War economy was defined to an extraordinary extent by the rapid and irreversible increase in the size and influence of private corporations. Businessmen had discovered the advantages of combination, of vertically and horizontally extending their enterprises and controlling competition through pooling their resources in legal trusts. According to the historian Richard L. McCormick, one of the unintended consequences of large-scale industrialization and the organization of trusts was "the unorganized public's dawning sense of vulnerability, unease, and anger in the face of economic changes wrought by big corporations. Sometimes, the people's inchoate feelings focused on the ill-understood 'trusts'; at other times, their negative emotions found more specific, local targets in street-railway or electric-power companies." The Hearst papers articulated this "vulnerability, unease, and anger" more powerfully and persistently than any other public medium in the 1890s.[46]

Will Hearst had inherited his antitrust sentiments from his father and the California Democrats. George Hearst's political career — and that of just about every other Democrat in the state — had been built upon opposition to the largest, most powerful trust in the West, the Southern Pacific Railroad or SP, as Californians were accustomed to calling it. The Octopus, as novelist Frank Norris referred to the railroad in his novel of that name, held in its tentacles the people of the state, wherever they lived, however they made their livings. "The SP offered the most obvious instance," the historian Kevin Starr has written, "of what was grossly wrong with California: a very few of the super-rich virtually owned the state — its land, its economy, its government — and were running it as a private preserve." The Big Four monopolists, Leland Stanford, Mark Hopkins, Charles Crocker, and Collis Huntington, all of whom had emigrated from the East — three from upstate New York — with the Forty-Niners, had built for themselves an interlocking empire of "railroads, steamship companies, land holdings (vast acres were granted by the federal government as a subsidy and spur to railroad construction), irrigation projects, hotels and urban real estate." The foundation and guarantor of their wealth was their manipulation of the political system. Generous bribes, insider business opportunities, free passes and hotel rooms, and campaign contributions had bought them control over the state Republican party, the legislature in Sacramento, the judiciary, and the big-city Democratic bosses and machines. Leland Stanford himself had served as governor and represented the state — and his railroad — in the United States Senate.[47]

Will Hearst, like his father before him, had battled the Southern Pacific in the *Examiner,* hiring as editorialists two of its most caustic critics, Ambrose Bierce and Arthur McEwen, the tall, blond, fiercely independent and combative Scotsman, who was every bit as brilliant a polemicist as Bierce but much further to the left. For McEwen, Leland Stanford's election to the Senate had been nothing less than "an indictment of the intelligence and moral character of the people of California."[48]

When Hearst moved to New York, he took McEwen with him to write the trustbusting editorials he had specialized in at the *Examiner.* In San Francisco, there had been only one major octopus of a trust, the Southern Pacific. In New York City, there were several. With monopoly control over ice, water, gas, power, transit, and insurance, the trusts wielded enormous economic power which, like the SP in California, they used to buy political influence. The citizens of New York, as the Hearst papers reminded them daily, were doubly victimized by the trusts. As consumers of public services, they were forced to pay too much for their gas, power, coal, ice, milk, even water — all of which were under the control of the trusts. As citizens they were deprived of voice, vote, and the wherewithal to protect themselves from the monopolies. Those who worked for the trusts were three-time losers.

Hearst had assumed control of the *New York Journal* at a time when the trusts were consolidating their hold on the city's economy. By late 1896, as the depression that had persisted since 1893 began to lift and as the population of the city burgeoned, there was a growing, inexorable demand for more sewers, tunnels, bridges, roads, streetcars, and electric lighting. The Republican legislature in Albany and the board of aldermen in New York City responded to the demand as they always had: by awarding the trusts exclusive franchises for twenty-five years, with an option to renew for another twenty-five.

Hearst and his papers kept a careful eye on the process, ever alert to new swindles, new payoffs, new "grabs" by the trusts and their lackey politicians, who were paid handsomely for their help — in cash and stock certificates. When, in late 1896, Mayor William Strong and the board of aldermen granted the Consumers' Fuel and Gas Company a franchise to tear up the streets of the city and lay entirely new and unneeded gas mains, Hearst hired a young attorney, Clarence Shearn, to enjoin the mayor and the aldermen from proceeding. Shearn's injunction was granted by Supreme Court Judge Robert Pryor on December 13, 1896. The *Journal* reported the news in a headline that extended clear across the front page, in bold type — the largest the paper owned — "WHILE OTHERS TALK THE JOURNAL ACTS!," with the word "acts" in double boldface. With this declaration, the *Journal* announced to the city that its political activism had not ended with the Bryan campaign, but would, in fact, become as integral a component of the newspaper as its crime stories. Shearn was kept on retainer at the paper to fight the gas, water, coal, and ice trusts in the courts. On December 9, 1897, the *Journal* announced that he had drafted an antitrust bill to abolish them entirely.

On December 3, 1897, Hearst marked the beginning of his third year in New York by celebrating the role he had carved out for his newspapers. The lead editorial that day was entitled "The *Journal's* Settled Policy":

Within the past year a new force has appeared on the side of good government in New York. . . . Above the boards and councils and commissions stand the courts, and by the side of the courts stands the New Journalism, ready to touch the button that sets their ponderous machinery in motion. . . . The *Journal* has adopted the policy of action deliberately, and it means to stick to it. It thinks it has discovered exactly the engine of which the dwellers in American cities stand in need. When it adopted the two mottoes, "While others talk the *Journal* acts," and "What is everybody's business is the *Journal's* business," it showed how the multitudes that are individually helpless against the rapacity of the few could be armed against their despoilers.

From this point on, Hearst would daily highlight the role his newspapers played in the life of the city, the nation, and the world. On December 20, 1897, to choose only one day at random, the *Journal* carried more than a half-dozen stories in which the newspaper was the chief protagonist. On page one, the top right-hand column reproduced a telegram from the lord mayor of London, under the headline: "Through the Journal He Sends Heartiest Greetings with Friendly Interest in the Prosperity of the Sister City." In the middle of the front page, another story, headlined "Spain's War on the Journal," claimed that the Spanish government was retaliating against the *Journal's* pro-Cuban activities by evicting it from its Havana offices and attempting to assassinate its representatives. At the bottom was an article about the New Year's Eve celebration the *Journal* was hosting to greet "the birth of the Greater New York." A story on page four told of a Professor Young who had written the *Journal* asking it to sponsor a "long distance fiddling match"; on page five was an announcement of "The Journal's $1,000 Prophecy Competition"; on page ten, an article outlining the *Journal's* plan to "establish a state institution for reception of child criminals."

The following day, December 21, a portrait of Kaiser William II of Germany appeared on the front page. The headline, "Kaiser Is Europe's New York Journal," reminded readers that the newspaper they were reading, like the German Kaiser, made history by "acting" instead of "talking."

Hearst had carved out for himself a unique place in New York politics. He was a reformer and an opponent of the trusts, a critic of Tammany Hall, and a loyal Democrat. There were obvious contradictions here, but Hearst chose to ignore them. To be a loyal New York Democrat in the 1890s was to be a backer of Boss Croker, the man who provided the trusts with the lavish contracts that permitted them to make a fortune by overcharging New Yorkers for transportation, water, gas, milk, power, and just about every other daily necessity. Born in Ireland, Richard Croker had risen through the ranks from volunteer fireman to chief sachem of Tammany Hall. He was a master of what George Washington Plunkitt called "honest graft." He "didn't steal a dollar from the city treasury, just seen opportunities and took them." No contract was let, no franchise awarded, no license assigned, no appointment made, no nomination secured, no policeman paid off without the Boss getting his cut. By the 1890s, Croker had pocketed a fortune in "honest graft," but with good government reformers, Albany Republicans, and crusading journalists keeping watch, he could not spend it as conspicuously as he would have liked in New York. Instead he relocated to the English countryside to enjoy the life of a country squire and raise race horses.[49]

Boss Croker returned home in 1897, to solidify his hold on the party and elect the first mayor of Greater New York, the consolidated city that included Brooklyn, Queens, Staten Island, and those parts of the Bronx that had been separately governed. Croker's candidate was Robert C. Van Wyck, an unknown and undistinguished judge. He was opposed by an equally nondescript Republican and two independent, anti-Tammany, reform candidates, Seth Low, the former two-term mayor of Brooklyn who was now president of Columbia University, and Henry George, the author of *Progress and Poverty,* founder of the Single-Tax movement, and arguably the most famous, if not the most widely read, radical in the country. With the support of New York's labor leaders, George had run for mayor in 1886 and though defeated by Tammany's candidate had polled more votes than the Republican nominee, Theodore Roosevelt. This time around, his chances of winning the election appeared excellent.

Ideologically, Hearst was closer to Low and George than he was to Van Wyck. Unwilling to abandon his father's political party, however, he supported the Democratic candidate, while publicly distancing himself from Boss Croker. "Please make an editorial saying the *Journal* is a Democratic paper," he directed James Creelman, his chief political writer and adviser, "and it believes the best way to secure good government is to fight for it within party lines. . . . There is no shadow upon the Democratic ticket except Croker and Croker . . . can be everywhere fought and overcome by good Democrats *within party lines.*"[50]

When Henry George died of a stroke four days before the election, Van Wyck's election was assured. Still, Hearst took credit for his victory in large part because the city's other newspapers, including Pulitzer's *World,* had supported either Low or the Republican candidate. In return for his papers' endorsements, Hearst had secured a plank in the Democratic platform calling for increased support for the public schools. When Croker and the Van Wyck administration reneged on their promise, Hearst sent Creelman to talk to the Boss. "Tell Mr. Croker," he instructed Creelman, "that the school plan was put in platform at *Journal* insistence and that when *Journal* supported Tammany we pledged Tammany's sincerity to our English and German readers [Hearst's German-language paper had also endorsed Van Wyck]. *Journal* would like to continue to warmly support Tammany as it is the democratic organization. I personally would like to be wholly friendly with Croker as he is an agreeable gentleman but the education of American children is not a question of party politics or even of personal friendship but of public duty. . . . I have asserted my friendship. Let Mr. Croker display his."[51]

On New Year's Eve, 1897, Will Hearst celebrated his new, self-proclaimed role as New York's favorite son by organizing a mammoth celebration to mark the amalgamation of the five boroughs into what would now be known as Greater New York. Nothing pleased Hearst more than staging a spectacular. His taste for the theatrical, his talent for self-promotion, and his love of modern technologies were all enlisted in planning the event. As the staunchly Republican *New York Daily Tribune*, still smarting from Tammany's victory in November, reported the next morning, "the spirits of disorder poured forth into the city streets and found their noisy and tumultuous way to City Hall Park, where the formal demonstration, held under the auspices of the *New York Journal*, was to be held. . . . *The Journal* offices were ablaze with colored lights, electric flags and all manner of illuminations. . . . The crowds came early. By nine o'clock they were packed in dense masses in the park." Though the weather was wintry cold and raining, it did not dampen the festivities Hearst had planned for the citizens of his newly adopted city. Choral groups from the city's ethnic societies and organizations sang before a panel of judges, which included the vaudeville impresario Tony Pastor. Floats and marching bands paraded under gleaming white magnesium searchlights. At 10 o'clock "the *Journal* showed its own special decoration — an oblong square of electric lights eighty feet long by forty feet" arranged in the Stars and Stripes. At midnight, the singers joined together in *Auld Lang Syne;* Henry J. Pain, the nation's most celebrated fireworks expert, set off a dazzling display of skyrockets, a battery of guns fired a deafening hundred-gun salute, and from three thousand miles away, Mayor Phelan of San Francisco pressed a magic button which sent an electrical signal across the nation to City Hall Park and "propelled the blue and white flag of Greater New York whipping up the staff of the City Hall cupola." "No one," the *New York Daily Tribune* concluded the next morning, "could hold a Roman candle to Hearst when it came to staging a spectacle."

$\text{\textinterrobang}\,7\,\text{\textinterrobang}$

"How Do You Like the *Journal*'s War?"

THERE ARE NO ACCOUNTS of Hearst's life nor are there histories of the Spanish-American War that do not include some discussion of the role of the Yellow Press in general and Hearst in particular in fomenting war in Cuba. Still, it is safe to say from the vantage point of one hundred years that even had William Randolph Hearst never gone into publishing, the United States would nonetheless have declared war on Spain in April of 1898. That Hearst has received so large a measure of credit or blame for that "glorious war" is a tribute to his genius as a self-promoter. It was Hearst who proclaimed the war in Cuba to be the *New York Journal's* war and he who convinced the rest of the nation that without the Hearst press leading the way there would have been no war.

The first Cuban revolution against Spanish colonialism had begun in 1868, when Hearst was five years old, and was only subdued after ten years of fighting. In early 1895, the rebellion was reignited after the United States imposed a new American tariff on Cuban exports that led to massive unemployment on the sugar plantations and economic hardship throughout the island. By the fall, the Cuban revolutionaries had freed enough territory from Spanish rule to proclaim their own provisional government. "The reports indicate that Cuba is likely to gain her independence," the *San Francisco Examiner* editorialized in August of 1895, "but not before many battles have been fought, many lives have been lost, much property has been destroyed." Concluding that Spain was prepared to "fight a war to extermination" in Cuba, the *Examiner* called on the government in Washington to protect the innocent men, women, and children of Cuba from the fate that had recently befallen the Armenians at the hands of the Turks: "It may not be our duty to interfere in Turkey, but we certainly cannot permit the creation of another Armenia in this hemisphere . . . Cuba is our Armenia, and it is at our doors . . . We are determined that no more butcheries and arsons shall be laid to our door. Cuba must not stand in the relation to us that Armenia does to England."[1]

In early 1896, Spain responded to the growing insurrection in Cuba by sending 150,000 troops to the island commanded by General Valeriano Weyler (soon to be known in the American press as "Butcher" Weyler). Weyler tried to quell the rebellion by herding Cuban peasants into concentration camps to prevent them from supporting the rebel armies with food and new recruits. Hundreds of thousands of Cubans were forced from their land to die of starvation and disease behind barbed wire. The suffering was unimaginable. Pulitzer's *World*, Dana's *Sun*, and the *Journal*, which were fed a steady diet of stories from the Junta, the rebels' unofficial diplomatic and publicity arm, covered the events in Cuba as if they were happening next door.

That Spain had no moral or political right to maintain a colonial empire in the New World was not, for Hearst, a matter of debate. But this was not the primary reason why the Cuban conflict was given a prominent place on his front pages. What made Cuba such a compelling story was the fact that events on the island lent themselves to Hearst's favorite plot line. Here was raw material for tales of corruption more horrific than any yet told. The villains were lecherous and bloodthirsty Spanish officials and army officers; the victims, innocent Cuban women and children; the heroes, crusading *Journal* reporters and their publisher.

"Credible witnesses have testified," read an editorial from December 1896, "that all prisoners captured by Weyler's forces are killed on the spot; that even helpless inmates of a hospital have not been spared, and that Weyler's intention seems to be to murder all the pacificos in the country. . . . The American people will not tolerate in the Western Hemisphere the methods of the Turkish savages in Armenia, no matter what the cost of putting an end to them might be. Twenty Spains would prove no efficacious obstacle in the way of a righteous crusade like that. Let us not act hastily, but let us act."[2]

In early 1897, Hearst offered Richard Harding Davis $3,000 a month plus expenses to serve as the *Journal*'s special correspondent in Cuba. Artist Frederick Remington was sent along to illustrate Davis's articles. The two were transported to Cuba — with a full crew of assistants — in Hearst's new steam-driven 112-foot yacht, the *Vamoose*, which he had purchased in the early 1890s and kept moored in New York. Unfortunately the *Vamoose*, though a magnificent-looking yacht and reportedly the fastest ship in New

York Harbor, was entirely unsuited for the mission. After three attempts at landing, the captain had to turn back. Davis was so frustrated at being marooned offshore that, as he wrote his mother, he lay on the deck and cried. The *Vamoose* returned to Key West, where Hearst wired his reporters an additional $1,000 to buy or lease another boat. Davis and Remington decided instead to take the regularly scheduled passenger steamer to Havana.[3]

Hearst made the most of his stars' heroic entry onto the battle-scarred island. In mid-January, the *Journal* reported triumphantly that its representatives had caught up with the insurgent Cuban army. Davis was outraged. As he had written his mother a few days earlier, not only had he not found any army in the field, he had in his entire time in Cuba not "heard a shot fired or seen an insurgent. . . . I am just 'not in it' and I am torn between coming home and making your dear heart stop worrying and getting one story to justify me being here and that damn silly page of the Journal's . . . All Hearst wants is my name and I will give him that only if it will be signed to a different sort of a story from those they have been printing."[4]

While Davis never did find any fighting, he was able to find enough material to write a few magnificent front-page stories on the devastation the war had visited on Cuba and its peoples. Frederic Remington was not so fortunate. Disgusted by the lack of action and his inability to find scenes worth illustrating, he telegrammed Hearst from Havana that he wished to return to New York. "Everything is quiet. There is no trouble here. There will be no war." Hearst, according to James Creelman, who wrote about the incident in his autobiography, answered Remington by return cable, "Please remain. You furnish the pictures, and I'll furnish the war."[5]

Though many pages have been written about these telegrams, there is no record of them outside of Creelman's 1901 autobiography. Hearst himself, in a letter to the *London Times* in 1907, referred to the intimation that he was chiefly responsible for the Spanish war as a kind of "clotted nonsense" which "could only be generally circulated and generally believed in England."[6]

Despite his disclaimers, Hearst might well have written the telegram to Remington, but if he did, the war he was referring to was the one already being fought between the Cuban revolutionaries and the Spanish army, not the one the Americans would later fight. There is no mention of or reference to American intervention in the telegrams; the groundswell that would lead to intervention after the sinking of the *Maine* had not yet begun. The war in question, the war Hearst may have claimed he would furnish, was the one between Cubans and Spaniards being waged in January of 1897, not the one that would be declared in Washington fifteen months later.

The question that is much more interesting than whether or not Hearst wrote the telegram is why its contents have been so universally misinterpreted. The answer is simple: Hearst, with his genius for self-promotion, so deftly inserted himself and his newspapers into the narrative of the Spanish-American War that historians and the general public have accepted the presumption that he furnished it.

Though Hearst tried his best to keep Cuba on his front pages, events conspired against him. By April of 1897, Cuba was no longer front-page news. Hearst focused his attention instead on the threatened war between Greece and Turkey, dispatching to the front a full complement of star reporters led by Stephen Crane, Julian Ralph, two "female correspondents," and a full "contingent of Greek couriers, translators, and orderlies."[7]

By the summer of 1897, peace having settled over Greece, Hearst and his editors were left without a viable front-page story cycle. They found it in August in Cuba where, as they reported in huge bold headlines and artfully engraved line drawings, Evangelina Cosio y Cisneros, the young and innocent daughter of a jailed insurgent, had been cast into an airless dungeon for daring to protect her chastity against the brutal advances of a lust-crazed Spanish colonel. Evangelina was the perfect heroine for Hearst's melodrama: a beautiful eighteen-year-old "Cuban Joan of Arc, with long black hair." As Creelman recalled in his autobiography — no doubt with some embellishment — Hearst, on hearing of Evangelina's plight, took command of the newsroom and barked out orders to the assembled editors and reporters:

> "Telegraph to our correspondent in Havana to wire every detail of this case. Get up a petition to the Queen Regent of Spain for this girl's pardon. Enlist the women of America. Have them sign the petition. Wake up our correspondents all over the country. Have distinguished women sign first. Cable the petitions and the names to the Queen Regent. Notify our minister in Madrid. We can make a national issue of this case . . . That girl must be saved if we have to take her out of prison by force or send a steamer to meet the vessel that carries her away — but that would be piracy, wouldn't it?"

"Within an hour," continues Creelman's account, "messages were flashing to Cuba, and to every part of the United States. The petition to the Queen Regent was telegraphed to more than two hundred correspondents in various American cities and towns. Each correspondent was instructed to hire a carriage and employ whatever assistance he needed, get the signatures of prominent women of the place, and telegraph them to New York as quickly as possible."

Hearst himself telegraphed the most prominent women in the nation, including Mrs. McKinley in the White House: "Will you not add your name to that of distinguished American women like Mrs. Julia Ward Howe . . . who are cabling petitions to Queen Regent of Spain for release of Evangelina Cisneros eighteen years old . . . who is threatened with twenty years imprisonment? She is almost a child, sick, defenseless, and in prison. A word may save her. Answer at our expense. William Hearst."[8]

Hundreds of responses followed — from Clara Barton, Mrs. Jefferson Davis, President McKinley's mother, and many more — each one of them reproduced on the pages of the *Journal.* While the *World,* citing the American consul general in Havana, screamed that the Cisneros story was more hoax than fact, and *Town Topics,* the weekly guide to gossip and politics in New York, echoing the opinion of the city's respectable classes, complained that the *Journal's* coverage was both "senseless and pernicious," Hearst continued to trumpet the story, with the focus shifted from what had been done to Evangelina Cisneros to what the *Journal* was doing for her.[9]

As it became apparent that Spain was not about to release Evangelina, Hearst ordered the reporter and adventurer Karl Decker to sail for Cuba and help Evangelina escape. Miraculously, with the help of some well-placed bribes, Decker succeeded in springing Cisneros from her dungeon and transporting her to New York City: "An American Newspaper Accomplishes at a Single Stroke What the Red Tape of Diplomacy Failed to Bring About in Many Months." In New York, Hearst dressed Evangelina like a princess in a long white gown, installed her in a suite at the Waldorf, and paraded her through the streets to a huge rally at Madison Square Garden, followed by a dinner at Delmonico's, a ball in the Waldorf's Red Room, and a trip to Washington, D.C., for a reception with President McKinley at the White House.[10]

Hearst's rescue of Cisneros was significant not because, as his supporters and critics would later argue, it embarrassed the Spanish and pushed the United States toward involvement in the Caribbean, but because it strengthened his sense of entitlement and bolstered his confidence that because he was acting on behalf of the American people, he could make his own rules — subverting, if need be, common sense and international law.

The Evangelina Cisneros rescue was a sideshow. The real story was being played out in Cuba, where the insurgents continued their battle for independence, and in Spain, where the new Liberal party government found itself caught between the Cuban insurrectionists, who demanded complete independence, and the Conservative opposition, army officers, Spanish landholders in Cuba, and colonial officials, who threatened civil war should the Liberal government cede the island to the Cubans. With no compromise possible, the war continued. American businessmen watched hopelessly as the Cuban economy disintegrated, trade halted, and tens of millions of dollars in American investments were rendered virtually worthless.

On January 11, 1898, antigovernment riots broke out in Havana, incited this time not by the Cuban revolutionaries but by Spanish army officers who feared that the government in Madrid might give in to the revolutionaries. President McKinley ordered the battleship U.S.S. *Maine* to sail from Key West to protect American interests on the island.

Two weeks later, a representative of the Cuban Junta appeared at the *Journal* office with a stolen letter in which Dupuy de Lôme, the Spanish ambassador to the United States, referred to President McKinley as "weak, vacillating, and venal." The Cubans had offered the letter to the *Herald,* but when the *Herald* editors delayed publication pending authentication, the rebels withdrew it and marched to Hearst's offices. The *Journal* published the letter next morning in an inflammatory English translation. The headline read, "Worst Insult to the United States in Its History."[11]

Under ordinary circumstances, Hearst could have wrung headlines out of this story for weeks, but events were now moving so fast he did not have to. On the evening of February 15, 1898, the U.S.S. *Maine,* under circumstances which even today are not entirely clear, exploded in Havana Harbor, instantly killing more than 250 of the sailors, marines, and officers on board. This event, if we are to judge only from the size of the headlines, became at once the biggest newspaper story since the assassination of President Lincoln.

According to Hearst's account, he was awakened with news of the *Maine*'s sinking by his butler, George Thompson:

> "There's a telephone call from the office. They say it's important news."
> The office was called up.
> "Hello, what is the important news?"
> "*The battleship* Maine *has been blown up in Havana Harbor.*"
> "Good heavens, what have you done with the story?"
> "*We have put it on the first page of course.*"
> "Have you put anything else on the front page?"
> "*Only the other big news.*"

"There is not any other big news. Please spread the story all over the page. This means war."[12]

While President McKinley convened a naval court of inquiry to determine the cause of the *Maine* explosion and newspapers across the country cautioned readers to await the gathering of evidence before jumping to conclusions, Pulitzer's *World* and Hearst's *Journal* determined, after only forty-eight hours, that the explosion had been detonated by a Spanish mine. "Destruction of the Warship *Maine* Was the Work of An Enemy," read the *Journal's* front-page headline on February 17, 1897. In the middle of the page was a drawing of the *Maine* in Havana Harbor with a mine placed directly underneath it. The caption read: "The Spaniards, it is believed, arranged to have the *Maine* anchored over one of the Harbor mines. Wires connected the mine with a powder magazine and it is thought the explosion was caused by sending an electric current through the wire."[13]

"*Maine* is great thing. Arouse everybody. Stir up Madrid," Hearst telegrammed James Creelman in London. Having determined that the Spanish were responsible for the explosion, Hearst positioned the *Journal* in the center of the story as the hero who would avenge the murder of the American sailors. He offered a $50,000 reward for the solution to the mystery of the *Maine* explosion, began a drive for a *Maine* memorial and contributed the first $1,000, devised a new "War with Spain" card game, enlisted a delegation of senators and congressmen to travel to Cuba on a Hearst yacht as "*Journal* commissioners," and implored his readers to write their congressmen. The combined circulation of the morning and evening *Journals* reached one million and continued to grow.

Pulitzer and his editors tried but failed to keep up with Hearst's newspapers on this, the biggest story since the Civil War. The *World* did not have the funds — or the Hearst-owned yachts — to send dozens of correspondents and artists to report firsthand on Cuba, nor did it have the staff to put out six to eight pages of articles, editorials, cartoons, interviews, and illustrated features on the Cuban crisis each day. The *Journal's* coverage was bigger, more spectacular, more varied, and more imaginative than that of any other paper in the city. There were dozens of stories on the *Maine* explosion, on the funeral procession for the *Maine* victims, on the mounting horrors in "Butcher" Weyler's death camps, on the findings of the "*Journal* commissioners" to Cuba. While McKinley awaited the report from his naval court of inquiry on the cause of the *Maine* explosion, the Hearst papers attacked the president together with Mark Hanna, the "conservative" newspapers that refused to join the crusade, and "the eminently respectable porcine citizens" who resisted the call to battle. To graphically demonstrate to the public how easy it would be to win this war, the *Journal* contacted America's most famous oversized athletes, including heavyweight champions James J. Corbett and Bob Fitzsimmons, baseball star Cap Anson, and champion hammer-throwers and wrestlers, to ask if they would consider joining a regiment of athletes. "Think of a regiment composed of magnificent men of this ilk!" the *Journal* gloated on March 29, 1898. "They would overawe any Spanish regiment by their mere appearance."[14]

"Whatever else happens, the *World* must go," declared *Town Topics* in early April. "It has been beaten on its own dunghill by the *Journal*, which has bigger type, bigger pictures, bigger war scares, and a bigger bluff. If Mr. Pulitzer had his eyesight he would not be content to play second fiddle to the *Journal* and allow Mr. Hearst to set the tone."[15]

When, less than two months after the *Maine* explosion, Congress passed a joint resolution demanding that Spain "relinquish its authority and government on the island of Cuba" and directing the president "to use the land and naval forces of the United States to carry these resolutions into effect," Hearst's *Journal* greeted the news, in headlines a full four inches high, "NOW TO AVENGE THE MAINE!" Five days later, on April 25, rockets were set off from the roof of the *Journal* building to celebrate the signing of the declaration of war and the *Journal* offered a prize of $1,000 to the reader who came up with the best ideas for conducting the war. A week later, Hearst, unable to contain his euphoria, asked on the very top of his front page, "How do you like the *Journal*'s war?"[16]

Though Hearst claimed that the war in Cuba was the *Journal*'s war, it was not. President McKinley had not asked for a declaration of war, nor had Congress granted him one, to please William R. Hearst. The "yellows" had been clamoring for war for several years, with no discernible effect, their strident voices balanced by more conservative Republican voices like Whitelaw Reid's *Tribune* and E. L. Godkin's *Evening Post*, which urged restraint. Hearst was a cheerleader not a policy maker. McKinley had his own sources of information in Cuba; he did not need a Hearst or Pulitzer to tell him what was going on there nor did he place much trust in what they had to say. According to the historian Walter LaFeber, he did not even read the "yellows." As John Offner, the author of *An Unwanted War*, has concluded, sensational journalism had "only a marginal impact" on the decision to go to war with Spain: "Hearst played on American prejudices; he did not create them. Although he and other sensationalists supplied many false stories, they did not fabricate the major events that moved the United States. . . .

Had there been no sensational press, only responsible editors, the American public nevertheless would have learned about the terrible conditions in Cuba [and] would have wanted Spain to leave."[17]

What prompted McKinley, Congress, and most of the business community to support intervention in early 1898, after resisting for so many years, was the recognition that Spain had lost control of Cuba and would not be able to regain it. Politically, McKinley could not afford to allow the Democrats to blame him and his party for so much human suffering and bloodshed so close to home. Economically, he could not allow the millions of dollars invested on the island to lie fallow or, worse yet, be lost forever should the Cubans oust the Spanish.

Hearst used every available means to put himself and his newspapers into the center of the war against Spain. He was not content with covering the hostilities in print alone. He wanted the Hearst name to be attached as well to the latest news medium, the moving-picture "actualities" or "visual newspapers" that the Biograph and Edison companies were exhibiting in New York's vaudeville halls.

The day after the *Maine* explosion, the Biograph Company recaptioned old footage of the battleships *Iowa* and *Massachusetts* as the *Iowa* and the *Maine* and showed it in vaudeville theaters across the country. The audience response was overwhelming. "There was fifteen minutes of terrific shouting," the *New York World* reported from a Chicago vaudeville hall, "when the battleships Maine and Iowa were shown in the biograph. . . . The audience arose, cheered and cheered again, and the climax was reached when a picture of Uncle Sam under the flag was shown on the canvas."[18]

Hearst offered space to Biograph cameramen on the *Anita*, one of several yachts he owned or chartered to transport reporters to Cuba, and entered into a partnership with the Edison Company to produce "war pictures" for exhibition in New York's vaudeville theaters. The Edison cameramen were transported to Cuba on another Hearst news yacht, the *Buccaneer.* Reporter Karl Decker, the savior of Evangelina Cisneros, sailed with them as their guide. Seventeen different "Edison-Journal views" were produced, several of them moving pictures of Hearst's yacht, captioned "*New York Journal* War Correspondents on Board." Though short-lived, the *Edison-Journal* War Pictures were invaluable to Hearst, as they associated the *Journal* with Edison, the most important name in moving pictures, and brought the paper free advertising in every vaudeville hall where the *Edison-Journal* films were shown.[19]

* * *

With the official declaration of war, the U.S. Navy — such as it was — joined the battle. Admiral William T. Sampson blockaded Havana Harbor with the North Atlantic Squadron, which consisted of two battleships, seven torpedo boats, five gunboats, and a handful of cruisers and monitors. On the other side of the globe, Commodore George Dewey sailed his seven warships and two unarmed colliers toward the Philippines to capture or destroy the Spanish fleet moored there.

With events occurring thousands of miles away and no effective means, short of the telegraph, of getting information back to New York, the newspapers embellished the official bulletins from Washington and stole items from one another which they published as "exclusives." Charles Michelson, a Hearst correspondent stationed in New York City, recalled in his autobiography how he and his colleagues, when they reported on Dewey's May 1 victory in Manila Bay, "blew up the short official bulletin. It was a shameless bit of fakery, but all the newspapers were doing it."[20]

Because the Hearst papers had the most reporters in the field, their dispatches were most often stolen, especially by Pulitzer's editors at the *World*. Brisbane found a way to make the *World* editors pay for their sins by slipping into an early edition of the *Evening Journal* "an item to the effect that in a naval bombardment . . . an Austrian artillery man, Colonel Reflip W. Thenuz had been slain." The story was picked up by the *World*, which carried it through some twenty or more editions without crediting the Hearst papers. The next day the *Evening Journal* announced on its front page that it had planted the story of the Austrian artillery man to trap the *World* editors: Reflip W. Thenuz was an anagram for "We pilfer the news."[21]

As the volunteers boarded trains for Tampa en route to Cuba, Will Hearst did his part by preaching the martial virtues in his editorial columns. Unfortunately, the more he exhorted American boys to battle, the more awkward became his own position on the sidelines. *Town Topics*, in particular, was relentless in its attack on the man it now referred to only as "Willieboy" or "Willie the Worst."

"It is a good little time that little Willie has in this sweet town of ours," Colonel Mann, editor, owner, and chief gossip, wrote under his pen name "The Saunterer" in mid-April:

> It was after burning up Broadway with two warm babes and a hot hansom . . . that Willie proceeded to Park Row the other night and penned an editorial "To the Boys of America." It was a beauteous thing. It glittered with the rheto-

ric that comes from resting in the laps of the lovely. . . . If this war of ours presents great opportunities to the boys of America, why, oh Willieboy, do you linger where the laps and the lobsters sing their siren songs? . . . Boy, you Willieboy, you, standing to-day just at the verge of long trousers, do you know what war is? It is hell. Go to — war, Willie!

He himself, the Colonel averred, took "not the slightest interest over Hearst's personal conduct." He rambled on:

My vague allusions to his ways of sultanic languor and sybaritish luxury, to his frantic imitations of Oriental schemes of festival, to his general and presumably enjoyable disregard of the tiresome conventions of sedate society, had no other object than the illumination of my comments on the inconsistency of his course in damning and slandering and cursing men and women for possibly wanting to do as he actually does. . . . For a man who lives in a house that is not only glass, but that is open as to doors, windows and roof at all hours of the day and night, to be hurling lumps of pitch and mud at others is something too much for patience. . . . I hold that if sloth, idleness, loose gayety, riotous extravagance and general demoralization of manners and morals are to be publicly pilloried, the editor and proprietor of the *Journal* is not the person appointed and anointed for the mission.[22]

We don't know if Hearst paid any attention to Mann's taunting. From all accounts, he could have stopped them by paying off Colonel Mann who, it was said, made as much money from bribes as he did from publishing. Still, the criticism had to have rankled if only because it exposed a real problem.

For personal and professional reasons, Hearst did not want to spend the war in New York City. War was the ultimate test of masculinity. It demanded courage, resolution, discipline, and daring. Men who called for war in peacetime but shirked their responsibilities in wartime were not real men, as Assistant Secretary of the Navy Theodore Roosevelt explained to the press on resigning his position to accept a commission as lieutenant colonel in the U.S. First Volunteer Cavalry, nicknamed the Rough Riders: "I want to go because I wouldn't feel that I had been entirely true to my beliefs and convictions, and to the ideal I had set for myself if I didn't go."[23]

Though Will Hearst, now thirty-five, was not as obsessed with proving his manliness as Roosevelt, he could not abide the thought that Teddy, more than four years his senior and more successful at Harvard, had gotten a head start by volunteering for duty in Cuba. If for no other reason than to protect his image from those who might compare him to Roosevelt, he had to find a way to action on some battlefield.

Late in May, after Roosevelt had accepted his commission with the

Rough Riders, Hearst wrote President McKinley offering to equip, at his own expense, a cavalry regiment — horses, uniforms, arms, supplies, everything. He asked in return, with uncharacteristic humility, that he be permitted to join his regiment as "a man in the ranks." The president politely thanked him but declined his offer. Having been turned down by the army, Hearst offered the navy "as a gift, without any conditions, whatever, my steam yacht *Buccaneer*," fully armed. This time, he asked that he be appointed "to a command on this boat" and promised that he would take and pass whatever examinations were necessary for a commission.[24]

In making these offers, Will paid no attention to cost. As Edward Clark, Phoebe Hearst's treasurer, wrote her on June 9, Will's offer to arm his yacht for navy service was going to cost $5,000 to $10,000, which he did not have. Phoebe was furious. She was concerned not just about the money, but about her foolhardy son who was trying so hard to put his yacht — and himself — in the line of fire. Clark reassured her that she need "have no anxiety as to his safety." If his plan ever came to fruition, he would sail to Cuba in the company of the United States Navy. Moreover, Cuban waters had been "practically rid of Spanish gun boats and the small boats are not likely to be detailed to participate in any engagements as they would be useless."[25]

Incapable of waiting on the sidelines while the navy considered his proposal, Hearst initiated his own military maneuvers in May on learning that a Spanish fleet was being assembled at Cádiz to recapture Manila from Commodore Dewey. Without consulting the Department of the Navy or Congress or the White House, the young publisher cabled James Creelman in London to "make necessary preparations, so that in case the Spanish fleet actually starts for Manila we will be prepared to buy or charter some English tramp steamer . . . and take her to some narrow and inaccessible portion of the Suez Canal and sink her where she will obstruct the passage of the Spanish fleet. I do not know that we will want to do this, but we may."

Creelman recognized at once that Hearst's request violated international law — newspaper publishers were not supposed to establish naval blockades — but set to work anyway. Fortunately, the Spanish reinforcements were soon recalled and Hearst's plan to blockade the Suez Canal abandoned.[26]

The plan was sheer madness and probably impossible to pull off. But it was no more daring than the rescue of Evangelina Cisneros from a Spanish jail — and that had succeeded. What was evident once again was that

Hearst believed he could claim the right to act in what he saw as the public interest, even when doing so violated national policy and international law.

In early June, the navy accepted the gift of Hearst's yacht, the *Buccaneer,* though without authorizing him to sail on it. When the *World* charged that the navy had commandeered the boat because the *Journal* had violated American law by using it to carry dispatches back and forth from Cuba, Hearst sued Pulitzer for half a million dollars. As proof of his innocence, he published the letters to McKinley in which he had volunteered his money, his yacht, and his services.[27]

Realizing belatedly that the only way he was going to get to Cuba now was on his own, Will Hearst appointed himself a war correspondent and telephoned Creelman to charter a steamer and secure press credentials for him. In mid-June of 1898, Hearst boarded the *Sylvia,* a refitted steamer leased from the Baltimore Fruit Company and reequipped for the trip south with printing presses, dark rooms, medical supplies, food fit for a king, and enough ice to resupply the American military hospital in Cuba when it ran out. He was accompanied by a boatful of cooks, stewards, illustrators, telegraphers, pressmen, editors, colleagues and friends, including James Creelman, Jack Follansbee, and George Pancoast. Also on board, traveling incognito, were the Willson sisters, Millicent and Anita, the chorus girls Hearst had been escorting around town for the past year and a half.[28]

Billy Bitzer, the Biograph cameraman who had been filming from the *Anita,* the first Hearst yacht to reach Cuban waters, was invited to transfer to the *Sylvia,* when it arrived in June. In his autobiography, Bitzer recalled his surprise at discovering that among the passengers on Hearst's ship were "two pretty young ladies who were sisters. . . . The *Sylvia* had just arrived that morning, and they were all anxious to go sightseeing. This would be difficult if the girls were seen by the sailors on the battleships, so to prevent this, the girls donned male attire. We were in the delirious state of being under fire in war time, and we got more friendly than we would have at home; the crew mixed with the guests and vice versa."[29]

After stopping off in Kingston, Jamaica, to restock supplies, the *Sylvia* landed on the southern coast of Cuba just days before the American invasion of the island. The printing equipment was transferred to a temporary plant at Siboney, a hamlet on the southern coast, where at least two editions of the *Siboney Journal* were printed and distributed to the grateful troops.[30]

Edward Marshall, a *Journal* reporter already stationed in Cuba, had a few days earlier been seriously wounded at the front. Worried that Phoebe had by now read about Marshall, Hearst cabled her on arrival that he was "at the front and absolutely safe so don't worry. Since poor Marshall was shot the General has made strict rules limiting newspaper men to certain localities . . . so there is no opportunity for any of us to get hurt even if we wanted to." He had sailed to Cuba, he explained, not to satisfy a lust for adventure, but because "the standing of the paper will profit by my being here."[31]

He was right of course. While every other newspaper, including the *World*, had reporters in Cuba, none covered the war with the bravado and extravagance of the Hearst crew. Hearst took his self-appointed role as war correspondent very seriously. He visited American and Cuban military leaders on the island and reported back to the *Journal* in a series of articles written with clarity, style, and the assurance of a seasoned correspondent. Hearst's writing had no histrionics, little purple prose, and a remarkable lack of sentimentality or flag waving.

In a memoir of the war, Charles Johnson Post, a former *New York Journal* cartoonist who had enlisted, recalled his shock at encountering the publisher on the road to San Juan Hill. The troops had halted at a clearing where he noticed, sitting in the shade of a large thick-leaved tree, a man on a horse:

> The horse was not big but the man was, and tall: his legs and white socks hung well below the horse's belly. Dressed in black civilian clothes as if he had just stepped over from New York, he wore a jaunty felt-brimmed straw hat with a scarlet hatband and a scarlet tie to match. It was William Randolph Hearst. . . . We hailed him joyously — he was someone we knew! "Hey, Willie!" The hail went up and down the column, and it was all friendly. Someone from New York! He never moved a muscle. Always poker-faced, he never cracked a smile. If he thought we were jeering he was wrong. We were just glad to see someone from home. James Creelman, the correspondent, came galloping back from ahead and conferred with Hearst. . . . Creelman turned in his saddle and called out to us: "Boys, you're going into battle. Good luck!" Then he spoke and turned to Hearst. Hearst made a gesture in our direction with his scarlet-banded hat. He almost smiled. "Good luck!" he called mildly. "Boys, good luck be with you," and then he stiffened again.[32]

Hearst and Creelman were, at the time, headed toward El Caney where the Spanish commanded a stone fort and several blockhouses. Not fully understanding the lay of the land — and the position of the Spanish troops — Hearst's entourage, on arriving at El Caney, strolled up the hill toward the Spanish fort. Only when the American soldiers, lying prone on the ground to escape Spanish gunfire, shouted at the civilians to make themselves scarce, did those in the Hearst party realize that they were walking toward the Spanish fortifications.

James Creelman drew fire from the Spanish soldiers and was wounded. Waiting for medical assistance, half-conscious and in great pain, he felt a hand on his "fevered head" and looked up to see William Randolph Hearst leaning over him, a "straw hat with a bright ribbon on his head, a revolver at his belt and a pencil and note-book in his hand."

"'I'm sorry you're hurt, but' — and his face was radiant with enthusiasm — 'wasn't it a splendid fight? We must beat every paper in the world.'"[33]

Hearst got his story and, while Creelman was lying on his litter on the beach waiting for the medics, reboarded the *Sylvia* and set off for Jamaica to file his exclusive, leaving not only Creelman but Jack Follansbee behind to fend for themselves. He returned to Cuban waters, a day and a half later, on the morning of July 3, just in time to witness the defeat of the second Spanish armada. With an arrogance that had become second nature by now, Hearst and his party boarded one of the burning Spanish warships, took notes, and collected souvenirs. They were chased back to their steamer by American marines who swarmed up the *Sylvia*'s gangplank as if it were an enemy ship.

Years later, Hearst told the story with boyish enthusiasm, as if describing an incident of trespassing:

"What were you doing on that ship?" said the officer in charge.

"Just looking about, sir, at the results of the battle," said your columnist meekly.

"Can't you mind your own business?" said the officer.

"Not very well, sir, and be good newspapermen," we replied with returning confidence.

The point of Hearst's story seemed to be that the marines had no business interfering with Hearst's news gathering — even though a war was going on around them. In recounting this incident — as he had the story of Creelman's wound — Hearst took enormous pleasure in describing his defiance of common sense and the marines.

As the marines departed the *Sylvia*, they warned Hearst to return to his yacht and stay out of trouble. Instead of remaining on the perimeter, as directed, he ordered the *Sylvia* closer to the shore where he had spied, through his state-of-the-art binoculars purchased for the occasion in New York, a group of men, "more naked than clothed," washed up on the beach. In a scene straight out of opera buffa, Hearst in his white yachting outfit and white captain's hat, with a revolver in his hand and a notebook in his pocket, boarded the *Sylvia*'s launch and was rowed to shore, racing all the way with a marine boat headed in the same direction. Fortunately for Hearst, the marine boat was farther out to sea and capsized before it reached the shore. Hearst bravely threw off his shoes — one report said his pants as well — and led his crew onto shore, where they discovered that the naked men were Spanish sailors who had abandoned their burning ships. "Battered and bruised, half clothed, half drowned, half starved," the Spaniards were delighted to be taken prisoner and helped Hearst turn his launch around so they could all go back to the *Sylvia*.

It being the Fourth of July, Hearst asked his prisoners, now safely aboard the *Sylvia*, to give three cheers for the American sailors on the nearby warship *Texas*. They obliged — with gusto — whereby Mr. Hearst "ordered that these prisoners should have plenty to eat and drink and [be] clothed in the best we could give them."

This was precisely the kind of situation that Hearst had dreamed of on his way to Cuba. He had not only maneuvered his reequipped fruit steamer into the thick of the action, he had taken his own prisoners. His only problem now was finding a place for them. He tried to locate a navy officer who would accept delivery, but the captain of the *Oregon*, the first ship he approached, refused:

> "Keep 'em," said the bluff Captain. "You took 'em. You can take care of 'em." . . .
> None of the battleships seemed to want our prisoners. . . .
> Finally, we encountered the *Harvard*, a converted cruiser. . . .
> Your columnist delivered the prisoners to an officer . . . on board the *Harvard*.
> We knew that no one would ever believe that we had taken twenty-nine Spanish prisoners, so we demanded a receipt.[34]

The story, as Hearst told it forty years later, was laced with self-deprecating humor. But the 1898 dispatches he telegraphed to his newspapers from Cuba were delivered straight, with Hearst describing his capture of twenty-nine sailors in the matter-of-fact understated tone of the veteran war correspondent. The result was more than he had hoped for. The former "Willie the Worst" was praised not only by his own newspaper but by politicians and publishers from coast to coast. Even the *New York Times* applauded his courage and his patriotism, though not without a trace of mockery.

"We observe that the proprietor of our esteemed and enterprising yellow contemporary *The Journal* has carried his characteristic enterprise into Cuban waters," the *Times* said in an editorial. "He has there, with his own hand, so to speak, captured some twenty survivors of the *Maria Teresa,* huddled on the beach, and turned them over to the proper authorities. This is the most genuine as well as the most legitimate increase of circulation, so to speak, which he has of late achieved, and is a subject for honest pride, beyond the fear of rivalry."[35]

In his rush to get to Jamaica to file his story, Hearst had neglected to get medical assistance to Creelman who, while he never publicly complained about Hearst's having abandoned him, was hurt by his boss's indifference. On July 5 he wrote Hearst in desperation, not knowing where the publisher was or when he would get the letter:

> Dear Mr. Hearst,
>   After being abandoned without shelter or medicine and practically without food for nearly two days — most of the time under constant fire — you can judge my condition. My shoulder was as you know. That I am here and alive is due simply to my own efforts. I had to rise from my litter and stagger seven miles through the hills and the mud without an attendant. . . . Mr. Follinsbee stayed one night with me and got a fever. We are both here without cloths. I must get to the United States in order to get well. I expect no gratitude but I do expect a chance for my life.
>
> Faithfully yours,
James Creelman[36]

Hearst remained on the *Sylvia,* commuting from Cuban waters to Jamaica, where he cabled his stories and telegrams back to New York. Taking advantage of his newfound respectability, he unmercifully attacked his opponents in New York, especially E. L. Godkin of the *New York Evening Post.* On July 10, he addressed a telegram to the *Daily News,* the one-cent Tammany paper in New York City, responding to a letter to the editor from Godkin, who had pointed out an error in one of his articles from the front. Hearst had reported that Cubans had "beheaded" forty Spaniards; Godkin insisted, correctly, that the number was four. Hearst counterattacked brilliantly, attributing his mistake to an "error made in transcribing my dispatch at the cable station." He then castigated Godkin for being "Spanish at heart" and one of the "skulkers" who had gotten "as far away from the front of the war as possible." Hearst concluded by reminding the readers of the *Daily News* that the *Evening Post's* editor was foreign-born and that his paper had indulged in such "treasonous utterances" that the "boys of Camp Black" had "kicked [its] unhappy correspondent bodily from the field."[37]

In one brief telegram, Hearst had managed to get even with a major critic who had accused him rightfully of an egregious error and endear himself to the plain people of New York whom he hoped to entice to buy his *Evening Journal*.

All told, Hearst was on assignment in Cuba for over a month. On July 19, two days after the surrender of the ranking Spanish general in Cuba, he cabled his mother that he was ready to return to New York City: "Don't worry. Everything is over here now, and we are coming home."[38]

III

Publisher, Politician, Candidate, and Congressman

❧ 8 ❧

Representing the People

Hearst sailed back to New York City in July. Instead of returning to the house on Lexington Avenue which he shared with Arthur Brisbane, he moved into a private suite of rooms at the Waldorf. "I hope you are getting along well," he wrote James Creelman, who was recovering from his war wounds at his home in Ohio. "I feel like hell myself. I sit all day in one place in a half trance and stare at a spot. I'm afraid my mighty intellect is giving way. Anybody can have Cuba that wants it."[1]

Complaining of this sort was entirely uncharacteristic for Hearst, who never revealed his interior thoughts to anyone other than his mother. That he was now telling Mr. Creelman that he felt like hell was highly revealing. "I guess I'm a failure," he wrote his mother at about this time:

> I made the mistake of my life in not raising the cowboy regiment I had in mind before Roosevelt raised his. I really believe I brought on the war but I failed to score in the war. I had my chance and failed to grab it, and I suppose I must sit on the fence now and watch the procession go by. It's my own fault. I was thirty-five years of age and of sound mind — comparatively — and could do as I liked. I failed and I'm a failure and I deserve to be for being as slow and stupid as I was. Outside of the grief it would give you I had better be in a Santiago trench than where I am. . . . Goodnight, Mama dear. Take care of your self. Don't let me lose you. I wish you were here tonight. I feel about eight years old — and very blue.[2]

Nothing had turned out quite as he had expected. There had been no parades or congratulatory telegrams to welcome him back to New York. Unlike Teddy Roosevelt, who had returned a national hero and been drafted by the Republicans to run for governor of New York, Hearst was in the same position he had been in before he sailed for Cuba. He had squandered the opportunity of a lifetime. Had he sailed into New York Harbor in uniform, as had Teddy Roosevelt, he might have been thrust into the political spotlight and offered his party's nomination for governor. Unfortunately, while Roosevelt had led a charge up San Juan Hill and tricked the public into thinking he had singlehandedly won the war in Cuba, Hearst had done nothing more heroic than command a converted steamer from Baltimore. That he had proved to his journalist colleagues that he was capable of writing good copy from the front was of no political consequence whatsoever.

His disquiet on returning to New York was exacerbated by the sorry state of his finances. His newspapers were now the largest selling dailies in the city, but they were also losing more money than ever. While the news from the fronts had boosted circulation, the new revenue did not begin to cover the added costs of putting out special war editions, sending correspondents to Cuba and the Philippines, and cabling back their dispatches to New York. It was rumored that Phoebe was so disturbed by her son's fiscal mismanagement that she had decided to replace him as *Journal* publisher with S. S. Carvalho, his managing editor.[3]

Hearst kept his job in the end, but was forced by his mother and her accountants to institute cost-cutting measures, including layoffs. Knowing that it would be far easier to make money if he and Pulitzer called a cease-fire in their circulation wars, he reopened the peace negotiations that had been stalled for over a year and in August agreed with Pulitzer to "stop the unfriendly utterances between the *World* and the *Journal.*" In October, the two publishers began negotiations for a comprehensive settlement.[4]

Hearst's spirits were buoyed somewhat by the return of the American troops from Cuba in early August and the opportunities this afforded for Hearstian promotional stunts. He took the lead in raising money to commemorate the "*Maine* martyrs"; hosted a "*Journal* Carnival Night" at Coney Island to honor wounded veterans with a glorious fireworks display; and campaigned for a "complete holiday" to greet the return of the American fleet from Cuba. When on August 20 the fleet sailed into New York Harbor, he dispatched his yacht, the *Anita,* to greet it and floated a giant hot-air balloon over Grant's Tomb with color-coded confetti to signal New Yorkers on its progress. Red confetti meant that the fleet's ships were leaving Staten Island, green and white denoted their progress through the harbor, and "brilliant showers of red, white and blue, followed by all colors of the rainbow" signaled their arrival.[5]

As he went back to work at his newspapers, Hearst's depression lifted but not enough to dispel the restlessness that had dogged him since his return from Cuba. In defeating Pulitzer in the New York circulation wars — as he had the De Youngs in San Francisco — he had accomplished his goal. That his New York newspapers were not yet making money did not disturb him. He was confident that they would in short order begin to repay their investment. Having done all he had set out to do as a newspaper publisher, he was anxious now to move into electoral politics. His father had waited too long to make the move and had died in the Senate. Hearst set his sights higher. He intended to end his political career in the White House.

His political ambitions were no secret to anyone, certainly not to his mother and close friends. Since Harvard, he had made it clear that he intended to combine careers in journalism and politics. Now, in 1898, having reached the age of thirty-five, the time had come to throw his hat into the ring. No one among his immediate circle had any doubts but that he would accomplish his goal in the end. "Will is simply marvelous," his friend Orrin Peck wrote Phoebe from Munich where he was still living and painting. "It is only a question of time when you will be doing the honors in the White House as the mother of the President — now mark my words and keep the dust off of 'our Emeralds' for the occasion."[6]

That Theodore Roosevelt, who was less than five years older, was already so far ahead of him only whetted Hearst's ambitions. It is impossible to measure the depths of his loathing for Roosevelt, who had preceded him at Harvard, been a member of many of the same clubs, including the prestigious Porcellian, been elected to Phi Beta Kappa, and graduated at age twenty-one. Roosevelt, he was convinced, was now and had always been a charlatan, skilled only at manipulating the press. He was the same preening aristocrat — though now in uniform — that he had been the year before when Hearst's *Journal* attacked him for wearing pink shirts and a tasseled silk sash instead of a vest.[7]

For a brief time, Will contemplated running for governor as a Democrat against Roosevelt and did his best to convince Phoebe that while the campaign would cost a great deal, it would be money well spent: "Brisbane is sure the nomination will do the paper an *immense* amount of good. He says just think how it would help the *World* if Pulitzer were nominated and elected governor of the state of New York. Would there be any doubt in our minds as to how that would dignify the *World* and raise it in public esteem, especially if he gave a good administration? . . . That is a fair way to look at it." Fully aware that Phoebe feared for the future of her investment in the New York newspapers, he informed her that he had "decided to put Brisbane in as publisher of the Morning and Evening papers. . . . I shall give [him] full authority to make changes we discussed. . . . We believe we can bring the loss down. . . . Advertising can be increased $300,000 so that for the year of 1899 I will show you a *Profit* on the *Journal*."[8]

Though Phoebe promised him the funding he required, Hearst did not run for governor in 1898, for the simple reason that no one bothered to ask him to. For him to have even contemplated getting the Democratic nomination for governor only three years after arriving in the state was a sign of remarkable hubris, but not uncharacteristic of the man.

Unable to assail Roosevelt from the campaign trail, Hearst went after him in his newspapers. Under Brisbane's leadership, the Hearst papers organized a brilliantly coordinated campaign of ridicule, seamlessly linking news reports, editorials, and editorial cartoons to reduce Roosevelt to size. While Homer Davenport and the *Journal's* core of cartoonists portrayed Colonel Teddy as an overgrown playacting child, with prominent front teeth, rimless spectacles, and a Rough Riders uniform, Hearst's editorial assassins, led by Brisbane, excoriated him for accepting the nomination of the boss-dominated state Republican party. "There is no humiliation to which Mr. Roosevelt will not submit that he may get the nomination for Governor," read an editorial from September 22. "The Theodore Roosevelt that was, was a humbug. The Theodore Roosevelt that is, is a prideless office-seeker."[9]

When Roosevelt was narrowly elected in November, Hearst was disappointed but not discouraged. He was already, it appeared, looking ahead to 1900, and William Jennings Bryan's second run for the presidency. Although he was unknown outside of San Francisco and New York and had never run for electoral office or held any appointive position, he had set his sights on running for vice president on Bryan's ticket. In August of 1899, he asked his mother to entertain Bryan when he visited California:

> I know you don't like Bryan and don't approve of his politics, but he is coming to California and this gives us an opportunity to approach him in a way in which he is rather susceptible — socially. He is really a fine man, although an extreme radical. . . . Anyhow, there is something which I know you always considered — the opportunity to make your offspring solid with a power in politics. . . . It is very important that he should be very close to me and to the *Journal.*[10]

Though he was already preparing for his entry into electoral politics, Hearst did not neglect his newspapers. When his attempts to negotiate a peace settlement broke down, Pulitzer went back on the attack, charging Hearst with having violated Associated Press guidelines by reusing wire items received at his morning *Journal* (which had an A.P. franchise) in the *Evening Journal* (which did not). While Hearst was in California visiting his mother, Pulitzer's lawyers hauled one of his top editors into court to testify in the A.P. suit. On his return to New York City, Hearst was tailed by process servers until they caught up with him and compelled him to testify as well. Hearst was outraged by Pulitzer's tactics. Through Carvalho, he made it clear that he did not "propose to be annoyed or prosecuted personally" in this way. He was willing to fight Pulitzer on the newsstands, but was not going to stand idly by as Pulitzer's agents trailed him through the street like a common criminal. Mr. Hearst, Carvalho wrote his counterpart in the Pulitzer organization, "desires me to convey notice . . . if you are willing to listen to it — to this effect: that if this course is persisted in and Mr. Hearst is compelled to appear before this referee, which is most unfair, the case not even being on trial, he *will terminate all relationship existing between the World and the Journal.* . . . and furthermore, he will begin a personal assault on Mr. Pulitzer in the columns of 'The Journal,' making it as personal and as powerful as he can."[11]

The hostility and sniping between the Hearst and Pulitzer camps would continue on and off for the next year. Only with the improbably successful strike of the New York newsboys in December of 1899 were the two publishers compelled to cooperate with one another.

During the Spanish-American War, Hearst and Pulitzer had raised the wholesale price of their papers from 50 to 60 cents a hundred. The newsies did not complain at the time because they were selling more than enough papers to compensate for the price hike. They were also convinced that the price increase would last only as long as the war itself. When they discovered a year later that Hearst and Pulitzer had no intention of rescinding the wartime price hike, they went out on strike. The *Journal* and *World* editors laughed off the children's strike — at first. But they found themselves outsmarted and outnumbered as the newsies succeeded in organizing a metropolitan boycott of the Hearst and Pulitzer dailies. Led by the Brooklyn Union's District Master Workboy, Spot Conlon, attired in his pink suspenders, the Brooklyn boys marched across the Brooklyn Bridge to join forces with their Manhattan comrades. Together, the boys not only shut down street circulation of the afternoon *Journal*s and *World*s in Manhattan, Brooklyn, Long Island City, and up and down the Atlantic seaboard, but they enlisted the public in their crusade by staging a series of parades, open-air rallies, and a huge mass meeting at the New Irving Hall.

As the evening *Journal*s and *World*s disappeared from the streets and advertisers demanded rebates, Hearst's and Pulitzer's editors were left with two choices: to accede to the boys' demands or use strong-arm tactics to get their papers back in circulation. They chose the latter, and directed their circulation managers to tour Bowery flophouses and assemble a brigade of bums to replace the boys in the streets. At the urging of Don Seitz, Pulitzer's chief lieutenant, Hearst agreed to stop criticizing the police in his pages if they offered the scabs protection. In the end, it made little difference. The newsies persuaded the Bowery bums to pocket the bonuses they were offered and dump the papers in the trash. Hearst and Pulitzer, with no conceivable way now of getting their papers on the street, conceded defeat and offered the boys a compromise settlement, which they accepted.[12]

Hearst's intention to enter the political arena was made manifest in the frequency with which his name now appeared in his papers. If in San Francisco and during his first years in New York, the Hearst name had appeared only on the masthead, it was now regularly seen on the front and editorial pages. Though still without an office to run for, Hearst was sounding very much like a candidate. He orchestrated a vicious attack on McKinley's secretary of war, Russell Alger, and the commissary general, Charles P. Egan, for poisoning American soldiers with "ancient" and "diseased" beef. In signed editorials, he joined the national debate over annexation of the Philippines by declaring for "retention" in the name of what he called "the Jeffersonian principle of national expansion."[13]

While taking a position on every significant foreign policy issue, he did not neglect domestic issues. In early 1899, in a series of signed editorials, he published "An American Internal Policy." Clearly looking ahead to national office, he offered a domestic program which was a brilliantly conceived amalgam of urban progressivism and Western populism. Like the Populists, he called for the direct "Election of Senators by the People" instead of by state legislatures; advocated the substitution of an income tax for the hated tariff which protected Eastern industry by raising the price of imported goods; and demanded currency reform, without explicitly endorsing the free coinage of silver. The remaining planks of his program spoke to issues raised by the urban progressives. He proposed that government be given new powers to regulate and control the growth of the "Trust Frankenstein"; called for "public ownership of public franchises"; and demanded "National, State, and Municipal Improvement of the Public School System."[14]

Hearst used the power of his press to organize as well as editorialize. He campaigned for city-owned public transit systems and led fights against the gas trust and the water trust, both of which, he claimed, were stealing from the public by charging inordinate prices for resources which ought rightly to be owned and regulated by the city.[15]

By early 1900, a little more than eighteen months after his return from Cuba, his crusade for municipal ownership and against the trusts had won over even his most caustic critics, like Colonel Mann, the editor of *Town Topics*, who publicly congratulated him for exposing the depredations of the ice trust:

> William Randolph Hearst and his colleagues . . . have earned the profound gratitude of all patriotic citizens, not only in New York City, but throughout the length and breadth of the United States. The *Journal's* exposure and pursuit of the criminal officials who betrayed the people in the interest of the Ice Trust will stand for many years as one of the most splendid and useful achievements of the modern newspaper. The *Journal* has made this fight against corruption in high places not only with zeal and determination, but with intelligent and skillful employment of resources. Mr. Hearst and his colleagues have done a great work, and they have done it with exhilarating thoroughness. I congratulate them.[16]

Still an outsider — with no position or standing in the city, state, or national Democratic party — Hearst had only one link to the electorate and the Democratic officials who chose candidates: his newspapers. To establish himself as a force in the national party and a potential running mate for Bryan in 1900, he needed to find a way to make his voice heard outside of New York and San Francisco. The most effective and efficient way to do this was by starting up a new newspaper in the nation's second largest city, Chicago.

Phoebe was outraged when Will asked her for the money required to buy a Chicago daily. "I have been feeling greatly depressed and did not feel like writing," she confided to Orrin Peck while she was traveling in Europe in May of 1899:

> Will is insisting upon buying a paper in Chicago. Says he will come over to see me if I do not go home very soon. It is impossible for me to throw away more money in any way for the simple reason that he has already absorbed almost all. In a few months there will actually be no money and we must then sell anything that can be sold to keep on. It is *madness*. I never know when or how we will break out into some *additional* expensive scheme. I cannot tell you how distressed I feel about the heavy monthly loss on the *Journal* and then to contemplate starting another nightmare is a hopeless situation. I have written and telegraphed that *no* argument can induce me to commit such a folly as that of starting another newspaper.[17]

Phoebe was really concerned that her son was following in the irresponsible footsteps of his father and investing money in new ventures before the old ones paid out. It took almost as much money to start up a newspaper as it did to dig a new mine. Although Will was confident, as George Hearst had been, that each of his investments would eventually pay off, Phoebe was not so sure. She had spent much of her marriage worrying about her husband's finances. She did not want to spend her old age worrying about her son's.

This time around, not even Orrin Peck was ready to defend his friend's actions. "I cannot understand Will's demand," he wrote Phoebe in response to her letter. "As you say, it is madness. He doubtless wishes to control the press of the U.S. That's alright but the main thing is to get the present established *Journal* under control. It's like dashing along a mad road with runaway horses and trying to harness in another. I see the situation is most desperate and makes one simply ill."[18]

Smart enough to recognize defeat when it came, Hearst didn't push his request — for the time being. When he asked again, a year later, the circumstances would be such that Phoebe would be unable to refuse a second time.

In November of 1899, Hearst set off on another of his grand tours, this time of Europe and Egypt, with Millicent and Anita Willson, chaperoned by their parents, as part of the entourage. George Willson, the former vaudeville hoofer, was now on the Hearst payroll, managing benefit performances to raise money for a *Journal* monument to the *Maine*. On leaving Europe in mid-March, Hearst reported to his mother that his vacation had been a great success. He was again "happy and well. My nervousness is gone, my stomach is getting into good condition, I sleep well and life is worth living again. . . . I shall be home soon now and ready to work hard once more."[19]

When he returned to the States in April 1900, he was contacted by Bryan's allies on the Democratic National Committee. As newspapers were not just the principal, but practically the only, effective campaign medium, Bryan and the Democrats were at an enormous disadvantage in the Middle West, where almost all of the big-city dailies were owned by Republicans. To reduce the odds against them, they asked Hearst to start up a daily newspaper in Chicago. They further asked him to serve as president of the National Association of Democratic Clubs, in which role they hoped he would produce and distribute campaign literature. There was no mention of the vice-presidential nomination nor would there ever be.

The invitation to establish a Chicago paper was a godsend, as it provided Hearst with a reason to petition his mother again for start-up funds, this time in the context of loyalty to his, her, and Senator George Hearst's party. With Phoebe in accord, he accepted the party's assignments, though not without a bit of strategic complaining.

"The undertaking is big and the prospect of another period of work and strain is not pleasant to contemplate," he telegrammed Bryan on May 19, 1900. "Still I am most anxious to please you and to be of service to the party. I would like to know how important you consider such a paper, what real benefit to the party it would be. If the good accomplished would compensate for effort and expense, etc. These things being determined I suppose the satisfaction of being of some value would lead me to disregard all other considerations."[20]

In May, Hearst invaded Chicago with his trusted associates from New York. S. S. Carvalho found quarters for the new paper in the aging but enormous building on Madison Street that had housed the Steuben County Wine Company; Arthur Brisbane arrived to edit the first issue; Andrew Lawrence, who had been with Hearst since San Francisco, was put in charge of the business and circulation departments. In six weeks' time, Hearst's team had set up an editorial office and a printing plant and hired a full staff of editors, reporters, typographers, compositors, and illustrators. The most difficult task they faced was getting the city's distributors, dealers, and newsboys to sell the new daily on the street. Most had ties to the *Chicago Tribune* and were loath to carry a competitor. Only with the assistance of the Annenberg brothers, Max and Moses, who were hired away from the *Chicago Tribune,* and the small army of thugs they brought with them, was Hearst able to get his new paper to potential readers.[21]

Democratic party officials had hoped that Hearst's new daily would be on the streets in time for the fall campaign. Hearst went them one better and had the first issue of his *Chicago American* ready by July 4. Having done Bryan and his party an enormous favor, Hearst extracted all he could in return. When Bryan agreed to publish an open letter on the front page of the debut issue of the *Chicago American,* Hearst provided him — through James Creelman, who had returned to work after his wounds healed — with explicit instructions on what to say and how to say it.[22]

"Please ask Mr. Bryan in his letter to the *American* to refer to the Work done by the *Journal* in the former campaign and to allude to the fact that the *American* was started not merely to make money but to provide at the request of Democratic leaders a Democratic paper for that large and important section of country. Ask him kindly to say that the name is a good one and fits the *Journal's* well known reputation for staunch Americanism. I hope all these things he will find to be true and may consequently legitimately speak of them." As published, Bryan's letter followed Hearst's suggestions, almost word for word.[23]

When Bryan was nominated for the presidency in St. Louis the following day, the hall was flooded with copies of the *Chicago American*. Hearst telegraphed his congratulations in the jocular, personal tone one might employ with an old friend: "Your nomination was not wholly a surprise to us but we are all very happy over it . . . and eager to aid in the great fight and be in the van at the hour of victory. Command us Colonel."[24]

The 1900 campaign for the presidency would be the lead story in Hearst's and every other daily newspaper through November. There was, in Hearst's mind, no contradiction between the imperatives of running a campaign and publishing a newspaper. Well-written partisan political coverage sold more newspapers than dry, distanced "they were here and said this" stories. The 1900 campaign story was plotted like his other continuing front-page features. The villains were McKinley and the wealthy Cleveland industrialist Mark Hanna who pulled his strings; the aggrieved innocents were the American people; the rescuing hero was William Jennings Bryan, with his crusading armies of Democratic candidates and campaign workers.

The crassly melodramatic plot could be presented in a variety of formats: feature stories, interviews, editorials, and front-page cartoons. Homer Davenport brought back his drawings of a grotesquely overweight, ghoulish Mark Hanna with dollar signs all over his coat. Frederick Opper, the equally brilliant cartoonist whom Hearst had hired away from *Puck* in 1899, produced a series of "Uncle Trusty" and "Willie and his Papa" cartoons, featuring a fat, balding businessman with a bulbous nose and dollar-sign slippers as The Trusts, Hanna as a nursemaid, and McKinley and Teddy Roosevelt, his running mate, as the obedient sons.

While in years to come historians and Hearst biographers would emphasize the Davenport and Opper caricatures of Hanna and McKinley, the politician portrayed most cruelly in the Hearst papers was Theodore Roosevelt. Opper caricatured him as an ugly boy on a hobby horse, with glasses, huge teeth, and a Rough Rider hat, who bullied McKinley and made him cry. In one cartoon, Nursemaid Hanna and The Trusts asked Willie (McKinley), "What Ails You This Time?" Willie answered, "We're playing Republican campaign trip, and Teddy's making all the speeches from the rear platform, and he says I'm merely a brakeman." Other cartoons ridiculed Roosevelt's war record, his tenure as police commissioner, and his passions for the West and for hunting.[25]

Hearst's newspaper attacks on McKinley, Roosevelt, and Hanna constituted only part of his contribution to the Democrats. He also gave Bryan between $10,000 and $15,000 of his own — or Phoebe's — money, and turned out an enormous quantity of campaign literature: pamphlets, special editions of his newspapers, and a campaign book, all abundantly illustrated by his cartoonists.[26]

Hearst was too smart and too ambitious to remain in the background for long. Bryan had envisioned the National Association of Democratic Clubs, which he asked Hearst to chair, as little more than a network of grassroots organizations that would provide the volunteer labor needed to distribute campaign literature, hold a few local rallies, and watch the polls on Election Day. Hearst had other ideas. He installed Maximilian F. Ihmsen, the chubby, rumpled, curly-haired, walrus-mustachioed political reporter who had been his chief Washington correspondent, as secretary of the National Association, and with Ihmsen's help, enhanced its role until it functioned almost as a shadow Democratic National Committee, organizing conventions of loyalists and public rallies across the country.[27]

As president of the National Association of Democratic Clubs, Hearst sponsored his own Bryan rally in New York City. When he learned that Tammany's Boss Croker was planning a separate rally to welcome Bryan to New York, he informed James Creelman that he was willing to defer his "show" until Croker had held his. In his new role as party leader, Hearst was prepared to go out of his way to ingratiate himself with the Tammany boss whom he had in the past repeatedly criticized for allowing the trusts to rob the people of New York. "Find Creelman," he wired an associate in New York City, "and tell him to get fine interview with Croker about plans for receiving Bryan, management of state campaign, chances of carrying state . . . want very agreeable interview: Get good picture. Old gentleman makes very distinguished appearance with gray hair and frock coat as he stands gavel in hand behind chairman's desk. Suggest you get a photograph . . . Tell Croker I have to go Chicago for few days but if there is anything he wishes done in paper or club to tell you or Ihmsen in my absence."[28]

Though Hearst had tried to be accommodating to the Boss, Croker was not willing to cede any authority to the young publisher who, without a single ward leader or district behind him, was acting as if he were the Boss's equal. Instead of coordinating his Bryan rally with Hearst's, Croker stole the speakers Hearst had already contacted. Hearst was furious. Another man might have admitted that he had been outsmarted and let it go without causing further trouble with a rival as powerful as Richard Croker. But Hearst could not abide being double-crossed. "Please see Ihmsen," he telegraphed James Creelman from Chicago, "and organize to make the meeting . . . the biggest thing ever. . . . Croker is jobbing us. He has asked all the speakers he learned we were going to have to speak first at his meeting. Please stop this. It is not fair. I postponed our meeting to please him, deferred announcing our meeting lest it should interfere with his . . . He is not acting in good faith and I resent it. America is full of good speakers. If he takes ours I will remember it against him. If we cannot be good friends we had better be active enemies."[29]

Bryan lost again in 1900, by a larger margin than in 1896. Hearst won — on several counts. Immediately after the election, he hired William Jennings Bryan as a special correspondent and sent him on a European tour — all expenses paid — thereby putting the "Great Commoner" in his debt. He also retained his position as president of the National Association of Democratic Clubs, and with Max Ihmsen's help began at once to reconfigure it into an organization dedicated as much to his own future in politics as to his party's. With his new newspaper in Chicago, the nation's second largest city, Hearst now had a commanding presence in the nation's heartland, as well as in the biggest cities on the East and West Coasts.[30]

On June 29, 1901, exactly two months after his thirty-eighth birthday, Hearst's portrait appeared on the cover of the inaugural issue of *Editor and Publisher*. He was identified as "The Foremost Figure in American Journalism." As he had promised his mother, his forays into politics had enhanced his reputation as a publisher. But there was trouble ahead.[31]

Before, during, and after the 1900 presidential campaign, the Hearst papers ceaselessly, almost monotonously, attacked President McKinley. When, in February of 1900, Kentucky governor-elect William Goebel was shot dead in an election dispute, Ambrose Bierce marked the occasion by suggesting in verse that the bullet that killed Goebel had not been found because it was "speeding here / To stretch McKinley on his bier." In April 1901, only days after the second inauguration, Arthur Brisbane outdid even Bierce in a lengthy editorial about the felicitous consequences of past political assassinations. "If bad institutions and bad men," he concluded, "can be got rid of only by killing, then the killing must be done."[32]

Hearst later insisted that he had pulled the editorial after reading it in the paper's first edition. James Creelman claimed that Hearst sent him, as an emissary, to apologize to McKinley for the editorial. Neither action would have been characteristic of Hearst, for whom all was fair in politics and journalism, so long as one did not intrude on a candidate's personal life. In the long run, whether or not Hearst apologized for this particular editorial was of no consequence, as he had been attacking the president for years.

Long before Leon Czolgosz approached President McKinley in the Temple of Music at the Buffalo World's Fair, with a handkerchief that looked like a bandage wrapped around his right hand, the evidentiary chain had been forged that would later be used to link Hearst to the president's assassin.

It was of course preposterous to claim that the half-mad assassin who pulled a revolver from his handkerchief and shot and killed William Mc-Kinley in September of 1901 had been moved to murder by an editorial published six months earlier in English, which he could not read — or by a stanza in Bierce's poem, published twenty months before. As Bierce himself recalled, his four lines on McKinley "took no attention" when they originally appeared. It was only after McKinley had been shot that "the verses, variously garbled but mostly made into an editorial, or a news dispatch with a Washington dateline but usually no date, were published all over the country as evidence of Mr. Hearst's complicity in the crime."[33]

With an assassin too incoherent to make a real villain, the Republican press went after its favorite left-wing bête noire, William Randolph Hearst, accusing him of having poisoned Czolgosz's mind and pulled the trigger for him. Across the country, but especially in places like New York City where competing newspapers were anxious to cut into Hearst's circulation, boycotts were started, anti-Hearst pledges circulated, and Hearst publicly accused of murder. According to Cora Older, who wrote his authorized biography, the publisher, who was in Chicago at the time of the assassination, began keeping a gun in his desk: "So many threats were made against his life, that when boxes of purported gifts arrived, Hearst had them burned for fear of bombs."[34]

The New-Yorker, a weekly magazine not to be confused with the unhyphenated journal founded in 1925, claimed that Hearst was held in such disrepute that the "Maritime Exchange, the New York Athletic Club, and other respectable organizations" excluded his morning and afternoon papers from their reading rooms: "Hearst will either have to print decent newspapers or get out of the business . . . As for Hearst personally . . . his reclamation and elevation to the plane of honorable men is not to be thought of. He will always remain the degraded, unclean thing that he is, shunned by every honest citizen, and for whose wandering feet there shall be no resting place where the American flag rises and falls upon the breeze."[35]

It was not only competing editors who held Hearst personally responsible for the bile and violence that saturated political journalism and, it was now claimed, had contributed to the climate that inflamed McKinley's assassin. As Vice President Theodore Roosevelt wrote his good friend Henry Cabot Lodge on September 7, when it was still believed that McKinley might recover from his wounds, "every scoundrel like Hearst and his satellites who for whatever purposes appeals to and inflames evil human passion, has made himself accessory before the fact to every crime of this nature."[36]

For perhaps the first time in his life, Hearst was forced onto the defensive. As a rather blatant attempt to establish his patriotic bona fides, he changed the name of his New York morning paper to the *American and Journal*, and later on dropped the *Journal* entirely from the title. The abuse became so intense that he was forced to write his mother to reassure her that he would, in the end, weather the storm: "All that distresses me is the fear that you will be hurt by the wicked assertions in hostile newspapers. I don't believe those attacks have the slightest effect except to lower the papers printing them. In New York all the people are in front of the *Journal* bulletins and are very friendly, cheering any favorable news. All merchants understand or did motives of assailants and stand by us. In fact as far as I can see the attacks have absolutely no effect whatever except to gratify the people already unfriendly to the *Journal*." While he conceded that he and the *Journal* had "a great many enemies," he wanted his mother to remember that they also had "nearly a million friends."[37]

While the Hearst papers would recover quickly, Hearst himself would have a more difficult time undoing the damage that had been done to him personally. His newspapers' attacks on McKinley had been intemperate and vicious, though no more so than those of other newspapers on other candidates, and probably much less so than the Republican papers' attacks on Bryan. What distinguished Hearst from his competitors was that his invective was better illustrated, better captioned, more pointed, and probably more effective.

In the aftermath of the McKinley assassination, Hearst absented himself from electoral politics, but remained active as publisher and editorial director of his newspapers in San Francisco, New York, and Chicago. With major daily and Sunday newspapers in the nation's most populous Eastern, Midwestern, and Western cities, he was already well on his way to establishing the nation's most powerful publishing empire.

The Hearst papers in San Francisco, New York, and Chicago shared news items, features, and editorials each day, and they all included the *American Humorist*, Hearst's color comic supplement, on Sundays. On moving to New York in 1895, Hearst had leased his own "wire" to move news, features, and editorials back and forth between the *Journal* and the *San Francisco Examiner*. In 1900, he added Chicago to this wire, laying the foundation for what would become his own wire service, the International News Service. In 1902, he added a second newspaper in Chicago, the morning *Examiner*, to supplement his evening *American*.[38]

All of this cost money, millions of dollars of it. Phoebe, reluctantly, lent her son the capital he needed, but kept careful track of every dollar. As her accountants and business advisers testified in a court hearing on her estate in 1921, while Phoebe believed that her son was entitled to half the senator's estate, she felt obligated "to exercise restraint over him." Instead of settling a sum of money on him, she lent him funds for business purposes. By 1902, she had loaned him a total of $8 million to purchase and upgrade his New York and Chicago papers. According to Hearst's own testimony, she then canceled that loan: "She told me that she felt that I was morally entitled under the terms of my father's will to half the estate, and she proposed to — with proper regulation on her part and decision as to amounts — let me have the necessary funds to establish my papers, but that she naturally wanted me to exercise more caution thereafter in the use of funds, and I did exercise more caution."[39]

When that same year, 1902, the *Philadelphia Record* was put on sale, Hearst was interested, but backed out in the end, no doubt because Phoebe having just forgiven him $8 million of debt was not about to advance him any more money. Hearst's major competitor for the Philadelphia paper was Adolph Ochs, the owner of the *New York Times*, who wrote to express his gratitude to Hearst for having abandoned Philadelphia: "I write to let you know that I am not unmindful of the significance of such a manifestation of good will. . . . I hope that when you do make your appearance in Philadelphia, your presence there may not endanger my properties, but that the pleasant relationship that now exists between us in New York may extend to Philadelphia; that we may find Philadelphia as we find New York — large enough for both of us."[40]

The two publishers were already, at this early date, entering into a sort of mutual admiration society. They had much in common. Both had bought failing New York papers, Hearst in 1895, Ochs the following year, and despite the predictions of almost everyone in the city, had turned them around. Ochs had had the more difficult time, but had succeeded in tripling circulation to 75,000 in 1898, when he lowered the price of his daily from three cents to a penny. Though his daily was still dwarfed — in advertising inches and circulation — by the Pulitzer and Hearst papers, which had combined evening and morning circulations in the vicinity of half a million, Ochs was unconcerned. Unlike Hearst and Pulitzer, he had no interest in securing a mass audience.

The *Times* did not entertain its readers. It did not illustrate its news stories or plot them as minimelodramas. Its columnists, reporters, and editorial writers were not known for their prose styles. It did not publish fiction or political cartoons or comics. Ochs's self-proclaimed task as a newspaper publisher was to inform, not to entertain. As he announced when he bought the *Times* on August 19, 1896, his goal was to give "thoughtful, pure-minded people . . . all the news, in concise and attractive form, in language that is parliamentary in good society" and to give that news "impartially, without fear or favor, regardless of any party, sect or interest involved."

Though he claimed, as Hearst did, that his was a nonpartisan newspaper, it was every bit as committed to Republican party candidates, platforms, and principles as Hearst was to Democratic. The difference in their political coverage was one of style. Hearst took his political stands proudly — and loudly. He was an advocate, an enthusiast. Ochs was not. He devoted many more inches of space to Republican candidates than to the Democrats, but covered their campaigns in a flattened, distanced prose quite unlike the adulation the Hearst papers lavished on the Democratic candidates they boosted in their news and editorial pages.[41]

Because Hearst and Ochs published very different papers for very different audiences, they did not compete with one another and would remain on good terms until Hearst entered politics.

Hearst returned to active politicking in the fall of 1902. He had, he wrote his mother, been approached by "a faction of the Democratic party usually very powerful [which] has asked me to allow them to present my name for Governor. They say I will be nominated. I don't think I will be. Still it is an alluring proposition because if a Democrat is by chance elected Governor of New York he stands the best chance of being the Democratic nominee for president in 1904. It would be ridiculous for me to consider such a possibility if there were any really big men in the field but there are not any."[42]

While the idea of running for governor in 1902 certainly appealed to Hearst, the party leaders never seriously considered his candidacy. He was too young, too inexperienced, too identified with Bryan, and too much a radical to be nominated for state office. He was, on the other hand, too rich and powerful to be ignored entirely. To demonstrate in advance the Democratic party's gratitude for Hearst's financial and editorial support in the upcoming campaign, he was given the nomination for the congressional seat from the Eleventh District left vacant by the death of the incumbent, Amos J. Cummings, coincidentally a former journalist.[43]

Hearst's nomination was greeted with little buzz in the New York dailies, even his own. Only the weekly gossip sheets paid much attention to the notion that the boy publisher and man-about-town might soon be campaigning for public office. The *New-Yorker*, which billed itself as "A Journal Mainly About Interesting People," found the prospect immensely amusing:

I understand that the Sassafras Sisters [Millicent and Anita Willson] are to join with their patron and protector, W. R. Hearst, in a personally-conducted campaign for Congress. . . . In serio-chronic roles they achieved immortal glory and annexed themselves to the Hearst leg — no, to the Hearst millions — and they are proposing to make partial payment of their debt of gratitude by hop, skip, and jumping through the district which is to be disgraced in Congress by the yellow degenerate. Old man Sassafras, who in his day did stunts as an "eccentric dancer," is expected to renew his youth during the next month and contort for the advancement of the political ambitions of his brevet son-in-law. . . . With the aid of the Sassafras family the debauchee of journalism expects to be rag-timed into Congress . . . To spindling "Billy" the pain of it will be that he cannot secure a certificate entitling the Sassafras Sisters to seats by his side during the session of Congress. Flanked by the ravishing demoiselles he could do great execution among the statesmen. . . . One of his former most intimate friends and associates, by the way, tells me that the political bee is buzzing very loud in the Hearst bonnet. He has made up his egotistical young mind that sooner or later he is going to be the first Socialist President of the United States.[44]

Befitting his new role as candidate — and no doubt to counter adverse publicity like that in the *New-Yorker* — Hearst remade himself from top to bottom. Years before, his mother's friend Clara Anthony had predicted that he would not succeed until he had broken from the "trammels and traditions of his present life. . . . If a blast of dynamite could extirpate most of his present advisers and he be allowed to be himself, he would develop as God meant he should. I hope I'm not barbarous but I would like to see Jack Follansbee for one break his ugly neck, and every other fawning sycophant that exploits Will follow suit."[45]

While Will was not willing to follow this course to the letter, he was now convinced that he had to do something to make it appear as if he were no longer the spindling Billy the *New-Yorker* took such delight in ridiculing. He shaved off his mustache and replaced his loud collegiate ties and checked suits with a long, black frock coat and broad-brimmed soft black hat. The frock coat gave him the appearance of physical weight and spiritual gravitas. Cloaked in black, with ghostly pallor and a cold, hard stare, he resembled a modern-day grim reaper.

Though with Tammany's backing his election was guaranteed, Hearst campaigned vigorously. According to the *New-Yorker,* which gave his campaign front-page coverage as if there were no other that November:

> The Yellow Fellow has knocked the hoops off his money barrels and is spending it like water. His campaign for Congress in the Eleventh District is a record-breaker in that respect . . . He is housing droves of labor skates from Chicago, sand-lotters from San Francisco and spellbinders from other camps at the Hoffman House and supplying them with richest food and viands. I do not know where he has his imported musicians staked out, but they, too, are living on the fat of the land. He has billed his district like a circus and established headquarters galore. Every man and thing in the district that money can hire or buy is on his pay-rolls or his deeds in his strong box.[46]

The capstone of the campaign was a rally at Madison Square Garden on October 27 that the *New York Times* labeled "the most important meeting" of the campaign. Hearst reportedly spent $10,000 alone on the premeeting fireworks display that began at dusk in Madison Square Park. The dust and smoke from the fireworks display was so great that, according to the *New York Sun,* "many a dinner at the hotels around the Square" was irretrievably "spoiled." Following the fireworks came a full-throttle outdoor band concert which must have disturbed the diners yet again. At 7:30, the doors to the Garden were thrown open to the 10,000 Democrats who had secured free tickets to the rally. The arena had, the *Times* reported, never been "more brilliantly decorated . . . From every available pillar, post, and balcony were strung out the red, white, and blue in reckless profusion, while from the girders were hung hundreds upon hundreds of American flags." Not content with traditional campaign paraphernalia, Hearst arranged for a special electrical sign behind the speaker's stand which spelled out in electric bulbs: "Congress Must Control the Trusts." The rally continued in high gear until the candidate took the podium. As the *Sun* reported rather kindly the following morning, "Hearst's voice is that of the ordinary man in daily conversation. In the Garden the strongest voices find it hard to satisfy all parts of the house. . . . Mr. Hearst had not gone far when the deepest bass [in the rear in the audience] cried: 'Give it to 'em, Billy. I only wish you had my voice.'" Fortunately, Hearst's speech was a brief one. He was followed to the podium by Eugene Schmitz, the orchestra leader who had been elected mayor of San Francisco, former governor James Budd of California, former vice president Adlai Stevenson of Illinois, Senator Charles Culberson from Texas, Senator Edward Carmack of Tennessee, chairman of the Democratic National Committee James Jones, and several labor leaders, a rather impressive assortment of speakers for a Congressional candidate running virtually without opposition.[47]

Though Hearst had accepted Tammany's nomination and imported a phalanx of Democratic stars to appear beside him in Madison Square Garden, he had no intention of playing by the established rules of political partisanship. William Randolph Hearst — as a candidate for office, he had begun using his middle name — was bigger than the Democratic party. On November 3, the day before Election Day, the *Evening Journal* called for a Democratic victory but quite pointedly declared that "the political struggle this year is not a struggle between two American political parties. It is a conflict between the trusts and the people."[48]

Hearst was not simply the candidate of the Democratic party, but the self-proclaimed candidate and champion of the working and immigrant peoples of New York and the nation. He published a German-language newspaper, supported Irish independence, and sympathetically reported on events of interest to the Russian-Jewish communities. And he would continue, as publisher and politician, to reach out to these communities. In 1903, in a stroke of journalistic brilliance, he dispatched Irish nationalist Michael Davitt to report on the massacre of the Jews in Kishinev, Russia. Two years later, his newspapers featured an on-the-scene account by Maxim Gorky of the Red Sunday massacre in St. Petersburg in 1905, and helped raise funds to aid victims of the pogroms.[49]

Hearst was elected to Congress in November of 1902 by more than 15,000 votes, which his papers proclaimed was the largest plurality ever recorded in the Eleventh District. Two days later, he issued his first manifesto. Lecturing Democratic party leaders from his editorial-page throne, he declared that the Democratic party would, in future, only be "victorious," as he had been in the Eleventh District, by associating "itself intimately and sincerely with the working people of this country . . . [and] embody[ing] in itself the fundamental ideas that give power to the unions, that give justice and victory to union efforts . . . The man who does not indorse [the demands of labor for shorter hours and better pay] has no right to call himself a Democrat, he has no place in the Democratic party."[50]

The message was the same one he had been articulating since his nomination. He had graciously accepted Tammany's nomination, but he was not going to Washington to follow orders or be a "team player." Bryan's second defeat had left the party with a leadership vacuum which Hearst intended to fill.

His moment of triumph lasted only that long. To celebrate his victory, he held a huge fireworks display in Madison Square, as he had done so often before. This time, something went wrong. "As the election excitement was at its height in Madison Square shortly before 10 o'clock," the *New York Times* reported the next morning, "a terrific explosion of fireworks occurred, transforming in an instant the entire east side of the park into a scene of death and carnage which a battlefield could scarcely have surpassed in its horror. . . . The solid ground shook as with an earthquake, and then for a large space there was nothing to be seen save mangled forms of women and children and some men lying dead and distorted or creeping away to the outskirts of the bloody plain, while the air was rent with the shrieks of the wounded and dying and the crash of falling wood, glass, and iron from wrecked buildings."[51]

A dozen spectators were killed at once, scores of others injured. Hearst's victory celebration had been transformed in an instant into a scene of unimagined horror. Though he had not lit the fuse, he was held responsible for the pain, the wounds, the deaths. The district attorney quickly, perhaps too quickly, absolved Hearst of legal culpability, but the case did not fade away, in large part because it highlighted one of the persistent slurs on Hearst's character: that he refused to take responsibility for his actions. Immediately after the fireworks accident, Hearst departed for an extended trip to California to visit his mother, his grandmother, and the *Examiner*. He left his attorneys behind to sort out his mess.

While back in New York his newspapers celebrated his electoral triumph and hinted at higher offices to come, Will attended to personal matters on the West Coast. He had decided to marry Millicent Willson, who was now twenty-one, and he wanted to explain his decision to his grandparents, whom he expected to be supportive, and his mother, who he knew would not be. According to Phoebe's niece and Will's cousin, Anne Apperson Flint, Phoebe was so "terribly upset" at her son's decision to marry the chorus-girl daughter of a Brooklyn hoofer that she took to her bed. Though she tried her best to talk Will out of the marriage, she recognized early that she was fighting a losing battle. Her boy was forty years old now and a congressman, and she had no allies — George having died and Orrin Peck having already accepted Will's invitation to be his best man.

Despite Phoebe's fears that her boy was marrying beneath his class, Millicent Willson was, in fact, the perfect companion for him. She was a stunning-looking woman, rather tall, with unblemished pale skin, dark hair, and piercingly dark eyes. She was also devoted to Hearst and having been with him for five years now, knew him as well as anyone else.[52]

The conventional wisdom, enshrined in dozens of articles and several biographies, is that Will Hearst married in 1903 for propriety's sake, that, having embarked on a political career, he needed to put an end to the rumors about his private life. Unfortunately, instead of putting rumors about his personal life to rest, his marriage to a Brooklyn chorus girl with whom he had been consorting for several years provoked more whispering about his morals — or the lack of them. "Mr. 'Billy' Hearst's marriage has been pretty much discussed the past week," the *New-Yorker* commented the week of the wedding, "and the general opinion seems to be, among men at least, that it has very effectually put a stopper upon his political aspirations . . . The 'first lady in the land' must, even in the eyes of the proletariat, be fashioned of other material than that which goes to the formation of a 'Sassafras Sister.'" The item concluded its political epitaph for Hearst by stating that should he ever run for president, it "would take only about three weeks for the cold facts to be brought by the opposition managers to the consciousness of every voter in the country. Mr. Hearst has signed his political death warrant."[53]

Hearst married Millicent Willson because he could think of no other way to continue their relationship. For the immediate future, he would be spending a great deal of his time in Washington and on the campaign trail. It was one thing to cavort with a chorus girl half his age in New York City, on vacation in Europe, or on a yacht in the waters off Cuba. It was quite another to live openly with her in the nation's capital.

The wedding ceremony was scheduled for late April 1903 at Grace Church in New York City with only family and a few friends in attendance. Will invited Phoebe to be part of the wedding and to accompany the couple on their honeymoon trip to Europe. Because there were only "single berths" available to bring her to New York City, Will leased a private railroad car for her. When Phoebe complained that she had other engagements that might interfere with her going to Europe with them, Will offered to delay the trip until she was ready. He even proposed to invite her friend, Mrs. Peck, on the honeymoon caravan.[54]

Phoebe never did arrive for the wedding, claiming she was too ill to travel East. She did however send a telegram and an emerald brooch, for which she was promptly thanked. "Your lovely telegram made everybody very happy," Will informed his mother the day of the wedding. "Bishop Potter officiated. He asked after you. He kissed the Bride and says that he wanted to know her better and that when we returned he would help her keep tabs on the Groom. He was extremely kind and pleasant. . . . We send the greatest love to you."[55]

Everything had gone off well, as Hearst later wrote his mother at great length:

> The chantry was very beautifully decorated with colored roses and apple blossoms. Our wedding was cheerful and not to be mistaken for a funeral. Some thirty of our friends were present. The bell rang, Orrin and I stepped out to the altar. The bishop looked very grand and solemn. Anita came up with Millie and her pa. They didn't have any bouquet. I had forgotten to bring it, Millie didn't mind. She stepped up alongside me trembling and frightened. The Bishop married us. Then he kissed Millie quite a smack and patted her on the head . . . Then I kissed Millie and the audience *applauded*. The bishop hushed them and appeared to be rather shocked but wasn't. We went away after shaking hands with everybody. All seemed pleased.

After the ceremony, the wedding party retreated to the Waldorf where Oscar, the famed maitre d'hôtel, served breakfast in the Astor dining room, while Will retreated downstairs to telegraph his mother.[56]

In the early afternoon, Will, Millicent, Orrin Peck, and their entourage drove to the docks to board the *Kaiser Wilhelm II*. A process server was waiting for them — ever since the fireworks disaster in November, Hearst had been followed by them — but Carvalho got rid of him.[57]

The first stop on the honeymoon tour was London, where Hearst on landing sent his mother another telegram, expressing yet again an almost pathetic gratitude for her present to Millicent which, he said, was the climax of their wedding day. Millicent was even more flattering in her telegram: "I can never thank you enough for your kind telegram and your beautiful present. We hope you will come abroad soon. We will try hard to make you as happy as you have made us."[58]

From London, the wedding party moved on to the Hotel Wagram in Paris. Again, Will wrote his mother a long letter, filling in new details about the wedding and thanking her a third time for her present. The letter concluded with a postscript from Millie who, Will informed his mother, "wants to add a line to tell you how fine she thinks you have been. I tell her you are finer than that when she shall come to know you — and I think you will find that she is nicer than you can imagine, when you know her better. We are all pretty nice folk aren't we?" There followed yet more thank-yous from Millie.[59]

Will Hearst was not a reflective man, but even had he been, it would have been difficult for him to sort out the many strands in his relationship with his mother. When George Hearst left his entire fortune to Phoebe, he irretrievably compromised her future relationship with her son. From that moment, Phoebe's role as mother was eclipsed by her position as feudal overlord of the Hearst estates. Whatever the reasons for the strange ritual of avoidance and approach that was played out on Will's wedding day and honeymoon, it followed the pattern that had been established long before.

On returning from Europe, the newlyweds traveled to Mexico to visit Jack Follansbee, who lived there, and tour the Hearst estates. They then took the train west to California to meet Will's grandparents in Santa Clara and Phoebe at her vacation home in Pleasanton, forty miles east of San Francisco. It did not take long for Millicent to win Phoebe's approval. If Will had not married a woman well placed in New York or San Francisco society, he had married one who was willing to go out of her way to be attentive to her mother-in-law. "Quite a number of people like her," Phoebe wrote Janet Peck in March of 1904, about a year after the marriage. "Will is very happy and Millicent is a good wife."[60]

❦ 9 ❦

"Candidate of a Class"

A NEW LIFE BEGAN at age forty for William Randolph Hearst, publisher and politician. It was as if the previous fifteen years had been prologue for what was to come. The boy publisher with the loud ties and a chorus girl on either arm had been replaced by the black-coated congressman who traveled only in the company of his demurely dressed wife.[1]

Hearst had been elected to Congress in November 1902, but had no intention of staying there for long. Immediately after his election, he began laying the groundwork for the 1904 presidential nomination. Like others in the Bryan wing of the Democratic party, Hearst believed that the radicals' victory at two successive nominating conventions had firmly — and permanently — placed the party in their hands. The question was who would represent the radicals and their party in November 1904. There were no candidates from the Bryan wing of the party with national appeal and few with regional appeal. It was into this void that Hearst strode. He had no doubt that he would be elected president, if not in 1904, then four years later. William Jennings Bryan had been nominated after two terms in Congress. Why not William Randolph Hearst after one?

Instead of taking the traditional route to the 1904 convention and organizing party regulars outward from his home state, Hearst detoured around the New York Democratic leaders, whom he considered both hostile and increasingly irrelevant. Unlike other candidates for office, he did not need the support of the party to get his message to the voters, distribute campaign literature, organize rallies, or get voters to the polls on Election Day. His newspapers provided potential voters with a full discussion of the issues on which he was running and a day-by-day commentary on his campaign; the Hearst fortune gave him the wherewithal to set up his own independent political organization.

All through the campaign, he would be dogged by accusations, as his father had been twenty years earlier, that he was buying delegate votes. Estimates of the amount of money Hearst spent ranged from $25,000 a week during the campaign season to $2,000,000. It is possible that some of this money went to bribing politicians. Most of it, however, was spent on building a campaign organization that was entirely independent of the Democratic party and loyal to him alone.

"In his unique campaign, Mr. Hearst has certainly set a few marks in politics," the political commentator of *Leslie's Monthly* noted in the spring of 1904. "None of his chief managers . . . are politicians of note. Most of them are newspaper men connected with his various publications. His press bureau is run by John W. Keller, once a newspaper man and recently charity commissioner of New York." Max Ihmsen, his former Washington correspondent who had organized the National Association of Democratic Clubs, was in charge of logistics; Arthur Brisbane formulated campaign strategy; Lawrence O'Reilly, who had worked for Brisbane and Carvalho, served as his private political secretary. Hinting broadly that Hearst was buying delegates, if not with bribes then with high-priced entertainments, the *Leslie's Monthly* commentator referred to his "expensive headquarters" in the Hoffman House in New York and the ways in which he wined and dined potential supporters in Washington, D.C.:

> Backwoods statesmen and country editors and their wives, first provided with free transportation to the capital, sit at Congressman Hearst's family board and enjoy hospitality of a lavishness beyond their maddest dreams. Politics *a la Hearst* are dished up between courses, and gifts of value — such, for instance, as solid gold pins bearing Mr. Hearst's portrait — are forced upon departing guests. Considering everything, Mr. Hearst has accomplished a great deal. He is the only man who ever ran for president with nothing to start on but his own right of suffrage at the polls.[2]

There was no ambiguity about what he stood for. For years, he had been hammering away at the trusts and defending working people and their unions. A rich and successful businessman, he assured the voters that he was beholden to no party and no financial backers. As Arthur Brisbane explained in an April 6, 1904, letter to the editor of the *New York Herald,* the source of Hearst's popularity was transparent:

> The American people — like all people — are interested in PERSONALITY. If they are asked to vote they want to know whom and what they are voting for. . . . If any man casts a vote for Hearst for President he will know that Hearst is answerable only to him. Hearst has gone back to the old-fashioned American

plan. He appeals to the people — not to a boss or a corporation. . . . Not even the most venal of newspapers has suggested that anybody owns Hearst, or that he would be influenced by anything save the will of the people in the event of his election.

To provide himself with additional outlets to get his message to potential voters, Hearst established a new morning paper in Los Angeles, the *Examiner*, and an evening paper in Boston, the *American*. Each of these papers was added to the Hearst "wire" and carried the same editorials, feature articles, and Sunday supplements. It is impossible to know how much it cost Hearst to start these new papers or where he got the money. With successful newspapers in New York, Chicago, and San Francisco, and with Phoebe having forgiven his $8 million debt in 1902, it is quite likely that he was able to borrow money from the banks for his new ventures.

The Hearst campaign started out as little more than a construct of the Hearst newspapers, but the more it was reported on, the more substance it acquired. As early as February of 1903, *Town Topics,* the gossip weekly with a strong interest in politics that spoke for the conservative faction of the Democratic party in New York State, felt obligated to comment on the rumors of Hearst's candidacy — all of them first planted by and then reported on in his newspapers. Although Hearst had shown "administrative ability in the management of his numerous and popular newspapers," *Town Topics* believed he was too young for the presidency and suggested it might be better if he waited four years before running.[3]

Through the summer and fall of 1903, the Hearst papers created the appearance of a groundswell of enthusiasm for the Hearst candidacy, transforming random remarks, inconsequential gestures, and simple hospitality into expressions of enthusiastic support. Day after day, there appeared dozens of items on the Hearst campaign, on the endorsements he was receiving, the "Hearst committees" that were being formed, the enthusiasm that greeted his candidacy everywhere in the nation. In July, it was reported that Hearst had been endorsed by several printers' unions and the letter carriers. President Roosevelt responded to news of the latter endorsement by firing off a confidential letter to his postmaster general, Henry Clay Payne, "Any man who has had any share in introducing resolutions endorsing Mr. Hearst . . . should be removed at once from the service." Civil service employees, he reminded Mr. Payne, were forbidden to engage in political activities.[4]

In August of 1903, *Editor and Publisher,* also getting its news from the

Hearst press, reported that a group of labor leaders had met in Washington to plan a convention for June 1904, the prime purpose of which was to "nominate a candidate for president, preferably William R. Hearst of New York, as a man pre-eminently worthy to be the people's choice for president."[5] Hearst's strategy was now clear. He expected to inherit Bryan's supporters in the West and Middle West, and add his own endorsements from urban machines and labor organizations in the Northeast. While this might still not give him enough delegates for the nomination, it would guarantee him a voice in selecting the nominee and make him the leading candidate in 1908. Because the first session of the Fifty-eighth Congress was not scheduled to convene until November of 1903, Hearst was able to spend the entire year following his election to Congress traveling across the country — by private railroad car with an entourage of advisers — looking for opportunities to present himself as a serious candidate. When there was no invitation to be garnered to a state or county fair or a meeting of some local Democratic club, Hearst and his advisers invented reasons for their visits.

In late October of 1903, Hearst organized and paid for what his newspapers referred to as a "Congressional Trip by Special Train Through the South-Western Territories in the Interest of Statehood." He escorted three senators, seventeen congressmen, and assorted photographers, reporters, political advisers, and their wives on a twelve-day circuit of press appearances, from Chicago to Missouri, Kansas, Colorado, New Mexico, Arizona, and Texas, with a brief side trip to Mexico.[6]

At each whistle stop, Hearst and his guests posed for group pictures and were greeted by local dignitaries, territorial governors, mayors, school children, and marching bands. Uncharacteristically for a politician, Hearst never made a speech. Still, he was the center of attention wherever he went, literally standing head and shoulders above everyone else, outfitted dramatically in his standard political uniform: a black three-piece suit, white shirt, conservative tie, white carnation in his button hole, full-length, double-breasted black overcoat, and black shoes. For evening public receptions, he wore a tuxedo. Only at the end of the trip, as he entertained his guests in a tiny restaurant in Hermocillio, Mexico, did he exchange his black frock coat for a light-colored suit jacket and a loud plaid tie.[7]

Hearst reporters and photographers accompanying the party telegraphed stories back to his newspapers each day. "Congressman Hearst is a great favorite among the people of the great Southwest and his many acts of charity have made him one of the best known figures of the West," the *New York Evening Journal* reported on October 20, 1903. "It is probable that no man could come to Arizona who would be more enthusiastically received or who could make a more profound impression upon the people." The paper reported in a sidebar that the people of Atlanta were looking forward to the congressman's visit there to celebrate "press day" at the Interstate Fair.[8]

In January 1904, Hearst officially declared his candidacy for the presidency in an "interview" with reporters from the *Chicago Daily Tribune* and the *New York Herald,* two of the nation's most respected Republican papers. The interview was still a relatively new reportorial form with no fixed parameters. Hearst, who did not like to be questioned in person, answered questions submitted in advance. He had nothing new to say about the trusts, the major topic of the interview. He emphasized that he was not proposing the elimination of all trusts and combinations, only the "bad" ones, a position which was neither terribly radical nor very much different from President Roosevelt's. Where Hearst differed from Roosevelt and from every Democrat with a national reputation was in his unequivocal support for labor unions. Without unions demanding higher wages, he argued, the nation might well move in the direction of "China and India where rich mandarins and rajahs lord it over starving populations." Unions were good not only for working people, but for the economy as a whole. The "prosperity" of the merchant, manufacturer, farmer, book publisher, theater owner, and actor — this was Hearst's list — depended on the purchasing power of the mass of the people:

> Poverty-stricken people do not eat beef or mutton; they do not buy woolen clothes in profusion. They have not enough for life's real necessities; nothing at all for the books, the travel, the pleasures that should accompany genuine national prosperity. Wide and equitable distribution of wealth is essential to a nation's prosperous growth and intellectual development, and that distribution is brought about by the labor union more than any other agency of our civilization.[9]

Apart from Eugene Debs, who would run for president in 1904 on the Socialist party ticket, no candidate for office had a record of support for labor as straightforward and consistent as Hearst's. But then, no candidate had a father like George Hearst, who had spent the better part of his life in the digging fields. Though the senator had died a millionaire many times over, he had not struck it rich until his fortieth year and didn't retire from the mines until his sixtieth. As Cora Older put it in her biography, no doubt following the line laid down for her by Hearst himself, "Conquest of fortune was not easy for George Hearst."[10]

Forced to choose between men who, like his father, worked with their hands to eke out a living, and those who sat back at leisure and profited from the labor of others, Hearst had no difficulty siding with the former against the latter. As Ambrose Bierce, who had earlier left Hearst's employ, remarked in 1912, "in matters of 'industrial discontent' it has always been a standing order in the editorial offices of the Hearst newspapers to 'take the side of the strikers' without inquiry or delay." The Hearst papers backed railroad workers in California, steel workers and coal miners in Pennsylvania, streetcar workers in Brooklyn. He was so committed to labor's right to strike that *Town Topics* declared at the onset of a steelworkers' strike in 1901 that Hearst should be held accountable for any violence that might occur: "If he could be hanged more than once, the number of times should correspond with the list of those who are more than likely to fall victims of his malevolent counsels. If the present strike does not attain the worst phases of which such affairs are capable it will be through no fault of his."[11]

For his past support of organized labor and striking workers, Hearst expected to receive organized labor's backing for his candidacy. And he did. But his invocation of the rights of labor did not sit well with the party's leaders or the business community. It was one thing to publish a daily newspaper that supported the right to strike. It was far different to elevate support for unions into a political principle.

Hearst's critics had tried at first to laugh his candidacy to death. But they realized quickly enough that he was in earnest and dangerous. In January of 1904, Franklin K. Lane, a California Democrat whom Hearst had earlier refused to support for governor, wrote a friend from San Francisco that the Hearst "boom [was] increasing. That it is possible for such a man to receive the nomination, is too humiliating to be thought of." In February, Mayor Harrison of Chicago called a meeting of Cook County leaders to plan an anti-Hearst strategy before it was too late.[12]

The personal attacks began in San Francisco in February 1904, when the *Star,* a weekly that specialized in politics and scandal, published the first in a series of scurrilous poems recounting in verse the tales about Sausalito Bill that had circulated a decade earlier, when Will Hearst and Tessie Powers had sailed up, down, and across San Francisco Bay in Hearst's yacht.

> What's the matter with Bill?
> He's the limit still.
> His Sausalito ark
> Was the real thing after dark,
> When the corks made

A fusillade,
And the guests, promiscuously vying,
Were trying,
After their wines and beers,
To kick down the chandeliers,
And the soubrettes sweet
Stood on their heads and waved their feet. . . .
And there was nothing to do but drink
And so forth — "so forth" having in't
All that the press declines to print.

The poem continued for another four stanzas, ending with Sausalito Bill in the White House, holding prize fights and poker games, with "blue" vaudeville shows every Sunday night.[13]

The following month, the *Star* ran a second poem, this one more scurrilous still, called "The Message from Bill: A Nightmare Dream in Which the Unspeakable Bill, as an Impossible President, Informs Congress How Honorable Diplomats Ignore Him and Self-Respecting Americans Ostracize Him."[14]

The *San Francisco News-Letter,* another weekly which specialized in political scandal, published a series of political cartoons reminiscent of those Hearst himself had used to ridicule McKinley and the Republicans in 1896 and 1900. Hearst was pictured as a ghoul juggling bombs, a stampeding ass, and a college boy in a beanie. He and the smaller figures who surrounded him were covered with captions rich in allusions to past scandals.[15]

On the first of March, the *New York Evening Post,* among the oldest and most distinguished newspapers in the nation, legitimized the assault on Hearst's character by joining in with a vicious editorial, "The Unthinkable Hearst." After professing its reluctance to "speak of the Presidential candidacy of William R. Hearst" because it was "one of those things that 'need much washing to be touched,'" the editorial went on to describe the "darker and more fearful" aspects of the Hearst candidacy in lurid detail:

It is well known that this man has a record which would make it impossible for him to live through a Presidential campaign — such gutters would be dragged, such sewers laid open! We can only refer to the loathsome subject. Let those who want a hint of the repulsive details turn to the *Congressional Record* of January 8, 1897. There they will find a speech by Representative Johnson of California showing the kind of millstone that will be hung around Hearst's neck if he were ever to come before the voters. . . . We are convinced that it is only necessary to set forth the facts in order to make an end of this unspeakable candidacy. Hearst's record will crush him as soon as it is known. . . . It is not a question of policies, but of character. *An agitator we can endure; an honest radical we can respect; a fanatic we can tolerate; but a low voluptuary trying to sting his jaded senses to a fresh thrill by turning from private to public corruption is a new horror in American politics.*[16]

Other men might have retreated from public life in the face of such an onslaught but Hearst remained almost oblivious to it. The accusations were repeated often enough to gather about them the texture of truth. There was sufficient money available — from unnamed and untraceable sources — to reprint and distribute anti-Hearst campaign literature across the country. The *San Francisco News-Letter* circulated thousands of extra copies of its "Hearst issue"; the *Evening Post* editorial, "Unthinkable Hearst," was reprinted in bulk and "sent to every editor, every educator, every clergyman, every public man in the South."[17]

Whatever the psychic toll, William Randolph Hearst had strutted onto the public stage and would remain there for the next half century. Ridiculed, feared, or adored, he would, from this point on, be impossible to ignore. He had become a new kind of political celebrity, his fame based equally on rumors about his personal life and the image he had cultivated as a knight on horseback come to rescue working people from the trusts.

In March, the first delegates to the national convention were chosen in Rhode Island. To the dismay of conservative Democrats and journalists around the country, Hearst won six of eight seats. The *New York Times,* which under Adolph Ochs had become an outspoken opponent of the Bryan wing of the Democratic party, sounded the alarm. In its lead editorial on March 12, 1904, "The Ambitions of Mr. Hearst," the paper asserted that while Hearst would never get the nomination, "the work he and his organizers are doing and the money they are spending . . . will have a certain effect, an evil effect, upon the body politic and upon the fortunes of the Democratic party. . . . He makes his appeal solely to restlessness and discontent. . . . He represents the sterile policy of agitation, nothing more. That is to say, Mr. HEARST stands for absolutely nothing but the arraying of class against class in the United States."

"It cannot be said that his Presidential boom is a thing of mushroom growth," the *Forum* reported in April of 1904. "Its blossoming may have been a surprise; but, as a matter of fact, the seed was planted more than two years ago, and there has been careful watering and fertilizing ever since. . . . His agents have been in almost every State; his position as president of the National League of Democratic Clubs has brought him into close and intimate association with party workers; while the attitude of his papers upon labor questions has secured him the support of the laboring classes in every section of the country. . . . He will be the only candidate who will go to St. Louis [for the nominating convention] with an organization behind him."[18]

Like a modern-day celebrity, Hearst was both omnipresent and elusive. The *New York Times* in an April 8, 1904, article about the "would-be President" reported that his "face and figure" had become "familiar to the galleries." Whenever he appeared on the floor of the House, "a whisper of 'There's Hearst!' rushes through them, and everybody looks at the candidate." Still, while images and representations of his own and his enemies' making were omnipresent, Hearst kept his distance from the public. He was personally shy and professionally wary. Perhaps because he knew how the press worked, he never spoke informally or off the record and did not invite the press to his home. He remained, as Lincoln Steffens would characterize him in his 1906 profile in the *American Magazine,* a "man of mystery" — to the press as well as the public. Did he have any ideas of his own? Did he write his own articles and speeches or edit his paper? Was he Brisbane's puppet or merely another rich man looking for a vocation in politics? The more journalists investigated, the less they learned. No one knew the man; no one, in fact, knew anyone who had ever had a serious conversation with him.[19]

His critics and the few journalists who remained neutral on the "Hearst question" assumed that his reticence, his shyness, his unwillingness to give interviews or speeches were signs of incapacity. A reporter from the *Chicago Record-Herald* who had accompanied the candidate on a campaign trip through the South found him tongue-tied: "He could not, at least did not, open his mouth. He was as inane as he looked . . . One of the men who rode with Hearst nearly the whole of one day and tried to talk with him thus relates his experience: 'I could not carry on a conversation with the man. He did not seem to know anything. He had no views, at least he did not express any. He was not only shy, he seemed to be deficient in his thinking department. . . . I was, too, forced to the conclusion that nothing came out because there was nothing inside, and that he has brains only when Arthur Brisbane and his other brilliant men on his staff are at hand to make and express ideas for him.'" The reporter from the *New York Times* assigned to penetrate the Hearst mystery disagreed. If Hearst had little to say to reporters, it was because he was "bashful," not because he had no ideas: "He suffers in the presence of the men he meets. Personally, from all accounts, he is a kindly and courteous gentleman, considerate of those about him, gentle in his dealings with men."[20]

Hearst had swept into Washington in the fall of 1903, leased the mansion within sight of the White House that had been occupied by McKinley's secretary of war, Elihu Root, demanded and won a seat on the prestigious Labor Committee after bombarding the House leadership with letters of support from labor leaders, and then left town. He had more important things to do than waste his days in a House of Representatives run from the top down by the Republican majority leader "Uncle Joe" Cannon and the Democratic minority leader John Sharp Williams of Mississippi, neither of whom thought much of or paid much attention to the freshman congressman from New York's Eleventh Congressional District.

"He goes the usual road of new Congressmen, sought only by his own little clique of friends, as is the custom with all legislative tyros," the *New York Times* reported of Hearst in April 1904. "He is not a 'mixer,' and the majority of the Democrats are as aloof from him, as he from them." He missed most roll calls, made no speeches, and appeared on the floor only when one of his pet projects was being debated. He was much more active in committee work. He attended "all the meetings [of his Labor Committee] at which testimony has been taken and has participated in them . . . At these hearings Hearst frequently asked questions and made suggestions designed to bring out the organized labor side of the issue." Louis Brownlow, a Washington-based journalist, attended one hearing at which Hearst testified on behalf of his bill for "government ownership of the railroads." The committee room was full of reporters who, like Brownlow, had come to see Hearst "flounder in disgrace." They were completely disappointed, Brownlow recalled in his autobiography: "Mr. Hearst, without notes, first made an oral presentation of his ideas on the problem and the solution that he had proposed in his bill. Then the questions began to come. No doubt most of the members of the committee had had the same notion that I had, but Hearst was too much for them. He knew his subject — from his point of view, of course — and he answered easily, quickly, succinctly, and in very good humor."[21]

Hearst's pet project was a bill mandating the eight-hour day for railroad workers and government employees. When the Republicans decided to bottle up the bill in committee, Hearst countered by attempting to add an eight-hour proviso to a naval appropriations bill, and surprised everyone by appearing himself in the House chamber. Then, according to the *New York Times* reporter covering the debate, there took place "one of the strangest scenes ever witnessed in Congress, and one absolutely without precedent":

> Without uttering a word except in a whisper, sitting on the small of his back with one knee in the air, and apparently having nothing to do with the debate, for three-quarters of an hour [Hearst] kept the House in a turmoil. . . . The old-line Democrats looked on silently at the curious scene. The members of the "Hearst Brigade" would come over to their chief one after another and get their assignments. Immediately afterward the man assigned to the work would arise and throw a new bomb into the Republican side. All this time the chief never changed his position except once, when he walked around to give an assignment personally to Mr. Livernash [a congressman from California], who was formerly a reporter on Mr. Hearst's San Francisco paper. Throughout the fight, the unversed and unsophisticated tourists in the galleries never suspected that the silent man sitting crouched in his chair had anything to do with the fight, much less that he was the head centre of it. He played on the House like a piano, and succeeded amply in his purpose to put the Republicans on record against the Eight-Hour bill. . . . It was an extraordinary sight. He and his handful of supporters were the whole show, and no debate so run has ever been witnessed in the House. It was unique. . . . When it was over and the Eight-Hour bill was beaten, Hearst put his hands into his pockets and lounged out. The scene no longer interested him, and when the roll call came on the passage of the bill he was absent.[22]

The Hearst bandwagon rolled merrily along through the winter and early spring of 1904, picking up support in the Middle West and the West, wherever the Bryan forces remained intact. As the *New York Times* explained to its readers in an April 1 editorial, "The Hearst Disease," the publisher was winning delegates by "appealing with equal fervor and greater recklessness to the very prejudices and passions aroused by the utterances of BRYAN . . . Here and there Democrats are found, in some States many Democrats, who, having welcomed Mr. BRYAN as the great deliverer, now acclaim Mr. HEARST as the appointed continuer of his work." Fortunately, the *Times* continued, the Democrats showed signs of "beginning to expel the Hearst poison" and uniting behind the candidacy of Judge Alton Parker of New York, "an old-school Democrat." Judge Parker was firmly in the grip of the conservative, anti-Bryan wing of the party.[23]

The Hearst camp responded to the relentless editorial criticism in the *Times* with an editorial in the morning *American* and the *Evening Journal* on April 7, accusing Adolph Ochs of being in the pay of Judge Parker's chief supporter, the Wall Street financier August Belmont. Though Belmont was, as charged, a *Times* stockholder — as was J. P. Morgan — there was no evidence that either of them had interfered in the paper's editorial policy. There was no excuse for the anti-Semitic imagery the editorial employed in portraying Ochs as "an oily little commercial gentleman [who had come] cringing into Mr. Belmont's office, with oily smiles, obsequiously curved shoulders and nervously rubbing his hands." Until now, the Hearst papers, unlike Dana's *Sun*, for example, had not stooped to this sort of caricature in criticizing Pulitzer or Ochs. In the heat of political battle, however, Hearst's editorial writers had begun to bring out all the weapons in the "populist" arsenal, including attacks which linked Wall Street financiers like Belmont — and their supporters like Ochs — to international Jewish conspiracies led by the Rothschilds. The anti-Semitic thrust of the attack was contradicted, but not erased, a few paragraphs down by the description of the publisher as "an ordinary type of the very ordinary man, who is as respectable as he dares to be, and whose opinions are given to him by his stockholders."

Contrary to the assertion by Susan E. Tifft and Alex S. Jones in *The Trust*, their book on the Sulzberger and Ochs families, Hearst did not write or sign this editorial. On April 7, the day it appeared, he was, according to his own newspapers and the *New York Times*, in Washington, introducing a resolution calling on the attorney general to furnish Congress with evidence his office had acquired in 1902 of "a conspiracy in restraint of inter-State trade among the anthracite coal railroads." Still, even though Hearst had taken a leave from day-to-day control of his newspapers for the duration of his campaign, he remained responsible for their editorial policies. He may not have personally approved and certainly did not write the anti-Semitic slurs against Ochs, but he never apologized or retracted them or muted the attacks on August Belmont as a Rothschild agent.[24]

From April 7, the day the anti-Belmont, anti-Ochs editorial appeared, to April 22, there was an uncharacteristic silence about Hearst's whereabouts or activities in his and the opposition newspapers. We can only assume that he spent these two weeks in New York City with Millicent who, on April 10, gave birth to their first son, George Randolph Hearst. The birth of his first son and child may have been kept out of his newspapers because he did not wish to call attention to his private life or to his marriage the year before. As both mother and son were healthy and there were plenty of servants and family members to look after them, Hearst returned to Washington on April 22 in response to a written invitation to testify before the House Judiciary Committee.

According to the *New York Times*, reporting on April 23, the hearing had been called solely "to learn whether or not Representative William R.

Hearst can make a speech." If the intention was to embarrass Hearst publicly, it failed. Hearst appeared in the hearing room as requested, with his attorney Clarence Shearn, and "many documents and legal works. When Chairman Jenkins announced that the hearing was open, Mr. Hearst arose. He was pale, but self-possessed. He wore a frock coat with silk facings; a puff tie of blue with white stripes, and gray trousers with a very faint stripe in them. He kept his coat buttoned, and thrust his hand into his trousers pocket, where it incessantly played with a bunch of keys or a knife while he spoke." Though he had few specifics to offer the committee about the antitrust conspiracy he had accused the coal companies and railroads of engaging in, Shearn, who followed him, provided the facts and figures. At the conclusion of the hearing, "the Hearst resolution was referred to a subcommittee. . . . When the meeting was over Mr. Hearst was found in the corridor, standing by a window, with his hat and gloves in his hand, patiently waiting for Mr. Shearn."

By mid-April, the campaign for the Democratic nomination had reached a critical stage with the convening of the New York state convention in Albany. Though Hearst realized that he had no chance of winning a majority of the New York delegates, he expected to pick up enough to keep his bandwagon rolling. When it became apparent that ex-Governor David Hill had the votes to "instruct" all the delegates to vote for the candidate who won the majority, thereby assuring that Parker would leave Albany with seventy-eight delegates, Hearst zero, his campaign advisers panicked. Though Hearst was, at the time, in New York City with Millicent and their newborn son, he had to have been in touch with his campaign officials, who were stationed in the Ten Eyck hotel. With "great secrecy," the Hearst camp in Albany prepared and distributed a manifesto charging that Parker was August Belmont's candidate and demanding that the delegates "maintain" their "manhood" by repudiating "the alien pawnbroker who came to our shores just before the Civil War as the representative of the Rothschilds and as vice consul of a petty European state." The attack was so blatantly anti-Semitic and so vicious that Belmont almost withdrew his name as an at-large delegate. While Hearst did not personally write this manifesto and would not himself have resorted to such anti-Semitic references, his subordinates were acting under his instructions and, no doubt, with his knowledge. They were, one and all, furious at the political shenanigans in Albany and determined to do whatever was necessary to rescue Hearst's candidacy from the party professionals. Their efforts to win support for Hearst by smearing August Belmont failed entirely. The convention voted, in the end, to instruct all seventy-eight delegates from New York to cast their ballots for Judge Alton Parker.[25]

The defeat in New York, as feared, slowed the Hearst bandwagon to a crawl. It all but came to a halt the following week when William Jennings Bryan, who had still not endorsed a candidate to succeed him as the Democratic nominee, spoke at the Second Regiment Armory in Chicago. The Hearst camp was convinced that Bryan would endorse the publisher and had packed the house with Hearst supporters. But Bryan, perhaps still harboring the impossible dream that a deadlocked St. Louis convention would turn to him for a third time, endorsed no one. As the *Chicago Daily Tribune* reported on April 24 in a front-page story, Bryan devoted his entire speech to condemning the conservative wing of the party and its candidate, Judge Alton Parker. The *Tribune* reported that "except for a passing reference in the Nebraskan's opening remarks and for a sporadic cheer or two in the audience, the name of William Randolph Hearst went unmentioned." Without Bryan's endorsement, Hearst had no hope of securing the votes he needed for the nomination. He fought on, hopelessly now, but unwilling to concede defeat, winning a few more delegates in Illinois, but losing in North and South Dakota, Texas, Oregon, Minnesota, and Montana. The fact that he was headed for inevitable defeat did not silence his critics. His appeal to class division, his support of the unions, and his attempt to bring together rural populists with the urban working class was too incendiary to ignore. In late May, long after the Parker forces had lined up sufficient votes to handily win the nomination, *Harper's Weekly,* still unwilling to let down its guard, declared that Hearst's remained the most "audacious" candidacy the country had ever seen:

> Mr. Hearst has no particular desire to become the Democratic candidate. . . . He wants to be the candidate of a class, and since classes have not hitherto been recognized as existing in this country, he has bent his energies and given his own talent and hired clever men of specious minds and spent freely of his money in an endeavor to create one. His newspapers are characterized by appeals to ignorance and prejudice, to hatred of the rich simply became they are rich . . . to socialism, discontent, and envy, to the basest of human passions. From the standpoint of a patriot, a lover of his country, the great and free, although still experimental republic, this is dastardly work. One shudders to contemplate the logical conclusion of its successful continuance.[26]

The Democratic nominating convention met in St. Louis during the week of July 4. Hearst, who had been campaigning in Chicago with Millicent (we don't know where two-month-old George Randolph was), returned to

Washington to await the delegates' decision. The reporters who had expected fireworks in St. Louis were sorely disappointed. Hearst canceled the contract for one hundred and fifty rooms at the Jefferson Hotel and called off the huge demonstrations planned on his behalf. As the *New York Times* reported on July 3, 1904, "Hearst Boom Noiseless. Divested of Its Clangor As It Reaches St. Louis."

Though his opponents, up until the last minute, expected him to disrupt the proceedings by denouncing the party or bolting it entirely, he behaved admirably, taking the high road to defeat. He did not criticize the undemocratic, boss-ridden procedures — like the unit rule — that he was convinced had robbed him of the nomination; he condemned neither his opponents nor Bryan; he declined to consider the nomination of the Populist party; he insisted that no matter what occurred in St. Louis, he would remain a loyal Democrat. Privately, he held his fire out of the belief that he would, if not now, then in 1908 or 1912, be elected president because his antitrust, antimonopoly, proworking class philosophy provided the nation with the only alternative to class warfare.

The Hearst delegates, as his papers reported in full, did their best to make sure that the Democratic platform adopted in St. Louis included progressive planks like those advocating the direct election of senators and jury trials in labor injunction cases. Hearst permitted his name to be put into nomination by Delphin M. Delmas, a San Francisco lawyer who had been an ally of his father, and Delmas dutifully delivered a stirring speech about Hearst, "the foremost living advocate of the equality of man . . . the champion of the rights of toil, the foe of privilege and monopoly." Clarence Darrow, the progressive lawyer whom Hearst had hired to serve as his newspapers' general counsel in Chicago, seconded his nomination, asking the delegates to look beyond the convention hall and consider the needs and wishes of "the countless millions who do their work and live their lives and earn their bread without the aid of schemes or tricks. . . . Sometime when the fever of commercialism has run its course, when humanity and justice shall once more control the minds of men, this great party will come back from the golden idols and tempting fleshpots, and once more battle for the rights of man." Following the nominating speeches came an obligatory but spirited demonstration, which, according to the Hearst papers, lasted a full forty-three minutes; according to the *New York Times*, it was a still impressive thirty-eight minutes.[27]

At 5:45 in the morning, the first ballot was completed. Hearst received 204 votes; Parker, 667, nine votes short of the two-thirds which he needed for nomination. There was no need for a second ballot, as sufficient delegates switched their votes to Parker to guarantee his nomination.

Hearst returned to New York, Millicent, and his son George in July. "The baby is undergoing singular transformations," he proudly informed his mother. "He has grown until he weighs considerably over twelve pounds. His hair is getting lighter daily until it is almost blond and perhaps he will turn out a tow head after all. His face has grown longer and he is developing a nose instead of the push button he started out with. I shall take some more pictures of him in a few days."

That, unfortunately, was about the only thing that was going right with his life. "I have had an awful siege here," he admitted to Phoebe. "I have stopped giving the slightest attention to politics and have been working truly day and night to straighten things out" at his newspapers and with his finances, both of which had deteriorated while he was on the campaign trail:

> I get to bed about three and frequently am up at five again walking the floor and trying to think things out. I have not had one night's sleep since you left. As a result I am pretty sick and miserable and blue and if I didn't have the family constitution I would be well along with nervous prostration or loco-motor ataxia. . . . My eyes have gone wrong and I have had to . . . get fitted for glasses. Imagine your dutiful son with big lamps on his nose. Milly is well but pretty tired too as she spends most of her time at night rubbing my head and trying to put me to sleep. If we get through the summer I suppose things will be better but if any of us get through the summer we will be lucky. Anyhow the baby is well and don't seem to worry much. He will have his little troubles in time, I suppose.[28]

Not even Hearst's money could save his young wife and baby from the stifling heat that engulfed New York City. (This was to be the first — and last — summer the Hearst family would spend in New York.) As Millicent wrote to Phoebe in Pleasanton, California, the heat had become so punishing and the baby "so restless and fretful" that Will had, in desperation, rushed out "and bought five electric fans and eight buckets full of ice and tried to cool the room the baby was in. When everything got going it sounded like a flying machine and looked like a cold storage warehouse, but didn't feel any cooler than before. Will was so hot carrying the ice upstairs and fussing with the electric fans that I think he raised the thermometer several degrees." His attempt to cool off their home having failed,

Will moved his family into the Netherlands hotel for the duration of the heat wave.[29]

In August, Will's world came crashing down around him. He had been on a merry-go-round for more than a year, commuting back and forth from Washington to New York, running a political campaign and serving in Congress, trying, at the same time, to oversee his publishing empire and spend time with his wife and newborn son. Exhaustion and depression took their toll. For one of the few times in his life, he had literally run himself into a corner.

"The work and worry about the papers and campaign and everything broke Will down and we had to come to Mt. Clemens to take the baths and to get a rest," Millicent wrote Phoebe from the Michigan spa in August. "We expect to be here about two weeks, but I don't know whether we shall stay so long or not. The papers get in every morning and there is always something the matter with them. I think we shall have to go someplace where there are no papers. We may run up into Canada."[30]

Will also wrote his mother from Mt. Clemens, but betrayed no hint of the breakdown Millicent had mentioned. On the contrary, his letter was as maniacally cheery as the ones he had written her from Cambridge, twenty years earlier:

> I have found a place that beats Carlsbad all to pieces. The waters are nastier, the place is duller, the food is worse and if possible there are more Jews. I am sure people ought to get cured here of anything they ever had. All I am afraid of is that I may lose my own diseases that I am used to and acquire somebody's else that will be new and unfamiliar and perhaps embarrassing. . . . We all bathe in the same bath tubs and interchange greetings and ailments in the most intimate and agreeable way. I don't know what I have drawn yet and I shall not, of course, for awhile, but I rather suspect that I have added eczema scrofula and the itch to my present collection. . . . The baby is at the beach. . . . He is a smart little thing, if I, who am chiefly responsible for his abilities, do say it myself. Milly also admits it. He weighs nearly sixteen pounds now and about fifteen and a half of that is *brain*. You see he does take after his father and his father's ma, doesn't he?[31]

In late summer, Hearst returned to New York. In October, he accepted renomination for a second term in Congress. He had no taste for the campaign trail in his local district, having spent the previous year running for president. It didn't much matter. His surrogates flooded his district with campaign literature and he was easily reelected in November. Judge Alton Parker had no such luck. While Hearst watched from the sidelines, endorsing the Democratic nominee but doing nothing on his behalf, Judge Alton Parker was outvoted by Theodore Roosevelt by twenty percentage points, the largest margin in American history. Even Bryan, in 1900, had been able to poll 1.3 million votes more than Parker did in 1904.

In nominating Judge Parker for the presidency, the conservative Democrats had, Hearst believed, made it clear that they did not want to be identified with working people. The result was a debacle for the party, a Pyrrhic victory for radicals like Hearst, and a triumph for Gene Debs and the Socialists, who had polled over 400,000 votes, 3 percent of the total. No one knew yet what Parker's defeat and Debs's vote tally meant for the future. The common wisdom, as dispensed by the national press and summarized in *Current Literature,* was that the Democratic party would "be reorganized — perhaps to the point of obliteration." The question that was being asked across the country was who would reorganize it, Bryan or Hearst?[32]

§ 10 §

"A Force to Be Reckoned With"

HEARST RETURNED TO WASHINGTON in December of 1904 for the lame-duck session of the 58th Congress. Recovered from his post-Convention depression, he was on track again, pointed toward the 1908 nominating convention. The fact that party leaders had passed him over to nominate Alton Parker, who had no chance of winning, confirmed every one of his suspicions. The Democratic party, at the local, state, and national level, had become as corrupted by money as the Republican. He had been mercilessly attacked during the campaign — and would continue to be attacked — because he dared to speak this truth to the American people. "The corporations," he wrote his mother in 1905, "control the Democratic machines quite as much as they do the Republican machines and anyone who is really opposed to the corporations must count upon opposition from the machines of both parties."[1]

In Congress, as elsewhere, he made his own rules, refusing to allow himself to be compromised or to contribute in any way to legitimizing the collection of boodlers and bagmen that held power. He proudly skipped 168 out of 170 roll calls in his first term, voted only 26 times in his four years in the House, and very rarely attended floor debates, even on the bills he had sponsored. He became instead a scold, a provocateur, a modern-day Jeremiah. He took extreme positions and refused to budge. He introduced new bills mandating his old causes: an eight-hour day for government workers, investing circuit courts with jurisdiction to enforce antitrust laws, providing federal funds for roads, requiring the direct election of senators, outlawing railroad rebates, establishing a parcel post system, regulating towing at sea, and increasing the powers of the Interstate Commerce Commission.[2]

None of this legislation had any chance of getting out of committee and he knew it. His aim was not to make better laws, but to convince voters that their government, as constituted, was incapable of meeting their needs and that he alone was capable of rescuing it from the stranglehold of trust-controlled and corrupted politicians.

Other candidates for national office might need political parties to advance their causes. Hearst did not. Bryan's betrayal had convinced him — if he needed further convincing — that he could not trust any professional politicians. Having been viciously attacked by the conservative element in his party and betrayed by the Bryan "radicals," he had no choice but to go it alone. As Frederick Palmer concluded in the three-part series on "Hearst and Hearstism" published in *Collier's* in 1906, Hearst represented "a strange, new element that presents to us a startling possibility. His is the first one-man party to have gained anything like national headway in the history of our democracy. . . . His power has been gained purely by advertising himself and his propaganda in his own daily editions. . . . He is a celebrity who is guaranteed four million readers every day. This is the largest continuous audience that any American public man has ever possessed."[3]

No one, it appeared, was neutral about Hearst. He had gathered around him a group of ten or twelve congressmen, referred to disparagingly as the "Hearst brigade," two of whom, Champ Clark of Missouri and John Garner of Texas, he would later support for the presidency. Outside of these few, he was distrusted and disliked on both sides of the aisle.

He devoted most of his energy during the lame-duck session that lasted from December to March to attacking his fellow congressmen, especially the Democrats, for being in the pay of the trusts. Congressional Democrats who refused to get behind the "Hearst bill" which would have increased the powers of the Interstate Commerce Commission to regulate railroad rates were assailed in his newspapers for not being "real Democrats" and for putting the interests of the railroads ahead of those of their constituents. When Representative John A. Sullivan, a second-term Democrat from Massachusetts, either on his own or at the behest of party leaders, remarked that had Congressman Hearst been truly interested in the legislation he sponsored, he would have appeared on the floor on behalf of it, the *New York American* attacked him as "a bald, red-nosed young man [who] revealed his hitherto unsuspected presence in the House" by asking some questions which showed he knew nothing of the hearings at which Hearst's bill had been discussed. The *American* attributed Sullivan's ignorance to either "congenital incapacity or indifference to the people's rights."[4]

On February 13, Representative Sullivan sought and received unanimous consent to state his case on the floor of the House. He was, he explained, not in the habit of replying to newspaper criticism, but this was different, as "the proprietor of the newspaper was also a Member of Congress" who was trying to silence those who disagreed with him by assaulting them in his newspapers. To protect the integrity and dignity of the House, Sullivan declared that he intended to discuss from the floor the "motives beneath" the article that had smeared him. He began by impugning Hearst's masculinity — a "manly man" would have criticized him face to face "instead of hiding under the cover of . . . cowardly newspaper attacks." In criticizing Hearst, he alluded to "the case of the moral degenerate who insolently casts his eyes upon the noblest of women whose virtue places them beyond the contamination of his lust." He assailed Hearst as a socialist; pointed derisively to his record of absenteeism; hinted that he did not speak in Congress because it might violate his "monarchical dignity" or reveal that his voice was neither "sonorous" nor "manly"; and referred to the Hearst papers' attack on him as a "scheme of political assassination which has been marked out by a Nero of modern politics."

Though Hearst had not been in the room when Sullivan began his oration, he appeared before it was completed, and asked for the floor to respond. To the charge of absenteeism, he pleaded guilty — with an explanation. "I do not know any way in which a man can be less effective for his constituents and less useful to them than by emitting chewed wind on the floor of this House. [APPLAUSE]." He concluded his ad hominem, ad-libbed attack on Sullivan by recalling, to the amazement of his colleagues, an incident from his own past. "When I was at Harvard College in 1885, a murder was committed in a low saloon in Cambridge. A man partly incapacitated from drink bought in that saloon on Sunday morning . . . was assaulted by the two owners of that saloon and brutally kicked to death. The name of one of the owners of that saloon was John A. Sullivan, and these two men were arrested and indicted by the grand jury for manslaughter and tried and convicted. I would like to ask the gentleman from Massachusetts if he knows anything about that incident and whether, if I desired to make a hostile criticism, I could not have referred to that crime?"

The House exploded into disorder. Mr. Butler of Pennsylvania demanded that the Speaker end the debate at once. When the chair ruled that Hearst still had the floor, Butler interrupted to remind the Speaker that "the gentleman from New York [had] inferentially charged the gentleman from Massachusetts with either having murdered some one or conspired to murder." That, he insisted, was clearly out of order. The Speaker agreed. Hearst replied that he was finished anyway.[5]

Congressman Sullivan admitted the next day that he had indeed been indicted for murder, as Hearst had charged, but had received a suspended sentence because he was only seventeen years old. He served out the rest of his congressional term and then retired from politics.

Hearst newspapers everywhere followed the Chief's lead in attacking politicians who, they claimed, were in the pay of the trusts. In Los Angeles, they assailed city officials for floating a water reclamation bond issue that would have enriched the local oligarchy of real estate speculators. In Chicago, they blasted former Mayor Carter Harrison and aldermen "Hinky Dink" Kenna and "Bathhouse John" Coughlin for taking bribes from the streetcar barons. In San Francisco, they attacked Democratic Boss Ruef and Mayor Eugene Schmitz for accepting bribes from local traction companies.[6]

In New York City, the Chief's home base, the Hearst papers concentrated their fire on Mayor George B. McClellan, Jr., the elegant, aristocratic, Princeton-educated son of the Civil War general and Democratic nominee for president in 1864, who they claimed was in the pay of the gas trust. George McClellan was the first in a long line of politicians whom Hearst turned on after endorsing. He was not a particularly "dirty" politician, but neither was he a crusading antitrust reformer. Hearst, relying on his power as a publisher, expected that he could compel the politicians he supported to keep the promises he believed had been made to him. When these politicians didn't or couldn't live up to his expectations, "he thrust them from his bosom the better to lambaste their buttocks." The words were those of Nat Ferber, who grew up on the Lower East Side and went to work for Hearst because he admired him and wanted to join him in battle against the "predatory interests." "Instead of taking the orthodox newspaperman's position, which is no position," Ferber wrote, "I took sides and shouted from the housetops, a cause for every housetop. The gas company, the traction companies, the beach barons, the food purveyors, in their attempts to raise their respective tariffs, found in me a watchful adversary lustily shouting 'Stop, thief!'"[7]

Hearst used all the resources at his command to fight McClellan and the gas trust. He directed his attorney Clarence Shearn to enjoin the city controller and mayor from paying any rate increases to New York Consolidated Gas, attacked McClellan daily in his editorials, and unleashed his political cartoonists against the mayor, the gas trust, Tammany, and its new boss, Charles Murphy, who had succeeded Richard Croker.

In response to charges that he was attacking McClellan because he planned to run against him in 1905, the *New York Evening Journal* declared that "Mr. Hearst has neither the desire nor the time to act as mayor. A man publishing newspapers in New York, Boston, Chicago, San Francisco, and Los Angeles, is fairly well occupied with public questions. . . . The Hearst newspapers are fighting municipal corruption in all the cities where they are published. Mayor McClellan's pet gang of Gas Thieves is but one of the Gas Thief gangs that the Hearst newspapers deal with."[8]

This much was true. Hearst was fighting the trusts in every city in which he owned a paper; and he did not want to run for mayor — New York City mayors did not get elected to the presidency. Still, he had made up his mind to deny McClellan a second term by running a candidate against him. As McClellan was sure to get the Tammany nod for reelection and Hearst refused to support a Republican, he directed Max Ihmsen, his chief political operative, to organize a new anti-Tammany reform party, the Municipal Ownership League.

Hearst was indefatigable. While organizing his third party, battling McClellan and the gas trust, and making as much trouble as he could in Congress, he continued to expand his publishing empire. In May of 1905, he concluded negotiations to buy *Cosmopolitan,* his first general-interest magazine, for $400,000, more than twice what he had paid for the *Journal* ten years earlier.

His advisers had been unalterably and unanimously opposed to the venture. Newspaper publishers did not publish magazines. The two media had dissimilar audiences, distinct production and editorial requirements, and very different distribution practices. Hearst went ahead anyway, convinced that he could succeed with a monthly as he had with a daily.

His timing was impeccable. He bought *Cosmopolitan* — he had started up *Motor* for automobile enthusiasts two years before — at the onset of the golden age of American magazines. Like its competitors, *Collier's, Everybody's, McClure's, Leslie's,* and the *American Magazine, Cosmopolitan* was making a great deal of money publishing the type of slashing exposés on political corruption that would soon be referred to as "muckraking." Hearst increased the number of stories on politics and current events, imported from his newspapers his most incendiary political writers and editorialists, like Ambrose Bierce and the future Socialist party candidate Charles Edward Russell, and added to them social activist novelists like Jack London and Upton Sinclair, and Socialists and Socialist sympathizers like Robert Hunter, Morris Hillquit, and David Graham Phillips.

Where his newspapers attacked political corruption at the local level, he intended to use *Cosmopolitan* to attack it at the top of the political hierarchy: the United States Senate. He tried first to enlist Charles Edward Russell, who had worked for him as writer and editor in New York and Chicago, to write an extended exposé on corruption in Washington. When Russell proved unable to take the assignment, Hearst turned to the novelist David Graham Phillips and offered him a Hearstian sum to write the article. After several months of research and writing, Phillips turned in a draft which was edited, set in galleys, and rushed to Hearst for final approval. Hearst was horrified to discover that Phillips had written an exposé that was too wild even for his taste. At two o'clock in the morning, he telegrammed *Cosmopolitan*'s editor to pull Phillips's article off the presses because it lacked sufficient documentation to withstand the criticism it was sure to receive. "We have merely an attack. The facts, the proofs, the documentary evidence are an important thing, and the article is deficient in them . . . We want more definite facts throughout. Supply them where you can. Then run the article if you want, and we will try to get the others later." Note here the limits of Hearst's journalistic fact-checking. He was willing to run the article first — and substantiate some of the facts thereafter.[9]

The rewrite was better. It was published — with great fanfare — in the March 1906 issue of *Cosmopolitan*. On the cover was a ghoulishly grinning photograph of New York's Republican senator, Chauncey Depew, over the caption, "Depew's joviality and popularity, according to Mr. Phillips, have cost the American people at least one billion dollars." On the next page was a second photograph of "Depew at close range," captioned, "Here is the Archetypal Face of the Sleek, Self-satisfied American Opportunist in Politics and Plunder." Hearst marketed the piece as only he could — with billboards, advertisements, and self-congratulatory editorials in his newspapers. The result exceeded his every expectation. *Cosmopolitan*'s circulation jumped by 50 percent. When President Theodore Roosevelt attacked the new journalism and coined the term "muckraking" in a speech at the Gridiron Club and then again at the laying of the cornerstone of the new House Office Building, there was no doubt in anyone's mind that he was talking about Hearst.[10]

It was no accident that Hearst bought *Cosmopolitan* within months of allying himself with progressive reformers like Samuel Seabury and organizing his Municipal Ownership League in New York City. All of these ventures were intended to broaden his readership — and political constituencies. Though comparatively low-priced at ten cents, *Cosmopolitan* was not for common laborers or recently arrived immigrants or for the vast majority of those who read the *Evening Journal* or Hearst's other evening papers on their way home from work. Having successfully conquered the "low" end of the market, Hearst was now returning to the "middle" ranges.

If in publishing and politics Hearst was reaching out to new social groupings, the same could not be said of his personal life. He had entered New York as an outsider and remained one. Even more than Teddy Roosevelt, he was considered a traitor to his class, though the identity of that "class" was in some dispute.

New York society had never been as homogeneous or closed as Boston's or Philadelphia's, but it had become ever more fragmented with the infusion of new money like Hearst's. There were, observers noted in the 1890s, already five distinct social elites: three British-American Protestant groupings, a German Christian, and a German Jewish. Hearst, the Western publisher of "yellow" journals and son of a Forty-Niner, and Millicent, the dancer daughter of a vaudeville hoofer, did not fit neatly into any of them. Hearst had, on coming to New York, joined a few clubs, including the prestigious Union Club and the American Yacht Club, but he had been asked to leave or had resigned voluntarily. After 1900, his name no longer even appeared in the Social Register.[11]

Hearst reveled in his outsider status. Even at the White House, where he and Millicent were invited in 1905, he assumed the role of scorned and scornful outsider. All the other guests, he wrote his mother, had "belonged largely to the class of vulgar rich who seek to conceal ill-breeding and stupidity behind an affectation of self-confidence that amounts to brazen effrontery. The women stared at the passing line from behind the barrier of ropes and through diamond studded lorgnettes. I despise lorgnettes. They are bad enough when they shield blinky, squinty eyes but oh, the insolence of diamond studded lorgnettes behind which ignorance and vulgarity take refuge. There is nothing to compare with it in hardihood unless it be the brutal indifference of the tenderloin lady who is 'drunk and glad of it.'"

Hearst proudly informed his mother that his and Millicent's visit to the White House wasn't "all the society we have been doing." But from the tone of his letter, it was quite clear that he was far from taking his social obligations seriously: "We went to Mrs. Depew's reception to meet Mr. and Mrs. Vanderbilt and we went to Mrs. McLean's dance. Milly danced and I sat in a row of old ladies and talked about the past when we were young and 'did *so* enjoy anything of this kind, don't you know.' Presently we had supper and I foraged for an elderly dame with an ample waist and an appetite to match. Then I rebelled and went off and sat with Milly."[12]

Phoebe was, at the time, in Paris, where she had relocated during her son's campaign for the presidency, no doubt to escape the unrelenting attacks on his morality. She would remain there for most of the next two years. Will wrote her a chatty letter in early 1905. He had, he wanted her to know, "had some bone taken out of my nose . . . It's a great nuisance going round with a featherbed up your nose as I have had to do ever since the operation but I guess the wadding will be taken out in a day or two and I hope that then I will be able to breathe some. The operation didn't hurt any. I was all cocained up . . . but the thing has been a nuisance since and I leak like a defective hose." He was, he continued, glad that Phoebe's Paris house had a "garage . . . I hope to heavens I can come over soon and use it some. I hope you are well again. Please be careful and don't take risks and overdo. You are not any younger than I am."[13]

In April of 1905, as promised, two large automobiles, with their chauffeurs, arrived to park in Phoebe's Paris garage. In May, after several false starts, Hearst appeared with Millicent, Baby George, sister-in-law Anita, his mother-in-law, and a full staff of personal secretaries and maids. Phoebe welcomed them with varying degrees of warmth: she was especially pleased to see her grandson, but loath to spend any time at all with "Old Mrs. W.," as she referred to Millicent's mother.

After a brief stay in Paris, Millicent and Will took a side trip to London with Phoebe and then left with the baby for an extended motor tour of Spain. Buried in a cardboard box marked "Ephemera" in the Peck family papers at the Huntington Library is a photograph taken on the Spain trip, which Phoebe must have sent to her friend Janet Peck. The handwritten caption reads, "Millicent took this — Mr H and George in shadow." Hearst is wearing a light summer suit with a full-brimmed hat. He is standing straight up with a stein or mug in his hand, playing to the camera.[14]

The Hearsts did not return to the States until September 1905, at which time they signed a lease on a grand new apartment at the Clarendon on 86th Street and Riverside Drive. Will had decided to give up his four-story Lexington Avenue townhouse; it was no longer large enough for a growing family and for his collections of stained glass, arms and armor, tapestries, sculpture, antique furniture, and decorative art objects, which had been expanding steadily since he had left college.

Instead of moving northward and resettling in a new and larger townhouse or mansion on Fifth Avenue, he confirmed his self-imposed status as a social outsider by moving across Central Park to the West Side and renting an apartment in the Clarendon, one of the first multifamily dwellings built for permanent residents.[15] The Clarendon was attractive because of its location on the Hudson River, with a yacht club nearby, and because of the size of the apartments. "Apartments are arranged two on a floor, consisting of ten to twelve rooms and four bath rooms to each apartment," the offering advertisements declared. "The servants' quarters are cut off with a separate entrance from the public hall, thus giving the same privacy one would have in a private house. Separate servants' elevator lands tradesmen, etc. direct to kitchen door." Hearst rented three floors, at a rent of approximately $24,000 a year, about $450,000 in 1990s currency.[16]

Part of the reason he chose to rent an apartment was financial. While Phoebe continued to bankroll Will's political campaigns and, according to his son Bill, Jr., contributed $10,000 a month to cover their living expenses, she was not willing to give him the money he needed to build his own home. As Millicent reminded her mother-in-law, rather bluntly calling attention to their financial plight, they had decided to live in rented quarters "until Will gets enough money to build a house on his lot. I guess we will stay there — in the apartment — for some time." Their new home, fortunately, wasn't "like an ordinary flat, cut up into little rooms but it has a number of fine big rooms and even the bed rooms are not so very bad. The view is really better than we could hope to get from a private house for we are on the tenth floor facing the river and can look up and down the Hudson for miles. Right in front of us is a little yacht club and there are always a number of pretty yachts anchored about it — and if Will ever gets that money that we refer to we may have a motor boat of our own — at any rate if we have nothing more than we have now, we will be very pleasantly situated and very comfortable in the flat."[17]

Though Charles Francis Murphy, Richard Croker's successor as head of Tammany Hall, was in speech and appearance more of a diplomat than his predecessor, he did not take kindly to Hearst's decision to organize a Municipal Ownership League to do battle with Mayor McClellan. In August of 1905, while Hearst was vacationing in Europe, Boss Murphy announced without fanfare that Charles V. Fornes, president of the board of aldermen, would be the Tammany candidate for Congress from the Eleventh District, in November of 1906. He did not mention that Hearst already held that seat. Although Hearst had no great love of Congress, he was not prepared to surrender his seat without at least a token show of his political strength. As the *New York Times* reported on August 10, Congressman Hearst had decided to "make a contest for renomination. . . . As a first step Mr. Hearst has completed arrangements to give every man, woman, and child of the district a free trip to Coney Island, including admission to most of the Luna Park shows. . . . Thousands of tickets are being distributed through the district by Hearst agents." The *Times* was wrong. Hearst had no intention of returning to a do-nothing Congress. He had every intention, however, of wresting political power from Boss Murphy and Tammany in New York.

On returning from Europe on September 30, 1905, he set to work at once looking for a candidate to run on his Municipal Ownership League ticket against Mayor McClellan in November. His first two choices were Judge Samuel Seabury, the thirty-one-year-old progressive reformer, author of a lengthy booklet on the benefits of public ownership, and an early supporter of the Municipal Ownership League, and Charles Evans Hughes, the attorney who had headed the New York State Assembly's investigation of the gas trust in 1905. When both declined to run, Hearst, unwilling to let McClellan be reelected without a contest, decided to run for mayor himself. He was taking an enormous gamble. The odds against any third-party candidate defeating a sitting Tammany mayor in a three-party race were extraordinarily long. Moreover, should Hearst lose decisively — as was likely — he would forfeit any chance he might have had of convincing voters and party officials to back him for the presidency in 1908. With the help of battle-hardened veterans of earlier Hearst crusades — Arthur Brisbane, Max Ihmsen, Clarence Shearn, and Jack Follansbee, who returned from Mexico to help out his friend — Hearst nearly accomplished the impossible.

His first miracle was the October 12 convention of his Municipal Ownership League, which was managed so spectacularly that even the opposition newspapers were forced to take the party and its candidate seriously. "If enthusiasm counts for anything," the *Times* reported the next morning, "the regular party organizations will have to reckon more seriously with the third ticket than they thought up to last night. The crowd at Carnegie Hall far exceeded the attendance at the Democratic or the Republican City Convention. . . . In less than fifteen minutes after the doors of the hall were opened the place was filled. The police handled the crowd so well that there was no disorder. For the benefit of those who could not get inside overflow meetings were held." This was not, the *Times* reported, the "tin bucket" brigade of workingmen whom Hearst had attracted to previous rallies: "There were hundreds of well-dressed and apparently well-to-do citizens on the platform and on the main floor of the hall."[18]

The campaign began the next morning when the first Hearst expedition got hopelessly lost in Williamsburg, Brooklyn, and had to ask a policeman for directions. But after this initial misstep, everything seemed to fall into place. Hearst had become a terrific campaigner. If, as a candidate for the presidential nomination, he had been reluctant to speak in public, he now seized every occasion he could, buoyed by the enthusiastic crowds he drew all over the city. When his opponents claimed that he was incapable of saying anything not written for him in advance by Arthur Brisbane, he discarded his text and spoke extemporaneously. He had conquered his shyness, learned to project his high squeaky voice beyond the podium, mastered the call-and-response format that was a staple of city politics, and managed to give each of his audiences precisely what it had come to hear.

Hearst delivered the same message wherever he went. He was beholden to no one but the people. If elected he would institute municipal control and ownership of municipal services and exclude the trusts from the business of providing the city with water, transportation, ice, gas, and electricity. Without the trusts, there would be no source of boodle for the grafters; Tammany and the bosses would be eliminated from city politics and municipal government returned to the people. As the Hearst caravan moved through the city, its every step was ballyhooed before and after the event in the morning *American,* the *Evening Journal,* and the German-language *New Yorker Morgen Journal.*

Hearst's campaign for mayor was such a good story that even the opposition papers reported it as enthusiastically as he did. "William Randolph Hearst drove through the lower east side last night in a procession of triumph, the like of which has not been seen in New York in many years," Pulitzer's *World,* which did not endorse Hearst or any other candidate for mayor, reported on October 31, a week before the election:

> He made five speeches to audiences that were limited only [by the] size of the halls, while outside the doors there swarmed many thousands of people, cheering wildly at the slightest excuse and waiting patiently until he reappeared so they could escort him to the next meeting place. This extraordinary enthusiasm over an individual has had its like but once before in the political history of the east side [the year before when President Roosevelt visited Little Hungary]. Mr. Hearst had a reception so enthusiastic in its cheers, so fanatical in its appearance of devotion, so vigorous in its declarations of voting for him that all the calculations of politicians about the east side were upset.[19]

The Socialist party was so disturbed by the excitement which Hearst was generating in working-class and immigrant districts that, ignoring Tammany and the Republicans entirely, it implored potential voters not to be misled by this purported "friend of labor," this "Moses" who promised to lead working people out of the wilderness to practical "socialism" via municipal ownership. Hearst was, the Socialists reminded their followers, just another capitalist.[20]

Hearst's popularity among the city's working people reached such heights that the newspapers in early November predicted that whoever won, Hearst would take over Tammany Hall after the election. The Democrats continued to fire away, accusing him of every imaginable crime, including McKinley's assassination. The Tammany-run *Daily News* published a cartoon with the ghost of McKinley pointing a finger at a fleeing Hearst and "displayed [it] in huge posters on fences and dead walls, all over New York City. . . . The Tammany managers tried to send out 300,000 copies of it on postal cards to voters, but they were barred from the mails as scurrilous matter."[21]

Tammany's attempts to portray Hearst as a lunatic anarchist accelerated in the last week of the campaign. Bourke Cockran, Tammany's star orator, declared at a huge rally at 14th Street and Union Square that Hearst had to be defeated because he represented "every appeal to passion that we have observed during the last nine years. Every incitement to murder, every encouragement to riot; every disposition to array class against class; every assault upon property and every insinuation against virtue, all those forces which have raised him to the position which he occupies. [Hearst was] an apostle of riot, an advocate of disorder, a promoter of Socialism. [His election] would be such a pronouncement of anarchy and riot that the very foundations of society would be shattered and the whole fabric of social order reduced to ruin."[22]

Unfortunately for Tammany and the Republicans, radical-baiting like this had no effect on the electorate. In his whirlwind month-long tour of the city, Hearst had managed to be seen and heard by thousands of voters. The truth was that, in person, Hearst did not resemble a bomb-throwing monster or a wild-eyed opportunist. He dressed like an undertaker, was soft-spoken, affable, and courteous. Instead of trying to disguise himself as a man of the people, he pointed to his wealth and social position as an argument for his solidity and his honesty: "I am not in this election because I have any itch for office or because I want the salary, but because I want to accomplish something for your benefit and win your approval."[23]

Hearst's ability to project his message in person and then reproduce it in print was winning him votes all across the city. The *New York Times,* which had dismissed his candidacy entirely three weeks earlier, on November 3 asked loyal Republicans to abandon their candidate and vote for McClellan to block a Hearst victory: "The diversion of Republican votes from Mr. IVINS [the Republican candidate] is now the only way to diminish the Hearst vote and the Hearst danger." Colonel Mann of *Town Topics,* who had also dismissed the Hearst candidacy, similarly implored his readers, who, he acknowledged, looked upon "elections as an unmitigated evil or at least a distasteful function, the duties of which they are ready to shirk," to get to the polls and vote for McClellan.[24]

The Sunday before the election, the *New York Herald* declared in its pre-election survey that Hearst's enormous strength in Democratic districts had the pollsters confused: "Herald's Poll Shows Party Lines Thrown to the Winds. . . . Mayoralty Contest a Bewildering Puzzle. . . . Conservatives Drift to McClellan While Wage-earners Rally to the Independent Standard."[25]

Hearst scheduled no campaign appearances on the Sunday preceding Election Day, but offered his supporters instead a free concert at Madison Square Garden by the Metropolitan Opera House orchestra. The concert attracted a crowd of 50,000, with 500 policemen to keep order. Fifteen blocks away at the Hippodrome between 43rd and 44th Streets, Tammany was holding its own rally, also with overflow crowds. Only the presence of a huge police contingent prevented bloodshed in the streets as a thousand Hearst supporters, unable to get into the Madison Square rally, marched north to confront the Tammany supporters.[26]

The next morning, November 7, in its Election eve editorial, "For the Defense of the City," the *New York Times* called its readers' attention to the Hearst rally that had been held the night before:

> There were from 15,000 to 25,000 persons inside the Garden, and according to varying reports from 10,000 to 20,000 or more in the streets surrounding the building. There was unbounded enthusiasm for Mr. HEARST. . . . These are matters of which no prudent man will fail to take note. What do they mean? They mean that every phase and kind of discontent and dissatisfaction has been marshaled under the leadership of Mr. HEARST, and that the number of voters in his following is so large as really to threaten his election to the office of Mayor.

W. R., as he was now referred to by his closest friends — it was the perfect compromise between the informal Will and the much too formal William — awoke early on Election Day and was at the polls by 6:45, with Arthur Brisbane and a coterie of supporters to cheer him on. The pre-election polls, the worried newspaper editorials, and the crowds that had greeted him were proof positive that he had gotten his message across. There seemed little question but that he would poll enough votes to defeat McClellan and Ivins, the Republican candidate.

He returned to his home for a few hours' sleep — he was not used to getting up at such an ungodly hour — and was driven to the Hoffman House, still his political clubhouse. Max Ihmsen, his campaign manager, who had warned him the night before that Tammany would do whatever it had to to steal the election, was already apoplectic. The reports from the field were worse than even he had expected.

All over town, there were instances of voter fraud, of poll watchers being chased away, of delays in reporting returns, of unopened and uncounted ballot boxes disappearing or being delivered to the wrong addresses or mysteriously turning up in a barber's shop, a tailor's shop window, and the East River. It was, the *Independent* declared, "the most extraordinary election ever witnessed in New York City."[27]

"Hearst watchers from the districts of Charles F. Murphy, 'Johnny' Oakley, and 'Big Tim' Sullivan," the *New York Times* reported on November 8, the next morning, "came into the Hearst headquarters at the Hoffman House last night with bandaged heads. Some carried their arms in slings. At about ten o'clock in the evening a report was received that the returns were being held back from these districts." While Hearst poll watchers were being intimidated and worse — the *Times* reported that one, an R. Little, had "had a finger chewed off and his face cut" — Tammany flooded the polls with repeaters.

Hearst remained outwardly calm, dispatching new poll watchers to replace the bruised and beaten, requesting the superintendent of elections to send in deputies, and gathering testimony from his men in the field for possible legal action.

By midnight, the returns indicated that McClellan was going to outpoll Hearst by a few thousand votes. Hearst, "pale with anger," according to the November 8 *New York Times,* demanded a recount. "We have won the election. All Tammany's friends, all Tammany's corruption, all Tammany's intimidation and violence, all Tammany's false registration, illegal voting and dishonest count have not been able to overcome a great popular majority," Hearst told reporters. "The recount will show that we have won the election by many thousands of votes. I shall fight this battle to the end."

"For once," reported *The Literary Digest,* "the greatest exponent of 'yellow' journalism has uttered a statement, sensational tho it is to the last degree, that stands unchallenged by many of the most conservative papers in the city . . . The local press generally . . . believe that the evidences of fraud, corruption, intimidation, and force in several instances are too positive to be ignored."[28]

There were few doubts that Tammany had stolen the election, but even fewer tears were shed at Hearst's defeat. The day after the election, the *Times,* simultaneously with reporting on the numerous instances of voter fraud, editorially congratulated the city's voters on defeating Hearst: "Their votes have spared the city the humiliation, the trials, and the dangers of a four years' management of its affairs by a peculiarly reckless, unschooled, and unsteady group of experimenters and adventurers . . . It is certain that the election of Mr. HEARST to be Mayor of New York would have sent a shiver of apprehension over the entire Union."[29]

Hearst put together a bipartisan team of politicians and civic leaders, with Republican candidate Ivins prominent among them, to demand a recount. He held demonstrations throughout the city and attacked Tammany more furiously than during the campaign, vowing to put those who had participated in vote fraud behind bars. Though in the first few days after the election Hearst was confident that the results would be thrown out, if not immediately in a recount, then through court action, he was wrong. There was no recount. While newspaper editorials and reformers prattled on about the sanctity of the ballot box, Tammany got away with robbery. On December 27, 1905, George Brinton McClellan was officially reelected as mayor of New York City. His plurality, in an election in which almost 600,000 votes had been cast, was 3,472. Though Hearst continued to contest the election, in the end, neither the courts nor the state legislature were willing to overturn an election, unseat a sitting mayor, and replace him with William Randolph Hearst.

Even if one accepted the final returns as accurate, which few did, it was clear that Hearst had turned a political miracle. Running for mayor as the candidate of a third party that had not celebrated its first anniversary, he had polled almost twice as many votes as the Republicans, robbed the Socialist party of half the votes it had polled in the previous election, and beaten Tammany in its own backyards. The most dramatic defections were on the Lower East Side, where Jewish and German voters deserted to Hearst in large numbers. Hearst had also, as McClellan would acknowledge in his autobiography, done extremely well "among what has since become known as the white-collar proletariat, the clerks, small employees, and small shopkeepers."[30]

"Whether or not Mr. Hearst is to be seated as mayor," the editors of *Current Literature* had concluded in December 1905, "the vote he received has startled the country and is variously interpreted." Was the vote primarily a protest against Tammany, a statement in favor of municipal ownership, a sign of support for Hearst, or some combination of all three? It didn't quite matter. William Randolph Hearst, *Harper's Weekly* declared without equivocation, had become "a force to be reckoned with."[31]

New York City politics would certainly never be the same. Until Hearst came along, Tammany had, for the most part, been able to ignore the Republicans and third-party reformers. Despite their occasional success in municipal elections, the reformers were, as Boss Plunkitt so eloquently put it, no more than "mornin' glories — looked lovely in the mornin' and withered up in a short time, while the regular machines went on flourishin' forever, like fine old oaks." Hearst was different. He and his newspapers spoke in a language New York City's voters listened to. The attention he paid to immigrant communities, combined with his support for striking workers and his demand for reforms that would lower the price they paid for milk, ice, gas, and local transit, had paid off handsomely on Election Day.[32]

Even before the campaign was over, Hearst's call for municipal ownership of public utilities had aroused so much public support that his opponents had no choice but to agree with him. McClellan, recognizing the effectiveness of Hearst's attack on Tammany, had to distance himself from Boss Murphy during the campaign and declare his independence after Election Day. Boss Murphy was so disturbed by Hearst's strength in the wards that Tammany had always controlled, that from this point on he nominated reform-minded candidates like Judge William Gaynor of Brooklyn and championed political and social reforms similar to those Hearst advocated. According to John Buenker, the author of *Urban Liberalism and Progressive Reform,* much of the important reform legislation of the Progressive Era was supported, if not introduced, by city machines and bosses. In New York City, this did not occur until — and, it is safe to say, because of — the Hearst challenge.[33]

§ 11 §

Man of Mystery

H<small>EARST HAD LOST</small> the mayoral election of 1905 because he had not been ruthless enough. He had been taken to school by Boss Murphy, but he was a good student. In defeat, he had witnessed the use of a new set of dirty tricks. Never again would he be caught by surprise.

He was, ironically, more venerated as a politician and candidate after defeat than before. He had run a comparatively clean campaign, built a political organization from the ground up, polled well over 200,000 votes, and transmuted a constituency of readers into voters. His organization remained intact, as did his newspaper empire and Phoebe's fortune.

There were no doubts as to his next move. Tammany's theft of his election had confirmed his belief that the political system was hopelessly corrupt and required a savior. He had entered the election with a protean messiah complex which was now fully developed. He was no longer just another candidate running for office; he was the "movement's" candidate, the people's candidate, the hero on the white horse who had come to town to clean up the mess and drive out the bad guys.

In a letter to Arthur Brisbane on the first of December, he characterized his defeat not in personal terms, but as "a tragedy to the people." Fortunately, as he reminded Brisbane, "the laborers and immigrants became involved — really involved" in the campaign, which meant that next time around he was sure to be successful: "I believe more than ever that our movement will succeed. . . . Our next effort will be the most important thus far . . . We will run for Governor as planned."[1]

If the New York City mayoralty was not on the path to the presidency, the governorship was. There was no doubt in Hearst's mind that should he win the Democratic nomination, he could easily defeat anyone the Republicans put forward. But how was he going to get the nomination of the party he had just run against? How was the people's candidate going to become the party's candidate? There was a simple solution. Hearst would use his 200,000 votes to blackmail the Democrats into nominating him. If they did not, he would run on a third-party line and siphon off enough Democratic votes to guarantee a Republican victory.

Hearst spent the winter and spring of 1906 more frantically active than ever: overseeing his expanding newspaper and magazine empire, meeting with the labor leaders in Los Angeles who had been instrumental in convincing him to start up the *Examiner* in 1903, traveling to Chihuahua, Mexico, to inspect his ranchlands, commuting to Washington to serve out the final session of his second and last term, taking the train to Albany to lobby for new municipal ownership bills.[2]

"For the last two months we have been living on the trains," Millicent wrote Phoebe in March, "going from Washington to New York and from New York to Boston and back again. I wish we could settle down somewhere for a few days and just keep still, but I do not see any signs of it and I suppose we will rush around on the trains until it is time to rush over on the steamer and then rush around in an automobile until we come home again."[3]

Though Millicent couldn't have known it at the time, her life was going to become even more hectic in the coming months. On April 18, 1906, Hearst, as usual sleeping late into the morning, was awakened by a call from the *American* informing him that the wire had just flashed a story about a San Francisco earthquake. Hearst warned the editor not to "overplay it. . . . They have earthquakes often in California." Then he went back to bed.[4]

The earthquake was only the beginning of the disaster for San Francisco. It was followed by a series of uncontrollable fires which destroyed nearly two-thirds of the city, including the Hearst building which housed the *San Francisco Examiner*. Hearst relocated the *Examiner* across the Bay in the *Oakland Tribune* building and telegraphed William Howard Taft — who as secretary of war was in charge of the disaster area — to ask permission to clear away the rubble so that he could begin at once to construct a new *Examiner* building.[5]

Edward Clark was dispatched to San Francisco as his plenipotentiary, while Hearst concentrated his attention on Congress and introduced joint resolutions providing "relief for earthquake and fire sufferers" and funds to "replace public buildings destroyed" by earthquake and fire. He raised additional money in New York for disaster relief by sponsoring benefits at the Casino, the Hippodrome, and the Academy of Music.[6]

While others, including his mother, grieved over their losses, Hearst, the eternal optimist, saw in the disaster the perfect opportunity to replace the destroyed eight-story *Examiner* building with a new one twelve stories high "with a six-story tower on top of it." Edward Clark, Phoebe's adviser, warned her by letter against giving Will the funds he requested for what was a rather extravagant building project. Constructing a new office building might be "beneficial to the paper, but from an investment standpoint it would certainly not be to your advantage." In a second handwritten letter marked "Confidential. Please destroy immediately," Clark explained further why he opposed lending Will any more money: "Mr. H . . . is in danger. He owes nearly $2,000,000, none of it pressing at this time but from $100,000 to $250,000 may have to be paid before long. Next year he has notes aggregating $750,000. . . . He is an able newspaper man but does not look ahead in financial matters. I will write you more fully as soon as I can from S.F. and if any thing urgent will cable."[7]

In May, Will traveled with Millicent and their son, George, to survey the earthquake and fire damage. "We are going to the hacienda and will spend summer trying to straighten things out in San Francisco," he telegrammed his mother in Europe. "It is a bad situation. . . . Why don't you come home and spend the summer with baby and us? He is fine big boy and very interesting. You would have lots of fun. Can't you come?"[8]

Though she was devoted to her grandson, Phoebe did not visit with him — or with his father and mother — that summer. She had no desire to be drawn into a debate with her son on the advisability of spending millions to erect a new *Examiner* office building. When, in June, she was called back from Paris to meet with Edward Clark on urgent business matters, probably having to do with losses suffered during the quake, she stayed only a week before returning to Europe. "Please don't write home that I am going to New York for I do not think it best for me to go to California," she wrote Mrs. Peck. "If Wm and my friends knew that I was going to NY they might find fault if I failed to go west. So it is best not to speak of it."[9]

All summer long, W. R. and Millicent wrote Phoebe in Paris. Their letters were invariably upbeat, designed in part to reassure her that it was safe to invest in San Francisco real estate. "Everybody is confident that a bigger and better city will rise from the ashes of the old one," Milly wrote on July 30, 1906. "Will thinks the fire will really be a benefit to San Francisco as most of the buildings destroyed were out of date rattletraps and the insurance money will allow modern buildings to be put up in their places. Then the expenditures of two or three hundred million dollars in San Francisco within the next few years will make the city a boom town . . . Will says we can all be cheerful about the *future* of San Francisco but the present is a little bit gloomy."[10]

In the end, Phoebe found it impossible to deny her son — and her hometown — a new office building. Work was begun almost immediately to clear away the rubble and erect a new twelve-story building at Third Street and Market, where the old one had once stood.

In late summer, the Hearsts returned to New York City. They had "had such a lovely trip out West," Millicent wrote Phoebe, forgetting for the moment that an earthquake had devastated the region, "but as soon as we get back we are in all kinds of trouble again — politics and lawsuits and business troubles and everything that is disagreeable and annoying."[11]

To his wife's dismay, Hearst returned to the campaign trail in September — for the third time in three years. He was running for governor as the candidate of the Independence League, the successor to his Municipal Ownership League. In mid-September, the state Democratic party, recognizing that it could not elect a governor with Hearst running on a third-party line and drawing off a substantial portion of the downstate vote, gave him its gubernatorial nomination. In a ruthless display of ambition and opportunism, Hearst accepted the Democratic nomination and turned his back on his Independence League.

Hearst's candidacy quickly became the political story of 1906. The nation's number one radical had come in out of the cold and was now the nominee of a major political party for an office that was one step away from the White House. Magazines across the country rushed into print with stories on the "Hearst phenomenon," the "Hearst movement," the "Hearst problem," the "Hearst myth," the "Hearst record," and the "Satanic Majesty of Hearst." "All over the country all sorts and conditions of men are asking 'What about Hearst?' And nobody seems to know," Lincoln Steffens wrote in *American Magazine.* "We approach, in more senses than one, a national question when we ask who, what, where is the reality behind the mystery of William Randolph Hearst, the unknown?"[12]

Steffens began his article by refuting the most prominent Hearst myths. The publisher did his own writing, ran his own empire, was nobody's puppet, and was in "deadly earnest" about his political crusade. His goal, simply stated, was to "restore democracy in the United States." There was,

Hearst explained to Steffens in an interview conducted during a long train ride from Chicago to New York, nothing terribly "radical" about his politics.

If Hearst wasn't a radical and didn't believe in socialism, as he assured Steffens he didn't, then why, Steffens asked in his article, was he so feared by the "plutocrats." The answer was obvious: if Hearst did "literally the things he says he will do, it means that this child of the privileged class will really try to abolish privilege in the United States!"

The more difficult question was why he was so feared and distrusted by reformers who agreed with him about the need to curb the power of the trusts. They feared him, Steffens argued, because while he spoke about restoring democracy, he wasn't really a democrat. Dedicated to securing power to do as he thought best and subordinating every means to that end, Hearst personified "the old spirit" that the reformers were trying to change. He listened to no one, trusted no one:

> W. R. Hearst is as hard to see and as inexpressive as E. H. Harriman [the railroad magnate] and Thomas F. Ryan [the streetcar king], who, like him, are mysteries. Hearst's self-reliance is theirs and their methods are his. He uses force as they do, and the same force, money . . . as a substitute for persuasion, charm, humor, pleadings. . . . He does not work with; he does not support . . . the other leaders of reform. He does not know who they are. Mr. Hearst is not a part of the general reform movement; he simply has a movement of his own. This isn't democratic, that is plutocratic; autocratic. Mr. Hearst is a boss.[13]

Appearing simultaneously with the Steffens profile was one by James Creelman, Hearst's past and future employee, who painted a very different portrait of the publisher and politician. Where Steffens found Hearst cold, humorless, and friendless, Creelman reported that he was, on the contrary, "the most placid of humans and finds plenty of time for play. It is hard to believe that this smooth-faced, soft-spoken and tranquil young man of forty-three years who idles in the restaurants, lolls amiably in automobiles, and generally studies the American people from the standpoint of the vaudeville theater, is the master-mind of a movement that keeps a large part of the nation in an uproar."[14]

Both Steffens and Creelman had written accurately about the man they had interviewed for their articles. Deliberately attempting to counter the image of the rich playboy, Hearst had, on entering electoral politics in 1902, cultivated the new dour persona which he displayed to Steffens. Creelman, who had worked with Hearst, traveled to Cuba with him, and visited him at home, knew a very different man.

Upton Sinclair, who also wrote about Hearst at this time, did so without the benefit — or distraction — of a personal interview and without attempting to understand his character or motivations. "There is no man in our public life today who interests me so much as William Randolph Hearst," Sinclair declared in *The Industrial Republic*, his book-length argument for socialism. "I have been watching him for ten years, during the last half-dozen of them weighing and testing him as the man of the coming hour. . . . He stands the best chance of being the candidate of the Democratic party in 1912; and . . . the man who secures that nomination will, if he does his work (and for him to fail to do it is almost inconceivable) write his name in our history beside the names of Washington and Lincoln." Just as Abraham Lincoln had in 1860 delivered the nation from "chattel slavery," so, Sinclair declared, would Hearst rescue it from "wage slavery" in 1912.[15]

Sinclair was not alone in believing that Hearst would one day soon become president. If elected governor in 1906 — and this was a distinct possibility — he would be set on the path to the presidency traveled by Grover Cleveland, the last Democratic president, and the current incumbent, Theodore Roosevelt, both of whom had been governors of New York.

"Hearst's nomination," Roosevelt wrote his friend and confidant Henry Cabot Lodge of Massachusetts on October 1, "is a very very bad thing. . . . I cannot blind myself to his extraordinary popularity among the 'have-nots.'" The danger to the party — and the republic — of a Hearst victory in the gubernatorial contest was so serious that Roosevelt intervened in state politics to make sure that the Republican nomination went to Charles Evans Hughes, the one Republican with antiboss, antitrust credentials as noteworthy as Hearst's.[16]

Even with Hughes as the Republican nominee, Roosevelt feared that Hearst might be too strong to defeat. "Hearst's nomination drives all decent-thinking men to our side," he confided to Cabot Lodge in late September, "but he has an enormous popularity among ignorant and unthinking people and will reap the reward of the sinister preaching of unrest which he and his agents have had so large a share in conducting."[17]

"The labor men are very ugly and no one can tell how far such discontent will spread," he continued in another letter the following week. "I am horrified at the information I receive on every hand as to Hearst's strength on the East Side among laborers and even among farmers. It is a very serious proposition. . . . There has been during the last six or eight years a great growth of socialistic and radical spirit among the workingmen."[18]

"We must win by a savage and aggressive fight against Hearstism and an exposure of its hypocrisy, its insincerity, its corruption, its demagogy, and in general its utter worthlessness and wickedness," he warned Congressman James Sherman, chairman of the Republican Congressional Committee. "Hearst's nomination is of such sinister significance as to dwarf everything else," he added that same day in a letter to Charles Sprague Smith, the reformer president of New York's People's Institute.[19]

From his citadel in the White House, Roosevelt obsessively plotted out every step in the Hughes campaign. He urged Hughes to pay more attention to "the great Catholic population of the State." He suggested that "at least one Catholic [be placed] on our judiciary ticket" and that Attorney General Mayer and Jacob Schiff be asked to campaign among Jewish voters. To attract more Jewish voters to the Republican party, he offered to nominate the first Jewish cabinet member, Oscar Straus, a Democrat, if Straus agreed to support Hughes against Hearst. Straus accepted Roosevelt's offer.[20]

While Roosevelt in Washington was secretly devising strategies to defeat him, Hearst was crisscrossing the state by private railroad car and automobile with his wife and child. He gave so many speeches — in a premicrophone era — that he developed recurrent sore throats and periodically lost his voice entirely. On October 17, he woke up in Oswego County on the shore of Lake Ontario, then "swept in a northeasterly curve . . . through four rock-ribbed Republican counties." In Watertown, he spoke from the platform of his private railway car, before being chauffeured into town to speak in a rented hall, a theater, and an opera house.[21]

Though now in his early forties, Hearst retained a surprisingly youthful face and figure. He was clean-shaven with a broad, plain, but not unhandsome face, his brown hair cut short and parted in the center. While he often smiled in public and was unfailingly polite, his campaign photos show a stern figure, dressed immaculately in a dark suit, the image softened only by the cherubic, smiling two-year-old George Hearst posed beside him. The rumors of unbridled sexual appetites, of tyranny and rapaciousness did not mesh with the image of this gentle giant, with a voice pitched so high it sounded almost girlish. He was not oily, whiskered, or red-faced like the stereotypical political boss; nor was he a grossly overfed society degenerate like the recently disgraced and murdered Stanford White or scabrously thin like the robber baron John D. Rockefeller.

While he toured the state like an old-fashioned "pol," Hearst was putting together a campaign that was as up-to-date as the motorcars he drove to his speaking appearances. In early October, the *New York Times* reported that the Hearst campaign would be addressing the state's voters with talking machine records and moving pictures:

Mr. Hearst, accompanied by one of his campaign managers, went to a talking machine place in Broadway. He spent upward of an hour there closeted with a machine and a mechanician who changed the cylinders as the flood of Mr. Hearst's oratory required. . . . As Mr. Hearst talked at the graphophone against the trusts and other things a moving picture man caught Mr. Hearst's gestures. Within a very few days moving picture outfits by the dozen, together with talking machines and the cylinders containing Mr. Hearst's speeches will be sent up State in charge of reliable agents, who will visit all the out-of-the-way places, where a real campaign speech is rarely heard . . . and where the farming population . . . will gladly drive many miles to listen to a talking machine and see a moving picture show. Mr. Hearst's moving picture and talking machine shows will be free.

The use of talking pictures in a political campaign in 1906 — twenty-one years before Al Jolson sang in *The Jazz Singer* — was revolutionary in itself. What made it even more remarkable — and effective — was the way the Hearst team coordinated the new communications technologies with the old ones. To get potential voters to see his moving pictures, Hearst advertised them in his new illustrated weekly newspaper, *Farm and Home.*[22]

There was no way to avoid the Hearst message. The morning *American* and the *Evening Journal* circulated throughout the state, as did *Cosmopolitan; Farm and Home* was given out free at state and county fairs in rural areas; the German-language *Morgen Journal* and the Yiddish-language *Jewish American* (which Hearst began publishing in mid-October and closed down after the election) reached thousands more voters in New York City. For those beyond the reach of his print media, there were the talking pictures, slide shows, and graphophone "canned" speeches, accompanied by free vaudeville.[23]

Hearst was spreading his message — that he was the only true "Democrat," that his Republican opponents were beholden to the trusts — and the voters were listening. A reporter from the *Outlook,* a conservative journal of opinion that opposed his candidacy, reported on the coalition of misfits, including many former Republicans, that Hearst was assembling. The converts included men from every social station: "the man who is embittered by class feeling and wants vengeance; the man suddenly roused against the unjust power of certain corporation managers, and about ready to accept any candidate who is vociferous in promising remedies; the unobtrusive socialistic workingman; the natural bigot who has fallen under the spell of

Hearst; and the rather shiftless, thoughtless loafer who follows the herd to which he belongs."[24]

As Hearst picked up support on the campaign trail, the attacks upon him intensified. Lincoln Steffens, seldom at a loss for words, confessed in his *Autobiography* twenty-five years later that he could not "describe the hate of those days for Hearst."[25]

Ten days before the election President Theodore Roosevelt, responding to the request of the English editor John St. Loe Strachey for information about Hearst, sent him a three-and-a-half-page letter, with "Personal & Private" scrawled along the top. Roosevelt wrote:

> It is a little difficult for me to give an exact historic judgment about a man whom I so thoroly dislike and despise as I do Hearst . . . Hearst's private life has been disreputable. His wife was a chorus girl or something like that on the stage, and it is of course neither necessary nor advisable, in my judgment, to make any allusion to any of the reports about either of them before their marriage. It is not the kind of a family which people who believe that sound home relations form the basis of national citizenship would be glad to see in the Executive Mansion in Albany, and still less in the White House . . . He preaches the gospel of envy, hatred and unrest. His actions so far go to show that he is entirely willing to sanction any mob violence if he thinks that for the moment votes are to be gained by so doing. . . . He cares nothing for the nation, nor for any citizen in it . . . If the circumstances were ripe in America, which they are not, I should think that Hearst would aspire to play the part of some of the least worthy creatures of the French Revolution. . . . He is the most potent single influence for evil we have in our life.[26]

Roosevelt did his best to broadcast rumors about Hearst's immorality by forwarding to his Republican opponent, Charles Evans Hughes, "a number of papers which I have received from a California friend, a Democrat . . . who believes Hearst to be a corrupt and insincere demagog . . . I think you can get some valuable hints from these papers, and I believe your manager should act on them at once and get hold of the men and of the documents mentioned." The papers were probably the San Francisco weeklies which had attacked Hearst so viciously in 1904.[27]

As Election Day approached, rumors of Hearst's immorality began appearing in opposition newspapers and magazines. The *Outlook* reminded voters that Hearst had "led a life of looseness and extravagance in San Francisco" and that his manner of life in New York City had been "a matter of concern to those interested in him politically"; the *New York Evening Post* resorted to classical allusions comparing him to three of history's greatest charlatans, Paracelsus, Cagliostro, and Alcibiades.[28]

While Hearst ignored the attacks, as he had in the past, he worried that his mother would not be able to. "Those articles are outrageous but don't read them," he warned her. "Any kind of success arouses envy and hatred. The best punishment is to succeed more. I shall try to do that. . . . Don't let us bother about the liars and blackguards. If a dog barked at me in the street, I would be foolish to get down on all fours and bark back."[29]

In late October, Roosevelt, who had done his politicking behind the scenes, agreed to go public. Instead of speaking himself, which would have been quite unseemly for a president, or condemning Hearst in an open letter as his friend Jacob Riis suggested, he dispatched Elihu Root, the current secretary of state and former secretary of war, to New York to speak on his behalf. With less than a week to go before the election, the secretary of state mounted the podium at a Republican rally held in his hometown of Utica, and spoke to the crowd:

> I say to you, with the President's authority, that he regards Mr. Hearst to be wholly unfit to be Governor, as an insincere, self-seeking demagogue, who is trying to deceive the workingmen of New York by false statements and false promises. I say to you, with the President's authority, that he considers Mr. Hearst's election would be an injury and a discredit alike to all honest labor and to honest capital, and a serious injury to the work in which he is engaged of enforcing just and equal laws against corporate wrong-doing.

And this was just the preamble. As reporters from every paper in the state gathered to hear the speech in person, while editors with advance copies in their possession prepared the text for the next morning's front pages, Root dropped his bombshell. He announced to the voters of the state that President Roosevelt considered Hearst complicit in the crime of the century, the assassination of President William McKinley:

> In President Roosevelt's first message to Congress, in speaking of the assassin of McKinley, he spoke of him as inflamed "by the reckless utterances of those who, on the stump and in the public press, appeal to the dark and evil spirits of malice and greed, envy and sullen hatred." . . . I say, by the President's authority, that in penning these words, with the horror of President McKinley's murder fresh before him, he had Mr. Hearst specifically in mind. And I say, by the President's authority, that what he thought of Mr. Hearst then he thinks of Mr. Hearst now.[30]

While the next morning Hearst's newspapers bitterly caricatured "Root, the Rat," every other paper in the state displayed his attack prominently on the front page. Hearst was thrown on the defensive. Instead of continuing his own attacks on the Republicans and the trusts, he had to defend himself against the charge that he was an anarchist assassin. The day after Root's appearance, Hearst made sixteen separate campaign speeches across the state. There were, unfortunately, only four days remaining before Election Day and that was not enough time to make voters forget Roosevelt's and Root's accusations. At the final campaign rally at Madison Square Garden, with Millicent and two-year-old George prominently exhibited in their box seats, Hearst reminded voters that unlike other candidates, he did not need the money the state paid its public officials, but asked only for the opportunity to serve them in Albany. He concluded by thanking them for their friendship and confidence.[31]

On November 6, New York's voters, enjoying perfect weather, went to the polls. Hearst slept late on this Election Day and arrived at the polls a bit after noon. He was not confident of victory, as he had been the year before. Though it quickly became clear that he had been beaten, he refused to concede. On the contrary, the *New York Times* reported the next morning that Max Ihmsen had telegraphed Hearst's supporters at eight in the evening to notify them that he had been elected by 50,000 and alert them to guard the upstate ballot boxes carefully. Shortly after midnight, the first edition of the *American* declared that Hearst had been elected by 20,000 votes. Two hours later, at 2:30 in the morning, Hearst conceded defeat. Charles Evans Hughes had been elected governor by slightly more than 60,000 votes out of a total of almost 1.5 million.

Hearst left town in a private railway car for St. Louis, en route to Mexico for a vacation with his wife and his son. Physically and emotionally exhausted, he was reported to have gotten into a shouting and shoving match with Joseph Pulitzer, Jr. during a visit to the offices of Pulitzer's St. Louis newspaper. We don't know the cause of their dispute, though it may well have had something to do with Hearst's comment to reporters that he intended to establish a daily newspaper in St. Louis. Later that day, according to a November 17 report in the *New York Times*, Hearst met up with young Mr. Pulitzer again at the Hotel Jefferson:

For a moment the two seemed to be conversing in a friendly way . . . when suddenly Mr. Hearst seemed to become somewhat excited. His head bobbed up and down emphatically as he spoke to Mr. Pulitzer, and all who were watching were wondering what was going on. Then Mr. Hearst walked away a few feet, took off his overcoat, laid it on the railing, and returned to where Mr. Pulitzer was standing. Mr. Hearst folded his arms and again began speaking to Mr. Pulitzer in emphatic fashion. Suddenly, without either man having raised his voice loud enough to be overheard, Mr. Pulitzer struck at Mr. Hearst two blows, which the latter warded off with his two hands . . . As it was, it was a very pretty little bout, and Mr. Hearst certainly showed some knowledge of the manly art of self-defense, for when the boy first struck at him, apparently without warning, he was prepared for him.

In a calmer moment during his layover in St. Louis, Hearst, questioned by reporters about his recent defeat, attributed it to the "treachery of the Democratic organization in the state. McCarren, of Brooklyn [the Democratic boss], and McClellan of New York City knifed me. That's all there is to it." He was "not so much interested in politics any more," he confessed. "'I'll have considerable more time now to devote to newspapers,' he laughingly added."

The numbers demonstrated that he had indeed been betrayed by the city's Democratic leadership, who had not gotten out the vote for him. But it had been his own fault. Though he had accepted the nomination of the Democrats, he had tried throughout the campaign to distance himself from his party and its leaders. This was not a winning strategy. He had already alienated the reformers who had backed his candidacy on the Independence League ticket. When he turned on the Democrats as well, he was left on his own. He had "greatly changed in the last few years," the former Boss Richard Croker told a *New York Times* reporter on November 18, ten days after the election. "Now, apparently, he is controlled by the idea that he is greater than the Democratic Party. . . . He is a slave to passion and egotism. His creed is that everybody who is for him is an angel, while everybody who is against him is a demon."

Though he had lost another election, he had held on to much of his working-class constituency. "It is perfectly evident that several hundred thousand voters are under the Hearst spell," the *New York Times* had editorialized on November 7, the day after the election. "Labor in this election has accepted Mr. Hearst. It has evidently paid little or no attention to what was said against him. It will continue to listen to his appeals."

"On the whole," *Current Literature* concluded in its review of the 1906 elections, "the majority of the American papers are of the opinion that Mr. Hearst has by no means been ended as a potent political factor."[32]

❧ 12 ❧

Party Leader

"I WAS PRETTY MUCH TIRED OUT and discouraged and disgusted with everything," Hearst wrote his mother in late 1906, "so I left New York and came to Mexico City for a few days. . . . We are not having a very good time in Mexico. . . . Every day since our arrival the weather has been cloudy and windy and very disagreeable. Our only consolation is that it is probably worse in the East, — but it surely must be better in California. The baby, or rather the boy for he had got over being a baby, has a little cold and is not well and that adds to our worries. . . . I could tell you all about the campaign but what is the use. I was beaten, and beaten by alleged democrats. The corporations control the democratic machines quite as much as they do the Republican machines and anyone who is really opposed to the corporations must count upon opposition from the machines of both parties. . . . I am greatly obliged to you for having helped me and regret that I did not win out for the satisfaction of all but I couldn't do it and I am pretty much worn out in the hard fight I made. I hope to be able to write a more cheerful letter soon when I get over the stings of defeat and get my business back in some sort of shape."[1]

After Mexico, Hearst, Millicent, and young George took the Southern Pacific west to Glendale and then switched to the coastal route north to San Luis Obispo, the station nearest the Hearst property at San Simeon, where they vacationed in the white ranch house with green shutters that George Hearst had built in 1878. Hearst's mother was still in Paris. "We have just arrived in God Blessed California," Will wrote her on a postcard. "The light is real sunlight, *not* artificial light, the heat is real sun heat, not steam heat, the Colorado river is real mud, the Yuma desert is real dirt, and the Indians are mostly real dirt, too. . . . I think California is the best country in the world and always will be no matter who comes into it or what is done to it. Nobody or no thing can shut out the beautiful sun or alter the glorious climate." The card was signed "Hurrah for dear old California."[2]

From San Simeon, Will and his family traveled north to Phoebe's Hacienda in Pleasanton, and after spending a few days there took the train back to New York. George was left behind with the servants to await his grandmother's return. Phoebe, as we shall see, had become an aggressively active grandmother. She had converted the bedroom next to hers at the Hacienda to a child's room and expected George to spend at least as much time with her in California as he did with his parents in New York.

From New York, Will wrote his mother a glowing letter about his stay at San Simeon: "I am exceedingly fond of the ranch as you know. We had a glorious time there — a perfectly *splendid* time. . . . We camped out and fished and rode horseback. I wish I were there now. . . . It is awfully hot and disagreeable here in the East. I wish I could spend more time in California. We had such a good time there particularly on the ranch. I am going to save up and build a cabin down there just big enough for you and the baby and me. Then I suppose you will go to Abyssinia and stay a year and a half."[3]

Though he had promised Phoebe that he would not run "for any office in many years," he refused to give up his crusade against the trusts and the politicians who protected them. Having concluded that the Democratic party was beyond redemption, he had made up his mind that it had to be destroyed. His vehicle would be the Independence League, which he planned to transform into a national political party. There were already active Independence Leagues funded and organized by Hearst in New York, Massachusetts, California, and Illinois, the states where he published newspapers. Max Ihmsen was directed to set up more Leagues in more states, pointing toward a national campaign in 1908.[4]

Hearst's notion that his Independence League might in a very short time grow to rival or displace one of the major parties was not implausible. The Republican party had, only fifty years before, emerged from minor-party status to elect a president. Nationally, the Populists had polled over a million votes in 1892 and, with Bryan as the candidate in 1896, effectively taken over the Democratic party; the Socialists had meanwhile increased their vote for Eugene Debs from 80,000 in 1900 to 402,000 in 1904. There were, of course, problems inherent in building a political party so closely associated with — and controlled by — one man. As Samuel Seabury noted in his diary, Hearst was so obsessed with the corrupting influence of money on party politics that he had convinced himself that the only way to protect the purity of his party was to keep it firmly "in his control or in the control of his friends." While Seabury sympathized with Hearst's fears, he recognized that as long as the Independence League remained Hearst's fiefdom, it would never attract the reformers who were its natural constituency: "If the organization is autocratic many good men, in sympathy with its aims, will have nothing to do with it."[5]

Because there were no major offices at stake in New York in 1907, Hearst chose the most important of the minor ones, sheriff of New York County, and nominated Max Ihmsen, who was his chief political operative, to run against the Democratic nominee, the saloon keeper and Tammany chieftain Big Tom Foley. As had become his usual autumnal routine, Hearst spent the first three weeks of October motoring across Manhattan, Bronx, Queens, and Brooklyn to assail Tammany in four and five speeches a day. The transcripts of every speech appeared, verbatim, in his newspapers the next day, alongside cartoons of thuggish-looking political bosses doing business with equally thuggish-looking businessmen and exposés about Tammany corruption, centered on "Nigger Mike," Tom Foley's chief of staff, who, the Hearst papers claimed, was a fugitive from justice, having fled a warrant for arrest as a "repeater."

In mid-October, news of the campaign was bumped from the front pages by the "panic of 1907." Cash and credit were already in short supply after a stock market plunge in August, when the attempt of two speculators to corner the stock of a copper company with the help of a major New York trust company resulted in a run on the New York banks. While J. Pierpont Morgan worked on a rescue plan in the library of his New York townhouse, Hearst, with outstanding debts and mortgages all across the country, retreated to the Clarendon to await the outcome. To help the nation — and himself — and stop the run on the banks, he published a signed front-page appeal for calm, urging his readers not to join the lines "of the panic-stricken" and withdraw their money. "There has been a campaign on and a panic and Will has been in both," Millicent wrote Phoebe on October 29. "One night Will was trying to learn his speech in time to go to six meetings while Jerome [the New York district attorney] was trying to arrest him for criminal libel and Edward Clark was explaining how everything was going to pieces in Wall Street and we would all be broke in the morning. Will went out without his dinner and wouldn't eat anything when he came back and I thought that was too much and made him stop speaking for a few days. Edward has been up to the house every day for the past week. Will thinks the situation has cleared somewhat but he never leaves the telephone until after banking hours. The course of the paper has made many friends among business people and Edward says that the day Will printed his signed statement he was the most popular man on Wall Street."[6]

By early November, the immediate crisis having been resolved, Hearst returned to the campaign trail. While he continued to attract huge and enthusiastic crowds everywhere he went, they had come to see him, not to commit themselves to voting for his surrogate, Max Ihmsen, who, with no experience and no following, didn't stand a chance against Tom Foley. Hearst didn't even bother to vote on Election Day, disappointing the photographers and reporters who had gathered to meet him at his polling place. Ihmsen and every other candidate who ran on Hearst's Independence League line were soundly defeated. His only victory was in Massachusetts where the Independence League candidate for district attorney in Suffolk County won his race.[7]

The election over, Hearst concentrated his attentions again on his newspapers, his finances, and his family. Millicent was pregnant with their second child. "In about ten days, if all goes well," he wrote his mother in California in early 1908, "there will be another heir to the Hearst millions — and all we will need then will be the millions. The finances are not very cheerful yet but things are improving some and we are gradually getting the debts paid. . . . Forty thousand we will pay off the day after tomorrow and then we will have nothing but the hundred and fifty thousand . . . that is pressing. The banks we will pay off gradually and our spare change will be devoted to satisfying the poor people who have been so unfortunate as to sell us things during the past few months. We will have to be careful about paying some of them. I am afraid the shock might be fatal in certain cases."[8]

On January 27, 1908, Millicent gave birth to William Randolph Hearst, Jr. The pregnancy had not gone well. Millie, Hearst wrote his mother, had been "somewhat worried because the promised baby doesn't seem to be in the right position." The plan had been for Millie, George, and the newborn baby to spend the rest of the winter with Phoebe at the Hacienda. But unlike his older brother, George, now almost four, Bill, Jr. was not a healthy child and was not able to travel West until the spring. "I was puny and sickly from the start," Bill, Jr. recalled in his memoirs. "It was only a year before I got pneumonia. Mom and Pop didn't think their young offspring was going to make it. I did, but was plagued with one illness or another much of my life."[9]

In April or May, Millie boarded the train for San Francisco with her four-month-old son, two nurses, and her father and sister. George had been sent

West earlier. In Chicago, Millie turned around and returned to New York, while the nurses and her father accompanied Bill, Jr. to his grandmother's Hacienda in Pleasanton.

Hearst wanted his boys to grow up as Californians, and as Phoebe was delighted to raise them — with the help of a squadron of nurses and tutors, presided over by a German governess — he left them in her care for extended periods of time. Phoebe's ninety-two room Hacienda, on two thousand acres of land forty miles east of San Francisco, became the boys' second home. She built a fifty-foot playhouse for the two older boys and when John, the third Hearst son, was born in 1909, had her architect, Julia Morgan, design a two-story, freestanding "Boys' House" for them, with thirteen large rooms upstairs and a gigantic playroom, complete with pool and billiard tables, reading rooms, and places for visitors downstairs.[10]

During the summer, Phoebe took her grandsons to Wyntoon, her estate near Mount Shasta just south of the California-Oregon border. For young boys, Wyntoon, situated in the mountains at the edge of the McCloud River, was even more exciting than the Pleasanton Hacienda. Phoebe had been introduced to the region in 1899, when she visited her friend and lawyer, Charles Stetson Wheeler, who had built a hunting lodge there. When Phoebe asked if she could buy some of his property, Wheeler refused, but offered her instead a ninety-nine-year lease on the understanding that she would erect a modest structure in the woods. Phoebe had other plans. She hired Bernard Maybeck, a founder and chief practitioner of what Lewis Mumford referred to as the Bay Region Style. Maybeck, a master at combining wood and stone into romantic rustic structures that meshed perfectly with their landscapes, designed a seven-story Gothic German stone castle that looked as if it had been lifted from a fairy-tale version of the Rhine. It was artfully sited, just above the flowing river, with tall pine trees towering above it. The castle was completed in 1904, the year of George Hearst's birth.[11]

George and Bill, Jr. stayed with their grandmother at Pleasanton and Wyntoon from April through November of 1908. Only Millicent, it appeared, was unhappy with the arrangement. "Milly is much worried about Brother William," Will telegraphed his mother in mid-November, "and I think it would be a good idea if you could send us a telegram every Sunday telling her all about the children. It does not cost anything to send it over the special wire [the news service cable that connected the Hearst papers], and it relieves her mind. I hope the babies are well and that you are too." The following week, apparently not having heard anything in the meantime, he renewed the request. "Milly interrupts to ask if you will not please have some pictures taken of Brother William and George and send them to her. She is getting very lonesome for the children and I suppose we will have to go West soon."[12]

The battle over who was going to raise the Hearst children would continue for the rest of Phoebe's life. Because Will was occupied with his newspapers and the campaign trail and because Phoebe didn't completely trust Millicent to hire the right people to care for her grandchildren, she kept them in California as long as she could, and bristled when her son or daughter-in-law hinted that she was usurping their responsibilities. "Don't you think I show considerable confidence by leaving my children away from me half the year which most parents don't do?" Hearst wrote her in 1915. "I must continue, however, to take some natural interest in them, to ask information and make recommendations for their welfare."[13]

From three thousand miles away, Hearst gave his mother directions on how to raise his children, as he gave his faraway editors instructions on how to write their editorials. He set the basic ground rules, the "policy" which he expected others to adhere to. "Warn the children," he telegrammed her just before July Fourth sometime in the early 1910s, "not to be gay with firecrackers and please don't let them have airguns yet. Paper only the other day had news items to the effect that two children had been wounded and one blinded by these airguns. Let them throw rocks at the birds. The exercise will do them good." He was worried that George, who he feared was "something of a jackass," might drown himself or kill himself with a pistol or lead William astray. "Don't let George get too independent . . . he may grow up to be as bad as I am," he telegrammed her in 1913 when George was nine, after a trip West to deposit the boys for the season.[14]

Though Will was a more responsible parent than his father had been, he was always a distant one. He spent little time with his boys and instead delegated authority for rearing them — to Phoebe, to Millicent, to the headmasters of the boys' boarding schools, and then to the publishing executives the boys worked for. According to Bill, Jr., his sons all suffered from the neglect: "All of us in the family felt he should have given us more of his time. My brothers and I felt we needed the reassurance of his presence and more personal guidance while we were growing up."[15]

Phoebe had expected her son and Millicent to join her and the boys in Pleasanton for their 1908 summer vacation, but Will decided to vacation in Europe instead. "We are only going abroad for six weeks," he explained to his mother by letter. "I suppose I will have to do some talking in September and October [during the upcoming 1908 presidential campaign] and that is really hard work so a little rest and change will do me some good. I would not get a real rest in California because I would get political telegrams and newspaper telegrams every day in addition to having the affairs of the California papers to attend to. So we thought we would take the little trip first and then come out later."[16]

From on board the *Lusitania,* Millicent wrote Phoebe to apologize. The change in plans hadn't, she insisted, been her idea, but her husband's: "You say that I am like Will and never tell you about our plans. As a matter of fact we never have any plans. Will thinks he is going to do one thing one day and another thing another day and when the time comes we don't do either but something entirely different. We didn't know until the last moment whether we would go abroad or go out West or take a trip to Canada."[17]

Such was life with Will Hearst. After six weeks abroad, he and Millicent returned home on the Cunard luxury steamer *Lucania* on July 25. That same day, they boarded the Twentieth Century Limited for Chicago, where the first national convention of Hearst's Independence party was being convened. The Republicans had already nominated William Howard Taft for the presidency; the Democrats, William Jennings Bryan; the Populists, Tom Watson; the Socialists, Eugene Debs; and the Prohibitionists, Eugene Chaffin. Each of these parties had a constituency, a permanent party organization, and a recognizable candidate. Hearst's Independence party had none of these. Still, oblivious to the effect another losing campaign might have on his political reputation, Hearst plunged ahead, hoping that he could come up with a presidential candidate in 1908 who could win enough votes to keep his third party in the news until 1912 when he intended to run for president again.

On July 27 at 8:25 in the evening, as always a bit late, William Randolph Hearst entered Chicago's Orchestra Hall and strode down the main aisle to take his seat at the platform. Twenty minutes later, he mounted the podium to deliver his address. The convention then proceeded to its main business. Thomas Hisgen, a manufacturer and dealer in kerosene and axle grease from Massachusetts, was nominated for president; John Temple Graves, a Hearst employee known for his small size and large vocabulary, for vice president.[18]

Because "Honest Tom" Hisgen could not possibly draw a crowd by himself, Hearst accompanied him everywhere on the campaign trail. With nothing particularly new to say, he found it impossible to get coverage anywhere except in his own newspapers, until in mid-September, he publicly revealed that he had in his possession "legal evidence and documentary proof" that John Archbold, who had been running Standard Oil since John D. Rockefeller's de facto retirement, had bribed prominent U.S. senators to influence elections, appointments, and legislation.

While Hearst announced that the Archbold letters had just come into his possession, he had in fact secured them almost four years earlier. Late in 1904, a young man named Charles Stump had appeared at the offices of the *New York American* with letters and telegrams from Archbold, which he claimed had been rescued from the wastepaper basket by Willie Winkfield, the janitor who worked in his office. Stump had tried to sell the letters to the *World*, and when he was rebuffed visited the Hearst papers. They too refused to buy, but gave him instead a list of 200 prominent Washington politicians and told him that they would pay for letters addressed to any of them. Over the next three months, Winkfield went through Archbold's files with his list of names in hand. Letters addressed to the men on the list were taken to the *American*'s offices and photographed before being returned to the Standard Oil offices.[19]

Hearst had kept the existence of these letters secret, waiting for the perfect moment to disclose them. On September 17, 1908, without advance warning to anyone, he pulled a sheaf of papers from the inside pocket of his frock coat during a rally in Columbus, Ohio, and began reading letters which he claimed, according to the *New York Daily Tribune*'s report the next day, "had been written by John D. Archbold, of the Standard Oil Company, to Senator J. B. Foraker, of Ohio, referring to legislation pending in Congress, and mentioning two inclosures of checks, one for $15,000 and another for $14,500."

Aware now that he had the full attention of the press, Hearst read two more letters the next day at a rally in St. Louis, one from Archbold to Republican Senator Foraker, the second from Archbold to Governor Haskell of Oklahoma, a Democrat, who was serving as Bryan's campaign treasurer. Archbold issued a curt statement dismissing Hearst's allegations as "pure fiction." Senator Foraker acknowledged that the letters were authentic, but claimed that the payments referred to compensation for work he had done for Standard Oil as a private citizen. Governor Haskell claimed that the Haskell referred to by Archbold was not him, but "another Haskell who had relations with Standard Oil." Such unbelievable answers were more than enough to keep the story going for another day or two.[20]

Hearst, a master of the continuing front-page exposé, now had the national press corps following his every step. And so began his strange journey across America, letters in hand, Hisgen trailing behind. From podiums in Memphis, New York City, El Paso, Los Angeles, and San Francisco, Hearst pulled letters out of his pocket and read them aloud to his audiences — and reporters — frightening politicians everywhere who feared that they too might be mentioned in Archbold's correspondence.[21]

Hearst was in his element once again, the center of attention, entertaining large crowds everywhere with his mixture of self-deprecating charm and bombast. Hearst's revelations remained big news through September and into October. But his reappearance in the headlines did not translate into support for his Independence party candidates. He had succeeded in reminding American voters that their political leaders were on the take. But having destroyed their confidence in the major political parties, Hearst had nothing to offer them in return: no vision, no alternative politics, no viable candidates. What voter, no matter how disaffected he might have become with Taft and Bryan, was going to elect Hearst's candidate, a dealer in axle grease, to the highest office in the land? While Hearst cannot be blamed for the decline in voter turnouts that had begun earlier in the century, he was contributing daily to the perception that the political system was so corrupt it didn't much matter who was elected. In 1896, 79% of the electorate had voted for president; in 1908, only 65% of those eligible voted; by 1912, the percentage would decline to 59%.[22]

When the votes were finally counted on November 4, 1908, the Republican candidate, William Howard Taft, was the winner. There were many losers, most prominent among them William Jennings Bryan, who for the third time suffered defeat by a landslide. At the bottom of the vote totals stood the Independence party with 86,000 votes, a third of them in New York City. Debs and the Socialists, in comparison, had polled over 420,000 votes; the Prohibitionists, over 250,000. While the November 5 *New York Daily Tribune* reported that Independence party officials had acknowledged that their totals "were much smaller than they had expected," Hearst had already, the day before the election, declared himself satisfied, whatever the vote totals. His Independence party, win or lose, had "laid the foundations for great reforms. It has made history. It has . . . sown the seeds for a rich harvest in future achievements." What he didn't say was that the defeat of Bryan in 1908, coupled with Judge Alton Parker's resounding defeat in 1904, left the Democratic party leaderless for 1912, a vacuum he intended to fill.[23]

There is a coda to the Archbold letters story. Two weeks after the election, Hearst wrote his mother that he had been summoned to the White House for a secret meeting with President Roosevelt. "I don't know what it is all about, but I doubt if it is a matter of importance. I suppose Roosevelt will touch on Standard Oil letters. Maybe that is the important thing he wants to see me about. He is mentioned in some of them." This, unfortunately, is all we know about the meeting. Neither Hearst nor Roosevelt ever again referred to it.[24]

Having spent the last five autumns on the campaign trail, each year doing worse than the year before, Hearst might, one would think, have been ready to retire from politics, but he was not. In October of 1909, he announced that he was running for mayor of New York City on his Independence party ticket. His major opponent was Judge William Gaynor of Brooklyn, whose reputation for independence, opposition to the trusts, and lifelong advocacy of municipal ownership of public utilities was such that Hearst had tried to enlist him to run for mayor on the Independence party line. The fact that Tammany had nominated Gaynor was an ironic tribute to Hearst's political success. He had so frightened Tammany in 1905 that its boss, Charles Francis Murphy, had been forced to nominate a man like Gaynor in 1909 instead of the usual party hack.

Tammany having stolen his candidate and his issues, Hearst was left with no basis on which to campaign except personality, which was far from his strongest suit. He accused Gaynor of improperly supporting horse-racing interests while on the bench and vilified him as a paranoiac, a liar, an intellectual hypocrite, a demagogue, a fanatic, an agitator, an old man, and for being "mentally cross-eyed." Gaynor and Tammany assailed him, in turn, for trying to buy his elections as he bought his newspapers, for advertising himself "as though he were a patent medicine or a nostrum," and for being hypocritical, dishonest, and immoral, with a face that, Gaynor confessed, "almost makes me puke."[25]

As part of its assault on Hearst's character, Tammany published an anonymous forty-eight-page pamphlet entitled *The Life of William R. Hearst,* with cartoons reprinted from the San Francisco scandal sheets of 1904, describing in exhaustive detail every blemish on his reputation, beginning with "the record of duplicity, deception and depravity which made his name a by-word in California." The concluding "indictment" pulled out all the stops:

> Buying newspapers with his millions, he debauches the press, prostitutes writers to the service of his personal ambition, and degrades and disgraces the profession of journalism. He violates every propriety, tramples upon every

principle of justice, invades the sacred precincts of the home and contaminates the air of the fireside with the foul breath of suspicion, to gain circulation for his malodorous sheets. He appeals to the evil passions of the weak and the malignant and strives to ruin that which he cannot rule. . . . Such is the pampered pet of fortune who, to gratify his monumental egotism, has slandered all who scorned his bribes, betrayed every cause he has espoused, turned traitor to Democracy and dastard to his political comrades and whose criminal journalism may boast as its most conspicuous achievement the assassination of President McKinley by one of its feeble-minded dupes. It is to New York's everlasting shame that a man with such a record could be seriously considered as a candidate for Mayor — it is the duty of every earnest, patriotic citizen to see to it that his impudent assumption is properly rebuked.[26]

The attack on Hearst's character struck a chord with New York's voters. Had Hearst been able to distinguish his position on political corruption from Gaynor's, he might have stood a chance, but Boss Murphy had chosen the perfect candidate to run against him, a white-haired judge with a sterling reputation for integrity. Still, Hearst's attack on Tammany was so effective that when, on November 2, 1909, New York City's voters went to the polls, they elected every anti-Tammany, reform candidate on the ballot, with one exception. They chose William Gaynor over William Hearst by a margin of almost 100,000 votes. Hearst polled 75,000 fewer votes than he had in 1905 and came in third, behind Gaynor and Otto Bannard, the Republican candidate for mayor. Hearst claimed victory anyway, congratulating himself on having swept Tammany's candidates for every office except mayor. He had indeed played an indisputable and indispensable role in defeating Tammany, as even the *New York Times* recognized in a November 6 editorial.

In mid-December, the city's reformers, led by Charles Sprague Smith, the Columbia professor who headed the People's Institute, recognized as much and honored William Randolph Hearst at a dinner in the ballroom of the Astor Hotel. Hearst soaked up the praise and delivered yet another in his repertoire of thunderous anti-Tammany speeches. But the appearance of vigor was deceiving. He was worn out by campaigning, unhealthy, and dangerously overweight. Millie and Phoebe agreed that he needed a complete rest cure or as close to one as he would permit.[27]

Late that winter, W. R., Millicent, five-and-a-half-year-old George, two-year-old Bill, Jr., and John Randolph, the latest addition to the family, who had been born during the campaign, boarded a private railroad car for an extended California vacation. After depositing the children in Pleasanton,

W. R. and Millicent took the train south to Los Angeles where the *Examiner* was sponsoring an international aviation exhibition. Hearst, invited to fly with a French pilot, squeezed his huge two hundred plus pounds into the monoplane, which miraculously took off without difficulty. He was so impressed by his flight that he offered a prize of $50,000 to the first person to fly a plane from one coast to another.[28]

In Los Angeles, Hearst visited a doctor who, he wrote Phoebe, advised him to take a rest cure: "I tried to joke him about it but he refused to be funny. He said American businessmen had no sense — that they knew how to take care of their money but not of their health. I told him that I didn't know how to do either but he declined to smile. He said very solemnly, 'Either rest and get well or work and be a chronic invalid.' I began to have creepy feelings up my back so I said I guessed I would rest."[29]

From California, Hearst and Millicent traveled south to Mexico and then, after retrieving the children in Northern California, returned briefly to New York. On May 11, 1910, they sailed for Europe on the R.M.S. *Mauretania.* From the ship Hearst wrote Phoebe a long, newsy letter about her grandchildren, who, he claimed, were the delight of the ship. "All these people like the children. I don't know what they think of *us.*" The Hearsts remained abroad for five months.[30]

After an absence from New York of more than eight months, W. R. returned from Europe in August of 1910, in time for another campaign season. The remnants of his Independence party had nominated him to run for lieutenant-governor and he had accepted, no doubt because without his name on the ticket, there was no hope whatsoever of his party getting any press coverage outside his own papers. On arriving in New York, he announced that he had a new set of secret documents with him that "he intended to read as the campaign went on." Independence party officials promised that it was going to be a "hot campaign." It was not. Hearst had no secret documents. He tried to keep up appearances, made a few speeches in New York City, and used his newspapers to denounce both major parties and their candidates for being corrupt, boss-ridden, and beholden to the trusts.[31]

Unfortunately, no one was listening anymore. Hearst and his Independence party running mates were soundly defeated. In New York City, Hearst polled under 50,000 votes for lieutenant-governor, less than half what he had polled in his unsuccessful race for mayor against Judge Gaynor the year before.[32] Such was the inglorious end of Hearst's electoral career, his "last hurrah" as an independent. In his concession statement, he said little about his future or that of his Independence party, but graciously congratulated the Democrats on their electoral sweep and expressed his "hope that the Democratic party will fully realize the expectations of its supporters and fully respond to the requirements of the citizens." He closed his statement with his customary declaration of victory: "I feel that I am the victor in this campaign . . . I carried on a campaign for which I need not be ashamed."[33]

§ 13 &

Hearst at Fifty: Some Calm Before the Storms

Without shame or remorse or a hint of contrition at having spent five of the last six years maligning the Democratic party, its leaders, and its candidates, Hearst declared in the fall of 1911 that he was a Democrat again. His announcement was timed to serve notice that he intended to play a role in the selection of the party's nominee for president in 1912. Though he recognized that there was little chance that he would be nominated by the Democrats for anything — at least for the foreseeable future — he allowed himself to dream of possible scenarios, like a deadlocked convention, in which the party's leaders would turn to him. He was, in fact, considered by many, including Congressman Cordell Hull of Tennessee, to be a strong possibility for the nomination. While making it clear that he would, if called, accept, Hearst did all he could to advance the candidacy of his old ally, Congressman Champ Clark of Missouri, and to block that of the governor of New Jersey, Woodrow Wilson. Clark was a Western-style progressive on issues like railroad regulation and the trusts; Wilson a stiff-necked patrician who wrote books and gave lectures on the superiority of British political institutions.[1]

In 1912, perhaps in preparation for the presidential campaign, Hearst had added a Southern newspaper to his political arsenal. With the acquisition of the *Atlanta Georgian,* he owned daily newspapers in every region of the nation and six of its largest cities. His magazine empire was growing even faster. The circulation of *Cosmopolitan,* which had been around 400,000 when he bought it, had grown by 1912 to three-quarters of a million. He had, in 1911, acquired *Good Housekeeping* and the *World Today,* which he renamed *Hearst's Magazine.* In 1912, he bought *Harper's Bazaar.* While neither *Good Housekeeping* nor *Harper's Bazaar* were employed in the attack on Wilson, *Hearst's Magazine* published "The Real Woodrow Wilson," a scathing "exposé" by Alfred Henry Lewis, who had made his name attacking robber barons for Hearst's *Cosmopolitan.*

Wilson was not particularly thin-skinned for a politician, but even he was overwhelmed by the barrage in Hearst's newspapers and magazines. "William R. Hearst has 'decided' I am not to be nominated," Wilson told his audience at a campaign stop in Chicago on April 6. "What an exhibition of audacity. What a contempt he must feel for the judgment and integrity of the American people. But it is delightful to realize the people of Illinois on next Tuesday will decide who is to be nominated and Mr. Hearst — a non-resident — can only have his say in his newspapers."[2]

Unfortunately for Governor Wilson, that "say" was a significant one. Wilson lost the Illinois primary to Clark by almost three to one. When the Democratic nominating convention convened in Baltimore in July, Hearst's candidate, Champ Clark, led Wilson by more than one hundred votes on the first ballot. Only as it became apparent that Clark could not muster the two-thirds vote required for the nomination did the convention turn to Woodrow Wilson, who was nominated on the forty-sixth ballot and elected the following November.

Though Hearst had, in the end, endorsed Wilson for the presidency, he wasted little time before going on the attack again. Less than a month after the inauguration, in a letter to the editor of the *Washington Post* which was reprinted the next day on his editorial pages, Hearst assailed Wilson for delivering his message to Congress in person, like a Federalist or, worse yet, a British prime minister; for getting "his degree of doctor of philosophy by an essay which contended flagrantly in the face of fact that the English parliamentary form of government was superior to the American Congressional system"; for admitting that he got "his information on world events from the columns of the London Weekly 'Times'" instead of an American newspaper; and for being "an English free-trader."[3]

While Hearst sniped at Wilson on a continual basis, his first substantive disagreement with the president was over Mexico, where the Hearst family owned several huge estates, the largest of which was Babicora in the state of Chihuahua in the northwest. Since the 1880s, the Hearst family — with other American businessmen and landowners — had enjoyed a cordial and profitable relationship with President Porfirio Díaz of Mexico, who had made sure that boundary and title disputes over their Babicora ranch were adjudicated in the Hearsts' favor.[4] When in 1911 it became clear that Díaz, after thirty-four years of dictatorial rule, was no longer able to protect American business interests, Hearst called for American intervention.

Díaz was overthrown and succeeded by Francesco Madero. Unfortunately for Hearst, Madero, whom Hearst hoped would be able to restore order and protect American investments, proved unable to control the revolutionary forces he had helped unleash. In July and then again in October of 1912, the Hearst ranch was placed under siege by Mexican peasant revolutionists and only rescued, at the last minute, by the Mexican army. Madero himself was overthrown by General Victoriano Huerta in February of 1913. The following month Wilson was inaugurated and Hearst began editorially petitioning him to intervene in Mexico. "There is only one course [to] pursue," he wrote in a November 1913 editorial. "That course is to occupy Mexico and restore it to a state of civilization by means of American MEN and American METHODS."[5]

As in so many other matters, W. R. in his Mexican policy enjoyed the luxury of believing that what was good for the Hearsts was good for the nation. As Parker H. Sercombe, the former president of an American bank in Mexico City, confidentially wrote William Jennings Bryan, now Wilson's secretary of state, in 1913, "The activity of the Hearst papers to foment war between this government and Mexico can be easily understood, for in the event of a protectorate or annexation, the value of the Hearst properties would be so much enhanced as to make a profit to the estate of not less than *10* million dollars."[6]

With the self-confidence of a Westerner who knew more about Mexico and Mexicans than Wilson would be able to learn in a lifetime, Hearst criticized the president's every action. When Wilson sent American marines to the port of Veracruz in April of 1914, the Hearst papers attacked him because the landing was not a prelude to full-scale intervention. When Wilson accepted a proposal from neutral Latin American countries to arbitrate the dispute with Mexico, Hearst accused him of humiliating the nation and making "the ruling power on this continent . . . the plaything of cunning, unscrupulous Mexicans and their South American sympathizers." Only armed intervention would "compel peace and enforce order," Hearst explained in a June 1914 interview with a German newspaper which was reprinted in all his newspapers. "I think that the Mexicans are far enough advanced to govern themselves under ordinary conditions, but not far enough advanced to give themselves as good a government as the United States could give them. . . . Our citizens have great interests there, and a great number live, or did live, and conduct business in Mexico. The complete anarchy there, lasting for several years, has been injurious to the interests of our country as a whole and disastrous and destructive to the lives and property of our citizens in Mexico. General Sherman said: 'War is hell.' But anarchy is also hell."[7]

On April 29, 1913, the Hearsts celebrated the Chief's fiftieth birthday and their tenth, "tin" anniversary with a luxurious dinner served on tin plates. The menus were engraved on a thin scroll of tin and the drawing rooms decorated with orchids and spring flowers. Having been excluded or having excluded himself from New York society, Hearst established his own social world by bringing together in the Clarendon old family friends, publishing and political associates, and overachievers from industry, politics, and show business. Their guests, the *New York Times* reported on April 29, included a wide social swath of Hearst employees, Democratic politicians, corporate leaders like Elbert Gary, the chairman of U.S. Steel, along with the art dealer Sir Joseph Duveen, the Broadway actress Nell Brinkley, the vaudevillian Elsie Janis, the radical suffragist Inez Milholland, and a large number of unaccompanied women.

As Orrin Peck, W. R.'s oldest friend, who stayed with the Hearsts often, confided to his sister in 1913, he was astounded at Hearst's continual motion: "My but Will is a busy one here — telephone rings about every minute. People trying to make appointments, [New York Governor William Sulzer] is in the drawing room with him now. . . . Tomorrow night Will and Milly give a big reception after dinner and serve a fine supper. After the theater last night — Will took his mother home and then [took his guests] out to Shanley's and then to Martin's — for supper and entertainment — my such crowds — and heat and smoke — and it was gay."[8]

When, in the early 1910s, New York went dance mad, with men and women of all ages and on every step of the social ladder doing the turkey trot, grizzly bear, bunny hug, and other dances to ragtime, W. R. invited the city's most popular dance team, Irene and Vernon Castle, to the Clarendon for dinner and dancing. After dinner, Irene Castle recalled in her autobiography, the Hearst butler "rolled up the rugs in the drawing room and turned on the gramophone. Vernon danced with Millicent Hearst while I danced with W. R. He had a very keen mind and if I showed him a step *once,* he remembered it. He also had that spring in his knees that is vital to a good dancer, and we thoroughly enjoyed the evenings we spent at his house." Castle, who was at the time regularly visiting the homes of New York's social elites, was impressed not only by the Chief's dancing, but by his refusal to dress his servants in uniforms. In "a day when everybody's chauffeur wore uniforms, very dressy, noticeable uniforms with frogs and braid and fur collars," Hearst's chauffeur wore a brown business suit.[9]

Retired from the campaign trail, Hearst spent more time than ever at the Clarendon on 86th Street and Riverside Drive. It was here that he held his business meetings, entertained friends, family, and publishing colleagues, and exhibited his favorite artworks. Hearst had originally leased the top three floors of the building and the roof garden, but as his family and art collection expanded, so did his need for additional space. In 1913, he asked his landlord for permission to lease the eighth and ninth floors and make extensive renovations throughout, including raising the ceiling on the top floors to accommodate a new oversized tapestry he had brought back from Europe. When the landlord refused Hearst permission to make these changes, he bought the building from him. The price was reportedly close to $1 million; Hearst borrowed $525,000 of it from the Mutual Life Insurance Company.[10]

Hearst, now free to do as he pleased, redid the top five floors. "The renovation," according to Andrew Alpern, author of *Historic Manhattan Apartment Houses,* "included replacing a large portion of the building's roof with a giant raised skylight room to illuminate the rooms below, and destroying all traces of the original two-apartments-per-floor room configurations. The two-storied living room he created was a cavernous affair with heavily carved woodwork, a huge stained-glass window and recessed cabinets to house a collection of oversized silver salvers. There was a Georgian dining room, a French Empire bedroom and bits and pieces of almost every other architectural and decorating style that ever existed. Perhaps the most archetypal 'Hearstian' room, however, was the triple-height vaulted stone hall." The massive gallery housed pieces from his medieval armor collection.[11]

For Bill, Jr., the Clarendon "was like a royal palace . . . The top two floors were made into a banquet hall for parties and a ballroom for dancing. The ballroom had a balcony at each end. . . . Our parents weren't home very much. When they did entertain, they didn't want five noisy boys roughhousing underfoot. They also were concerned about all the valuable paintings, statuary, and armor in the place. So we boys lived downstairs. . . . We had governesses, nannies, and private tutors. . . . We saw Mom virtually every day during our grade-school years. My father, like many other parents, would step in when we had study or deportment problems, but, for the most part, we came under the direction of others. We were really a type of American aristocracy, styled along the lines of the British upper class. In those days, many wealthy American parents allocated time to their children only when there was good reason and available time."[12]

The Clarendon had something for everyone in the family: lots of playing room for the boys, exhibition space and a private office for Hearst, a ballroom and formal dining room for Millicent's entertaining. The only problem with the property was the proximity of the New York Central railroad tracks on the other side of Riverside Park. Complaining that the noise made when freight cars were shunted from one track to another was so loud he could not sleep, even with double windows, and that the stench from the cars that carried livestock was unbearable, Hearst demanded that the New York Central stop using the tracks north of 72nd Street as a railroad yard. When the railroad refused to bow to the adverse publicity Hearst showered on it in his newspapers, he took the company to court. It would take years, but Hearst, in the end, won his war and forced the New York Central to stop switching or storing freight cars north of its yard, above 72nd Street.[13]

Although there was as yet almost no mention of Hearst's art holdings in the press, by the time he moved into the Clarendon, he had already assembled one of the most impressive collections in the country. Collecting was a passion that ranked for him just below journalism and politics. Part of every day was devoted to visiting galleries, attending auctions, or corresponding with his dealers and representatives in New York, London, and the major European art capitals. As one of their best customers, he was given advance notice of every auction and sale and bombarded with mailings, catalogues, and brochures, which he somehow found time to study. When in the spring of 1907, to cite but one example, the American Art Association auctioned off the contents of architect Stanford White's New York City residence after White had been shot and killed by Harry Thaw, the husband of the actress Evelyn Nesbit, with whom he had had an affair, Hearst was one of the chosen few invited to attend and bid. According to Wesley Towner, author of *The Elegant Auctioneers,* he spent a good deal of the time bidding against John D. Rockefeller, Jr. The two millionaires fought "like schoolboys over everything in sight. Hearst got most of the stained-glass windows and the Venetian weather vanes to supply San Simeon, but Rockefeller refused to be outbid on the Spanish oil jars. They divided the Renaissance doorways and sarcophagi and came out even on the Caen stone well curbs, acquiring about a dozen or so each. Hearst paid the highest price — $320 — for the only one capable of drawing water, a medieval contraption complete with windlass and a leaky bucket." Before the auction was over, Hearst had also outbid the producer David Belasco for an immense sixteenth-century celestial globe and paid $8,000 for a "ceiling with personages identified as 'Angels Bringing Tidings of Christ's Birth.'"

The ceiling can be seen today in the Doge's Suite sitting room at San Simeon.[14]

Hearst collected art not for investment purposes or because he felt any great need to show off for others or because, like J. Pierpont Morgan, he believed in a "gospel of wealth" and wanted to assemble an art collection to share with the less fortunate. Hearst collected because he took an enormous pleasure in possessing, accumulating, and living among things of beauty. The money he earned from his newspapers and magazines he regarded as his to spend as he saw fit. And spend it he did. He had still not learned — or perhaps refused to learn — the art of double-entry bookkeeping. When he saw an item he wanted, he bought it, regardless of whether he had the money in the bank to pay for it. His spending had always been extravagant, but as he approached the age of fifty, it ballooned out of all proportion to his income.

Now that he had a number of extremely profitable publishing properties, he found it relatively easy to borrow on his own instead of going to Phoebe for money, though he did that as well. Convinced that his publishing revenues would grow faster than the interest on his debts, he bought whatever he wanted — real estate, art, newspapers, magazines — on credit, and delegated Edward Clark, who now looked after his as well as Phoebe's funds, to find the money to meet his obligations. When he had exhausted his own credit, he borrowed more by getting his mother to cosign his loans and mortgages. "Will worries her — with his investments," Orrin Peck wrote his sister in 1914, "too many of them that don't pay — some of them at a loss of over $125,000 a month — Think of it if you can — I never knew there was so much money in the world — and always looking for her to sign for him — It is simply killing her." In 1915, Hearst, who already owed his mother $722,000, borrowed an additional $556,000 from her. In 1916, he borrowed another $350,000, bringing his total debt to nearly $2 million. Phoebe's response was to write off the old debt of $722,000.[15]

Though Hearst was deeply in debt, it was not because his publishing empire was not earning a great deal of money. His newspapers, especially the older ones in New York and San Francisco, had finally been put on a paying basis. His magazines, particularly *Good Housekeeping* and *Cosmopolitan*, were doing quite well. The Hearst publishing empire had also discovered the benefits of syndication. To supply his newspapers with news, features, editorials, photographs, and the Sunday comics, Hearst had established his own rudimentary wire and feature services. By the mid-1900s, he had begun to sell those services to subscribers in cities without Hearst newspapers. In Washington, D.C., his representatives, operating out of the Munsey building, claimed that they gathered and distributed advance copies of speeches, reports, and "other documents of important character" to "two hundred morning and evening daily papers . . . from Boston to San Francisco and Portland, Oregon." By 1908 the Hearst Sunday comics were appearing in more than eighty newspapers in fifty cities. In the spring of 1909, Hearst formed the International News Service (I.N.S.) to coordinate these syndication services. In 1915, he directed Moses Koenigsberg, a man with an ego as large as his boss's — and a girth even larger — to split off a separate feature service, which Koenigsberg, rearranging the letters of his own name, incorporated as the King Feature Service.[16]

Eddie Hatrick, who was in charge of photo syndication for I.N.S., had purchased a moving-picture camera for himself in 1911 or 1912 to experiment with news pictures. Pathé, the French company which was at the time the world's largest movie producer, had already introduced an American edition of its newsreel, the Pathé Weekly, in the summer of 1911; the Vitagraph company had followed almost immediately with the Vitagraph Monthly of Current Events. Neither Pathé nor Vitagraph nor any of their competitors succeeded in making money. It cost a great deal to gather quality location footage, and timely distribution remained a serious problem. Still, Hatrick was not discouraged. In 1913, he took moving pictures of Woodrow Wilson's inauguration and sold them to Harry Warner, a future founder of Warner Brothers, who got them into the theaters the day after the inauguration. I.N.S. earned a profit of $2,000 from the venture, thereby demonstrating to W. R. that there existed a lucrative market for moving news pictures. Hatrick was authorized to enter into negotiations with Colonel William Selig, a small-time producer of fiction and topical films in Chicago, to produce Hearst-Selig "news reels."[17]

Hearst and his executives at I.N.S. had every expectation of succeeding where their predecessors had failed. The Hearst name had, by the early 1910s, achieved the status of a brand name signifying sharp, snappy, accessible, and entertaining news and features. Attaching "Hearst" to the title of a "news reel" and advertising that reel in the Hearst papers would introduce the new medium to millions of potential viewers who, it was hoped, would then pressure their local theaters to subscribe to the service. The advertising for the Hearst news pictures implied strongly that while other companies might fake their news pictures, the Hearst-Selig News Pictorial could be counted on to get the true story because it was "operated by the trained news gatherers of Hearst's great International News Service which covers the entire globe." "No such combination of the best trained newspapermen in the world, working hand in hand with a matchless producing company, has ever before been known," read an advertisement in *Motion Picture World.* "No staging, no make-believe, no 'play acting' — just the actual drama of life with its heroes, unconscious of their audience, snapped in the great crises of the world's events and their every look, every gesture, every movement brought from the uttermost ends of the earth and flashed upon your theatre screen."[18]

With loyal newspaper and magazine readers in every section of the country, the Hearst publications controlled a national network capable of reaching more Americans on a regular basis than any other advertising medium, especially on Sundays, when circulation picked up and the paper, instead of being discarded, was kept around for the whole family to read during the following week. The fact that the Hearst papers were reaching millions of Americans every Sunday — not the ten million Hearst claimed, but a very substantial number — was not lost on the moving-picture industry. While Hearst was starting up his newsreel with Selig, Pathé entered into a partnership with him to publicize its films. We don't know what the financial arrangements were, but it is likely that Pathé paid a premium to get the Hearst papers to run "novelizations" of its forthcoming films as Sunday features. "Pathé Pictures and the Hearst Papers," read the double-page ad in the February 28, 1914, issue of *Moving Picture World.* "The greatest combination ever effected in the Business, *Pictures* and real *publicity*. By an exclusive arrangement with the world's greatest newspaper organization Pathé Pictures' stories will be told in the Hearst papers the same day they are released. Let your patrons know you run these films."

The following month, Pathé and Hearst coproduced *The Perils of Pauline,* starring Pearl White as a young girl whose ambition is to become a serious writer. For twenty episodes, Pearl/Pauline literally chases her dream — and is chased by her departed father's male secretary who is trying to steal her inheritance. The film was shot and edited by the Wharton Brothers in Ithaca, New York, an ideal location for filming "cliffhangers" because of its own steep cliffs, perilous waterfalls, and rushing rivers. Hearst took an interest in the project from its inception.[19]

Morrill Goddard, his Sunday editor, who was asked to recommend a writer for the project, suggested his brother, Charles, a New York playwright. Charles prepared a 500-word synopsis which his brother edited. Then the two of them took it to Hearst at the Clarendon. Hearst had a number of questions and some suggestions, including, it seems, the title for the serial. On leaving Hearst, according to John Winkler, a Hearst biographer, "Charles Goddard remembered that a copy of the outline had not been left with Mr. Hearst. 'Oh, he doesn't need a copy,' commented Morrill Goddard confidently. 'He has one in his memory.' Weeks later, after the entire script had been completed, Mr. Hearst reminded the author that he had never done anything about the spirit of an Egyptian Princess which, in an early episode, had emerged from a mummy case. Although of minor importance this was the only loose end the playwright had forgotten to tie up." When the scripting was completed, Hearst turned his attention to the filming of the serial. In mid-April, a photograph of the Chief in his wide-brimmed black Stetson and long black overcoat "watching the making" of one of the episodes appeared in the *New York Dramatic Mirror*.[20]

Though *The Perils of Pauline* was neither the first nor the most accomplished of the serials, it is still the best known, and established Pearl White, until then the almost anonymous heroine of dozens of Westerns, as a leading Hollywood star. The free publicity given it in Hearst's newspapers had a great deal to do with the serial's success. On the day before each serial episode was introduced in the theaters, the Hearst papers carried the illustrated story of that episode as a Sunday feature. When the entire serial had been released, Hearst's International Publishers published the complete narrative as a hardcover book. Alan Dale, Hearst's theater critic, "reviewed" the episodes in his newspapers. The reviews were then recycled as trade-journal advertisements, under the headline "More Than Ten Million People Read the Story Every Sunday." As an added incentive to get his readers to see his serial, Hearst offered thousands of dollars in prize money to those who correctly answered questions about the episodes.[21]

Like other Hearst products, the Hearst-Pathé serials were bigger, bolder, brighter, and more exaggerated than anything viewers had seen before — with more thrills, stunts, and chases, plus a spectacular cliffhanger ending every week. First as Pauline, then in three separate serials as Elaine (*Exploits of Elaine, New Exploits of Elaine,* and *Romance of Elaine*), Pearl White traveled across the world by every imaginable means of transportation, including airships, balloons, racing cars, and yachts, fighting off an assortment of pirates, gypsies, sailors, cowhands, renegade Indians, mad scientists, Clutching Hands, and poisonous snakes. In the final *Elaine* series, scripted while Europe was at war, Pearl White was pitted against Marius Del Mar, played by Lionel Barrymore, a villainous foreigner who was trying to destroy America's coastal defenses and conquer the nation.[22]

As soon as the series was completed, Hearst and his film executives began scripting their second "war" serial. *Patria,* starring Irene Castle, would be filmed in 1916 and distributed to the theaters in early 1917.

The Hearst name was omnipresent in the nation's movie theaters in the mid-1910s. He not only produced weekly newsreels and serial films, but had become a supplier of animated films, or cartoons, that were based on his Sunday comic characters. Winsor McCay, whom Hearst had hired away from the *New York Herald* in 1911, had earlier tried to make and distribute animated films based on the characters he drew for Hearst. When W. R. found out, he was enraged with McCay not only for moonlighting but for exploiting a product that Hearst had paid for and owned. In December 1915, when Hearst signed a new agreement with Vitagraph to coproduce and distribute his newsreels, he agreed to provide animated shorts to follow the news items and set up his own animation studio at 729 Seventh Avenue in New York City, with Gregory La Cava, the future director of *My Man Godfrey* and other feature films, to manage it. One by one, with the help of the best animators in the business, Hearst turned Maggie and Jiggs, the Katzenjammer Kids, Krazy Kat and Ignatz Mouse, Happy Hooligan, Maude the Mule, Parcel Post Pete, Judge Rummy, Joys and Glooms, Jerry on the Job, and Tad's Daffydils into moving-picture stars.[23]

IV

Of War and Peace

❧ 14 ❧

"A War of Kings"

"THE WAR IN EUROPE seems to us in America one of the most terrible and one of the most unreasonable things that has ever happened in the world," Hearst cabled Lord Northcliffe, publisher of the London *Times,* and Lord Nurnham, publisher of the *London Daily Telegraph,* in early September 1914.[1]

"This is a war of kings," he informed his countrymen in a signed editorial on September 3, "brought on by the assassination of a king's nephew, who is of no more actual importance to modern society than the nephew of any other individual, citizen or subject, in all Europe. . . . In the histories of more enlightened ages, the rulers responsible for this war will not be described as heroes, but as homicidal maniacs, as traitors to the sacred trust solemnly imposed upon them to promote the happiness and protect the lives of their people. There is no glory in murder and robbery, and war is but organized authorized piracy and manslaughter."

That the European powers had been unable to settle their differences short of war was proof positive that the Old World was mad. Neutrality was the only sane option for the United States. This was Hearst's position, and, he was sure, that of the American people. "The allied newspapers, publications and news services controlled and directed by Mr. Hearst KNOW the sentiments and feelings and opinions of the American people, day by day, as no one else knows them," his editorial pages would proclaim on January 5, 1916. Hearst saw his role to be that of a clairvoyant, bringing to the surface, prearticulating, and giving voice to an often inchoate and unorganized public opinion. It was his responsibility to discern what the people thought and then to disseminate that thought back to the people and forward to their governments. To shirk such responsibility in the face of world crisis was unthinkable. He was the people's tribune, their intermediary with Washington and the capitals of Europe.

In early September, Hearst asked Lords Northcliffe and Nurnham in London to join with him in using the power of a united press to stop the European war while it was still in its infancy. The press, and only the press, could "end this war, and end all wars," Hearst wrote his English counterparts in a letter he published on his own front pages on September 10, 1914. "I think the press can appeal to the people, to your people, to our people and to all other people, as no other influence can. I believe that if the appeal is made now to the press of all nations, and by the press of all nations, the war can be stopped and will be stopped."

There being no reply from London, Hearst went ahead and launched his own peace offensive with huge open-air rallies in Golden Gate Park in San Francisco and at Grant's Tomb in Manhattan. Attending the New York rally were clergymen, politicians, representatives of pacifist organizations, the Sixty-Ninth Regiment band, and three hundred girls from Washington Irving High School who sang "'The Star-Spangled Banner,' 'Angel of Peace,' and other songs appropriate to the occasion. . . . All the girls carried flowers, which they laid at the tomb," the *New York Times* reported the next morning.[2]

Though President Wilson had called for neutrality — and Hearst applauded him for it — no one opposed the war with Hearst's fervor. As a transplanted Californian and a student of history, he possessed a unique perspective on global politics. The war in Europe was, he explained to his readers on September 3, "that most dreadful of all wars — a civil war." No matter which side won, Western civilization would be the loser, and Japan and Asia the victors.

Hearst feared no European power as much as he did Japan. Ever since the victory of the Japanese in the Russo-Japanese War of 1905, Hearst and his newspapers had been warning their readers in San Francisco to beware of the "yellow menace." In September of 1905, the *Examiner* had, according to the historian Roger Daniels, "printed a cartoon showing a Japanese soldier casting his shadow across the Pacific onto California." A little more than a year later, on December 20, 1906, the front page of the *Examiner* alerted San Franciscans to the presence of "Japanese spies" in their midst.

JAPAN SOUNDS OUR COASTS
Brown Men Have
Maps and Could
Land Easily

Now, in September of 1914, Hearst renewed his warnings and extended them to the rest of the nation. Japan, he reminded his readers over and over again, had a world-class navy, had established beachheads in the Pacific, in Hawaii, and on the American West Coast, and was poised to extend its sphere of influence west to Europe and east to North America. It was imperative, he warned his readers, that warfare among the Occidental nations cease before Europe was weakened to the point where it was no longer able to defend itself. It was even more imperative that the Americans remain neutral so as to conserve their resources for the forthcoming battle with the Japanese for supremacy in the Pacific.[3]

While Hearst had, for the moment, put his presidential ambitions on hold, he intended to play a dominant role in setting his nation's foreign policy from his vantage point as the nation's leading publisher. His immediate objective was to end the hostilities in Europe but, if that proved impossible, to at the very least keep the United States out of war. If, in pursuit of those objectives, circulation had to be sacrificed, so be it.

Hearst never shied away from sensation-grabbing headlines that might increase circulation, but he refused to be a pawn of the British and French propaganda offices and run the stories of German atrocities in Belgium which they were peddling, with great success, to American newspapers. "It would be much more complimentary to our national intelligence and information," he wrote in a February 2, 1915, editorial, "if American publications and American citizens would drop sentimental talk about 'martyred little peoples,' 'Huns at the gates' . . . and all that sort of manufactured excuse, and recognize the truth that Europe's struggle is simply a scramble of Europe's financiers, military and naval aristocracies and throned rulers to rob one another of trade, profit and territory."[4]

When, in the late summer and autumn of 1914, Europe's young men marched off to war, it was universally believed, as the English historian A. J. P. Taylor has written, "that it would be an affair of marches and great battles, quickly decided. It would be over by Christmas." By the spring, those assumptions had been discarded. As both sides settled into a war of attrition, each stepped up its efforts to deprive the other of the food and military supplies that were essential to sustain life on the home front and the battlefield. The British, with their stronger navy, had an easier time establishing their blockade and interdicting American trade with the Germans. The Germans were forced to use the threat of their U-boats to slow American trade with the Allies.[5]

On May 7, 1915, after repeated warnings, a German U-boat sank the British ocean liner *Lusitania*, which was carrying a cargo of munitions as well as 128 American passengers. President Wilson responded immediately by demanding that Germany cease its U-boat campaign. Secretary of State Bryan insisted that the president also protest the British blockade. When Wilson resisted, Bryan resigned, becoming at that moment a hero in the Hearst papers for standing up to the British.[6]

The Hearst papers, on May 8, 1915, denounced the German attack on the *Lusitania* as "a deed of wholesale murder," but they also condemned British calumny and harangued Wilson for not doing enough for peace. Almost alone among American newspapers — Colonel Robert McCormick's *Chicago Tribune* being the dominant exception — Hearst's editorials argued that the American government had no right to demand that Germany cease its submarine warfare while the British maintained their blockade.

Convinced now that he was fighting on the side of the angels against not only the president and his cabinet, but against the business and banking interests that required an English victory to protect their investments, Hearst and his papers opposed granting loans to the British or permitting American manufacturers to sell them armaments. Alone on the parapets, fighting a holy war to protect the peace from the alliance of Anglophiliac politicians and murderously greedy manufacturers and bankers, Hearst employed every resource he controlled to frighten the American people into agreement with him. The cartoonist Winsor McCay was reassigned to the editorial page where, under the supervision of Arthur Brisbane, he drew almost a cartoon a day, posing wistful Uncle Sams, stoic Founding Fathers, animalized Japanese warlords, and grasping top-hatted businessmen in front of nightmarish Gothic landscapes of war and devastation. Hearst portrayed his call for peace as the only just, the only moral, the only Christian position in a world gone mad with war. McCay's cartoon on March 9, 1916, portrayed Jesus with uplifted arms. "Let Us Nobly Serve Ourselves and Mankind by Organizing Peace," read the caption.

As the war progressed, Hearst's anti-English, pro-German news coverage and editorials left him increasingly isolated. Nat Ferber, a reporter at the *American,* recalled in his autobiography that in 1916,

> one had need of great fortitude even to serve him. His delivery men were greeted by bonfires made of the papers they were attempting to distribute. As for the Hearst reporter, few were the assignments on which his ears didn't ring with the abuse heaped upon him.
>
> "You work for that man Hearst," was the usual greeting. "Get the hell out of here."
>
> Usually this was followed by the slamming of the door in the reporter's face.[7]

The more Hearst's coverage outraged the majority of the population, the more popular he became among immigrant New York voters. To the German-American community he was a hero for his political views and his continued publication of a German-language newspaper. The Jewish community remained in his camp because of his vigorous protests against Russian anti-Semitism. His popularity among Irish-Americans soared as he assailed the British and celebrated the Irish nationalist Sir Roger Casement, whom he compared to John Hancock and John Adams, and other signers of the Declaration of Independence. When Casement was hanged by the British as a spy, the Hearst papers' eulogy for their hero so outraged Edith Wharton that she tried to get out of a contract with *Cosmopolitan,* which had bought the rights to serialize her new novel, *Summer.*[8]

In October of 1916, the English government, charging that Hearst's European war correspondents had deliberately falsified their dispatches, denied his International News Service the use of the British mails or cables to transmit reports to the United States. "I will apologize for nothing, retract nothing, alter nothing," Hearst responded in an open letter published in all his newspapers:

> The act of the English censors is wholly unjust and unjustifiable. . . . I am convinced that the exclusion of the International News Service is . . . due to the independent and wholly truthful attitude of the Hearst papers in their news and editorial columns. . . . I will take a personal pleasure in giving our readers and clients the most complete information of the utmost truth and value, and in getting it from more trustworthy sources than the biased and bigoted English censorship affords.[9]

Barred from transmitting his dispatches from England, Hearst had no choice now but to rely on his correspondents in Germany to provide the bulk of his war coverage. William Bayard Hale, the former *New York Times* reporter who had worked for the Wilson administration in Mexico and was now chief German correspondent for the International News Service, made an arrangement with the German government to transmit I.N.S. dispatches by "wireless" from a radio station in Nauheim to a receiving station in Sayville, Long Island. German officials willingly supplied Hale, not only with access to government officials in Berlin, but with moving pictures for his newsreel service. One of the first full-length war documentaries shown in the United States was the *History of the World's Greatest War in Motion Pictures,* assembled and produced by Hearst-Selig from German footage.[10]

The German government was so intent on getting its pictures into

American theaters that when in mid-1915 demand appeared to slacken, it secretly established its own company — the American Correspondent Film Company — to publicize, distribute, and exhibit its films. The man in charge of the American operation, Dr. Karl Fuehr, wrote to Berlin in August and again in October of 1915 that he was in touch with the Hearst organization

> in order to bring about an agreement, which would make available to us without any cash outlay the colossal power of the Hearst papers in the United States for our film matters. . . . The advantages of such a combination under our control are indeed so apparent in view of the well-known power and executive ability of Mr. Hearst and his chief associates that we do not need to discuss them. It is sufficient to mention that Hearst personally owns seven of the most important American newspapers in the East as well as the West, including also one well known paper published in German. . . . An especially interesting point is that the Hearst papers are controlled by a 100% American and are themselves out and out American. They are read by all classes of the population and by all nationalities which will be especially useful to us in the quiet and widespread dissemination of our ideas.

Though Hearst agreed to distribute the German war footage and share half the profits, before signing any agreement he wanted full assurance that he would have a monopoly on German war pictures. Fuehr contacted Berlin to see if Hearst's terms were acceptable, adding that they appeared to him to be quite justifiable on account of the great power possessed by the Hearst papers. In the end, for reasons that are not entirely clear, the deal was never consummated.[11]

Instead Hearst and Edward Hatrick, who was now in charge of his moving pictures, sought to arrange for their own cameraman, Nelson E. Edwards, to take war pictures from behind the German lines. In December of 1915, Hearst wrote a personal note to Count Johann Heinrich von Bernstorff, the German ambassador to Washington, asking for his help in the matter. The two met several times at the Clarendon and apparently got along quite well. Von Bernstorff was, like Hearst, very much a bon vivant. He was already on good terms with many publishers and politicians and was having an affair with Cissy Patterson, whose family owned and operated the *Chicago Tribune*.[12]

Von Bernstorff needed Hearst to broadcast to Americans the message that the Germans were not brutes; Hearst needed von Bernstorff to gain access to German news and moving pictures. Both got what they wanted. Thanks to von Bernstorff's assistance, Nelson Edwards was granted permission to cross the border from Holland into Germany to collect war footage for the "Hearst News Pictorial."[13]

Though Hearst made full use of his access to German officials to disseminate the German side of the story, he did not neglect material from other sources. As Count von Bernstorff explained in a confidential report to Berlin in December of 1916, the Hearst newspapers, though friendly to Germany, could not "be regarded as blindly pro-German, for they publish a good deal that can hardly be desirable for us."[14] Side by side with pro-German dispatches from William Bayard Hale in Berlin, the Hearst front pages reported on German espionage rings in the United States and published anti-German diatribes like the one by Rudyard Kipling that appeared on February 7, 1916, under the headline, "Exterminate Entire German Species, Urges Kipling."

These reports from the front, pro-German or pro-English, were all written from a particular point of view. The Hearst papers did not subscribe to the view that "objectivity" in a journalist was either possible or desirable. It certainly did not make for readable stories. When questioned after the war by a Senate subcommittee investigating German propaganda efforts, Hearst's senior editor, Bradford Merrill, acknowledged that Dr. Hale had been "sent to Berlin . . . expressly to write the German side of the war, precisely as the *American* sent other distinguished correspondents to get [other] sides of the war. It was Dr. Hale's duty to send the German Government's own interpretation of every important event and the views of the foremost German statesmen."[15]

What Hearst refused to recognize through the early years of the war was that by unapologetically presenting the German side of the story, he was treading on dangerous ground. If in New York and Chicago, Irish, German, and Russian-Jewish immigrants saluted his anti-British, pro-German coverage and editorials, elsewhere he was viewed as consorting with, if not supporting, a future enemy.

As long as his reporters and editorialists wrote as he wanted them to, few questions were asked about sources or motivations. Hearst never much cared how his reporters got their stories. What counted was the final product. If, in the 1890s and early 1900s, he had surrounded himself with radicals, progressives, and not a few socialists, he now brought into his inner circle writers, editors, and businessmen who were as pro-German as he was. What he did not know was that several of them were in the pay of the German government. Karl Fuehr, with whom he had negotiated for German newsreel footage, was not the owner of an independent film company, but a German government employee. Bolo Pacha, the French newspaper publisher whom Hearst entertained at a special dinner at Sherry's in March of 1916 and invited to his apartment to discuss newsprint contracts, was a German agent sent to New York to collect funds to establish a pro-German newspaper in Paris. William Bayard Hale, his chief International News Service correspondent in Germany, had been paid by the German government since the war began.

While assailing the Wilson administration for being too bellicose in Europe, Hearst continued to attack it for being too pacifist in Mexico. Nothing short of armed intervention, he was convinced, would secure a lasting peace in Mexico and permanent protection for American landholders and investors. The revolution which had been launched against Porfirio Díaz in 1910 had entered a new stage in 1914–15. Venustiano Carranza had succeeded General Huerta as president, but he too had been unable to restore peace or unify the nation. His major opponent was General Francisco Pancho Villa whose army was strongest in the northern provinces, including Chihuahua where Hearst's Babicora ranch was located. In December of 1915, Villa and his army, under siege by forces loyal to President Carranza, seized and looted the Hearst ranch. Five of Hearst's employees were taken prisoner and one, an American bookkeeper, was killed before the rebels were ousted. Hearst instructed his editors, through Than Vanneman Ranck, who was in charge of foreign coverage, to condemn the Wilson government "for its failure to do anything in Mexico," but not to mention the Hearst family holdings there.[16]

When in early March 1916 Pancho Villa raided Columbus, New Mexico, and killed seventeen Americans before retreating into the Chihuahua mountains, President Wilson ordered Major-General "Black Jack" Pershing to pursue him into Mexico. The Hearst papers applauded the incursion as the first step toward a full-scale invasion that would eventually lead to the conquest and annexation of Mexico. "At Long Last Our Flag Has Been Saluted," read the March 10 *New York American* headline. Pursuing the story as only it could, the Hearst organization assigned a newsreel cameraman to the Pershing forces and enjoyed an exclusive on moving-picture coverage until the competition complained of the monopoly to the secretary of war, who directed the Hearst organization to share its footage.[17]

For the next few months, the Hearst papers, while insisting on American neutrality in Europe, called for continued involvement in the Philippines and armed intervention in Mexico. "Our army should go forward into Mexico first, to rescue Americans, and, secondly to redeem Mexicans,"

Hearst declared in a signed front-page editorial on May 3. "Our right in Mexico is the right of HUMANITY."

His demands for intervention were so bellicose and his opposition to the Wilson administration so strident that the Bureau of Investigation in Washington, the forerunner of the F.B.I., launched an investigation of rumors that Hearst, either on his own or in cooperation with German agents, was smuggling arms into Mexico to support a counterrevolutionary coup. In the fall and summer of 1916, the Bureau sent undercover agents to San Simeon, Pleasanton, and Chihuahua, Mexico, to look for arms and ammunition stockpiled for shipment to Mexico. The agent assigned to San Simeon got himself hired as a ranch hand so that he could ride over the thousands of acres of Hearst land to locate any hidden ammunition storage areas. After searching the entire ranch — or so he said — making small talk over campfires with Hearst's ranch hands, and investigating the San Simeon wharves, the agent reported no sign of the ammunition. Agents sent to Hearst's holdings in northern California and Mexico also found no evidence of smuggled arms. But they kept looking nonetheless.[18]

Hearst's contempt for Wilson was so personal and so intense that he was prepared to do anything possible to deny him reelection. Overlooking for the moment that his old nemesis Theodore Roosevelt was more adamant than Wilson on the subject of American support for the British against the Germans, Hearst tried to persuade him to challenge Wilson for the presidency. Though Hearst, unlike T. R., was unalterably opposed to the United States entering the war in Europe, he was as staunch an advocate of "preparedness" as the ex-president. Hearst was convinced that the best, perhaps the only, deterrent to aggression or invasion was a strong army and navy. Like Roosevelt, he never let an opportunity pass to assail President Wilson for neglecting his duties as commander in chief.

In April of 1916, the Chief asked Roosevelt to lunch. T. R. graciously declined, inviting Hearst to visit him instead. "I look forward to seeing you," he telegrammed Hearst, as if they were old, dear friends. "Meanwhile, I am going to commit the frightful misdeed by sending you a copy of my book. This is a violation of the principle laid down to me by my uncle . . . many years ago when he said he had done a good many mean things in the course of his life, but he had never asked anyone to read one of his books."[19]

Hearst responded immediately with the same courtly grace. "You do not have to ask me to read your books. I read them without being asked. I am particularly pleased, however, to have the book you mentioned as a present from you. I am looking forward to our talk on Wednesday next."[20]

The friendly exchange of messages continued all spring, with Hearst at one point inviting Roosevelt to write for his newspapers or, failing that, to choose "any one on our papers who you propose as representative . . . to report your acts and utterances fully faithfully and sympathetically."[21]

In June, Hearst assigned himself to cover the Republican national convention in Chicago, hoping that he might be able to engineer a Roosevelt nomination. The Republicans instead nominated Supreme Court Justice Charles Evans Hughes, who had defeated Hearst for governor ten years earlier. W. R. toyed with the notion of supporting Hughes against Wilson and on July 1 instructed Joseph A. Moore, the Canadian publisher whom he had hired to run *Good Housekeeping* and then made the head of his magazine division, to prepare a series of articles on Hughes, including a "nice personality of Mr. Hughes and his family" for the October *Cosmopolitan*, an article on Mrs. Hughes for the September *Good Housekeeping*, and a third piece on Hughes for the August issue of *Hearst's*.

Hearst waited as long as he could before issuing a rather tepid endorsement of Wilson for reelection. No matter how much he despised him, he could not bring himself to openly support a Republican for the highest office in the land.[22]

With the European countryside transected by trenches, Hearst was forced to cancel his annual motor tour of Europe. Though his mother had very much hoped he would spend the summer of 1915 at her Pleasanton Hacienda, he deposited the two youngest boys instead and with Millicent, eleven-year-old George, his friend Orrin Peck who was visiting from Munich, and a small army of friends and servants, took the train south to the family's cattle ranch in the Santa Lucia mountains near the old whaling village of San Simeon.

The Chief, as he was now referred to by those who worked for him — W. R. was used only by his closest friends and associates — took vacations seriously. Though he had never been willing or able to plan anything far in advance, that did not mean that any detail was left to chance. Every excursion was carefully planned, the motor routes laid out, the private railway cars leased, the rooms booked, the servants and chauffeurs retained before he and his party arrived. He never traveled alone, but only in the company of a full entourage of family and friends, whose way he paid and whose itinerary he chose.

His Los Angeles editor, Dent Roberts, with Mrs. Roberts and her secretary, had been delegated to make the preparations for his trip to San Simeon. Though this was to be a camping vacation, Hearst did not expect anyone to have to rough it. On the contrary, he imported all the luxuries of the best European hotels to "Camp Hill," the elongated ridge, 1,600 feet above sea level, where he intended to pitch his tents. The preparations for a Hearst camping vacation were so extensive that, according to his cousin Anne Apperson Flint, they "upset the whole running of the ranch. He'd call off the cowboys to bring horses and wait on him and to set up this establishment. . . . When he came out there in the summer . . . he arrived and commanded."²³

By the time Hearst and his party arrived for their summer 1915 stay, the cowboys had erected a small village of Venetian-style canvas tents, the size of cottages, with brightly colored awnings. One of them was set aside for the dining room; the others, with living and sleeping quarters, were fully furnished. Oriental rugs were placed over the wooden floors. "The floored tents were all up and dining table set," Orrin Peck wrote his sister in a letter describing their arrival at the top of the hill. "Mrs. Dent Roberts's secretary had been here a week and got things in shape. Cooks and all. . . . Our drinking water is brought up every morning also ice from the Ranch House. . . . Dear old Will is very sweet and kind — looks about 35 — (days when he's not worried over telegrams or dunning bills)."²⁴

The more time Hearst spent at San Simeon — and he would vacation there through the war years — the more he grew to love the land. In 1917, he wrote Phoebe from Camp Hill,

> I am out here to jam as much health into my system as possible, and I really feel, Mother, that this is the place to do it. I can take long rides over these beautiful hills; I can camp out in the pretty spots beside the creeks, in the valley, or in the little hollows on the mountain tops; I can go fishing in the streams, or fishing and boating on the sea. It seems to me that anything that can be done anywhere is all assembled and ready to be done on the ranch. I get a great vacation here, and I need it, as you know. I get great enjoyment here, it is a relief to the mind, and I get further away from business than I would anywhere else. . . . I feel so immensely better today than I have felt at any time for the past three months, or, indeed, for the past year, that I know I am going to be able to do everything in a few days and get the usual benefit from my vacation here. . . . We like the all-outdoors part of it. We go to bed between 9 and 10 o'clock, get up between 6:30 and 7 — 6:30 this morning — and make the most of the long day and good solid sleep at night. It is great stuff, and I really feel that NY is like one big office building and that you do not really get out to breathe good air and get good sunshine until you get at least west of the Mississippi.²⁵

"I love this ranch," W. R. continued, in another note to his mother, apologizing once again for taking Millicent to San Simeon instead of spending the summer with her at Pleasanton. Although the Hacienda was beautiful in its own way, it did not, he tried to explain to Phoebe, afford him the same kind of total escape that he found at San Simeon:

> I love the sea and I love the mountains and the hollows in the hills and the shady places in the creeks and the fine old oaks and even the hot brushy hillsides — full of quail — and the canyons full of deer. It's a wonderful place. I would rather spend a month here than any place in the world. And as a *sanitarium!* Mother it has Nauheim, Carlsbad, Vichy, Wiesbaden, French Lick, Saratoga, and every other so-called health resort beaten a nautical mile.[26]

At the age of fifty-two, W. R. was to be a father again, this time, he hoped, of a baby girl. "We think Phoebe or Elbert, we can't tell which, will arrive about Christmas and we want you surely to be here for the festivities," he wrote his mother on October 22, 1915. Six weeks later, on December 1, he wrote again, "We cannot call them Phoebe because they are not of that persuasion but we could call them Phoebus and Apollo for just at sunrise two of the loveliest boys you have ever seen were born to Mr. and Mrs. William Randolph Hearst."[27]

The twins, Randolph and Elbert, whose name would later be changed to David, spent their first winter and spring in New York before being shipped out West to their grandmother for the summer and fall. As usual, Phoebe would not part with them as promised and Hearst had to take the train West in November to retrieve them. En route, he telegraphed mock instructions to the babies to prepare for his arrival:

> Get up early and eat your bacon and eggs with your lonesome front teeth and meet us at Oakland Friday morning. This is Thanksgiving Day and you ought to be thankful that you have such a dear devoted Grandma, such kind nurses, such nice noisy brothers, such a handsome father, and such a loving mother. Here is long life and much happiness to you and to all. Now rise up on your hind legs, drink a bumper of imperial granum, look embarrassed and make a proper speech in reply. Say as Tiny Tim said, God Bless us every one.

The telegram was signed "Pop."[28]

Although his letters and telegrams were like this one, full of good cheer, there were problems in New York which Phoebe knew nothing of. Millicent Willson, the adoring, compliant sixteen-year-old chorus girl that W. R. had fallen in love with twenty years before, had matured into a formidable woman of thirty-five, with five children, the largest apartment on the West Side to preside over, and social aspirations of her own. As Bill, Jr. recalled years later, his father and mother were becoming "incompatible. . . . She liked Society with a capital 'S' and he didn't . . . And he was bored with the kind of parties she liked." While W. R. still held society in contempt and dressed his chauffeur in a plain business suit, Millicent had dismissed her male servants when they refused to wear liveries.[29]

W. R. was very much a man about town, a habitué of what would later be known as café society, that promiscuous mixing of Broadway, society, and newspaper folk in the city's nightclubs and after-hours joints. When in town, he never missed a night at the theater. "He always was a stage-door Johnny, just always," his son Bill Jr. recalled in his oral history. "He always used to take us backstage at the Ziegfeld *Follies*." After the theater and a visit backstage, there were dinners at Delmonico's or Sherry's or Rector's and late-night parties in the theater district or West Side apartments like that of the actress Elsie Janis and her mother. Hearst attended many and hosted a few himself in the rooms he leased at the Bryant Park Studios at 40th Street and Sixth Avenue within walking distance of the Broadway theaters.[30]

It was at these gatherings that men about town, like Hearst, met Broadway's most eligible actresses and chorus girls. The girls of the chorus were fresh, young, all-American (no blacks or Jews), fun-loving, athletic. According to the historian Lewis Erenberg, they no longer embodied the "image of sinful womanhood," but instead "combined a sensuality with niceness."[31]

The attraction of such girl-women for middle-aged, overworked, overweight businessmen like Hearst was obvious. And vice versa. Though many of the girls lived with their parents, as Millicent and Anita Willson had, they sought the freedom that could only come with an income greater than their wages from the chorus line. It cost money to dress well, to go out — and to appear as glamorous offstage as you did onstage. The best solution for the girls who were not going to become headliners was to locate a suitable "patron" among the stage-door Johnnies that came calling and sent their cards and gifts backstage.[32]

Sometime after Christmas of 1915, not many weeks after Millicent had given birth to the twins, W. R. Hearst came calling on Marion Davies, an eighteen-year-old chorus girl who was performing in the new Irving Berlin musical, *Stop! Look! Listen!*, at the Globe Theater on 46th Street and Broadway, six blocks from his bachelor studio.

Marion, at eighteen, was already a veteran of the chorus line. The youngest daughter of a moderately successful Brooklyn lawyer, Bernard Douras, she had followed her older sisters Ethel and Reine into show business, borrowing the name Davies from Reine, who had adopted it first because it made for a much better stage name than Douras. In *Stop! Look! Lis-*

ten!, Marion was featured in the production number "The Girl on the Magazine Cover." While the male lead sang in front of a giant reproduction of a *Vogue* magazine cover, Marion and three other girls from the chorus walked off the page to join him in an elaborately staged song and dance number.[33]

The show opened in December of 1915. Hearst, who saw every musical comedy that played in the city, attended it with his friend and fellow publisher, Paul Bloch, who may have been dating Marion at the time. Bloch and Hearst sat in the second row of the orchestra section, Hearst's favorite seats. "In later years, Marion chose to forget that she was featured in a revue as early as 1915," her biographer, Fred Guiles, has written, "since it would have made her only fifteen years old by her calculations, but to a greater extent out of deference to Hearst. Their friendship was supposed to be secret that year of their meeting."[34]

"He sent me flowers and little gifts, like silver boxes or gloves or candy," Marion recalled in the taped reminiscences that were later published as *The Times We Had.* "I wasn't the only one he sent gifts to, but all the girls thought he was particularly looking at me . . . The next thing that happened — I was asked to have some special photographs made at Campbell's Studio." The photographs were for Hearst's Sunday theater section; Marion's mother had accompanied her to the studio and fixed her hair for her. "I had two or three pictures taken before I saw Mr. Hearst," Marion went on. "It was hard to see past the bright lights, and he was sitting right under the camera. He was dressed very conservatively, in a dark blue suit. If his suit had been in any other kind of color, I might have seen him sooner. . . . When we got out in the studio, Mr. Hearst had left. He hadn't meant any harm, and he owned Campbell's Studio. But he had the most penetrating eyes — honest, but penetrating eyes. He didn't have a harmful bone in his body. He just liked to be by himself and just look at the girls on the stage while they were dancing. I think he was a very lonesome man."[35]

There are other stories of Marion's and Hearst's first meeting, but in all of them, Hearst's approach is circuitous, never direct. However they met, by the spring of 1916 they were seeing each other regularly, at parties, dinners, and gatherings at Hearst's suite near the Broadway theaters.

Though Hearst had never been particularly good at keeping secrets about his private life, he tried hard this time. He did not want to hurt Millicent, nor did he want rumors of his relationship with Marion to get back to his mother. Unwilling to give up Marion, he had no choice but to learn to lead a double life. Occasionally those lives intersected, as he must have known they would. Anita Loos, who would later write screenplays for

Hearst and publish in his magazines the stories that would become the basis for her best-selling novel, *Gentlemen Prefer Blondes,* was present at one of these occasions:

> It was during the early stages of his romance with Marion. She and I had been seated to W. R.'s right and left at dinner in a hideaway he kept at the old Beaux Arts [Bryant Park Studios] apartment building. Now it so happened that I'd been asked by W. R.'s wife, Millicent, to dine the very following evening at the legitimate Hearst home on Riverside Drive. When dinner was announced I was embarrassed to find myself again seated next to W. R. But as I took my place he observed with the first twinkle I ever saw in those pale eyes of his, "Well, Nita, we seem to be meeting under rather different circumstances, don't we?"[36]

Marion was at the time eighteen years old, though she looked younger, with strawberry blond hair, worn long, in flowing curls. She was not a classical beauty — her nose was a bit too big, her teeth not perfect. But her bright blue eyes, her perfect complexion, a girlish vitality, and a flirtatious smile more than made up for such minor imperfections. She was relatively tall — about five foot six — and willowy thin, which may also have appealed to Hearst, who at fifty-two was becoming increasingly pear-shaped. Marion spoke with a noticeable stammer; it only added to her charms.

The first documentary evidence we have of their relationship is found in the theater pages of Hearst's *New York American,* where photographs and news items about Marion Davies, still a relatively unknown chorus girl, began to appear in early 1916. On February 7, Marion's photograph was published over a brief news item. "Rumor has it that Miss Marion Davies of the *Stop! Look! Listen!* company . . . may soon join the ranks of film beauties. Miss Davies coyly denies that she is going to be a photoplay star, but her friends declare otherwise." The following Sunday, the drama page included another photograph of "Miss Marion Davies of *Stop! Look! Listen!*" In May of 1916, a story in the *New York American* announced that because of Miss Davies' beauty and talent, she had been "the first of the new Follies beauty crop to be selected by Mr. Ziegfeld" for his upcoming show. She had, the article continued, shown such promise that Mr. Ziegfeld had "commissioned the librettist to write a special part for her in the book of the new production."[37]

From this point on, interviews, news items, and photographs of Marion Davies appeared regularly in the Sunday drama sections of the Hearst papers. Though Hearst may have been trying to be discreet, his relationship with Marion had to have been known to his editors, photographers, and reporters, who took every opportunity to report on Marion's blooming career.

As W. R. had become something of an authority on chorus girls — he had married one — there was nothing unusual in his calling the attention of his editors to a "pretty" face on Broadway. Hearst's drama pages were, in fact, crowded with photographs of actresses and chorus girls, puff pieces on their careers, and friendly reviews. In early 1915, before he ever met Marion Davies, he had directed his editors to publish only favorable dramatic reviews: "I am wholly averse to old style dramatic criticism and believe merely in dramatic reviews and interesting accounts of dramatic performances with only most kindly and considerate criticism of performances. In other words I don't want dramatic critic. I want dramatic reporter who will give entertaining account of performance, quote bright lines and consider on the whole the viewpoint of public rather than perverse view of a blasé dramatic critic."[38]

Even with his papers' penchant for photographing actresses and giving them favorable notices, the treatment afforded Miss Davies became remarkable. With the help of the favorable publicity she was receiving in the Hearst papers, Marion's career blossomed through 1916. Her name was not yet in lights, but she was on her way to becoming one of Broadway's better-known chorus girls. On October 8, 1916, Hearst's *New York American* carried a picture of Marion Davies while an item in the "Motion Picture Trade News and Studio Gossip" column listed her as one of the "fashion stars" who would be "posing in the latest creations for the Hearst International News Pictorial." Later that winter, when Marion and her friend Justine Johnstone were invited to audition for roles in *Oh, Boy*, a musical comedy by Guy Bolton and P. G. Wodehouse with a score by Jerome Kern, they arrived at the audition in a limousine, wearing mink coats and diamonds. When the show went on tour in the spring, Marion's hotel suites grew larger and larger as the company moved farther west. On the last stop of the tour, in Cleveland, Marion threw an extravagant cast party with champagne, caviar, a full buffet, and a five-piece orchestra for dancing. There was no doubt in anyone's mind as to who had paid for it.[39]

Although Hearst did all he could to promote Marion's career on Broadway and invited her to "pose" in his newsreels, he did not cast her in his serial films. She was too young, too inexperienced, and too unknown. As in his other businesses, he recruited experienced or "name" stars like Pearl White and Irene Castle.

Hearst did not begin producing moving pictures because he wanted to make a star of Marion, but because it made good business sense. Decades before the word synergy entered corporate discourse, Hearst was putting the concept to work, exploiting his products in several different media forms. His news stories were recycled in newsreel form — and vice versa; his Sunday comics were turned into animated cartoons; each episode of his serial films was "novelized," run serially as a Sunday newspaper feature, and then published in hardcover. The next step was to adapt the fiction he bought for his magazines for feature films and publicize those films in his newspapers and magazines.

In the summer of 1916, his International Film Service, which was already making serial films and weekly episodes of the "Hearst International News Pictorial," released its first feature film, *Jaffery,* under the Golden Eagle Feature label. The film had been produced by the Frohman Amusement Corporation. That fall, International Film Service released a second film, this one produced by the Superb Pictures Corporation.

In October of 1916, anxious to produce his own films instead of merely releasing those produced elsewhere, Hearst directed Joseph A. Moore, the head of his magazine division, to instruct his magazine editors to "get moving picture options on all stories and try to monopolize all best fiction and all best moving picture material." In December he wrote Moore again, emphasizing how important it was that they begin to corner the market on commercial magazine fiction: "A great story ought to make circulation and prestige for the magazine and to be valuable as a moving picture asset, and as a book asset thereafter."[40]

That fall, Hearst personally contacted D. W. Griffith, the most famous and successful producer and director in the country, with an offer "to start some sort of business arrangement." Though Griffith was unable or unwilling to enter into a partnership with Hearst, the Chief graciously promised that he would "do everything I can for *Intolerance* [Griffith's latest film] anyhow."[41]

Marion Davies was not a part of any of these early moving-picture ventures. She did not star or have a role in any of Hearst's serial films or in the four Golden Eagle features that were released by the International Film Service. Her first film, *Runaway Romany,* had been produced by her brother-in-law, George Lederer, and financed by Paul Bloch. Marion played Romany, a rich man's daughter kidnapped by gypsies. Though neither she nor the critics thought much of her acting, Hearst screened her film and found her performance promising enough to offer her a film contract for five hundred dollars a week for one year with an option. "I signed it," Marion remembered, "because on the stage I was only getting forty-five or fifty dollars a week."[42]

As a player in musical comedies and reviews, Marion had to spend a good deal of time on the road in places where Hearst could not easily visit her. As a film actress, she could work closer to home, in New York and New Jersey. This was, however, not the only reason why Hearst signed her to a film contract. To succeed in moving pictures, as he had succeeded in the newspaper and magazine business, he needed a leading lady to play the Mary Pickford–like roles that were popular with audiences. On screen, Marion radiated alternating images of fragile innocence and gritty independence, much like Pickford. Her stammer might have held her back on stage, but it would not be a problem in moving pictures that had not yet learned to speak.

W. R.'s affair with Marion Davies was played out against the backdrop of a European war which daily moved closer to American shores. In December of 1916, President Wilson responded to a German peace feeler by asking both Germany and England to publicly state their war aims so that he might mediate a peace settlement. When the Allies rejected Wilson's offer of mediation — the Germans had simply ignored it — the Hearst papers attacked their "veiled insult to the President of the United States." American entry into the European war now became a more distinct possibility.[43]

With no hope now for a negotiated peace, Ambassador von Bernstorff, on January 31, 1917, informed Secretary of State Robert Lansing that German U-boats were, the next day, going to renew their attacks on merchant vessels bound for the British Isles, including ships of neutral countries like the United States. The Germans recognized that by placing American vessels in harm's way they were forcing Wilson to declare war. Still, they expected that their blockade of England would bring the war in Europe to an end before the Americans were able to mobilize.

As American intervention in the war grew closer, the Hearst papers' editorial rhetoric grew more heated. Declaring that they spoke for the majority of "plain, every-day, hard-headed and clear-thinking Americans [who] are not deceived by cheap declamation and cheaper cant about Europe's war," the Hearst papers repeated over and over that neither Germany nor the American people wanted war. "Let Us Firmly Resolve That Under No Circumstances Will We Waste Our Wealth and Slaughter Our Youth in the Wars of European Alliances," declared the editorial headline on February 9, 1917. A week later, in a particularly strident editorial, "Let Those Who Have to Pay for War Decide Whether They Shall Go to War," the Hearst papers demanded that war not be declared until the people had been polled "upon the question [in a national referendum]. And the women should vote as well as the men." The advocates of war in Europe, the editorial contended, were aged politicians "Who Will Not Run the Slightest Risk" of getting hurt. Elihu Root, Roosevelt's secretary of state, Hearst's readers were reminded, though nineteen years of age in 1864 "did not enlist. . . . WHEN THE NATION'S LIFE WAS AT STAKE. . . . We protest against war being forced on the nation by men who had neither the patriotism nor the courage to fight for the nation in their own youth. The shirkers and slackers of 1861 have no right to be the jingoes of 1917."

From Palm Beach, where he was vacationing at The Breakers with his family, Hearst cabled Solomon Carvalho, who had run his newspaper empire since coming over from Pulitzer twenty years earlier, with daily instructions on the next morning's editorials. While he believed strongly that Germany's violation of American shipping rights as a neutral was not a cause for war, he dared not champion peace while German U-boats were attacking American ships. To cover himself against charges of disloyalty, he hid behind the flag, instructing his editors to "run little American flags to right and left of date lines on inside pages," print masthead titles in red, white, and blue, and run "the verses of the Star Spangled Banner as originally written" across the top of the editorial pages.[44]

As war with Germany was now all but inevitable, his editors scurried to protect themselves — and their chief — from charges of disloyalty or treason. Caleb Van Hamm, an editor at the New York American, urged Hearst by telegram in late February to "check or stop Hale dispatches [from Germany]. They come by wireless and surely are picked up. Despite your well-known attitude of neutrality these dispatches are so worded as to permit the interpretation that Berlin is dictating our policy. I fear we are drifting into a situation akin to the false McKinley one only accentuated many fold. With profound respect I urge we check Hale and all agencies that tend to throw discredit upon our declared attitude of sturdy Americanism."[45]

Van Hamm was right. Every dispatch from Germany was being forwarded by the navy from the radio station in Sayville, Long Island, to the Military Intelligence Division of the War Department and the Bureau of Investigation. The case against Hearst was being built, cable by cable.

❦ 15 ❦

"Hearst, Hylan, the Hohenzollerns, and the Habsburgs"

EARST GREETED AMERICA'S ENTRY into the European war by festooning his front and editorial pages with flags and opening "enlistment bureaus" in the "six great cities" his papers served. Still, he made it clear that this declaration of war, unlike the one against Spain in 1898, was not a cause for celebration.

As if from Mount Olympus, he and his newspapers looked down upon the war effort and saw only frailty, ignorance, and inevitable tragedy. Employing the rhetoric of defeatism, Hearst insisted that because successive administrations had failed to build the modern navy that he had been calling for editorially since 1898, the American war effort was doomed to failure. "It is no secret that we are almost wholly unprepared for real warfare," read the editorial published on April 3, one day after Wilson had called for a declaration of war. "That is no fault of the Hearst newspapers. We have argued and pleaded for preparedness for twenty years. Most of that time our reward was the sneers and the jeers of the unthinking and the foolish."

Given America's lack of preparation for war and the ever-present danger posed by the Japanese, Hearst argued strenuously against providing America's allies, particularly the British, with any material assistance. To leave America defenseless by shipping food, military supplies, and soldiers to fight a war in Europe, he declared on April 13, was nothing short of madness. "In these circumstances of uncertainty . . . there is only one possible course that is sensible, and that is to keep every dollar and every man and every weapon and all our supplies and stores AT HOME, for the defense of our own land, our own people, our own freedom, until that defense has been made ABSOLUTELY secure. After that we can think of others nations' troubles. But till then, America first!"

* * *

The official surveillance of Hearst that had begun the year before was stepped up now, as officials in the War Department and Bureau of Investigation looked for the "smoking gun" that would tie Hearst to the German government. When the Bureau received a report from Phoebe's niece, Anne Apperson Flint, who was staying with Phoebe while her husband served in the army, that five of her aunt's employees at her Pleasanton Hacienda were pro-German, agents from the Military Intelligence Division of the War Department were sent to investigate. When a tip was received that the two maps with "Arabic hieroglyphs" in a *New York American* cartoon might contain encoded information intended for the Germans, the Bureau of Investigation looked into it. When neighbors reported that Hearst's lawyer in Boston, Grenville MacFarland, had purchased a thousand rounds of ammunition, employed a German woman, and received phone calls from Washington, the Military Intelligence Division of the War Department instructed agents in Boston to initiate a full-scale investigation. When an anonymous letter was received in the San Francisco office of the Bureau of Investigation charging that the Hearst newspapers were being "subsidized by the German government and that the hanging of the American flag around the office of the *Examiner* is a mere bluff to divert suspicion," the Bureau assigned Customs Inspector Mencke to investigate. Mencke found nothing out of the ordinary. "The *Examiner's* office," he reported, "shows every evidence of being most loyal and it is giving their whole-hearted support to our Government. They have a recruiting station right in their office."[1] Though none of the rumors were ever substantiated, Hearst's enemies kept looking.

The first sign of trouble came from an entirely unexpected source. Six months before the declaration of war, Hearst's grandest serial film to date, *Patria,* had opened to generally good reviews and a strong box office. *Patria,* like so many other films produced in 1916, was a "preparedness" serial about a Pearl White–like adventuress who saved her dangerously unprepared country from an invading military force. Instead of being anti-Hun, like every other "preparedness" film, it was, as the *New York Telegraph* declared in its November 20 review, "frankly anti-Mexican and anti-Japanese in line with William Randolph Hearst's policies." The heroine of the story, Patria Channing, played by the ballroom dancer Irene Castle, is the sole survivor of a patriotic American family of munitions makers. When Japanese and Mexican spies incite a strike at her plant, she foils it by granting her workers' demands, in return for their agreement to volunteer for military training and stay away from foreign agents. In the final episode, "For the Flag," she and her men, armed with her weapons, turn back the invading Mexican cavalry, led by Japanese soldiers.

The film was virulently racist, as were almost all the films of the 1910s which featured Japanese actors or characters, but there had been no complaints by reviewers or censors until April of 1917, when Japan, which had in 1914 declared war on Germany, became an American ally. Within days of the American declaration of war, the commissioner of the Department of Licenses in New York City demanded that *Patria* be withdrawn from distribution because it was critical of Japan. The commissioner, supported by the second assistant secretary of state, asked Pathé, which distributed the serial, to "voluntarily withdraw the films from display . . . through patriotic motives." Hearst and Pathé agreed to reedit the film to remove the most blatantly anti-Japanese images. The new version was screened and put back into circulation. But this was not the end of the story.[2]

On June 1, Secretary of Commerce William Redfield asked President Wilson to personally request that Pathé withdraw *Patria* from the theaters because a "'business friend'" had told him that the film inflamed "the idea of suspicion toward Japan." Three days later, Wilson wrote the Pathé executive in charge of distributing the serial that he had "seen portions of the film entitled 'Patria'" in Keith's Washington, D.C., vaudeville palace and was disturbed by the character of the story. It is extremely unfair to the Japanese and I fear that it is calculated to stir up a great deal of hostility which will be far from beneficial to the country, indeed will, particularly in the present circumstances, be extremely hurtful. I take the liberty, therefore, of asking whether the Pathé Company would not be willing to withdraw it if it is still being exhibited."[3]

Pathé responded immediately, informing the president, without mentioning Hearst's name, that his International Film Company had invested "a great deal of money . . . in the making, advertising and marketing of this picture" and that the film had already been reedited once. The State Department counsel informed the president that the federal government had no legal grounds for censoring the film or withdrawing it from circulation, but Wilson wrote the Pathé representative again, asking that the company voluntarily reedit or withdraw the serial as a favor to him and the nation: "It would seem desirable to omit all those scenes in which anything Japanese appears, particularly those showing the Japanese and Mexican armies invading the United States, pillaging homes, kidnapping women and committing all sorts of other offenses. I trust that this will be found possible, and if not, I again venture to ask whether you are not prepared to withdraw the film entirely from exhibition."[4]

Though Wilson had no desire to negotiate directly with Hearst or his representatives, the Pathé executives' refusal to proceed without the publisher's approval forced President Wilson to discuss the matter with Hearst's attorney and adviser, Grenville MacFarland. MacFarland assured Wilson in writing that the changes he had requested would be made, "though with great difficulty." All images of Japanese kimonos, costumes, servants, interior fittings, flags, and military uniforms would be eliminated from the reedited version which would be sent to the State Department "for further inspection." While MacFarland, following Wilson's lead, did not refer to Hearst directly in his letter, he must have infuriated Wilson by suggesting that those who disapproved of the propaganda in *Patria* reminded him "of the very respectable Athenian citizens who denounced Demosthenes for attempting to disturb the amicable relations of Athens with the friendly power of Macedonia."[5]

Patria, now in its second revision, was screened in October of 1917 by representatives of the State Department and the Japanese Embassy who found it improved, but still objectionable. Secretary of State Lansing suggested that the film be returned for another round of alterations, but Wilson refused to push the matter further. *Patria* had, after almost a year in the theaters, already reached its audience, and the president knew that he had no legal grounds for proceeding against Hearst nor did he want to ask him for any more favors.[6]

The controversy over *Patria* may have alerted Hearst to the troubles ahead. In May of 1917, Arthur Brisbane, no doubt with the approval and financial backing from his chief, bought the *Washington Times* and launched a one-man campaign to convince the Wilson administration that Hearst was on its side. In the fall, Hearst authorized his attorney, Grenville MacFarland, to arrange a private meeting for him with the president. MacFarland wrote Wilson a personal letter describing the ways in which the Hearst papers were "helping the great cause" and asked Joseph Tumulty, Wilson's secretary, for "permission to bring over some day next week Mr. Hearst for a little informal talk." In the event that the president was unable to meet with Hearst, MacFarland asked that the fact that he had suggested the meeting "be kept confidential." Wilson tersely replied that it was "out of the question for me to see Mr. Hearst on any business of any kind and I would be very much obliged to you if you would convey that intimation to Mr. MacFarland so that this suggestion might be as if it had never been made."[7]

There was little Hearst or his editors could do now to alleviate the Wilson administration's suspicion that they were traitors to their nation. In early October, T. V. Ranck, his editorial director, traveled to Washington on a goodwill mission with a Hearst reporter by the name of Andersen who supposedly had information about events in Germany to report to the War Department. Captain Dick Slaughter of the Military Intelligence Division interviewed Andersen and informed his commanding officer that he had been

> very careful to keep both Ranck and Andersen under my eye at all times while they were in the building, so that I am sure that they got nothing out of Military Intelligence on which to base an article or a statement. . . . I am convinced that Hearst desires to use the Military Intelligence for the purpose of showing how loyal he is in submitting articles to the Military Intelligence before publishing them. . . . I am convinced that Ranck desires to "plant" Andersen as an officer in the Military Intelligence to work in the interests of Hearst.[8]

Ironically, as Hearst discovered, the same lack of enthusiasm for the war which caused him such trouble in Washington had enormously enhanced his popularity in New York City. His nonstop assault on the English — at one point, he demanded that no American troops be sent to Europe until the "500,000 English slackers" in the United States had been "shipped straight to the fighting lines in Flanders" — combined with his crusade against the "disloyal defamation" of antiwar dissenters and German-Americans had boosted his standing among Irish, German, and Jewish-American voters. He was once again being spoken of as a possible mayoral candidate against John Purroy Mitchel, who had in 1913 defeated Tammany's candidate for mayor and was running for reelection in 1917.[9]

As Hearst had no interest in the mayoralty, when the Democrats nominated Judge John Hylan of the Brooklyn County Court, a nondescript but perfectly presentable candidate, to run against Mitchel, Hearst endorsed him. Mitchel and his supporters immediately seized upon Hearst's endorsement as the major issue in the campaign. A vote for the Democrats, they claimed, was a vote for "Hearst, Hylan, the Hohenzollerns, and the Habsburgs." The charge that Hearst was a German sympathizer and Hylan his willing puppet was taken up by his opponents everywhere. The *New York Times*, in its editorial the week before Election Day, referred to him as "the spokesman of the Kaiser in this country." J. M. Beck, a politician, lawyer, and stridently pro-English propagandist, "denounced" Hearst at Carnegie Hall as "the 'fountain head' of the pro-German propaganda in the United States which has as its purpose the destruction of the morale of the American people." The *Times* published Beck's speech, verbatim, on its front page, under the boldface headline, "Nation's Greatest Menace."[10]

In October 1917, in the midst of the mayoral campaign, Merton Lewis, the Republican attorney general of New York, leaked information to the *New York Tribune* that Hearst was under investigation for his ties with Bolo Pacha, a Frenchman who was being tried in Paris as a German spy. Pacha, who had been in New York the year before, ostensibly as the representative of a French newspaper, had given a dinner for Hearst at Sherry's and Hearst had reciprocated by giving him a farewell party at the Clarendon. While French and American officials had sufficient evidence to indicate that Pacha was a spy, they had nothing to link him to Hearst. Hearst denied Lewis's charges and threatened him with a slander suit. Lewis refrained from leaking any more information to the press, but opened a new investigation and detailed a special deputy, who happened to be a convicted felon, to interview employees and residents of the Clarendon where Hearst was alleged to have met with German spies and agents.[11]

Intelligence-gathering agencies on two continents were now sharing information in an attempt to uncover evidence against Hearst. The French provided testimony from their interrogation of Bolo Pacha; Naval Intelligence contributed the complete text of all dispatches wired between Nauheim, Germany, and Sayville, New York; the attorney general's office in Albany offered reports from the field agents and volunteers who had interviewed Hearst's Riverside Drive neighbors, chauffeurs, doormen, and elevator boys; the Military Intelligence Division and the Bureau of Investigation in Washington added gossip and hearsay picked up by agents and volunteers across the country.[12]

Even with unlimited resources at their disposal and the absolute certainty that Hearst was guilty of something, the investigators after more than a year of searching were unable to uncover any proof of treason or disloyalty. The closest they came was a working hypothesis that Hearst had accepted German money because he was in financial difficulties. According to General Churchill, who was the Military Intelligence Division's liaison with A. Bruce Bielaski, chief of the Bureau of Investigation, Hearst was having trouble paying for newsprint and his mother was threatening to withdraw support. This much was probably true, but had been for decades. It did not constitute a motive for treason.[13]

The cumulative effect of these investigations on Hearst's editors and writers was devastating, as they too were placed under suspicion of disloyalty and treason. "One of the gravest allegations lodged against me," recalled Moses Koenigsberg, who ran Hearst's feature service, "was 'the maintenance of secret relations with W. R. Hearst.' . . . Despite its absurdity, the complaint nettled me. It was at the height of a country-wide series of attacks on Hearst. Denounced by countless enemies in print and speech as pro-German, he was burned in effigy in several cities. Copies of his newspapers were gathered at public places in different states from time to time and piled on bonfires." When Koenigsberg reported to Hearst that he was being investigated by the ultrapatriotic American Protective League, Hearst only laughed. "'What is the matter?' he asked banteringly. 'Can't you stand an investigation?' Then, with a mischievous smile, he added, 'I just love to be investigated.'" That, Koenigsberg continued, "was a boast without reservation. No man had a keener sense of publicity values than Hearst. He approved the judgement of the theatrical ham who rated 'a bad notice better than no notice.' But unlike the actor, he could and did turn adverse mention to immediate account. He welcomed attack. It was a pretext for the expression of his greatest talent. No publicist of his generation surpassed him in polemic writing."[14]

While Hearst laughed off the attacks or responded with his own, the charges of disloyalty were having an effect on his business. In January of 1918, he warned Joseph A. Moore, the head of his magazine division, that because his newspapers were losing money, the magazines had to take up the slack: "Mrs. Hearst and I will have to get a good deal of our personal income out of the magazines . . . Mr. Moore, we must make money out of these magazines. I am not conducting them merely for an artistic success. I do not think anything is successful that does not pay and pay well." In a telegram sent the next day, he provided Moore with specifics: "I want to get $10,000 a month [a little more than $100,000 in today's currency] — $5,000 for Mrs. Hearst and $5,000 for myself — out of the magazines in the way of regular salary. We work hard enough, I think, to get this, and I want it paid regularly. You must consider this in your budget."[15]

As had become their custom, Hearst and Millicent spent their winter vacation at The Breakers in Palm Beach. Not coincidentally, Marion and her mother were also vacationing in Palm Beach that winter, as the *New York American* reported on February 28, 1918, in an item headlined, "All Palm Beach at Feet of Lovely Marion Davies." Hearst had grown too fond of Marion — and perhaps too jealous as well — to let her out of his sight for any length of time, even during his vacation with his wife. For at least the third time in his life, he had fallen in love with the wrong woman. Twenty years earlier, he had dated another Broadway chorus girl half his age; twenty years before that he had "kept" a Cambridge waitress as his mistress. But instead of treating these women — and now Marion — as disposable playmates, he had fallen in love with them.

In early May, Hearst and Millicent left New York City again for a brief vacation at the spa in Mt. Clemens, Michigan, that they had been visiting regularly since the summer of 1904. Even in Michigan, on vacation with his wife, W. R. felt compelled to stay in touch with Marion, if only by letter and telegram. In one telegram from Mt. Clemens he wrote, referring to himself in the third person,

> Billy says he is not chasing petticoats and doesn't like them. He says the reason he doesn't like them is because the dearest and sweetest thing that he knows in all the world doesn't wear them. Billy says his idea of perfect attire is a sort of filmy combination of pink silk and lace and that he would follow that inspiration forever as the fanatic Moslems followed the trousers of Mahomet. Billy sounds kind of mushy and not wholly moral to me but the poor fellow is madly in love and is not altogether responsible.[16]

Hearst returned from Michigan to oversee the publicity campaign for Marion's new picture, *Cecilia of the Pink Roses.* The film was produced by the Marion Davies Film Company, though it had been paid for by Hearst. According to a June 12, 1918, article in the *New York Sun,* the film was so promising that Lewis J. Selznick had not only agreed to distribute it under his Select Picture Corporation, but had paid a premium for the right to do so. *Moving Picture World* reported in its June 15, 1918, issue that Selznick had agreed to release five more Marion Davies films after *Cecilia.* Selznick was not banking on Davies' star quality alone. He — and the rest of the industry — knew that Hearst intended to back her films with every resource he owned. As Colonel Mann's *Town Topics* reported on June 3, well before the film opened, the city was already

> plastered with lilies and other flamboyant advertising material of Marion Davies, who has been making movie appearances here recently. This advertising, which must have cost a fortune, is reported to have been done by William Randolph Hearst, who is deeply interested in the movie business and believes that in Miss Davies he has another Pickford. Last winter, the Hearsts entertained the Davies girl at Palm Beach, together with the Dolly Sisters, and no one will be more disappointed than the newspaper magnate at the failure of his new star to impress the critics and enthuse the audiences.[17]

Colonel Mann was incorrect — but devilishly so — in claiming that the Hearsts, plural, had entertained Marion at Palm Beach. To guarantee that no such items would appear in future, Hearst instructed Joseph Moore to begin advertising in *Town Topics,* in effect paying Colonel Mann *not* to write about him and Marion.[18]

* * *

In the spring of 1918, as American soldiers engaged the enemy on the bat-tlefields of France, the Chief acceded to the mounting assaults on his loyalty by discontinuing publication of his German-language newspaper. The *Deutsches Journal*, formerly the *Morgen Journal*, had in November of 1917 added *New Yorker* to its title, reduced the *Deutsches* to unreadably small letters, and adopted the tag line, "An American Paper printed in Ger-man on behalf of American Unity and Universal Democracy." Unfortu-nately, in the increasingly hostile atmosphere of 1918, not even these con-cessions were sufficient to remove distrust. On April 21, 1918, the *New Yorker Deutsches Journal* announced in English that it was suspending publication in a "supreme sacrifice in behalf of AMERICAN UNITY."[19]

The following month, Congress passed a sedition act, imposing harsh penalties on anyone using "disloyal, profane, scurrilous, or abusive lan-guage" about the flag, the army, conscription, or the government. The Chief's response was to write and sign a lengthy editorial detailing every patriotic action his papers had taken since the war began.[20]

It was already too late. The new legislation emboldened his enemies to attempt to destroy him one more time. The attack was led by the *New York Tribune*, the staunchly Republican newspaper that had been on the oppo-site side of Hearst on every issue. With information leaked from the state attorney general's office and the encouragement of officials in Washington, the *Tribune* on successive Sundays from April through June of 1918 pub-lished a scathing six-part attack on Hearst's loyalty that was, in effect, a brief for prosecuting him under the new legislation.[21]

Widely circulated in pamphlet form under the title, "Coiled in the Flag — Hears-s-s-s-t," the *Tribune* series argued on the basis of war coverage and editorials in the *New York American* and *Deutsches Journal* that Hearst was a German sympathizer and traitor to his country. Each of the six articles was preceded by a boxed scorecard:

Since the United States entered the war the Hearst papers have printed:

> 74 — attacks on our allies
> 17 — instances of defense or praise of Germany
> 63 — pieces of antiwar propaganda
> _1_ — deletion of a Presidential proclamation
> Total 155

— or an average of nearly three a week, while America has been engaged in the life and death struggle with civilization's enemy.[22]

Adopting the practice Hearst himself excelled at, the *Tribune* followed its exposés with news items describing their effect. On July 1, it ran a story about a patriotic anti-Hearst rally in Methodist churches in Chatham, New York. There were stories on July 2 about the anti-Hearst button that had been designed by an army lieutenant and was in demand "in many states." That same day the *Tribune* reported that the boycott of Hearst papers had spread to Great Barrington, Massachusetts; Port Jervis, New York; and Rutherford, New Jersey, which had proudly refused "to Be Prussianized By the Hearst Trust." On July 17, the *Tribune*'s front-page headline read, "Charge Hearst Employee Sold Secrets of U.S." On July 22, the paper reported that a "dead Prussian soldier at Hill 304, Verdun," had been found with a copy of a German newspaper with extracts from a Hearst editorial. On July 31, it was reported, again on the front page, that Deputy Attorney General Becker had released a letter from the hanged German spy Bolo Pacha which "Named Hearst as 'My Friend.'"[23]

That same month, July 1918, the state Democratic party of New York convened in Saratoga to choose candidates for state office. All year long, there had been rumors that Hearst, building on support in the Irish, German, and Russian-Jewish communities, was going to run for office again. Judge Samuel Seabury, once Hearst's principal ally, was so outraged by the possibility that he asked for the floor to introduce a special resolution:

> Resolved, that this conference of Democrats . . . as an earnest of their loyalty, repudiate every truckler with our country's enemies who strives or has striven to extenuate or excuse such crimes against humanity as the rape of Belgium, the sinking of the *Lusitania* and the German policy of assassination by submarines; who seeks or has sought to sow dissension among our allies, or who now seeks to capitalize by election to public office, the latent treason whose total annihilation is the most pressing need of the hour.

The resolution named no names, but Seabury acknowledged to reporters that "I meant Hearst when I proposed the resolution." It passed by a large margin, ending all discussion of a Hearst nomination. Al Smith was nominated for governor and, with Hearst's endorsement, was elected in November.[24]

In the fall of 1918, Garet Garrett, an assistant editor at the *Tribune*, prepared a brief charging Hearst with treason under the Espionage Act of 1917 and traveled to Washington, D.C., to outline his case to Attorney General Thomas Gregory. In October, a federal grand jury sitting in New York City interviewed Garrett and subpoenaed a copy of his brief. While Garrett insisted that he had "evidence tending to show treasonable activities" on Hearst's part, he was unable to produce any. The case against Hearst was dropped. Still the suspicions lingered.[25]

Through it all, Hearst did very little to defend himself. Convinced that he had been correct in opposing American entry into the war and thereafter to urge a negotiated peace, he was not about to surrender his right to speak his mind to his readers. When, in November of 1918, after more than four years of war, an armistice was signed, Hearst alone greeted the moment not with congratulations for the nation's leaders or a prayer of thanksgiving for its soldiers, but with another angry warning: "Since the entrance of America into the war I have unquestionably acquiesced in the wisdom of the decision of our Government to make war on the side of the Allies." Peace now having been "finally declared, I resume my rights to opinion . . . subservient only to the interests of my own people and my own country."[26]

He was more convinced than ever — and made his opinions known to his readers — that the leaders of the European nations and President Wilson had been criminally insane in their refusal to heed his warnings. Millions had been killed, nations destroyed, Bolshevism unleashed, the cause of Western civilization set back, the Japanese emboldened, and to what end? The only victor, he argued, was the British Empire, which had emerged intact because the American government had protected and preserved it.

The Treaty of Versailles, with its League of Nations covenant, was, for Hearst, the final confirmation of the war's futility. The leaders of the allied nations, including President Wilson, Hearst informed his readers in a signed front-page editorial on January 26, 1920, had "preached to their peoples that the war was a crusade for democracy, for liberty, for the self-determination of nations and the independence of peoples; that it was a crusade against imperialism and militarism." But once their dynastic war was won, they devised "a treaty and a covenant of nations which repudiated every pledge they had made and violated every preachment they had uttered."[27]

The conferees in Paris had allowed Japan to retain the Shantung peninsula in China, which it had occupied since driving the Germans out in 1914. In so doing, they had rewarded Japanese militarism and invited a second generation of wars in Europe. Even more stupidly, they had rearranged the map of Europe, dividing up the Austro-Hungarian Empire and ceding German land to Poland and Czechoslovakia: "To revert to small states in Europe is distinctly a step backward. . . . It means not more liberty, but less individual freedom, less tolerance, less progress, more jealousy, more conflict, more acts of oppression like these massacres of the Jews." The May 1919 pogroms in Poland were, for Hearst, only the first "instance" of what he regarded as the "evil results of dividing Eastern Europe into a number of inconsiderable, irresponsible, states whose main idea of liberty is license to commit excesses."[28]

If Wilson had merely participated in writing a flawed peace treaty, Hearst felt, that would have been bad enough. But he committed an even more serious error in attaching the League of Nations covenant to the treaty. Article X of the League covenant provided for collective force to be used against any nation that violated the sovereignty of another. In practical terms this meant that the United States, in joining the League, was offering its services as global policeman to protect the territorial status quo in Europe. Should Europe once again be drawn into suicidal civil war, the United States would be bound to send troops to rescue it. As Hearst wrote to Harry Haye Tammen, the co-publisher of the *Denver Post*, "I do not consider it a league to keep us out of war but a league to get us into war. A man does not keep himself free from the small pox by going to bed with four other people who have it; and we cannot keep free from war by tying ourselves up with nations like England, France, Italy and Japan, which have the war disease in its worst form."[29]

Instead of wasting the nation's time, energy, and dollars by tying its future to that of Europe, Hearst, with Western senators like Hiram Johnson of California, urged Wilson to pay more attention to Asia, where the Japanese had accumulated new power, resources, and territory:

> The great problem before the white races is not whether boundaries of white nations in Europe shall run this way or that way, but whether Japan shall absorb and organize Asia for the conquest of the World . . . Who shall say that the stupidities and jealousies of the white peoples, which have reached an unbelievable degree of madness and blindness, shall not some day create a situation which will arouse the yellow races to succeed? . . . The Japanese situation is a genuine danger, more immediately to America, but ultimately to the whole white world. Upon us will fall the first burden of the battle for the white man's civilization.[30]

"The battle against the League of Nations" was, Cora Older declared in her 1936 authorized biography, "the most important of [Hearst's] many campaigns during his life as a journalist." "Other editors might have carried on my other campaigns," Hearst told Older, "but there was no one else with so many newspapers actively interested in defeating the League of Nations . . . If it had not been for my papers, this country might, through the League of Nations, have become involved in war."

When, in November of 1919, the treaty was defeated in the Senate, the Hearst papers responded with an editorial headlined "Thanks Be to God, This Nation Has Indeed Had a New Birth of Freedom."[31]

Peace had returned to Europe, but the charges against Hearst were too numerous, too widely publicized, and too often circulated by high government officials to be quickly forgotten. In December of 1918 a subcommittee of the Senate Judiciary Committee held hearings on "foreign propaganda, espionage, and intrigue in the United States during the World War." The result was another round of front-page headlines tying Hearst to German spies. While the hearings were in session, Mayor John Hylan of New York, with characteristic fealty, publicly invited Hearst to serve on a committee of citizens to welcome the returning veterans to American shores. The public response was overwhelmingly negative. Beginning in December and continuing through March of 1919 when the ships landed, the non-Hearst New York papers ran daily stories condemning Hylan and Hearst. The mayor tried to control the damage by enlarging the size of the welcoming committee to 5,000 members, but he refused to publicly disinvite Hearst.

Opposition newspapers tracked the protest against Hearst from New York City to South Dakota, Ohio, and Pennsylvania where state legislators had forwarded resolutions to Congress demanding that the disembarkation point for the troops be shifted away from New York Harbor so that Hearst would not be present to greet the returning troops. In Washington, the Military Intelligence Division monitored the threatening letters sent to Mayor Hylan, including one from a Private Robert W. Owens who suggested that in the interest of Hearst's personal safety the mayor "take particular pains to see that Hearst is not on the reviewing stand when Battery B 341 Field Artillery passes by. We have been over here in the land of hell, hate, and Hun and are in no mood to deal softly with such a slimy Hun sympathizer as Wilhelm Hearst."[32]

The Chief went on the offensive, charging that his enemies were part of the "large Tory element in this country, which seems to think now as it thought in the days of the Revolutionary War — that the only way to be pro-American is to be pro-English." Specifically named among those enemies were Rockefeller, Morgan, and Du Pont. To show his patriotism and court veteran support — and because he believed it was the right thing to do — Hearst wrote signed editorials demanding that all soldiers be demobilized immediately with a six-month bonus.[33]

When the *Mauretania* arrived in New York Harbor with the first contingent of returning veterans, Hearst was there to greet it. As Nat Ferber, at the

A family portrait from the mid-1920s, when Hearst began spending most of his time on the West Coast. The twins, standing in front, were born in December 1915. (*Copyright © Hearst Castle™/Hearst San Simeon State Historical Monument™*)

Hearst with Julia Morgan, his San Simeon architect, 1926
(*Marc Wanamaker/Bison Archives*)

Casa del Monte, or B house at San Simeon, where Hearst and his family
stayed during the summers of 1921 and 1922 (*Marc Wanamaker/Bison Archives*)

"La Cuesta Encantada" at San Simeon, circa January 1948
(*Copyright © Hearst Castle™/Hearst San Simeon State Historical Monument™*)

St. Donat's, Hearst's castle in Wales, purchased in 1925 (*San Francisco Examiner*)

Hearst occasionally opened the grounds, including the pool, to the public
(*San Francisco Examiner*)

Ocean House, the estate in Santa Monica that Hearst bought for Marion Davies in 1926 (*Copyright © Hearst Castle™/Hearst San Simeon State Historical Monument™*)

Beacon Towers, or the Belmont House, in 1917–18. Hearst bought this home in Sands Point, Long Island, for Millicent in late 1927. (*Suffolk County Vanderbilt Museum*)

Cinderella House at Wyntoon, Hearst's estate in northern California (*Kimberly Lake*)

W. R. and Millicent Hearst at a costume ball at the Ritz in New York City, April 28, 1927 (*San Francisco Examiner*)

Hearst with Winston Churchill, who was visiting him at the time, and
Louis B. Mayer, on the MGM lot, September 1929
(*Marc Wanamaker/Bison Archives*)

Giving a radio address on "Painful and Painless Taxation," June 3, 1932
(*Marc Wanamaker/Bison Archives*)

time a city reporter for the Hearst papers, described the scene, Hearst, who "might have faced the meeting with trepidation, was jubilant. Placing one arm about Gene Fowler, a fellow reporter, and the other around me, he skipped with us, schoolboy fashion, down the deck, the earflaps of his 'Sherlock Holmes' cap flapping in the wind."[34]

On March 26, 1919, the first major contingent of veterans, the soldiers of the 27th Division, paraded up Fifth Avenue, greeted by crowds so large that the police lost control and several spectators were injured. On the reviewing stand at 82nd Street and Fifth Avenue, they were greeted by Mayor Hylan, flanked by Governor Al Smith and Acting Secretary of the Navy Franklin D. Roosevelt. Hearst was nowhere to be seen. Then, according to the *New York Times,* as the column of soldiers approached the stand, "the place that had been occupied by Mr. Roosevelt was taken by William Randolph Hearst, and thereafter Mr. Hearst received with the Mayor the salutes of the regimental battalion and company commanders as they passed the stand."[35]

In his first two decades as editor and publisher, Hearst had focused his attention and, he hoped, that of his readers, on the intertwined issues of the trusts and political corruption. But, in the course of the Great War he had been forced to direct his gaze outward to encompass questions about America's role in the world beyond its borders. His position was unambiguous. He was unalterably opposed to American involvement in European affairs and would be for the next thirty years. When, in December of 1919, the Wilson administration sent American troops to Russia to join the fight against the new Bolshevik regime, Hearst protested:

> The Russian people have thrown off the yoke of the Czars and of the corrupt and cruel nobility and have established a democracy — not a perfect democracy, but a form of democratic government that will develop daily into a better democracy . . . Why should President Wilson, without authority of Congress, without the approval of the American people, send our American boys to the snows of Siberia to endure the hardships of military service . . . in order to try to fight down an infant republic and to reestablish an autocracy of despotic Czars, corrupt and conscienceless nobles and cruel Cossacks?[36]

While American politicians and publishers criticized the Bolsheviks for being German agents, making a separate peace, confiscating and nationalizing private property, and, most incredibly, as the *New York Times* reported in October of 1918, requiring eighteen-year-old girls to register at a government "bureau of free love," Hearst cautioned restraint. In December of 1918,

Gerald MacFarland, speaking for Hearst in a *Boston American* editorial —
which was clipped and filed by agents at the War Department's Military Intelligence Division — urged Americans to withhold judgment on the
Bolsheviks until they knew more:

> This newspaper does not know the truth about Russia. For all we can say posi-
> tively the Bolsheviki leaders may be saints or crooks or just ordinary men. But
> we can say this with certainty, that the great majority of people keep them in
> power, and that for more than a year there has been a vast conspiracy to slan-
> der them, and that there is a good ground for suspicion that men who have to
> be lied about continuously in order to make them appear bad are not so very
> bad after all.[37]

Hearst's opposition to administration policy on the Soviet Union posed
so serious an obstacle toward establishing a national consensus that Briga-
dier General Dennis E. Nolan, General Pershing's chief of intelligence in
Europe, wrote the War Department in June of 1919 to suggest that new
pressures be applied to Hearst to join the anti-Bolshevik campaign. "Indi-
cations," he wrote, "are that Hearst is eager at this time to bid for absolu-
tion." Nolan was mistaken. If Hearst blamed himself for anything, it was for
not speaking out loudly and forcibly enough to prevent American involvement in a costly, bloody, and senseless war. He would, he pledged to himself
and his readers, not allow this to happen a second time.[38]

Hearst's antagonism to what he now called "Wilsonian internationalism"
remained at so high a pitch of intensity that he declared, in a front-page editorial in the fall of 1920, two years after the armistice, that he would support James Cox, the Democratic nominee for president in 1920, only if he
threw off the Wilson yoke. When Cox refused to do so, Hearst, for the first
time in his life, endorsed a Republican, Warren G. Harding. The paramount issue in the election, he declared, was "the defeat of the Wilson foreign league."[39]

V

A Master Builder

❧ 16 ❧
Building a Studio

P HOEBE, NOW IN HER SEVENTIES, refused to allow old age to slow
her down. She remained an active member of the Pacific Coast Field
Committee of the YWCA and a leader of the Women's Board which
helped to organize the 1915 Panama-Pacific International Exposition in San
Francisco. Though she did not publicly support the National Women's
Party, she worked closely with its leader Alice Paul and was a cofounder
with her of the National Mothers' Congress. In the summer of 1916, while
her son called for military preparedness in his daily newspapers, Phoebe accepted an invitation to join the "preparedness" parade in San Francisco
scheduled for July 22. Ignoring the threats of violence — and the bomb that
was thrown during the parade and killed nine or ten marchers — Phoebe
Hearst, at age seventy-four, dressed in white, wearing a flowered hat, a
parasol in one hand, an American flag in the other, marched the entire
route of the parade at the head of the women's contingent.

In December of 1918, one month after the German surrender ended the
Great War, Phoebe traveled East to spend the Christmas holidays with the
Hearsts at the Clarendon. Though seventy-six years of age and suffering
from a nasty cold, Phoebe still found time for shopping, visiting with
friends, dining out, attending the opera, and traveling to New Haven to
visit her niece, Anne Apperson Flint, who had returned from Pleasanton
when her husband, a professor of surgery at Yale, left military service. In
late January, exhausted from her travels, Phoebe was forced to take to her
bed, but after a few days' rest she was well enough to travel West by private
railway car, accompanied by her grandsons Bill, Jr. and John, Edward Clark
and his wife, and the usual entourage of servants.[1]

During her stay in the East, as Hearst later testified at a hearing on the estate taxes, his mother had entered the sitting room where he was reading
his newspapers and asked him about his finances: "I told her they were

pretty fair considering the war conditions, but that I had to borrow some money and that I might have to borrow some more. . . . She said her own affairs were not in any too good condition and that I must be careful and not call upon her for further help, because she would not be able to give it to me."[2]

W. R. was putting the best possible gloss on his financial situation. Advertising had plummeted during the war and his newspaper circulation had been affected by the adverse publicity and boycotts his enemies had incited. Instead of retrenching until his newspapers began to earn money again, he had gone deeper into debt to finance his moving-picture business. The combination of debts owed his mother and those incurred by the Star Company, his primary holding company, made it impossible for him to seek further credit from the banks, which he required regularly to refinance outstanding loans. In February of 1919, Phoebe bailed him out again by agreeing to write off the $1.8 million (equivalent to almost $19 million in today's currency) he owed her because, as she put it, "the existence of these obligations would naturally embarrass and hamper you in making representations to your bankers."[3]

On returning to California in February, Phoebe found enough strength to sit up for several hours a day dictating letters, visiting with friends, and making plans to take her grandchildren to Wyntoon for the summer. But as the weeks wore on, she grew weaker instead of stronger. It was becoming clear now that what she had thought was a simple cold was the influenza that the soldiers had brought back from Europe. By mid-March, her condition had deteriorated to the point where her physician, Ray Lyman Wilbur, who was at the time president of Stanford University, contacted her son in New York. A nurse was engaged and Phoebe's local doctor put on call. On March 26, as Hearst was making his stealth appearance on the reviewing stand to greet the returning veterans, her condition took a turn for the worse and she developed pneumonia. W. R. and Millicent boarded a train to California the next morning. They arrived at the Hacienda on March 31. Phoebe brightened on seeing her only son and seemed to recover, but within a week had relapsed again.[4]

On April 13, Easter Sunday, at 4:30 in the afternoon, Phoebe Apperson Hearst died in her sleep. "This was the first time that I had looked death in the face," her grandson Bill, Jr. recalled in his memoirs. "I wept for days. The whole world had fallen and crashed into smithereens for this eleven-year-old boy. I could not envisage life without her." We have no first-person record of William Randolph Hearst's reaction to his mother's death, only the words of his authorized biographer, who may have interviewed him on the subject. "It was," Cora Older wrote of the Easter Sunday his mother died, "the most melancholy day in Hearst's life."[5]

For the next three days, Phoebe's body, dressed in a lilac dress, her casket surrounded by flowers, was placed on view in the Music Room of her Hacienda. Private services were held for family and friends at the Hacienda, followed by a public funeral at the Grace Episcopal Cathedral in San Francisco, with the governor of California an honorary pallbearer. For those not able to attend either ceremony, a musical service was held later in the day in the Civic Auditorium. Phoebe was buried at the Cypress Lawn Cemetery, south of the city, in the family mausoleum beside her husband. The day of her funeral, all activities were canceled at the University of California at Berkeley, where she had been a regent and major benefactor. According to the *New York Times,* the California Superior and Justice Courts were also closed down as was the Federal District Court, the first time a woman was so honored.[6]

Phoebe's death left her only son bereaved — and extraordinarily rich. She had bequeathed half a million dollars in gifts to friends and other members of her family and $60,000 to the University of California at Berkeley for Phoebe A. Hearst scholarships. The *Examiner* building in San Francisco was left to her grandchildren, as were the proceeds from the sale of her Pleasanton Hacienda. Wyntoon was given to her niece. Everything else — the land in Mexico, the "cattle ranch" at San Simeon, and the family's other real estate, stocks, and bonds — went to her son and heir. Edward Clark estimated the total value of the estate at $7.5 million, worth around $75 million today; the *New York Times* put it at between $5 and $10 million — a considerable amount, given that Phoebe had, since her husband died, donated more than $20 million to charities and forgiven her son another $10 million in debt.[7]

At age fifty-six, William Randolph Hearst finally came into his patrimony.

By 1919, Hearst's film companies had produced several very successful serials, hundreds of newsreel episodes, and almost a dozen feature films. With the arrival of peace in Europe — and perhaps the expectation that he would soon inherit the money rightfully due him — Hearst was ready to take the next step forward in the film business and set up his own studio. When, in January, D. W. Griffith, Charlie Chaplin, Mary Pickford, and Douglas Fairbanks announced that they were going to establish their own film company, United Artists, Hearst proposed that they enter into a partnership with him. In a telegram to Max Ihmsen who, now that Hearst's political career was on hold, had been moved to the *Los Angeles Examiner*, the Chief set forth the terms of the partnership. Hearst would distribute their films and in return get 50 percent of the gross proceeds, out of which he would cover all costs of distribution and promotion. "We have no interest in this matter from a small view point," he informed Ihmsen. "We are the biggest institution of publicity and promotion in the world with all our magazine and newspaper services, news films, feature services, etc. We are only interested in this combination of stars because that is the biggest thing of its kind in the world."

When the "Big Four," as Hearst referred to them, declined his offer, he was not in the least discouraged. As he had earlier told Ihmsen, the main advantage of a deal with United Artists would have been the "association with these big stars." He was convinced, nonetheless, that with or without them, he would be able to establish himself as a major power in the film business.[8]

His next approach was to Adolph Zukor, the bearded and diminutive Hungarian fur-dealer who had entered show business as part owner of a penny arcade and moved on to become the nation's top producer, distributor, and exhibitor of feature-length moving pictures. Hearst proposed to Zukor an arrangement under which he would establish his own independent film studio in Manhattan, Cosmopolitan Productions, and produce features which Zukor would distribute. Although Hearst had no experience running a studio and, just short of his fifty-sixth birthday, was rather old to begin a new career, Zukor gladly joined forces with him. On March 22, 1919, five days before Hearst took the train to California to visit his ailing mother, the picture industry trade journals announced that the two moguls, one of the press, the other of the screen, were entering into a partnership. The announcement and the advertisements that followed it reminded the industry that while Hearst's new company, Cosmopolitan Productions, had not yet made any pictures, it entered the marketplace with an enormous advantage over its competitors. "This company," reported *Motion Picture World*, "controls motion picture rights to the works of the greatest authors writing today. Just a few of these names include John Galsworthy, Elinor Glyn, Robert W. Chambers, Rupert Hughes. . . . The publicity possibilities of the Cosmopolitan Productions are enormous owing to the special alliance with such magazines as *Cosmopolitan, Hearst's, Good Housekeeping, Harper's Bazaar, Motor,* and *Motor Boating,* besides newspapers whose circulations run up into the millions."[9]

As Hearst's trade-journal advertisements told potential exhibitors, Cosmopolitan Productions features would arrive presold. The vast majority of these early pictures were based on material that had already appeared in the Hearst magazines. This was especially important in the era of silent films. Audience familiarity with story lines and characters made it much easier to tell stories without extensive subtitles. The tie-in between *Cosmopolitan* magazine and Cosmopolitan Productions, the multipage spreads in the trade journals proclaimed to the exhibitors, was creating "a new class of motion picture patronage. Every *Cosmopolitan* reader and their myriad friends, and the countless thousand friends of these friends will want to see the characters — those they enjoyed so much in print — live. Better arrange to take care of your regular patrons and then book a few extra days to handle the new business the picture is bound to bring you."[10]

With the energy and commitment of a man half his age, Hearst set out to create for himself a position in the moving-picture industry as exalted as the one he occupied in publishing. By late April, he was already in high gear. From California, where he had returned to settle his mother's estate, he wrote Joseph Moore, who had been promoted again, this time to corporate treasurer and de facto head of his New York business office, that their paramount need was for "more directors . . . Twenty-four pictures a year means five or six directors and as many stars. . . . We need directors that we can depend upon and that belong to us. We have a big contract with Zuckor [sic] and we should organize to fill that. After we have done that and produced our twenty-four per year we can think about additional pictures with other companies."[11]

He had suggestions to make about every aspect of the business, but was most concerned with Miss Davies' pictures. In June of 1919, he wrote William LeBaron, the former magazine editor he had installed as general director of his film company, with his thoughts on the scenario for Marion's next picture, *Restless Sex,* based on the Robert Chambers novel about a wealthy and restless New York society girl that had been serialized in *Cosmopolitan* magazine: "I think the scenario should not depart too far from the book, but I think Miss Davies should continue to represent the kind of admirable young girl parts for which she is establishing a reputation."[12]

"He was very interested in her," Allan Dwan, one of Marion's early directors, recalled, "and he'd come around and see how things were going, invite us all to lunch — the whole afternoon would be gone before we'd get back to work — which didn't bother him much. . . . He was a nice guy."[13]

To make sure Marion got the best possible scripts written for her, Hearst contacted screenwriter Frances Marion, who had written several films for Mary Pickford and become one of Hollywood's busiest and most highly paid screenwriters: "Would you consider contract as writer and director at

Cosmopolitan Studio, New York? Salary two thousand dollars a week." The telegram was signed W. R. Hearst. Frances took the train east at once. She had expected that her meeting with Hearst would take place in his office and was surprised to be directed to meet him instead at the Bryant Park Studios:

> A liveried doorman had been told of an expected guest and given my name. I was ushered into an apartment and left in the hall. From behind closed doors I could hear the wild throbbing of jazz. The door was opened suddenly by Marion Davies. "Hi, Frances, come in, we're just t-teaching W. R. how to sh-shimmy!" Surrounded by girls, Mr. Hearst stood in the middle of the floor . . . He was somewhat breathless. "Welcome," he said. "They call this dancing! I feel as if I were riding a bucking horse without the horse."[14]

Though Marion was a star of the first magnitude at Cosmopolitan Productions, she was not the only one. Because Hearst intended to establish a major studio of his own, he needed several female stars in his company. Marion would play the ingenue/Mary Pickford roles; Alma Rubens, whom he promoted almost as extensively as Marion, would be placed under contract to play the romantic heroines. In the fall of 1919, Hearst made several trips to Los Angeles to scout out the additional actresses needed to fill out the casts of the twenty-four pictures he intended to produce his first year. In a series of lengthy telegrams to Joseph A. Moore — who had become, by default, his chief adviser on the film industry — Hearst offered capsule summaries of the actresses whose work he had previewed, including Ethel Barrymore, who he declared was "too self-conscious for screen." Elsie Ferguson, who had appeared in six different society melodramas in 1918, was, he thought, "tremendously expressive [and] absolutely best for *Cosmopolitan* stories." Alice Joyce, a Vitagraph star since 1916, was a "competent, dignified star." Phoebe Foster, he was "convinced will be good despite somewhat unsatisfactory test. All best screen people say tests are not conclusive. Personality in actual play is what counts. . . . You must have something to make a star. You can't make a silk purse unless you have the silk. . . . Regarding directors," he reminded Moore once again, "I want none but the best."[15]

While the Chief appeared to be having the time of his life scouting actresses in Los Angeles, Joseph Moore was left behind in New York to try to find a way to pay for it all. Moore tried his best to warn the Chief that they were already seriously overextended, but Hearst paid him no heed. Though Phoebe's will would not be probated until October, he no doubt counted on her assets to bail him out of whatever difficulties he got himself into. It was Moore's job, in the meantime, to watch over the bottom line. In September of 1919, he warned the Chief that "the financial situation at the International Film Company [the parent company of Cosmopolitan Productions] is really in very bad shape." If Hearst intended, as planned, to expand film production "on a large scale and build up an enormous payroll, I am afraid," Moore wrote, "that we are going to have trouble financing it." Moore agreed with Hearst that it was necessary to sign actresses and directors to long-term contracts. Directors capable of churning out several features a year were in short supply and receiving not only large salaries *but* a percentage of the profits as well.[16] Since Hearst refused to share his profits, he had to pay extravagant per-picture fees to his directors. Fully aware that the Chief was spending too much money on his films, Adolph Zukor had written in August to suggest that Paramount, which already distributed Cosmopolitan films, produce them as well. This, Zukor wrote, would not only save the Chief money, but "very materially assist in the developing of [Marion Davies'] talent," which Zukor knew meant a lot to Hearst.[17]

Hearst asked his chief film executive in New York to thank Zukor for his "kind offer," but inform him that he preferred to run his studio by himself:

Making pictures is fundamentally like making publications. It is in each case an endeavor to entertain and interest, enlighten and uplift the public. In fact the same material is used more and more in both publications and pictures. If a man knows good material and knows the public all he has to learn is the technique of either profession. I think I have learned various things in the publishing business that will be of value in the motion picture business . . . If I am right then I ought to be able to develop something good and something distinctive, something that expresses my own purposes and personality. I feel that I must work that out myself.[18]

Hearst knew precisely how he wanted to proceed. He had no interest in producing cheaply made "program" pictures for the cramped storefront theaters that littered the streets of every American city. He intended to produce quality "class" pictures for the white-collar workers and professionals who were readers of his magazines and patrons of the dollar vaudeville palaces and higher-priced theaters. In publishing, he had made his fortune by extending the audience for daily and Sunday papers downward into the working classes. In moving pictures, he would extend the audience up the social ladder by producing pictures so stylish and expensive-looking that even "society" would flock to them.

Following on the success of D. W. Griffith's *Birth of a Nation*, the industry had begun to label its most lavish products "super-specials." Hearst expected that every film produced by his company would be handled by Zukor as a super-special and booked into legitimate theaters at $1 or more a ticket. "You know, you have told me from the beginning that you want me to make super-specials," he wrote Zukor in response to the complaint that he was taking too long to deliver his films for distribution. "Very good pictures like all very good products, cannot be made hastily, any more than they can be made cheaply. I want you to realize that we spend a great deal of time and care on these pictures, as well as a great deal of money. I can easily make more hasty pictures and make a great deal more money for ourselves and a great deal less for you. I don't think you want me to do that and I don't want to do it because I have an ambition to make the best pictures that you distribute, which is some ambition."[19]

As his newspapers and magazines were distinguished by their layout, design, and use of graphics, so would his pictures be marked by superior and costly settings and visual effects. Hearst brought to this project a lifetime of experience with visual display. He had been schooled in Charles Eliot Norton's art appreciation courses at Harvard and had, for a half century, been a habitué of the finest galleries and museums of Europe. His private rooms and offices were filled with expensive European paintings, sculpture, architectural artifacts, rugs, wall coverings, and the finest furniture. To make certain that his films were designed with the same degree of elegance and extravagance, Hearst hired as his art director Joseph Urban, a designer equally at home, as Hearst himself was, in elegant drawing rooms and Ziegfeld's *Follies*.

Joseph Urban had been born and educated in Vienna. After a distinguished career as an illustrator, architect, interior decorator, and theater designer, he had traveled to the United States in 1904 to design the interior of the Austrian Pavilion at the St. Louis World's Fair. He returned again in 1911 to serve as artistic director for the Boston Opera Company. When the company folded in 1914, Urban was unable to find work in wartime Europe and relocated to New York where he became the chief designer for the Metropolitan Opera and Florenz Ziegfeld's *Follies*. He had designed the set and lighting for Marion's number, "I Left Her on the Beach in Hawaii," in the 1916 edition of the *Follies*.[20]

Urban offered Hearst everything he was looking for: European sophistication and professionalism combined with a flair for the spectacular. Although he had misgivings about taking on a position that might interfere with his work for the Metropolitan Opera and limit his trademark use of bright colors, Urban accepted a long-term contract to become the artistic director for Cosmopolitan Studios. He was to be paid the princely sum of

$1,286.98 a week for the first year (equivalent to about $10,000 a week in to-day's money) and $1,442.31 a week for the second and third years of his con-tract. If Hearst chose not to renew for an additional three years, Urban was to get another $25,000. Urban was also given permission to continue his work for the Metropolitan Opera and, with Hearst's approval, to design fu-ture editions of Ziegfeld's *Follies*.[21]

Hearst hired Urban to provide his films with a distinctive look, one that radiated expense, sophistication, and "class." His purview was to include not only set design but costuming, makeup, and lighting. "The directors and cameramen received Father warily," Gretl Urban, his daughter and chief assistant, recalled in her unpublished autobiographical notes:

> Here was this new Hearst favorite, who was famous for color and knew abso-lutely nothing about black and white and silent films. . . . Hearst arrived at Fa-ther's office the evening of our first day there and welcomed Father with as much friendly warmth as his unfortunate personality permitted. He had Bill LeBaron [his chief studio executive], Luther Reed [a screenwriter], and a cou-ple of directors with him and told them that from now on Urban would be in complete artistic charge for all productions. . . . He made no secret that he was proud to have Urban as the head of his Cosmopolitan studios.[22]

Because Hearst had been unable to sign directors and screenwriters to long-term contracts, the only permanent presence at the Cosmopolitan studios in New York City was Urban. Even Marion Davies appeared in only half of Hearst's films. Urban designed almost all of them. As Hearst later admonished Joseph Moore, "Don't lose Urban under any circumstances. He makes the high spots in our pictures. There are lots of directors but only one Urban."[23]

The Chief went out of his way to accommodate Urban. The affinities be-tween the two men were striking: they were roughly the same age; both were large and physically imposing; each appeared in public only in formal wear — no matter what the weather; and each had fallen in love with a younger woman, though only Urban had deserted his older wife to marry his mistress. With a new wife, a new home, and a workshop in Yonkers, Ur-ban had precious little free time to share with Hearst and Marion. Still, he did occasionally agree to join them for their weekend cruises on Hearst's newest and most spectacular yacht, the 205-foot *Oneida*. Hearst made use of the *Oneida* on both the east and west coasts, moving it back and forth through the Panama Canal. In New York, he had it outfitted with a projec-tion system so that he, Marion, Urban, and others from the studio could view the week's rushes while cruising the Hudson. When he learned that

Urban disliked sailing but enjoyed swimming, "he had the Captain rig up a huge net which with long beams could be lowered from the deck," his daughter recalled. "Hearst presented it as a special surprise and was childishly pleased when Father dived into it with a joyous shout." Urban's wife Mary recalled similarly that Hearst went out of his way to make her husband comfortable. "If Urban expressed a wish for duck and champagne," during his stay on board the *Oneida*, "they had duck and champagne until the gang rebelled and he expressed another wish for something instead of duck."[24]

"Beside Father, me, and Marion," Gretl recalled, the *Oneida* cruises usually included "Bill LeBaron, Luther Reed, and the film director of the moment. We were the visible ones. The invisible ones were Marion's mother and sister who were never seen after their arrival and whom Father called 'the Mourners at the Feast.' They must have been mighty uncomfortable below deck in warm weather and were probably much relieved when Hearst one day decided that Father and I were chaperones enough. 'Such nonsense' [Father] used to say. 'Millie knows all about this clandestine business and is probably glad to have him out of the house.'"[25]

﴾ 17 ﴿

Builder and Collector

LTHOUGH HEARST HAD ENJOYED camping out at San Simeon
during the war years, he was, at age fifty-six, ready to build a permanent vacation home for himself at "the top of the hill at the
ranch. . . . the loveliest spot in the world." That spot, which he called Camp
Hill, was 1,600 feet above sea level, connected to the village of San Simeon
below by five miles of winding, rutted cattle paths. George had left Phoebe
— and Phoebe would leave Will — almost 60,000 acres of land nestled between the Pacific Ocean and the Santa Lucia mountains, halfway between
Los Angeles and San Francisco. Looking inland from the Pacific, one sees
first a strip of sandy beach, dunes, and bluffs, then an elongated stretch of
grassland, rising imperceptibly into rolling hills of green in winter and
spring, more yellow and brown in summer and fall, dotted with clumps of
sage, laurel, and live oak. The hills slope gently at first, before giving way to
steep, rugged ridges and peaks. Camp Hill, an elongated, oval ridge, was located well below the summit of the Santa Lucia mountains, but far enough
up the hill to provide respite from the summer heat that regularly consumed the grasslands below. The views from the ridge were spectacular: below was the coastal plain, San Simeon, and the Pacific; on either side, rolling green hills; directly above, the Santa Lucias.

In the spring of 1919, Hearst met with the architect Julia Morgan in her
suite of offices on the thirteenth floor of the Merchants Exchange Building
in San Francisco. Walter Steilberg, a draftsman in the Morgan offices who
overheard the Chief's conversation with Miss Morgan because "his pitch
was very high, so it carried," said that Hearst wanted her to "build something up on the hill at San Simeon . . . 'The other day I was in Los Angeles,
prowling around second-hand books stores,' Hearst told Morgan, 'and I
came upon this stack of books called Bungalow Books. Among them I saw
this one which has a picture — this isn't what I want, but it gives you an idea

of my thought about the thing, keeping it simple — of a Jappo-Swisso bungalow.' He laughed at that, and so did she."[1]

Julia Morgan was the perfect choice for the Chief. She was frail-looking, only five feet tall, and weighed no more than one hundred pounds, but she was as indefatigable as her employer. "Wearing tailored suits and French silk blouses," her biographer Sara Boutelle has written, "she clambered over scaffolds and descended into trenches to make sure that the walls and drains met her high standards. The head of a busy, prosperous practice, she worked quietly and alone. . . . Devoted to her career, she seems never even to have considered marriage, although she had many friends among her fellow students, clients, and colleagues." Her work was her life.[2]

Miss Morgan had studied civil engineering at Berkeley (there was, at the time, no architecture school there) and then traveled to Paris, where she became the first woman to be accepted by and receive a degree from the Ecole des Beaux-Arts. On her return to California, she worked alongside two of the state's most distinguished architects, Bernard Maybeck and John Galen Howard, the official architect of the Berkeley campus. By the time W. R. engaged her, she was nearing fifty, had done a considerable amount of work for Phoebe, including work at Pleasanton, and had won several important commissions for private homes and public buildings in the Bay Area, on the Berkeley campus, at Mills College in Oakland, and in downtown San Francisco, where she rebuilt the Fairmont Hotel which had been destroyed in the 1906 earthquake.[3]

Hearst had at first discussed building a "simple" bungalow at San Simeon because he could afford no more. When his mother died in April of 1919, however, everything changed. "I don't think it was a month," Steilberg recalled, "before we were going on the grand scale. . . . The general scheme was evolved very soon of a big master house. He wanted that to dominate the group. Then the three . . . guesthouses."[4]

Hearst was, as always, in a hurry. In mid-August 1919, he wrote Morgan from San Simeon where he and the family were spending what they hoped would be their last summer in tents: "Mrs. Hearst anxious to have main building built first as that provides both sleeping rooms and assembly rooms. Would like to see the axes established and the rooms staked out before we leave. Say about middle of September." The Chief expected the "big master house" in which he planned to live with the family to be finished by the following June — in time for their summer vacation — with the smaller guesthouses completed by the end of 1921. Because the major obstacle to meeting this schedule was going to be moving building materials up the winding, muddy, five-mile wagon road from the foot of the hill to the summit at Camp Hill he set to work at once improving it. "I am having the road bettered," he wrote Morgan in September on returning to New York, "but we will have difficulty in getting heavy things up the hill in slippery weather. We should get them up *now*."[5]

It would have been easier building a house on a desert island in the Pacific than on the hillside Hearst had chosen. "The experts told Pop that it couldn't be done," his son Bill, Jr. recalled in his autobiography:

> No one could build an adequate foundation for a large home up there on the crest of that steep hill overlooking the Pacific and the little village of San Simeon. There was no proper building material available — no lumber, no nearby steel or iron. Even if such materials were carried by boat to the pier, a rising, curving road would have to be constructed out of the wilderness. And it was more than a five-mile pull up the 1,600-foot grade to the mountaintop. Wet winter weather could make such a twisting route treacherous to climb, especially with heavy, unstable loads. Where would the skilled workmen come from? Where would they be housed? How would they be fed? And where would sufficient drinking water be found?[6]

All his life, Hearst had accomplished the impossible, and he saw no reason why he could not do as he pleased on his hillside. He was deterred only by a serious shortage of cash. His mother had left a large estate, but after dispensing more than a half million dollars to her friends and relations and paying the $1 million estate tax, there was not enough to build a dream house, especially one on a rocky isolated hilltop that was a considerable journey from San Francisco, the nearest source of building materials and skilled labor. Hearst had estimated the cost of construction at fifty cents a cubic foot for 156,000 cubic feet in the main building. When he discovered that he had underestimated the size of the building and the cost by half, he cabled Morgan to "wait more definite figures before giving instructions to proceed." Morgan replied that she would "do my very best to keep the cost down, but as you know, both the times and the local conditions are full of uncertainties."[7]

In late September, Joseph Moore in New York wrote Hearst that "the financial situation at the International Film Company" was in such bad shape that he had had to divert $40,000 from other Hearst enterprises to meet the weekly payroll and expenses. By October, Hearst's inability to pay his bills had reached the point where his long-time accountant, Henry Bicknell, resigned after twenty-three years of service. "There seems to be a lack of appreciation of the fact that payrolls, paper bills, trade acceptances and other immediate obligations must be met with daily cash payments," Bicknell wrote Hearst. The accountant had spent his life with Hearst holding back payments and adopting a series of "expedients to meet these demands." He was no longer willing to do that.[8]

Two days after receiving Bicknell's letter, Hearst authorized Morgan to begin work again, but on the smaller "bungalows" instead of the more expensive main building. Three would be built at once, others in the future. For the time being, these were referred to as Houses or Cottages A, B, and C. Later each would be named for the view from the front window. House A, which looked out on the Pacific, would become Casa del Mar; House B, which faced the mountains, Casa del Monte; House C, which looked west toward the setting sun, Casa del Sol. In a three-page, single-spaced letter mailed in late October, with his own annotated drawings attached, the Chief outlined the new construction program. He wanted the bungalows, small houses, or cottages, as they were alternately referred to, sited lower on the hill than originally planned, with their sitting rooms repositioned for maximum views. "The main thing at the ranch is the view," he reminded Morgan. If his drawings were not clear, would "take the train and come west [to] locate the houses exactly." He had, he told Morgan, also made "considerable changes in the interior arrangements." He had enlarged the "closets, because we need them for trunks as well as clothes" and the bathrooms, dressing rooms, and bedrooms in House A, where his family would live until the main building was constructed. He suggested that the large fireplace in House B — the cottage across the plaza from the one his family would be occupying — be replaced with "a Della Robbia bas relief in blue and white, or blue and white and yellow, against the white background of the wall." In response to Morgan's query about the floors, he directed her to use wood instead of tile or concrete, except in the bathrooms which he wanted tiled, floor and ceiling, in white. "Paneling, however, or ceilings, doors or window frames, beams or anything else, which appears to be of wood, should be made of composition [a plaster product that could be painted brown to simulate wood], by all means. In the first place, the composition is cheaper, as it can be cast in any number of duplicates; in the second place, it is non-inflammable; and in the third place, the rats will not eat it, and they will eat anything of wood." Although California-bungalow architecture featured ceilings "open up to the roof," he did not want that style ceiling "in the living room or anywhere. I think flat-beam ceilings, moulded and decorated, are much richer and more home-like."[9]

By early November, Morgan was able to report that her on-site superintendent, Mr. Washburn, the young builder she had imported from Monterey, had "his camp ready and is hauling sand and gravel so that in another two or three weeks things should be pretty well assembled" and construction could begin. Washburn had earlier had rock from Camp Hill tested and the reports, Morgan told Hearst, had shown that it "will make a remarkably fine grade of concrete. I believe it will be economy when the time comes to build the main building, to quarry a good part of the rock needed from under the main building itself — using part of the 'hole' resulting for your basement."[10]

Morgan's toughest job, for the moment, was getting building materials to the old whaling village of San Simeon and then up the hillside. Shipments by water from the Bay Area, the closest source of supplies, had been delayed by a waterfront strike. Only in December did the first lumber for the cottages arrive after a long journey. The lumber had been purchased in Portland, then transported via railway to Oakland where, once the strike was settled, it was loaded onto the *Cleone*, "a very disreputable old coaster," Morgan called it, "carrying cement, . . . nails, reinforcement bars for concrete, ready roofing and a second-hand band saw, and rock crusher." Unfortunately, by the time the lumber arrived, the rains had made the wagon road too slippery to use. Morgan had to not only rebuild it, but find more powerful trucks to haul the materials up the hillside. When she finished with the roadway, she rebuilt the pier so that larger steamers could dock and unload there.[11]

Though Morgan was consistently upbeat in her letters to Hearst, she was, she wrote him in April 1920, plagued by a persistent "shortage of every kind of material and of workmen." All of the workmen she had hired in the winter had left, a few before they had unpacked: "Some stayed a week or more. They all agreed that the living conditions, money and food were all right, but they 'didn't like feeling so far away from things.'" She wrote again, in mid-May, that she had found it "necessary to provide board, lodging and transportation in order to get men in any of the trades, crafts or even plain labor. The cost of temporary shacks, tents, bedding, kitchen and dining outfits, etc. has been heavy . . . The chef says he is the most important man on the mountain and while one does not like to hear it too often, the latest cook is a find."[12]

Hearst approved all of Morgan's attempts to keep the workmen happy, with one exception. When, in the spring of 1921, he learned that some of the crew had been hunting and fishing on the property, he sent off an uncharacteristically harsh letter to Morgan: "Impossible to allow men on Hill to wander over the ranch or to fish or hunt . . . If you hired a plumber to fix your bathroom you would not expect him to be wandering around your parlor or reading your books in the library. We do not even allow indiscriminate hunting or fishing by guests on ranch. . . . Please definitely instruct Washburn I am sorry but a very definite stand is necessary in such matters to protect the property."[13]

Morgan was now spending almost every weekend in San Simeon. On Friday evenings, she booked an upper berth (the upper afforded her room to work on her portable drafting table) in a sleeping car on the southbound eight o'clock Lark. The train arrived at San Luis Obispo at 2 A.M. After a bowl of milk and bread, she began the long trip by automobile over paved and unpaved roads to the ridge on Hearst's mountain. On Sunday evening, she took the train back north, arriving in San Francisco at dawn.[14]

The tiny architect and the tall, overweight publishing tycoon made an odd couple, but they worked well together. Hearst provided Morgan with recommendations not only for the size, shape, and siting of the main buildings and the surrounding cottages, but for furnishing the houses and landscaping the hillside. Millicent was, through the early 1920s, the third partner in this enterprise. In his instructions to Morgan, Hearst referred to her regularly and when he did not, used the pronoun "we" to suggest that he had consulted her on the question at hand. Though he was seeing Marion regularly in New York, visiting her on location, spending time with her at his apartment at the Bryant Park Studios, and enjoying weekends in good weather cruising the Hudson on the *Oneida,* he had no intention of abandoning Millicent and his five boys. His vacation home on Camp Hill was to be a family home. He would spend his summers there, while Marion remained in New York, filming her moving pictures.

While Morgan's construction crew worked on the exterior of the three guest cottages, Hearst, Millicent, and Morgan began to design the main building, which would become known as the castle or the big house — Casa Grande. This was to be Hearst's personal front page, his signature on the landscape. He wanted to build in a style that was indigenous to California, but agreed with Morgan that the Mission style of early California Spanish architecture was too primitive. Like other wealthy Californians, he was drawn to a "neo-Mediterranean," "Spanish Colonial" style that looked for inspiration not to early California but to the southern Spanish Renaissance. Though this style "had no historic association with California, or rather with the Spanish architecture in California," he asked Morgan rhetorically if it would "not be better to do something a little different than other people are doing out in California as long as we do not do anything incongruous?"[15]

It made perfect sense that Hearst, having decided to build himself a dream house — surrounded by dream cottages — in a "city on the hill" in Southern California, would look to a Mediterranean model. As the historian of California Kevin Starr has written, Mediterraneanism at the turn of the century represented an essential ingredient of the California dream:

> It challenged Californians to achieve something better in the manner of American living: to design their cities and homes with reference to the poetry of the past and in harmony with the land and the smiling sun. It asked them to bring their gardens to ordered luxuriance. . . . Here in California, Mediterraneanism suggested, might emerge a people living amidst beauty . . . a people animated by a full play of sense and spirit.[16]

A defining component of the Mediterranean style, as incorporated in the San Simeon design, was the integration of architecture and landscape, house and garden. The esplanades, walkways, and plazas became essential design elements, intended, as Hearst wrote Morgan in December of 1919, to "bring all the structures together into a harmonious whole." In February 1920, he wrote Mr. Fairchild, the editor in San Francisco who was acting as his business agent at San Simeon, that he wanted "all paths, pergolas, terraces, etc. finally finished with the planting by May first. I propose coming west, living in houses and superintending planting and such details."[17]

Though Morgan worked with a succession of landscape designers and gardeners, she was responsible for the overall plan. Hearst had chosen to build his Mediterranean village 1,600 feet above sea level but well below the highest peak of the Santa Lucias. The hilltop was rugged, steep, and very rocky, dotted here and there with some California laurel and coast live oaks. Though the views were extraordinary, the landscape was not spectacular enough for Hearst. To improve it would, in the end, require almost as much time, effort, and funding as it did to build the cottages and Casa Grande. First the ridge had to be entirely regraded and terraced. Then topsoil had to be brought up the hill and water piped down from natural springs. Where the ground was too rocky to dig, workmen used pickaxes to open crevices, inserted sticks of dynamite and set them off, then filled the holes with topsoil. Only after the ground had been thus prepared could the trees, shrubs, plants, and flowers be hauled up the five-mile curving roadway to their final destinations.

The first shipment of plants, mostly geraniums and roses, arrived on the hillside from a nursery in Santa Barbara in early 1921. Through January and

February, Hearst and Morgan exchanged correspondence on the "color floral scheme for houses." Each of the guesthouses was to have its own garden with its own color scheme. Hearst's cottage would be planted in pink and white to set off the dark blue and white frieze tile. The garden in front of House C would be crimson and deep yellow; the House B garden would be planted in blue, light yellow, and orange. Hearst proposed that bougainvilleas be planted to climb up the walls and terraces of House A and that oleanders, heliotrope, and red, white, and yellow French flowering cacti be placed in the courtyards of Houses B and C. Elsewhere on the hillside, he asked Morgan to consider "flowers like hollyhocks . . . some flowering trees like magnolia, flowering eucalyptus, and blue flowering tree seen in Santa Barbara. Advise Italian cypress for certain effects . . . Don't think I like ivy for bedding. It is too black and buggy."[18]

W. R. asked his old friend the artist Orrin Peck to work with Morgan on laying out the gardens. While he was in residence at San Simeon, Orrin also became Morgan's chief consultant on the fireplaces, which Hearst said were emitting too much smoke. Peck, who had no other visible means of support — and had probably not received a regular allowance since Phoebe's death — was delighted to have work. Will, in turn, was delighted to have his oldest friend back from Europe.

No one amused him as much as Orrin and no one got along as well with the women in his life. Orrin had, in the fifty years he and Will had been friends, been close to Phoebe — and Will's chief defender — as well as to Tessie, Millicent, and now Marion. By the time he relocated to San Simeon, he was approaching sixty and, though apparently in good health, stouter than ever from a lifetime of good eating. In early 1921, he took a break from his work on the hilltop to visit a friend in Los Angeles. While there he suffered a fatal heart attack.

Orrin's death, following by only a few years that of Jack Follansbee, who had died of alcoholism in a New York sanatorium in December of 1914, deprived Hearst of his two oldest, closest friends. Although in the years to come, he would establish personal relationships with several of his longtime editors, Brisbane chief among them, no one would replace Follansbee and Peck. He had grown up with them, traveled with them, and been defended by them when his mother complained about his indiscretions. Follansbee had been his partner in Mexico and, for a brief time, his roommate in New York; Orrin Peck had been his best man and accompanied him and Millicent on their honeymoon. They had always been there when he needed them. He would sorely miss them.

* * *

Through the winter and spring of 1920, while Morgan was building his cottages and landscaping his hillside, Hearst was shopping for art, furnishings, and architectural elements for his rooms, courtyards, and terraces, which he transported to the West Coast in private railway cars. The first carload arrived in March, the second on May 18. While the cottages were being finished, the material was stored in warehouses at the foot of the hill. On May 23, Hearst wrote Morgan that he had "bought some more stuff at the last auction sale of the season. I am sending it in a third car, which should arrive in about a month from date." There followed a single-spaced two-page letter describing what he had bought and where he wanted it placed. The pair of excellent doors and matched window grills were for House A; the two pairs of matched doors with Renaissance panels and a window grille for House B; the two fine Hispano Moresque columns of the twelfth century were for the loggia of House C, the big stone mantel with the grotesque figures, the twenty-six rather plain iron and glass lanterns, the Gothic stalls, Gothic pictures, and the large, square fifteenth-century Italian sideboard were for the trophy, living, and dining rooms of the main house whose foundation had not yet been laid.[19]

Had he chosen to, Hearst could have furnished every room in Casa Grande with items in storage from his own and his mother's art collections. He preferred not to. Collecting was his oldest and his most constant passion. Through good times and bad, since his first trip to Europe with his mother, he had been a compulsive shopper, hungry to possess every object of beauty he came across. Hearst did not rely on "experts" to tell him what to buy and why. Like J. Pierpont Morgan, the collector he most resembled in the catholicity of his tastes and the money he spent to indulge them, Hearst did not limit himself to one scholarly adviser, or to one specific period, one genre, or a single standard of taste. And like Morgan, he never sought to strike a bargain for anything he wanted. He bought from every major dealer and gallery in Europe and New York City. Alice Head, who was in charge of his magazine company in London, was his primary buyer in the British Isles and Paris. Luigi G. Gallandt worked as his agent on commission in Italy. Arthur and Mildred Stapley Byne, who had spent their lives writing about and collecting Spanish art, scouted for him in Spain. Karl von Wiegand, his chief correspondent in Germany, oversaw Eastern and Central European acquisitions.[20]

"The question of getting good art objects in Austria, Hungary, and Russia is very important to me," Hearst wrote von Wiegand in March of 1921, "and I think it would be well for you to employ or retain, with additional payment for each definite assignment, some experts on armor, pictures, tapestries, etc." He had discovered quite by accident that the Vienna Hof Museum was selling off some of its pictures: "If things are to be sold, I suppose I might as well be a bidder for them as anyone else. So kindly take steps to get the fullest information and let me know in ample time."[21]

While American millionaires had for a generation been transporting European art across the Atlantic, never before had the contrast between European indebtedness and American prosperity been as great as it was in the 1920s. Not only individual works of art, but entire monasteries, castles, and country estates were being auctioned off by impoverished nobles and clerics who had been deprived of both wealth and standing in the aftermath of the Great War. "At the present time a good many things are being forced into the market by the money stringency among the former nobility and aristocracy," von Wiegand wrote Hearst from Germany in the fall of 1921. "Every conceivable thing in the way of art, gold- and silverware, pearls and diamonds, is constantly being offered me or submitted to me with the request whether I know any Americans who would be interested in purchasing such things."[22]

No one, especially in Central Europe, had been spared the ravages of war, not even the man who was chancellor of Germany from 1900 to 1909. In October of 1922, von Wiegand informed Hearst that he had just had dinner with "Prince and Princess von Bülow. . . . One time one of the world's most famous statesmen, Bülow, like hundreds of other Germans is financially in a bad way, and is compelled to sell some of his priceless treasures." The situation was much the same in Spain, where the Bynes reported to Julia Morgan in the fall of 1925 that there was no "question about the willingness of the Spanish Lords, Dukes, and Marqueses to sell their properties, nor is even the question of getting State permission so serious." The only problem Hearst might encounter in removing artwork from Spain, the Bynes warned, was that "the villages or towns in which the edifices are situated [might] rise up and through the press carry on a campaign against you."[23]

Hearst was not concerned. He had no qualms whatsoever about stealing away European art treasures at bargain prices. Just as the Romans, two thousand years before, had signaled their ascendancy in the Mediterranean world by stripping the Greek isles of their treasures, so would twentieth-century Americans like Hearst celebrate their empire's newfound prominence. From Hearst's vantage point, the wholesale transmigration of art and antiquities to his New World was an act of creative rescue. Europe was dying or, more accurately, destroying itself through war, revolution, and financial irresponsibility. As it could no longer be counted on to protect its treasures, it was best they be carted away to San Simeon.

Directly after the war, the Chief had, through the Bynes, purchased a derelict stone monastery in Burgos, Spain. "It was used as a storehouse for wine vats," Hearst wrote Lawrence O'Reilly, his personal secretary in New York, "and was so dirty and reeking with bad smells that nobody could visit it. It is still, I understand, used for the same purpose. It is not being guarded or protected or preserved." When word got out, however, that Hearst had bought the monastery, the Spanish authorities declared it "a public monument" and forbade its removal. Furious at the Spanish government's interference, Hearst directed O'Reilly to "get Secretary [of State] Hughes to communicate to the Spanish Government about it and see if the matter could not be straightened out in some way. Please see what can be done? Suppose you go down to Washington and see Ned McLean [the owner of the *Washington Post* and a good friend of President Harding] to help you. He is very influential with the administration." The Spanish government may have stood firm in this instance, as there is no known record of this particular monastery having been shipped or received.[24]

Following the example set by the architect Stanford White, arguably the foremost American interior designer of his era, Hearst favored a generic European historicism that transcended spatial, temporal, and stylistic boundaries. He considered the European past as a resource to be plundered and rearranged, not a sacrament to be revered. To slavishly restore or recreate European designs was to diminish the significance of the American present.

Like Bernard Berenson, the foremost art critic of that day, who had attended Harvard with him and also studied with Charles Eliot Norton, Hearst believed that "the end of art was delight." He did not need the refracted glory of the art object to bestow on him the aura of culture. He had such faith in his own taste that he felt no compunction about improving upon the old masters, when he deemed it necessary to do so. After seeing a photograph of the sixteenth-century "Fountain of Venus" by Niccolò Tribolo, probably in Edith Wharton's *Italian Villas and Their Gardens,* he directed Morgan to have two copies of the fountain carved in marble and installed on either side of the lower terrace of Casa del Mar. Tribolo's fountain had been topped by a hefty Venus, posed rather awkwardly on one leg, wringing out her wet hair. Hearst improved upon it by substituting statues of svelte, athletic-looking, flapper-style nymphs sculpted by a contemporary German artist.[25]

Like most collectors of his generation, Hearst bought regularly, though not exclusively, from the art dealer Sir Joseph Duveen, who maintained establishments in New York, London, and Paris. In May of 1926, Joseph Duveen wrote him an unctuous letter about some twelfth-century stained glass that was being sold by "Mrs. O. H. P. Belmont [Oliver Hazard Perry Belmont] who was, you know, W. K. Vanderbilt [Alva Vanderbilt]. . . . Now my dear Friend, this is something stupendous and you are going to have it. If by chance you are in her neighborhood (as I know you travel about so much) before I return, I can arrange for you to see it because the house is for sale, and it is on that pretext that you can see the glass. I assure you you will be amazed. After all, forty years ago one could find such things, but they are becoming increasingly scarce." Duveen, who was sailing to Europe with Mrs. Belmont, promised to negotiate with her for the stained glass. He assured Hearst that he was "not going to make any profit out of this matter. You will have the glass at the price I pay for it."[26]

We don't know if Hearst ever bought Mrs. Belmont's stained glass, but the following year he purchased her Sands Point estate for Millicent.

Hearst was also a regular customer of the American Art Association and the Anderson galleries, which would later be merged into the Parke-Bernet Galleries. One of his favorite pastimes was gallery shopping. Emile Gauvreau recalled in his memoirs that soon after being hired by Hearst to edit the *Mirror* in the late 1920s he accompanied him on a visit to a 57th Street gallery in Manhattan. Hearst spent the next few hours "immersed . . . in hundreds of photographs of medieval fireplaces, castles in Scotland, interiors of paneled rooms, paintings and statuary. He bought that afternoon, apparently by looking at pictures, the rooms of an entire French cloister of the seventeenth century and asked my opinion of a sixteenth-century fireplace, every stone of which was to be transported from abroad."[27]

Though unfailingly cordial, the Chief was not an easy man to do business with. One of his least ingratiating habits was that of visiting dealers, reserving pieces, and then forgetting to pay for or release them, forcing the dealers to pester his subordinates to find out what he intended to do.[28]

Besides buying directly from dealers, galleries, and auction houses in New York and during his European tours, Hearst was one of the world's great catalogue shoppers. Every dealer and auction house, Duveen's included, spent huge sums of money producing guides to their collections, which were sent to Hearst wherever he happened to be. Hearst put aside time from his other duties almost every day to review the piles of catalogues, brochures, memoranda, letters, and photographs sent to him.

Those items he was interested in bidding on were marked in the catalogue with a red ring around the number of the lot. The catalogue was then forwarded to Chris MacGregor in New York, who was authorized to bid on the marked items. As Joe Willicombe, the imposing-looking former *New York American* reporter who had become Hearst's personal secretary in the early 1920s, informed MacGregor, it was MacGregor's job "to get all the things he has marked, unless they go to outrageously high prices . . . Do not make the mistake I made the first day I attended of letting some get away from me under the impression that the prices were high . . . Just get them, unless you are sure someone has rigged you up to rob you."[29]

When, as happened occasionally, Hearst or his surrogates were outbid, he directed MacGregor to find out who had bid against him. Though Hearst didn't care much about the money involved, he had no desire to get into bidding wars with men as wealthy as he was. Duveen was occasionally called upon to mediate between the titans, most of whom were his customers. In June of 1927, Hearst wrote Duveen to apologize for having outbid Clarence Mackay, another multimillionaire who had inherited a mining fortune, at a recent auction. Both had bid up the price of a helmet which Hearst eventually purchased: "I did not have in mind any conflict with Mr. Mackay. . . . I do not know whether it is possible or desirable to have an arrangement with Mr. Mackay on sales, but if it is desirable, we should have a little more definite understanding."[30]

No matter what the circumstances, Hearst never paid cash, offering personal "notes" instead. His patronage on these terms was a mixed blessing — especially as he delayed paying on his notes. The Bynes had such trouble getting paid that at one point Arthur Byne informed Julia Morgan that they had decided to do no more business with Mr. Hearst. He wrote her at some length:

Since my first disastrous dealings with him I have found out a great deal about him from dealers in Paris. He makes a business (and incidentally considerable gain) of holding people off for years and then settling on his own terms. . . . When I say all this I don't mean that I am not willing to cooperate with you and Mr. Hearst; in fact nothing would give me greater pleasure. But my first experience . . . proved to me that I must above all protect myself first in dealings with Mr. Hearst. I have never had a word from him though I have written innumerable letters. There is no use in sending me a cable "BUY ETC. ETC." when the amount involves thousands and thousands of dollars; I have not the money and there is no reason why I should employ it if I had. Furthermore Mr. Hearst is utterly unknown in Spain for which reason he can't buy here on credit as elsewhere.[31]

In early 1927, the treasurer of the American Art Association turned down Hearst's request to extend repayment of his bill for an additional year. At the time, Hearst owed the auction house a quarter of a million dollars and at least that much to consignors from whom he had purchased objects at A.A.A. auctions. The treasurer threatened to notify "these consignors that Mr. Hearst is not taking care of the obligations he assumed when he agreed to buy from them. . . . If you will pardon my saying so," he wrote Albert Kobler, Hearst's New York editor who was also his intermediary with the galleries, "I do not believe that Mr. Hearst would like to have us put him in this position." Hearst offered to return the pictures he had purchased. Unwilling to take back merchandise already sold, the auction house accepted the Chief's terms for payment.[32]

Hearst had, by the early 1920s, become so notorious a spender that he had to use aliases and agents to avoid the escalation in prices that occurred when it was known that he was bidding on an item. This need for subterfuge had unintended consequences for art historians. For decades, it had been known that Antonio Canova had sculpted three versions of his *Venus*. One was purchased by Lucien Bonaparte and then, in 1816, sold to Lord Landsdowne. It was later resold at auction in 1930 to a George Willson and thereafter "lost" forever. What was not known was that the George Willson who purchased it was Hearst's father-in-law and the missing *Venus* was not lost but on view in the Assembly Room on the ground floor of Casa Grande.

Hearst's collecting tastes were widely eclectic. His collection ranged from the extraordinary to the ordinary and mediocre. It was probably weakest in paintings. Unlike other collectors of his day, Hearst had no special interest in paintings — except for Madonnas, which he seemed to buy by the dozens.[33]

Dealers like Sir Joseph Duveen, while only too happy to take Hearst's money, never considered the publisher a serious collector. Hearst, wrote S. N. Behrman, "was what Duveen termed an accumulator, rather than a collector. . . . In Duveen's opinion, Hearst's collateral interest in ibexes, llamas, and Welsh castles kept him from attaining the rarefied heights on which he himself liked to operate."[34]

At any given auction or sale, he could be counted on to buy in numerous different categories. According to Wesley Towner, author of *The Elegant Auctioneers*, a history of the Parke-Bernet Galleries and the auction houses that preceded it, Hearst bought dozens of different items at the Stanford White auction in 1907; a knife and fork from the sale of the Chicago streetcar magnate Charles Tyson Yerkes' collection in 1910; shoe buckles, snuff

boxes, whist counters, and wine glasses from an auction of George Washington's relics in 1917; a pair of paintings by minor sixteenth-century primi-
tives at a 1926 estate sale of Viscount Leverhulme, the Lever Brothers soap
king; and what seemed like carloads of bridal chests, slant-top writing
desks, Sheraton canopy bedsteads, old New England wagon seats, silver,
pewter, and a Chippendale mahogany highboy at the auction of Philadelphia wool merchant Howard Reifsnyder's collection in 1929.[35]

To receive, catalogue, and store his purchases from abroad, Hearst had
leased a five-story warehouse in the Bronx, on 143rd Street near Southern
Boulevard. He would purchase it outright in February of 1927. Lawrence
O'Reilly, who had been his political secretary through the 1910s, was originally put in charge. When O'Reilly died in 1922, he was replaced by Chris
MacGregor, a former reporter, who had proved himself trustworthy as the
boys' chauffeur and babysitter. Miss Schrader, who had been Hearst's personal secretary at the Clarendon and still worked out of an office there, kept
track of the accounts in New York City.[36]

Hearst's art collecting operation had, by the early 1920s, become so extensive that he formed his own company, International Studio Arts Corporation, as a wholly owned subsidiary of his chief holding company, to
purchase his art for him and, when necessary, clear customs. Though the
bulk of Hearst's collection was stored in the Bronx, where MacGregor and a
staff of twenty, including clerks, photographers, bookkeepers, packers, han-
dlers, and customs clearers, received artwork from Europe and stored, catalogued, and shipped it West, Hearst had items squirreled away in facilities
all across the city, including a huge garage he owned around the corner
from the Clarendon, at 325 West 85th Street, and space in commercial storage facilities on 42nd Street, opposite the Grand Central terminal, on 52nd
Street and Seventh Avenue, and on East 61st and East 55th Streets. He
owned additional warehouses and storage facilities in San Simeon, San
Francisco, and Los Angeles.[37]

With so many objects stored in so many different locations, it was often
impossible for him to find what he was looking for. In July of 1921, Hearst
decided that he wanted to ship West a "big painting of Napoleon in imperial robes" which he had bought twenty years before in Paris. He delegated
O'Reilly in New York to track it down through Wells Fargo, which had
shipped it, and "Daquin," the French dealer "who used to buy for me." We
don't know if it was ever found.[38]

Record-keeping problems were complicated by the steady inflow of new
materials. In June of 1921, Joe Willicombe was informed by George Thomp-

son, the Chief's valet, that Mr. Hearst wanted the things he bought at Anderson's, a New York gallery and auction house, sent up to the Clarendon, and the things he bought at Clarke's, another dealer, sent out West. Willicombe, confused because Hearst hadn't been at Anderson's in months, asked him what items he was referring to. The Chief drew a blank. Days later, he remembered that he had dropped into Anderson's months earlier — without Willicombe — and bought "a couple of Egyptian bronzes."[39]

§ 18 §

Marion, Millicent,
and the Movies

HEARST SPENT ANOTHER SUMMER VACATION in California in 1920. With two political conventions to cover, San Simeon under construction, five children, one wife, and one mistress, there was too much to keep him occupied in the States for him to resume his annual summer motor tours of Europe. He arrived at San Simeon, with the boys and Millicent, in late July for a family vacation on Camp Hill. Unwilling to be separated from Marion, however, even for the summer, he moved her to Los Angeles, installed her in the Hollywood Hotel — with mother and sisters as chaperones — and leased space at Brunton Studios so that she could complete her latest movie, *Buried Treasure,* a confused story of reincarnation, Spanish galleons, and pirates. To the despair of Joseph Moore, his corporate treasurer, who complained vociferously that he could not afford to pay for space in Los Angeles while carrying "an enormous studio overhead" in New York, the Chief also made arrangements for Marion to shoot her next film, *The Love Piker,* in Los Angeles.[1]

Though Hearst had pushed Miss Morgan as hard as he could, she had not been able to complete any of the guesthouses. He, Millicent, and the boys were forced to spend another summer — he hoped their last one — in their Venetian-style tents. The hillside, Bill, Jr. remembered, was covered with "workmen and their little tents and their little wooden shacks. . . . There was an administration tent where the Big House is. And it was three or four times the size of the other tents, but the same material. Very dark green, dark heavy canvas." At one end of the big green tent was the dining table, at the other there were "a couple of projection machines" which threw film images onto a "big screen outside about thirty, fifty feet away . . . or more, one hundred maybe."[2]

Hearst was preoccupied with moving pictures that summer. When he wasn't working with Marion on her movie career, he was writing, producing, directing, shooting, and acting in his own home movie at San Simeon. "The Lighthouse Keeper's Daughter" starred Millicent as the daughter who was abducted by cowboy villains. W. R. played the hero who rescued her on horseback. The film was a mock Pearl White serial with lots of horseback chasing, a scene of abduction and rescue on the open seas, fires, bombs, villains, and cowboys. His sons ten-year-old John and eleven-year-old Bill, Jr. did the special effects and lit the sulfur flares to make the smoke for one of the explosions, almost asphyxiating themselves in the process. Hearst's guests and ranch hands played the minor roles.

Millicent, as the damsel in distress, was in almost every scene. Though in her late thirties, with five small children, she looked much younger — athletic, trim, and very much at ease in front of the camera. Hearst, her rescuer, cut a slightly ridiculous figure, too old and overweight to easily play the part he had given himself. The film was a delightful spoof of the cowboy melodramas which were then all the rage, with Hearst's intertitles, in rhyming verse, offering a running tongue-in-cheek commentary on the film and the filmmaker.

> The tense excitement strains
>   One's very vitals.
> It takes a lot of brains
>   To write these titles. . . .
> The hero has the fattest part
>   And gets the greatest glory
> But that's because he runs the ranch
>   And also writes the story.
>
> Dog gone it! I don't want
>   To utter strictures
> Or run down other great
>   Directors' pictures
>
> But Griffith, Ince, and Dwan
>   Have never seen
> A thing as good as this
>   Flashed on the screen.
>
> You watch and see
>   I'll bet you will agree
> With me.

The film ends with Hearst doing a Spanish fandango for his guests, with Millicent looking on. They embrace and kiss.

He loves the dainty maiden
And our hero never misses
An opportunity to greet
His darling girl with kisses.[3]

Looking at this home movie today, it is difficult to believe that all the time he was making it with Millicent as his star, he was stealing away to the south to rendezvous with his mistress. Because he could not bring Marion to San Simeon, dared not meet with her in Los Angeles, and was, according to her biographer Fred Guiles, jealous of the attention she was receiving from younger men in Hollywood, Hearst had rented a large private estate for the two of them in a lemon grove just outside Santa Barbara, halfway between Los Angeles and his ranch. To provide himself with a legitimate reason for spending time in Santa Barbara, he had also rented office space there and even considered building a studio.[4]

The year 1920 had been good, though not profitable, for the Hearst film companies. It had cost Hearst a small fortune to construct his own moving-picture studio on the site of the former Sulzer's Harlem River Park Casino between 126th and 127th Streets on Second Avenue. The space was large enough to shoot two features at once. There was also a spacious wood-paneled office for Hearst — which he rarely occupied — and offices for Urban and assorted Cosmopolitan Productions executives; dressing rooms for Marion and the stars; cubbyholes for the directors; and lots of storage space for the art, antiques, and furniture that Hearst bought at auction and had trucked to the studio to add "class" to his pictures.

Hearst's team of publicists, including M. R. Werner, a future biographer of William Jennings Bryan, were headquartered at the studio, their appointed task to find or invent items for the daily press and the trade journals. Werner interviewed "actors, actresses, and directors. If their lives were not colorful enough or were too colorful, we had to take liberties with them. We manufactured innocent habits for men who really preferred whiskey to their mothers. . . . We made Alma Rubens a direct descendant of Peter Paul Rubens." Louella Parsons was not yet on the Hearst payroll, but Marie Manning, who as Beatrice Fairfax wrote a "love and advice" column, the cartoonist Harry Hershfield, the reporter Nellie Bly, and the Hearst papers' favorite psychologist, Hereward Carrington, visited the studio regularly. "They praised our pictures in words and drawing," Werner recalled, "and every Hearst paper ran most of the stuff. We were allowed carte blanche. All the Hearst papers in the United States — and there were quite a few of them in those days — had to print practically everything we sent them about Cosmopolitan pictures, and all of them published full-page advertisements day after day during the run of one of our pictures in their towns."[5]

Unfortunately, though unlimited publicity might have helped the Hearst pictures at the box office, it couldn't guarantee their success. Of the five *Cosmopolitan* features released in 1920, only one, *Humoresque,* was a hit. Directed by Frank Borzage with a screenplay by Frances Marion, *Humoresque,* like almost all of the Hearst films produced that year, was based on a *Cosmopolitan* story by Fannie Hurst, this one about a Russian-Jewish family on the Lower East Side of Manhattan. Alma Rubens, Hearst's "brunette," was chosen to play the lead, though Vera Gordon, the veteran of the Yiddish stage who played the "Jewish mama," stole every scene. The film, designed by Joseph Urban, was a first-class tearjerker, about a poor immigrant boy who, with his mother's love and encouragement, becomes a brilliant concert violinist, enlists in the Great War, returns wounded, and is nursed back to health — and the concert stage — by his fiancée and his mother. The happy ending was required by Zukor and Hearst. It had not been part of the original story.

Neither Hearst, who produced the picture, nor Zukor, who distributed it, were particularly enthusiastic about the project. "If you want to show Jews," Zukor told Frances Marion — or so she claimed, "show Rothschilds, banks and beautiful things. It hurts us Jews — we don't all live in poor houses." Despite Zukor's fears, the film not only was a commercial success but was awarded a 1920 *Photoplay* Gold Medal that was presented to Hearst, "because," as the magazine explained, "no picture can be greater than its producer. It takes the producer's faith, foresightedness, money, and appreciation to make a great picture."[6]

Hearst would have agreed entirely. He had put together the team that made the picture and given the designer Joseph Urban carte blanche to spend whatever he wanted on it. Urban brought an operatic sumptuousness to the three-dimensional sets he built for Hearst's cavernous studio on Second Avenue. He had quickly become, as Hearst had expected when he hired him, the most important man on the set and in the Cosmopolitan studios in New York. He was now doing not only the set design, but the lighting, costuming, and makeup as well. When he refused to make another film with Alma Rubens because he found her difficult to work with, no doubt because she was already under the influence of the heroin that would kill her, Hearst removed her from the picture she was scheduled to shoot. She remained on the payroll, however, fueling unsubstantiated and untrue rumors that Hearst continued to support her because he had had an affair with her. He refused to fire her because, as he wrote Joseph Moore, he had already "put a lot of advertising behind her and helped create her with our audiences." It was not "easy to get good leading women. . . . Remember we must have the right type, not blonde or ingenue but good looking, dignified and sufficiently good actress."[7]

Although Urban got his way in the Alma Rubens matter, he was never entirely comfortable working for a man who was always watching over his shoulder, often from the balcony above the studio floor. While Hearst seldom interrupted rehearsals or filming, he reviewed rushes, demanded that the director's print be sent to him for approval, and freely made suggestions for casting, design, costuming, and filming. In May 1921, when Hearst proposed a number of retakes on *Enchantment* — in which Marion played a flapper in an updated version of *The Taming of the Shrew* — Urban, exhausted, refused.

"I am very sorry that you are tired, and I know that you must be," Hearst wrote Urban after this standoff. "You work very hard; in fact you have overworked, and we all realize that. . . . You ought to take a good vacation . . . It is well for you to have your nerves in first class condition because this is certainly a trying business. However, my policy is to go smiling through all kinds of difficulties and you must adopt the same policy both for your own sake and for the sake of the institution. . . . You know I have as much personal interest in the success of these pictures as anybody connected with them. I feel as deeply the necessity for making them popular successes as anyone can."[8]

To make further amends and to provide Urban with the vacation he badly needed, W. R. invited him and his daughter, Gretl, to join Marion, her mother and sister, and an entourage of film people for an extended cruise on the 205-foot *Oneida*. While he told his guests that they were sailing only as far as Baltimore and would return at the end of the weekend, he had planned an extravaganza of Hearstian proportions. When, at cocktails on Sunday afternoon, Urban casually remarked that instead of heading home for the work week, they appeared to be sailing in the wrong direction, W. R. "gave one of his rare toothy grins and said: 'Surprise, surprise! The weather's ideal for a nice sea voyage. I have decided we're all going to Mexico.'"

Because none of his guests had been prepared for a long cruise, Hearst had the captain dock the boat at New Orleans, where he treated them to a shopping spree. Though W. R. spent a good deal of the trip going through the great mass of papers he had brought aboard, he was an energetic host and wanted his guests to see everything. In Galveston, Texas, the party disembarked from the *Oneida* and boarded a private railroad car for the six-hour trip to San Antonio and then south into Mexico. At Tampico, Mexico, they rejoined the *Oneida,* which had been sent on ahead, and sailed south to Veracruz, where they boarded another train to Mexico City. In no apparent hurry to get back to New York, Hearst personally escorted his guests through every small Mexican village along the route. Only Marion was left behind during each of these expeditions, "for fear of gossip even when we went to stretch our legs in some godforsaken tiny hamlet," Gretl Urban recalled in her unpublished reminiscences. "In those days Marion was kept under wraps, albeit rather elaborate ones." After visiting Mexico City, the party returned north to Galveston where the yacht was waiting for them. Anxious to get back to his wife, Urban took the train to New York.[9]

The first direct evidence we have that Millicent knew about her husband's relationship to Davies is from the fall of 1921, only months after their yacht cruise to Mexico. Hearst had stayed behind in San Simeon in the summer of 1921, after Millicent and the boys returned to New York. In November, he traveled to Mexico to inspect his Babicora ranchlands. While there, he received a telegram from Joseph Moore with a query from Millicent about the newspaper advertising for *Enchantment,* Marion's new film, which Millicent thought excessive for a film which hadn't yet opened. Hearst telegrammed back asking Moore to explain to Millicent that the prerelease advertisements had been necessary "to comply with Paramount requirements and to give any picture chance for success." He hoped that Millicent would understand this. He wanted her "to be satisfied."[10]

She was not. Five days later, Moore reported to the Chief that Millicent had insisted "all advertising be distinctly on picture and not on star." Hearst responded calmly that he could not permit that. If the Hearst papers in New York ran advertisements that were different from those placed in other publications, it "would cause unpleasant comment in scandal sheets."[11]

Two weeks later, Hearst discovered that the advertisement of *Enchantment* that had appeared in his New York papers had omitted any mention of the star, as Millicent had demanded. He was furious. "This is ridiculous and wrong," he telegrammed Moore in New York. "I thought I made clear that advertisement in our papers were to be the same as in other papers' advertising. Star and photoplay as usual. Has this been done or not? Please promptly proceed to do so now. I cannot allow anybody to run my business but myself. I do not care what the results may be. I intend to manage my own affairs my way. Run all advertising now and hereafter exactly as when I prepared it." By return mail, Moore defended himself by explaining that the *Enchantment* ads had been altered only in the New York papers and only because "of your telegram to the effect you wanted Millicent to be satisfied."[12]

From California, where Hearst returned from his Mexican trip in mid-November, he wrote Moore what he must have hoped would be his final letter on the subject of Millicent's demands and Marion's advertising. This time, his tone was conciliatory, almost apologetic. He had made a mistake in trying to placate his wife: "I am very sorry I interfered . . . but I wanted to please and I thought success would not be needlessly impaired. I was wrong. Advertising was utterly emasculated. It is obvious that outside matters cannot be allowed to interfere with business or else our business will be ruined. . . . Hereafter go right ahead on purely business basis doing what is best for the pictures and allowing no interference from anyone. This telegram is your authority which you can use as required. Can you come west and talk important matters over with me? Perhaps we can go east together."[13]

While Hearst's tone in this letter is almost confessional, his use of the word "emasculated" to describe what had happened to his advertising is telling, as is his insistence that his promotion of Davies was based on purely business concerns. He was not, he tried to convince Moore as he had convinced himself, promoting Marion because she was his mistress, but because she was his star.

W. R. was reunited with his family in December of 1921, when he returned East, after a six-month absence, to spend Christmas with his family. He and Millicent were already leading almost entirely separate lives. She had plenty to do in his absence. Millicent Hearst not only ran a household of five children and dozens of servants in one of the largest private apartments in New York, she had also embarked on a career of her own in society. During the war, she had taken a prominent role in several charities. She served as chair of the Mayor's Committee of Women on National Defense. She organized a campaign to secure a better designed and equipped "soldiers kit" for the boys in the trenches and was a founding member of the Free Milk Fund for Babies. She played a large role in arranging a victory celebration for soldiers returning from Europe, and raised funds for an orthopedic hospital clinic in Brooklyn that treated wounded veterans. While Hearst's reputation during the war was under siege, Millicent's only improved. The former chorus-line dancer and daughter of a vaudeville hoofer had not only become more reputable than her husband, but her standing as a philanthropist had grown to the point that in the summer of 1921 and again in 1923, her name would be floated as a possible candidate for a seat in Congress.[14]

It may well have been during the 1922 Christmas holidays that Bill, Jr. witnessed one of the few scenes of open marital discord in the Hearst household. Millicent, Bill, Jr. recalled in his memoirs, confronted W. R. "with the fact that she knew he was seeing another woman. Mother was very upset and my father tried to calm her. Suddenly she took off her wedding band and threw it on the floor, declaring, 'If this is all you think of our marriage, keep it!' She stomped out of the room and remained secluded for several days. When Mom returned, she was wearing her ring. She and Pop pretended the incident never took place, but apparently he never forgot it."[15]

Perhaps to compensate Millicent for the pain he was causing and to demonstrate his commitment to the family, Hearst consulted with her regularly in planning their family vacation home at San Simeon. In the months to come, Hearst's letters to Julia Morgan were filled with references to Millicent's wishes. There was no area of design, landscaping, or construction in which Millicent did not feel competent to make suggestions. In March of 1922, she asked that Miss Morgan add a billiard room for the boys. In late August, she complained that there was "not apparently adequate steel reinforcement of big building." In September, she demanded — and her husband agreed — that the guesthouses be redesigned and rebuilt so that each bedroom had a bathroom of its own.[16]

At the same time that they were designing their vacation home in California, W. R. and Millicent were embarking on a renovation of their Clarendon apartment so immense that it would take two full years to complete. Whatever had been said — or left unsaid — about their marriage, it appears that they decided to proceed as if Miss Davies did not exist.[17]

Hearst had embarked on two extraordinarily costly ventures — building San Simeon and the Cosmopolitan studios — at the worst possible time. The economy was in turmoil, buffeted by a severe postwar depression and a succession of strikes that involved over four million workers — one-fifth of the industrial workforce. For newspaper publishers, the economic downturn was exacerbated by the precipitous end of wartime price controls and the resulting threefold increase in the price of newsprint between 1916 and 1921. The effect on the Hearst papers, the nation's leading purchaser of newsprint, was, Joseph Moore telegrammed the Chief in April of 1920, severe enough to threaten "the very existence of our newspapers."[18]

While Moore warned that "the financial situation of your various Companies is in an alarmingly serious condition," the Chief went blithely on, spending money like water. According to Gene Fowler, who worked as a reporter for the Hearst papers through the 1920s, "Mr. Hearst had less regard for money, as such, than anyone else of his financial size. Arthur Brisbane once said that his chief was the only man he ever knew who could not get along on less than ten million dollars a year."[19]

Though already the proud owner of the *Oneida*, the Chief directed Lawrence O'Reilly in May of 1921 to look into buying him "a sea-going steamer . . . or a passenger steamer or even a freight steamer . . . preferably an oil-burner or boat with Diesel engines." When he learned that publisher Frank Munsey had bought a "castle" in Germany, he directed his chief correspondent in Germany, Karl von Wiegand, to find a "really fine castle" for him in Bavaria, the Tyrol, or Austria, this at the very same time he was spending hundreds of thousands of dollars annually constructing his castle at San Simeon.[20]

The Chief had no compunctions about spending millions of dollars because he considered every bit of it earned income. He subscribed to the labor theory of value — with an ironic twist. Because wise business executives contributed considerably more "value" than common laborers, they deserved more in the form of recompense. "It is certainly a fact that 'the laborer is worthy of his hire,'" he wrote in a 1918 editorial, "but it is equally a fact that the manager, the inventor, the promoter, the developer, the director, the executor, or whatever word you call the creating head of an enterprise, is worthy of HIS hire." The example he gave to prove his point came directly out of the Hearst family saga: "The men who dig in the ground for gold are worthy of their share of the gold found; but the man who tells them where to dig in order to get the gold is of determining importance and is worthy of liberal compensation. Wars are won by GENERALS; not merely by armies."[21]

Wherever he was, recalled Jimmy Swinnerton, his friend and cartoonist in San Francisco and New York, Hearst "worked harder than any of his men." As he traveled often, living virtually a bicoastal existence through the early 1920s, he carried his "office" with him. When in New York, he held most of his business meetings at the Clarendon. Short, round George Thompson, who had waited on him twenty years before at the Hoffman House, had graduated from valet/butler to gatekeeper. It was his task — one he seemed to enjoy — to keep Hearst's visitors waiting until he, "George Tom," concluded the Chief was ready to see them.[22]

While Thompson presided at the Clarendon, Joe Willicombe was required to travel with Hearst wherever he went, often at literally a moment's notice. "No indication yet of when or where we are going," Willicombe wrote Lawrence O'Reilly, his friend and predecessor as Hearst's secretary, in June of 1921. "Get all kinds of hints. Saturday it looked like Chicago direct and then to the Coast. That was the first indication. Yesterday Chief said he would be in town only 'a few days more.' This, of course, for your personal information, if you can make anything out of it." Willicombe was on duty twenty-four hours a day, with pad and pencil at the ready. He had made himself indispensable to the Chief because he knew shorthand, needed very little sleep, was willing to be on call every hour of the day or night, was intensely loyal and thoroughly discreet. Although few of Hearst's friends, Marion especially, had anything good to say about Willicombe, the Chief trusted him more than anyone else in his family or employment. Whenever Hearst had a message for his editors, publishers, film executives, art dealers, or family members, he dictated it to Willicombe, who knew the current whereabouts of everyone in Hearst's universe and how to get a phone call or cable to them. The workload was inhuman, but Willicombe never complained. In February of 1921, he apologized to O'Reilly for having sent him so long a letter with so many instructions: "Mr. Hearst shot a number of messages for you at me in between a flock of letters that he unloaded on me as soon as I got in to-day. I'll give them all to you in this one letter, if you don't mind."[23]

The division of labor in the Hearst organization was clear. It was Hearst's job to spend whatever he wanted. It was treasurer Joseph Moore's job to find the money to pay the bills. It was his publishers' and editors' job to make the money that Moore would transfer to Hearst's personal accounts to pay his bills and his and Millicent's generous allowances. That Phoebe had left her son several million dollars did not make matters easier. Her bequests to friends and family and $1 million in estate tax liabilities had quickly depleted the estate of liquid assets.

To meet the Chief's mounting obligations — construction costs at San Simeon were consuming some $25,000–$30,000 a month (equivalent to $230,000–$280,000 a month in 1990s currency) — Moore had borrowed from the New York banks until, in May of 1920, the banks had refused to extend him any more credit. He got additional credit to pay off the still outstanding $250,000 deficit by using as collateral Hearst's shares of stock in Cerro de Pasco, a Peruvian copper mining company that he had inherited from his mother.

Having, with this transaction, exhausted all available sources of credit,

Moore suggested that Hearst try to reduce his deficits by cutting back production at his movie studio. Hearst scornfully rejected his treasurer's recommendations. "Production," he lectured Moore, "is necessary for profit." If Cosmopolitan Productions made fewer moving pictures, it would earn fewer dollars. "We must make twelve pictures per year under the Zukor contract and we should make at least six more to sell."[24]

Still, he agreed with Moore that something was amiss. He was making good moving pictures. If they failed to make money, it had to have been because his control over his pictures ceased at the moment the finished negatives were delivered to Adolph Zukor and Paramount. His inability to control every aspect of the picture business — from production to distribution and exhibition — and his dissatisfaction with the way Zukor was distributing Marion's films never ceased to trouble the Chief. His moods veered abruptly from heady optimism to resignation and defeat. On October 7, 1920, after receiving a congratulatory letter from Zukor on his most recent film, *The World and His Wife*, which was, like *Humoresque*, doing well at the box office, Hearst boasted to Moore that he was "glad to learn from Zukor that public agrees with my views. Am pretty good judge of public taste in Journalism and policies, may be in pictures too." A day later, his mood had darkened considerably. He had, he wrote Moore, decided to "close the film company in a month or two. I don't think it can ever make any money and I am tired of it."[25]

Hearst was convinced that Marion's films were not making money because Zukor was not getting them to the audiences they were intended for. Instead of selling them to theater owners, one at a time, Zukor grouped them into "blocks" with other Paramount pictures and distributed them sight unseen. This meant that theater owners who wanted to exhibit Hearst's superior, high-class Cosmopolitan Productions starring Marion Davies could not do so unless they also bought the cheap, inferior pictures that were block booked with them.

When, in the summer of 1921, it came time for Hearst to renew his distribution agreement with Paramount, the Chief directed Moore to inform Zukor that he would only re-sign the agreement if he was permitted to "make other arrangements with other companies" to release Miss Davies' pictures as "special presentations." "You understand without my stating it," he telegrammed Moore, "my reasons for being interested in these pictures and why they are peculiarly important to me."[26]

Hearst was not used to entering a negotiation in the role of supplicant. As the negotiations for a new distribution agreement dragged on through the summer and into the fall, Hearst became increasingly frantic, almost paranoiac about Zukor, who he feared might be cheating him in some way. The most courteous of men under usual circumstances, Hearst, when crossed, turned into a brutal bully. Never one to do his dirty work for himself, he delegated his subordinates to make and carry out his threats. In a flurry of 4 and 5 A.M. telegrams from San Simeon to New York, Hearst directed Joseph Moore in New York to warn Zukor and Paramount that negotiations had to be completed at once "in friendly or unfriendly way as they see fit. . . . The unfriendly way will give them the biggest exposé they have ever had with civil suits and possible criminal prosecutions with the assistance of the government. I prefer the friendly way if it can be had right."[27]

While negotiating with Zukor, Hearst directed Moore to open discussions on a possible distribution deal with United Artists, the company that Douglas Fairbanks and Mary Pickford had established in partnership with Charles Chaplin and D. W. Griffith. In September 1921, Moore wrote Hearst that it looked "as though we are going to be able to close with United Artists on the four star pictures you mentioned. . . . [Marion was always referred to as "star."] This looks good. The best news however is Zukor now wants to do everything you ask."

Zukor had taken Hearst's threats to heart. Already under investigation by the Federal Trade Commission for his block-booking practices, Zukor could not afford to have Hearst as an enemy, fight off a public lawsuit, and defend himself from the campaign against him the Chief implied he was ready to launch in New York, Los Angeles, Washington, D.C., and everywhere else he owned a newspaper. In the end, Zukor gave Hearst what he wanted. All he asked in return was that the Chief use his influence with "his friend in Washington," President Warren Harding, to solve Paramount's antitrust problems.[28]

The new agreement gave Hearst a higher percentage of the box-office take and Zukor's promise to release Marion's films as "super-specials." Hearst, for his part, agreed to give up the $30,000 monthly "advance" Paramount had been paying him, though Moore pointed out that without these funds coming in, he would have to divert funds from other sources to finance film production. In giving up Zukor's $30,000 monthly advance, the Chief had effectively ransomed his film company in return for special treatment for Marion's pictures.

❧ 19 ❧

A Return to Normalcy

THE POSTWAR RECESSION that had rocked Hearst's business empire — and made life so difficult for Joseph Moore, who had to pay the bills — was as short-lived as it had been severe. By 1922, the American economy had embarked upon an extraordinary seven-year growth cycle. The business boom was stimulated by the beneficent tax policy that President Warren Harding's secretary of the treasury, the Pittsburgh industrialist Andrew Mellon, shepherded through a Republican-dominated Congress. Maximum tax rates for individuals were reduced from a wartime high of 77 percent to 24 percent, excess profits taxes were abolished, and lower rates were set for capital gains. Hearst benefited additionally when Secretary Mellon's appointees at the Income Tax Bureau reduced his tax liabilities for the war years by some $1,737,097.[1]

Taking full advantage of the economic boom and Republican tax policies, Hearst went on a buying spree. In 1921, he purchased two evening papers — the *Times*, in Detroit, and the *Record*, in Boston — and a morning paper, the *Post-Intelligencer*, in Seattle. In 1922, he added an evening paper, the *Herald*, in Los Angeles to complement his morning paper there, and a morning paper, the *Herald*, in Washington, D.C., to complement his evening paper. And he started up three new dailies, the *Oakland Post-Enquirer*, the *Syracuse Telegram*, and the *Rochester Journal*.

Hearst, who never paid cash for anything, borrowed recklessly to make each of these purchases. By the end of 1922, he had exhausted his working capital to pay off existing debt obligations and was still a half million dollars short of meeting them all. "We are absolutely at the end of our string in manipulating finances," Moore telegrammed the Chief on December 29, 1922.[2]

Hearst responded by blaming Moore for allowing him to borrow more than he could repay. "You should be more cautious and conservative," he telegrammed his treasurer. "If I am disposed to embark in a new enterprise, you should have the figures to show me whether or not we can afford to undertake it. . . . I am of a promoting temperament. My disposition is to expand. . . . What I want is to have somebody advise me not to expand before things become disturbing, and to keep expenses down on the various papers and not merely get agitated about them after they have gone up."[3]

Moore was hardly to blame. Time and again, he had tried to rein the Chief in, to stop him from buying a paper mill, to plead with him to cut back film production, to demand that he fire Alma Rubens, who was getting too high a salary for too little work. In the long run, Hearst's decision to buy new dailies would pay off handsomely, but in the short run it had pushed the corporation to the brink of bankruptcy.

While Moore was left to hunt for funds to meet payrolls and to plead with lenders for patience, Hearst continued to buy newspapers. In early 1923, he took out more than $5 million in additional loans and mortgages to buy the *Baltimore American* and the *Baltimore News* from Frank Munsey. When Joseph Moore suggested a year later that he reduce that debt by selling his morning paper to the owners of the *Baltimore Sun,* the Chief, apparently forgetting his previous advice to Moore to rein him in, responded again with anger: "What you propose is last ditch remedy disastrous to our prestige and stimulating to our opposition everywhere. It might do much more harm than good. Any dub can confess failure and throwing up sponge is not generally considered evidence of courage as much as of incompetence."[4]

By the summer of 1923, the Chief was so overdrawn on his New York accounts that he was asked to take his business elsewhere. "Yesterday the president of the Chase National Bank sent for me," Joseph Moore telegrammed Hearst in San Simeon in July, "and after going over the situation as regards our accounts there, which showed the *American* account overdrawn, the *Journal* account overdrawn, the Cosmopolitan Finance Corporation account with an extremely small balance, the Star Company account with a balance of $2500 and a total loan of $800,000, he asked if we would not kindly take the account into some other bank. He tried to be extremely courteous but said they could not go on with an account which was continuously in such bad shape."[5]

Five days later, Hearst received another telegram with even worse news. Moore warned him that they were going to have to come up with $1 million in the next sixty days to pay off outstanding loans in New York *and* an additional $700,000 for obligations in Chicago. And this without any help from Chase National Bank, formerly their chief source of credit. In a panic,

Moore wrote John Francis Neylan, the publisher of Hearst's *San Francisco Call*, to ask him to look into the possibilities of borrowing money from San Francisco banks. Neylan, an Irish-American attorney from San Francisco with strong ties to progressive Republicans in California, had moved steadily up in the Hearst ranks to become a sort of editor in chief for his West Coast papers. As canny in financial dealings as in political, he would soon replace Moore as Hearst's chief financial adviser.[6]

Neylan did his best to secure new sources of credit for the Chief. Unfortunately, Hearst was so overleveraged that no banker in his right mind would have extended him further credit except as a personal favor. This, as Neylan recognized at once, was bound to have an effect on his newspapers' editorial independence, especially since Hearst's chief source of funds on the West Coast had been Herbert Fleishhacker, president of the London and Paris National Bank in San Francisco, whom Neylan had been attacking for months in the pages of the *San Francisco Call*.

Because San Francisco's future growth and prosperity depended on its securing additional water, the city's business and political leaders had been coveting Hetch Hetchy, a valley in northwest Yosemite through which the Tuolumne River flowed. If the valley were dammed and an aqueduct built, it would supply the city with abundant water and hydroelectric power for decades to come. San Francisco's progressives, Neylan among them, were determined to secure full municipal ownership and control of Hetch Hetchy water and power. They were opposed by the business and banking communities, led by Fleishhacker, a board member of several of the transit and power trusts, who hoped to be able to privatize at least some of the Hetch Hetchy resources.[7]

When Neylan suggested that there might be a conflict of interest if Hearst borrowed money from a man his newspapers were in the process of attacking, Hearst reassured him that there was no need to worry. "Regarding Mr. Fleishhacker," he wrote Neylan in October of 1923, "do not be at all alarmed. . . . We owe him some money. If we do not want to owe it to him, we could owe it to somebody else — if we need to owe it at all. . . . I do not always agree with him in his policies — he does not always agree with me in my policies. But I think we agree a good deal and have a sufficient respect for each other's opinions. . . . There are occasions like in the Hetch Hetchy matter where we have to take a stand which is opposed quite generally by the ultra-conservative, by big financial interests in the community. But if we are fundamentally right in these occasional important crusades, we preserve the respect even of these people — all the more so if we give an exhibition of the paper's power."

Hearst was signaling to Neylan that he would support crusades, but only if they were occasional and pursued with moderation. "It is easy," Hearst continued, "to lose the respect of all the judicious elements of the community by too captious criticism and too much quarreling. We are not the only good citizens in the community. Our way of doing things is not the only way of benefitting the community. Undoubtedly the great enterprises which these big financial interests create, and you may say constitute, are in themselves benefits to the community. We want to realize those facts and not disturb things more than is necessary to secure an honest conduct of these enterprises."

It had to have been painfully obvious to Neylan that, with this memorandum, Hearst was signaling a significant shift in editorial policy. No longer would the Hearst papers take an unequivocal stand for municipal ownership. No longer would they employ the language and images that had been their stock in trade. Hearst closed his memo with what sounded at first like an apology but was instantly transformed into a defense of his actions: "I suppose you think I am a poor progressive; but I am not. I want to see progressive achievement more than mere progressive display. I want our powerful newspapers to cooperate with other powers whenever that cooperation means most for the benefit of the community."[8]

Through 1924, as the fight over the privatization of the Hetch Hetchy project continued in San Francisco, with Neylan leading the forces advocating municipal control, Hearst warned him not to go too far in criticizing Fleishhacker. "It is not right to . . . make reflections upon him or his enterprises. Please try to conduct our fight with a little more consideration. Mr. Fleishhacker is entitled to consideration not merely because he is our friend — although he certainly is that — and that should make us treat him with fairness at least — but also because he is an important citizen in the community, deeply interested in the welfare of the State and City, and entitled to his views on this question even if they differ from ours . . . In any event let us maintain the pleasant relations we have always maintained, without any reflection upon Mr. Fleishhacker or his enterprises."

This letter, from February 1924, closed rather ominously with the Chief informing Neylan that "Mr. Fleishhacker has been talking to me" in New York City: "Please get in touch with Mr. Fleishhacker when he returns and let him tell you what he has been telling me and then please write me as above suggested, and oblige."[9]

Fleishhacker had traveled to New York to talk about the Hetch Hetchy project and to discuss a new financing strategy for the Hearst corporations. It was, ironically, Neylan, the progressive, who had first come up with the idea to raise money, much as the government had during World War I, by selling small-denomination bonds to the public. For this plan to work, Hearst required the services of bankers and brokers who would underwrite the issue and assist him in marketing his bonds.

The basis for a Hearst-Fleishhacker alliance was obvious. Hearst needed Fleishhacker to sell his bonds, while the banker needed the Hearst newspapers to promote his plans for Hetch Hetchy. After meeting with Hearst in New York, Fleishhacker returned to San Francisco and began negotiations with Neylan. Hearst urged Neylan to listen to Fleishhacker's arguments, which Neylan did. In the end, however, Neylan was convinced that there was no way to reconcile Fleishhacker's demands for privatization of Hetch Hetchy with the Hearst papers' policy of municipal control. He promised Hearst that he would provide space for Fleishhacker's views in his news columns, but reiterated his view that the Hearst newspapers should continue to press for municipal control of public utilities, as they had for the past forty years.[10]

On the bond issue, there was no disagreement between Fleishhacker and Neylan. With Fleishhacker as principal selling agent on the West Coast, Neylan launched a national campaign to sell Hearst's bonds to the public. The opening salvo, on April 24, 1924, was an article by B. C. Forbes, who had continued to write for the Hearst press after starting his own magazine, *Forbes*, in 1917. Under the intriguing headline "W. R. Hearst May Offer Securities to the Public," Forbes reproduced the text of a purported interview he had conducted with Hearst.

"Our business has grown," Hearst was reported to have told him. "We deal so directly with the public in our business that I have sometimes thought of giving the public an opportunity to become security holders. Something along this line is in mind, but I have no definite announcement to make, at least not yet."

Forbes concluded his article with a decisive endorsement of the forthcoming bond issue: "It is a safe bet that if Mr. Hearst should decide to give the public a chance to acquire securities based on such gold mines there would be a stampede to buy them."[11]

On April 26, a second article by Forbes appeared in the Hearst newspapers, again boosting the forthcoming bond issue. On April 29, the official offering statement appeared in newspapers across the country. That morning, in his front-page editorial column, Arthur Brisbane declared, "These bonds are SAFE. Buy them, if you have money that you would like to invest with absolute safety . . . You can invest any amount from $100 to $100,000." Brisbane confided to his readers that he had already contacted his friend Herbert Fleishhacker in San Francisco and bought $200,000 worth of bonds for himself. In a separate article on the financial pages, Fleishhacker told Hearst's readers that the bonds were backed not only by "a security conservatively estimated by experts at more than $40 million," but also by the personal guarantee of William Randolph Hearst, which means that "in addition to the properties . . . all of his vast assets become part of the pledge that makes the issue gilt-edged."[12]

Hearst's strategy of selling bonds to his readers in small denominations was immediately successful. A week after the initial offering, the *New York Times* reported that "virtually all of the $12,000,000 bond issue had been sold . . . Eighty percent of the Eastern sales were in lots of $1,000 or less, a half of this total having been lots of $500 each and less."[13]

The growth of the Hearst publishing empire in the 1920s was extraordinary and unprecedented, as was the amount of debt accumulated to underwrite that expansion. With his financial problems temporarily solved by the infusion of new capital, Hearst returned to the marketplace to buy more newspapers. He had already purchased three newspapers in 1921, five more in 1922, and the *Baltimore News* in 1923. In 1924 he added another three, the *Albany Times-Union,* the *San Antonio Light,* and the *Milwaukee Sentinel.* It was more difficult now for Hearst to engage in the virulent populist trustbusting, anti–big business, anti-capital rhetoric that had defined his newspapers' editorial policies since the 1880s. Without the cooperation of bankers in New York and San Francisco, the Hearst empire would long ago have collapsed and he knew it. The Chief did not temper his rhetoric merely to court favor with bankers to whom he was indebted, but because he had long before begun to identify the national interest with the Hearst interests. If the free flow of capital — from bankers to business — was good for the Hearst empire, then it was also good for the nation. The same logic applied to national politics. If, as seemed to be the case, the Republicans in Washington were pursuing policies that helped Hearst extend his publishing empire, then they were performing a national service and should be commended for it.

During the twelve years that the Republican presidents retained Andrew Mellon as secretary of the treasury Hearst would find it difficult to support a Democrat for the presidency. Mellon not only kept income tax rates low, but he and the other Republicans who occupied the center of power in Washington in the 1920s subscribed to the same laissez-faire economic theories that Hearst had begun to enunciate in his signed editorials. If, in years past, the Chief had been an opponent of the Republicans because they were too close to the business community, he now supported them for the very same reason and forbade his editors and reporters to criticize them for being too close to corporate leaders. In 1922, when *Hearst's Magazine* ran a story criticizing Harding's secretary of the interior — Albert Fall, the architect of the Teapot Dome scandal — Hearst complained to Arthur Brisbane, who contacted the editor on the Chief's behalf.

"There is an article in *Hearst's Magazine,* much to Mr. Hearst's displeasure, unfriendly to Secretary Fall," Brisbane wrote. "I haven't seen it, but Mr. Hearst wires me that he objects to its publication, and asks me to obtain in Washington material for an article, illustrated, in all of our papers such as might please Secretary Fall, and at the same time let the public know of the good work that he is doing."[14]

Eighteen months later, when Norman Hapgood, whom Hearst had hired as editor of *Hearst's International,* attacked Andrew Mellon for not enforcing Prohibition laws more strictly, Hearst telegrammed Joseph Moore at 3:35 in the morning to ask him to rein Hapgood in.

"I think Mellon is an excellent Secretary of the Treasury and a fine man and that he is very earnestly trying to give good administration," Hearst told Moore. "I think we are unfair to the man and I think the tone of article is truculent and unnecessarily offensive. It would be a great relief to me if Mr. Hapgood could accept my viewpoint that personal attacks of this kind are out of place in a monthly magazine of dignity and importance and literary character as [is] Hearst's."[15]

As part of his 1920s expansion, Hearst had, in 1924, reluctantly and belatedly, entered the tabloid market in New York City, starting up the *New York Daily Mirror* to compete with the *New York Daily News,* which Joseph Medill Patterson and Robert McCormick, the owners of the *Chicago Tribune,* had begun publishing in June of 1919. The term tabloid referred to a newspaper that was published in small-size pages. Most early nineteenth-century newspapers had, in fact, been tabloids out of necessity because it was difficult to get enough newsprint to publish larger papers. The tabloid format returned to prominence in England in the early 1900s when Alfred Harmsworth, later Lord Northcliffe, established the *Daily Mirror* as a women's newspaper, then converted it into a fully illustrated, half-size newspaper. Harmsworth's tabloid, filled with highly condensed, sensational stories about crime and scandal, was an enormous commercial success. By 1909, its circulation approached one million.

While insiders had long predicted that Hearst would be the first American publisher to put out a tabloid-sized, illustrated newspaper, he had resisted doing so because he was not comfortable with the format. He had no interest in publishing a picture newspaper that had little room for the political coverage, columns, cartoons, and the editorials that he cared so much about. Newspaper publishing remained a calling as well as a business enterprise for Hearst. He was in it for the influence his papers brought him and the public service he still believed he was performing as a big-city publisher. As he wrote Arthur Brisbane in a 1928 telegram complaining about the New York newspapers' lack of interest in the local public schools, "Artie, if we don't improve the schools in New York we don't deserve to publish successful newspapers there. There is nothing in just getting circulation if we don't do anything with it."[16]

Hearst delayed entering the tabloid market in New York as long as he could, though he did, in 1922, reduce one of his Boston papers to tabloid size. He tried at first to pay McCormick and Patterson to cease publication of their *New York Daily News*, because he did not want to have to compete with it. When they refused either to stop publishing or to sell the *Daily News* to him, he was left with no choice but to start up his own tabloid.[17]

It was already too late. By the time the first issue of the *Mirror* appeared, the *News* had been in operation for five years and had built a circulation base of more than three-quarters of a million readers. When Hearst and his New York editors tried to position the *Mirror* as the brash young tabloid on the make, they were trumped by Bernarr Macfadden, the millionaire body builder, promoter, and publisher of *True Story*, who three months after the *Mirror*'s appearance established a tabloid of his own, the *Evening Graphic*. Macfadden's evening tabloid was so sensational, so heavy on sex and crime, and so light on news, that it barely qualified as a newspaper. Still, it stole circulation from Hearst's *Evening Journal* as well as from the *Mirror* and his morning paper, the *American*.[18]

In 1924, in the midst of his newspaper buying spree, Hearst was asked by *Editor and Publisher* if it was his "intention . . . . to possess one hundred newspapers in the United States." He answered, quite truthfully, that he had no "plan to possess any more newspapers. . . . But occasionally somebody wants to get rid of a paper and tries to sell it to me, and if I think I can see a way to make it a success, I am very likely to take over the job and try out my program."[19]

Hearst's empire had grown so rapidly that he could now claim, with only some exaggeration, that almost seven million American families, or one out of every four families in the entire United States, regularly read a Hearst publication. Millions more read Hearst syndicated features in their local newspapers. Like Rockefeller in oil and Zukor in moving pictures, Hearst had effectively used the threat of competition to force newspapers across the country to subscribe to his feature and news syndicates. According to Moses Koenigsberg, the head of King Features, publishers who declined to subscribe to the Hearst services were subtly warned that if they did not, Hearst might be compelled to establish a daily of his own in their home cities.[20]

At one time or another during the 1920s, the Hearst papers syndicated work by the fiction writers Fannie Hurst, Elinor Glyn, Mary Roberts Rinehart, Edith Wharton, and Rex Beach; the reporters Damon Runyon, Gene Fowler, and Lowell Thomas; the financial columnist B. C. Forbes; the society writer Cholly Knickerbocker; the Hollywood gossip columnist Louella Parsons; the tennis champion Helen Wills; and many internationally known writers, among them Gabriele d'Annunzio, Rabindranath Tagore, Oswald Spengler, Maxim Gorky, Vicente Blasco Ibánez, and Hendrik Willem Van Loon. In the middle 1920s alone, the Hearst papers serialized and syndicated Bruce Barton's *The Man Nobody Knows* and Henry Ford's *The Great Today and Greater Tomorrow;* the "letters" of Theodore Roosevelt, Queen Victoria, Joseph Conrad, Sarah Bernhardt, and Woodrow Wilson; the "life stories" of Mabel Normand, Rudolph Valentino, Jack Dempsey, Gene Tunney, David Belasco, and Benito Mussolini; and "Batting Tips" by Ty Cobb. The cartoons by artists under contract to King Features included George McManus's *Bringing Up Father,* Harry Hershfield's *Desperate Desmond,* George Herriman's *Krazy Kat,* the sports and dog cartoons of TAD, Billy De Beck's *Barney Google,* Russ Westover's *Tillie the Toiler,* E. C. Segar's *Casper* and *Popeye,* Chic Young's *Blondie,* together with the drawings of Rube Goldberg, Frederick Opper, and others.[21]

Though Cosmopolitan Productions, his film company, continued to lose money, Hearst had made true his boast to Adolph Zukor and was producing films that were winning acclaim from the critics and at the box office. His first big hit was *When Knighthood Was in Flower,* a fictional account of the life of Mary Tudor, based on the bestselling historical romance by Charles Major which had twenty years earlier been made into a Broadway play starring Julia Marlowe. Mary Pickford and Douglas Fairbanks, among others, had tried to get the film rights to the property, but only Hearst was able to meet the price demanded by Major's widow.

Knighthood was the film Hearst had always wanted to make: a glossy, costumed extravaganza that showed off Marion Davies' skills as an actress and his as producer and studio head. He had originally asked D. W. Griffith to produce it, but when he declined chose Robert Vignola, a veteran director who had worked on several of Marion's earlier pictures. The film cost an unprecedented $1.5 million. Joseph Urban, with an unlimited budget, designed sets of operatic grandeur, including, according to Randolph Carter and Robert Reed Cole, his biographers, "two blocks of a street in old Paris, a Gothic cathedral, part of London's Billingsgate district, and the tower of London. The set for the Paris scenes was at the time the largest indoor set ever built, consisting of thirty-two complete buildings, or at least their façades." The scale of the production was such that it occupied no less than three different studios at the same time: Hearst's 127th Street studio, Zukor's facility in Astoria, and the Jackson studio in the Bronx. Three thousand extras were employed for the crowd scenes.[22]

Marion worked harder than she ever had to make Hearst proud. "I had to learn fencing," she recalled in her recorded reminiscences. "I was supposed to be disguised as a boy, and I'm in an inn in England . . . and they think I'm not quite a boy . . . So I had a drink and ate the meat, with my hands, and then somebody said, 'How about a duel?' So then I had a duel — with five or six men. . . . Well it took four months to rehearse that scene . . . I was so stiff I couldn't walk, but the director thought I walked just like a princess."[23]

Hearst leased the Criterion Theater on Broadway for the opening and hired Victor Herbert to compose a "Marion Davies March" to be played as an overture. To make sure everyone on Broadway knew about the film, he bought space at the Times Square triangle at Broadway and 47th Street and erected a billboard with a painting of Marion so huge that *Variety* commented on it in its review of *Knighthood*.

The reviewers, as usual, lavished praise on Cosmopolitan's publicity campaign and Urban's designs, but this time they also singled out Miss Davies for special commendation. "While this is a fine picture for all concerned," wrote the *Variety* critic, "it is a finer one for Marion Davies for *When Knighthood Was in Flower* implants this handsome girl right among the leading players, those who can act — something mighty few beautiful women of the screen ever accomplish. . . . Cosmopolitan will gloat over this production. . . . *When Knighthood Was in Flower* is a fine big and splendid mark on the not-so-long roadway of filmdom to date."[24]

The film ran for months in the movie palaces — at two dollars for the better seats — before being put into general release in February 1923. Special booths were set up in theater lobbies and department stores to sell *When Knighthood Was in Flower* souvenir books, enlarged stills printed in sepia, and portraits of Miss Davies in full costume.[25]

Though it is impossible to know if the film ever recovered its $1.5 million costs, there was no doubt that *Knighthood* was a hit. Its success at the box office convinced Hearst that his instincts had been right, that the public would pay premium prices for costumed spectaculars produced by Cosmopolitan, designed by Joseph Urban, and starring Marion Davies. For years to come, whenever anyone expressed doubts about his producing skills or Marion's acting, he was able to point to *Knighthood* in rebuttal.[26]

Having triumphed with *Knighthood*, Hearst was determined to replicate that success with another historical costume drama, *Little Old New York*, also adapted from a Broadway show. Shooting began in late December of 1922 and was on track until a fire damaged Cosmopolitan Productions' 127th Street studio. Hearst promptly relocated production to Fort Lee, where the sets were rebuilt and the costumes remade.[27]

Joseph Urban, once again given permission to do as he pleased, constructed what *Moving Picture World* called the largest and most remarkable indoor set ever used in a motion picture. A replica of the *Clermont*, Robert Fulton's steamboat, was sailed down the East River to the studio, and fire wagons were reproduced from models at the New-York Historical Society. The artist Gustav Brock was hired to hand-color individual frames in two sequences — when Miss Davies blushed after hearing a risqué story and when the flag was hoisted over the *Clermont*. It took thirty hours of labor to color eight seconds of film.[28]

Marion again played a spunky, irrepressible, headstrong girl, this time poor and Irish. When her brother, who had somehow inherited a fortune, dies before he has had a chance to claim it, Marion disguises herself as a boy and invests money in Robert Fulton's steamboat. She falls in love with her American cousin, who learns at the end of the film that "Pat Day" is a girl, thereby legitimizing the affection he has felt for him/her.

"Marion Davies is to *Little Old New York*," *Variety* wrote, "what Times Square is to all of the country — the centre of attraction. Her performance will sell this film when it reaches the picture houses." The only problem with the film was that Hearst, committed to producing a super-special that could be offered to the public at premium prices, made it much too long.[29]

The year 1923 was a banner one for Cosmopolitan Productions. In addition to Marion's hits, Hearst's studio produced Lionel Barrymore's *Enemies of Women; The Love Piker*, with Ziegfeld star Anita Stewart and a screenplay by Frances Marion; and *Pride of Palomar*, based on an anti-Japanese novel, which did "wonderful business" — in great part, as a California theater owner told *Moving Picture World*, because it took "a nice slap at the Japs." Even before *Little Old New York* opened, Hearst had made movie history by having three different pictures playing on Broadway at the same time.[30]

In August, *Little Old New York* premiered at the Criterion Theatre in Columbus Circle, which Hearst had leased, renamed the Cosmopolitan, and hired Joseph Urban to redesign for the opening of Marion's new film. The opening was a grand success, though Marion worried throughout that the five-tiered chandelier Urban had finished installing just hours before the curtain might fall and kill audience members sitting beneath it. Mayor Hylan, a full contingent of Astors and Whitneys, and every important show business celebrity in the city attended the premiere. Hearst was discreetly absent, as he would be for all of Marion's premieres. Arthur Brisbane presided in his place.[31]

Little Old New York was an even bigger hit than *Knighthood*. *Screenland* rated it the third biggest box-office success of 1923. With three big hits almost in succession and two of them starring Miss Davies, Hearst had finally entered the first rank of moving-picture producers. He cut loose at last from Adolph Zukor to start up his own distribution company, Goldwyn-Cosmopolitan, in partnership with Joe Godsol, the head of Goldwyn Pictures. In November, he announced that he was going to expand film production in New York City by building three new studios large enough to film super-special costume dramas.[32]

Although he had spent a good deal of time with Marion in 1923, Hearst had also been an attentive husband. In April, he and Millicent celebrated their twentieth wedding anniversary with a costume dance at the Clarendon. The guest list, crowded with titled foreigners and society folk, was Millicent's. There were no publishing or show business people in attendance and only one or two politicians.[33]

Hearst and Millicent spent the summer of 1923 at San Simeon, probably with all five of their sons, and their winter vacation at The Breakers in Palm Beach. Hearst did what he could to make Marion's life comfortable while he was out of town, instructing his private secretary, Joe Willicombe, to put his yacht at her and her sisters' "service and call" during the summer: "Think they should live on it. Kindly see them and boat frequently to make sure everything going well."[34]

With Marion in New York, Palm Beach was impossibly dull. Only days after his arrival, the Chief was telegramming Joseph Moore in New York to inquire "what [was] going on. It is terrible down here. Nothing to do. I want something to worry about." Within a week, he had begun to complain about the Florida weather: "This is an awful burg — with all your snow and slush in New York, according to reports, you can believe me you are better off than we are in this balmy climate — for the climate is about all there is here — nothing else; there's nothing else here."[35]

Hearst occupied himself by working, as he did on every vacation. "Busy as a deuce since we got here and of course all the way down on train — and still at it," Willicombe wrote Christy MacGregor in New York, on their arrival. "Haven't been in for a swim once." In Palm Beach, Hearst met with Joe Godsol, his partner at Goldwyn-Cosmopolitan, who was looking to sell Goldwyn Pictures to the highest bidder. Hearst entertained the idea of buying it, but he was short of cash and unable to consummate a deal. Godsol sold the company to Marcus Loew, who combined Goldwyn Pictures with Metro Pictures Corporation and hired Louis B. Mayer as vice president and general manager. The new company, Metro-Goldwyn (the Mayer would be added later), was incorporated in the spring of 1924, with Hearst's and Godsol's distribution company folded into it.[36]

Hearst and Marion had become valued commodities. With Joseph Urban providing the set designs, costumes, and lighting, and the Chief choosing the properties, directors, and screenwriters and supervising scripting, production, and publicity, Marion was on the verge of becoming a major picture star, and Hearst a respected producer of Davies' super-specials and Cosmopolitan features. Marcus Loew, Louis B. Mayer, and Mayer's new chief of production, Irving Thalberg, were delighted to welcome him, his star, and, of course, his nationwide publicity machine, to their new company.

❦ 20 ❦

Another Last Hurrah

IN APRIL OF 1922, Hearst was asked by the editor of the *Brooklyn Eagle* to comment on the rumors that he was going to run for governor of New York. He replied that he was now "a rancher, enjoying life on the high hills overlooking the broad Pacific. If you want to talk about Herefords, I will talk to you — but not about politics. I have no ambition to get into politics unless there be some special reason, and I don't see any special reason."[1]

He was a modern-day Cincinnatus who preferred his farm to the statehouse. If summoned, however, he would agree to answer the call to public service. While the Chief was not as obsessed with the presidency as some of his biographers have portrayed him, he had not entirely given up hope that the nation would one day call on him to serve as its chief executive. A lifetime of journalism had deepened his conviction that politicians were, with few exceptions, mendacious, corrupt, and incompetent. The country needed a leader who was not tainted by the political process and was not dependent on the largess of machine politicians or big businessmen.

While denying that he had any interest in the gubernatorial nomination, Hearst delegated William J. Conners, a Buffalo publisher, and Mayor John Hylan of New York to organize political support and Joseph Moore and Edward Clark to buy two upstate newspapers, the *Syracuse Telegram* and *Rochester Journal*.[2] It was an opportune time to reenter the political arena. Former Governor Al Smith, the most popular Democrat in the state, had retired from politics in 1922 after being defeated for reelection. With no one else on the horizon as a possible gubernatorial candidate, Hearst considered the nomination his for the asking.

Perhaps because he had been spending more and more time in California — and as a gift to Millicent who much preferred Europe to San Simeon —

Hearst took her and his three oldest boys to Europe in the spring of 1922. It was to be another Hearstian grand tour, the first since before the war, with a full entourage of servants, family members, friends, and business associates, included among them Guy Barham, the publisher of Hearst's Los Angeles paper, and his wife. The Hearst party sailed for Europe on the *Aquitania* on May 23.[3]

Marion Davies, according to her biographer Fred Guiles, set off in the same direction a week later. Arriving in London, she was met by J. Y. McPeake, a white-haired Irishman with pince-nez glasses whom Hearst had hired to start up a British version of *Good Housekeeping*. McPeake put Marion in an elegant suite of rooms halfway across the city from the Savoy, where Hearst and his family were staying. While Hearst met with publishing associates and, with Millicent, visited Prime Minister David Lloyd George for luncheon at 10 Downing Street and Lord Beaverbrook at his country home, Marion was entertained by McPeake in London.[4]

Hearst's — and Marion's — vacations were interrupted in mid-June when Guy Barham was rushed to the hospital with stomach pains and died after an emergency operation. Hearst accompanied Barham's body back to New York on the *Olympic*. His butler, George Thompson, and his sons John and Bill, Jr. sailed with him. Marion returned to New York at the same time — Fred Guiles tells us — on the same ship as the Hearsts. Millicent and George Hearst, the oldest son, remained in Europe to continue their vacation.[5]

On the Saturday after Marion's return, her sister Reine gave her a welcome-home party at her Freeport, Long Island, vacation home. The party ended abruptly just before midnight when Oscar Hirsch, identified in the newspapers as "a wealthy electrical manufacturer," took a bullet in the mouth from his wife Hazel's "pearl-handled revolver." The wound was not serious. The next morning, according to the newspaper accounts, Oscar and Hazel not only kissed and made up, but, according to their attorney, "vehemently declared . . . that they will never again taste a drop of intoxicating liquor."[6]

The story would have merited no more than a back-page mention in the Long Island papers had the Davies sisters not been involved and had Marion, on Hearst's advice, not had her attorney telephone the New York papers to say that she had not been at the party. On the Monday after the shooting, almost every non-Hearst newspaper in the city carried some version of the "Rich Man Strangely Shot" Oscar Hirsch story on their front pages, the *Daily News* with a photograph of "Miss Marion Davies, screen beauty." When the Freeport story died a natural death without Marion being further implicated, Hearst had to have been enormously relieved. In the midst of his campaign for the gubernatorial nomination, he didn't need a whiff of new scandal to set off the retelling of old ones.[7]

On returning to New York with Guy Barham's body, Hearst announced that he would be staying for only three days before sailing to Europe to rejoin his wife. Five days later, the newspapers declared that he had changed his mind and would be traveling to California instead. He did neither, but stayed behind in New York until July 15 when Millicent returned from Europe on the *Mauretania*. Now in full campaign mode, Hearst met her on the gangway, accompanied by Grover Whalen, New York City's Commissioner of Plant and Structures, a welcoming committee appointed by Mayor Hylan, and the Police and the Street Cleaning Department bands.[8]

The Chief never did get to San Simeon that summer. His nomination for governor was put in jeopardy when a convention of anti-Hearst Democrats assembled in Syracuse in July to publicly denounce him and ask Al Smith to run against him in the primary.[9] Hearst's candidacy posed as great a danger for political and business leaders in 1922 as it had in 1904 when he ran for president for the first time. He was still, from the podium at least, an uncompromising foe of corporate power, the trusts, and the corrupt politicians who refused to take them on. His candidacy threatened to reopen questions about the future of American capitalism and the role of the state which politicians and corporate leaders alike considered resolved.

After two decades of debate and agitation, the rise and fall of Populist, Progressive, and Socialist parties, and innumerable strikes and lockouts, a corporate-liberal consensus had finally been achieved. It was now the accepted wisdom — in the board rooms and in Washington — that the role of government was not to supersede or control the corporation, but to legalize and legitimize it by regulating its excesses.

Hearst was determined to rip apart this consensus by reviving the discourse of the 1890s, redefining the trusts as corrupt and un-American, and arguing that government officials had not only the right but the responsibility to replace them with municipally owned and operated utilities. On June 25, more than four months before the election, the *New York Times* warned its readers in an editorial to stand guard against the "wide open democracy which Mr. Hearst has been advocating in his newspapers for a generation." To get himself elected, the *Times* predicted that Hearst would mobilize "the footloose in politics . . . the ultra-progressives and semi-radicals." Once elected he would make matters worse by providing voters with unwarranted and unnecessary new powers to oversee their elected officials: "direct primaries for the nomination of candidates to all offices, inauguration in this State of the initiative, referendum, and recall of public officials [and] the recall of judicial decisions."[10]

Each of the initiatives would, not coincidentally, have the effect of weakening the political parties while enhancing the power of the press. With "initiative, referendum, and recall," Hearst would be able to legislate through his newspapers by identifying issues, rousing public opinion, and organizing his own campaigns to pass laws, recall officials, and overturn judicial decisions. Control of the daily press — and a newsreel service — was, in the days before radio and television, tantamount to control of public and political discourse. And that control, combined with Hearst's unquestioned ability to speak directly to the voters, posed a threat to the Republic. As William Church Osborn of Putnam County, a leader of the "Stop Hearst" forces, declared in early July, "There is a monopolist in this country who seeks to control the sources of information which are vital to the healthy life of our Republic. This man has driven his shafts throughout the country into the secret and abnormal strata of poor humanity, and has drawn from the shafts poisonous and sickening stuff, which he has distributed daily to the people of the United States for his own profit and his own power."[11]

In the end, Hearst was done in by the leaders of his own party, who persuaded Al Smith to come out of retirement and run for governor. Hearst agreed to withdraw from the race if the party would nominate him instead for the open Senate seat. Though Boss Murphy was willing to consider this possibility, Smith vetoed it. He had been publicly feuding with Hearst since 1919 when the publisher, after supporting him for governor, turned on him immediately after his election and accused him of supporting the milk trust in its attempt to raise milk prices in New York City. Even his aged mother, Smith recalled in his autobiography, had been disturbed by "the most dastardly and infamous cartoons widely circulated through the city, depicting me as the fiend of the milk trust, willing to starve helpless women and children for the extra pennies wrung from the poor."[12]

Smith got his revenge at the Democratic nominating convention in July of 1922. As the *New York Times* reported the morning after the delegates had chosen their nominees, the convention had struck "a death blow to the political hopes of William R. Hearst by eliminating him as a candidate for any place on the ticket and virtually reading him out of the party . . . Most of the leaders believe that this will be the final attempt of the publisher to make forcible entry into the party . . . The opinion most frequently expressed was that 'Hearst is through'; that the party 'is well rid of him and his meddling' and that he 'should be kept out.'"[13]

Everyone but Hearst himself had reached the same conclusion: that at age fifty-nine he was finished in politics and would peaceably retire to California or Palm Beach. But the Chief was not ready to concede defeat to Al Smith, who was elected to another term as governor in 1922, or to Boss Murphy and Tammany Hall, who had stood firmly with Smith against him. In 1923, the Chief ran his own independent slate of candidates for the State Supreme Court. They were soundly defeated. "Good-bye to Hearst Waved by Tammany . . . Never, Never Is the Wigwam to Consider Him a Friend Again," read the postelection headlines on the front page of the *New York Times*. The chairman of the Democratic state campaign committee declared that "Hearst's usefulness to any party is a thing of the past"; Boss Murphy announced that he was barring all Hearst papers from his home and asked all New Yorkers to do likewise: "It is to be hoped that our decent, clean-thinking men and women will not hereafter tolerate in their homes the lying, filthy newspapers under the Hearst management."[14]

Still, Hearst was not done. In June of 1924, he joined forces with his old foe, William Jennings Bryan, against his new foe, Al Smith, who was the leading candidate for the Democratic presidential nomination. To demonstrate to the Democratic leadership that he was willing to play a major role in the upcoming election if his candidate, William McAdoo of California, was nominated, he hosted a gala reception for six hundred prominent Democrats at the Ritz-Carlton. "The entire first floor of the hotel was transformed into a conservatory by towering palms, orange trees, rambler roses and ferns," the *New York Times* reported the morning after the event. "The Palm Court, the main dining room and the Japanese Garden were held for the reception, and two orchestras, Paul Whiteman's and Eddie Elkin's, provided the music. . . . At midnight, a divertissement was given, the performers including . . . Clifton Webb and Will Rogers. Supper was served in the Japanese Garden."[15]

The balloting for the presidential nomination began five days later on June 30. When after several days and forty-two ballots, Smith and McAdoo remained deadlocked, Bryan, fearing that the rural, anti-Smith delegates would run out of money and leave town, asked the Chief for funds to help out "the delegates that may be pressed for money." Hearst agreed to pay room and board for one hundred of them, but informed Bryan, through Brisbane, that he wanted to keep the entire matter secret.[16]

After the ninety-ninth ballot, Smith and McAdoo withdrew and the convention nominated corporation lawyer John Davis on the 103rd ballot. Hearst condemned the nominee as a puppet of Wall Street and, with Millicent and the Hylans in tow, left for San Simeon.

Determined not to have anything to do with Davis and the Democrats but unwilling to switch to the Republicans, Hearst was consigned to political limbo. "There seems to be no special reason why we should be particularly partisan in the coming campaign," he wrote his editors in a lengthy memo on July 10. "It should be possible to print a paper which Republicans and Democrats and LaFollette [the progressive governor of Wisconsin] followers would all not only be able to read, but would like to read on account of its fairness — a paper to which these various factions would turn to get the TRUTH of the political situation." Hearst wanted his editorial writers to begin addressing their readers as they would friends in conversation. Cartoons should be "light and amusing and inoffensive. Avoid bitter personalities."[17]

Hearst tried to maintain his nonadversarial, nonpartisan posture even when in the summer of 1925 Al Smith and Tammany took revenge on him by running James J. Walker, a Tammany loyalist, in the mayoral primary against his protégé, Mayor John Hylan. From San Simeon, the Chief directed his New York editors to run Hylan's campaign, but without making it "bitter and antagonizing. We may ridicule Walker a little at times if he makes absurd statements but don't lose our temper. Keep cool like Coolidge and win like Coolidge."[18]

Smith and Tammany accused Hylan of being Hearst's puppet and attacked Hearst as a California immoralist and interloper who spent his days "loafing in the splendor and grandeur of his palatial estate on the Pacific Coast." Hearst, unable to resist the call to battle, let loose a polemic as explosively effective as any he had written in his youth: "The distinguished Governor of the great State of New York has taken three days laboriously to prepare a vulgar tirade that any resident of Billingsgate, or any occupant of the alcoholic ward in Bellevue could have written in fifteen minutes in quite the same style, but with more evidence of education and intelligence. The Wall Street friends of Governor Smith have enabled him to remove his domicile and his refined person from the neighborhood of the Bowery, but he still reverts in manner of thought and of expression to the familiar localities of Five Points and Hell's Kitchen, if this may be said without undue offense to these historical localities."[19]

None of this, unfortunately, did Hylan much good. He was defeated by Walker in the primary by well over 100,000 votes. In a front-page signed editorial published the day after the primary, Hearst urged Hylan to continue the fight against Tammany by running for mayor as a third-party, reform candidate. Privately, he said in a telegram to Joseph Moore that it was time now for Hylan to "retire from politics."[20]

VI

The King and Queen
of Hollywood

❦ 21 ❦

"Do You Know Miss Marion
Davies, the Movie Actress?"

THE RULES OF CELEBRITY JOURNALISM in the 1920s were not the same as they are now. Publishers of daily newspapers maintained a gentlemanly pact to keep stories of illicit sexual relationships out of their pages, unless they hit the courts. Divorce trials and crime news therefore received extensive coverage. Once a scandal reached the police blotter or the courtroom, publishers could write about it without the fear of libel suits.

W. R. had been with Marion for almost a decade and their names had only once appeared in print together — in a brief item in Colonel Mann's *Town Topics.* Now that Hearst's mother was dead and his political career on hold, he had no reason to fear adverse publicity. He had already been accused of every imaginable crime, including treason. Still, if he cared little about his own reputation, he was determined to protect Millicent's and Marion's.

On July 23, 1924, William J. Fallon, the flamboyant Broadway lawyer whose clients included Nicky Arnstein and Arnold Rothstein, went on trial for fixing the jury that had acquitted the stock swindlers Edward Markle Fuller and William Frank McGee. Fuller and McGee had been protected by Tammany and Big Tom Foley, who had received substantial kickbacks for their efforts. The evidence against all of them was so overwhelming that Victor Watson, the editor of Hearst's *New York American,* was convinced the juries had been tampered with and put his top investigative reporter, Nat Ferber, on the case. After a great deal of digging, Ferber turned up a former associate of Fallon's, three-hundred-pound Eddie Eidlitz, who agreed to testify that Fallon had fixed the juries. To make sure that Eidlitz didn't change his story, Watson had him sequestered — at Hearst's expense

— in a Brooklyn hotel, where he was wined, dined, and visited regularly by his girlfriend. Fallon went into hiding. When discovered, he said he had secret information on Hearst's private life and that he had fled because Hearst and Watson were out to get him.[1]

The Fallon trial was too big a story to ignore. Every paper sent its top reporters to the courthouse. On July 23, the attorney representing Fallon opened the proceedings by asking prospective jurors if they knew William Randolph Hearst or "Miss Marion Davies, the motion picture actress." According to the front-page story in that day's late edition of the *Daily News*, when the prosecuting attorney objected that the question about Miss Davies was irrelevant, the presiding judge had it stricken from the record, but not before every court reporter in the city had jotted it down on his pad.[2]

By the time Fallon took the stand in his own defense, his trial had become the hottest show in town. The *New York Herald* reported in its page one story on August 7, 1924, that Fallon "faced the jury" from the witness stand and "calmly related an amazing story of organized persecution and intrigue, intended, he said, to bring about his ultimate ruin. . . . Fallon testified that William Randolph Hearst, multi-millionaire publisher, had ordered his destruction 'at all costs' after learning that Fallon possessed the birth certificates of a motion picture actress's children."[3]

Hearst had become a victim of the methods he had employed to boost circulation in his newspapers. Daily newspapers loved trials because they provided an ongoing story line that almost always led to an eventful climax — the verdict. Through the early twentieth century, press coverage had consisted in large part of verbatim transcripts of testimony. Hearst had helped to reconfigure the trial story into a more reader-friendly and headline-grabbing format. The trial narratives he presented on his front pages were plotted as melodramas with little men and women struggling against big, bad, and always corrupt officialdom.

While the Hearst newspapers tried to place Fallon in the role of villain, the attorney brilliantly turned the tables and, from the witness stand, convinced the jury that he was the injured victim and Hearst the villain. In the end, Fallon was acquitted of all charges. Although Fallon testified in court that he had in his possession the "birth certificates" of twins born to Hearst and an unnamed moving-picture actress, he never produced them. Still, the rumors that Marion had given birth to a set of twins fathered by Hearst would remain in currency for the rest of their lives. No birth certificates were ever found nor were witnesses to any birth ever produced. Had these twins been born, it was inconceivable that Marion and W. R.

would have abandoned them or hidden them away. According to Marion's closest friends, she would have readily given up movie stardom to raise Hearst's children. As Evelyn Wells, who knew both Marion and W. R. personally, told William Swanberg, "Believe me, if Marion had one child by Hearst, she'd have worn it around her neck."[4]

Marion may have gotten pregnant at some time during her long liaison with Hearst, but if that were the case, the probable outcome would have been an abortion, the preferred solution for unwanted pregnancies in Hollywood. Alice Marble, the great tennis champion who visited often at San Simeon in the 1930s, recalled in her oral history that when Marion and her friends hid away in Marion's dressing room where the women gathered to drink in secret, they would talk about their abortions. Fred Guiles, Marion's biographer, thinks it quite probable that she had several abortions. That at least was the impression she gave a member of her family who, desperate to help out a friend who had "gotten a girl into trouble," asked Marion for advice. "Marion lightly told her relative to give the name of Dr. So-and-So. 'He took care of all of mine,' she said, and she wasn't laughing." The story rings true, but Guiles followed it with the reminder that "Marion was a cool lady with a joke, and after a few martinis she often would say just about anything good for a laugh or a shock."[5]

To ride out the storm which Hearst knew would accompany Fallon's testimony, he moved Millicent to San Simeon, and Marion to a rented mansion on Bedford Drive in Beverly Hills. He was worried about Marion's career. There was little tolerance in 1924 for movie stars who brought adverse publicity to the industry. Hollywood had still not recovered from the scandal that had erupted only a few years earlier when the starlet Virginia Rappe was found dead of a ruptured bladder after a night of sex and booze at Fatty Arbuckle's hotel suite in San Francisco. Only months after the Arbuckle scandal, the industry had been rocked again when director William Desmond Taylor, who was having simultaneous affairs with the actresses Mabel Normand and Mary Miles Minter, was found shot to death in his Hollywood mansion.

Because of Fallon's testimony, Marion's name and photograph were splashed across the pages of non-Hearst papers all over the country. Reporters camped out at her Beverly Hills home hoping for an interview. Joseph Urban, who was at the time in Hollywood, wrote his wife in Yonkers that the Fallon case had become the talk of the dinner parties.

According to Fred Guiles, Hearst, "sick with apprehension, on an impulse sent off a letter to Marion, written on the cheap, yellow-lined pad he so often used for memos, telling her that he had decided to go out of moving pictures. His reasons were, he said, that the work was too hard and the compensation too little." Marion, he claimed, would do better without him. Throwing caution to the winds, Marion called him at San Simeon to beg him to reconsider. If he retired from moving pictures, she would too. She had, she reminded him, only become a movie star to please him. Hearst wrote back that if Marion wanted him to, he would continue to produce her moving pictures. He cautioned her, however, to keep a low profile until the uproar over the Fallon trial subsided.[6]

Still worried about the fallout from Fallon's testimony, Hearst kept Marion on the West Coast through the fall and into the winter. When Millicent and the boys left for New York at the end of the summer, he stayed behind at San Simeon. With Marion nearby, his private secretary Willicombe at his side, and telephone and cable access to Neylan in San Francisco, Moore in New York, and his publishers and editors across the country, there was no need for him to return to New York to conduct business.

This was not the first time he had lingered on the West Coast after Millicent had taken the train east with the boys. In past years, he had returned to New York by November, Christmas at the latest, but in 1924 he remained in California through the autumn, winter, and into the spring, commuting back and forth from San Simeon to the suites of rooms he kept on permanent lease at the Ambassador Hotel in Los Angeles and the Palace in San Francisco.

Because San Simeon was the family's vacation home, Hearst did not permit Marion to visit him there during the nine months he lived in California in 1924 and 1925. Instead, he bought her a white stucco mansion at 1700 Lexington Road in Beverly Hills. To protect them both from prowling journalists, the deed was in the name of Mrs. Rose Douras, Marion's mother, who had moved with her to California.

With her mother and sisters still acting as chaperones, Marion settled into her new mansion. "That's where we had the most fun," she recalled in her memoirs. "Mr. Hearst stayed there too." Though the mansion was more than spacious, Hearst hired a crew of carpenters and masons to attach a ballroom to it. When Joseph Urban arrived in Hollywood in the fall of 1924, Hearst hosted a "wonderful welcome party" for him at Marion's new house. Urban wrote to his wife that the guests included Douglas Fairbanks, Mary Pickford, and director Tom Ince. It hadn't taken long at all for Marion and W. R. to establish themselves in their new community.[7]

Conveniently located at the top of a hill, just off Sunset Boulevard and a short ride from the studios, Marion and her sisters, with Hearst's occasional assistance, presided over the gayest social scene in Los Angeles. According to Louella Parsons, who was Marion's houseguest on several occasions, "Rudy Valentino, Charlie Chaplin, John Barrymore, Mary and Doug, the lovely ill-fated Alma Rubens, Harry D'Arrast, and Harry Crocker belonged to the coterie who met several times a week at Marion's house." From the moment that Marion moved to Beverly Hills, Charlie Chaplin recalled, "the film colony enjoyed an era of Arabian Nights. Two or three times a week, Marion gave stupendous dinner parties with as many as a hundred guests, a melange of actors, actresses, senators, polo players, chorus boys, foreign potentates and Hearst's executives and editorial staff to boot."[8]

There were masquerades, weekday and weekend parties, and smaller Sunday gatherings around the swimming pool. Whatever the day, whatever the hour, the Victrola played, couples danced, and there were card games into the dawn. The parties were especially lively, Chaplin remembered, on those occasions when Hearst was away at San Simeon, San Francisco, or New York. Marion "would gather all her friends at her house . . . and we would have parties and play charades into the small hours. Then Rudolph Valentino would reciprocate at his house and I would do the same at mine. Sometimes we hired a public bus and stacked it with victuals and hired a concertina player, and ten or twenty of us would go to Malibu Beach, where we built a bonfire and had midnight picnics and caught grunion."[9]

With a succession of solid hits — and Hearst's publicity machine behind her — Marion had become an attractive commodity in Hollywood. In early July, Adolph Zukor asked if Hearst would be interested in coproducing James Barrie's *Peter Pan*, with Marion as the possible lead. Because James Barrie had his mind set on Lillian Gish as Peter, Marion would have to "test" for the role. Hearst rejected the offer outright. Marion was a star now. He was not going to allow her to audition for anyone.[10]

Concerned that Marion's ascendance toward Pickford-like stardom would be stalled if she did not return to work immediately, Hearst leased studio space at United Artists so that Marion could shoot her next film, *Zander the Great*, in California. Frances Marion was hired to adapt the 1923 stage play, which had starred Alice Brady; Louis B. Mayer, who had been brought in by Marcus Loew to manage his new conglomerate, helped finance the film, which would be the first Cosmopolitan feature to be released by Metro-Goldwyn.

Hearst consulted regularly with Frances Marion and made several suggestions for the scenario. When shooting began, he visited the set regularly, and had the daily rushes messengered to him wherever he happened to be, even in San Simeon. By mid-September, the film was well under way, but Hearst concluded that it was not up to the standards of a Cosmopolitan Productions feature. He abruptly closed down production, destroyed the existing footage, and wired Joseph Urban to take the next train West to redesign the production.[11]

Shooting on *Zander,* now under Urban's supervision with a new director, George Hill, continued through the fall. Only Marion appeared unperturbed by the turmoil on the set. Though she often had trouble getting up in the morning after a particularly strenuous party the night before, she enjoyed herself once she got there. Her old friend from Broadway, Hedda Hopper, at the time a not very successful film actress, played her mother.

Marion's double Vera Burnett remembered that Charlie Chaplin "used to come on the set quite frequently" while Marion was working on *Zander.* Under ordinary circumstances, he would have been engrossed in his own work, but he had suspended filming on *The Gold Rush* because his leading lady and soon-to-be wife, Lita Grey, was pregnant. While Lita waited out her pregnancy at home with her mother, Charlie showered Marion with attention. Chaplin, who was notorious in Hollywood for flitting from one gorgeous woman to another, found Marion captivating for the same reasons Hearst had: she was beautiful, unpretentious — especially for a movie star — and funny. She was also unattached during the long stretches that W. R. spent at San Simeon.

"They seemed to be very enamored of each other," Vera Burnett remembered. "They had told me if I saw Mr. Hearst come in, just to let them know. Also, they told Jimmy Sweeney, who was the prop man, to immediately notify them and Mr. Chaplin would go out the back door." In her unpublished diary, Mary Urban recounts the story of the "evening on the lot when the moving picture group got out of hand. Hearst was away and they started to play. A lion's den was a set constructed for one of the pictures and Marion and Charlie went inside the set and some one performed a mock marriage. . . . Everybody got into the act and the cameraman started to shoot. The picture itself was being shot under the direction of Luther Reed [one of Hearst's screenwriters], and he was furious. Urban went haywire trying to gather up all the film and destroy it before some enterprising person got it to Hearst."[12]

While the daily press continued to stay away from stories about Marion and Hearst, there was no such prohibition on gossip about Marion and

Chaplin. "Charlie Chaplin, the real sheik of Hollywood," Grace Kingsley wrote in a *New York Daily News* column on Sunday, November 9, 1924, "seems to be dividing his attention between two young things these days. One is his lovely leading lady, Lita Grey; the other is Marion Davies, Cosmopolitan star. . . . Marion Davies and Charlie Chaplin have attended several big dinner-dance parties together. The last one was a Halloween party given by Elinor Glyn at the Biltmore." The following week, Kingsley wrote almost the same column, this time with photographs of Chaplin and Davies: "Charlie Chaplin continues to pay ardent attention to Marion Davies. He spent the evening at Montmartre dining and dancing with the fair Marion the other night. There was a lovely young dancer entertaining that evening. And Charlie applauded but with his back turned. He never took his eyes off Marion's blonde beauty. Miss Davies wore a poudre blue dinner dress and small blue hat and looked very fetching indeed."[13]

Hearst, of course, was partly responsible for Marion's wandering off. She was thirty-five years younger than he was and unlikely to go into seclusion while he was away at San Simeon every weekend. During one of Hearst's visits to San Simeon, Marion, according to her friend Gretl Urban, arranged to go away for the weekend with Charlie Chaplin. Hearst, who found out about their plans though he was hundreds of miles away in San Simeon, directed Joe Willicombe to follow their car and bring Marion back "without fuss and without scandal," which he did. Marion later told Gretl that the "incident was never mentioned by Hearst."[14]

To make up to Marion for choosing San Simeon over her almost every weekend, Hearst spoiled her when he was in Los Angeles, hosting lavish entertainments for her and her friends at 1700 Lexington and taking them on luxurious cruises on the *Oneida*, which he had had sailed through the Panama Canal and now moored in San Pedro Bay. One of these weekend cruises, to Catalina Island, included Luther Reed, Bill LeBaron, a Cosmopolitan Productions executive, Anita Stewart, who was starring in a Cosmopolitan feature, Charles Chaplin, and Gretl, Mary, and Joseph Urban. Marion decided to hold a costume party. Hearst, as usual, gave her what she wanted, though according to Gretl Urban, "Everyone except Marion was utterly bored at the idea." Hearst landed the yacht on Catalina Island and his guests went shopping for their costumes. "Marion and Anita bought themselves some little-girl dresses. Charlie Chaplin put on one of my dresses, and I put on one of his suits. Bill LeBaron wore a dark robe and said he was a monk. Luther Reed borrowed a rather fancy negligee of Mary's, while Father and Mary just wrapped themselves in blankets and said they were Indians. Hearst, not in costume, had the boat decorated with Japanese lanterns, and, crackpot idea or not, we all had a good time as we sailed along." Chaplin was, as usual, the life of the party. "Unexpectedly, Charlie Chaplin suddenly stood up in the prow of the lounge where we were sitting and started reciting 'To be, or not to be,'" Gretl remembered. "He had us all spellbound, his handsome head silhouetted against the evening sky. It was an extraordinary, deeply moving experience, everybody forgetting that he was wearing a dress." Later that night, Gretl stumbled upon Charlie "making love to Marion in my cabin. To ease the embarrassment I laughed and told Marion I was glad she was having a little playacting fun."[15]

Another yachting trip was planned for the following week, this time to San Diego in honor of the forty-third birthday of Thomas Ince, one of Hollywood's top producers and directors, with whom Hearst was negotiating a coproduction deal. According to Gretl Urban, who was a guest on the *Oneida*, the cruise was uneventful, the mood "pleasant and relaxed, the food and drink . . . the best, the sea smooth and the night balmy. We sat on board until midnight, then all went to bed." During the night, Mary Urban, Joseph's wife, heard groans from Ince's cabin and awoke Dr. Daniel Carson Goodman, one of Hearst's Cosmopolitan executives. "Ince was in great pain and vomiting profusely," Gretl Urban recalled. "I don't know whether Dr. Goodman was much of a doctor, but he diagnosed it as a severe heart attack. We headed immediately for San Diego. When the anchor was dropped, we all stood around as a launch was lowered. In front of us, Hearst warned Dr. Goodman not to let anyone ashore know that his patient had come from the *Oneida*. . . . The unfortunate Goodman, upset by the sudden tragedy . . . completely lost his head and fabricated so many impossible tales and acted so super-discreet that the press and everyone else ashore were convinced he was covering up some horrendous crime."[16]

Ince was taken to his Hollywood home, where he died the next day. Though the news of Ince's death was a big story in newspapers across the country, only the *New York Daily News* mentioned that he had been stricken on Hearst's yacht. The *Daily News* story also linked Hearst to Davies by suggesting that "Miss Davies [had] issued the invitations for the yachting party" and adding that although the *Oneida* was "said to be listed . . . under the name of International Film Corporation, it has been regarded . . . as the personal yacht of Miss Davies." Complete with photographs of Hearst, Chaplin, Davies, Goodman, Elinor Glyn, and Margaret Livingston, who was rumored to be Ince's mistress, the *Daily News* story took up most of the third page of the afternoon edition, then disappeared entirely from later editions.[17]

Stories began to percolate through Hollywood that Hearst, in a fit of jealous rage, had murdered Ince. The absence of hard evidence made it easier to invent new rumors. In the years to come, Hearst would be accused of poisoning Ince, shooting him, hiring an assassin to shoot him, fatally wounding him while aiming at Chaplin — and, most recently and ridiculously, in an article published in 1997 in *Vanity Fair*, of accidentally stabbing him through the heart with Marion's hatpin, causing an instant, fatal heart attack. Today, seventy-five years after Ince's death, there is still no credible evidence that he was murdered or that Hearst was involved in any foul play.[18]

While it was true that Hearst had done his best to keep Ince's presence on the *Oneida* a secret, he had done so not to cover up a murder, but because he did not want the press or the local police investigating his yachting party with champagne flowing in flagrant disregard of the Prohibition laws.

Ince was buried in Hollywood on November 21 after a private funeral. Marion, Chaplin, and a number of Hollywood stars were there to pay their respects. Hearst was not. He had left Los Angeles and, he hoped, public view, for an extended stay at San Simeon. The Ince case, coming as it did only four months after the Fallon accusations, frightened him. The wall he had put up around his private life remained in place, but he could not be certain that it would withstand another assault. He retreated to San Simeon and summoned Joseph Moore, his treasurer and chief financial adviser, and Ray Long, who ran his magazine division, to meet him there. Sobered perhaps by the Ince tragedy, he paid attention this time when Joseph Moore warned him about the rapidly increasing gap between corporate expenses and income. He agreed to cut costs by merging *Hearst's Magazine* into *Cosmopolitan* and closing down film production in New York City.

The decision to close down his 127th Street studio was difficult but inevitable. With Marion making movies on the West Coast, there was no reason to maintain a costly production facility in New York. Though he intended to continue to produce Marion's pictures, he was ready to merge his Cosmopolitan Productions into a major studio and hand off the headaches of managing his own production facilities. After extensive negotiations with every major company in Hollywood, in March of 1925 he signed an "extremely advantageous" deal with Metro-Goldwyn, which already distributed his pictures. The arrangement, he wrote Moore in New York, not only relieved him of all expense in producing moving pictures, but it put him in a position where he ought to make a half million dollars a year. He would be paid for the rights to the *Cosmopolitan* magazine stories, and get 40 percent of the profits on *Cosmopolitan*-based films: "They attend entirely to the production and all I have to contribute is a reasonable amount of promotion, which is left entirely to my discretion, and a sufficient number of good stories." Marion's salary was raised to $10,000 a week for forty weeks a year, $6,000 of it paid by the studio, the remaining $4,000 by Hearst who, in return, received one-third of the profit from Marion's pictures.[19]

Though Louis B. Mayer now held what was arguably the top management position in town, he was still a relative newcomer to Hollywood, having arrived in 1918 from New England, where he had made his fortune as a theater owner and film distributor. Mayer had signed a lucrative deal with Hearst for two critical reasons: because it made good business sense and because he believed that by associating with the likes of Hearst he would raise his own status and that of his company. In San Francisco and New York the Hearsts had been regarded as parvenus, but by Hollywood standards they were American aristocrats. For second-generation Jews like Mayer who, as Neal Gabler has written, "regarded themselves as marginal men trying to punch into the American mainstream," W. R. was an American colossus. He was the son of a millionaire miner and senator. He had gone to Harvard, traveled widely in Europe, and was a collector of fine art, a confidant of presidents, and a native-born Californian who looked at ease in the saddle.

"Towering above him," Mayer's daughter Irene recalled, "Hearst would place his hand on my father's head for emphasis and pat it as he spoke, calling him 'Son.' They were certainly an incongruous pair. Hearst tall, portly, a man with light blue eyes and a high-pitched voice who appeared not to have too much on his mind, and whose inner self never seemed to surface; my father stocky, compact, dynamic."[20]

In the middle 1920s, Hollywood was struggling to establish itself as more than just a movie set, more than a mirage of glittering surfaces. Fame and fortune were transient commodities. The real power in the industry was in the East where the bankers made the major decisions. Studio bosses like Louis B. Mayer were constantly looking over their shoulders. Their power was local, ephemeral, that of lesser feudal lords beholden to distant princes. Hearst was different. He had been a vital force in California before movies were produced and would remain one whatever happened to the industry. His empire was not built on celluloid.

There was another reason why Mayer was pleased to absorb Cosmopolitan Productions into Metro-Goldwyn. He was convinced, as Hearst was, that Marion Davies was a legitimate, bankable star. In April 1925, he publicly welcomed her to the studio by presenting her with a ceremonial makeup box. The photograph of the two of them, transmitted by telegraph wire from California to New York, marked the official beginning of their partnership.

Soon afterward, putting aside his otherwise inviolable "puritanical instincts," Mayer took his wife and daughters and went calling on Miss Davies who was, at the time, living in a rented summer home in Santa Monica, just down the beach from the Mayer family. "Considering Dad's propriety," Irene Mayer Selznick wrote in her autobiography, "I am at a loss to explain how he reconciled our being exposed to Marion."[21]

Of all the "queens" on the Metro-Goldwyn lot, and there were plenty of them, including Norma Shearer, Joan Crawford, Lillian Gish, and Greta Garbo, only Marion had her own palace. When she arrived at Culver City, Marion recalled, all the dressing rooms on the lot had been located "in a wooden building. . . . The women were on the top floor. . . . The men were underneath, and there was a sign 'No Men Allowed to Go Upstairs.'" Only one of the women's dressing rooms had its own bathroom and although it had been promised to Marion, Lillian Gish had stolen it away. Either Marion complained to Hearst or Hearst on his own decided that she should have her own dressing room. In May, a month after he signed with Mayer, W. R. asked Joseph Urban "to design immediately a bungalow for Marion Davies outside the Goldwyn lot." Urban had a week to draw up the plans and send them to the Goldwyn people who were going to execute them. He visited Hearst's warehouse in the Bronx to pick out furniture and artwork, only to be told that it would cost a minimum of $700 to uncrate the items he wanted to look at. It didn't much matter. Although Hearst, Marion, and everyone else on the lot persisted in referring to the building as a bungalow, it was in fact a self-contained fourteen-room mansion, with living quarters on the top floor and Hearst's office and a banquet-sized dining room on the ground floor.[22]

Hearst was more comfortable in Hollywood than he had ever been in New York. He arrived without his past trailing after him. Hollywood didn't know or care about his feud with Al Smith or blame him for the excesses of yellow journalism. And, in this town without history, no one remembered that he had opposed the World War or had been accused of being a German spy. There was no doubt just as much whispering, but there was much less moralizing about his private life. Hollywood in the 1920s and 1930s was filled with Svengalis who advanced the careers of women they loved and admired: D. W. Griffith and Lillian Gish, Joseph Schenck and Norma Talmadge, Irving Thalberg and Norma Shearer, Joe Kennedy and Gloria Swanson. Marion had become a Hollywood favorite — no one was going to fault Hearst for being in love with her.

Zander the Great was released the month after Hearst signed his agreement with Mayer. It was Marion's twenty-first moving picture and arguably her best. She had by now learned to master silent-screen acting, without histrionics but with just enough exaggeration to demonstrate the requisite emotion. In *Zander,* her versatility was astonishing. She played Mamie, a freckle-faced, pigtailed orphan who is taken in by a kind woman and her young son, Alexander, or "Zander" for short. When the mother dies, Marion takes Zander on a journey through Arizona to find the boy's father, meeting up with a series of adventures along the way.

At Hearst's request, writer Frances Marion added dramatic scenes to the film to show off Marion's acting talents and invite comparisons with Mary Pickford and Lillian Gish. The references to "Little Mary" — including Pickford's trademark curls and white dress — were so explicit as to be embarrassing. The film ended with a Griffith-like scene stolen from *Orphans of the Storm,* in which Marion, like Lillian Gish, is tied to a tree during a punishing desert sandstorm. The reviews were good, the box office solid.[23]

Marion returned to New York in May of 1925 for the *Zander* premiere. She was met at the train by her friend Louella Parsons, who described her homecoming in Hearst's entertainment newspapers as if it were the biggest, perhaps the only, news in town. Miss Davies, Louella wanted her fans to know, was not only one of the screen's brightest stars, she was also one of its most intelligent.

"'What are you reading?' I inquired, wondering which of the new novels she found absorbing enough to clutch so tightly. 'The Life of Socrates,' she replied; and then, with her eyes dancing and her face wreathed in smiles, she said mischievously: 'If you hadn't known me so well, wouldn't you, with your years of experience interviewing motion picture actresses, say I was posing for the press by pretending to read highbrow literature?' 'Is that why you have hidden [it],' I inquired. She laughed and naively admitted she did not want anyone to accuse her of pretending to be a bluestocking." Louella concluded her column with more thoughts on Miss Davies' knowledge, her quiet, unpretentious ways, her unfailing sense of humor, her brains, her naturalness, her common sense and her ability to see things in their true light, and her talents as an actress.[24]

Hearst traveled to New York with Marion, though to save Millicent any possible embarrassment he arrived separately and claimed that he had returned for business reasons and to help out Mayor John Hylan, who was running for reelection. (This was the election in which Hylan was defeated in the primary by James Walker.) As was his custom, he was out of town for the premiere of *Zander* at the Capitol Theater, this time taking the train to Washington, D.C., to consult with his editors and have lunch with President Coolidge, with whom he had become quite friendly. There is, unfortunately, no record of their discussions.[25]

Since the Clarendon was still being renovated, Hearst moved into the suite at the Ritz-Carlton that had become the de facto family home and served as his New York office. He met here with Alice Head who was in charge of the English edition of *Good Housekeeping* and *Nash's*, the British magazine he had purchased in 1910. The day after her arrival in New York, Head was summoned to have dinner with Hearst and Millicent at the Ritz-Carlton. She put on her very best white and silver dress, thinking that she had been invited to a formal dinner party, but was instead served a "simple and homely gathering in the Hearst private apartment." After dinner, she and Hearst sat down to talk together, Head recalled in her autobiography: "He listened with close attention to everything I had to say, made friendly comments, told a few funny stories. . . . In appearance, he is a tall, big man of imposing presence, he has blue eyes (*I* don't think they are cold), the most beautiful teeth in the world for a man of his age . . . a gentle voice and a ready smile." Hearst casually informed Miss Head that he was interested in buying "a country home in England, and that if ever Leeds Castle in Kent or St. Donat's Castle in Wales were for sale, I was to let him know. He had seen pictures of both of them in *Country Life*, and was interested in purchasing one or the other."[26]

Miss Head returned to England and set off to find her Chief a castle. When St. Donat's, an eleventh-century, 125-room castle on 13,000 acres, fourteen miles west of Cardiff, came on the market, she notified Hearst by telegram and he directed her to buy it. "I felt a kind of sinking when I realized what we had undertaken," Head recalled. "I knew that the cost of upkeep would be heavy, that the responsibilities in connection with it would be onerous and that I had involved myself in something quite outside the normal duties connected with a publishing house. But I had already begun to acquire something of the Hearst outlook upon life, and to be concerned with the ownership of a beautiful and historic Castle seemed to me to be a tremendous lark."[27]

Hearst spent very little time in New York that spring. On May 21, Millicent gave a Gypsy Ball for the ambassador to Spain in the Crystal Room of the Ritz-Carlton — which had been redecorated for the occasion by Joseph Urban. There was no mention in the press of W. R. as host or guest. By early June, he and Marion were back in California.[28]

⸙ 22 ⸙

Family Man

I N 1991, forty years after his father's death, Bill Hearst, Jr. broke the family's silence about the breakup of his parents' marriage and W. R.'s relationship with Marion Davies. It was his mother, he said, who precipitated the breakup. Since meeting Marion Davies in 1915, Hearst had been living two separate but adjacent lives: with Millicent and the boys at the Clarendon and San Simeon and with Marion at his suite of rooms at the Bryant Park studios and at her home on Lexington Road in Beverly Hills. He would, it appeared, have been content to continue in this lifestyle had Millicent "not forced him to make a choice: Marion or her. It was an ultimatum. My father then knew he couldn't have what he wanted — his wife and family, and Marion too."

The final breakup occurred during the family's summer vacation at San Simeon. The year was probably 1925. "Pop said that he had to go to Los Angeles on business," Bill, Jr. recalled in his memoirs, "but someone told Mom that he had seen Marion. After he returned, she had packed and left for New York."[1] This was not the first time that such a scene had been played out.

"When I arrive he is always sweet and charming, but never stays more than a few hours," Millicent later told Charles Chaplin. "And it's always the same routine: in the middle of dinner the butler hands him a note, then he excuses himself and leaves the table. When he returns, he sheepishly mentions that some urgent business matter needs his immediate attention in Los Angeles, and we all pretend to believe him. And of course we all know he returns to join Marion."[2]

Millicent forced the "Marion" problem into the open and signaled that she would no longer pretend it did not matter to her. This, Bill, Jr. believed, was a fatal mistake. His father had to this point made no commitments to

Marion and was not living with her. "It was still possible that Mother could have prevailed. But she would have had to be patient."[3]

One sympathizes with Bill, Jr., who loved and respected his parents and, at age eighty-three, was still mourning their breakup sixty-five years earlier. Still, it is difficult to agree with him on this. By 1925, Hearst had been with Marion for almost a decade and had no intention of giving her up. Their relationship was, if anything, stronger than it had been. Forced to choose between his wife and his mistress, Hearst sought a third way. He had no intention of giving Marion up, nor was he prepared to let Millicent go. Divorce he considered out of the question. However amicable, it would have ruined his already precarious financial status by forcing him to yield assets to Millicent. It would also have set off an avalanche of negative publicity. Once the matter reached the courts, there would be no stopping editors and reporters from dragging him, Marion, Millicent, and the boys through the mud.

W. R. got his way. He continued his affair with Marion, but remained married and on remarkably good terms with Millicent. "They didn't have any formal parting of the ways," Bill, Jr. recalled in an oral history taken at San Simeon. "There was no announcement, there was no divorce, there were no proceedings. There wasn't anything. There was just that Pop was spending more time away from home . . . out in Los Angeles."[4]

Outwardly all was peaceable. Millicent never betrayed her hurt or her anger to anyone other than her sister and her parents, who kept her confidence. In the course of the next quarter-century, when Marion came up in conversation, Millicent, her son Bill recalled, "usually refrained from comment. If she was forced to refer to Davies, she called her 'the woman.'"[5]

After their decision to lead separate lives, Millicent visited W. R. at San Simeon in October of 1925. Two months later, the family was reunited there for Christmas and their first dinner in Casa Grande. George, who was now twenty-one, took the train from San Francisco where he lived with Bill, Jr., who was attending high school in Berkeley. The two boys made quite a contrast. George was overweight and drinking far too much; Bill was blond, blue-eyed, thin, and very handsome. From New York City came the ten-year-old twins, probably still in short pants, their brother John, who was sixteen, and their mother.

"It was a very festive occasion," Bill, Jr. said of that first dinner in the big house. "The guests, surprised and even stunned by the array of great art, were swept up in the beauty of the room. . . . That was the last Christmas we had dinner together as a family. My mother had a big Christmas party for local youngsters before we returned to New York. Then Marion Davies moved in openly."[6]

In the end, Millicent and W. R. were in accord. She too understood the way the press worked. Once divorce papers were filed, the daily papers would be given legal cover to dig into every corner of her, Marion's, and W. R.'s past. To save the children and herself from the embarrassment that would inevitably follow, she agreed to Hearst's terms.

There were, of course, enormous advantages to remaining Mrs. William Randolph Hearst. To mention only the most obvious, as Mrs. Hearst, the former Millicent Willson had access to the society pages of the *New York American*. Her Boswell was Maury H. Biddle Paul of the Philadelphia Biddles, who wrote Hearst's society columns under the name Cholly Knickerbocker. Paul boosted Millicent's career in society with the same persistence that Louella Parsons boosted Marion's in Hollywood. Because Hearst's papers combined society and film news in the same section, the Paul and Parsons columns appeared on the same page, with Paul providing news of Millicent's latest benefit for her Milk Fund and Parsons the latest talk of Marion's triumphs in Hollywood. To forestall any embarrassing juxtaposition of stories, Hearst's editors made sure that Millicent's and Marion's name never appeared together on the same page on the same day. In April of 1925, for example, items on Marion's new film ran on April 9 and 17; items about Millicent's Milk Fund appeared on April 10, 15, and 16.

"My mother's outlook took two different roads" after the separation, Bill, Jr. recalled in his memoirs. "She began to spend money lavishly and sought a new life as a matron of New York society." Millicent had been enlisted into charity work during the Great War to bolster her husband's deteriorating reputation. But she found that she was good at it and, in the postwar years, devoted more and more time to it. Her pet project was the Free Milk Fund for Babies, which had been founded under her name in 1918. With her husband's help — and Maury Paul's frequent mentions in his society columns — Millicent was able to raise a good deal of money at theater benefits. The funds were used to buy pasteurized milk and during the summer months, when unspoiled milk was at a premium, dispense it from milk booths to anemic children.[7]

With her five boys now out of the house — George and Bill in San Francisco, John, Randolph, and David in preparatory schools in the East — Millicent had more time to devote to her charities and to spending money, her best revenge on her husband, who continued to pay all her bills. One of her closer friends during this period and for the rest of her life was the celebrated hostess Elsa Maxwell. For thirty years, Millicent said nothing about the humiliation she had suffered when W. R. left her for Marion. Several years after W. R.'s death, while dining with Millicent and Elsa, Cole Porter told the story of his first sighting of Millicent, a quarter-century before, at Tiffany's buying a string of pearls for a sum running to six figures. Millicent confirmed the story. "'I bought the pearls,'" she told Porter and Maxwell. "'Some women buy a new hat when they're angry. I bought the finest string of pearls in New York. You see,' she added with a wistful smile, 'I was awfully angry, but I got over it a long, long time ago.'"[8]

From 1925 until W. R.'s death in 1951, he and Millicent remained husband and wife, raised their children together, communicated by telephone, telegram, and cable, saw each other on a regular basis, and jointly entertained friends and business associates. In April of 1926, only months after their Christmas dinner together at Casa Grande, Hearst took the train East and hosted a gala dinner with Millicent for his publishing executives. Two weeks later, the two held a party at the Clarendon to celebrate their twenty-third wedding anniversary and his sixty-third birthday. Hearst would return to New York in December of 1926 and 1927 to spend Christmas at the Clarendon.[9]

Though Millicent would not let the boys visit San Simeon after Marion moved in, she continued to vacation at the ranch, carefully coordinating her visits so as not to intrude on W. R.'s life with Marion. "The co-existence between Marion and Mrs. Hearst was mutually understood," Charles Chaplin remembered. "When it was nearing time for Mrs. Hearst's arrival, Marion and the rest of us would discreetly leave or return to [Los Angeles]. Millicent had no illusions. . . . She often talked confidentially with me about the relationship of Marion and W. R., but never with bitterness. 'He still acts as though nothing had ever happened between us and as if Marion doesn't exist,' she said."[10]

Millicent was reluctant to give up the pretense that she and her husband were still living together. On January 12, 1926, an article about Millicent appeared in the *New York American* stating that she had "passed the autumn and early winter at her estate, 'Las Estrellas,' at San Simeon, California." Hearst wrote Joseph Moore in New York with an angry reprimand and correction. "I do not like the article. . . . I do not know who wrote it, but I would like to know, and also why it was written in the way it was. It says that Mrs. Hearst has 'passed the autumn and early winter at her estate, 'Las Estrellas,' at San Simeon, California.' In the first place, the name of the estate is not 'Las Estrellas.' In the second place, it is not Mrs. Hearst's estate. It is peculiarly mine, free even from community ownership under the laws of California because it is my inheritance. However, I have not, of course, any objections to having it referred to as 'our estate,' but I do not like to be so wholly excluded from it." Moore apologized, telegramming Hearst that the offending captions had been "practically dictated" by Mrs. Hearst.[11]

W. R. and Millicent were never out of reach of one another. "There was hardly a week," Bill, Jr. recalled, "that he didn't write a letter, send a telegram, or speak with Mother on the phone." They exchanged greetings and gifts on one another's birthdays. "Hope you have happy birthday," Hearst telegrammed Millicent from Los Angeles on July 16, 1926. "Do you want pick out a present at the shops or do you want me to send a check? Think latter is more sensible under circumstances."[12]

Millicent, it appeared, never quite accepted the fact that she had been permanently replaced by Marion. And Hearst, it is just as clear, never wanted her to. In September of 1926, Millicent asked that a portrait of Hearst be taken out of storage in the Bronx and hung in the library on the ninth floor of the Clarendon. In early 1927, she telegrammed Hearst from Palm Beach, where she was vacationing, to suggest that they travel to Europe together. "Allie Mcintosh [one of Millicent's society friends] would like us to take Lady Mountbatten's house for May and June in London. One thousand weekly. Thinks we would have interesting time. What do you say?" That same day, W. R. received a telegram from another of Millicent's friends, Marjorie Jones: "Millicent and I have decided that you must take us abroad as promised for May and June. Lots of love. Please answer."[13]

In the end, Millicent had to tour Europe alone. Her vacation ended abruptly when she caught typhoid fever in Paris. "Heavenly day, where have you been to get typhoid," W. R. cabled her from San Simeon. "Let us know how you are getting on. Everybody well and send love."[14]

Like two old friends, husband and wife continued over the years to chat long-distance about family, acquaintances, real estate, politics, even sports. When Gene Tunney defeated Jack Dempsey for the heavyweight boxing championship in September 1926, W. R. telegrammed Millicent in New York, "Wasn't it wonderful to have a good loyal Marine win instead of a slacker?"[15]

Millicent continued to take an interest in the family business, serving as a roving ambassador of sorts during her frequent travels in Europe. In the summer of 1927, when she visited Rome, Hearst asked her to give his regards to Mussolini, whom he was trying to recruit to write for his newspapers. During her visit, Millicent must have asked Il Duce for his help in finding Italian marble and marble carvers for San Simeon. On July 18, 1927, Hearst telegrammed Julia Morgan to ask her to relocate the draftsmen who were working in the Bay Area on the drawings for the marble work so that he could meet with them at San Simeon: "These have been hanging fire for some time. We can finish them here quickly and send them to Mussolini and get all the finished material back by April 1 and begin erecting them this coming spring."[16]

Though he had separated himself by three thousand miles from his wife and children, W. R. was not prepared to let go of them entirely. He had chosen not to live with Millicent anymore, but he still cared for her. This is not to say that he acquiesced to her every demand. While paying her bills and settling a munificent allowance on her, he continued to insist that she learn to live within her budget — something he had never managed to do. He also scolded her for abusing her position and asking for too many special favors. He telegrammed her in Paris in the summer of 1926 to demand that she stop asking Hearst officials abroad to pay any bills: "They are not authorized to do this and [it] embarrasses them greatly. I will pay return steamer reservations . . . You are being supplied with ample funds for other requirements. Love." In 1930, when she innocently asked for copies of Charlie Chaplin's photograph for the boys, he replied angrily, "That is a ridiculous request. We have overtaxed the courtesy of the various companies by getting pictures for myself, yourself, George, William, John and everybody connected with the family. We will have to stop what amounts to an imposition."[17]

Raising his sons was important to Hearst, but never his first priority. Although he always sent them presents for their birthdays, he never chose them himself but asked Millicent or Joe Willicombe to do so. There were also long stretches of time in which he remained entirely out of reach. "His silences toward us were often difficult to understand and bear," Bill, Jr. recalled. "The only reasonable explanation that I have been able to come to over the years was his far-flung company and other responsibilities. . . . In not spending more time with his wife and children, my father made the biggest mistake of his life. It left an emptiness in all of us."[18]

After extended silences, the Chief would fire off a long letter to one or the other of his boys, filled with advice and warnings to straighten up. Like his mother before him, W. R. interfered at a distance in every aspect of their private lives well into their adulthood. George, at age twenty-three, was lectured by "Pop" on his weight: "You are getting dangerously stout. Health is important, and if you do not take pains to keep from getting dangerously fat, you are going to pop out some time soon with fatty degeneration of the heart or kidneys or something of that kind." Bill, Jr., at twenty-nine, was criticized for getting sick: "I am sorry that you are ill. Have you gone back to drinking and smoking. . . . Keep yourself in good condition. Do not drink. Do not smoke. You can have fun in LOTS of ways which will not injure your health."[19]

All his life, he was terrified that his sons would grow up to be irresponsible. None of his boys, as Randolph Hearst explained in an interview years later, had "the talent or the drive of the old man" — and they all knew it. Nor, as Bill, Jr. wrote in his autobiography, did they ever come close to their father "in disciplined working habits." He desperately wanted them to be able to take over the publishing empire he had built from the ground up. "Pop repeatedly warned us that he would not treat us like a rich man's sons. Each of us was told he would have to prove himself to my father's satisfaction."[20]

Still, no matter what he might say or write, it became clear to the boys quite early that their father would give them what they wanted. "I expect something more of you than to be playboys," he wrote the twins at the Lawrenceville School in New Jersey. "You will have to work and work hard. You might as well be learning how to work now. You have got to get an education that will make you able to take care of yourselves. . . . If you are not trained for the contest that is ahead of you, you are likely to bring up the rear of the procession."[21] But when the twins did poorly at school, Hearst excused their failures. "I have read the headmaster's letter about Randolph, and I suppose David, too," he wrote Millicent:

> There is nothing very surprising in this. These boys are simply behaving as the others did. We may not approve of their behavior, but it is characteristic of the clan. They do not take kindly to education. This is probably a defect, but Brisbane says, "It takes a good mind to resist education." . . . I wish they would learn something, but apparently they will not. . . . The school is probably too strict with them. . . . They are simply more or less untamed and untamable. . . . At any rate, I would not worry about them. . . . If they do not get along at that school, we will put them in another school and give them all the education they will consent to absorb.[22]

Having paid little attention to formal schooling in his own life, W. R. could not quite bring himself to demand that his boys do so. "None of us completed college," Bill, Jr. wrote in his memoirs. "That did not seem to bother Pop, since he was not graduated from Harvard. George spent a year at UC Berkeley; John dropped out of Oglethorpe, Randy left Harvard; and David didn't go to college at all. I left UC Berkeley after two and a half years."[23]

As they left school, Hearst apprenticed them all to trusted executives in his publishing companies, who were expected to watch over them, teach them the ropes, and report on their progress to their father. When the boys made a decision he did not agree with or, worse yet, abdicated their responsibilities, he lashed out, showing little mercy. "Some of my brothers," Bill, Jr. wrote in his memoir, "were surprised and, at times, shocked at what they perceived as a hard-nosed attitude on our father's part when it came to work. Pop tested the ability of each of us to perform, independent of our being his sons. Coming of age was a very disturbing time for each of us. We had been sheltered from many of life's cruelties, despite various warnings by Pop that making a living was no easy business. Most of us felt we needed more time and greater warning from him before facing the problem of a career. The working world came as a cold and perhaps even cruel blast of new air. My brothers felt that Pop treated us harshly."[24]

George, the oldest, had the roughest time of all. At age nineteen, after leaving Berkeley, he was given his first position at the *San Francisco Examiner*. When he proved himself uninterested in or incapable of doing any work there, his father ordered Joseph Moore to fire him, in a fashion. "George can continue drawing his wages," Hearst wrote Moore, "but do not want him around any more. He gets soused all time and is terribly sick after every drunk and useless for days. Besides being alcoholic disgrace, this last time he got drunk and missed train and I have nobody to do his work. Am awfully sorry but I must get reliable man."[25]

George was given another chance. When he failed again, Hearst delegated John Neylan, his West Coast lieutenant, to take charge. "In regard to George Hearst," Hearst wrote Neylan, "he is apparently too lazy to occupy a position by himself and do any work. So there is one of two things to be done with him; either put him in the Fleishhacker bank for a year or two, until he gets an acquaintance with business methods — and I think this is the best thing to do — or else put him back under your care and make him work. . . . Do as you think best." After three years of failure on the West Coast, George was finally shipped East to New York City in 1926 to serve as president of the *New York American*. He was then twenty-two years of age.[26]

There was no way George or any of the other boys could possibly succeed. When they slacked off, they were criticized by their father for being bums. When they tried to take their work seriously, they were criticized for overreaching. "Sousa said anybody could conduct my band for a while," W. R. wrote George in the fall of 1927, after he had been sent back West to take over the *Examiner* again. "What he meant was he had his band well trained but that it would soon begin deteriorating unless careful superintendence was kept up. I think *Examiner* is beginning to deteriorate."[27]

Having failed to demonstrate any talent at all for the publishing business, George was quickly superseded as heir apparent by his younger brother Bill, Jr., who, after leaving college at age twenty, joined the *New York American* as a City Hall reporter. He soon worked his way up the hierarchy under the tutelage of editor Edmond Coblentz, until he was, while still in his twenties, named publisher of the *American*. Although W. R. complained about Bill's playboy antics, his love of fast cars and planes, his drinking, and the time he spent in nightclubs, he was much gentler with him than with George. "Please keep out of airplanes, Bill," he telegrammed him in 1927, when he was nineteen years old. "Am afraid you will break your neck just as you are getting to be useful newspaper man. Am serious about this."[28]

This is not to say that Bill, Jr. was spared his father's complaints. "There are two kinds of cartoons appearing . . . that I find very objectionable," W. R. wrote him at the *American*. "One is the kind reflecting on colored people and the other takes contemptuous attitude toward the poorer classes who do menial work. I wish you would kindly stop these absolutely both in the daily and in the Sunday papers." The following week, Bill, Jr. received a second telegram from San Simeon: "Please try to understand instructions and advice that I give you. I may not always have time to explain them, but you can generally depend on the fact that my experience is greater than yours. Of course Victor [Watson] and all the others try to tell you that you are right. I try to tell you the TRUTH."[29]

Hearst's most vexed relationship was probably with John Hearst, his third oldest son. Perhaps the most gifted intellectually of all the boys, with movie-star good looks and a surfeit of charm, John was a constant disappointment to his father. After a checkered academic career in various prep schools, he enrolled in Berkeley, but was asked to leave when he failed to attend class. Though W. R. had accepted the other boys' scholastic failures, he was furious with John:

> Your failure to attend school makes it necessary for me to end your futile attempts at education. You will not go to college. You will resign from . . . school and go to work on some newspaper in San Francisco immediately. You will surrender your automobile or sell it, because I will not give you any money to take care of it. You will probably be better able to get along on some other pa-

per than any one of my papers, because I do not want you merely to be a dependent in journalism and be as big a failure in journalism as you have been in your studies.[30]

By the fall, Hearst had agreed to give John a second chance at college, this time at Oglethorpe University, near Atlanta, where Hearst had the previous May received an honorary degree. Though the Chief had not appeared to care much whether any of his other sons attended college, he did not know what else to do with John, who was not yet eighteen and much too young and immature to take a position at one of his father's newspapers or magazines. "Well here I am Alabamy bound much to my disgust," John telegraphed his father in San Simeon. "But as you say quote much must be sacrificed in the quest of knowledge unquote. Don't forget it. Won't be long before I am a year older and as a birthday gift to myself I became engaged to Dorothy. Love from your well meaning but blundering son John."[31]

The woman John referred to was Dorothy Hart, "the belle of her social set in Los Angeles," according to Irene Selznick, and "one of the most beautiful girls in Southern California. . . . She could stop traffic." Both sets of parents objected to the marriage: the Harts, according to Sally Bedell Smith, the biographer of Dorothy's second husband, William Paley, because John's father lived openly with his mistress; the Hearsts because John was uneducated, unemployable, and barely eighteen years of age. After weeks of telegrams and letters back and forth from John, who wanted his father's help, "Pop" gave in. John promised to delay his marriage and concentrate on his schoolwork. W. R. bought him a "lovely ring" to give to Dorothy and instructed the editor of his Atlanta newspaper to give him the money he needed to make his first and subsequent payments on a new car.[32]

Despite his promises, John dropped out of school to marry Dorothy Hart in December. After a lengthy and expensive honeymoon, he returned to New York, still only nineteen years of age, to take a position as president of the Hearst company which oversaw *Town & Country, Harper's Bazaar*, and a few other magazines. The following fall, John tried to justify his new title and $100,000 salary by sending his father a lengthy memo with suggestions for the magazines. W. R. turned most of them down and corrected John's spelling errors.[33]

While Millicent's major complaint about her boys was that they didn't write her often enough, W. R. could not countenance their spending habits. "These young people," he wrote Millicent in the fall of 1930, "are all as mad as March Hares on the money question and seem to think there is no limit to the bankroll. . . . I am sure that if George had not had so much money he would not have got into the trouble he has got into. All work and no play may make Jim a dull boy, but no work and all play makes Jim all kinds of a jackass. I want you to get our youngsters together and tell them I am going to shut down on the money supply . . . These nincompoops are never satisfied and are being ruined by living far beyond their means and mine. Please read them a lecture and make them keep their expenses down."[34]

Try as he might to rein in his sons' spending, the Hearst example spoke much louder than his threats. The boys, following in their father's footsteps, continually ran into debt and called on their parents to bail them out. This they did, as had Phoebe before them, but never without complaining.

ও 23 ৯

Dream Houses

"**M**ARION DAVIES WILL SOON MOVE into her beach house at Santa Monica," Louella Parsons wrote in her September 6, 1926, column. "It is the largest house on any southern California beach. . . . Even Marion doesn't know how many . . . rooms there are."[1]

Four months earlier, on returning from New York City, where he and Millicent had celebrated their twenty-third wedding anniversary and his sixty-third birthday, W. R. picked Marion up at her Beverly Hills mansion for a drive to the Santa Monica beach. They stopped close to the spot where Aimee McPherson, the nationally known radio evangelist, had been seen for the very last time before she had vanished earlier in the week. A huge wave swept toward them and almost knocked Marion over. W. R. took her up to higher, safer ground. Did she like the spot she was now standing on? he asked her. When she replied that she did, he told her he would build a home for her there.[2]

The Santa Monica beach, far enough from Hollywood to shelter its residents but near enough to comfortably commute from, had become the favored home for the movie colony's elite. Jesse Lasky, Louis B. Mayer, Sam and Frances Goldwyn, Norma Shearer and Irving Thalberg, Mildred and Harold Lloyd, and Doug Fairbanks and Mary Pickford already lived there in luxurious mansions that were emblematic, they hoped, of their royal stature in Hollywood. Marion's beach house dwarfed them all.[3]

Irene Mayer, who lived with her parents down the strip, recalled in her memoir that, as Hearst's and Marion's "great mansion began to assume its overpowering position on the beach," she became "increasingly fascinated, and . . . constantly drawn to have a look at what was going on." Her "Uncle William," whom she was fond of because Hearst always found time to talk to her when he visited the Mayer house, invited her for a tour around the site. "My visits came to be almost definite appointments. As we parted, he would announce when he would be there next. He never said he expected me, but when I showed up, he'd say he'd been wondering where I was."

Hearst, delighted to have someone to talk to about his new project, especially a smart and attractive twenty-year-old, lectured Irene "about Georgian paneling, original brasses, and a lot more about mantels and overmantels than I ever had need to know." Irene became his "companion in his housebuilding, since Marion never bothered to come. . . . He had a passion for building. . . . We never discussed anything but details of the architecture, the imports, and what was to be done about the pool. The pool was begun several times; he increased its length, changed its depth." When the pool was finally completed, Hearst invited Irene Mayer to baptize it with him. On the appointed day and time, Mayer appeared at Hearst's mansion:

> I didn't get the welcome I expected because he was upset. . . . There was a problem which appeared minor (to me): Uncle William didn't have a bathing suit. He covered all the rooms upstairs and I devoted myself to the basement, which was temporarily a supply depot. It was piled high with enormous cartons of bathing suits, every size except his. . . . Someone must have gotten hell, because even standing by the pool I could hear his high-pitched voice. . . . When he returned, he was quiet and frightening. . . . Coldly, he asked me to conduct the so-called ceremony by myself; he would observe. It was no fun to mount the big board, swim the length, and come up to an unsmiling Uncle William. I fled down the beach, pained for the poor man who had been so humiliated.[4]

By the time it was finished, Ocean House, according to Marion's biographer Fred Guiles, had cost Hearst $7 million — $3 million in construction costs and $4 million more in furnishing and artworks. "It almost got to be as big as the White House," Marion recalled. "Bigger, maybe. Just like you build with little blocks, he added on and on. But little blocks wouldn't have cost the money."[5]

Ocean House at Santa Monica (or the beach house, as it came to be called) consisted of a U-shaped three-story white Georgian colonial-style mansion, surrounded by four other buildings in the same style. Behind the central mansion was a 110-foot heated, saltwater swimming pool, lined with Italian marble and traversed by a Venetian marble bridge. To the right were the tennis courts. Hearst and Marion lived in the main house and did their entertaining there. The other four houses were occupied by Marion's family, long-term guests, and thirty-two full-time servants. There were 110 bedrooms and 55 bathrooms in the complex. As at San Simeon, every bedroom was part of a suite, with a sitting room and private bathroom. Marion and W. R. had their own suites, connected by a hidden door.

Busy as he was with his own castle at San Simeon, Hearst supervised the construction, interior decoration, and furnishing of Marion's new home. Though Julia Morgan did not design the structure, she was enlisted to help decorate and furnish the interior. "When we come to the decoration of the interior of the beach house," Hearst wrote Morgan on June 15, 1926, "in order to prevent too much similarity in the ten bedrooms [in the main house, which was built first] I think it might be well to have on the top floor for instance, one Dutch bedroom, one French bedroom, etcetera. . . . On the top floor we might want to let the beams show [something he had ruled out at San Simeon], and get a little different type of treatments, all in the 18th century period, however. . . . Do we use these vacuum cleaners on the Hill? I would like to provide means of using them at the beach. Also have house telephones, radio connections, etc."[6]

Hearst purchased and imported entire rooms from different parts of Europe and installed them at the beach house. Three of the public rooms in the main building, "each more than sixty feet long," according to Anne Edwards, writing in *Architectural Digest* in April 1994, "came from Burton Hall in Ireland. There was a ballroom from a circa 1750 Venetian palazzo and a tavern from an inn in Surrey dating from 1560. . . . Going from one room to another was somewhat like an abbreviated tour of grand European houses — English, French, and Spanish predominating. The artworks displayed had no feeling of a collection."[7]

There were dinner parties at Marion's every night of the week when she was in town and all-day swimming parties on the weekends. "On Saturday," the actress Louise Brooks remembered of a weekend visit in April of 1928, "there were twenty people to lunch, forty were added in the afternoon to swim in the Venetian pool of white marble which separated the house from the ocean, and forty more were added for the buffet supper served on the porch overlooking the pool." On special occasions, like Hearst's birthdays, which after 1926 would be celebrated with Marion in California, huge canvas tents were erected to accommodate up to 2,000 guests.[8]

If her husband's increasingly expensive, quasi-public relationship with Marion caused Millicent discomfort, she did not exhibit it. Marion Davies might be the queen of Santa Monica; Millicent ruled over a much larger and more important social empire in New York City.

Millicent received an allowance of $10,000 a month (equivalent in buying power to more than $95,000 in today's currency) from Hearst's International Magazine Company. Hearst's companies also paid for her living expenses at the Clarendon, her winters at The Breakers in Palm Beach, summers in Europe, and Septembers at San Simeon. All that Millicent lacked to keep up with her society friends in New York was a between-season residence that was not too far from Manhattan.[9]

In the autumn of 1927, a little more than a year after construction had begun on Marion's beach house, W. R. bought his wife the beachfront estate at Sands Point, Long Island, that had been owned by Mrs. Oliver Hazard Perry Belmont, the former Alva Vanderbilt. Short of cash, he directed Jack Neylan to find the first $100,000 payment for Belmont House, which, he told Neylan, had been bought at Mrs. Hearst's insistence.[10]

The estate, also known as Beacon Towers, had been designed by Richard Howland Hunt of the firm of Hunt & Hunt, the architects of choice on Long Island's North Shore. Mrs. Belmont, who had previously commissioned the Hunts to build a $3 million fairy-tale French mansion at 660 Fifth Avenue and the $11 million Marble House at Newport, outdid herself on the eighteen acres of beachfront property she purchased in Sands Point. Beacon Towers was one of the strangest and most magnificent dwellings on Long Island. Built directly on the Sound, it was part Norman fortress, part Loire Valley manor house. Though Millicent's neighbors included Vincent Astor and Daniel Guggenheim, and there were glorious mansions up and down the north shore, when F. Scott Fitzgerald wrote *The Great Gatsby* in 1925 he modeled Gatsby's mansion on Mrs. Belmont's 140-room medieval castle.

"The desired effect," writes Robert B. King, author of *The Vanderbilt Homes*, "was to awe and overwhelm the eye: the building rose from the beach of Long Island Sound with no lawn to taper and balance its extreme height: rather the building seemed to rise out of the sea itself, reaching five stories into the sky. The house's exterior was left unadorned of embellishments or detailing. Rather, battlements and balconies protruded from its mighty mass, while turrets, towers, and gables rose upward from all directions." To keep out intruders, Mrs. Belmont built a stone wall around the estate. When the North Hempstead Town Board questioned her right to block access to the beach, she bought an additional five and one-half acres of beachfront land and the lighthouse that stood on it.[11]

Millicent was, she wrote W. R. in October, delighted about Belmont House, but she agreed with her husband that renovations were necessary before they could move in. The roof had to be raised, the windows enlarged to let in more light, the lighthouse converted to a guest cottage. Though Millicent suggested that the "inside" be left alone, Hearst had ideas here as well. According to Robert King, Hearst removed "the oppressive medieval-style murals of St. Joan [and] the grilled-iron gateway and heavy doors.

Archways were installed in their place, and extraordinary medieval stone fireplaces brought over from Europe were added. A carved oak dining room was purchased [from Scotland and] decorated with paintings by Sir Joshua Reynolds and with gold consoles and mirrors from a mansion near London."[12]

The *New York Times,* in its report on the sale of the home, noted that it had been purchased as a "'between season' home" for the Hearsts, plural. This was certainly Millicent's intention. "When are you coming on so you can make some changes," she wrote her husband in early October 1927, just before they took title. "I think it would be delightful for us all to be there in early spring. Think you would enjoy it. Twins tickled to death. They now want a boat. When do you think you and A. B. [Arthur Brisbane] will be coming?"[13]

Though W. R. was already overseeing the construction of Ocean House in Santa Monica and Casa Grande at San Simeon, he took complete control of the renovation and decoration of Millicent's new estate. When, in the spring of 1929, Emile Gauvreau, the future editor of the *New York Daily Mirror,* met Hearst for the first time at Sands Point, he was invited to help him uncrate furniture. "While we talked," Gauvreau recalled, "Hearst and I hacked away at crates, pulling excelsior from early American pieces such as highboys, benches and chests. Various periods were represented in card tables, candlestands, wing chairs, love seats and what not. I admired the flat surface decorations and wood inlay work of some of the furniture and my remarks seemed to please the publisher who felt the lacquered areas with a certain fondness."[14]

While Hearst was intimately involved with Marion's and Millicent's estates, and with St. Donat's, his castle in Wales, his first passion remained San Simeon. It was here that he spent the greatest portion of his time and his corporations' income from the middle 1920s on. Hearst had learned, from his father perhaps, that if one had the patience to wait and did not panic as debt piled upon debt, investments wisely made in the past would pay off handsomely in the future. His newspapers, like his father's mines, had required an enormous initial outlay, with a time lag of years before they began to turn a profit. By the middle and late 1920s, the papers he had purchased earlier in the decade — and refused to sell when urged to by his financial advisers — had begun to pay back their investments, and more.

Having substantially reduced his expenditures on his moving-picture studio and entered into what appeared to be a lucrative coproduction deal with MGM, Hearst found himself with more money to spend than ever before. Other businessmen might have saved some of this newfound income for future investments or some sort of rainy-day fund, but Hearst did not. Income was for spending; investment capital, when needed, could always be borrowed.

As his disposable income grew ever larger, his imagination ran wild. Though he had learned to read plans, the finished product seldom matched his expectations. Time and again, he would visit a recently constructed or renovated room at San Simeon and decide that mistakes had been made, that the plans which he had approved had not been correct, that the proportions were all wrong, the ceiling too low, the fireplace at the wrong end of the room.

Walter Steilberg, one of Julia Morgan's assistants, was present during the completion of the work in House C, Casa del Sol, in the early 1920s. "The fireplace," Steilberg recalled in his oral history, "had been located on the long side of one of the living rooms. He came in, and I was there when he said, 'No, I don't like it there. Take it out and move it over here.' It was all built! Chimney going up to the roof, and everything, and the foundation went to hell and gone down the hillside. I was also there when, six months later, Hearst said, 'No, that was a mistake. We shouldn't have moved it from where it was. Take it out of there and put it back where it was.' I think he enjoyed it like a small boy, in a way."[15]

This type of decision making was almost routine. Nothing he built was ever left alone for long. In July of 1922, he purchased some Roman temple fragments and had them installed in his new rose garden. In 1923, he instructed Julia Morgan to construct a reflecting pool in front of the temple fragments and plant it with night-blooming water lilies. In 1924, he asked her to enlarge the reflecting pool into a swimming pool for his boys. The following spring, he had the swimming pool enlarged. When the enlargement was finished, he decided he wanted the pool lined with marble. In 1928, he had dressing rooms and an extended Neptune Terrace added. Three years later, he would rip up everything and redesign the entire structure for a third time.[16]

Hearst disliked stasis. As soon as something was completed — or neared completion — he began planning improvements or replacements or shifted his attention to an entirely new project. In April of 1927, as the marble was being installed in his newly enlarged Neptune Pool, he decided that he needed another pool, elsewhere on the property, and wrote Morgan:

> We could put a big hot-house down where we were going to build the Persian Garden, and in the middle of this hot-house we could have a big pool about

the size of our present pool. In the hot-house, sufficiently back from the pool, we would have palms, ferns, and whole lot of orchids. . . . The temperature of the hot-house, and of the pool, too, would be warm on the coldest, bleakest winter day. *We would have the South Sea Island on the Hill.* . . . Towards the sea there should be a big rest room, and a loggia. Here we could serve toi or poi, or whatever the situation called for. The pool, of course, would be the main attraction; and we might put a turtle and a couple of sharks in to lend verisimilitude. This, except for the sharks, is not as impractical a proposition as it might seem. It is merely making a hot-house useful, and making a pool beautiful.[17]

Hearst carried around in his head the blueprints for every room, terrace, and plaza at San Simeon. When he saw something that might fit, he bought it. As his income expanded during the 1920s, so did his expenditures on his art collections. "A great many very fine things will be arriving for the ranch — some of them have already arrived," he warned Miss Morgan, from Los Angeles, in February of 1927. "They are for the most part of a much higher grade than we have had heretofore. In fact, I have decided to buy only the finest things for the ranch from now on, and we will probably weed out some of our less desirable articles. I had no idea when we began to build the ranch that I would be here so much or that the construction itself would be so important. Under the present circumstances, I see no reason why the ranch should not be a museum of the best things that I can secure."[18]

For four decades Hearst had collected treasures and stored them away in his warehouses. He was now ready to undertake the laborious but rewarding process of relocating his most prized possessions to the West Coast. On an almost daily basis, he cabled Chris MacGregor at his Bronx warehouse or Miss Schrader, his personal secretary whose office was at the Clarendon, with instructions to locate and pack a particular painting, windowpane, architectural element, rug, or piece of porcelain for shipment in the next railroad car to San Simeon, via San Luis Obispo. Working for the most part from memory, he described the pieces he wanted, hoping that MacGregor would know where to find them in the five-story warehouse in the Bronx. When MacGregor located the item requested, he had it unpacked and photographed, with its dimensions recorded on the back of the photograph. The photograph was then mailed West. Only after Hearst received the photograph and approved final shipment was the item crated for shipment.

When enough material to fill a full railroad car had been assembled, a detailed list of the contents of that car was mailed to San Simeon, with a summary sent by wire. Each item, each list, each lot and packing case was sequentially numbered. To make sure that Hearst's instructions were followed exactly at each stage of the process, a copy of every letter or telegram sent from San Simeon to the Bronx was forwarded to Miss Schrader at the Clarendon, who was instructed "to keep them on file and make sure, by sufficiently frequent inquiry, that instructions have been or will be carried out."[19]

While Casa Grande was under construction, Hearst lived in House A, Casa del Mar. There were two bedrooms with adjoining bathrooms on the upper floor, one for him, one for Millicent, with a sitting room in between that Hearst may have used as his office. We don't know where Marion stayed when, sometime in the spring of 1926, she replaced Millicent as Hearst's de facto West Coast wife and hostess at San Simeon.

"I'd go up on weekends," Marion recalled in her memoirs, "and there'd be twenty or thirty guests, possibly forty or fifty. The train would leave Los Angeles at eight-fifteen and arrive at San Luis about three in the morning and we'd motor on up. We'd come back on Sunday to be at work Monday." Hearst's guests would be met at San Luis Obispo by a fleet of limousines which would transport them for the ninety-minute drive over dirt roads to San Simeon. "When we arrived we'd have breakfast and a rest. Luncheon was about two-thirty and dinner about half past eight at night. Saturday night we'd watch a movie. Before breakfast on Sunday we'd play tennis or go horseback riding — the usual things, the sporting life routine. Or we'd swim. . . . W. R. would come out and join the guests and go swimming. And he played tennis and went horseback riding. He was excellent at riding."[20]

W. R. was, by the middle 1920s, well into his sixties; Marion was not yet thirty. The last thing he wanted was to coerce Marion and her friends into traveling a full day to spend two days with him at the ranch, if they were going to end up being bored there. He began making additions to San Simeon until it was not simply the most beautiful place on earth but the most fun.

In April of 1926, he informed Miss Morgan that he was going to be doing more entertaining at the ranch and that she should hire extra servants. In July, he asked her to purchase the biggest and best Frigidaires available. "We have all the electric power we need and these big Frigidaires will make the temperature almost anything you please. You can freeze meat solid if you want to. They also make . . . ice and if we have enough Frigidaires . . . we would not have to transport so much ice as we do now." In August, he directed her to install Victrolas and radios in the Assembly Room, to construct dressing rooms near the pool, and to rebuild the tennis courts which, in their current state, did "not correspond in sumptuousness with the rest of the establishment." The following February, he instructed her to refit the rooms in the guesthouses with sound-proofing in the walls and ceilings: "It keeps people in the bed rooms from being annoyed by the phonographs and radios and maniacs in the parlors."[21]

Swimming, tennis, hiking, picnicking, and sightseeing were apparently not sufficient diversions for his guests, so, in the fall of 1927, he asked Miss Morgan to add "a polo field . . . on the lower part of the ranch . . . I think this could be combined with a flying field. I want these made very LARGE and very GOOD and with a small stand for spectators." The flying field would be built, but not the polo field, probably because none of Hearst's guests played polo.[22]

One of the attractions on the hillside was the largest privately owned zoo in the world. "W. R. wanted the animals around because it was picturesque," Marion Davies remembered. "And he thought the zoo might entertain the guests."[23]

At first, he bought only animals that could live in his fields without having to be caged: elk, white fallow deer, and a herd of bison which he purchased for $1,000 a head from a Missouri refuge. Species that could not live together were segregated in their own special preserves. In October of 1925, Morgan wrote him that the reindeer had arrived and the man who delivered them had suggested that they be separated from the buffaloes and bulls. Though they would eventually be able to graze on the native grasses, Hearst was told that he would have to buy Iceland moss for them to eat until they were used to new food.[24]

W. R. retained Richard A. Addison of the San Diego Zoo to buy wild animals for him. Addison traveled regularly to Boston and New York City to purchase animals off the ships transporting them from Africa and other countries. The animals were then loaded onto private express railway cars for the trip to San Luis Obispo, where they were offloaded onto trucks for the final journey to San Simeon. Julia Morgan telegrammed the Chief in July of 1927 that the latest shipment of animals had arrived "in beautiful shape. I had to rub my eyes last night when out of the semi-darkness staring at the lights were grouped three ostriches, five zebras, five white deer, two with big horns, a llama, and some speckled deer. All in a group! The giraffes are a beautiful specimen."[25]

Because the animals needed shelter and safe feeding places — and because Hearst wanted his guests to see them — he directed Morgan to build a set of "exceedingly picturesque log houses and put them in certain picturesque locations not far from the main road. Watering troughs can be put adjacent and feeding rooms established in connection, so that the animals will congregate at places where they can be seen from the road." He was especially concerned with the giraffes whom he wanted "transferred from where they are. Nobody yet who has come to the ranch has seen the giraffes."[26]

By 1928, an inventory of his zoo listed over three hundred animals, including twenty-seven antelope, five kinds of deer, forty-four bison, three cougars, five lions, two bobcats, a leopard, a cheetah, three kinds of bears, a chimpanzee, three Java monkeys, a tapir, sheep, goats, two llamas, two kangaroos, and a wallaby. There were special kennels for the dogs that Hearst bred, a lion den, bear pits, and a house for Marianne, the elephant Hearst bought in 1929 and named after Marion's first role in a talking picture.[27]

A walk down the hillside to the zoo at feeding time was an obligatory part of every stay at the ranch. Zoo stories became an ingrained element in the San Simeon folklore. Marion herself told stories about Doris Duke being chased by a spider monkey, about the lion who clawed young David Hearst, and the bear that chewed off the tip of a guest's finger — "and she had gloves on."[28]

Hearst had a warm spot in his heart for all his animals, the large and the small. He directed his staff to trap mice live and set them free on the grounds. When, in the spring of 1929, Hearst's zookeeper informed him that a kangaroo had been killed, probably by a predatory yak, the Chief urged him not to condemn the yak out of hand. The kangaroo, he suggested, might have been killed by another animal or run over by an automobile. He did not, in any event, want the yaks punished or the kangaroos isolated from the rest of the animals: "Let us not do anything as yet until we have some further experience."[29]

If for the first six or seven years, the Hearst weekend guest list had been top-heavy with publishing associates, after 1926 it was reconfigured into something quite different. Marion, who loathed being alone, was accustomed to being surrounded by an entourage of family and friends. Because W. R. wanted her to enjoy herself at the ranch, he gave her carte blanche to invite whomever she wanted to spend the weekend with her there.

W. R. and Marion were the oddest of Hollywood couples. Hearst, especially, was a complete enigma to some of his guests. Often the tallest man in the room, with vivid blue eyes and a life-long habit of staring unblinkingly at his interlocutor, he struck many visitors to San Simeon as cold and distant, even a bit frightening. "There was always a little aura of the mysterious and awe about him," King Vidor remembered. "He seemed to be suspicious of strangers, and did not meet people very well," Frances Marion recalled in her oral history.[30]

Marion was as friendly and voluble as W. R. was distant and reserved. "She was a delightful hostess," the Hearst newspaper reporter Adela Rogers St. Johns recalled in an oral history. "She wasn't formal but very gay and very warm."[31] Every week, Marion and her secretary, Ella [Bill] Williams, whose office was at the MGM Culver City Studio, put together the next weekend's guest list and made the phone calls. Hearst, of course, had his own names to add. Together he and Marion were assembling a new California aristocracy of the amusing, witty, beautiful, and accomplished that included Marion's old friends from the *Follies* and her new friends from MGM, prominent studio executives, established and on-the-make stars and starlets, reporters, publishing tycoons, politicians, bankers, and writers. "We left the Southern Pacific station at 6:30 on Friday night," the actress Colleen Moore recalled of her first visit to the ranch, in 1927. "With me on the train was Hedda Hopper (who was still playing bit parts in movies), Julanne Johnston [a silent-screen actress], Constance Talmadge, King Vidor and Eleanor Boardman, Adolph Menjou and his wife Katherine, Eileen Percy and her husband Eric Busch (of the Busch breweries), Bebe Daniels and Jack Pickford, Jack Gilbert, Irving Thalberg and Norma Shearer . . . Arthur Brisbane and Damon Runyon."[32]

Though San Simeon was now W. R.'s business headquarters — and he invited his top executives to meet with him there — he much preferred to surround himself with people he found interesting. His favorite guests seemed to be his younger reporters. Adela Rogers St. Johns, who had begun writing for Hearst publications in 1913, was invited to the ranch for the first time in the middle 1920s, to meet with Ray Long, the head of Hearst's magazine division. Joe Willicombe had called her directly in Los Angeles to say that the Chief was, that evening, driving north to the ranch and would be happy to take her with him.

"He picked me up," St. Johns wrote, "and we went along quietly beside the Pacific Ocean. . . . Mr. Hearst far in one corner of the big luxurious limousine, me in the other." At Los Alamos, they stopped at a roadside diner "and sat on stools and Mr. Hearst said he recommended the ham and eggs or the chili." At San Luis Obispo, the fog got so bad that Hearst took over from the chauffeur and drove the rest of the way north to San Simeon. They arrived early in the morning. "Mr. Hearst bowed and told me a courteous good night and thanked me for my company. A maid was waiting in my room, the blaze of a wood fire in the huge fireplace was at the moment more important than art treasures and the light gleaming from behind silent shades, and silver sconces gave the peaceful and comforting effect of candlelight. . . . I thought to myself, This is a life I shall be glad to have known. I shall realize that people who have always had it and take it for granted are different from other people; they can be worthy and strong and accept their obligations, or they can be indulgent and selfish but they are *different* from people who scramble for money."[33]

In June of 1926, after a weekend filled with guests, most of them from Hollywood, Hearst sent Julia Morgan a handwritten note, apologizing because "all those wild movie people prevented me from talking to you as much as I wanted to. . . . Nevertheless the movie folk were immensely appreciative. They said it was the most wonderful place in the world and that the most extravagant dream of a moving-picture set fell far short of this reality. They all wanted to make a picture there but they are NOT going to be allowed to do it."[34]

Though most of the guestrooms in the castle would not be habitable until the late 1920s, the major public rooms — the Assembly Room, the Refectory or dining room, and the Morning Room — were in use by 1927. Then as now, Hearst's castle — or Casa Grande as it was referred to at the time — was San Simeon's front page, its billboard. It is difficult to find the right terms to describe this massive structure placed on the hillside where all sightlines led. In exterior design and interior layout, it resembles a cathedral much more than a castle. But unlike either, it is built of reinforced concrete covered with a veneer of Utah limestone so artfully applied that no one could guess that the structure was not made of stone.

Castles are, in effect, enclosed military fortresses; Casa Grande is not. It had no parapets or moats. Instead of being closed off to the world, the entranceway offered access across a beautifully landscaped terrace with a small pool. In the final analysis, Casa Grande invites comparisons with medieval castles *and* Gothic cathedrals because it incorporates and projects both lay and ecclesiastic power. Hearst, at San Simeon, was building a monument to himself, a visual representation of his place in the world. In form and function, Hearst's hillside village of guesthouses looking upward to Casa Grande resembled nothing quite so much as a medieval township. The villagers in their cottages were dependent on the lord of the castle for all services. There were no kitchens, refrigerators, or dining facilities outside the big house. It was not possible to get a cocktail before dinner, a midnight snack, or even a cup of coffee anywhere but in Casa Grande, as Adela Rogers St. Johns, who became a regular guest, discovered on her first visit. "This was almost the only thing I found difficult," she recalled:

All the years I went there, sometimes I spent weeks at a time, I had to get dressed, walk paths between white statues and flowering trees to the Castle for my coffee . . . At home I had coffee the moment I opened my eyes. I once asked Marion Davies about this incongruous bit amid the luxury, the meticulous service, and extravagant indulgence by which guests were surrounded. She said W. R. did not approve of breakfast in bed. If people did not *get up* and *get dressed* they might frowst away hours that could better be spent *outdoors*. He thought, Marion said, that the wonderful walk through morning dew and freshness with the sparkle of the sea below and the mountain air blowing from above the Sierras was a good way to start the day. I'm sure it was but at the time I thought I could have appreciated it more with one cup of coffee.[35]

Though a shy man, W. R. had never been comfortable with solitude. He was most at home in theaters, restaurants, and newsrooms, engulfed in crowds of strangers. At San Simeon, where there were no urban amusements, no public theaters or restaurants of any kind, Hearst had to engineer a social environment to meet his particular needs for controlled sociability. He did so by constructing a social setting which directed all activity toward Casa Grande, over which he presided. The library, the movie theater and Billiard Room, the Assembly Room where cocktails were available before dinner, and the Refectory or dining room were all located there. Just beyond were the pools and the tennis courts.

While Hearst and Julia Morgan often referred to the guesthouses as cottages, they were anything but. The smallest, Casa del Monte, had ten rooms; Casa del Sol had eighteen rooms on three levels surrounded by its own gardens; Casa del Mar had eighteen rooms. Only when compared to the looming four-story, 115-room, 38-bedroom castle/cathedral that dominated the hillside could these Mediterranean-style villas be characterized as cottages.

Unlike Casa Grande, with its towers defiantly reaching beyond the highest point of the hillside to touch the sky, the villas were built into and became part of the sculpted landscape. Though they were all multilevel structures, the sides facing Casa Grande were only one story in depth, so as not to compete with the grandeur of the castle.

Hearst designed his gardens and terraces as "outdoor" rooms for reading, chatting, even doing business. Alice Head, who managed Hearst's magazines in England, visited San Simeon a few times in the 1920s and recalls having her meetings with the Chief in "a quiet spot in the garden [with] other Hearst executives lurking in the bushes, awaiting their turn. . . . One scribe, after his first visit to the Ranch, wrote as follows: 'The place is full of worried editors dodging the kangaroos.'"[36]

Because the exterior was to be as fully lived in as the interiors, Hearst made sure that every inch of ground on the hillside was carefully planned before it was planted. Plantings were color coordinated and designed so that something would be in bloom twelve months a year. "We would propagate from five hundred to seven hundred thousand annuals per year," Norman Rotanzi recalled. "There was a complete change in the gardens at every season."[37]

Norman Rotanzi, one of Hearst's orchard men, relished his meetings with the Chief. "You really felt at ease around him," Rotanzi said. "He knew all the names of the plants and most of the pests we have to deal with. The gardeners were sort of his pets. He would like to come out and stroll around and talk to everybody. And it didn't make any difference who he had with him — Winston Churchill, or the president of U.S. Steel, or whoever it was, he would always introduce you to these people."[38]

Hearst was like a little boy at San Simeon, happy with his new toys, but inconsolable and impossibly cranky when something broke. When, in February of 1927, he returned to his hillside after a month's absence and was assaulted by a ferocious storm, he inundated Camille Rossi, Morgan's construction supervisor, with a list of weather-proofing improvements he wanted made "promptly." "Please realize Mr. Rossi that these are not merely things which ought to be done some time. They are things which we positively must do just as soon as possible. . . . Let's have COMFORT AND HEALTH before so much art. The art won't do us any good if we are all dead of pneumonia. Let's make it possible to be warm and comfortable."[39]

When everything was not set right — immediately — the Chief dashed off a second letter to Rossi:

> We are drowned, blown and frozen out. . . . Everybody has a cold. All who could have left and the few who remain are eagerly waiting a chance to get out. . . . Of course the houses are wonderful to look at but one cannot live on looks alone. Living in them is like living in a palatial barn. . . . Let's make what we have built practical, comfortable and beautiful. If we can't do that we might as well change the names of the houses to pneumonia house, diphtheria house and influenza bungalow. The main house we can call the clinic. I am not coming back to the hill until we put the small houses at least on a livable basis.[40]

His letters to Julia Morgan alternated between complaints about what had already been built and visionary plans for new construction. In February, in the midst of his torrent of complaints about leaky doors and windows, he forwarded to Morgan his friend Jimmy Swinnerton's suggestion that they build an artist's studio "between the towers of the third floor of the north wing." Morgan warned that a studio on the third floor might "unbalance the Patio . . . and bring the roof line" too high. She suggested instead that the studio be housed elsewhere.[41]

Hearst agreed to leave the North Wing alone — for the moment — but he would never give up trying to improve the buildings and the landscape on what was now referred to as "La Cuesta Encantada," the enchanted hill. Like the cathedral which can never be finished, San Simeon would remain a work in progress for as long as Hearst lived.

§ 24 &

Businesses as Usual

W ITH THE ARRIVAL of the New York City tabloids, the *Evening Graphic* and the *Daily News*, Hearst's role as publishing's bête noire was eclipsed. Not only were his papers no longer as outrageous as they had once been — and certainly not as lowbrow or spectacularly vulgar as the tabloids — they had, according to H. L. Mencken, become as staid and predictable as the *Philadelphia Public Ledger*. Instead of battling "the corruptions of wealth, whether political or social, with an immense fury and a superb technical virtuosity," the Chief had become another Coolidge sycophant. "His present ignominious presence in the Coolidge band-wagon," Mencken lamented, "is, in more than one way, a public calamity. For there was never a time in American history when the old-time Hearst was more needed than he is needed today. . . . The American daily press, with Hearst leading it in a devil's dance, was loud, vulgar, inordinate and preposterous — but it was not slimy and it was not dull. Today it is both."[1]

There were, for Hearst, no more dragons to slay — or at least none that he was interested in slaying. He was comfortable with Calvin Coolidge in the White House, Andrew Mellon at Treasury, and the brokers and bankers whose loans and bond issues had made it possible for him to expand his business empire. Though he had been accused of many things in his life, including anarchism, socialism, and rabid radicalism, Hearst was at bottom a classic liberal who believed, with Coolidge, that that government which governed least governed best. Hearst had never wanted to break up the large corporations; he had only wanted to force those that were cheating the public to behave, play fair, and stop buying politicians. He was now, in the 1920s, persuaded that they were doing so. He was not, of course, the only one who looked at big businessmen differently than he had thirty years before. The cartoon image of the business leader as an unscrupulous, predatory robber baron had been transmuted into a portrait of a benevolent corporate prince.

Mencken had spoken precipitously when he accused the Hearst papers in 1927 of having lost "all their honest frenzy" and the Chief of growing "respectable, personally as well as professionally." Hearst was actually between crusades. Though he was in agreement with the Republicans' domestic policies, particularly on taxes, there was one point of friction. He found Presidents Harding and Coolidge and Herbert Hoover, their secretary of commerce and potential successor, too Wilsonian for his tastes.

While the primary focus of the Republican administrations had been prosperity at home, Presidents Harding and Coolidge had recognized that domestic prosperity was dependent on prosperity in Europe, which required peace and political stability. Using economic leverage to the maximum, the Republican administrations had compelled European agreement to a series of disarmament treaties which, they hoped, would prevent a postwar arms race, ease financial strain, and encourage European nations to pursue peaceful means to resolve their conflicts.[2]

Although he would not have been familiar or comfortable with the label, Hearst was very much an isolationist. This was not an unpopular position in the 1920s. As the Senate had repudiated both Wilson's 1920 League of Nations initiative and bills put forward in 1923 and 1926 under which the United States would have joined the World Court, Hearst's position on foreign affairs was very much in the mainstream.[3]

Like the Western and Midwestern progressive senators William Borah of Idaho, George Norris of Nebraska, Robert LaFollette of Wisconsin, Arthur Vandenberg of Michigan, Robert Taft of Ohio, and Hiram Johnson of California, Hearst's isolationism was selective. He was opposed to political and military intervention in European affairs, but not in the Caribbean, Central or South America, or in the Pacific. He was also very much a unilateralist and against the United States entering into "entangling alliances" of any sort in any region of the world.[4]

He opposed disarmament treaties because they limited America's freedom to do as it pleased with its armed forces and navy; he was against international economic agreements like the Dawes Plan which reduced German reparations because they compromised American prosperity and independence by tying the American economy to Europe's; he was against multinational diplomatic treaties like the 1928 Kellogg-Briand Pact because it pledged its signatories to avoid war by acting in concert with one another to settle international disputes. And he was unalterably opposed to

American participation in the World Court. The Court was an organ of the League of Nations and membership in it, he argued, would bring the United States one giant step closer to membership in the League, involvement in European affairs, and another war, paid for by another income tax.[5]

Although the coming of the tabloids in the middle 1920s made Hearstian yellow journalism look more respectable in hindsight, it had not done Hearst's bottom line much good. As *Time* magazine had reported on August 15, 1927, the *American* was "weakening. The terrible tabloids have out-Hearsted Hearst and the morning New York field in screams and scandals is dominated by the *Daily News*."

Fully aware that the tabloids were eating into his circulation in New York City and might, in the near future, do so in other cities, Hearst cautioned his editors to condense their news stories: "The average man in the street wants to read all the news of importance . . . presented to him briefly as well as brightly. There are so many things to occupy the time of every man, woman and child in America these days that no one ever has a great deal of time to give to any particular matter."[6] Still, while he wanted shorter news stories, he was not willing to follow the example of the tabloids and substitute photographs for text. "Pictures that do not have news value," he warned his newspaper executives, "do more harm than good. . . . *The mass of pictures in a newspaper should have definite news value or else they should not be in the newspaper.*" He was also uncomfortable with the tabloids' penchant for attacking celebrities every bit as viciously, if not more so, than politicians. "Please, Phil," he telegrammed Phil Payne, his editor at the *New York Mirror,* after a particularly scurrilous attack on Gloria Swanson, "be more kindly to people and try make friends of them. Nearly everybody I know is weeping on my shoulder because of way *Mirror* roasts them. Can you not get some good natured reporters on staff?"[7]

This is not to say that there wasn't a steady decline in the quality of the Hearst papers, especially the evening editions and the *New York Mirror.* The international and national coverage was no longer as well-written or as complete, the front pages were no longer laid out as cleanly as they had been, there were too many thick, bold headlines, and on the inside pages ads usurped space that should have been devoted to news items.

The Hearst papers had always specialized in crime stories, the more heinous and bloody the better, but while earlier these stories had also called attention to the role of political malfeasance and police incompetence in fostering criminality and derailing justice, that subtext had largely disappeared. If Hearst had earlier built a readership and political constituency among his working-class and ethnic voters by presenting himself as their ally in the battle for a safer, more livable city, he now attempted to hold on to that constituency by practicing a sort of identity politics. Gone were the crusades against the trusts and the bosses, against corrupt machine politicians and judges. In their place were rather blatant attempts to appeal to ethnic groups by hiring their "heroes" to write columns.

As part of his never-ending and never successful attempt to compete with the *Daily News,* Phil Payne at the *Mirror* asked for Hearst's permission to commission the world's most famous Italian, Benito Mussolini, to write a regular column. "Believe a Mussolini signed editorial exclusively in the *Mirror* would mean hundred thousand extra daily circulation for us in New York," Payne telegrammed the Chief in February of 1927. "Mussolini is constantly seeking to influence American public opinion. That is why I think he will do the job for nothing. What do you think about it?" Hearst replied that he thought the Mussolini idea was great. Unfortunately, Mussolini had already signed an agreement with the United Press syndicate, which was at the time Hearst's major competitor, to write "opinion pieces." To get Il Duce's articles, Hearst had to buy them from the United Press, which he reluctantly agreed to do.[8]

Payne had more luck with his "Jewish" columnist. In February of 1927, he wrote Hearst at San Simeon that he had been able to sign on Rabbi Stephen S. Wise to do a column for the *Mirror.* Hearst was delighted. As he had earlier advised Lee Ettelson, the editor of the *American,* his other New York morning paper, it was "very important to have the support of the Jewish people in New York." The *New York Times,* he feared, was doing a much better job "looking out for the interests of the Jews — possibly because Mr. Ochs is a Jew; but although we are not, it is the policy of the *New York American* to deplore any race prejudice and to promote good feeling among all creeds and classes and protect the interests of every worthy cause."[9]

Instead of attempting to represent the people in their fight against the bosses and the trusts by seeking injunctions or organizing demonstrations, the Hearst press in the 1920s had begun to rely on "stunts" and contests to attract new readers and hold on to old ones. The *Mirror* outdid itself, month after month, in this regard. In the fall of 1927, Phil Payne engineered his most spectacular — and last — circulation stunt for Hearst. Caught up in Lindbergh fever with the rest of the nation, Hearst had offered to sponsor an entry of his own in a contest to fly the Atlantic, nonstop, to Rome. When Phil Payne announced that he was joining the crew of "Old Glory," the Hearst plane, in its trans-Atlantic flight, the Chief argued against it. To prove to Hearst that "Old Glory" was flight-worthy, Payne took Millicent up for a ride from the Old Westbury, Long Island, field that Lindbergh had used. Millicent immediately telegrammed Hearst her enthusiastic endorsement: "I know the boys will make Rome in Old Glory. Think this is a most wonderful ship."[10]

Hearst remained opposed to the plan and just days before departure telegrammed Payne that he would back the flight "only if the Government [assumed] authority and responsibility." Receiving no answer from Payne and fearing the worst, Hearst sent another telegram, this time to Mitchell Shiber, an editor at the *New York American*. "Rush Extra. Get this message by telephone to Phil Payne wherever he is immediately and confirm by telegram, quote, 'Do not let Old Glory hop off except under Government sanction per telephone message to Coblentz last night, unquote.'"

It was already too late. "Old Glory" had taken off as scheduled and crashed in the Atlantic with no survivors. Hearst, deeply embarrassed and ashamed that the life of his editor had been lost in so obvious a circulation stunt, published his correspondence with Payne in the *American*.[11]

Although Hearst had balked at risking a life to win circulation, in the spring of 1927, when he was presented with a golden opportunity to thrust himself — and his newspapers — back into the headlines, he had grabbed it. Edward Clark, his financial adviser and the overseer of his Mexican properties, had discovered a cache of secret documents that "proved" that Mexican president Plutarco Calles was not only a Bolshevik, but had, with Russian support, fomented and financed the 1926 Nicaraguan revolution. Hearst was interested in the documents and directed Clark to secure them. If authentic, they would not only discredit the new Mexican government, which Hearst and most other American landowners and businessmen heartily distrusted, but win circulation for his newspapers.

Ever since the overthrow of Porfirio Díaz and the onset of the Mexican Revolution in 1910–1911, W. R. had been arguing that American intervention was necessary to restore "order" to Mexico and safeguard American investments. He had temporarily made peace with Mexico during the presidency of Álvaro Obregón, who had won his confidence by revalidating his title to his Mexican properties. But Calles, on succeeding Obregón in 1924, had not only refused to endorse his predecessor's agreements, but had threatened to expropriate the property of American oil companies and in 1926 had provided material support to Augusto César Sandino and the army of insurgents that was attempting to overthrow the pro-American government in Nicaragua.[12]

President Coolidge and his secretary of state, Frank Billings Kellogg, branded Calles and his government as Bolsheviks, but they had no intention of intervening in Mexico. Instead, Coolidge appointed Dwight Morrow of J. P. Morgan and Company as ambassador to Mexico to negotiate a comprehensive settlement with Calles. By the time that news of the secret documents reached Hearst in the spring of 1927, tensions between Mexico and the United States had been thoroughly defused.

Hearst, on receiving the documents from Miguel Avila, the Mexican-Texan who claimed to have stolen them, dispatched Edward Clark to South Dakota to show them to the vacationing President Coolidge. When Coolidge refused to examine them — as did Secretary of State Kellogg who was also contacted — Hearst realized that he had no choice now but to proceed to try to authenticate them on his own. Victor Watson, the editor of the *New York American,* suggested that Miguel Avila be planted in the Mexican consul-general's office in New York to see if he could locate more corroborating documents. It was ludicrous to entrust the thief who had stolen the documents with the task of authenticating them, but Hearst agreed with Watson's plan. Not surprisingly, Avila found a new cache of "secret" documents in New York that supposedly confirmed the authenticity of the ones he had brought with him from Mexico City.[13]

On November 14, the Hearst dailies began publishing the documents, which they claimed established beyond doubt the existence of a Mexican plot against the United States. Every day for the next three weeks, they published a new set of Mexican documents in translation, complete with facsimiles, commentaries, illustrations, and editorials. Curiously enough, given the Chief's later preoccupation with Russian Bolshevism, the articles had little to say about the role of the Soviets in this anti-American Bolshevik conspiracy. On the contrary, it was made clear in the first installment that "the Hearst papers . . . have no special antagonism towards [the Russian] government . . . and that the Russian people's right to establish their own government should not be interfered with by other governments."[14]

The Bolshevik villain in all the articles was the Mexican president Calles. On November 16, the Hearst papers charged Calles with funneling $1 million to Nicaragua to finance an anti-American insurrection; on November 17, with paying $25,000 to the Russian legation in Mexico City to defray the costs of communist propaganda and $30,000 to "Pablo Polivichi, a communist propaganda expert" to print propaganda-filled textbooks for Mexican children and conduct a propaganda campaign among the Indians of Guatemala; on November 18, with transporting three thousand boxes of rifles and cartridges to the Nicaraguan rebels; on November 19, with transferring $100,000 to a Comrade Litvinoff in Russia for Bolshevist propaganda purposes. The secret Mexican documents plastered across Hearst's front pages disclosed a widening conspiracy emanating from Mexico to support Bolshevists around the world, from Communists in China to striking dockworkers in England to Ernest Gruening, the editor of the *Nation* (and the future senator from Alaska).

Only the Hearst papers paid any attention to the story, until on December 9, during the third week of exposés, the Chief released his most "newsworthy" document. Signed by the controller-general of Mexico, it authorized the payment of $1.15 million to four United States senators, ostensibly bribes to support pro-Mexican legislation. The senators' names were blacked out in the facsimile, although Hearst claimed that the original, in his safe, revealed them.[15]

By blacking out the names of the accused senators, Hearst shielded himself from libel suits and forced the Senate to act on his charges. As Senator David Reed of Pennsylvania explained on the floor of the Senate, as long as Hearst's story "appears in print untested, uninvestigated, undenied, the honor of every member of this body is at stake." A five-member Senate investigating committee was promptly empaneled to investigate his charges. On December 15, Hearst appeared before it to deliver all of his documents, including the one which named the four senators accused of taking bribes from the Mexican government. Displaying no sign of unease or impatience, the Chief explained where he had gotten the documents and described the efforts his editors had made to authenticate them.[16]

Three of the four accused senators, William Borah of Idaho, Thomas Heflin of Alabama, and Robert LaFollette of Wisconsin, appeared before the committee to deny the charges against them. George Norris of Nebraska, who was too ill to attend the session, responded in an open letter to Hearst, asserting that the publisher had attacked these four senators because they had "all been prominent in the Senate in their opposition to interference by our government in the affairs of Mexico." Norris went on to say,

> You have testified before the committee that you have very valuable properties in Mexico. It is almost common knowledge that you were in favor of the overthrow of the present government. . . . For the sake of your financial investments, you were not only willing to ruin the reputation of honest and innocent men but you were willing to plunge our country into war with a friendly neighbor, and thus increase the army of widows and orphans and wounded and crippled soldiers. . . . The record which you made in this matter . . . dem-

onstrates that the Hearst system of newspapers, spreading like a venomous web to all parts of our country, constitutes the sewer system of American journalism.[17]

In his reply to Norris, published as usual on the front pages of his newspapers, Hearst displayed the polemical skill he had sharpened in previous battles with the likes of William Gaynor and Al Smith. He admitted that he owned $4 million worth of property in Mexico, but assured Senator Norris that had he cared to protect his Mexican investments, he would have kept his silence: "Certainly nobody but a perfect jackass — and Senator Norris is not that — at least not a perfect one — could imagine that my property holdings were benefited by losing the friendship and favor of the Mexican Government." He insisted that he held no animus against the four senators named in the documents: "Senator Borah, I have had occasion to support and commend you probably more than any man in the Senate. I do not know that I have ever supported Senator Norris, but then I cannot recall that he's ever done anything worth supporting."[18]

While Hearst was engaged in his front-page polemics with Senator Norris, the investigating committee recessed for the Christmas break, after putting the disputed documents in the hands of six handwriting experts — three selected by the committee, an additional three by Hearst. When the committee reconvened on January 5, W. H. DeFord, Hearst's counsel, informed it that Hearst's handwriting experts had unanimously determined that the Mexican documents were spurious. On January 11, the committee issued its final report on the matter, declaring that it had found "not a scintilla of evidence that any United States senator has accepted, or was promised, or was offered . . . or received money from the Mexican government." The story was buried in the *New York Times,* the *New York Herald Tribune,* and other non-Hearst papers. Only the Hearst press put it on the front page — under the subhead, "Hearst Not Criticized."[19]

For nearly a month, Hearst had published front-page articles based entirely on fictitious sources. He had libeled several nations, dozens of foreign statesmen, at least two prominent American journalists, Oswald Garrison Villard and Ernest Gruening, and four United States senators. And yet, as the *New York Herald Tribune* reported the morning after the final report was issued, neither the committee nor any of its members had seen fit to criticize Hearst. Outside of Senator Norris, everyone, it appeared, had accepted his claim that because he had "left the whole thing to his editors," he was not to be blamed.[20]

Though suspicions would later be voiced by Hearst's biographer Ferdinand Lundberg, among others, that Hearst had had a hand in the forgeries, there is no evidence to support this allegation. The records of the Military Intelligence Division of the War Department demonstrate clearly that, as soon as Hearst discovered that the documents had been forged, he sent his own agents into Mexico to find the forger.[21]

Despite all the signs to the contrary — including the misspellings and grammatical errors on almost every page of every "official" document — Hearst had accepted the documents as authentic because they confirmed everything he believed about Mexican radicalism and the necessity for American intervention. His editors, for their part, did not go out of their way to establish their authenticity, because they knew the Chief was anxious to publish them.

The investigating senators exonerated Hearst because they believed he was no longer exercising day-to-day control over his newspapers, but they were quite mistaken. Little, if anything, appeared in his magazines or papers — especially on the front page or the editorial page — without his approval. When one or the other of his editors dared venture off on his own, he was swiftly reprimanded. As the Chief had written in 1929 to C. S. Stanton, the editor of the *Herald-Examiner* in Chicago, in a blistering seven-page, single-spaced memo, "I have always been in direct charge of the editorial departments of my papers. . . . You will please conduct the paper in all its editorial departments according to the instructions which you receive from me."[22]

Although permanently ensconced in San Simeon, the Chief made all the decisions on editorial policy. "The editorials I write are not written as individual policies," he reminded Edmond Coblentz, the managing editor of the *New York American*, in December of 1929. "They are written to outline policies for the paper to be pursued at every opportunity thereafter until rescinded. They should not be regarded as 'sacred cows,' only inserted to please the boss, and therefore casually inserted and hurriedly forgotten; but as basic outlines of policy on which the newspapers are to be conducted. Will you please so regard them and will you please keep a scrapbook of them, and let the scrapbook serve as a guide to editorial writers?"[23]

Still, while Hearst had never given up control of his publications, he had learned over the years to isolate and distance himself from the more devious machinations of editors and reporters who went out of their way to get news that the Chief would want to print. "If there is any skullduggery, he does not want to know about it," Silas Bent wrote in the *Outlook* in January of 1928. "And so if a managing editor looked Hearst in the eye and told him that the Mexican documents were the goods and a whale of a story, that was enough. The publisher has all the yearning of a cub for a big beat; his fondness for sensational news has carried him away more than once."[24]

Following the Mexican documents fiasco, Hearst began a major reorganization of his newspaper division, not because his editors had blundered into publishing three weeks of stories based on bad forgeries, but because they were losing their circulation wars. While the circulation of his twenty-eight newspapers in 1928 still comprised more than 10 percent of the nation's total circulation on weekdays and almost 20 percent on Sundays, only on the West Coast did his papers dominate their local markets. While he continued to expand his total circulation by buying new papers, the mainstays of his empire — his big-city morning papers — were rapidly falling behind the competition. Between 1925 and 1928, the gap in Chicago between Colonel McCormick's *Tribune* and the Hearst *Herald-Examiner* had grown from 274,000 to almost 360,000. In Boston, Hearst's *Herald* was outsold by the *Globe* and the *Post.* In New York, the *American* had lost almost one-quarter of its circulation since 1925 and now ranked below not only the tabloids but the *Times,* the *Herald Tribune,* and the *World.*[25]

In early 1928, Hearst tried to remedy the failures in his newspaper division by making wholesale personnel changes. He shifted Victor Watson from the *New York American* to the *New York Mirror,* hired Frank Knox, a Michigan editor who had done an excellent job with the Hearst papers in Boston, to replace Bradford Merrill as general manager of the newspaper division, and asked Arthur Brisbane to take over the *New York American.*

Brisbane was reluctant to take on a new assignment. He had more than enough to occupy him with his daily column and his real estate deals. (He had just bought the Warwick Hotel on 54th Street and Sixth Avenue with Hearst. They also owned jointly several parcels of land on Columbus Circle and the Ritz Tower apartment house/hotel on West 57th Street.) Still, he could not say no to the Chief, who let him write almost anything he wanted in his front-page column and had made him, he claimed often to friends and colleagues, the highest-paid journalist in the nation, at $250,000 a year (equivalent in today's currency to about $2.5 million).

Exhilarated by the prospect of remaking his flagship paper with his oldest friend and colleague, Hearst invited Brisbane to San Simeon to discuss their new venture and deluged him with telegrams, at least four of which were sent to Kansas City to coincide with Brisbane's stopover there at ten fifty-five P.M.

In the coming weeks, the Chief would suggest changes in the front page, the layout, and almost every section of the *New York American*. He wanted better Sunday comics, a front-page "cartoon with editorial under it — such cartoon of course expressing the essence of editorial, a half-page daily serial of book of moment . . . set in large readable type . . . with some explanatory introduction and some comments," a full eight-page sports section during the summer months, an ongoing crusade to improve the public schools, a new "highly illustrated" front page for section two, more "paragraphic gossip and personal mention" in the society section, additional space for drama and moving pictures, a "women's page" with better fashions and "more class to interest best readers and impress advertisers," and a new "round the world" stunt, if possible with Lindbergh and Rickenbacker or Ruth Elder (the champion swimmer) competing against one another.[26]

If his morning papers were losing ground to the competition, his Sunday papers were holding their own. The Hearst color comics were still the best in the business. And his *American Weekly* Sunday supplement continued to attract readers with odd pseudo-scientific pieces like "Why Intelligent Children's Parents Ought to Have Intelligent Children; Interesting Experiments with Rats Seem to Settle the Long-Standing Scientific Dispute as to Whether Highly Developed Brains Can Be Inherited and If 'Dumb' Couples Are Likely to Have Rather Stupid Children" and its general-interest features on "How the Mysterious Mayans Made War" and the Prussian actress who "Played Suicide Role at the Theatre — Kills Herself Same Way."[27]

To broaden the appeal of his Sunday papers and enhance their reputation, Hearst added a new "March of Events" section in 1928. "The main purpose of the section," he advised T. V. Ranck, his Sunday editor, "is to create prestige."[28]

Week after week, the Sunday "March of Events" featured "Noted Writers" on "World Topics." Hearst paid top dollar for contributors and the dollar was strong, so that he was able to enlist almost anyone he wanted to write for him — especially retired European politicians. Hearst was not the first publisher to print columns like this — the Scripps-Howard syndicate had been buying and marketing articles by former English prime minister David Lloyd George and others since 1921 — but he was the first to create a Sunday section to feature them. From 1928 through the middle 1930s, Hearst bought, syndicated, and featured in his Sunday papers essays by Benito Mussolini, the former journalist who was now the Italian premier; English politicians, usually David Lloyd George or Winston Churchill; French statesmen, occasionally Aristide Briand but more often the former premier Edouard Herriot; and German political leaders, among them the former Chancellor Wilhelm Marx, Hermann Goering, Franz von Papen, and Adolf Hitler.

Though the bylines were impressive, the contents were less so. His editors, aware that Hearst was going to review every article they sent him, made sure that there were no surprises. Every article, as a result, came out sounding as if Hearst himself had written it. On September 23, 1928, David Lloyd George argued that the Allies should evacuate the Rhineland and stop violating Germany's sovereign rights. That same Sunday, the section carried an excerpt from Emil Ludwig's anti-war book, *Five Tragic Weeks.* The following September, the "March of Events" published another anti-war excerpt, this time from Leon Trotsky's *My Stormy Life;* an anti–World Court article by Senator Arthur Vandenberg; and an anti–League of Nations commentary by Benito Mussolini. "Speeches continue year after year in a never ending flow of oratory with beautiful platitudes recurring again and again," Mussolini reported of the tenth annual meeting of the Assembly of the League of Nations. "This is indeed a decade of marathons . . . There have been dance marathons, piano playing marathons, coffee drinking marathons and so on. Geneva is the diplomatic and oratorical marathon."[29]

As part of his attempt to boost the reputation of his papers, Hearst also ran articles on Sunday and occasionally on his editorial pages by H. G. Wells, George Bernard Shaw, Fannie Hurst, Will Rogers, Henry Morgenthau, and, for a short time after her husband's election to the presidency, Eleanor Roosevelt.

Of all the illustrious names that crowded Hearst's pages, none appeared more often than that of George Bernard Shaw — in large measure because his opinions on so many subjects were close to Hearst's. In 1906 and 1907, Hearst had reprinted Shaw's articles on women's suffrage, which they both supported, on religion, which they distrusted, and on Fabian socialism, whose basic tenets they both championed — at least at that time. During the Great War, their collaboration had been strengthened, since Shaw could be counted on to reinforce what Hearst himself had written about the follies of war. Between 1914 and 1921 alone, the *New York American* published over sixty articles by Shaw; seven more appeared in *Hearst's Magazine.* Through the 1920s, Shaw continued to write regularly for Hearst's morning newspapers and his magazines — on literature, the theater, boxing, Irish home rule, inhumane prisons, capital punishment, and on one of Hearst's favorite topics, the idiocies of English life and government.[30]

In 1927, Shaw decided to put together a series of articles commemorating the 100th anniversary of Beethoven's death and inquired of Hearst about publishing them in the United States. "Centenary of Beethoven's death on twenty-sixth demands article in every civilized newspaper," he wrote Hearst at San Simeon. "Brilliant articles by Arnold Bennett, Romain Rolland, myself, and others are going begging in America. Editors say, who is Beethoven anyway? Is he a Dutch Babe Ruth? Merrill [the executive in charge of Hearst's newspapers] handsomely promises not to bear malice against me for my foolish offer. Meanwhile Wireless [radio] prepares bushels of Beethoven. Can you do nothing to save the credit of American culture?"[31]

Hearst wrote back at once that he would be delighted to publish the series — at whatever price Shaw had proposed — and invited Shaw to visit him at San Simeon: "When can you come to America? You really should come. Let me herewith extend you formal and fervent invitation to be my guest and ride the range with me in California."[32]

Shaw declined: "If you had a nice desert island I should be with you by the next boat but I dare not face America just now as I am hard pressed with work so let us postpone. Thousand Thanks."[33]

Unable to accept no as an answer, Hearst wrote Shaw that he was "extremely sorry you cannot come now but am encouraged by your message and will try to find nice desert island but feel sure ranch is sufficiently isolated to be almost as satisfactory as desert island. Hope to have you visit us later."[34]

Shaw did visit Hearst at San Simeon, in 1933.

One of the cornerstones of Hearst's campaign to revive circulation was promotion. As he confessed to Arthur Brisbane, he had become "a nut on publicity . . . I think the promotion of our various newspapers should be watched almost as carefully as their news and editorial columns." Since taking over his father's San Francisco daily in the 1880s, he had employed every conceivable medium and device to promote his publications: billboards and posters, newsreels and serial films, stunts, service features, and contests. But these techniques belonged to the past; the future, as he tried to convince his editors and publishers, was in radio. Hearst's objective was to blanket the country with Hearst-affiliated radio stations and programs that would broadcast the Hearst brand name in news and entertainment to listeners who were not yet readers.[35]

"Let's have some one paper — preferably the *Chicago Herald-Examiner* — go into the radio promotion on as big a scale as possible and see what the results are," he proposed in June 1926 to the members of the executive council he had set up to coordinate the management of his newspaper empire. "I personally believe that radio promotion is the greatest promotion in the world today. Los Angeles is actually centered on the disappearance of Mrs. McPherson [Aimee Semple McPherson, the radio evangelist], whom nobody knows except over the radio."[36]

Hearst's enthusiasm was not contagious. When none of the publishers on his executive council were willing to divert even part of their promotion budgets to radio, the Chief focused his attention on his West Coast publishers, with whom he was in closer contact. "I think the *Examiner* should develop a really great radio program," he telegrammed the publisher of the *Los Angeles Examiner* in November 1926, "and should report all games and events of importance, and give bulletin news and lectures by important and amusing people, in addition to the best music in Los Angeles, not only from regular orchestras, but from special performers. I cannot get anybody to do what I think a newspaper should do on the radio. I hoped the *Examiner* here would show the way."[37]

Try as he might, the Chief was unable to galvanize his newspaper executives into sharing his opinion about radio broadcasting. "Our institution is years behind the times in radio," he warned the publishers on his executive council again in September of 1927:

> I wish council would devote sufficient number of serious sessions to radio to solve problem finally for our papers. Howard [Roy Howard, the head of the Scripps-Howard newspaper chain] paid twenty-five thousand dollars for exclusive right to radio Dempsey Tunney fight. Every radio in the United States listened in and all heard as much about the Scripps-Howard papers as about the fight. This was the greatest advertisement I know of. It is astonishing how many people talked about it even people who did not know much about newspapers. The effect on . . . advertisers must have been very great. I don't have to dilate on value to those who understand universality of radio especially with younger generation. We must constantly use radio especially for big occasions of all kinds. It must be as much a part of our service as our wire service or our picture service. . . . Employ best announcers and make our service attractive feature in every home. The first things to cover are news events. After that we can enlarge scope and add important musical features, etcetera. Please answer.[38]

Because sports programming was relatively cheap to produce, promised the largest national audience, and was a natural complement to the sports coverage in the evening papers, Hearst believed this was the best place to begin: "I would like to have all of our papers broadcast the world series. You can probably arrange with some local station to broadcast series for you but if not Howard Hogan of *Herald-Examiner,* Chicago, can make arrangements for you. Quick action is necessary so please don't delay."³⁹

It took him almost two years, but by mid-1928, the Chief was beginning to see the results of his continual prodding, if only on the West Coast. Not only had his newspapers there bought local radio stations, but they had tied them together into a statewide Hearst Radio Service that was effectively promoting the Chief's newspapers — and his politics. In September of 1928, the five Hearst radio stations on the West Coast proudly presented a full program of "G.O.P. oratory" as a public news service for his readers:

Turn on your radio this afternoon, twist the dial to KPLA and come with us behind the scenes of a great national political contest . . . For the first time in history the American public, to all intents and purposes, will be admitted to the inner sanctum of the party chiefs to see how campaigning is carried on, what a big job it is to make a president. . . . The program will be short, the speeches vigorous, straight-from-the-shoulder and very much to the point.⁴⁰

The daily newspaper, as Hearst tried to convince his publishers, could not expect to maintain its monopoly over cheap news and entertainment without going out of its way to attract new readers. "Our publishers themselves may not be interested in radio," he warned his newspaper executives in early January of 1930, "but certainly their children are, and the publisher should learn from his children what an important part radio plays in the life of the nation today. It is an effort to read a newspaper; it is no effort to listen to a radio."⁴¹

While Hearst struggled with his newspapers, his magazines continued to build circulation and churn out revenues. *Good Housekeeping,* the number one magazine in its field, had between 1920 and 1928 tripled its circulation to almost 1.5 million. Hearst was proud of his magazines, not only because they were moneymakers, but because, like his morning newspapers and Marion's moving pictures, they were patronized by a relatively upscale audience. He was also proud of their editorial independence. In June of 1929, David Town, an executive at his magazine division, suggested that an antitobacco article scheduled for *Good Housekeeping,* "The Attempt to Make Smokers of Girls," be canceled because it would generate "unfavorable reaction from an advertising standpoint." Hearst overruled him. "I have no objection to the article on cigarettes in *Good Housekeeping,*" the Chief telegrammed Town from San Simeon. "In fact, I am glad that *Good Housekeeping* has the independence to print such an article, and I think the extravagant effort of the cigarette makers to sell their stuff to men, women, and children is bound to bring a popular reaction."[42]

Cosmopolitan, though with a smaller circulation than *Good Housekeeping*, remained the flagship publication of Hearst's magazine division. With the era of muckraking long past, *Cosmopolitan* had turned increasingly to short fiction, articles by famous people, and political memoirs, like those Calvin Coolidge published on leaving the White House in 1929. It was resolutely middle-brow, and Hearst was determined to keep it that way. In August of 1929, he telegrammed the editor, Ray Long:

> In dummy just received there is article headed "Has An Unmarried Woman Right to a Child?" This article gives me cold chill. I think it will lose us many readers of better class. Don't think it has any place in *Cosmopolitan* and if not too late will you please cut it out. Never mind any inconvenience or expense necessary to omit article. I think it does not do any good to print articles that attract the more reputable and wholesome readers and then when we get them with Coolidge articles, offend them with articles of illegitimate child kind. You and I planned out entirely different kind of magazine. . . . Please try to get rid of that obnoxious article.[43]

The following day, he wrote Long a letter on the same subject:

> I hope we can agree on definite plan to make high grade magazine free from this kind of sensationalism. It's important to have consistent policy or we fall between two stools. I think we can succeed by being consistently entertaining and wholesome and Macfadden [publisher of the *Daily Graphic* and *True Story*] can succeed by being consistently sensational but I don't think we can mix sensationalism and conservatism and get anywhere. Of the two forms of success I would much rather have the more wholesome and reputable kind . . . I would like to see *Cosmopolitan* make circulation with its fiction and reputation with its special articles.[44]

The program Hearst had outlined for *Cosmopolitan*, the magazine, was identical to the one he had established for Cosmopolitan, the film company. He was interested in producing high-quality, high-priced features for the upper end of the moving-picture market. The commercial success he and Marion had enjoyed with *Knighthood* and *Little Old New York* had convinced him that there was a substantial audience for middle-brow costume dramas. Louis B. Mayer and Irving Thalberg, his head of production at Culver City, apparently agreed. In *Lights of Old Broadway*, Marion played an Irish immigrant in nineteenth-century New York; in *Beverly of Graustark*, she was a wealthy girl who is sent abroad to visit her cousin, a crown prince;

in *The Red Mill,* based on a Victor Herbert musical comedy, she played a Cinderella character in Dutch costume.

After the *The Red Mill* lost money, Irving Thalberg proposed that Marion's next picture be set in the present-day. He suggested an adaptation of *The Fair Co-Ed,* the musical which had starred Elsie Janis on Broadway. Hearst agreed and asked that George Ade, who had written the Broadway show, be brought in to adapt it and that Sidney Franklin, who had done a fine job on *Beverly of Graustark,* be hired as director.[45]

When Hearst discovered that Thalberg had rewritten Ade's treatment and hired Sam Wood, a "B" director, instead of the more respected and higher-priced Franklin, he was outraged. "Sorry you thought I was cranky yesterday," he telegrammed Mayer at the studio on July 14, 1927, a day after he had visited to complain in person, "but I was much disturbed. . . . I felt I was an orphan and nobody cared for the poor darned little thing [Marion's next picture] so I was going stay up here on ranch rest of my life and let you feel sorry when I died. However I have talked to Irving this morning and feel little more cheerful. Can't we make definite arrangement about Franklin that will allow Marion to have him . . . Won't you please let me hire him. Be a good old fellow and let me do this."[46]

Thalberg apologized to Hearst for the confusion and confessed that he had had to replace Franklin because he "absolutely point blank refused to make college story of any kind." He had mistakenly kept this information from Hearst and, on his own, reworked the screenplay and hired a new director "because I didn't want to load you with all the worries of producing pictures that I thought you wanted to get away from. . . . I don't know of anyone I have tried to please more than you, including Louis [Mayer] or Marcus [Loew] or Nick [Schenck] and it hurts me to think that you felt like a little orphan when I have been trying to be both a father and a mother to you. Warmest regards."[47]

In the end, Hearst conceded defeat, though he never forgave Mayer or Thalberg for foisting Sam Wood on him and putting Marion in what he thought was a cheap-looking comedy. When Mayer asked him to provide *The Fair Co-Ed* with the same kind of publicity he had given Marion's other MGM pictures, the Chief agreed, but only grudgingly:

> I will give good publicity to *The Fair Co-Ed* but I would prefer not to do any-
> thing very extraordinary, as I do not think it is an extraordinary picture. . . . I
> cannot see that it is necessary to have the star get hit in the face with a book,
> fall off a fast moving vehicle on her head, and get kicked in the pants, in order
> to get yap laughs. . . . I think slap-stick stuff is small town stuff, not worthy of
> your best star nor of your best pictures. I think a star who can do *Little Old*

New York and *Quality Street* ought not to have to do Mack Sennett slap-stick stuff. I will put extraordinary publicity behind *Quality Street* because I am proud of it, and because that is the kind of pictures I want to make even if I have to make them myself.[48]

Despite his complaints — and the difficulty he had working in partnership with anyone — Hearst got on well with Mayer and Thalberg and made sure all the MGM executives, stars, and pictures received positive publicity — and lots of it — in his newspapers. In February of 1927, when the Loew and Mayer families vacationed together in Palm Beach, Hearst directed Moses Koenigsberg, the head of King Features, to "please send out good pictures and pleasant stories about them to our papers, morning and evening, with instructions to print." When Mayer was indicted for participating in a fraudulent stock deal, Hearst kept the news out of his papers until the indictment was dismissed and then directed his publishers to carry the announcement of the dismissal in "a conspicuous position . . . and through all editions."[49]

Since MGM had no newsreels to distribute with its features, the Chief volunteered to start up an MGM newsreel, though he was already under contract to produce one for Universal. Make them "livelier and more entertaining," he directed Eddie Hatrick, his chief film executive. "The news reels should be built on the same lines as tabloid newspapers: all stuff brief bright and newsy."[50]

The start-up costs associated with a second newsreel pushed Hearst's film business further into debt. His share of Marion's salary and the upkeep on her bungalow were already costing $10,000 a week against an income of $5,000 from his share of the profits. In the summer of 1927, Hatrick warned Hearst that he would have to either cut back expenses or shift money from his publications to cover the deficit incurred at the studio.[51]

Alternating, as he always had when it came to the film business, between reckless optimism and despair, the Chief countered Hatrick's downsizing proposal with one of his own. He proposed that Hatrick move to California, hire "several strictly first class men," and build an "organization" to oversee Hearst's moving-picture interests. To Hatrick's suggestion that it might not be possible to make money producing the kind of expensive costume dramas the Chief wanted Marion to star in, Hearst reminded him, not for the first time, that before coming to MGM, he had, on his own, "tried to make notable pictures and was reasonably successful. Moreover, the idea that we constantly lost money was a mistake. Some years we made money, as I know from my income taxes . . . So it is possible to make money on notable pictures, and furthermore, they are mainly the kind of pictures that I am interested in."[52]

Hearst's optimism lasted no more than a month. "Am discouraged with moving picture situation," he wrote Hatrick in October of 1927. "We are giving lot of attention and general promotion and absolute advertising and getting little or nothing. I do not care what arrangements you make but we have got to have some revenue if I am to continue interested in this business."[53]

The Fair Co-Ed, despite Hearst's objections, made a profit of $131,000. Marion's next two films, *Tillie the Toiler*, based on a Hearst comic strip, and *Quality Street*, lost a total of $252,000, not because they were not adequately promoted or well made, but because Hearst's productions cost twice as much to make as MGM's other features. Perhaps to wean Hearst from his expensive costume dramas, Louis B. Mayer asked King Vidor to direct Marion's next film. Vidor's previous film, *The Crowd*, was still "on the shelf," because it was so unlike anything that MGM had ever produced or distributed that no one knew how to market it. Vidor recognized that if he wanted to continue to make innovative films like *The Crowd*, he would have to do the studio's bidding. Besides, as he recalled in his memoirs, he did not consider "directing Miss Davies . . . an unpleasant chore. . . . I considered her to be a most accomplished comedienne."[54]

Hearst had been trying to get Vidor to work on Marion's films ever since he had directed *The Big Parade*, a mildly anti-war film that had impressed the Chief and done well at the box office. Vidor was as likeable as he was talented and a regular at San Simeon and at Marion's beach house, where he was married to his second wife, Eleanor Boardman. (It was to have been a double wedding, but Greta Garbo never showed up to marry John Gilbert.)[55]

Vidor's first film with Marion was *The Patsy*, a contemporary comedy of manners, in which Marion played Patsy Harrington, an oppressed younger sister with a brutish mother and an adoring "Pa," who was Hearst's age. The film, with Vidor in control, took only twenty-seven days to shoot, cost half as much as Marion's previous film, got great reviews, and turned a profit of $155,000. Marion was, for the first time, given free rein to display her comedic skills and her talent for mimicry in brilliant parodies of the actresses Mae Murray, Lillian Gish, and Pola Negri.[56]

Though Hearst gave Vidor more leeway than he usually allowed Marion's directors, because he trusted him to refrain from any vulgar slapstick, he was, as always, omnipresent on the set. "W. R. sat on the set with a screen around him," recalled Eleanor Boardman, "and he'd dictate to somebody for the *Examiner*, or one of his newspapers, and wait for her, hold her hand on the way home, take her hand the next morning, and drive to the studio. Spend all his time with her. Devoted."⁵⁷

The Patsy did so well at the box office that Mayer asked Vidor to make another contemporary comedy with Marion, this one adapted from a stage play about an actress that MGM had purchased a few years earlier. With writer Lawrence Stallings, who had written *The Big Parade* and *The Patsy*, Vidor turned the "unreadable" script he had been handed into a brilliant Hollywood satire. *Show People* was based loosely but recognizably on the life of Gloria Swanson who had "started out as a Mack Sennett bathing-beauty . . . and then become the Marquise de la Falaise de la Coudray." The "gimmick" that Vidor intended to use to accompany his heroine from her humble beginnings "as she rose to the heights" was a custard pie. "In her early slapstick days Marion would be a target for custard pies," Vidor wrote in his autobiography. "Later when she became the snooty countess and started to upstage all her old comrades, a lowly actor would bring her to her senses by hitting her in the kisser with an expertly tossed meringue. Here was our story, beginning, middle, and end. We were wildly enthusiastic. When we told it to Louis B. Mayer, who sort of mother-henned the Hearst activities, he looked rather dubious. He told us to go to San Simeon and see if we could sell it to W. R."

Vidor and Stallings drove through the night and arrived at the ranch in time for breakfast. "Later that afternoon we told W. R. and Marion our Hollywood story. At the end Marion cheerfully piped up in her best voice, 'I like it.' But the Chief was silent." After dinner, Vidor tried to find out from Marion why Hearst had "frozen up and gone gray-faced at some point in the recitation of the scenario," but Marion claimed she didn't know. When Stallings and Vidor got back to the studio, Mayer informed them that Hearst was not going to allow Marion to take a pie in her face. When Vidor refused to write the pies out of the script, Mayer arranged an opportunity for him to convince Hearst of their importance. Vidor did his best, acting out all the parts in the film before a roomful of MGM executives and Hearst. When he had finished, everyone in the room applauded. "There followed several moments of silence as all eyes turned to Mr. Hearst. Presently the great man rose and in a high-pitched voice said, 'King's right. But I'm right, too — because I'm not going to let Marion be hit in the face with a pie.' With this simple proclamation he walked out of the room, settling the issue for all time." Vidor, unwilling to abandon the project entirely, was forced to come up with a "compromise symbol . . . a forceful stream from a siphon bottle." With reservations, Hearst allowed the film to go forward. Still uncertain as to how the Chief might react to the final scene, Marion arranged with the publisher of the *Los Angeles Examiner* for W. R. to be called away to a conference as the siphon scene was filmed. "As soon as his limousine had driven away, the prop man came forth with the fire hose."[58]

Show People was a huge success, grossing over a million dollars, and turning a profit of $176,000. Unfortunately, by the time it was released in November of 1928, the era of silent comedy was already over. Having achieved success in silent films, Marion — and Hearst — would have to start all over again in the talkies.[59]

❧ 25 ❧
A New Crusade: Europe

"**H**OOVER SAYS he cannot go to ranch on account of other engagement so I am having luncheon with him here tomorrow," W. R. wrote Millicent from Los Angeles in September of 1926. "I think he is cautious gink, too cautious ever to be elected to anything."[1]

Herbert Hoover and his friend and chief advocate in Hollywood, Louis B. Mayer, had been trying for years to enlist Hearst's support for a Hoover presidential bid. As secretary of commerce, Hoover had helped Hearst secure a satisfactory wavelength for a radio station he and Louis B. Mayer wanted to establish in Chicago. Despite his efforts, Hearst was unwilling to support him or any candidate for public office whom he associated with Wilsonian internationalism. Hoover had not only served in the Wilson administration, but had advocated American entry into the League of Nations and the World Court. To block Hoover's nomination, which appeared assured when Coolidge declined to run for another term, Hearst, in the summer of 1927, directed his Washington correspondents "to consider [Secretary of the Treasury Andrew] Mellon as one of the most important presidential candidates and to so handle the news."[2]

Mellon had no chance, even with the support of the Hearst newspapers. In June, Hoover was nominated at the Republican National Convention in Kansas City, which Hearst attended. His opponent in November would be Al Smith who, in spite of Hearst's opposition, had won the Democratic nomination.

Although the Chief in the end supported Hoover for the Republican nomination, he did not immediately endorse him for the presidency, but, according to John Winkler whose 1955 biography of W. R. was written with the cooperation of the Hearst family, waited until Hoover visited him and pledged support for federal highway and development projects which the Hearst papers had been advocating for years.[3]

Before sailing for Europe — with Marion and several of her friends whom he planned to escort on a motor tour of the continent — Hearst made clear the editorial position he wanted adhered to in the campaign to come. Although he had in late June directed Brisbane to have the cartoonist Winsor McCay draw several half-page cartoons showing Al Smith posed with Tammany Tigers and disreputable-looking New York barkeepers, bums, and machine politicians, he quickly thought better of it and instructed Brisbane to tread more carefully in the upcoming campaign. "Could we not maintain our independence," he telegrammed him on July 4, 1928, "by satirizing some things in Democratic party and some things in Republican party, not making cartoons personal at all but merely satirizing conditions or policies."[4]

Hearst was attempting to construct a new political role for himself and his newspapers. Though he did not intend to follow the example of Adolph Ochs and keep his political opinions to himself, he was no longer content with the style of political partisanship that had characterized his advocacy journalism. "Think news services should be told that they should print all political news," he instructed Frank Knox, the general manager of his newspaper division, on July 13, the week before he sailed to Europe. "Attitude of Hearst papers is one of general friendliness to Hoover, to a continuation of the administration's policies under which country seems to be prosperous and people content. We are going to be just and fair and print all the news and make no violent campaign, but that is our attitude."[5]

Although he was unalterably opposed to Smith's candidacy, Hearst refrained from joining the attack on him as a "wet" or a Catholic. When asked by a reporter about Smith's Catholicism, Hearst reacted angrily that "religion has so little place in politics that I refuse to discuss it. I would not vote for or against a man because of his religion. I think we should have at least some regard for the framers of the Constitution, who believed in a spirit of tolerance and freedom of thought."[6]

On July 20, 1928, Hearst and Marion left for Europe, Hearst on the *Olympic*, Marion on the *Ile de France*. To make sure that no luggage was misdirected, Joe Willicombe had Chris MacGregor meet their twenty-six trunks at Pennsylvania Station and guide them to the proper ship.[7]

Marion's sisters Rose and Ethel, her niece Pepi Lederer and nephew Charlie Lederer, and Papa Ben, who joined the group in Italy, were part of the entourage that summer, every penny of their expenses paid for by Hearst. According to Marion's biographer, Fred Guiles, Hearst also brought with him to Europe two of Millicent's relatives, Sadie Murray and her daughter Anita, Lloyd Pantages, whose family owned a chain of movie theaters, and society columnist Maury Paul, as well as Harry Crocker of the San Francisco banking family, who had taken on the role of court jester, crony, confidant, and traveling secretary.[8]

On arriving at the Hotel Crillon in Paris, Hearst contacted Alice Head, the head of his English magazine division, and invited her to join the party. "I duly presented myself at the Crillon," Head said in her memoirs, "with a small suit-case packed for the week-end only, but I did not see my home again for six weeks, which is but as a day to my esteemed Chief." She went on:

> He told me at dinner that we were going to make a brief motor tour to some of the most interesting spots in France and that we should be starting about midday the next day. Four large touring cars were drawn up outside the hotel the following morning and we set forth, first to Versailles, and then to Rambouillet and Chartres. As we came out of the cathedral, Mr. Hearst remarked: "Well, children, shall we dine here or shall we go on to Tours?" One of the girls in the party replied, "We don't care *where* we dine, but we *must* find the ladies' room." The ladies' room in Chartres, when found, proved to be exceedingly primitive. So we went on to dine in Tours and we stayed there for two or three days while we visited the chateaux of the Loire.

From Tours, the Hearst party went on to Vichy, Grenoble, the Riviera, Monte Carlo, and south into Italy. W. R. and Marion led the procession, sitting in the backseat of their car; Marion's maid sat up front with the chauffeur. "As the party included some extremely beautiful and attractive girls from Hollywood dressed in the smartest of summer frocks from Magnin's," Miss Head recalled, "the arrival of our cars in French villages always caused something of a sensation. The whole countryside used to turn out to watch our arrival and departure, and there was much photography of the beautiful and attractive members of the party. On one of these occasions Mr. Hearst took my arm and said: 'We're *much* the most important people, but nobody wants to photograph us!'"[9]

Most of the time on tour was spent in cathedrals, chateaus, galleries, and art museums, where Hearst, trailed by his guests, joined his handpicked guides in explaining the wonders of the artwork on display. "At night, at dinner, Mr. Hearst examined us on what we had seen during the day. But he was," Alice Head remembered, "very indulgent if we made mistakes." Although she and Harry Crocker were enchanted by everything Hearst pointed out to them, Marion and her friends were bored by most of it and exhausted by W. R.'s pace. Sixty-five years of age and portly, the Chief was indefatigable. "He took the trips to Europe very seriously," Marion remembered:

> W. R. always maintained that if people wanted to go to Cannes or Biarritz or places in Paris to have fun, they could just as well do it in New York or any restaurant. He thought that if you went to Europe, you had to see Europe and understand educationally what the history was. There was no time for any jollities or frivolities in Europe. If anybody wanted to go to a nightclub, he'd say, "This is an educational tour. If you don't appreciate it now, you never will." So everybody would pretend to be on their toes, but I'd know they weren't listening. . . . I couldn't blame him for being impatient with people. He was trying to teach us something, and we didn't want to learn. He might as well have been hitting his head up against a stone wall.[10]

While Hearst made the big decisions, Marion was in charge of room assignments. With Willicombe's and Crocker's help, she also arranged — and rearranged — the seating in the touring cars. "Some guests wouldn't like each other, and they'd want to change cars; we had that all the time," Marion remembered.[11]

Though the tour was laid out in advance, Hearst was always changing the plans. In 1928, he extended their stay in Florence from three days to three weeks. Then, to reinvigorate Marion and others who had become exhausted by his art tours, he arranged for the party to drive directly from Florence to Venice for a fortnight at the Hotel Excelsior on the Lido. "After nearly four weeks' continuous travel and sight-seeing," Alice Head recalled, "the days on the beach at the Lido were a real refreshment. We had several cabanas and I greatly enjoyed the early morning bathing. . . . In Venice, all the shopkeepers and glass-blowing institutions seemed to be on the look-out for Mr. Hearst. He was the grandest shopper the world has ever known and on these holiday trips he turns himself into a kind of perpetual Santa Claus."[12]

Even Marion never got used to the Chief's extravagances. "Once we were driving in France," she recalled. "There were about twelve cars. W. R. had a chauffeur named Hall who got a little drunk that day over the wine at lunch. We were passing through a small out-of-the-way village near the coastline when he hit a goose. Mr. Hearst said [to the chauffeur], 'You're fired. But first take the goose and go back to the house and say that it was killed. Then I'll drive.'" Though W. R., according to Marion, was a "wild driver," he got them all safely to their next stop, Bordeaux, where, Marion later learned, he "arranged for that woman [whose goose had been killed] to have a new car, a Renault. He had it delivered to her with a goose inside."[13]

Wherever he traveled, Hearst was afforded the privileged treatment reserved for heads of state and given private audiences with national leaders. On this trip, he was invited to luncheon with the French foreign minister, Aristide Briand, at the Quai d'Orsay and he took Marion Davies with him. The French were, at the time, negotiating a bilateral treaty with the English under which England would be permitted to expand its navy and France its land forces. As the Americans were opposed to the expansion of the British navy and the Germans to the expansion of the French land forces, the exact nature of the treaty was kept secret.[14]

Hearst was in contact with French politicians who were opposed to the pact because they feared it would exacerbate tensions with the Germans. They offered to secure a purloined copy for him, hoping that premature publication would scuttle the treaty. We don't know how the document finally got to Hearst, but delivery may have taken place at the luncheon Briand gave. In her memoirs, Marion claimed that she stole the document — which she said was wrapped in a ribbon — from an open safe and gave it to Hearst. The story is hard to believe, although it is possible that Marion was somehow involved in the cloak-and-dagger handover of the stolen pact, and had tried to protect Hearst. In any event, two days after the luncheon with Briand, the secret Anglo-French pact was published, in full, in Hearst's American papers.

That same day, the Chief departed for England to avoid contact with the French police, who were investigating the theft of the document. Though his major correspondent in France was later arrested — as were the Frenchmen who had been instrumental in getting the document to him — the Chief was entirely at ease, delighted that he had not only broken a major story, but, in so doing, blocked the treaty from being signed. He had embarrassed the French and English officials who were engaging in precisely the sort of secret diplomacy that had played so large a part in precipitating the Great War.

On his arrival in England, he contacted Miss Head as if nothing of importance had occurred in Paris. With her and Sir Charles Allom, his architect for St. Donat's, he set off to Wales to visit his latest acquisition. It was, in many ways, the most spectacular of all his properties. St. Donat's was a medieval fortress, built originally in the eleventh century, and then rebuilt, reinforced, and extended in succeeding centuries. The structure had an irregularly shaped interior courtyard which Alice Head thought "rather like an Oxford College." Surrounding it were three-storied stone buildings, battlements, ramparts, parapets, guard towers, and an English gatehouse which served as the entrance to the entire complex. On the west, the castle overlooked a deep ravine; on the south a succession of enclosed terraced gardens led down to the shore of the Bristol Channel.[15]

Hearst, who had bought St. Donat's two years before and not yet seen it, was delighted with the exterior, but recognized at once that the interior would have to be entirely redone. The 135 rooms were small, dark, and airless; the bedrooms opened onto one another; and there were very few bathrooms. Sir Charles Allom, who been knighted for his redecoration of Buckingham Palace, took Hearst on a tour of the buildings. Hearst was able to stay only a night before departing again for London, but left, nonetheless, "with a complete mental picture. He was able," Alice Head recalled, on the basis of this short visit, to "instruct Sir Charles from California, to make comments and suggestions on the blue-prints that we submitted, and apparently he carried in his memory a perfect picture of the lay-out of the interior which I was not able to do until after a good many visits." On his return to the States, he dictated a twenty-five-page letter to Allom detailing precisely what he wanted done.

The tiny castle rooms in the North Court were, as he instructed, combined into "eight good bedrooms, each with a magnificent marble bathroom." A "princely banqueting hall" was constructed "with an armoury over it and a very beautiful bedroom suite with private sitting-room, over the armoury." When the interior had reached a state of reasonable repair, work began on the exterior. He built two tennis courts, a croquet court, and a 150 by-50-foot pool, fed by filtered sea water and adjoined by a "picturesque old cottage [with] dressing-rooms and . . . bathrooms with cold showers."

To furnish and decorate St. Donat's, Hearst dispatched scouts across the British Isles to find stone fireplaces, screens, and carved ceilings. According to Clive Aslet, author of *The Last Country Houses,* "Hearst's greatest quarry was Bradenstoke Priory, in Wiltshire. In 1929, the medieval tithe barn was taken down stone by stone amid great secrecy; the workmen did not even know who was employing them." When it was discovered that it was Hearst who had bought, dismantled, and removed the structure, "questions were asked in Parliament as to whether an American millionaire could be allowed to jumble the national heritage in this way. The SPAB [Society for the Protection of Ancient Buildings] was outraged. It went to the unprecedented lengths of putting up posters in underground stations showing before and after photographs."

Alice Head and Sir Charles found themselves in the position of having to defend the Chief. Sir Charles argued that Hearst was not destroying

but rescuing structures that would otherwise have been allowed to rot, unaware perhaps of the European treasures that were already rotting away
in Hearst's warehouses. This may, unhappily, have been the fate of the
Bradenstoke Priory. Though it was removed from its original setting and
transported to St. Donat's, it was never incorporated into the building. It
was eventually dismantled and shipped, stone by stone, to San Simeon
where it remained in unpacked crates until in 1960, it was sold to Alex Madonna, the owner of the Madonna Inn in San Luis Obispo.[16]

On his return to the United States in October of 1928, Hearst admitted to
the reporters who greeted him that he was "inclined to favor Mr. Hoover"
in the upcoming presidential election. Adopting, for the moment, a states-
manlike, nonpartisan pose, he added that he held nothing against Mr.
Smith, but simply believed that Hoover would be "better for the country."[17]

Herbert Hoover was elected in November and took office in March of
1929. As president, he continued to court Hearst's support as assiduously as
he had as a candidate. In September, Hoover invited Arthur Brisbane for "a
long talk" and informed him that he had given "the Income Tax department" instructions that "will be extremely useful to [the Hearst] organization." Brisbane reported to Hearst that the president was also "very much
interested in the matter about which you sent me word, adding the California Peninsula to the United States, the part now belonging to Mexico.
He told me confidentially, of course, that the pride of the Mexicans would
prevent them selling the land, but they might exchange it for territory. His
idea was that we might be able to buy British Honduras from the British,
give that to the Mexicans, plus a little money and get back in return that
strip 1,000 miles long on the Pacific, enabling us to control the bay inside."
Although Hoover had no intention of following through on Hearst's preposterous suggestion that the United States annex Mexican territory, he
was not prepared to dismiss it out of hand, for fear of angering the publisher.[18]

It was too late. In his inaugural address, Hoover had urged American
participation in the World Court, which Hearst was prepared to oppose
with every weapon in his arsenal. In December of 1929, the Chief wrote a
"letter of instructions" to all his publishers, directing them to "support the
various movements against the League Court, and the various organizations back of the movements throughout the country [and] to make the
League Court an issue in the coming senatorial primaries and elections,
and to support candidates, Republicans or Democrats, who are opposed to
our entrance into the League Court. . . . In every case do whatever is most

effective from the viewpoint of the cause; and let us try earnestly to accomplish results. . . . We do not want to make this merely a newspaper promotion campaign. It is a sincerely patriotic endeavor to prevent our country from making a mistake which may be disastrous."[19]

Hearst led the crusade against the World Court from San Simeon, marshaling all the forces he controlled, including radio. "Most important medium in your campaign against World Court is the radio," he wrote John A. Kennedy, the publishing executive in New York he had placed in charge of the project. "We should take every opportunity to use radio and we should take advantage of interest in senatorial campaign throughout country to have important national figures like Senator Johnson and Senator Borah speak on radio against World Court. Furthermore when Mrs. McCormick [Congresswoman Ruth McCormick, the sister-in-law of the *Chicago Tribune* publisher] speaks on World Court her speech should be broadcasted all over the nation."[20]

Hearst's political weapons were too many and too widely deployed for Hoover. By 1930, he owned twenty-six daily newspapers in eighteen American cities. His Sunday papers accounted for more than 20 percent of the total national circulation. There is no way of even estimating how many Americans saw his newsreels or listened to the radio programs or radio stations sponsored by his newspapers. With Hylan no longer the mayor, Hearst had lost control of local politics in New York City, but he was every bit as powerful as he had ever been in Los Angeles, San Francisco, Boston, Chicago, and congressional districts where his daily newspapers were read.

Recognizing that Hearst was going to fight the World Court to the end, Hoover surrendered. As Secretary of State Henry Stimson wrote in his private diary, the president explained to him that "the protocol had no hope whatever. Every congressman living in a district where there was a Hearst paper was sure to be against it."[21]

In June of 1930, Hearst and Marion docked at Southampton on the first leg of their annual summer tour of England. After a few days at the Savoy in London and a weekend of shopping, the Hearst party motored to St. Donat's, where they spent almost a month and celebrated the Fourth of July with an elaborate fireworks display. They then crossed the Channel, stayed a few days at the Hotel Crillon in Paris, motored to Bad Nauheim so that Hearst could take the cure, and from there to Munich where Hearst gave an interview to the *Frankfurter Zeitung* and attacked the Treaty of Versailles for subjecting the Teutonic peoples to the domination of non-German European powers, including France. After attending a performance of the Passion Play at Oberammergau, Hearst and his party motored to Lucerne and Interlaken, and then returned to the Hotel Crillon in Paris.[22]

No sooner had they checked into the hotel then two officials of the French Sûreté Générale approached Hearst in the lobby and served him with an order of expulsion for his role the year before in obtaining and publishing a secret government treaty. Edmond Coblentz, who was with him in Paris, later recalled Hearst's response:

> Immediately after receiving it Mr. Hearst asked me to ride with him in his automobile. There was silence for a moment while he sat strumming his fingers on his knees, a characteristic gesture when he was deep in thought. Then he said to me quietly: "The French government has ordered me to leave France."
>
> "What a foolish thing for them to do," I commented.
>
> "It was silly," he replied. "I am not remaining here. I am leaving this afternoon."
>
> I accompanied him to the Gare du Nord, where, seemingly unperturbed, he walked up and down the platform munching peaches. I waited, and when the train pulled out, I glimpsed him seated in his compartment writing in longhand.[23]

Hearst left Marion behind in Paris with her sisters and Maury Paul so that she could complete her fittings for the twelve thousand dollars worth of clothes she had ordered. From London, he triumphantly cabled a front-page editorial to New York, reporting firsthand on his expulsion from France:

> I have no complaint to make. The officials were extremely polite. They said I was an enemy of France and a danger in their midst. They made me feel quite important. They said I could stay in France a little while longer, if I desired, that they would take a chance on nothing disastrous happening to the Republic. But I told them that I did not want to take the responsibility of endangering the great French nation; that America had saved it once during the war, and I would save it again by leaving.[24]

Before sailing for New York with Hearst and the rest of the party, Joe Willicombe cabled Victor Watson, managing editor of the *New York American,* that the Chief was "dead set against any public demonstration in connection with his home-coming. He has sent radio messages to various organizations, the American Legion, the Disabled Veterans, earnestly urging that there be no public incident attendant upon his home-coming." The message, of course, was interpreted as meaning the exact opposite, and with Hearst's New York newspapers coordinating the event, a huge demonstration of support was organized for their conquering hero. Hearst's liner, the *Europa,* was met at the quarantine station by the steamboat *Hook Mountain* with a reception committee and band under the auspices of the Disabled American War Veterans, the *New York Times* reported on September 16, 1930: "The disabled veterans, many on crutches, wearing their old khaki uniforms and waving flags . . . cheered the publisher when he came on board." In addition to the veterans, Mr. Hearst was welcomed by a delegation headed by Senator Robert F. Wagner and several congressmen.[25]

Hearst was in his element now. After several press releases and a nation-wide radio broadcast carried by short wave to Europe, he embarked on a cross-country lecture tour to give his personal account of his expulsion — and the dangers of American involvement in European affairs. It was like old times again, except that he was no longer a candidate. In Boston, he was greeted by Mayor Curley; in Chicago, he spoke before a crowd of 100,000 at Soldier's Field; in San Francisco, he was met by the mayor and honored at the St. Francis Hotel, where he gave a radio address over the NBC network. Everywhere he went, he gathered headlines. His own newspapers treated him like royalty, with entire pages devoted to his comings and goings and verbatim accounts of his speeches. In St. Louis, it was reported that "Hearst for President — 100% American — No Foreign Entanglements — Independent in Everything — Temperance, not Prohibition" buttons had begun to appear everywhere.[26]

During his tour, bathed in glory and publicity, the Chief sounded only one sour note, complaining loudly in print and on the radio that he had not been suitably protected from the French by "our paid servants at Washington. . . . I still think if Theodore Roosevelt had been alive, or if Grover Cleveland had been alive, you would have heard . . . much about the value and validity and inviolability of the American passport, and of due and necessary respect for the rights and liberties of the American citizen."[27]

The facts were, as Secretary of State Stimson reported to Hoover, that the U.S. had not done anything to protect Hearst because the publisher had never asked for assistance. Furthermore, in expelling Hearst, France had been "entirely within her rights, and was following out well-understood international customs and that we, ourselves, had been perhaps the most extreme of all nations in excluding people for no other reason than we did not like them."

The entire incident and the way Hearst had capitalized on it to criticize the president, Stimson recalled in his diary, had made Hoover sore and doubtful:

He despised Hearst but he did not want to evidently have any trouble with him. I told him that in my opinion, so long as we did not take any official action, he could do what he pleased in regard to inviting Hearst to lunch, which was his suggestion. He said that he was not going to give anything formal, but that he had already had Hearst here at the beginning of his administration and that he might have him again here privately. I said that, in my opinion, he, the President, was entitled to make things as easy for himself as possible, and that if this would make things any easier with Hearst, as long as it was not official action . . . he could do what he pleased.[28]

The invitation was issued and accepted, but it did little to remove the distrust between the president and the publisher. On the contrary, Hoover's reluctance to publicly protest Hearst's expulsion confirmed the publisher's fears that the president remained an unreconstructed Wilsonian internationalist.

The Hearst victory tour ended in mid-October in Oakland, California. "Now," he told his audience at the conclusion of his speech, "I am going to board a train and go down to my ranch and find my little hide-away on my little hilltop at San Simeon, and look down on the blue sea, and up at the blue sky, and bask in the glorious sunshine of the greatest State of the greatest nation in the whole world." There followed a month of silence, at the end of which Hearst, on December 1, 1930, ended all speculation about his future by publishing an open letter to F. Champion, Jr., the man who claimed to have started the "Hearst for President" boom, graciously asking him to stop circulating the Hearst campaign buttons: "I have had my day in politics. It was not a very long day, nor a very brilliant one, but it was sufficient to convince me that my best opportunity for achievement was in supporting principles and policies and not in holding public office."[29]

§ 26 §

The Talkies and Marion

"WHEN I HEARD THE VOICE of Al Jolson, I thought, No. This can't be," Marion remembered. "There can't be talkies. I'm ruined. I'm wrecked."

On their return from Europe in October of 1928, W. R. and Marion had spent a few days in New York at the Ritz Tower. The biggest show in town that season was Al Jolson's second talkie, *The Singing Fool,* which Marion went to see with Maury Paul.

"When Jolson started singing, 'When there are clear skies . . .' I started to cry. The mascara ran all over my face. . . . When we went back to the Ritz Towers, I couldn't stop crying. . . . When W. R. saw me he said, 'What's the matter?' Maury said, 'Sonny Boy got her down.' I really thought I was finished. . . . No one thought I could talk, and I didn't think I could either. I stuttered."[1]

Marion was so terrified of making her talkie screen test that she contemplated quitting film altogether, but W. R. would not let her. Determined to make her as big a star in talkies as he had in silent films, he did what every studio head and agent in town was doing and hired speech and elocution coaches from Broadway to teach her to talk. Adela Rogers St. Johns was a visitor at San Simeon during this period. "As long as I live, I will remember when she was trying to learn to talk! She would go up in the library and [Hearst] had Margaret Carrington [a speech coach], and God knows not who, and good stage directors from New York come out. And they'd all go up there all morning and work with Marion on her speech. You know she stuttered very badly. She did! . . . She stuttered and it was very funny and she was trying to learn. Well, she would come down, and some days she would come roaring in and say: 'I'm not going to go any farther with this!' And then she would give you that speech about Romeo in the tomb, when he came to, and found Tybalt's bones. She'd say, 'Well, none of that makes any sense, I'm not running around memorizing this kind [of] stuff, saying this stuff all the time.'"[2]

In the end, Marion passed the talkie screen test Irving Thalberg gave all the MGM stars on contract. With a bit of sherry to fortify her, she threw away her script and ad-libbed brilliantly. Thalberg was delighted and of-fered to extend her contract. When W. R. saw the test, Marion remembered, he "started to cry. He said, 'My God, it's marvelous.'"[3]

The transition to sound took place with lightning speed. In September of 1928, Nick Schenck announced that two-thirds of MGM films produced during the next year would have sound sequences. That same autumn, the Chief, anxious to secure the best possible "sound" property for Marion, be-gan negotiations with Flo Ziegfeld for the music and talking rights for *Rosalie,* the Marilyn Miller hit, with music by George Gershwin and Sig-mund Romberg and lyrics by Ira Gershwin and P. G. Wodehouse. Romberg and Gershwin had a better offer elsewhere, but Ziegfeld who was in debt to Hearst for the publicity given his last musical, *Show Boat,* promised to de-liver the musical for $85,000.[4]

Hearst and MGM bought *Rosalie,* even given the steep price. Unwilling to fall behind in the race to sound, Hearst and Thalberg decided in the meantime to rescript and reshoot *Five O'Clock Girl,* the film Marion was al-ready working on, as a talkie. Frances Marion was called in to doctor the script, but resigned claiming that the adaptation which Hearst had person-ally selected was impossible to mend. Hearst and Thalberg proceeded nonetheless, then canned the talkie version after three weeks of shooting.

It was rumored that the film had been canceled because of Marion's speech defect, but Ilka Chase, who acted with Marion in her talkies, claimed that "she did not stutter when playing a scene." Marion went on to make dozens of films, radio shows, and speeches without any noticeable stutter or stammer. It is more likely that Hearst canceled *Five O'Clock Girl* because he did not want Marion to make her talkie debut playing a com-mon shop girl.[5]

Still awaiting the *Rosalie* script, Hearst commissioned Laurence Stallings to do a musical-comedy version of Vidor's *The Big Parade,* with Marion playing the role of Marianne, a French farm girl who falls in love with an American doughboy. The Chief previewed the picture at the ranch in the summer of 1929 and telegrammed Thalberg that the "work people on the hill laughed and cried and had a grand time. You certainly made a gorgeous picture out of unpromising material." *Marianne* did reasonably well at the box office.[6]

The success of *Marianne* convinced Hearst that he had been right to believe that, given appropriate projects, Marion would do very well in the talkies: "I think musical comedy is the best thing for the talkies and best thing for Marion . . . In fact I would like to see her do nothing but musical comedy; but of course I am willing to have an occasional straight comedy if you think best."[7] Because there were still problems with the *Rosalie* script (it would in fact never be produced), Hearst let Marion make another King Vidor film, *Not So Dumb*. Though Vidor had succeeded twice with Marion, Hearst refused to let him — or Thalberg — alone on the project. When the shooting was completed, he was sent a rough cut to view at San Simeon. "Here comes Groucho," he telegrammed Thalberg on October 14, after viewing the film and writing up the long list of changes he required. "Am entirely confident you are wrong," Thalberg answered within hours. "Strongly recommend getting audience reaction before any further eliminations or any further retakes. Would appreciate your telephoning me on receipt of this wire. Regards."

Hearst gave in — this time. "All right old man. It's your funeral. I am only a pall bearer." In the end, it was Hearst, not Thalberg, who was right on this one. Vidor's two earlier comedies with Marion, *The Patsy* and *Show People*, had earned profits of $155,000 and $176,000. *Not So Dumb*, which cost less to make than either of them, ended up with a loss of $39,000.[8]

Marion's next film was *The Floradora Girl*, a costume comedy which gave her ample opportunity to sing and dance. Hearst's reputation for meddling in Marion's films was by now so well established that director Harry Beaumont, according to Ilka Chase, who played Marion's friend in the film, "devised a simple and ingenious trick for keeping the boss from underfoot. When the red light is on outside the door of a sound stage it means a scene is shooting, and God Himself can't come in. Harry posted scouts at all the approaches to the stage, and as Mr. Hearst advanced upon it, he would promptly order the doors closed and would then rehearse his scene in peace while the mighty one cooled his heels. There was one sequence, however, where this ruse failed. The 'Tell Me, Pretty Maiden' scene was shot in *glorious* technicolor, and because of the blazing lights the stage got so hell-hot the doors couldn't be kept closed longer than five minutes at a time, and in would hop old Nosey Parker."[9]

Hearst was nosey, of course. Though he and Marion had been together for a decade, he was intensely jealous and, according to Marion's biographer, had her watched when he was out of town.[10] In the spring of 1929, returning from a brief business trip to New York and Washington, where with Millicent he had lunched with President Hoover at the White House, Hearst found a telegram waiting for him at his 9:55 stopover in La Junta,

Colorado, on the way home: "How about telling that engineer to put on some more steam. Am getting impatient. Can hardly wait for Sunday. Love, M."

W. R. wrote his reply on the back of the telegram: "I told the engineer and he is laughing. He says girls are like that. They are great jollyers. He says if he put on too much steam and got there too soon it not be wise. He says things like that have occurred. Anyhow why didn't you tell me something of this kind over the telephone during the last six weeks. I have been wanting to hear it. Out of sight out of mind. W. R."[11]

Before handing the telegram to Willicombe, Hearst crossed out the last three sentences, softening the meaning, but not entirely.

In his late sixties and desperately in love with a movie star just turned thirty, Hearst could not help but be anxious. Still, it was apparent to everyone that while Marion still engaged in brief flirtations, she was very much in love with her "Pops." As she confided to her good friend Eleanor Boardman, who was then married to King Vidor, "'I started out a g-g-gold digger and I ended up in love.'"[12]

"She was devoted to Mr. Hearst," Colleen Moore who "knew Marion very well" remembered. Theirs was "one of the great love stories of the ages. . . . I recall once seeing them walking through the pergola [at San Simeon], hand in hand. They stopped and he kissed her, ever so tenderly."[13]

"It was a great romance," Adela Rogers St. Johns agreed. "Marion adored W. R." If earlier she might have hoped that W. R. would divorce Millicent and marry her, she knew now that this would not happen and not only accepted the fact, but, as time passed, took a sort of pleasure in the sacrifice she had made. "She told him, in my presence," St. Johns remembered, "that he was not to divorce his wife, that she wouldn't hear of it, and she said, 'All right, you are a great man. You are a big man. You are one of the most important men in the world. Now it's all right for you to have a blonde ex-Follies girl–movie star for your mistress. That's all right. But you divorce the wife and mother of your five sons to marry a much younger blonde, and you're an old fool and I won't have it! I won't have you. . . . We love each other, we live together, this is all right. But I'm not going to have you make a fool of yourself.'"[14]

W. R. and Marion were now husband and wife in all but name. When Marion's mother died in January of 1928, Hearst provided her with the emotional and financial support she needed to hold herself and her family together. Sister Rose, who had been drinking steadily for years, required the most attention. In 1924, her estranged husband, George Van Cleve, who worked for Hearst, had kidnapped their daughter, Pat. Father and daughter remained in hiding for the next five years. Hearst hired detectives to search for them. After several misses, Van Cleve was found and Pat returned to her mother at San Simeon, but only briefly. Van Cleve was able to win legal custody of his daughter because of Rose's alcoholism.

In later years, there were rumors that Pat was not Rose's and Van Cleve's child, but Marion's and W. R.'s. But there has never been any evidence to support these rumors, aside from what some people regard as Pat's physical resemblance to Hearst.[15]

Although Hearst was infamous in Hollywood for nosing around the set, meddling in Marion's films, and pushing his films over budget, when it came time to renew his contract with MGM, he was courted by every studio in town. "W. R. Hearst stands in an important spot today in the highlights of the film industry," *Variety* explained on May 1, 1929. "Hearst with his pictures, newspapers and influence, is said to be looked at by several film combinations as a most desirable prospect. . . . From the first look of Hearst in pictures as a wealthy man with a film hobby who didn't care what it cost him, W. R. Hearst has grown to be a substantial part of the film industry."

The betting in Hollywood was that the Chief was going to sign with Warner Brothers. He had, in fact, secretly negotiated a contract with Jack Warner under which Marion would have been obligated to work forty-two weeks a year and make three pictures for a fee of $150,000 each. When Louis B. Mayer got wind of the proposal, he made a counteroffer that was even better. But the Chief, feeling that Mayer had not paid enough attention to him and Marion, was determined to make the move to Warner Brothers. The MGM proposals, he wrote Eddie Hatrick, who was negotiating for him, would "have been gladly accepted if they had been made at an earlier date. But . . . we are forced to conclude they were made because of the proposals of the Warner Brothers, and would not have been made otherwise. . . . We think it would be better for us to go elsewhere than to be in the position of securing from the Metro Company by duress a proposal which they would not willingly have made of their own accord. . . . I would like you to see Mr. Mayer and tell him these things. I just cannot do it myself. I am too fond of him personally to be able to present the situation in a logical way."[16]

Though the Chief would have preferred to move his film operations to Warner Brothers, in part because Jack Warner was prepared to provide him with the funds he needed to launch a new "sound" newsreel, while Mayer was not, he left the final decision to Marion. She chose to turn down the Warner Brothers' offer and remain at MGM.[17]

One of the reasons the Chief wanted to leave MGM was that it was in the process of being taken over by William Fox who had bought a controlling interest in Loew's, MGM's parent company, from Marcus Loew's widow. Fox, who had developed the first successful talking newsreels, was Hearst's major competitor in that market. Like Adolph Zukor, he was a Hungarian Jew who had entered show business by buying a penny arcade which he later converted into a movie theater. Unlike Zukor, however, he made no pretense of gentility and was not considered a giant in the industry. His deal for Loew's had come as a major shock to everyone in Hollywood, including Hearst. The only roadblock standing in the way of his merging his Fox Film Corporation with Loew's to form the largest movie complex in the world was Mayer's threat of an antitrust suit.

While Hearst remained loyal to Mayer and Thalberg, and had, according to *Variety*, earlier tried to buy MGM to protect their positions in it, he had no choice but to come to some understanding with Fox, if only because he controlled the patents on the sound system that Hearst needed to convert his newsreels to sound. Aware that Fox was going to require his help to navigate through his antitrust problems in Washington, the Chief sent Ed Hatrick to negotiate with him. The negotiations were held in secret, as Hearst had pledged his support to Mayer and Thalberg in their fight to keep MGM out of Fox's hands.

"Had talk with Fox on newsreel situation," Hatrick reported back in late June of 1929, "and he has an interesting proposition but it will take capital. . . . I would like to know if you expect to come east within the next three or four weeks as I believe it would be advisable for you to talk it over with Fox. . . . He seems very gratified we stayed on the Metro lot and is anxious to further cement the relations."

Fox's proposal, which Hearst accepted, was that the publisher buy "a substantial interest in the Fox Movietone Corporation." Hearst and Fox would continue to make and market separate newsreels for MGM, with Fox sharing the Hearst organization's news-gathering capacities and Hearst getting full use of Fox's sound-recording patents. With enormous fanfare, the Hearst Metrotone News debuted in October of 1929. The first program was representative of the "news" that would be presented for the next twenty years. The addition of sound strengthened the newsreel's capacity to influence public opinion and sway voters. The newsreel that talked — with an authoritative, one might say authoritarian, narrator's voice framing the action — was a much more persuasive instrument than its silent predecessor had ever been.[18]

Though the editorial opinions offered in his newsreels were more muted than those in his newspapers, they too ceaselessly promoted his politics and pet projects. In the first edition, there were moving pictures of the wedding of John Coolidge, the son of Hearst's favorite president; of the British army evacuating the Rhineland, which the Chief had advocated for some time; of Charles Schwab, the head of Bethlehem Steel, advocating a "Big Navy" proposal which Hearst supported; and of Mussolini, Hearst's Sunday columnist, reviewing the troops before the Tomb of the Unknown Soldier in Rome. Of more immediate interest to viewers may have been the preview of the upcoming World Series between the Philadelphia Athletics and the Chicago Cubs.[19]

To inaugurate his new venture, Hearst leased the Embassy Theater in New York City and converted it into an all-newsreel theater. "For the first time in history, the Newsreel is to have its own theater," the Hearst papers proudly announced on October 28, 1929, the day before the stock market crash. "The vast volume of news pictures flowing into the laboratories of the Fox-Hearst Corporation demanded additional outlet. Spot news will be a daily addition to the regular program, which will be changed weekly or semi-weekly. Every important event in New York City will be shown on the screen within a few hours after it takes place. Similarly every big event in the world will be rushed to the Newsreel Theater with all possible speed."[20]

Hearst's new contract with MGM only enhanced his stature in Hollywood. He was on excellent terms with every power broker in town, including Harry and Jack Warner, whose contract offer he had spurned, Louis B. Mayer, who retained control of MGM after William Fox lost control of the company in the 1929 stock market crash, and Will Hays, the former postmaster general, whom the studio heads had hired in 1922 as head of the Motion Picture Producers and Distributors of America. Though a large part of Hays's responsibility was protecting the studios from scandal and cementing better ties with Washington, his contacts and access to political power paled beside those of Hearst.

The Chief, never shy to use his influence on behalf of his friends, was called on regularly. In early 1929, he took up the movie colony's crusade against the income tax by asking Arthur Brisbane to write an editorial about the unjust tax treatment for actors and actresses who "make a lot of money for a very brief period," pay "enormous" taxes on it, and then are "fined for mistakes and assessed on back taxes and things of that kind until in many cases they are rendered practically destitute. Bill Hart paid 80 percent of his total possessions in back taxes. He is now off the screen and not making any money. . . . The situation is pretty bad, Artie, and a little vigor in the editorials might not be amiss."[21]

William S. Hart, the great cowboy star, was not the only Hollywood figure who had landed in tax trouble. That same year, both Marion and Irving Thalberg were also charged with income tax dereliction and threatened with heavy fines. Thalberg was particularly frightened, as he had been accused of fraud and informed that, if found guilty, he could go to jail. Hearst offered Thalberg the use of one of his Washington attorneys and assured him that "various newspaper and political friends will help when and as required." In a handwritten note mailed to Thalberg in Washington, the Chief promised that he would be exonerated in the end. "I personally don't believe that anyone is going to be hanged for not knowing what can or cannot be done with these damn complicated taxes. If there is any hanging or drawing and quartering to be done, the first to be executed should be the federal agents who take advantage of the technicalities and the confusion and the general ignorance of the tax question to overtax the public."[22]

Marion's case was similar to Thalberg's. She too was charged with underpaying her taxes and taking unnecessary deductions for, among other things, her makeup and automobiles. Unfortunately, her case was so complicated and took so long to adjudicate that by the time a decision was made in 1931, Hearst had broken with the Republicans and could not protect her. Marion was, in the end, charged with defrauding the government and required to deliver certified checks for $900,000 in back taxes and $110,000 in fines.[23]

A large part of Hearst's exalted status in the movie colony came from San Simeon. While other California millionaires had built glorious mansions along Sunset Boulevard, in the mountains, or at the seashore, Hearst had constructed a veritable Mediterranean village on the central coast. In its eclectic glories, its manic splendors, and its oversized, overwrought magnificence, San Simeon was, for the Hollywood community, a concrete representation of the Chief's ability to get things done.

Hearst was as proud of his achievements at San Simeon as he was of anything he had accomplished. In early 1929, Adolph Ochs, the publisher of the *New York Times,* visited Los Angeles and had dinner at the Ambassador Hotel. Hearst, who was also dining at the hotel, stopped by to say hello and sent a handwritten note to Ochs, suggesting playfully that he should relocate to California. "Seriously, it will add ten years to a very valuable life if you live part of your time in California. May I take you up to my ranch and show you what the country is like?"[24]

Ochs did visit the ranch and was so impressed by what he saw that he asked Hearst if he could send a reporter and photographer to do a story. Hearst agreed and in July of 1929, the *New York Times* published the first article on San Simeon, a two-page Sunday feature:

> A Renaissance Palace in Our West: On His Ranch in California, Mr. Hearst Has Brought Together Objects of Art from Spain, Italy and France. . . . It is all a long way from anything the old Spanish rancheros of the Central California coastline . . . ever dreamed of. Even the eighteenth-century Spanish mission friars . . . could hardly have imagined such ethereal white opulence as this, which was at once so full of museum-like magnificence and of charmed repose. But in such a fashion American wealth has brought to the 175,000-acre ranch of La Questa Encantada — The Enchanted Slope — the Renaissance spirit of building and collecting for the sake of beauty to be privately enjoyed.[25]

A new chapter was opening in the Hearst story. Although there had been occasional hints in the press about his art collecting, from this point on dozens of stories about his lifestyle, especially his compulsive buying and rebuilding, would make their way into print. Journalists who visited San Simeon could not quite decide whether the old man was an eccentric Medici-like relic of times past or a visionary businessman who knew better than most how to lead the good life.

"Atmospheres mingle on the Enchanted Hill," *Fortune* magazine reported in May of 1931:

> The stage is set with the treasures of Europe; jesters from Hollywood amuse; celebrities strut or peer curiously — but behind and beyond them all there is functioning a great chain of newspapers and their allied enterprises. To spread the gospel, there is a wireless and a telegraph office. Even more vital, perhaps, the telephone switchboard. It is an exchange in itself. Call it if you like. You merely ask for Hacienda, California. Through it you can reach any part of the estate.[26]

By 1929, the ranch had already become a must stop not only for Hollywood's stars, but for politicians, businessmen, and world leaders. In September of 1929, Winston Churchill, who had lost his position as chancellor of the exchequer with the defeat of the Conservative government in May, arrived for a visit. Winston's son, Randolph, every inch the snob, was prepared not to be impressed by San Simeon. But, as his diary entries show, he too was overwhelmed. On September 14, 1929, he wrote in his diary:

The ranch — for so it is termed in false modesty — comprises 300 square miles, stretching along 35 miles of sea. The house is absolutely chock full of works of art obtained from Europe. They are insured for sixteen million dollars . . . Hearst is reputed to possess an income of twenty million dollars. The house and grounds are by no means completed, though nine years have passed since it was started. Everywhere are workmen, motor lorries and pneumatic drills. The bathing pool has already been demolished twice, and now is entirely lined with black and white marble. The two or three acres surrounding it are in process of being paved in marble too. . . . One of the subsidiary houses possesses the most divine overhanging Moorish windows that can be imagined. Monasteries, palaces and castles throughout Europe have been and still are being ransacked for gems of one kind and another.

Because the theater had not yet been built, Hearst entertained his guests by showing the latest talking films in the garden on what Randolph referred to as a full-sized cinematograph apparatus.[27]

The Churchills spent four days at San Simeon, long enough for Winston to do some painting on the terrace, and inadvertently, according to his biographer, William Manchester, cause quite a commotion when a maid misheard him and interrupted Hearst in conference: "'Churchill is fainting!' she cried. 'He wants some turpentine!' Hearst rushed out to a terrace, where he found Winston painting, not fainting, awaiting a thinner for his oils and placidly puffing a fat cigar."[28]

From San Simeon, Hearst had the Churchill party driven to Los Angeles, where they were installed at the Biltmore Hotel. Intent on proving to his guests that California was as splendid and luxurious as any European capital — and much more fun — W. R. hosted a luncheon in Churchill's honor for 200 guests at Marion's MGM bungalow. Entertainment was provided by a twenty-piece orchestra and twenty-five chorus girls. At the conclusion of the luncheon, the Chief and Churchill made speeches that were recorded on sound and film and reprinted the following day in the Hearst papers.

After their royal reception at the MGM studios, the Churchills went deep-sea fishing on the Chief's yacht, were entertained at a luncheon for sixty at Montmartre Restaurant, and attended a swimming party and banquet at Marion's beach house at Santa Monica. Hearst had earlier asked Winston's son Randolph and his nephew, Johnny Churchill, to draw up a list of movie stars they might like to meet. The boys were astounded when every star on their list, except for Garbo, showed up at Marion's party.

"Charlie Chaplin and Marion Davies danced a pas de deux, the interesting thing being that Charlie's feet were so small he was actually able to step into Marion's shoes," Johnny Churchill remembered later. "Hearst, plump, rotund and hospitable, was in very good form. He contributed to the entertainment with a solo act in which he let his legs go wobbly and lurched his enormous frame across the room to the rhythm of the band."[29]

The Churchills accepted Hearst's bigamous relationships with nary a glance. Millicent was at the ranch when they arrived in mid-September and served as their hostess there. "I told you about Mrs. H. (the official) & how agreeable she made herself," Winston wrote his wife. "She is going to give me a dinner in N.Y. & look after the boys on their way through. At Los Angeles (hard g) we passed into the domain of Marion Davies; & were charmed by her. She is not strikingly beautiful nor impressive in any way. But her personality is most attractive; naïve childlike, bon enfant. . . . She asked us to use her house as if it was our own. But we tasted its comforts & luxuries only sparingly."[30]

At Marion's poolside party at Santa Monica, the Churchills were introduced to Hollywood's stars. At Millicent's farewell dinner at the Clarendon, they met New York's elites: the Astors, Vanderbilts, Goulds, Swopes, Condé Nasts, and some titled Europeans.

The dinner was, Millicent wrote her husband, "very successful. You should have been here for it."[31]

VII

The Depression

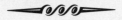

ৡ 27 ৡ

"Pretty Much Flattened Out"

M
ILLICENT'S PARTY FOR THE CHURCHILLS was held on a Saturday night in mid-October 1929. Her guests most surely did not discuss the stock market, but prices had been falling all month. On Tuesday, October 29, they crashed, losing in that one day of trading $14 billion in value.

Like President Herbert Hoover and many of the nation's business and financial leaders, Hearst considered the fall in stock prices a necessary correction. Six months earlier, he had written Brisbane that he was worried about the frenzy of speculation that had gripped the market. "The thing which ought [to] be stopped is fleecing of small investors who are lambs at mercy of the wolves because they speculate with insufficient funds and on small margins. Protecting these innocents by making such marginal speculation illegal would not only protect the people from robbery but would stabilize stock market and minimize chances of panic. France has made it illegal to speculate in food stuffs. America could and should make it illegal to speculate on margins."[1]

As stock prices continued to fall through early November, Hearst suggested that President Hoover offer the public some "reassuring utterance," while pursuing "vigorous action in stimulating the legitimate activities of the Federal Reserve." He was so convinced that the American economy was fundamentally sound that on the day he published his letter to Hoover, he telegrammed George Young, the publisher of the *Los Angeles Examiner,* that he wanted "to borrow a million dollars to buy stocks, and I wish you and Frank [Knox] would go out and see if I can get it."[2]

The fall in stock prices had not affected him because the bulk of his investments were in real estate. He had, during the 1920s, bought commercial properties in Atlanta, Baltimore, Los Angeles, San Francisco, and Chicago. He was, according to *Fortune* magazine, among the largest "realtors" in

New York City, with properties worth close to $41 million in 1935 or over half a billion in today's currency. Most of the real estate was owned by his various publishing companies or by dummy corporations set up by his real estate adviser, Martin Huberth; a not insignificant portion was held in partnership with Arthur Brisbane. Hearst's Manhattan empire included a block in Lower Manhattan between Catharine Slip and Market Slip which was occupied by his newspaper offices and plant; much of the land around Columbus Circle; significant portions of 56th, 57th, and 58th Streets from Madison to Sixth Avenue and of the Madison Avenue blocks between 82nd and 83rd and 54th and 58th Streets; several midtown hotels, including the Ritz Tower on 57th and Park and The Warwick on 54th and Sixth Avenue; and the Ziegfeld Theatre on 54th and Sixth. Hearst continued buying real estate after the market crashed. On November 8, a week after Black Tuesday, he closed on an apartment house on Park Avenue and East 58th Street. A month later, he purchased a huge plot of land in Brooklyn.[3]

Although confident that the market would eventually rise again, the Chief exercised some restraint. On November 15, he wrote to Alice Head in London, asking her not to proceed on the St. Donat's renovations without instructions from him. "We have all just been run over by a steam-roller here in America and feel pretty much flattened out. You have been reading about the stock market, of course. It is not that all of us are in the stock market — thank goodness I am not very heavily — but it does not look as if a collapse of this kind would do business any good. Therefore, the other day I cabled you that perhaps you might better stop work at St. Donat's after the work in hand was finished." No such orders were issued at San Simeon, where construction continued apace.[4]

The Chief's only concessions to the Depression came in early 1930 when he decorated the walls of his new movie theater at San Simeon with red damask instead of a more expensive green Majorcan velvet and authorized his representatives in New York to sell his two yachts moored there. One of them, the *Hirondelle,* which had been owned by Prince Albert-Honoré-Charles of Monaco, had been bought in 1923 and left unused at a Brooklyn pier since 1924. But even minor adjustments such as these were abandoned as the stock market began to rise again through the winter of 1930. In March, Hearst authorized the purchase of the Canova statue of Venus that is today on view in the Assembly Room at San Simeon. That same month, at a Christie's auction in London, he purchased an eighteenth- or nineteenth-dynasty Egyptian black granite bust of the lion-faced goddess

Sekhmet, which Miss Morgan combined with other Sekhmet statuary in a specially designed setting on the South Esplanade.[5]

While the nation suffered through the worst depression in its history, the Chief expanded his animal shelters and grottoes at San Simeon and added a new Celestial Suite and a recreation wing with a billiard room and a full-sized moving-picture theater to Casa Grande. He also completed the most spectacular ornament on the hillside, the Roman pool, built under the tennis courts behind Casa Grande, every inch of its walls, ceiling beams, and floors lined with mosaics of blue and gold inlaid glass tiles imported from Murano, Italy.

But he was still not finished. He owned a Mediterranean castle at San Simeon and a medieval fortress at St. Donat's in Wales. He had built a monstrous beach house for Marion in Santa Monica and bought Millicent the Belmont estate at Sands Point. In the winter of 1929–30, when his mother's German-style castle at Wyntoon in Northern California burned down, Hearst commissioned Bernard Maybeck and Julia Morgan to replace it with something grander. Phoebe had originally left the estate to her niece, Anne Apperson Flint, but W. R. had purchased it from her in 1925.[6]

Maybeck wanted to replace the seven-story castle that had burned down with a larger medieval one which would have two main towers and sixty-one Hearst-sized bedrooms. Julia Morgan, according to her biographer, Sara Boutelle, suggested an alternative design: "a 'Bavarian village' with three half-timber three-story guesthouses, each composed of four to eight bedrooms (each with its own bathroom) and two sitting rooms. These were to be placed around a large, grassy oval clearing in the middle of the forest, with the back of each house paralleling the river as it curved downstream." The Chief chose Morgan's plan. Early estimates — from 1931 — placed the preliminary cost of construction at $2 million (equivalent to almost $22 million in today's currency).

Wyntoon, which *Fortune* magazine would in 1935 refer to as the "new Hearst principality," was located on fifty thousand acres of alpine-like forest, with the McCloud River snaking through it. To the north stood the village green with three four-story wooden and stone mansions. The roofs are steeped, with bay windows, chimneys, and gables. Each of the houses overlooks the river on one side and the village green on the other. In the early 1930s, Hearst commissioned Willy Pogany, a muralist, magazine illustrator, and Hollywood set designer, to paint fairy-tale murals on the exteriors. The houses were named after the subjects of each mural: Cinderella House, Fairy House, and Bear House, where Hearst and Marion lived. Though the characters might be from old fairy-tale books, the execution was Disney-esque. There was nothing brooding, nothing foreboding about Hearst's Bavarian Village. Just below Bear House was River House, which had been built by Charles Wheeler, Phoebe's lawyer, who had owned the land on which Phoebe built her castle. Morgan remodeled River House into an additional guesthouse. Across the river were two entertainment houses, Bridge House, where movies were shown until the Gables with a full-sized theater was completed, and Tea House, with an outdoor terrace for dancing.

Wyntoon was Hearst's northern European estate, designed to house his collections of German art and serve as a summer retreat from San Simeon. Because Hearst intended to spend several weeks each year at Wyntoon, he set up a communications headquarters there, much as he had at San Simeon. Adjacent to Bear House, Morgan built a shingled bungalow which served as Joe Willicombe's home and office and what *Fortune* magazine called the "empire's nerve center." Here were located the telephone switchboards, telegraph facilities, and three operators who kept the switchboards open around the clock.

About a half mile down a winding road were the pool, the croquet court, and the Gables, a stone lodge built on the site of Maybeck's original castle with a dining room for sixty, a lounge with a great fireplace, and a theater for moving pictures. Across the river from the pool were the stables. A quarter mile further down the road was the Bend, the rustic stone lodge which had been the Charles Wheeler home. In 1934, Hearst purchased Wheeler's land and set to work enlarging the Bend by adding a mammoth entertainment hall, theater, and dining complex.[7]

Like their competitors, the Hearst papers lost revenue during the Depression — not from circulation, which remained steady, but from advertising, which dropped precipitously: by "15 percent in 1930, 24 percent in 1931, and 40 percent in 1933."[8] Though it might have been wise for Hearst to sell some of his weaker papers and consolidate his holdings, he refused to even consider the possibility.

Eleanor (Cissy) Patterson, the sister of the *New York Daily News* publisher Joe Patterson and cousin of the *Chicago Tribune* publisher Colonel Robert McCormick, tried to buy the *Washington Herald* from Hearst, but he refused to sell. Instead, he proposed that she edit the *Herald* for a nominal salary and a third of the net profits. His decision paid off almost at once, with dramatic increases in circulation and advertising. In 1931, rumors surfaced that Ned McLean, the son of John McLean, the publisher who had sold Hearst the *New York Journal* in 1894, was going to sell the

Washington Post. Cissy Patterson, not having given up her goal of owning a newspaper, tried to buy it in partnership with Hearst, but McLean refused to sell. Two years later, McLean having in the meantime pushed the paper into bankruptcy, the *Post* was sold at auction. Again Patterson and Hearst tried to buy it, but were outbid by Eugene Meyer, who had just resigned as chairman of the Federal Reserve.[9]

Ned McLean was not the only second-generation publisher who foundered during the Depression. Though Joseph Pulitzer's sons did better with their father's legacy, they were not able to weather the storm. By early 1931, frightened by the amount of money they were losing, they put the morning, evening, and Sunday *World*s up for sale. Hearst, too, was losing money in New York, but he could not let an opportunity like this one go by. Because he knew the Pulitzers would never entertain a bid from him, he entered into partnership with Herbert Bayard Swope, the former editor of the *World.* The two met clandestinely at Marion's MGM bungalow, her beach house in Santa Monica, and at Charles Chaplin's home in Beverly Hills. Hearst was willing to pay between $5 and $8 million for the morning and Sunday editions, which he intended to close down. He never got the chance. The Pulitzers sold instead to Roy Howard of the Scripps-Howard chain, who killed off the morning and Sunday editions and merged the evening *World* with his own *Telegram.*[10]

Though Hearst's *New York American* had been hemorrhaging circulation and advertising revenues more rapidly than the *World,* Hearst had no intention of shutting it down. On the contrary, buoyed by the 100,000 readers who moved to the *American* when the morning *World* was closed, the Chief set in motion yet another plan to reinvent his flagship newspaper by positioning it as a third choice between the ultra-serious, text-heavy *Times* and *Herald Tribune,* on the one hand, and the illustrated tabloids, on the other. There was, he was certain, room in the marketplace for a paper that was smart, well written, attractively illustrated, and filled with news stories condensed for busy readers, a paper not unlike the early *San Francisco Examiner* or *New York American.* Unlike the *Times* and the *Herald Tribune,* he would give his readers "brief stories and bright stories." Unlike the tabloids, he would continue to carry the strong features and opinion pieces that would establish the *American,* as its logo proclaimed it to be, "A Paper for People Who Think."[11]

Although he had the greatest respect for Adolph Ochs of the *New York Times,* who was not only weathering the Depression but adding circulation year by year, Hearst did not intend to follow his example. When Coblentz suggested that the *American* should eliminate its women's page because the

Times did not have one, the Chief resisted. "You mention the *Times* not having these things. I do not think that means a great deal. We have never run the kind of paper that the *Times* runs. The *Times* is an Ochs paper. Our papers are Hearst papers. There is a definite difference in everything, from political policies to news judgement, and character of the departments. In fact, it is desirable for us not to be like the *Times* but to be sufficiently different from the *Times*."[12]

As the former *Times* reporter Alva Johnson noted in a 1932 *Vanity Fair* article, though Hearst and Ochs had been publishing newspapers in the same city for more than thirty-five years, they had had "little effect on each other." Ochs saw himself as "a vendor of information." He kept his name and opinions out of his paper. Hearst, on the contrary, appeared before the public "as a minstrel and sage, ethical guide, social coach, financial adviser, confidant and strategist in affairs of the heart, culinary tutor, educator, house mother, prophet, purveyor of warm data on high life. . . . Every day of his life, he strives to exert his influence to the utmost."[13]

Instead of borrowing from the *Times*, Hearst, in early 1931, decided to go it one better and add a new feature, a contributors page — what would later come to be called the op-ed page — aimed rather directly at more educated and affluent readers. "The idea of the new page of contributions is to reach new class of people," he told Coblentz. "It is necessary to do something different with the *American* than we have been doing."[14] The heading of the new page, "Writers With Something to Say, Who Know How to Say it," was an apt description. A large number of these writers — Bertrand Russell, Aldous Huxley, G. K. Chesterton, and Rebecca West — were British. All were masters of the short-form essay. Huxley was among the most prolific. According to James Sexton, who edited a collection of these essays, Hearst contacted Huxley's American publisher in June of 1931 to propose that the author, who had just completed *Brave New World*, write a series of weekly articles "which would provide a very comfortable income." He was to be given a free hand as to subject matter. "It seems good money for not much work, and of a kind that might be rather interesting," Huxley wrote back to his publisher. He would, over the next four years, deliver 173 different essays on an extraordinarily wide variety of subjects: from "drugs, to pieces on travel, language, nature, entomology, medicine, art, books," dogs, communism, fascism, and current politics and political personalities.[15]

Hearst's daily opinion page was run opposite his editorial page. Each of his contributors was free to write on whatever he or she chose. The result was a remarkably diverse set of essays. On September 9, 1931, to offer just one example, Hearst published a column by Bertrand Russell, "In Praise of

Artificiality," in which Russell argued that "the praise of nature, in which our age abounds, is not itself natural; it is a reaction against too much artificiality. As a reaction it has its uses; as a theory of life, it won't do." Three days later, the page carried an essay by Huxley on "Bullfights and Democracy," in which he reflected — brilliantly — on the French government's bizarre decision to outlaw bull fights in which the bull was put to death, but let the events take place if the promoters paid a fine in advance.[16]

Unfortunately for Hearst, short essays by British intellectuals on his op-ed page did not make up for the steadily deteriorating news sections. The Hearst papers were weak in both local and international news. While Hearst's International News Service had bureaus in every major European city, they were staffed, for the most part, by writers and editors who were paid by the Chief to express his opinions. The same was true of his Washington coverage. Hearst set the editorial line which everyone was obliged to follow. If in the past he had been able to find able reporters willing to work under these conditions, that no longer appeared to be the case.

A. J. Liebling would remark after Hearst's death that he would be remembered for introducing "big money" into newspaper publishing. And that he had — paying his star writers, columnists, and cartoonists much more than the going wage in the industry. To recoup these costs, Hearst required each of his newspapers to purchase and publish, uncut and unedited, a large number of Hearst-syndicated columns, comics, features, and daily opinion pieces, like Brisbane's. His local editors, robbed of space and editorial budget, had to cut back somewhere and did: on reporters, columnists, and opinion writers. The result was apparent to anyone who compared the Hearst papers to their competitors. The Hearst papers looked much the same, as Liebling also remarked, wherever you were in the country. The Chief recognized the problem and urged his city editors to be more resourceful, but without adequate funds to hire reporters, there was little they could do.[17]

The Hearst papers' weakness in local and international reporting was, to some degree, compensated for by the strength of their syndicated columnists. Damon Runyon, who had been with the paper since the 1920s and had covered everything from sports to Mexican border disputes to the Lindbergh kidnapping trial, continued to write for the *American*. Walter Winchell filled his role as star columnist at the *Mirror*. Both were widely syndicated to other Hearst papers. So were Louella Parsons, Hearst's Hollywood reporter; Maury Paul, his society columnist; Robert Ripley, the author of the "Believe It or Not" cartoons; and a number of lesser names. When the *World* folded, Hearst tried to hire Walter Lippmann to write another syndicated column for him, but Lippmann signed on with the *Herald Tribune* instead.

The Chief's intellectual in residence remained Arthur Brisbane, but it was difficult to know whether he was an asset or a liability. Every Hearst morning paper was forced to run Brisbane in the far left column of the front page and pay the Hearst syndicate for the privilege. None were particularly happy with the arrangement.

It is difficult to describe but easy to parody the contents of a typical Brisbane column. He wrote on whatever happened to come into his mind that day, the only constant being his positive references to his friends and the stocks he had invested in. Each column contained several different items, usually including the kind of pseudo-scientific musings he had specialized in as a Sunday feature editor. David Starr Jordan, the president of Stanford University, coined his own word to describe Brisbane's musings: "sciosophy," which he defined as "systematized ignorance, the most delightful science in the world because it is acquired without labor or pain and keeps the mind from melancholy." Another commentator referred to his writings as "Brisbanalities." A. J. Liebling was particularly biting about Brisbane's "inspirational sapience":

> The kind of thing that would worry Brisbane . . . was the number of eggs produced by a female codfish. According to Brisbane, it was millions. Then he would multiply the number of eggs by the number of codfish, and point out that nature, which he always spelled with a capital "N," had thoughtfully provided a number of oöphagous fellow-creatures who kept the codfish population of the world within bounds. But what would happen if these monitors suddenly lost their appetite for eggs, he would ask. The world, within eleven months, fourteen days, and a number of hours that he ventured only to approximate, since he hadn't gone into the problem deeply, would turn into one vast uncooked codfish ball, with only the top of Mount Everest and possibly a small portion of San Simeon protruding from a limitless sea of cod-liver oil.[18]

And yet, there might still have been room, even given the Brisbanalities on the front page, for the type of morning paper Hearst envisioned, one that was "smart" and informative, but not as intimidating, weighty, or wordy as his nontabloid competitors. The problem was that Hearst, approaching seventy, had neither the time nor the energy nor the capital to invest in such an ambitious venture. While he had tried to create a reserve fund for new projects, it had long ago been exhausted. He was overextended with long-term and short-term debt, bloated payrolls, real estate mortgages, construction and renovation costs, and huge bills to art dealers and auction houses on both sides of the Atlantic. There was no ready capital available to invest in his morning newspapers nor, in the midst of the Depression, was it going to be easy to borrow money for this purpose.

This is not to say that Hearst was prepared to reduce his publishing empire or sell off his assets, as the Pulitzers had. On the contrary, he urged his local newspaper executives to spend more of their revenues on circulation campaigns and promotion. He continued to believe that the most effective way to recruit new readers was through radio. In April of 1930, he appointed Emil Gough of Los Angeles as his special assistant for radio:

> I think you should make a tour of the whole circuit and attend to various matters of prime importance in connection with the radio situation. The first thing of importance is to find the best possible man for radio editor of each paper . . . I am afraid that not all of our publishers realize the importance of radio. . . . It is fully as important as moving pictures. It is much MORE important than the drama. . . . The second matter for which you are making the tour is a matter that had been pretty thoroughly discussed with the publishers heretofore; namely, acquiring broadcast stations or making adequate connections with established stations and providing attractive programs.

That it would cost a small fortune to buy or build new radio stations did not concern the Chief at all.[19]

All his life, Hearst had been able to borrow capital whenever he needed it to refinance old debts and buy new properties. Jack Neylan, who had taken over as corporate treasurer on the retirement of Joseph Moore, had floated two successful multimillion-dollar bond issues in 1925 and 1927 and was, in 1930, prepared to raise more capital by selling stock in Hearst's corporations. In May of 1930, he had incorporated Hearst Consolidated Publications, Inc., in Delaware. In July, shares of preferred stock in the new corporation were offered to the public with the same kind of hoopla that had celebrated the Hearst bond issue of 1927. B. C. Forbes, Hearst's financial columnist, recommended the stock in his columns, as did advertisements prominently placed in all Hearst publications, each with a coupon, phone number, and illustration of a smiling mother and father holding their dividend check, their young daughter looking on. Playing upon the fears of Americans everywhere, the advertisements offered the Hearst stock as a Depression safety net, a sound and secure place to earn money in times of economic distress.

> Seven Per Cent with Safety
> is still available as
> Falling Interest Rates
> disturb

Fixed Incomes
FINANCIAL INDEPENDENCE
may be secured by the purchase of
Hearst Consolidated Publications, Inc.
7% Class A Shares
TIME is your greatest aid in the accumulation of MONEY
START TODAY

For those who could not afford the $25 it cost to purchase a share, a partial payment plan of $5 down and $2 monthly was available. Hearst company employees were offered the stock for $24 a share, the extra dollar allegedly paid by Mr. Hearst himself. Readers were regularly reassured that the Hearst publications would remain strong and stable forever, because their product was "an urgent public necessity in the face of all economic conditions."[20]

What the advertisements didn't say — though it was clear in the prospectus — was that the preferred stock carried no voting rights. These were lodged in the common stock, all of which was owned by Hearst's personal holding company. Only in the event that Consolidated skipped four consecutive dividend payments would the preferred stock holders be given voting rights to elect their own board of directors. The advertisements for the stock also didn't say where the money raised was going.

Because Hearst Consolidated had bought its properties — ten newspapers, the *American Weekly,* and a newsprint company — from Hearst's personal holding company for $50 million, a substantial portion of the funds raised through the stock offering was committed to paying off this debt to Hearst. Another portion was dedicated to paying off the bonds and debts owed by the individual properties which had been bought by Hearst Consolidated.

Hearst profited all the way round. Not only did his personal holding company get an immediate cash infusion, but because it owned all the common stock in Consolidated, it received a substantial portion of the dividends distributed. Between 1930 and 1935, $10 million of the $17 million paid in dividends went directly to Hearst's personal holding company.[21]

Although early advertisements said that "application will be made to list this Class A Stock on the New York Curb, and the Chicago, San Francisco and Los Angeles Stock Exchanges," this was never done. The notice disappeared from later advertisements. Hearst sold the stock himself through his newspapers. Remarkably enough, the absence of an open market for the stock was not a major problem through the early 1930s. As the advertisements promised, preferred shares of Hearst Consolidated, Inc., turned out to be reliable investments in an uncertain marketplace. Hearst had promised an enormous and safe interest rate and he delivered on that promise. That he also profited from the arrangement was not, at the time, cause for concern to anyone.[22]

Through the first year of the Depression, the Hearst papers refrained from criticizing Hoover's economic policies, perhaps because the Chief was in agreement with the president that the Depression was a domestic business crisis caused by excessive stock market speculation that would, given time, heal itself. On other issues, the Hearst papers were as active as ever through the early years of the Depression. Prodded by the Chief, his editors initiated crusades for improved public schools, prison reform, and "state hospitals and farms for the cure of narcotic addicts" and against crime, boxing, auto accidents, capital punishment, licentious theater, "the narcotics evil," and Prohibition.

Hearst's major policy initiative was the campaign against Prohibition. While Hearst had originally supported the 18th Amendment, as early as January 1925, he had begun to criticize it for breeding "law violators" and financing the underworld. Privately, he paid the law little heed. There was always a steady supply of the best beers at San Simeon, much of it shipped West from New York by Chris MacGregor. In February of 1927, for example, Joe Willicombe urgently telegrammed MacGregor:

As AB [Arthur Brisbane] is leaving Saturday or Sunday, you have little time to act on this matter — so get after it quickly and oblige. Chief says AB has way of getting Bass, and Rudolph [an unidentified employee] has way of getting the German. (I must necessarily make this cryptic.) Chief would like AB to get some Bass for here and would like Rudy to get some German also for here, same to be turned over to you for transportation. In communicating on the subject, you can refer to the Bass as the English and the other as the German or Germanic — I will understand. . . . And ask Rudy if he cannot get a real big shipment, even if it is down below over the border and we will try to engineer way to get it up.[23]

By January of 1930, Hearst was ready to launch a direct assault on Prohibition. In a signed editorial, he blamed the 18th Amendment for every ill that had befallen the nation since it was passed:

Prohibition has led to wide-spread invasion of the rights and liberties of a free people. It has substituted tyranny for liberty and despotism for democracy. It has violated the sanctity of the home, and made every man and every man's house and every man's family subject of a system of espionage that is only equaled by that of Russia. Prohibition has increased crime enormously, star-tlingly, dangerously . . . Prohibition has filled our jails with young boys, and has associated them with hardened criminals . . . Prohibition has corrupted our police system . . . Prohibition has divided our people into factions almost as bitterly hostile to each other as the factions that existed before the Civil War.[24]

He did not let up on this campaign until the Prohibition Amendment was repealed.

After a brief rebound in early 1930, the American economy continued to deteriorate. A spectacular drought brought ruin to much of rural America, turning huge sections of the Midwest into a dust bowl. Overall investment continued to decline. Unemployment increased, the banks began to fail, and breadlines to form. By January of 1931, there were in New York City alone, according to the historian Edward Robb Ellis, eighty-two breadlines serving an average of 85,000 meals a day, two of them operated and paid for by Hearst, one at Times Square, the other at Columbus Circle.[25]

The Hearst lines, as the songwriter Yip Harburg recalled, were the biggest in the city: "He had a big truck with several people on it, and big cauldrons of hot soup, bread. Fellows with burlap on their shoes were lined up all around Columbus Circle, and went for blocks and blocks around the park, waiting." At the time, Harburg was writing a show called *Americana*. In one skit, "Mrs. Ogden Reid of the *Herald Tribune* was very jealous of Hearst's beautiful bread line. It was bigger than her bread line. It was a satiric, vola-tile show. We needed a song for it." That song became "Brother, Can You Spare a Dime."[26]

In June of 1931, Hearst responded to the worsening economic situation by presenting his own plan for economic recovery in a speech delivered live from 11 P.M. to 11:15 P.M. over the eighty-two stations in William Paley's CBS Radio Network. The next morning, the speech was published in full on the front pages of the Hearst newspapers. In an aristocratic accent not unlike FDR's, the Chief called for the immediate expenditure of $5 billion to pro-vide public works jobs for the unemployed at prevailing wages. Offering his own version of the "underconsumption" thesis, Hearst claimed that con-sumer dollars had been withdrawn from the economy by the twin scourges of overcapitalization (too much money had been invested in unproductive speculative stock issues) and profiteering. For prosperity to return, there had to be a sharp increase in "the purchasing power of the masses."[27]

Though proposals for increasing government expenditure on public works had earlier been floated by politicians, citizens' groups, and Hoover himself, no one had come anywhere close to suggesting that the federal government should spend $5 billion that it didn't have at a moment in the nation's history when the deficit was rising to unprecedented levels. Hearst's plan was bold, imaginative, and in a great many respects quite similar to the public works projects that would, two years later, become the centerpiece of Franklin Roosevelt's New Deal.

Immediately following the Chief's radio address, the Hearst papers launched their print campaign for the Chief's $5 billion prosperity plan. On June 6, the editorial page cartoon by Winsor McCay, still Hearst's favorite illustrator, pictured a raft of unemployed men dressed all in black, afloat on a sea of money. The cartoon was labeled "Want in the Midst of Plenty"; the caption read, "There is plenty of money in the country, plenty of money in the savings banks. It should be spent to employ labor on a grand scale." To the left of the cartoon was the related editorial, "For a Prosperity Loan!," which referred, if only obliquely, to Hoover in its final paragraph: "The country is crying aloud for courageous national leaders who will formulate plans for using the nation's credit economically and effectively instead of star gazing and wondering why prosperity disappeared."[28]

The Chief fully expected that the Hoover administration would respond to his plan. As Hearst had reminded his listeners in his radio address, Hoover, as a presidential candidate, had "won many to his support [including Hearst himself] by the magnificent program of public improvements which he described as the main feature of his policy." All Hearst now asked him to do was to fulfill this campaign pledge. When Hoover, however, not only refused to endorse Hearst's recovery plan but paid it no attention whatsoever, the Chief lost his patience and began to turn on the president.

Two weeks later, Hoover committed what for Hearst was the unpardonable sin of approving a one-year moratorium on the repayment of European war debts. Instead of spending to put Americans back to work, he was, Hearst declared, taking money out of their pockets and giving it to Europe's bankers:

> I say that American taxpayers have enough taxes to pay on obligations they have already incurred, and that they should not be asked to pay any further the price of European war frenzy, and that any American politician who asks them to pay for past European wars or supply funds for future European wars should be impeached by the Congress of the United States and tried for treason to his people and his country. This plan for revision of war debts, with America paying the piper while war-mad Europe dances is purely a plan of international bankers, who make money through commissions out of spoliation of their countrymen.

Directly challenging the president, Hearst declared for Calvin Coolidge for the next president of the United States and hinted that if Coolidge were not available, he would throw his support to Franklin Roosevelt:

> The American people want a vigorous American in the White House, and they are going to have one — either a Coolidge or a Roosevelt. Not all the subsidies of foreign nations, lavishly spent in American politics by international bankers, are going to prevent American voters from electing the next time an American President who will stand staunchly for the interests of his own country and the welfare of his own people first, last and all the time.

From this moment on, seldom a day would pass without an attack by the Hearst papers on Hoover as incompetent, uncaring, and committed more to the welfare of the European economy than the well-being of his own people. On July 14, 1931, Winsor McCay's editorial-page cartoon figured the president as a bent old man in a dark suit, with his back turned on an endless "U.S. Bread Line," throwing a life raft labeled "moratorium" to a sinking Germany. The text of the adjoining editorial read, "Why Not Extend Economic Relief Here, Mr. Hoover?"[29]

The Chief was determined to let no occasion pass to demonstrate to the American public that Hoover was not on their side. In October, on returning from Europe, he directed Ed Coblentz in New York to "make well printed pamphlet of my first two letters from London against [debt] moratorium . . . please include my most recent article on Europe's endeavor to transfer war debt. Send to all members of Congress, governors of state, Mayors, Legislators." When the president called upon the churches in the fall of 1931 to do more for the unemployed and impoverished, Hearst reminded him caustically in a front-page editorial in all his newspapers that "conditions here at home are a Government problem; not merely a problem for churches and private charities. The American people do not want charity; they want work."[30]

§ 28 ೬

"An Incorrigible Optimist"

"W R. WAS AN INCORRIGIBLE OPTIMIST," Jack Neylan remembered, "the last man to believe in the Depression." While Hearst did not dispute the fact that millions of Americans were suffering, he refused to believe that there was anything fundamentally wrong with the economy. On December 23, 1931, as the nation prepared for the Christmas holidays, Willicombe telegrammed Hearst's editors with instructions that the "Chief would like all papers to avoid use of the word 'depression' as much as possible and certainly to avoid any emphasis on the depression." It was time, the Chief believed, to stop complaining and look ahead.[1]

Hearst's own spending and entertaining became more frantic, more spectacular, more lavish as the Depression worsened, as if to signal that he was too strong, self-reliant, and self-confident to be swayed by temporary economic dislocation. Through the early 1930s, he and Marion were well on their way toward becoming the new king and queen of Hollywood in place of Doug Fairbanks and Mary Pickford, whose reign was dissolving along with their marriage. (They were divorced in 1936.) The San Simeon guest lists continued to grow, limited only by the number of rooms on the hill. To accommodate additional guests and larger, more extravagant parties, Hearst ordered the completion of the eight new bedrooms under construction and laid plans for a Great Hall in the rear of Casa Grande. "I think this can be made the grandest hall in America," he wrote Julia Morgan in April 1932. "When this hall is not in use as a ballroom or a banqueting hall, it could be used to contain some of the important collections in cases in the middle of the room. We could also use a lot of armor there. . . . That is the scheme! Isn't it a pippin?" The letter was signed, "Your assistant architect."[2]

Even without the banquet hall/ballroom, which was never built, the Hearst-Davies weekends and parties were, according to the Hollywood gossip and historian Kenneth Anger, "the most extravagant the movie colony had ever seen; the Golden People grabbed at the chance of an invitation." The Chief outdid himself for birthdays — his and Marion's — for leave-takings and returns, and for Christmas and New Year's Eve.[3]

He and Marion did their Christmas shopping at San Simeon. Bullock's, I. Magnin's, and the other major Los Angeles department stores would send trucks full of possible presents to San Simeon, where they were unloaded and laid out on the floor of the Assembly Room. Marion and W. R. would go through the room carefully, picking and choosing the gifts they wanted to give that season.[4]

Come Christmas, Frances Marion remembered, "in that great baronial hall we called 'The Big Room,' there would be a towering pine with a mound of packages underneath. Cases of champagne would be brought up from the cellar and there were garlands of mistletoe hung overhead with wreaths of evergreen on the doors. . . . Mr. Hearst would have white deer brought up from the zoo and quartered on the tennis courts. They would have sleigh bells strapped on them and would jingle to the delight of the children. After dinner Mr. Hearst and Marion would pass out expensive presents. To one he would give a black pearl, to another a whole silver service, someone would get a diamond bracelet, emerald earrings, or some other thing of great beauty and value."[5]

The most famous parties were the masquerades Marion gave at her beach house or San Simeon to celebrate the New Year and W. R.'s birthday. Costumes were supplied by the Western Costume Company, which outfitted all the studios. "They would just call up and say, 'Send up a couple of costumers,'" King Vidor remembered. "I mean people, two or three, with trunks and trunks, racks of costumes, many more than were needed to costume the people there. So then you went up in the library. . . . and you'd go pick out your own costume. And it was very important that you did the best you could."[6]

On New Year's Eve 1932, Hearst and Marion held a "kids" masquerade at the Santa Monica beach house that was so extravagant even Louella Parsons felt obliged to make excuses and tell her readers that "the beauty of this party was that the costumes were inexpensive." Clark Gable came as a Boy Scout, Joan Crawford as Shirley Temple; Marion wore an incredibly short toddler's sun dress and a white bonnet.[7]

For Hearst's seventieth birthday, in April of 1933, the theme was the Old West; for his seventy-first, the guests came dressed in colorful Tyrolean peasant costumes. In the years to come, there were circus parties with a full-size merry-go-round from the Warner Brothers lot; a Forty-Niners party; Cowboy and Indian parties; a Civil War masquerade; a Midsummer Night's Dream party with a 125-piece orchestra supplied by Jack Warner; and a Your Favorite Movie Star party, where Gary Cooper came as Dr. Fu Manchu and Groucho Marx as Rex, the Wonder Horse.[8]

W. R. almost always dressed for the occasion — as President James Madison, a circus ringmaster, a Western gunslinger, a Tyrolean peasant — and always looked slightly ridiculous. Photographs taken at the parties show him in a jolly mood, feeding cake to his son Bill, posing next to Hedda Hopper, or standing for a picture with Irene Dunne, Bette Davis, and Louella.

Hearst's routine at San Simeon did not change significantly. According to his son Bill, Jr., W. R. usually rose "around ten or so. . . . He wore big silk nightgowns, heavy, heavy silk. And then in robes and slippers he'd paddle around. And he'd work in the morning . . . on the phone and make notes and stuff. Willicombe would send him in the mail."

Neither W. R. nor Marion appeared much before noon or had breakfast with their guests who assembled in the Morning Room, where staff took their orders. The food was served and eaten in the Refectory. "Breakfast was always just there. It was a buffet," Bill, Jr. remembered. "Boxes of cornflakes and cream and milk and sugar and honey and stuff on the tables. And then if you wanted eggs you just said what you wanted."[9]

Lunch was served, buffet style, at 2 P.M. in the Refectory, though once guests had filled their plates and taken their seats, they were attended by the butler. Colleen Moore recalled that both luncheon and dinner were served with the same "beautiful blue Venetian glass, Blue Willow china, paper napkins, and bottles of catsup, mustard, pickles, jellies, etcetera. I guess Mr. Hearst had to prove his place was a ranch after all. You know, we all used to wonder what became of the bottles and jars that were left half full at the end of the meal, because at the next meal there were always new ones, freshly opened."[10]

After lunch, Hearst's and Marion's guests were free to do as they pleased in the afternoon, though the Chief always tried to get them to go outdoors. Colleen Moore remembers gathering with friends in San Simeon sitting rooms before roaring fires, curled up in enormous sofas, to "gossip and talk, and pretty soon Mr. Hearst would come in. He would say, 'Come on now, get out and get the fresh air,' and he'd make us all go out and go horseback riding. It was just dreadful. Marion was terrified of horses, just terrified."[11]

For those like Marion and Colleen Moore who did not want to ride, there were card games and jigsaw puzzles — some of them specially designed by Parker Brothers — in the Assembly Room,[12] a library of books on the second floor, sunbathing on the terraces, swimming in the pools or at the beach at the bottom of the hill, visits to the zoo, and tennis, which had become something of a fad in Southern California in the 1920s. At San Simeon, almost everyone played. For those who arrived without the proper equipment, there were private dressing rooms near the courts with tennis rackets, shoes, and "whites" in every size. For the serious players, there were pros to hit balls with, including the champion Bill Tilden and the future champion Alice Marble. Tournaments were arranged for the weekends, with everyone involved as players or spectators. Hearst himself was an avid player and tried to take time out to play in the afternoon. Well into his seventies, with his Stetson on his head, he would stand in the middle of the court and expect his opponent to hit the ball back to him. He played with everyone — from actor Dick Powell to Alice Marble. As Joel McCrea recalled, the Chief "didn't run around much, but if he could reach the ball and hit it, he did."[13]

More than anything else, the Chief enjoyed talking about his art collections with anyone who was interested. Bill Apperson, the son of Hearst's cousin and ranch manager, Randolph Apperson, recalled in his oral history that when he showed an interest in the antiques and the paintings, Hearst, "was kind enough to give me some instruction, and to have discussions with me about it. Those were wonderful times down in the library on the second floor. . . . If there were other young people here with their families, they were always invited, so he'd have four or five of us together when he'd give these little lectures for us." Billy Haines, Marion's co-star in *Show People* who later became one of Hollywood's most important interior decorators, claimed that he learned most of what he knew from extended discussions with W. R. at San Simeon.[14]

Hearst also tried to find time to go horseback riding with his guests or take long walks or swim in his outdoor pool. Ilka Chase, who admitted in her autobiography that she had always found Mr. Hearst's presence "alarming," recalled the afternoon when "he scared me to death . . . in the swimming pool, where he looked like an octopus. . . . He dived in and came up quite near me, and the sight of his long head with the white hair plastered down over his brow by the water, and his strange light eyes gleaming on a level with my own, sent me thrashing to the far end of the pool."[15]

Hearst's favorite leisure activity was taking his guests on long horseback excursion-picnics to the far reaches of the ranch. Even in his seventies, the Chief loved nothing better than leading a party over miles and miles of trails, until they were all too tired to go on. "It really was a sadistic ride,"

King Vidor remembered. "He'd let people lie down for about fifteen minutes and then he'd say, 'Come on, up and at 'em! Let's go!'" Occasionally, he would take his guests on an overnight "picnic" to a specially chosen destination. These excursions were planned in advance with almost military precision. Cars loaded with food, ice, and champagne were sent ahead so that when the riders arrived at their location, there was a fully supplied minicamp waiting for them. "We went over the mountain," Eleanor Boardman remembered many years later. "It was a long way . . . We saw smoke coming up. When we got there they had a big bonfire going; there was a tent for every person with a card table and with a wooden floor. There was a screen door. And we slept. We went to bed early. Bright and early the next morning, he yelled 'Whoopee! Everybody up! I'm going down to that creek to clean that tooth.' Then we'd . . . get back into the same saddle again, a long trek home. . . . aching, hurting." That night, there'd be dancing "all around the dining room," with Hearst leading the way.[16]

Douglas Fairbanks, Jr., who was a regular guest at San Simeon, avoided these outings: "I was told that the discipline of the horseback riding was such that you always had to keep behind Mr. Hearst, that you could never ride on your own particularly. It was like a military parade, and I wasn't of the temperament that would take that. I had books to read, and there was water polo, in the pool."[17]

One of the few inviolable rules at San Simeon was that all the guests had to appear for cocktails at 7 P.M. in the Assembly Room. "The women wore dinner dresses, but the men did not wear dinner coats," Adela Rogers St. Johns recalled. "An awful lot of the men came in a hurry — they were actors and directors and big publishers. They didn't always have time to drag their dinner coats along. So that nobody who was traveling would ever be embarrassed, the men never saw Mr. Hearst in a dinner coat."[18]

While the guests awaited the arrival of their host and hostess, they drank their cocktails — no more than two per guest — did jigsaw puzzles, or chatted quietly. According to Merryle Rukeyser, the financial editor for the Hearst papers, one never knew when Hearst might appear: "Sometimes it would be nine, sometimes nine-fifteen, sometimes nine-thirty. In other words, if there was a calamity in New York, and he was on the phone, he wouldn't say, 'I can't talk to you, dinner's served.'"[19]

When the time came, the Chief and Marion would appear, god-like, from the wood paneling in the Assembly Room that concealed the entrance to their elevator. They entered the room together, then separated, each seeking out different guests or greeting newcomers. Though Hearst was unfailingly courteous, he did not easily suffer fools. If his guests had nothing to say or were pompous, he discreetly moved on. Gretchen Swinnerton, the wife of Jimmy Swinnerton, Hearst's old friend and a cartoonist from the early San Francisco days, remembered one evening when "the Carters, who owned Little Carter's Liver Pills, came up, and the old man drove W. R. nuts, practically. He was just a fuddy-duddy. . . . Mr. Hearst just didn't care for Carter's Liver Pills, I don't think. He wanted someone that he could talk to, who was more interesting on different subjects and things."[20]

Hearst remained in close contact with his eastern editors during cocktail hour and dinner. The "hotline" telephone in the Assembly Room, Adela Rogers St. Johns remembered, never stopped ringing. "The *American* would be beginning to go to bed, all morning papers would be approaching deadline, and whatever news would be breaking, and whatever decisions needed to be made about what to do, they would come through the phone to him, at that time."[21]

After cocktails, Hearst ushered his guests into the Refectory for dinner. It was Marion's job to arrange the place cards for the meal, but Hearst always changed them around. He and Marion sat facing one another in the middle of the long table, with their favored guests alongside them. "The longer you are there, the further you get from the middle," P. G. Wodehouse wrote a friend after his visit to the ranch. "I sat on Marion's right the first night, then found myself being edged further and further away till I got to the extreme end, when I thought it time to leave. Another day, and I should have been feeding on the floor."[22]

Although fine wines were always served at dinner, the waiters and the head butler, Albert, were instructed to watch carefully for signs of overindulgence. "If you gulped it down, four or five drinks at a time," Rogers St. Johns said, "you didn't get anymore. Albert had a weather eye, because if something went amiss Mr. Hearst would be very cross with him."[23]

The main course was generally red meat or fowl. "Poultry raised at the ranch included chickens, turkeys, pheasants, quail, guinea hens, partridges, geese and ducks. Hearst's favorite dish was pressed duck, cooked very rare and squeezed in a silver press." Much of what was eaten at the ranch was raised there, including all the vegetables and "nuts, oranges, lemons, grapefruit, tangerines, pears, apples, apricots, plums, peaches, nectarines, figs, and avocados. The estate also raised its own berries, persimmons, and kumquats." Hearst also received regular shipments of delicacies from San Francisco and Los Angeles, including lots of fresh fruits and vegetables, "Debeukelaer Cookies Mayfair Brand," which must have been a favorite as they were ordered often, and pounds of sausages, calf's liver, and sweetbreads. Willicombe regularly telegrammed an assistant in Los Angeles who telephoned the orders to Young's Market. The December 20, 1939, order, which Willicombe wanted sent out that evening, included "Xmas table decorations for 30 persons, 3 jars of anchovies, 24 crumpets, 6 pounds of prepared meats, 18 enchiladas, 12 tamales, 36 tortillas, 12 jumbo squabs, and 8 pieces of smoked Alaska cod, a brick of Kraft Old English, and a round of Roquefort."[24]

The food was prepared in a full-sized hotel-style kitchen, with a giant pressure cooker, a stockpot capable of making soup for sixty, three bread ovens, four regular ovens, a rotisserie, a griddle, a five-gallon ice cream freezer, a walk-in refrigerator to age meats from the cattle slaughtered on the ranch, and four walk-in vegetable coolers. The vegetables were topped with a simple Hollandaise sauce, the meat roasted or broiled and always served rare. "Hearst used to give me hell because I didn't like my meat raw," St. Johns remembered. "Roast beef, according to him, should be bright red, or you shouldn't eat it, and he used to scold me. I don't think I ever really sassed him back, but we had duck, and it was dripping. I said to him, 'This duck is going to walk right off your plate if you don't look out!' He said, 'Well that is the only way that it really tastes good.' And then he'd pour bottles of everything on God's earth on everything he ate!"[25]

Directly before and after dinner, there were games at the table and informal entertainments. "We played this game of 'who are they,' which was naming the initials, you did not have to say man or woman, of the silent movie stars," Alice Marble recalled. "And so we would go on all evening. This was a great dinner conversation thing, because all of these people were silent movie stars. . . . Everybody would have to get up and entertain. Mr. Hearst could yodel very well indeed. He always had his turn, and somebody told stories. Charlie Chaplin played his left-handed violin."[26]

The evening invariably concluded with Hearst and Marion leading their guests into the private theater for that evening's prerelease feature film that had been chauffeured up in the afternoon from Los Angeles and would be sent back on the midnight train from San Luis Obispo. There were fifty seats in the theater — with room for chairs in the rear for the help who came into the theater when they finished their work. Hearst and Marion sat up front. If the film was impossibly dull, Hearst, who had a direct line to the projectionist, would order up one of Marion's films, all of which were kept on hand.

Most of the guests retired after the film, though some played billiards or gathered in their sitting rooms to talk. Hearst went back to work. By the mid-1930s, he had centralized his work space in his Gothic Study on the third floor, where he worked at a library table under an arched ceiling, surrounded by almost 4,000 books, many of them first editions. It was here that he read his mail, looked over the day's newspapers, studied his catalogues, and dictated hundreds of telegrams: to MacGregor at the Bronx warehouse, his art dealers and agents, real-estate offices, newspaper publishers, magazine editors, political operatives and allies, movie executives, and his wife and children, wherever they might be.

Hearst's younger guests took his departure in his elevator as the signal they were waiting for to let loose. "When the cat was away the mice began to play and the young indulged in all sorts of harmless pursuits," David Niven recalled in his autobiography. "W. R. knew everything that went on and sometimes damage was extensive but nothing was said provided none of the three cardinal rules were broken — 'No drunkenness,' 'No bad language or off-color jokes,' and, above all, 'No sexual intercourse between unmarried couples.' This last was a strange piece of puritanism from a man living openly with his mistress, but it was rigorously enforced."[27]

Though Niven spent an evening at the ranch trying to find the "bedchamber" of the "very beautiful girl" who had driven up with him from Los Angeles, he was never caught and was invited back several times after this incident. Eleanor Boardman, one of Marion's closest friends, had no such luck. In her unpublished oral history of life at San Simeon, Adela Rogers St. Johns recalled the day when Marion "said to Eleanor Boardman and Harry D'Arrast [the film director whom Eleanor would later marry] 'You two have been misbehaving!' Well, they had been living together for some time. 'You have to go! I'll have the car here for you at five o'clock.' Then Eleanor Boardman turned to her and said, 'Look who's talking!' Marion said, 'If Mr. Hearst and I could marry, we would. That's the difference!'"[28]

The Chief tried to restrain his guests from drinking at the ranch. "He wasn't keen about people getting drunk and noisy," his son Bill, Jr. recalled. "If they made a scene of themselves in any way and if they were new, they wouldn't come again. There was a superstition, almost, that if they got stewed, let's say, or disgraced themselves that the next morning or that night when they returned to their room they'd find their bags packed, you know, which was the broad hint that they should leave the next day. . . . It was a running gag that you'd better watch yourself or you'd find your bags packed when you got back."[29]

Marion had been a heavy drinker since her teenage years in New York and, as she aged, found it harder and harder to hold her liquor. W. R. may have tried to limit her drinking by restricting that of his guests, but he failed — on both counts. Her friends and sisters, many of them heavy drinkers themselves, were expected to repay her hospitality by supplying her with liquor. "The smuggling of liquor became our daily pastime . . . It was fraught with suspense in which we used to dramatize W. R. as a spine-tingling bugaboo," Anita Loos recalled in her memoirs. "As soon as any houseguests arrived, a servant was waiting to unpack the luggage; bottles were confiscated, not to be returned until one's departure. But a well-placed bribe generally overcame that debacle."[30]

"There was one heartstopping occasion," David Niven wrote in his auto-biography, when Marion "opened her handbag upside-down during dinner and after a loud crash of broken glass, the unmistakable smell of Booth's gin rose from the stone floor . . . 'My new perfume,' she giggled nervously at W. R. He smiled indulgently across the table but the hurt and the fear were in his blue eyes."[31]

Hearst knew what was going on, but the most powerful publisher in the world was powerless when it came to saving the woman he loved. "When the drinking had got bad," Adela Rogers St. Johns remembered, "he used to have to watch her pretty closely . . . Marion, whom I adored, was an alcoholic. And we all knew it, and we all did our best about it. Like all alcoholics, she would go along quietly for some time and then suddenly this would all break loose. It was a great shame, it really was."[32]

Hearst played many roles in Hollywood, but the most peculiar perhaps was as its self-appointed moral watchdog. Though Hearst had spent his life opposing any form of press censorship, he had become an unrelenting critic of what he called "suggestive . . . and ultra-sex films." In June of 1933 and then again in October and the following July, he published signed editorials on the "demoralizing" effects of "sex pictures and crime pictures" on the American population; this at the same time that he was protesting any attempt by censors or the Hays Office to interfere with his own films.[33]

He was particularly outraged by the way film producers represented newspaper publishers and reporters on screen. In 1931, Warner Brothers released *Five Star Final,* with Edward G. Robinson playing an unscrupulous evening tabloid editor whose sensational exposés lead to tragedy. The Chief, who may well have seen the film as a direct assault on his papers' practices, directed a multidimensional attack that was so intense and effective that *Variety* commented on it at length in successive issues in November 1931. He was incensed, he wrote Jack Warner, with the "constant attacks upon the newspaper fraternity in films which portray reporters as drunkards and editors as unscrupulous rascals," especially at a time when the studios were importuning newspaper editors to support their campaign against censorship. *Five Star Final* was given negative reviews in all the

Hearst papers, and local editors, including Walter Howey in Boston, were deputized to call on their city officials and ask them to remove the film from the theaters. So powerful was the Hearst attack that two similar anti-press films in production were shelved.[34]

According to Colleen Moore, Hearst's power in the film community made him "as much of a legendary figure in Hollywood as D. W. Griffith. Although Mr. Hearst was a mild, even-tempered and congenial man, everyone was scared to death of him. He could even cow Louis B. Mayer, and that took some doing."[35]

He was not averse to using that power to help his and Marion's favorites. When Marion found out that Joel McCrea's option was not being picked up at MGM, she told Hearst about it. According to McCrea, Hearst appeared totally uninterested in the news. The next morning McCrea, who was at San Simeon, was handed a Western Union telegram directing him to return to Hollywood to see Louis B. Mayer at his office at MGM. At their meeting, Mayer blamed Thalberg for not re-signing McCrea and offered him a new contract with a $250 a week raise. "He stood up, came over and shook hands and said, 'You're an all-American boy.'" Later that day, McCrea was shown a carbon copy of the telegram that had changed Mayer's mind: "Dear Louis: I understand you just dropped an all-American boy named Joel McCrea. In my business . . . we never signed anyone under contract unless we thought they had possibilities. And we never let them go until we explored and found whether they did or not. Joel McCrea has never had a chance." It was signed William Randolph Hearst.[36]

Hearst had a soft spot for all-American, all-California cowboy types like McCrea. According to more than one San Simeon informant, after hearing Roy Rogers perform with the Sons of Pioneers at San Simeon, he decided that Roy, too, should be in movies.[37]

The Chief's primary energies in Hollywood were, as always, devoted to Marion. The most popular starring vehicles in the early 1930s for actresses of Marion's age, especially at MGM, were what the *Motion Picture Herald* referred to as "sin and succeed" pictures. The innocent childlike stars of the Mary Pickford silent era had been replaced by exotic sirens like Greta Garbo and Marlene Dietrich, and homegrown bombshells like Mae West and Jean Harlow. Even Norma Shearer, Mrs. Irving Thalberg, had graduated — if that is the right word — to adult "fallen women" dramas like *The Divorcee,* for which she won an Academy Award, and *A Free Soul,* in which she played Clark Gable's mistress. If Davies were to continue developing as an actress, she too would have to leap into roles which, in Molly Haskell's words, displayed her sexuality "front and center."[38]

Irving Thalberg, who had faith in Marion's versatility as an actress, believed that she could make the necessary transition and proposed that her next film be based on a Fannie Hurst story about a dime-store heiress who bore a striking resemblance to Barbara Hutton. Hearst reluctantly agreed, if only because he trusted Thalberg's taste and Fannie Hurst's stories. He changed his mind as soon as he read the script. "I do not think I made myself clear about *Five and Ten*," he wrote Louis Mayer in March of 1931. "I think Marion has great qualities as a comedienne and a character actress. I do not think she has any special qualities as a sex or sophisticated actress. . . . I think Marion should stick to her line; and I think that if you and Irving do not think her line has any chance at the Metro studios, you ought to tell her so frankly and let her either retire or go somewhere else if anybody else wants her."[39]

Had Hearst been able to come up with an alternative property for Marion, he might have been able to resist Thalberg indefinitely, but as he preferred not to let Marion remain idle for too long, he reluctantly approved the script of *Five and Ten*, complete with love scenes and adulterous romances. Marion, who had seen Leslie Howard on Broadway, selected him as her leading man, only to discover when he arrived at San Simeon for rehearsals that he was several inches shorter than she was. They spent three weeks rehearsing in a tiny theater at San Simeon — with Howard perched on a platform for their closeups — and Hearst watching in the back. As usual, he was convinced that Marion needed him, not only to choose her projects, but to rewrite her scripts and rehearse with her. "He would coach me, and we'd go over the scripts line by line," Marion recalled in her memoirs. "When I'd see him with a pencil, I'd say, 'Oh, Lord, don't change it. I've got it memorized.'

"He'd say, 'This little change won't bother you.'

"We'd rehearse it, and it would throw me off a bit. Lots of times he'd sit on the set, which would make me a little nervous."[40]

Five and Ten was released in July of 1931. Although the conventional wisdom, held by those who have not seen Miss Davies' films, is that W. R. did not permit her to be kissed on the lips, in *Five and Ten* she spends several scenes locked in awkward embrace with Mr. Howard. The only real passion displayed in the film, however, is in her kiss-and-fondle scenes with the actor who played her Hearst-aged father.

Hearst had been correct in predicting that audiences were not going to accept Marion Davies in a Jean Harlow hairdo and role. *Five and Ten* lost $274,000, more than any other film Marion had starred in.

In her next project, chosen by Hearst, Marion reverted to form and starred in an old-fashioned, sentimental drama, *Polly of the Circus,* in which she played a circus aerialist who falls in love with the Reverend John Hartley, played by Clark Gable. *Polly of the Circus* was released in February of 1932 and, with the assistance of Gable's charm as a leading man, turned a profit of $20,000, not much, but enough to confirm Hearst's conviction that he was a better judge of properties than either Mayer or Thalberg.[41]

All that spring, there were phone calls, meetings, and letters back and forth about Marion's next film. The Chief alternately cajoled and threatened Mayer and Thalberg to find a suitable starring role for Marion — or else. "I think Marion is one of your greatest stars and one of your most loyal ones. She has, of course, considered going elsewhere; but she has never GONE, and almost EVERY company has tried to get her to go. Her loyalty and ability ENTITLE her to big pictures. . . . In fact, Louis, we are not interested in little pictures any more. If we cannot have big ones, we might just as well go abroad and have a good time." Still smarting over *Five and Ten,* W. R. warned Mayer again that "Marion cannot do sex pictures. She does not look like a vampire. But she is marvelous in boy's parts . . . She is excellent as a waif . . . She does a fine college girl . . . She does inimitable characterizations . . . She is good as just a fresh American girl . . . and she is good in a sentimental story. Good Heavens, Louis, if this is so — and you know it is — she does not HAVE to do sex pictures; and your folks ought surely to find plenty of important stuff for a star of that ability and versatility to do. Do you not think so?"[42]

Marion was not without her champions at MGM, and, despite Hearst's fears, Mayer and Thalberg were among them, as was Frances Marion, the top screenwriter in Hollywood at the time, with two gritty Depression-era dramas, *The Big House* and *The Champ,* both huge commercial and critical triumphs, to her credit. Frances Marion, who was well aware of Davies' talents, had written a realistic, Depression-era, rags-to-riches drama for her about a chorus girl from the tenements. It was called *Three Blondes.* Hearst was so enthusiastic about the scenario that he wrote King Vidor to ask him to direct. Vidor liked the script, but had to turn down the project because of scheduling conflicts.

Three Blondes, Hearst was convinced, would establish Marion as the star of the 1930s. But changes were necessary. The script was too gritty, too hard-edged, with too many "rude awakenings." While he had more respect for Frances Marion than anyone else in the business, Hearst would not let her script alone. She resisted as long as she could, then left the project, claiming illness. In her place, Thalberg hired a new set of writers, including

Anita Loos, to punch up the dialogue for what would eventually be released as *Blondie of the Follies*.[43]

Film is a collaborative craft, but there were too many collaborators on this picture. Thalberg wanted a role for Jimmy Durante, Hearst wanted Marion to appear in every scene, Anita Loos wanted more humor, and Frances Marion had insisted her friend Zasu Pitts be given a part. The result was a hopelessly overplotted film. Marion again did a creditable job as Blondie, the slum girl who, with the help of a playboy admirer played by Robert Montgomery, gets a job with the *Follies* and then becomes the live-in lover of a Hearst-aged millionaire. As in most of Marion's recent films, the picture piled up such huge expenses it was impossible for it to make a profit, even if it had found an audience, which it did not.[44]

Unwilling to risk alienating Hearst and unable to think of any solution to the "Marion" problem, Thalberg and Mayer let him have his way on her next three films. In *Peg o' My Heart*, the "star," now in her middle thirties, played the teenaged daughter of a poor Irish fisherman in a Hearstian musical costume drama. The film, one of W. R.'s favorites, made a tiny profit.

To boost the box office for Marion's next musical, *Going Hollywood*, MGM borrowed Bing Crosby from Paramount. In Crosby, Marion found an actor who liked to drink almost as much as she did. With Crosby and Marion drunk a good deal of the day and hung over every morning, the shooting dragged on interminably. The film took six months of studio time, after several weeks of rehearsal at San Simeon.

In his autobiography, Crosby claimed that although he showed up on the set every morning at 9 A.M., Marion seldom appeared before 11. With her came an "entourage of hairdressers, make-up ladies, secretary and — a holdover from the silent days — a five-piece orchestra . . . to keep things lively and to entertain her between shots." At noon, after no more than an hour's work, Crosby and Davies repaired to her bungalow for a formal luncheon which "dawdled on until two-thirty. Then we went back to the set . . . About three the orchestra would launch into a few more *divertissements*. At five, we'd be ready to shoot the scene when Marion would suggest something refreshing. Nobody was ever loath, so, thus restored, we'd get the scene shot and start thinking about the next scene." According to Marion, W. R. not only permitted, but seemed to encourage such eccentricities. "He used to coax us not to work. I think he thought it was a waste of time. . . . W. R. didn't worry about the budget. He'd even call the set about a quarter to five and say it was time to quit. He'd be lonesome. He'd say, 'You've been working all day' — not knowing we'd done only one scene."[45]

By the time *Going Hollywood* was booked into New York City's Capitol Theater as the MGM Christmas special for 1933, it had run up costs of $914,000 to become one of the studio's most expensive films. Even with Crosby as its co-star, *Going Hollywood* lost over a quarter of a million dollars. Time was running out on Marion's career, as everyone except Hearst seemed to realize. Seven of her last nine films had lost an average of $175,000 each; her two hits had earned a total of $40,000.

Unwilling to put Marion into "sophisticated sex films" or light comedies, the Chief turned back to historical costume drama, the genre in which he and his star had originally made their mark. Marion's next film — and her last at MGM — was *Operator Thirteen,* in which she played an actress who becomes a spy and disguises herself as a mulatto. Gary Cooper was borrowed from Paramount to co-star.

For the first time in her screen career, Marion, alternating between blond actress and "dark-face" mulatto, looked ridiculous. Aside from some exciting Civil War battle scenes, which Hearst supervised, the film had little to hold the attention of the audience. *Operator Thirteen,* which cost almost as much as *Going Hollywood,* also lost a quarter of a million dollars.[46]

This would be Marion's and Hearst's final film at MGM. They had resigned with MGM in 1929 because they trusted Irving Thalberg's judgment more than that of anyone else in the business. But Thalberg was a sick man with a weak heart, as everyone in Hollywood knew. On Christmas Eve 1932, he suffered a serious heart attack, and in February sailed, probably on Hearst's advice, to Bad Nauheim, to recuperate at the Chief's favorite spa. When Thalberg returned to work, in July of 1933, it was as one of several "unit producers" at MGM. He would no longer supervise Marion's films from scripting through production. Worse yet, Hearst, unwilling to accept any other explanation for Marion's failures at the box office, suspected that with Mayer's connivance, Thalberg had begun to devote his limited energies to promoting his wife Norma Shearer's career, to the detriment of Marion and the other MGM stars. When Shearer was given the role of Elizabeth Barrett Browning in the screen version of *The Barretts of Wimpole Street* and then, less than a year later, chosen to play Marie Antoinette in the screen version of Stefan Zweig's biography, Hearst's suspicions were confirmed.

On November 1, 1934, Louella Parsons broke the news of what she considered "by far the most important motion picture deal of the year, in fact in many years." Hearst and Marion had left MGM for Warner Brothers. Jack Warner, in announcing the new arrangement between Warner Brothers and Cosmopolitan Productions, had praise for Marion Davies' talents as an actress and for William Randolph Hearst whom he and his brothers regarded "as the most important and uplifting influence, not only in the journalistic field, but also in the motion picture industry."[47]

The day after the contract signing Joe Willicombe telegrammed George Young, the publisher of the *Los Angeles Examiner:* "Chief says, the moving picture connection of the Hearst institution from now on is the Warner Brothers Studio. Anything that you can do to help Warner Brothers will be appreciated."[48]

§ 29 &

The Chief Chooses a President

On the evening of January 2, 1932, the Chief drove from Marion's beach house to Station KFI in Los Angeles to deliver a well-advertised national radio address. The topic was "Who Will Be the Next President?"

It was a foregone conclusion that Hoover would not be reelected. The only question was which Democrat would succeed him. The party had united behind New York Governor Al Smith in 1928, but the liberal/conservative split that had divided the Democrats since William Jennings Bryan's first run for the presidency in 1896 had not been entirely healed. The Bryanite/Progressive candidate with the most support in 1932 was Governor Franklin Delano Roosevelt of New York. Among the stop-Roosevelt candidates were Al Smith, Governor Albert Ritchie of Maryland, Newton Baker, Woodrow Wilson's secretary of war and now a successful corporate lawyer, and Owen D. Young, the chairman of the board of General Electric. Although Roosevelt represented the positions that Hearst had advocated all his life and had been promoted in the Hearst press as a potential presidential nominee after his reelection in 1930, neither Roosevelt nor anyone else knew whom Hearst was going to anoint as his candidate.[1]

Instead of speaking of the Depression or discussing the candidates' programs or qualifications, Hearst began his radio address with a history lesson: "In 1912 Champ Clark, a distinguished and a genuine Democrat, came before the Democratic Convention at Baltimore with the support of a popular majority." But the Democrats, Hearst went on, chose Woodrow Wilson instead. His politics not only led the nation into war, but cost the Democratic party its leadership in the nation. Hearst urged the Democratic party and the nation to learn something from history and in 1932 nominate a "sound and sincere" Democrat like Champ Clark instead of a visionary internationalist like Woodrow Wilson. His candidate was "John N. Garner,

Speaker of the House of Representatives . . . a loyal American citizen, a plain man of the plain people, a sound and sincere Democrat; in fact, another Champ Clark. His heart is with his OWN PEOPLE. His interest is in his OWN COUNTRY. . . . Unless we American citizens are willing to go on laboring indefinitely merely to provide loot for Europe, we should personally see to it that a man is elected to the presidency this year whose guiding motto is 'America first.' . . . Seldom in the whole history of the nation has the selection of a good AMERICAN for president been so important to the people as it is today. God guide us to choose wisely, so that this year of grace 1932 may be a happy New Year for us all."[2]

John Nance Garner, the congressman from Texas with the ruddy face and short-cropped white hair, must have been taken by surprise, like the rest of the nation, by Hearst's endorsement. In his long tenure in the House, Garner had given few speeches and sponsored little legislation, but he was well respected among his colleagues, though generally unknown outside of Washington and Texas. As a "dry," an unknown, and an uncommitted and unenthusiastic candidate to boot, he stood little chance of getting the nomination.

Before Hearst could even address these difficulties, he had to stop the Roosevelt bandwagon. Two days after his radio address, the Chief wrote Edmond Coblentz — the balding, bespectacled editor who had worked for him since the turn of the century and was now managing editor of the *New York American* — to gather evidence of Roosevelt's past support for Wilsonianism. "Please put men on this work that are accustomed to going through library files." Coblentz found what Hearst wanted and forwarded to San Simeon excerpts from Roosevelt's acceptance speech for the Democratic vice-presidential nomination in 1920. Armed with Coblentz's research, Hearst published a series of front-page editorials in January, citing Roosevelt's 1920 advocacy of American entry into the League of Nations as proof of his "internationalism" and criticizing him for not using the word "AMERICAN" enough in his speeches.[3]

Hearst found it easier to attack Roosevelt than to elicit any enthusiasm for Garner — even, it appeared, among his own editors. "Chief is very much interested in Garner," Willicombe reminded all Hearst editors and publishers in telephone messages delivered on January 23, 1932. "It is not merely a personal interest. He feels that it would be a great thing for our country to have for president someone who was primarily interested in America. Chief says he would be very much obliged if you could find means of helping Garner among the politicians of your state and neighboring states. He says he would like you wherever you can to send correspondents or political friends into neighboring states to help Garner, and he says he would also welcome letters from you from time to time stating how matters are progressing in Garner's interest, and what you are planning to do further."[4]

Several of Roosevelt's supporters, including Colonel Edward House, Wilson's former chief adviser, James Farley, the leader of the New York State Democratic party, Mayor James Curley of Boston, and Joseph P. Kennedy, tried to convince Hearst that Roosevelt was not and had never been a Wilsonian, but the attempts backfired when Hearst demanded in an editorial published in his newspapers on January 22 that the governor stop playing political "shell games." "I beg leave to say that if Mr. Roosevelt has any statement to make about his not now being an internationalist, he should make it to the public publicly and not to me privately. My experience has proved that a man who is running for office, and is not willing to make his honest opinions known to the public, either has no honest opinions or is not honest about them."

Roosevelt was trapped. If he placated Hearst, he would offend the Wilsonians in the party; if he did not, he would lose the support of the nation's most powerful Democratic publisher. On January 30, 1932, Louis Howe wrote to urge Roosevelt "to be sure and telephone Hearst." Howe had heard from friends in Atlanta that the publisher had succeeded there in "making some trouble in his violent attacks on you on the international subject. You may have to make a public statement before we get through, if this thing gets any more violent."[5]

Three days later, in a speech to the New York State Grange, Roosevelt publicly declared that he no longer favored "American participation" in the League of Nations and castigated "the European nations for indulging in an orgy of spending and not meeting their just obligations to the United States, the payment of war debts."[6] Roosevelt's conversion to Hearst's foreign policy came too late to satisfy the Chief. "Despite his rather feeble denial," Hearst wrote one of his editors, he was convinced that Roosevelt was "at heart an internationalist and that keeps me from being for him . . . I do not want anything except to see progressive democrat and good American named. I will not vote or work for reactionary or internationalist."[7]

All through January and February, the Chief sent off a steady stream of telegrams to his editors urging them to do more for the Speaker. When it appeared that Garner was unprepared or unwilling to file for the Nebraska primary, Hearst's operatives did it for him. The Chief's task was complicated by Garner's refusal to campaign on his own or cooperate with Hearst's team. "I have to work in dark with little or no information from

Washington," Hearst telegrammed Victor Watson, an editor in New York. "The reason is that our friend refuses to talk politics or devote any attention to any campaign or allow any manager to be appointed to coordinate efforts being made in his behalf. Consequently if we want to accomplish anything for him we have got to do it ourselves and in our own way . . . If Garner gets in the way he will be run over by his own boom. The people do not care what he wants. It is a question now of what they want."[8]

As Garner refused to organize his own campaign, the Chief did it for him: "There is just one way to carry the situation for Garner and that is by radio. If you can have right kind of people talk over radio and over various radios if you can get them, it will have great political effect."[9]

In the end, Hearst's support — in print and on the radio — was enough to make Garner a credible candidate and secure victory for him in the California primary. Combined with delegate support in his home state of Texas, and in Illinois, where Hearst also exercised enormous political clout, Garner amassed over one hundred delegates.

The Roosevelt camp was not worried that Garner would take the nomination, but that with a hundred delegates he would be able to deny Roosevelt a two-thirds majority, stalemate the convention, and force the party to turn to a dark-horse candidate like Newton Baker. Joseph P. Kennedy, who had known Hearst since the early 1920s when he tried to enlist him in a joint film venture, visited San Simeon in April to plead the case for Roosevelt. Kennedy warned Hearst, as had Mayor Curley and Jim Farley before him, that "Wall Street interests" were plotting to repeat the strategy they had used in 1924. They intended to deny Roosevelt, who already had a majority of the delegate votes, the two-thirds needed for nomination and then impose their own conservative candidate, either Al Smith or Newton Baker, on the convention.[10] Hearst listened but refused to commit himself to Roosevelt.

On June 30, at 4:28 in the morning, the roll of the delegates was called at the Democratic National Convention in Chicago. Roosevelt had a clear majority, but was one hundred votes short of the two-thirds he needed for nomination. Two more ballots were taken, but Roosevelt made up only eighteen of the votes he needed. Finally, after four hours of balloting, the convention adjourned. Their worst-case scenario unfolding before their eyes, Roosevelt's advisers were close to panic, fearful that if the governor wasn't nominated on the next ballot, the party would turn elsewhere.

All night long, the Roosevelt camp tried to reach Hearst by telephone. Joe Kennedy got through early in the morning, and was able to convince Hearst that if he did not release the delegates pledged to Garner, the conservative party leaders would succeed in using the threat of a deadlocked convention to thwart the role of the majority and nominate a candidate like Newton Baker. "I felt that there was nothing to do," Hearst later wrote Millicent, "but communicate with Speaker Garner and tell him the truth about the whole situation. He responded nobly. So we threw California and Texas, and by means of Mayor Cermak [of Chicago], Illinois also into the Roosevelt column and Governor Roosevelt was nominated." Few were surprised when Roosevelt chose Garner to be his running mate.[11]

The Chief took full credit for Roosevelt's nomination, though it is likely that the governor's first-ballot strength was such that he would in the end have secured his two-thirds vote without Hearst's intervention. Millicent, with whom he had been in touch throughout the campaign, was among the first to congratulate him on his victory. "Hope Roosevelt will realize how he got his nomination," she telegrammed him on July 2. "It was a great piece of strategy on your part . . . All send love."[12]

W. R. responded with a long letter, asking Millicent to carry a message for him to the nominee:

> I don't know how well you know Governor Roosevelt or Senator Farley, but if you know them well enough to consult with them as to how Roosevelt can best be elected, I wish you would do so. I am very anxious to see him elected. I am probably more of a Roosevelt man than any one imagines . . . I will work everywhere for him, in our papers and over our radios and in the newsreels. . . . I have some ideas and would like to submit them. First, I think the less debate we have in the campaign the better . . . I think the old-fashioned American way of a candidate retiring to his estate and allowing his friends to make his campaign for him is full of impressive dignity. . . . Second, I think — and this is important — that Governor Roosevelt has all the radical support that there is. He cannot gain any more by being additionally radical. What he needs is the support of certain conservative elements which should legitimately come to him. . . . Of course I am not suggesting any modification of policies. I never modify my own policies and I am the last man to suggest modification of policy to another person. But I think Governor Roosevelt is in fact properly conservative and I think that the reactionaries are the dangerous radicals.[13]

The Chief took every presidential election seriously, but he was particularly concerned with the outcome of this one. He feared — and he was not alone in having such fears in July of 1932 — that Herbert Hoover, pushed and pulled by Wall Street financiers, international bankers, and profit-hungry, shortsighted businessmen, might very well drive the nation's working people and farmers to the brink of rebellion by increasing their burdens and ignoring their pain. Those fears were exacerbated when, in July of 1932, Hoover called on the army to drive out the twenty-five thousand veterans who had marched on Washington in May and June to demand early payment of the bonuses that were due in 1945. Hearst had long been in support of the demands of the Bonus Marchers and was outraged when Hoover permitted General Douglas MacArthur to chase them from the nation's capital — with tear gas and drawn sabers — and burn down their encampments on the Anacostia Flats across the Potomac.

"I do not care if every paper in the United States comments favorably on Hoover's action," the Chief telegrammed Ed Coblentz in New York:

> I think it was the most outrageous piece of stupidity, if nothing worse, that has ever been perpetrated by the government. If the idea is to develop Bolshevism in this country, there is no better way of doing it. Certainly the action of the government cannot be excused or explained, if it had any other purpose in mind. . . . That is the way I feel about it, and I think our editorials should temperately express that view. . . . I feel like mourning not only the death of the veterans, but mourning the passing of American sentiment and democratic principles. I am afraid this despotic action on the part of the Government will tend to precipitate further conflict between Communism and Fascism which is already developing in the country and which threatens to eliminate the patriotic and Republican principles on which this nation was built.[14]

Hearst had become more and more of a conservative as he aged, for the very simple reason that he had more and more to conserve. He had sincerely meant what he had told Millicent in his letter, that he was a Roosevelt man because Roosevelt was "properly conservative and . . . the reactionaries . . . the dangerous radicals." As long as centrists like Roosevelt remained in control of the federal government, American democracy and capitalism would remain safe. The greatest threat to the future was not from the Left which remained weak and unorganized, but from reactionaries like Hoover who, in their insensitivity to the legitimate interests of America's working peoples, were pushing them into the arms of the Bolsheviks.

From July to November, the Hearst papers attacked Hoover so effectively that they literally frightened him into silence. When in late July Secretary of War Stimson suggested that the president give a speech commending the Kellogg-Briand Pact as a tool to safeguard the peace in Asia, where the Japanese had invaded Manchuria, Hoover vetoed the idea because he was worried about Hearst's editorial reaction. That evening, a disconsolate Stimson wrote in his diary that the president had become so frightened of Hearst that he was "bringing down the record of his Administration . . . to the pattern of what Hearst is going to say about it. That is what made me sad."[15]

While denigrating Hoover in print, Hearst promoted the Roosevelt candidacy in all his media outlets, including his newsreels. As Jane Collings has noted in her dissertation, images of a smiling, confident Roosevelt became a staple of the Hearst Metrotone newsreels:

> Campaign period segments would show FDR sitting casually outdoors in a wicker chair with his campaign manager, swimming with his grandchildren, or introducing his family to newsreel viewers — and letting his little granddaughter announce that the campaign's song was "Happy Days Are Here Again." While Hoover might be shown in a long shot, in a long black coat at a public event, FDR would be shown yachting under a voice-over announcing, "Rough or smooth — it's all the same to the governor who faces another journey on the stormy seas of politics."[16]

The message was transparent: here was a leader, an activist, a healthy, vibrant grandfather who would shepherd the nation to prosperity.

The campaign was running smoothly, but Hearst refused to take any chances. "I think no disaster could happen in this country as great as reelection of Hoover," he wrote Arthur Brisbane in late September. Three weeks before Election Day, from his hospital bed in Cleveland, where he was recuperating from a minor throat operation, Hearst directed Joe Willicombe to send Joe Kennedy a $25,000 check and ask that it be delivered to the Democratic national campaign fund "with Mr. Hearst's request that it be used for radio campaigning."

The campaign not only solidified Hearst's connection with Roosevelt, but with Kennedy as Hearst's conduit to Washington. Hearst's contribution, Kennedy informed him by return mail, was so large it had been matched by only two others: "I realize that this check coming to the Committee through me helps a great deal in having consideration [given] to any suggestion that I might want to make. You may rest assured, and this I want to say in order to go on record, that whenever your interests in this administration are not served, my interest has ceased."[17]

Franklin Delano Roosevelt was elected president on November 8, 1932. "I congratulate you on the greatest fight of your life," Jack Neylan wrote Hearst from San Francisco, "God Bless You. The American people will thank you some day." From New York came an almost identical telegram from Millicent. "You must be very happy and delighted today at this great victory. It certainly has been a great surprise to everybody here. I saw Roosevelt last night. He said he was going to telephone you. You are getting all the credit for this victory from everybody I meet."[18]

The Chief returned to California after his operation, in good health and better spirits. "What in Hades is the matter with your fellows, Roy," he telegrammed Roy Howard, the head of the United Press, after a U.P. reporter had called San Simeon to ask if Hearst had "passed on." "A couple of months ago I had a small operation about as important as having your tonsils removed and today one of your myrmidons telephoned up to ask me if I was dead. I had to leave a tennis game to tell this gink that I was alive and then I do not think he believed it. Now Roy stop this damned nonsense. I have never been sick in my life nor dead either. Moreover if you want to participate in a little light humor I will bet you one thousand dollars that I attend your funeral."[19]

The Chief had good reason to feel giddy. He had, after almost two decades in exile, come home again to the Democratic party. On November 14, just six days after the election, W. R. telegrammed Joe Kennedy with advice for the president-elect. He urged Roosevelt, who would not be inaugurated for another five months, to lay low and refrain from cooperating with Hoover on an interim recovery plan:

> Do not let the incumbent unload on our friend any part of his unpopularity or any part of the responsibility for those things which cause his unpopularity. I think it far better for our friend to go into office with a clean slate and with an impressive program for meeting the conditions which are then before him than it is to make some compromise program with the present incumbent which might deprive our friend of part of his prestige and of the opportunity to make the most of his great victory.[20]

Hearst also began forwarding to Kennedy his suggestions for Roosevelt's cabinet. He expected to play a major role — as unofficial senior adviser — to the president-elect and was apparently put off when Roosevelt declined to respond directly to his suggestions. Kennedy, his link to the president-elect, was also put in an uncomfortable position when Roosevelt neglected to follow through on his promise and invite Hearst to New York for private talks. In late December, Kennedy wrote Hearst to apologize for not having come West to see him while he recuperated from his throat operation. Declaring that his first loyalties were to the Chief, not the president-elect, Kennedy claimed that he was no longer in direct contact with Roosevelt: "My interest in politics and national affairs has not ceased. My contact ceased from the day a certain gentleman neglected to send a telegram to you urging you to come to New York which he told me he would do. In spite of my very close connections during the campaign I have never seen him from that day to this."[21]

The Chief's response was rather measured. He was, he telegrammed Kennedy, sending him "an opinion" on the cabinet through Ed Coblentz:

> I don't want to be intrusive but you said that distinguished gentleman wanted me to come East to express such views as I have. Therefore I thought an occasional view on something immediate which would not wait on my visit might not be amiss. If you think it would not be well received do not present it. I can always express my opinions through the papers. My only object in submitting them to him personally is the hope of being of some service. I believe it to be of immense importance to the nation that this Democratic administration should be successful. Therefore I am going as I told you [to] go to great lengths to support him regardless of minor differences of opinion. Consequently if he does not agree with the suggestions I submit I will in no sense be offended but in the hope of sometime submitting something of value will continue to give him my most careful thought, provided he so desired.[22]

There was nothing particularly radical in the eleven-point program the Chief presented to Roosevelt and began publishing daily on his editorial pages. He advocated a "Buy American and Spend American" campaign, increased tariffs, a larger merchant marine, the expansion of American air fleets and transcontinental railways, the completion of east-west and north-south automobile highways, and internal improvements of the nation's waterways and harbors.[23]

The centerpiece of his recovery program was, for the time being at least, his "Buy American" campaign. As Dana Frank has written in *Buy American:*

> Every day for two months, beginning December 26, the front pages of [Hearst's] twenty-seven newspapers trumpeted at least one, and often three or four, Buy American stories. Every day he wrote an editorial praising the idea. Every day he inserted the Buy American concept into smaller stories throughout his papers. His Hearst Metrotone News Service, meanwhile, carried the message into the nation's movie theaters. In one especially charming newsreel, entitled "Children Enlist to Aid 'Buy American,'" a bevy of endearing white children clutched American-made toys (including a black Mammy doll) and asked viewers to admire their "smart" American-made sailor suits. "My mother and dad say that everybody should buy American so lots of people will get jobs," a nervous little blond girl recited.[24]

Hearst was so committed to this campaign that he appeared in one of his newsreels to give his "Buy American" pitch. The footage was shot outdoors at San Simeon, with Hearst looking like a kindly grandfather, dressed warmly in hat and overcoat. To the accompaniment of military band music, the spot opened with the large block-lettered newsreel title, "'Buy American' to Help Prosperity says W. R. Hearst. Noted publisher launches nation-wide movement to aid U.S." The music ended, the title disappeared, and Hearst took up the screen, speaking confidently to the camera in his peculiarly high-pitched voice. Ironically for a "Buy American" campaign, the backdrop for his speech was the sixteenth-century Spanish wrought-iron door grille, which, with extensions made by Ed Trinkkeller, a Los Angeles artisan, stood at the front entrance of Casa Grande.[25]

In early January, Roosevelt invited Edmond Coblentz to his New York City townhouse to discuss Hearst's cabinet suggestions and his eleven-point program. The president-elect, Coblentz wrote the Chief after their meeting, was "very earnest in his expressed desire to talk with you personally, and suggested that you come to Warm Springs between the 20th of this month and the 4th of February, where he said he could confer with you at leisure and without interruption. . . . He thought you could come by way of New Orleans to Warm Springs and thus avoid any risk of running into cold weather. If I may be permitted to say so and if your personal affairs do not stand in the way, I feel you would be accomplishing a great good for the nation by acceding to his request. He said that he would have his plans on paper and would like to discuss them with you in detail.

"Unquestionably," Coblentz continued, "you would be able to crystallize many of his policies, which to me at present seem in a rather vague and nebulous state. You could give direction and force to many of his ideas. I think he needs your advice and I think the country would benefit by your personal contact with him."[26]

Hearst replied, in a note to Roosevelt, that while he was "sincerely anxious to make the trip East," his "tyrannical doctor" refused to let him do so. Hearst continued:

I have been following your course very closely and think I have a good general idea of your plans; and I can assure you that I am in hearty accord with those plans as I understand them to be. Doubtless if I had gone East I could have done but little more than express my great gratification at the result of the election, and my earnest desire to be of service in support of your soundly Democratic ideas. I have written Mr. Coblentz of the *New York American* and our other editors to this effect, and when you . . . are in New York, I shall ask Mr. Coblentz to discuss with you the effective course for the papers to pursue.[27]

Hearst's letter to Roosevelt reveals a good deal about what the Chief wanted from his relationship with the president-elect. We don't know whether he declined to go East because his doctors had truly forbidden it or because he was piqued at FDR's delay in making the invitation. But he was now demanding closer ties with the president than he had had with the candidate. In return, he promised the full support of his communications empire.

Hearst's interest in the president-elect's recovery plan was more than academic. The effects of three years of economic downturn were beginning to hit home. Not even William Randolph Hearst was immune to the effects of the Depression. While the Chief continued to hope that the economy would, in due course, heal itself, he was running out of time. In December of 1932, Jack Neylan, his financial adviser and unofficial second in command, arrived at San Simeon to urge the Chief to retrench and cut salaries across the board. Hearst's initial reply was that he'd "rather go broke than do that." Neylan insisted that there was no other option. His publishing revenues had declined to the point where they were no longer sufficient to pay off the interest on his loans and mortgages and meet his payrolls and publishing costs. The only way to forestall bankruptcy was to reduce expenditures and institute an across-the-board wage cut. Frightened by Neylan's facts and figures, the Chief authorized him to proceed.[28]

Tom White, who was the general manager of the newspaper division, had not been consulted and tendered his resignation immediately (though he later withdrew it). White, born in Ireland, had emigrated at age fourteen with his mother who had come to Chicago in 1893 to sell lace at the World's Columbian Exposition. His first job with the Hearst organization was selling newsprint, but he had risen from there to become head of the magazine, and then the newspaper division. Hearst trusted him as much as anyone in the organization, and would in 1934 make him its first general manager.

White was furious at the size of the reduction — 39 percent — and at Neylan's decision to implement it forty-eight hours after announcing it. "If Mr. Hearst and you would only examine our payroll," White wrote Neylan, "you will find that, except for your stellar people who will be largely immune anyway . . . you can put on the fingers of two hands the people who could stand an adjustment such as I am starting out to-day to place on everybody who will take it."[29]

Cutting the payroll by nearly $7 million was a significant step away from bankruptcy, but, unfortunately, far from sufficient. Hearst refused to sell any assets and the banks would not lend him any more money, so Neylan had to raise new capital by selling more Hearst Consolidated stock to the public. When he suggested that Hearst's employees be directed to sell stock as part of their job descriptions, White was infuriated and protested to Hearst:

> Utilizing the members of your organization to sell stock in your company, rather than in the performance of the duties for which they are engaged, does not appear to be sound. Sending these people out to sell stock on the heels of a general salary cut seems to me to be inopportune. If they are good editors, reporters, circulation men, or advertising men, they are all the more likely to prove poor stock salesmen. If they are poor stock salesmen, they will not help your stock sales nor your credit.[30]

We don't know what, if anything, came of Neylan's suggestion that Hearst's employees be enlisted to sell stock. Whatever the outcome, Hearst remained in desperate need of cash to meet his debt payments. Neylan, convinced that the only way to raise this cash was by selling more Hearst Consolidated stock, proposed to advertise over the radio and asked for the Chief's assistance in getting "some cooperation from Messrs. Brisbane, Forbes, Rukeyser, and other high-priced financial writers. . . . May I suggest that you write Cobbie [Edmond Coblentz] a letter suggesting to him that he interview these gentlemen and find out if there is anything in the rule book against an appropriate dignified reference to the securities of the institution from which they draw their salaries, particularly in view of the fact that these securities were honestly priced in the first place and have been earning and paying the interest or dividends for which the purchaser contracted."[31]

In the desperately long winter between the election and the inauguration of Franklin Delano Roosevelt in March, Hearst did all he could to prepare the president-elect and the nation for the task of recovery that lay before them. Shortly after the election, he was asked by MGM if he was interested in having his Cosmopolitan Productions unit produce a political parable about an activist president who rescues America from a devastating Depression. Hearst was no stranger to the political uses of moving pictures. Although the films he had produced for Marion were devoid of overt political messages, he had fifteen years earlier produced *Patria,* one of the first and most powerful American propaganda films. Moving pictures, he knew, could teach lessons while they told stories.

The film he agreed to produce, *Gabriel over the White House,* was based on a novel by an adviser to Lloyd George. Brought to MGM by the producer Walter Wanger, it was the kind of uncompromising attack on American political institutions that only an English liberal could have written. It portrayed American politicians, without exception, as venal, dumb, and mendacious.

The picture, as scripted by Wanger and his writers, with major input from Hearst, opened with Jud Hammond, a good-looking, good-natured party hack played by Walter Huston, taking the oath of office as president of the United States. By brilliantly incorporating documentary footage into the opening montage, Wanger alerted viewers that what they were about to see was more "real" than most moving pictures.

Days after his inauguration, on a trip to the Naval Academy, President Hammond takes the wheel of his car, and playfully trying to outrun the press, pushes the speedometer toward 100, goes over an embankment, and is mortally injured. When he returns to consciousness — after the intervention of the angel Gabriel — Hammond has been transformed from a Warren Harding–like hack who speaks in Herbert Hoover–like platitudes to a man of Lincolnesque stature who sounds like a Hearst editorial. With Gabriel looking over him — and writing his Hearst-like speeches — the new president spurns his mistress, fires his cabinet, dismisses Congress, personally greets a Bonus Army that has marched to Washington looking for assistance, ends Prohibition, establishes a gigantic public works/employment program, threatens foreign governments with war if they will not pay their debts and disarm, declares martial law, launches a war on organized crime, and brings prosperity to the nation and peace to the world.

The first draft of the script was completed in January of 1933 and forwarded to the Hays Office for approval. James Wingate, Hays's primary censor, was stunned by its political audacity. Though the novel on which the film was based had placed the story in 1950, muting its political message, the script which Walter Wanger submitted was set in the present and clearly alluded to recent inflammatory political events and personalities. Wingate told Hays and Louis B. Mayer that there were problems with the script which had to be corrected before the film could be released. Mayer assured James Wingate that there was nothing to worry about because "neither he nor Mr. Hearst would want to do anything that would weaken the authority of government or cast reflection upon any national administration, present or incoming." He invited Wingate to a preview scheduled "next week in a nearby town" to view the film with Mayer and Mr. Hearst and have a conference with them the following morning.[32]

Wingate, in the meantime, forwarded his list of script changes to Irving

Hearst, Marion Davies, and Charlie Chaplin at a charity event at the
Olympic Stadium in Los Angeles, 1932 (*Bob Board Collection*)

The Refectory at
San Simeon in the
mid-1930s. Marion's
empty chair, pulled
out on the left, is
across the table
from Hearst.
(*Copyright © Hearst
Castle™/Hearst San
Simeon State Historical
Monument™*)

Charlie Chaplin and Marion, holding her dachshund, in the San Simeon movie theater, 1933 (*Courtesy, Kobal Collection*)

Hearst and Marion enjoying a stein of beer during their 1934 stay in Germany. The woman between them is probably Eileen Percy, a friend of Marion's. (*Courtesy, Academy of Motion Picture Arts and Sciences*)

Hearst and Marion at San Simeon (*Bob Board Collection*)

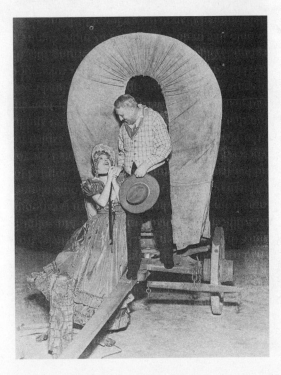

and at a Western
masquerade party,
1933 or 1934
(*Bob Board Collection*)

Hearst and Marion at Wyntoon, 1935

(*Copyright © Hearst Castle™/Hearst San Simeon State Historical Monument™*)

The Chief with one of his dachshunds (*Copyright © Hearst Castle™/Hearst San Simeon State Historical Monument™*)

Cutting the cake at the "circus" birthday party at Ocean House, 1937. Hearst is gazing across the room at Marion, in profile. (*Kimberly Lake*)

Hedda Hopper and
Hearst, dressed as James
Madison, at his seventy-
fifth birthday party, 1938
(*Courtesy, Academy of Motion
Picture Arts and Sciences*)

Hearst, Millicent, and their five boys at their last reunion at San Simeon, 1938
(*Courtesy, Bancroft Library, University of California, Berkeley*)

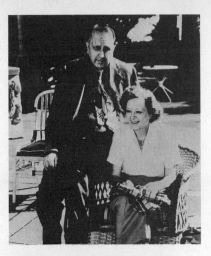

Hearst and Marion at San Simeon in
the mid-1940s (*Kimberly Lake*)

William Randolph Hearst, his son Bill, Jr., and his grandson,
William Randolph Hearst III, just before Hearst's death, 1951
(*Courtesy, Bancroft Library, University of California, Berkeley*)

Millicent Hearst, followed by George, Bill, Jr., John, Randolph, and David, leaving Grace Episcopal Cathedral after Hearst's funeral, August 15, 1951 (*San Francisco Examiner*)

Outside Grace Cathedral (*San Francisco Examiner*)

Thalberg, who was still in charge of production at the studio. "The preliminary portrayal of distressing conditions," Wingate wrote, "should be treated in such a way as not to overemphasize organized discontent. We, of course, feel nobody engaged in the industry would want to do anything that might foment violence against the better elements of established governments, particularly in these times of stress and unrest." As currently written, he doubted "whether any censor board would permit such outspoken vilification of existing governments."[33]

Thalberg assured Wingate that the script would be revised according to his specifications. Within weeks, he delivered a new draft to Wingate, which was still problematic. President Hammond's economic rehabilitation program, Wingate wrote Will Hays, still paralleled very closely the program laid down in the Hearst press.[34]

By March, news of the film — and Hearst's interest in it — had been leaked to the White House, where Roosevelt had the week before taken up residence. When Stephen Early, the president's press secretary, called Hays to express his concern, Hays, "in strictest personal confidence," assured the president that he was paying "personal preferred attention" to the matter and working closely with the studio.[35]

With the White House now involved, the stakes for MGM and the Hays Office were that much higher. Nick Schenck, who ruled the studio from New York, assured Early, as Hays had, that MGM was revising the script and that *Gabriel*, in its final version, would not only be acceptable to the White House, "but affirmatively serviceable. . . . You may be very certain that before the picture is released it will be free from all objectionable features, and will be presented to you for screening. As to all of this I will be glad if you will assure the President."[36]

Though the revised script was approved by the Hays Office, Hearst was unhappy. MGM, he feared, had done more than was required to mute the film's political message — perhaps, he hinted, because Mayer, a lifelong Republican, had tried to protect Hoover's image. "Dear Louis," he wrote Mayer on March 25, 1933:

I want to recommend to you the words of the English prayer book with reference to the picture *Gabriel*, "We have left undone those things which we ought to have done; and we have done those things which we ought not to have done." I can realize the necessity of complying with the President's request and putting the naval scene [in which Hammond bullies the leaders of the foreign governments into paying their debts] on a yacht instead of on a battleship and perhaps even the desirability of having the unemployed army in Baltimore, although they would have been much more dramatic in Washington.

Still there were a lot of alterations in the picture which were not requested by the government and which in my humble opinion were in no way necessary, and which detract from the story value and the dramatic value of the picture. . . . I think you have impaired the effectiveness of the President's speech to the Congress because you have been afraid to say the things which I wrote and which I say daily in my newspapers and which you commend me for saying, but still do not sufficiently approve to put in your film. . . . I believe the picture will still be considered a good picture and perhaps an unusually good picture. Nevertheless, I think it was a better picture.[37]

Recognizing that the *Gabriel* film with its activist president the hero, and its Harding/Hoover hack the villain, had done him a great service, Roosevelt congratulated Hearst personally. "I want," the president wrote the publisher in San Simeon, "to send you this line to tell you how pleased I am with the changes which you made in *Gabriel over the White House*. I think it is an intensely interesting picture and should do much to help. Several people have seen it with us at the White House and to every one of them it was tremendously interesting. Some of these people said they never went to movies or cared for them but they think this a most unusual picture."[38]

The film opened in early April to mixed reviews. Political columnists, including Walter Lippmann, had a "merry time" criticizing it, "most likely," the *Motion Picture Herald* noted, "to the profit of the box office." Lippmann, in particular, found the film objectionable because it represented "the infantile world of irresistible wishes. More specifically, it is a dramatization of Mr. Hearst's editorials."[39]

Gabriel did quite well. With a cost of only $200,000 — a quarter of the average cost of Marion's films — the picture turned a handsome profit. Even had it not, it would have accomplished Hearst's goal of getting his message across in a new medium to those who might not have read it in his newspapers. Money had to be appropriated to start up a gigantic public works program; the European nations had to be compelled to repay their war debts.[40]

VIII

New Deals and Raw Deals

§ 30 ❧

Hearst at Seventy

TIME MAGAZINE MARKED the Chief's seventieth birthday with a cover story. "The scandalous bad boy of only yesterday — the genius of a thousand melodramas" had outlived his sins. "Five years or so ago," *Time* reported, "it was the fashion to regard Hearst as a 'failure' and a 'tragic figure,' but . . . it is doubtful that so subtle a mind as Hearst's is trapped in tragedy." By returning to the mainstream, the Chief had enhanced his political powers. His positions on domestic and foreign policy appeared to be consonant with those of the newly elected president, Franklin Delano Roosevelt. Both supported increased funding for a big navy, opposed war debt cancellation, and favored spending on public works projects. Neither believed it a priority to balance the budget.[1]

The Hearst papers were as effusive in their praise of Roosevelt as they had been damning in their criticisms of his predecessor. The president returned the favor by providing the publisher with access to the White House and the illusion that he was going to be an important adviser. Two days after the inauguration, Hearst telegrammed President Roosevelt with yet another recommendation for an appointment. The president not only personally thanked the Chief for his suggestion, but invited him to visit the White House on his next trip East.[2]

On March 19, Hearst employed his favorite and most effective editorial device to bestow his blessing on Roosevelt. Winsor McCay's editorial-page cartoon pictured a smiling Uncle Sam leaning over Roosevelt's desk to shake hands as millions of Americans cheered. "Uncle Sam is delighted with his new Chief Executive, and well may be," the caption read. "The people cheer as they recover confidence. There is a man in the White House who knows how to ACT, and realizes that he represents the 123,000,000 people that elected him, not a small handful of befuddled financiers that prayed for his defeat."[3]

The following month, the Hearst papers celebrated Franklin Delano Roosevelt's "bold and sustained action" by calling for a new holiday, President's Day.[4]

In politics and journalism, as Hearst knew only too well, access was power. By the early 1930s, he had secured access not only to the president of the United States, but to the principal leaders of Europe whom he paid handsomely — in dollars — to serve as foreign correspondents for his March of Events Sunday section.

The Hearst newspapers had tried but failed to sign Benito Mussolini to a contract in 1927 and had, since that time, been purchasing his articles from the United Press syndicate. Millicent, who had visited with Mussolini in 1923 and 1927, arrived in Rome from Egypt, where she had been vacationing with two of her friends, in March of 1930. Hearst's offices in Rome planned her itinerary, found her and her friends accommodations, and notified the Chief when she arrived. Wherever she traveled, Millicent assumed the role of roving ambassador for the Hearst empire. From Rome, she cabled her husband with the suggestion that he relocate his two news services and his magazine and newsreel headquarters which were "scattered over Rome in small poor offices" to office space she had located opposite the Hotel Excelsior in the American quarter. Hearst apparently agreed with her suggestion. At the bottom of her telegram, Willicombe noted, "Concerning this the chief said quote 'I think I would like to do this. It gives us more dignity to have one big impressive establishment than to have a lot of little ones.'"[5]

Millicent's major task in Rome was to interview Mussolini for a feature article in Hearst's Sunday papers and negotiate a contract with him to write exclusively for the Hearst newspapers. Mussolini met with her in the great hall of the Palazzo Venezia where popes had once greeted their guests. "When I expressed to him my admiration of his work for Italy he thanked me with a smile which impressed me with its sincerity and its kindliness . . .

"'Do you know Ostia?' he asked me. On my replying in the negative, he seemed sorry and added: 'If you will allow me, I will take you to see the new excavations and the city by the sea which is coming into existence.'"

A few days later, Mussolini drove up to the Grand Hotel where Millicent was staying "in a four-seater Alfa-Romeo driven by himself." He asked her to sit next to him for the drive to Ostia.

After describing her tour of Ostia with Il Duce, Millicent concluded her article by informing Hearst's readers that "Mussolini is a great executive, a true leader of men, and the great works he has accomplished are his genuine fortification to a high place in history and in the hearts of his people."[6]

What she did not tell them was that she had offered him $1,500 an article (equivalent to about $15,000 in today's currency) to write for the Hearst papers.

Mussolini consulted with Madame Margherita Sarfatti, his mistress and ghostwriter, who was already negotiating a contract with Karl von Wiegand, Hearst's German correspondent. They agreed to accept Millicent's offer. "On April 24," Philip Cannistraro and Brian Sullivan wrote in their biography of Sarfatti, "Margherita signed a contract guaranteeing that she would deliver twelve articles by Mussolini in 1931 for $1,500 each. On behalf of Mussolini, Margherita agreed to write only on topics approved by the Hearst organization, especially on newsworthy current events. Margherita promised an option on the same arrangement for 1932."

Mussolini and Sarfatti's editor in New York was Than Vanneman Ranck, Hearst's editorial manager. Ranck, according to Sarfatti's biographers, did not have an easy time with the two, nor they with him: "Ranck upset Mussolini and Margherita by referring to them openly in telegrams sent to Rome. The Duce worried that informers or gossips might lurk among the employees of the Italian telegraph system." It was finally agreed that Mussolini would be referred to by the code name Albis, and Sarfatti by the name Romis.[7]

Though Hearst was proud to publish articles by the premier of Italy, dispatched from Rome "By Special Cable," Ranck had a great deal of trouble with the copy Sarfatti and Mussolini delivered to him. The prose was ponderous, the subjects dull, the copy late. Worst of all, it was often difficult to know what the premier was writing about. "Dark forebodings had hovered over the face of Europe for many weeks, and even the bright summer days could not bring out a ray of hope for the economic situation. The year, coming upon us relentlessly, could only be seen as a critical year in which order and restoration were bound to hang in the balance." So began his and Sarfatti's July 12, 1931, front-page article on President Hoover's war debt plan.

Though a few of the articles were rejected and several had to be rewritten, Hearst was, for the most part, pleased with them. When it came time to renew the agreement for a second year, he and Ranck proposed that Sarfatti and Mussolini deliver twenty-six articles for $1,000 each in 1932. The parties compromised, in the end, on a contract for eighteen articles at $1,200 each, which, given the increase in the number of articles and the fall in price of the Italian lira, left Sarfatti and Mussolini with considerably more money than they had received in their first contract. The 1932 set of articles were, like the first year's, consonant with Hearst's own editorial policies. Il

Duce and his ghostwriter argued that governments had a responsibility to assist the unemployed, blasted the Versailles Treaty, called on England and France to disarm, supported Germany's demand for "equality of armaments," and warned of "Danger from Far East Unless Disunity Among White Races Ends."[8]

Only toward the end of 1932 did Mussolini and Sarfarti begin to balk at the agreement they had signed to write only on subjects preapproved by Hearst and Ranck. In September, they turned down Hearst's proposal that they write about the failed disarmament talks in Geneva. And then in December of 1932, they broke one of the cardinal rules of the Hearst organization when, in their economic forecast for the coming year, they called on the United States to cancel European war debts. "I would not print Mussolini's article or any other propaganda for debt cancellation," the Chief cabled Ranck in New York. "And you must be very careful to see that articles from all these foreigners do not contain such propaganda."

Ranck, disturbed at Hearst's implying that he had not been careful enough in editing out propaganda, telegrammed the Chief the next day that "all foreign contributors have for years been instructed they must not write anything that could possibly be construed as debt-cancellation, pro–League of Nations, or any other kind of propaganda contrary to our policies and that if they did write such propaganda it would not be printed."

Ranck directed the Hearst representative in Rome to inform Sarfatti that they were not going to publish her and Mussolini's year-end article or any other that referred to American war debts. Sarfatti offered instead to write one on the role of women in Fascist Italy, but Mussolini refused to cave in entirely to Hearst's demands and ordered his ghostwriter to rewrite the year-end forecast article, which she did, this time eliminating any reference to war debts.[9]

Although highly appreciative of the exposure to American audiences and the money he was getting from Hearst (with which he bought his country house in the Romagna), Mussolini was no longer willing to abide by the rules the Chief had established. According to Cannistraro and Sullivan, Mussolini and Sarfatti knew in advance how Ranck and Hearst were going to react to their articles, as they intercepted all the cables sent back and forth from Hearst's office in Rome. Still they persisted in pushing their own agenda in their articles, instead of adhering to the Chief's.

In February of 1933, they suggested again that it would be wise for the United States to forgive European war debts. This time Hearst had had enough. "I would just as soon not have Mussolini article or any of these articles by foreign statesmen, if they are going to be employed for foreign propaganda against the interest of our country," he cabled Ranck. Mussolini, realizing belatedly that he had gone too far this time, agreed to rewrite the column.[10]

As the time approached for negotiating a new contract with Il Duce, Ranck questioned whether he was still worth the money and the trouble: "Am experiencing greatest difficulty with Mussolini not only in getting his material on time but in choice of subjects." Mussolini was now insisting that while Hearst had the "right to suggest topics, final choice rests solely with him. Agreement by us to Mussolini's point of view," Ranck continued, "would enable him to make us take any old pot-boiling topic that he pleases at any time at twelve hundred dollars per article. Not only has Mussolini been endeavoring to work off some very uninteresting subjects but in spite of all our admonitions has been providing some of them so late as to miss our [deadlines]. I can readily understand that some diplomatic topics are too delicate for Mussolini to discuss but that should not prevent him from getting together with us on subjects that he can cover and which are of interest to America."[11]

The Chief agreed: "Have noted that Mussolini has been less interesting of late . . . There is no reason why we should take and pay for dull stuff. . . . I think Mussolini will understand that if his political complications prevent his writing the articles that are interesting in the United States there is no reason why we should suffer because of that foreign situation."[12]

Though the Chief did not countenance insubordination from any of his writers, even those who were heads of state, as long as Il Duce produced articles, as he did in 1933, attacking France's foreign policy and defending Hitler, the Chief accepted occasional duds for publication, like "Mussolini Works on Farm, Visits Factories to Learn Needs of Italian Masses," which appeared on November 19, 1933.

When in 1936, Hearst learned that Sarfatti and Mussolini, who had declined to renew their contract, were negotiating with the *Herald Tribune* and the United Press, he offered them a raise to $1,750 an article for twelve articles. With the invasion of Ethiopia in the fall of 1935 and his intervention in the Spanish Civil War the following year, Mussolini had put himself back in the headlines. Though Hearst was prepared now to allow Mussolini to publish articles in other foreign journals — a right denied him in earlier contracts — he still insisted on preapproval of all topics. "Do not miss Mussolini," Hearst cabled Ranck in New York. "He is particularly important now and will be for the next couple of years. However I would rather pay him two thousand a week with the understanding that he write on topics of interest to America than half that amount on any other basis."[13]

In the realm of journalism, Hearst was the Il Duce; Mussolini, Hitler, Lloyd George, Churchill, and all the others were merely writers under contract. There was an enormous danger here, which Hearst quickly succumbed to. He could not resist the temptation to imply that his power as publisher denoted something more substantial, that in approving the topics and editing the words of his statesmen, he was influencing their thoughts as well.

Mussolini was not the only national leader who wrote for Hearst in the 1930s. General José Félix Uriburu, president of the Argentine Republic, and Emilio Portes Gil, president of Mexico from December 1928 to February 1930, were also among his foreign correspondents. When, on September 14, 1930, the National Socialist German Workers' Party unexpectedly won 6.5 million votes — it had polled only 800,000 two years earlier — to become the second largest party in Germany, the Chief offered and Adolf Hitler, the party's leader, accepted a contract to write for the Hearst papers. The fee was one thousand marks an article, equivalent then to about $240, far less than Mussolini was getting, but enough, according to Putzi Hanfstaengl, Hitler's foreign press chief, to enable Hitler to stay at the plush Kaiserhof Hotel when he went to Berlin.[14]

Two weeks later, on September 28, 1930, the first article by Hitler appeared. All that week, the Hearst papers had advertised on their front pages their upcoming exclusive: "Adolf Hitler's Own Story; He Tells What Is the Matter with Germany and How He Proposes to Remedy It." The article appeared in the Sunday March of Events section alongside a photograph of Hitler staring straight at the reader, arms akimbo, in full-length leather jacket: "Let not the world deceive itself, Germany will either become a free nation again or, losing faith in any other future, will be driven into the beckoning arms of Bolshevism. That is no mere phrase, no threat, no prophecy, but just a statement of fact, of the sentiment of the German masses of today. I know that sentiment as no other statesman or politician in Berlin."

The following Sunday, October 5, a second Hitler article was featured in the March of Events section. Hitler's pronouncements, though angrier and much more bombastic, echoed Hearst's own editorials about the injustices Wilson and the Allies had foisted on Germany with their Treaty of Versailles:

The Germany I lead — the new and coming Germany, the young Germany — is certainly not guilty of war, had nothing to do with making it, and upon

Germany no amount of legislative acrobatics can morally place the slightest responsibility. This being the fact, this new and young Germany which I lead does not propose to be convict labor for its entire own generation. . . . France can stand on her head, can invade Germany, and can create a still greater depression in the economic world by eliminating Germany. All that and more can happen and we shall suffer, but it will not break the determination of the young Germany I lead that there shall be a more reasonable and sensible adjustment of the unfulfillable burdens dictatorially imposed on Germany.

Though Hitler was for a time a favorite commentator of Hearst's because he produced headlines and delivered sharp, incisive copy, he fell out of favor because he was terrible at meeting deadlines. In December of 1931, Hitler promised Ranck that he would give the Hearst papers an exclusive on the next open letter he planned to send Chancellor Brüning. When he delayed delivery for three consecutive days, Ranck was furious, Hearst annoyed. "Hitler article losing value because so much Hitler material published in past few days," the Chief telegrammed Ranck in New York. "If he doesn't come through now, please cancel."[15]

Hitler was never quite broken in by Hearst and his editors. He continued to miss deadlines and withhold his promised exclusives. On December 30, 1931, Ranck telegrammed Hearst that Hitler, "after agreeing sell New Year's message to us for $500 and to withhold general publication until nine o'clock Munich time changed mind late tonight and gave out to all papers in Berlin for immediate publication without charge. . . . Have asked for explanation."[16]

Apparently the explanation, when it came, was enough to convince Ranck and Hearst to give Hitler another chance. "Hitler writing article blasting ratification any disarmament agreement in Geneva if unfavorable to Germany. Wants $1,000," Ranck telegrammed Hearst in San Simeon in late January of 1932. "As he's been writing profusely, some of it not vital, have offered $500 . . . provided he can make it stand up for . . . publication. Don't think it's worth more than that, do you?" Hearst cabled back that he thought that "Hitler writes interestingly and that article on disarmament question would be interesting in America. If you cannot get it for $500 better increase the bid." Ranck contracted for the article — we don't know at what price — only to be put off by Hitler, who continued to postpone writing it. "This," Ranck telegraphed Hearst, "in spite of our persistent efforts to get it. Will keep right after him."[17]

Hearst's access to Hitler, together with his public record of support of Jewish causes, prompted Hollywood's Jewish community to seek him out as a potential champion. In mid-January 1932, while Hearst and Ranck were negotiating to publish Hitler's articles, Carl Laemmle, the president of Universal Pictures, wrote Hearst at length "on a subject which I firmly believe is not only of great concern to my own race but also to millions of Gentiles, throughout the world":

> It is about the current political situation in Germany and the probable consequences to the Jewish population in that country in the event Hitler is successful, as seems likely, in getting control of the Government. I realize perfectly, Mr. Hearst, that the political situation in Germany is something that no other country, or foreigner, can consistently attack or even criticize. At the same time, I am convinced that the personal safety of the many thousands of Jews in Germany is of definite concern today to all reasonable, thinking people the world over; and it is strictly on that premise that I am presuming on your time and patience in submitting my own thoughts. . . . Speaking as an individual, I have been greatly worried for some time about the members of my own family in Germany. . . . I might be wrong, and I pray to God that I am, but I am almost certain that Hitler's rise to power, because of his obvious militant attitude toward the Jews, would be the signal for a general physical onslaught on many thousands of defenseless Jewish men, women and children in Germany. . . . As a man so sincerely and consistently the champion of human rights, there is none whose voice would carry more effectively to the consciences of all races alike than your own. As the foremost publisher in the United States, the moulder of the opinions of millions of thinking American people and the spokesman thereof, there is none in America whose influence and opinions would command more respect and consideration from Mr. Hitler than your own. . . . A protest from you would bring an echo from all corners of the civilized world, such as Mr. Hitler could not possibly fail to recognize.[18]

There is no record of any response by Hearst to Laemmle's letter. Hearst, we can only conclude, did not take the studio head's warnings very seriously. Though Hitler had made no secret of his obsessive anti-Semitism — it was a major theme in *Mein Kampf* and in his public speeches — his rhetoric had, according to his biographer Ian Kershaw, shifted somewhat in the late 1920s. His "anti-Semitism seemed now rather more ritualist or mechanistic. The main stress had moved to anti-Marxism." Still, as Kershaw reminds us, it was only the presentation of his ideas that had been modified. Hitler's pathological hatred of Jews remained unchanged.[19]

Six months after Laemmle's letter to Hearst, his predictions came true. In national elections held in late July of 1932, the Nazis increased their share of the vote to 37.4 percent, making them the largest party in the Reichstag. On August 30, Hermann Goering was elected Reichstag president. Ranck telegrammed the Chief for permission to pay Goering for a front-page article to be published on September 11, 1932, the day before he was scheduled to present the Nazi program to the Reichstag: "In line with our policy of getting strong articles from foreign contributors for first page news section Sunday papers would suggest Goering article for that position." Hearst agreed, sending Ranck into near ecstasy at their journalistic triumph. "In his article Goering tells precisely what the Hitlerites propose to do which includes forcing situation in Reichstag," Ranck telegrammed the Chief at San Simeon. "Last Monday he openly announced that no action would be taken by the Hitlerites until September 12. As this is the coming Monday, our article will be the first announcement of the Hitlerite plans. Mussolini [who also had an article in that Sunday's paper] comes out boldly with statement Germany is entitled to arms equality, the contrary attitude of France notwithstanding. So far as I can ascertain this is first announcement of this policy by Italy. Hearst papers thus become the official spokesman for the Hitlerites and for Italy on these two important situations."[20]

Because Hitler refused to abide by his agreements and deliver exclusive and timely copy, Ranck and Hearst recognized that they would not be able to count on him for regular contributions. Still, Hearst was able to maintain direct access to Hitler through Putzi Hanfstaengl, his foreign press chief, a well-connected, cultured six-foot-four-inch graduate of Harvard who counted himself a personal friend of the Chief. Hearst had known Hanfstaengl's mother, an American, and his father, an internationally known Munich art dealer, with whom Hearst had done business. Hanfstaengl had been close to Hitler since the early 1920s. Hitler had often visited Hanfstaengl's home to have dinner with him and his family and listen to Putzi play Wagner on the piano. Though Hanfstaengl was no longer part of Hitler's inner circle, he retained sufficient access to serve as Hearst's liaison.[21]

In seeking Hearst's support in 1932, Roosevelt had on several occasions declared publicly and privately that he was not an internationalist. The Chief had, in the end, taken him at his word. The first test of their understanding occurred with the opening of the International Monetary and Economic Conference convened in London in June 1933.

To Hearst's dismay, Roosevelt, who had inherited the conference from Hoover, not only agreed to participate, but placed at the head of the American delegation his secretary of state, Cordell Hull, a Wilsonian internationalist. Hearst was unalterably opposed to the United States entering into any sort of negotiations with the Europeans, at least until they had paid back their war debts. Like Roosevelt, he believed that the quickest way to revive the economy was to pump more money into it by inflating the dollar relative to the European currencies. When the European nations at the London Conference tried to get the United States to agree to a monetary stabilization plan that would have prevented it from unilaterally raising the price of the dollar, Hearst cabled T. V. Ranck, his editorial director in New York, that it was "desirable to dynamite this foreign situation. Please have cartoons made showing . . . Hull [and the other members of the American delegation] hauling down American flag and running up British flag and singing quote Great Britain is the Gem of the ocean unquote. Make other cartoons along same lines such as English pound eclipsing the American dollar. We have got to arouse American public to danger this country is in by surrendering so many advantages to foreign nations, especially England. We can probably do it best by powerful cartoons and brief editorials under them."[22]

Two days later, the Chief's anger at Roosevelt had reached the boiling point. "As a general instruction to writers of editorials," he wrote T. V. Ranck in New York, "would it not be well to begin to hold President Roosevelt responsible for some of the discredit and perhaps danger which the American representatives abroad are bringing upon this country. Mr. Hull, for instance is a most embarrassing Secretary of State — a vapid visionary, apparently willing to sacrifice the interests of the American people for his fantastic theories."[23]

President Roosevelt, acting almost as if he had read Hearst's telegrams, torpedoed the London Conference the next day by sending what the newspaper reports referred to as a "bombshell" message to London, denouncing the "old fetishes of so called international bankers." The Chief hailed the president's message, which effectively broke up the London Conference before any substantive agreement had been reached, as nothing less than "a modern declaration of independence."[24]

The first breach in the Hearst-Roosevelt entente occurred not because the president was an "internationalist," as Hearst had always feared, but because he was not the "conservative" the publisher had believed him to be. The centerpiece of the Roosevelt New Deal was the National Industrial Recovery Act (NIRA) which established the Public Works Administration (PWA) and the National Recovery Administration (NRA). Roosevelt allocated $3.3 billion to the PWA to get Americans back to work. While the sum was less than the $5 billion Hearst had called for in his 1931 recovery proposal, the Chief supported the initiative because he considered it a conservative recovery measure intended to pump money back into the economy. The NRA was another matter entirely. Not content with simple recovery measures, the president, Hearst feared, had been persuaded by his radical advisers to try and reform the economy through the NRA by reducing what they saw as the destructive competition and rampant overproduction that had been responsible for plunging the economy into the Depression in the first place.

The NRA was a new governmental agency established to persuade industrialists and businessmen to soften competition and limit production by signing industry-wide agreements or codes that would raise wages and reduce work hours. All his life, Hearst had advocated government regulation of trusts, monopolies, transit and traction companies, railways, and public utilities. But he had never imagined that such regulation would ever be extended to every industry in the nation, especially to newspaper publishing, which he believed was explicitly protected from government interference by the First Amendment. He was not only astounded then, but outraged when news leaked out of Washington that the NRA expected the newspaper publishers to draw up their own industry-wide code, with regulations on minimum wages and maximum hours.

"Please tell the President," he directed Ed Coblentz in New York, "that I consider his proposal to license the press under the NRA in direct violation of the Bill of Rights, that it is an abridgment of the freedom of the press guaranteed by the Constitution, and that I will fight his proposal with every means at my command, even if it means taking it to the Supreme Court of the United States, and even if it costs me every nickel I possess."[25]

When Coblentz relayed the Chief's message to Louis Howe at the White House, Howe, according to Coblentz, "put Frank on the phone." The president asked Coblentz to tell Mr. Hearst that there was nothing to worry about, that the NRA was not intended to curtail the freedom of the press. At this point in their relationship, Hearst trusted the president enough to take his word on the matter. Common sense dictated as well that Roosevelt was not about to enter into any protracted struggle with the newspaper publishers he so desperately needed to win to his side. Given the president's reassurance, Hearst joined with his colleagues in drafting an NRA industry code. As added insurance against government interference in their First Amendment privileges, the publishers appended an explicit guarantee that the constitutional rights of a free press could not "be abridged by the application of a licensing system or the use of injunctions to suppress a newspaper." On August 16, Hearst signaled his acceptance of the code by putting the Blue Eagle, the NRA logo, on the top of his front pages.[26]

Though he had festooned his papers with Blue Eagles, the Chief continued to worry about the precedent that had been established when the publishers agreed to cooperate with the NRA in setting prices and wage rates.

"Has it occurred to you," he telegrammed Coblentz on September 9, 1933, "that the NRA is really another form of taxation on business? Business is also worried about turning the whole country over to the labor unions . . . I think our experiment in Hitlerism is a failure . . . As a seer and prophet . . . I am bound to say that political complications may be looked for in 1934, and I am seriously worried about THAT."[27]

In October, still only seven months into the Roosevelt administration, he went public with his criticisms. On October 29, he published an open letter to American newspaper publishers in which he called on them to expose and oppose the NRA as "a menace to political rights and constitutional liberties, a danger to American ideals and institutions, a handicap to industrial recovery and a detriment to the public welfare." Two days later, he criticized it in another front-page editorial as "a measure of absolute State socialism [that was] not only not democratic [but] opposed to every fundamental conception of democracy and every principle of individual liberty on which democracy was based. . . . The blighting effect of the NRA policy," he insisted, "has been so complete that a justifiable interpretation of the letters NRA would make them read appropriately, 'No Recovery Allowed' . . . The people elected a Democratic Administration, not a socialistic dictatorship. The people approved the well considered proposals of the Democratic platform, not the theories of Karl Marx and the policies of Stalin."[28]

Hearst's language was intemperate, but then it had always been. He spoke in the hyperbolic rhetoric of newspaper headlines and cartoon captions. He did not mean his words to be taken literally; he scattered them like buckshot through his editorials in the hope that they would evoke in his readers the fear, distrust, and anger that he was experiencing.

The Chief was a true believer in the American dream which, for him, was founded on the twin pillars of representative democracy and free-market capitalism. His family history was testimony to the reality of that dream. His father had arrived in California with nothing but his native intelligence and capacity for hard work and, because of the existence of a free market, had amassed millions of dollars for himself and his family. His son, also through hard work and because of the free market, had been able to pyramid these millions into millions more. There had, in his father's and his lifetimes, been a succession of economic downturns, depressions, and panics, but the nation and its people had survived every one of them, as it would this one. There was, he was convinced, nothing fundamentally wrong with the economy that a one-time infusion of capital through a public works program could not cure. What the economy did not need was the government tinkering with it. If gently and conservatively tended, it would recover and continue expanding, as it had always done in the past.

Roosevelt and his advisers declined to defend themselves against Hearst's polemics. On the contrary, the president acted as if they remained the closest of friends and allies. Hearst was regularly invited to the White House for private discussions. When he was unable to make the trip himself, his editors were received and entertained in his place. The Chief responded to the president's gestures of friendship and respect by periodically declaring in public that despite his criticism of the NRA, he remained a Democrat and Roosevelt supporter.

Together the president and the publisher played a game of political tit-for-tat, a game in which both were extraordinarily skilled. In early December of 1933, after Hearst had delivered a series of particularly bitter anti–New Deal editorials and radio addresses, Arthur Brisbane sent a "private" telegram to the president, suggesting that he listen to Hearst's next radio broadcast and read the transcript in his newspapers the next morning. "You and millions of Americans will like Mr. Hearst's tribute in his broadcast to your efforts for the people." That same day, Brisbane delivered a separate letter to the White House, asking the president to reconsider a complicated trade provision about interest payments to American corporations in England, a provision that had a direct effect on Hearst's magazine holdings there. Roosevelt responded promptly that he was having the matter looked into by the federal trade commissioners, the attorney general, and the acting secretary of the treasury.[29]

Time and again, this scenario was played out, with friendly editorials proffered in return for presidential favors and vice versa. In March of 1934, Hearst forwarded to his chief correspondent in Washington his plan to improve the nation's inland waterways: "I would like to advocate this editorially. . . . Kindly see President about it to learn if he is inclined to approve it. There is no use shooting editorials unless project would meet with administration's approval."[30]

Never before had Hearst encountered a politician with the personal skills of a Franklin Roosevelt. But, then again, never before had Roosevelt encountered anyone as volatile — and powerful — as Hearst. In February of 1934, only two months after one of their friendly get-togethers at the White House, Hearst was back on the attack. In response to rumors circulating in Washington that Roosevelt was going to reject the NRA code that the publishers had agreed on and submitted to him six months earlier, Hearst linked the president to "the Mussolinis, the Hitlers, the Lenins and all of those who seek to establish a dictatorial form of government . . . by repressing the press; because nothing is so fatal to their plans and ambitions as general public knowledge of their purposes and proceedings which free publication affords." To emphasize the connection between Roosevelt's New Deal and European fascism, the Hearst papers began publishing articles by Mussolini under headlines like "U.S. Abandons Individual Enterprise, Adopts State Control, Says Mussolini: Duce Sees Many Similarities Between NRA and Fascist Government Operation."[31]

Roosevelt, of course, had no intention of curtailing the freedom of the press. In the end, he accepted the code submitted to him, but only after insisting that the clause guaranteeing freedom of the press that the publishers had appended to it was "pure surplussage. . . . The recitation of the freedom of the press clause in the code . . . has no more place here than would the recitation of the whole Constitution or of the Ten Commandments."[32]

The president was enraged at having been backed into a corner by Hearst and his colleagues. There had certainly been no excuse for Hearst's name-calling. But when Roosevelt not only capitulated to the onslaught but forgave Hearst for it, he provided him with further proof that he could write whatever he chose and still enjoy the president's favor.

Left to their own devices, Hearst and the other publishers might have found a way to live with the guidelines on maximum hours and minimum wages that the NRA code mandated. But the same law that had established the NRA had also explicitly declared, in Section 7a, that "employees shall have the right to organize and bargain collectively through representatives of their own choosing." As Arthur Schlesinger, Jr. has written, Section 7a raised more questions than it answered. Its meaning would "be determined in large part not by the words of the act but by the pressures management and labor could bring to bear on the process of interpretation."[33]

On August 7, 1933, Heywood Broun, the oversized columnist for the *World-Telegram*, took up the challenge of Section 7a in his syndicated "It Seems to Me" column. Broun, with his tousled hair, tie askew, always rumpled suit, and inimitable prose style, had, by 1933, become one of the nation's premier and arguably its most liberal columnist. He had begun his career on the sports desk at the *Tribune* and worked stints there as drama critic, war correspondent, and book reviewer before moving on to the *World* and its successor, the *World-Telegram*. In his column, Broun announced that "beginning at nine o'clock on the morning of October 1," he was going to do the best he could to organize a newspaper writers' union. "I think I could die happy on the opening day of the general strike if I had the privilege of watching Walter Lippmann heave a brick through the *Tribune* window at a nonunion operative who had been called in to write the current 'Today and Tomorrow' column on the gold standard."

Newspapermen across the country responded to Broun's announcement by forming local unions or "guilds." In December of 1933, the first national conference of the American Newspaper Guild was convened in Washington. Heywood Broun was elected president, a position which he would hold until his death.

Hearst had in the past supported blue-collar newspaper unions and, in turn, been supported by them in his campaigns for political office. For the time being, he was unwilling to reverse himself and go on record against the Guild. "I do not like to discuss these labor problems," he telegrammed T. V. Ranck in New York on December 19, 1933. "You are liable to offend some labor faction or offend the employers. Keep out of the whole mess."[34]

Four days later, the Chief suggested that an offer be made to Broun to move his column to the Hearst papers. When T. V. Ranck, who was an editor at the *New York American,* protested that Broun was highly dangerous and refused to be edited, the Chief answered that Ranck had nothing to worry about as Broun's columns would run in the *Mirror.* Broun chose in the end to remain at the *World-Telegram.*[35]

The Chief's politics, at age seventy, were defined more by his opposition to internationalism, big government, and the income tax than by anti-communism. In mid-1933, disturbed that the government was devoting too much time to fighting communist subversion and ignoring homegrown American fascists, he directed George Young, publisher of the *Los Angeles Examiner,* to prepare

> an editorial saying that fascism and communism are the two extremes of class government, equally tyrannous and equally opposed to our American form of democratic government, which is not government by class but government by the whole people. This government opposes communistic activities as threats against the American system. There is no reason why the government should not equally oppose fascist activities. In Los Angeles lately there have been fascist organizations created apparently with no opposition or objection on the part of the local government. But communistic demonstrations have been rigidly suppressed. I would like you to advocate either equal tolerance or suppression of fascism and communism by the government. And conclude by saying that if these disturbers and notoriety seekers want to wear some kind

of distinctive shirts, they do not have to wear black shirts or brown shirts, as the state makes a very distinctive blue shirt [the color of prison uniforms] and it might insist on these folks wearing them.[36]

The Chief, who had long supported diplomatic recognition of Russia, applauded President Roosevelt and Russian foreign minister Litvinoff in November of 1933 for negotiating the agreements that laid a firm "foundation for hearty cooperation between the United States and Russia in the support of common causes, including the promotion of the peace of the world."[37]

Through 1933 and into 1934, Hearst alternately and, it appeared, indiscriminately criticized President Roosevelt for flirting with "Hitlerism" and for proposing a "socialistic" NRA consistent with the "theories of Karl Marx and the policies of Stalin."[38] The only constant in his editorials was his fury.

By the spring of 1934, as the American Newspaper Guild's organizing campaign reached his newspaper offices, Hearst's anger was stretched to encompass his newspapermen who contemplated joining Heywood Broun in the Guild. "I think the most unfortunate thing that has occurred in Mr. Roosevelt's MISDEAL," Hearst told Tom White, the head of his newspaper division,

has been encouragement of the newspapermen to form guilds — and to support extreme radicalism. We are not only going to have trouble with the guilds interfering with the efficient conduct of the newspapers, but we are going to have eternal difficulty in keeping radical propaganda out of the papers, because every newspaperman as soon as he joins a radical guild becomes a radical propagandist. . . . I hardly believe that communism will succeed in this country, but if it gets strong enough it will develop into the formation of a fascist organization, and that is very likely to succeed. Either communism or fascism is destructive to democracy, and there can be no freedom of the press except under liberal democracy. These jackass newspapermen do not realize that if we had either communism or fascism we would have suppression of newspaper development [and] limitation of newspaper activity, with the painful result of the newspapers being very much less important, very much less prosperous, and very much less liberal as employers. In fact, most of these enthusiastic theorists who are now advocating the abolition of our democracy would find themselves and their jobs abolished with it.[39]

The Hearst newspapers had always spoken with one voice, Hearst's. A newspaper's writers' union would threaten that control by protecting writers who disobeyed his editorial dictates. On April 4, the same day that Hearst wrote White to complain about the Guild, Louis Burgess, an editorial writer and Guild member, was summarily fired from the *San Francisco Examiner* after inquiring when the paper was going to begin to adhere to the provisions of the NRA code. Six weeks later, Dean Jennings, another Guild member who worked as a rewrite man at Hearst's *San Francisco Call-Bulletin,* was denied the right to schedule his vacation so that he could attend the first Guild convention.[40]

Because Hearst's record on unionization had up to this point been so positive, even the Guild was taken unawares by the turnabout. According to Daniel Leab, the historian of the American Newspaper Guild, a resolution was offered at the 1934 national convention condemning Hearst for his opposition to the guilds: "For the record he was described as a 'son of a bitch,' but later in the convention the delegates adopted a less inflammatory substitute measure suggested by Hearst-employed newsmen, which attributed antiguild activities to the publisher's subordinates and invited him to meet with guild representatives."[41]

There was no reply from Hearst, who was at the time in Europe. When he returned in the fall, fifteen Guild members at Hearst's *San Francisco Call-Bulletin* who had been advised to resign or be fired wrote directly to the Chief, calling on his "sense of fairness." They too received no reply.[42]

Although the Hearst papers had never before paid much attention to communist subversion, in late March of 1934 as the Guild organizing drive reached the Hearst newspaper offices, they began publication of a front-page series of articles by Ralph Easley on "Soviet Power in America." Easley, the chairman of the National Civic Federation, was, when Hearst hired him, already notorious in journalistic circles for succumbing to the calls of kooks and cranks who made their living selling "secret" Soviet documents.[43]

His first story for Hearst was on the Department of Justice's decision to disband its counter-subversive force of "thirty well-trained, undercover men." Arthur Sulzberger of the *New York Times* and Geoffrey Parsons, the chief editorial writer at the *Herald Tribune,* had already turned the story down when Easley contacted Hearst with it. "If Mr. Hearst had not come into this situation," Easley wrote T. V. Ranck, Hearst's editorial manager, in early March, "nothing would have happened and our country would have been in a very serious condition. At the right time and place, I intend to give you some further inside information."[44]

Easley was soon afterward commissioned by Hearst, as he informed Milton Hershey, chairman of the board of the Hershey Chocolate Corporation and one of his chief supporters, to write a six-part series on "the radical situation in the colleges and schools [for] the Sunday editions of the Hearst chain of 26 papers. This series of six will be followed by ten articles on the industrial situation, showing the activities of the Third International in the labor unions, farmer organizations and so forth."[45]

Ranck and Hearst collaborated on editing the Easley articles. "Easley articles on Communism are subject to careful and intelligent condensation," the Chief wrote Ranck, two days before the first article was to appear, "but we must not lose the point of the articles. This is a crusade which we want to make effective." The first article was published on March 25, 1934: "'Soviet Power in America,' Slogan of Communist Drive. Students Called to International Meet This Year. 'National Student League a Funnel for Pouring Propaganda Into Schools and an Under-cover Tool in the Drive to Bolshevise American Youth,' says Easley." The following day, Easley's second article appeared: "Communist Plan for May Drive to Seize All Property in United States Revealed." Immediately below the headline, an editor's note in italics reported that this was "the first of a series of news features showing the startling progress of Industrial Communism in the United States. All the facts to be presented in these articles were obtained from documents, publications of the Communist Party, and specific reports from secret agents."

The articles had precisely the effect Easley had hoped for. "The Hearst papers all over the country," he joyfully wrote an associate in early March of 1934, "are stirring up the people on this Red situation pictured in my articles." The National Student League, he was happy to report, had begun to picket the *New York American* building "to protest the attacks made upon the League in my articles — all of which plays on our side."[46]

Hearst accompanied Easley's "news" features with a series of editorials criticizing Congress for not launching a "systematic investigation" of Red infiltration and for not calling for a "loyalty requirement for public school teachers." In May of 1934, the Chief outlined for Ed Coblentz an editorial he wanted written "saying that the thing to do with communists is to deport them. . . . They are chronic troublemakers. They are a destructive element purely, and we should get rid of them as we would of any vermin that are striving to undermine the foundations of our establishment. . . . It is time to call in the cockroach man."[47]

Hearst's seventieth year — and year one of the Roosevelt administration — ended much as it had begun, with Hearst attacking the New Deal and the president inviting him to the White House. After one of their get-togethers, Hearst sent the president as a present a "little silhouette of General Jackson" and an original Andrew Jackson letter. When FDR thanked him, the Chief sent a handwritten note and another present: "I am very pleased that you liked the little silhouette of General Jackson. I am sending another letter — an original — to go with it. This letter is not so lugubrious as the other and it relates to public affairs. . . . I have been doing a little work since I got back telling the business people how fine you are. I guess at your next election we will make it unanimous." The note was signed "Faithfully, W. R. Hearst."[48]

The gifts and visits notwithstanding, Roosevelt neither liked nor trusted Hearst. In May of 1934, he complained "vigorously" to Henry Stimson "of the dis-service which W. R. Hearst was doing to the country and the wide-spread influence which his papers in some twenty-two states . . . could do in holding a club over the members of Congress."[49] Still, the president could not afford to antagonize the most powerful publisher in the nation. Only days after complaining to Stimson about Hearst, Roosevelt met with the publisher at the White House. The Chief was so charmed and reassured by the president that at an impromptu press conference held just before he sailed to Europe, he had nothing but praise for the man and his policies. "In virtual reversal of his former attitude," the *New York Times* reported the next morning, "the publisher said he felt that every one should support the NRA and recovery measures so long as the measures did not 'tell you to do something you can't do.' He said he was in sympathy with President Roosevelt."[50]

❧ 31 ❧

Hearst and Hitler

A S HE DEPARTED on the Italian liner *Rex* for Europe in the spring of 1934, Hearst told the reporters assembled at dockside that he planned to "visit Italy first where he hoped to meet Premier Mussolini. . . . He said he did not know if he would see Hitler, but he would like 'very much' to meet the German Chancellor."[1]

Hitler had been appointed chancellor on January 30, 1933. Less than two months later, the Reichstag, Germany's national legislature, had passed an enabling law which gave him dictatorial powers. All month long, Nazi storm troopers, energized by Hitler's accretion of power, had accelerated their violence against the Jews. On March 23, as the Reichstag voted itself out of existence, that violence reached new and frightening levels, setting off a round of protests in the United States, Europe, and Palestine.

The Hearst papers reported in full on the Nazi violence and the growing anti-Nazi protest movement. Among the stories carried on the morning of March 24 were "Reich Assailed by Churchill for 'Ferocity,'" "Veterans Hear [New York Mayor] O'Brien Attack Intolerance," and "All Sections Join Fight on Nazi Violence: Christian Leaders to Speak at Jewish Protest Meetings." There was also a front-page article with the headline "New Yorker, Beaten by Hitlerites, Describes Conditions in Germany," a first-person account by Nathaniel S. Wolf of Rochester, who had been "beaten in Berlin by Nazi Storm Troops." The lead editorial was "'Hitlerism' . . . The world is horrified at the reports which are coming out of Germany. . . . If Hitlerism means pillage, cruelty and oppression, as well as tyranny, it is doomed — and Germany perhaps with it."

Events continued to spiral out of control over the next few days. On March 27, the American Jewish Committee announced that it was organizing an international boycott against German goods. Hitler retaliated by announcing a German boycott against Jewish businesses in Germany. Under pressure from, among others, Hjalmar Schacht, president of the Reichsbank, who urged him not to pursue an action that might further damage the already shaky German economy, Hitler restricted the boycott to one day.

While the American press, including Hearst's papers, criticized Hitler's boycott of Jewish-owned businesses as it had the storm trooper violence that preceded it, less attention was focused on the laws that were passed the following month barring Jews from the civil service, discriminating against jurists and doctors, and limiting the number of Jewish students in German schools and universities.

American reporters in Germany, including William Shirer and Karl von Wiegand of the Hearst organization, found it difficult to report on Nazi anti-Semitism. As Deborah Lipstadt, the author of *Beyond Belief,* has argued, they "felt sustained pressure both from readers and editorial boards, who wanted them to substantiate their information, and from the Nazis, who denied the veracity of their reports." The all-too-common responses to early stories of violence or discrimination against Jews were that they were fabricated or exaggerated. Some blamed the violence on unruly mobs or accused the Jews of having "caused their own suffering."[2]

Still, given this situation, Hearst's correspondents covered events in Germany as well as most American papers and better than many. On August 5, 1933, Karl von Wiegand reported on the complaints lodged by American journalists with the American ambassador, William Dodd, "against the manner in which German censors were delaying or refusing to pass news dispatches addressed to American agencies." On Sunday, August 6, the March of Events section carried two anti-Nazi articles, one by the former premier of France Édouard Herriot, entitled "Hitler Wants Era of Peace to Prepare Scientifically for War, Says Herriot. Sees Ruin in Amazing Policies of German Chancellor"; the second by Hearst's favorite European historian, Guglielmo Ferrero, who wrote of the danger posed by the "aggression of Nazis" in Austria. The following week, on August 14, 1933, the Hearst papers reported under a photograph of Mrs. Carrie Chapman Catt that her letter protesting the persecution of Jews in Germany had been signed by "9,000 Non-Jewish U.S. Women."

In mid-August, Hearst, concerned that Karl von Wiegand was sending home too many anti-Nazi dispatches, directed his New York editors to rein him in: "Von Wiegand articles and cables seem too incendiary. Think he should be instructed to send generally interesting news without partisanship."[3] By "partisan," Hearst meant critical. There was too much at stake to risk angering Hitler and losing access to him and his government. Still, the Chief, while warning von Wiegand, did not move him to another post, as he often did when he was displeased with his correspondents.

In October of 1933, when Hitler dramatically took Germany out of the international disarmament talks in Europe and withdrew from the League of Nations, the Hearst papers greeted the event as predestined: "The world may regret Germany's retirement from Geneva, but any world power that pretends to be surprised by this action insults the intelligence of thoughtful men everywhere. The course which Germany has taken has long appeared to be inevitable."[4]

Rather than condemning or questioning Hitler's action, Hearst and Ranck, Hearst's editorial manager, tried to get him to write about it for their Sunday papers. On December 19, Ranck informed Hearst that their Berlin office had cabled that "Hitler out of question to present Germany's side League crisis unless we willing pay him as much as pay Mussolini. Frankly," Ranck added, "do not believe he is worth as much as Mussolini. Do you? What would you think of Goering? Have informed Berlin article should be nine to ten hundred words."[5]

Hearst apparently agreed with Ranck. By 1934, Goering had replaced Hitler as the "German" insider/expert in the Hearst papers. Although Goering could not demand or expect the same fees as Hitler or Mussolini, he too was a tough bargainer, as William Shirer, who was a Hearst correspondent at the time, recalled in his memoirs: "We gave him a top price to begin with and he was always asking for more money for ensuing pieces. I must say he was genial enough about it, though persistent. 'Come on,' he would say. 'Your Mr. Hearst is a billionaire, *nicht wahr?* What's a thousand or two more dollars per article to him.'"[6]

As the Chief had told reporters at the pier when he left for his 1934 summer tour of Europe, he hoped "very much" that he would get a chance to meet Hitler. But first he had to take his annual motor tour of the continent. Accompanied by Marion; his three older sons, George, Bill, Jr., John, and their wives; Harry Crocker, who had become something of a traveling secretary; and the usual complement of business associates and Marion's Hollywood friends, Hearst toured the Spanish countryside in a caravan of seven open sedans. The group stopped off in Barcelona where everyone, except Marion and Hearst, went to the bull fights. Hearst had hoped to fly in the Graf Zeppelin from Spain to England, but was persuaded to use a chartered Fokker instead. The flight ended badly. According to Marion's biographer, the plane, when it reached England, was forced to land "in a hilly pasture, making a belly landing and killing eight sheep." Harry Crocker was deputized to find cars to drive the party to London. After a few days at the Savoy and a brief visit to Lord Mountbatten's country estate, Hearst and his guests drove west to St. Donat's, where they remained for a few weeks.[7]

While Hearst paused at St. Donat's, Hitler was making headlines in Germany. On June 30, 1934, in a sudden and brutal show of authority, he ordered the summary execution of his opponents within the Nazi party in what came to be known as the Night of the Long Knives, and then, citing the danger of internal dissension, proclaimed himself "responsible for the fate of the German nation," with the right to act, unilaterally, on its behalf.[8]

Like the rest of the American press, the Hearst papers harshly criticized the extralegal brutality with which Hitler had moved against his opponents. "I don't see how we can support the revolutionists," Hearst telegrammed Edmond Coblentz from St. Donat's with editorial instructions. "You might say however that [it] is a lesson in despotism. The German democracy has been destroyed and now instead of having peaceful democratic methods to decide differences of political opinion the Germans must resort to revolution with all its violence and bloodshed and with the cruel execution of the defeated leaders. America must be careful how it jeopardizes its democracy."[9]

Hearst wanted his editors to use the occasion of Hitler's coup to warn Americans against the dangers of despotism — in Germany and the United States. While he did not condone Hitler's usurpation of power in Germany, he was not about to focus his editorial wrath on the leader who he believed was poised to undo the injustices and right the imbalances of power created by the Versailles Treaty. Instead he used the narrative of Hitler's acceding to dictatorial powers as a cautionary tale for Americans. In mid-August, after the death of President von Hindenburg, German voters overwhelmingly approved Hitler's proposal to merge the positions of Reich president and Reich chancellor into a new office of führer and Reich chancellor, giving him de jure as well as de facto dictatorial powers. Hearst's editorial pages responded on August 29, 1934, by publishing an editorial cartoon of a swastika made of coiled fists. Over the swastika, in rainbow-shaped lettering, was the word AUTOCRACY. Under it were masses of faceless creatures, marked GERMANY. "What lesson," the caption read, "does the remorseless progress of autocracy convey to America? One lesson only: *'Democracy with all its shortcomings, is still the ark of free government!*

*America must be watchful and alert not to jeopardize its democracy! When we
see what despotism is and does we should realize that liberty is the most precious possession of mankind!*"[10]

Hitler's revolution in Germany shared headline space that summer with
news of labor unrest in the United States. In May, after local businessmen in
Minneapolis attempted to break a teamsters' strike by mobilizing their own
"citizens' army," violence erupted and the National Guard was called. That
same month, longshoremen in San Francisco went out on strike. On July
3, shipowners attempted to break the strike and open up the waterfront
by piercing the picket lines with a caravan of strikebreakers escorted by
seven hundred armed San Francisco policemen. The striking longshoremen fought back with "thrown objects — bricks, cobblestones, railroad
spikes — and their fists. . . . The police responded with gunfire." After a day
off to observe July 4, the battle was renewed on "Bloody Thursday." Two
people died, thirty were wounded by bullets, dozens more were clubbed,
stoned, and gassed. "The city became a camp, a battlefield," the organizer
and future novelist Tillie Olsen wrote of Bloody Thursday and the days that
followed. "The screams of ambulances sent the day reeling, class lines fell
sharply — everywhere, on streetcars, on corners, in stores, people talked,
cursing, stirred with something strange in their breasts, incomprehensible,
shaken with fury at the police, the papers, the shipowners."[11]

Hearst, at St. Donat's, was kept informed of events in San Francisco by
Jack Neylan who, on July 14, convened a meeting of the city's newspaper
publishers in his suite at the Palace Hotel. According to the California historian Kevin Starr, the publishers at that meeting agreed "to form a Newspaper Publishers Council to coordinate an antistrike campaign by the Bay
Area press. . . . The bound volumes of the Bay Area newspapers published
in mid-July 1934 reveal today just how blatantly the publishers and editors
followed Neylan's suggestion" that the strike had been taken over by sub-
versives, led by Harry Bridges, the thin Australian in the white longshore-
man's cap, who on July 16 called for a general strike of all San Francisco
workers. "San Francisco," Starr writes, was depicted in the *Examiner* and
the other San Francisco dailies "as a city on the verge of armed insurrection. Photographs of soldiers, tanks, and police are everywhere. . . . An *Examiner* photograph depicted a line of mounted police officers, wearing gas
masks, prepared to sweep Cossack-like into any mob that might material-
ize." Hearst, on vacation, learned all he knew about the strike from Neylan's
telegrams and the newspapers that were forwarded to him. Alarmed by the
accounts he received, he contributed to the hysteria by cabling home an ed-

itorial praising the way the English had brutally smashed the 1926 general strike in London.[12]

After only three days, the strike committee, frightened by the violence that had been unleashed, called off its general strike. Neylan telegrammed Hearst in triumph: "San Francisco crushed the general strike more thoroughly and promptly than London did [in 1926]. There has been no compromise of any character or description. As a San Franciscan you have a right to carry your head even higher than you did last week."[13]

Though the strike was over, the Red Scare that it evoked lasted much longer. The general strike in San Francisco which had been supported by the communists, combined with the violent clashes in Minneapolis and Toledo, at Kohler, Wisconsin, and elsewhere demonstrated vividly what could happen when an organized labor movement confronted an organized business community, supplemented by the police and/or the National Guard.

Hearst, traveling in his fleet of black limousines through southern and central Europe but never out of touch with events in the United States, could not help but compare the situation at home with that in Europe. Hitler had argued, in the pages of the *New York American* and elsewhere, that Nazism and Fascism had been brought into being as an antidote to Communism. The Communists were not strong enough to seize control of anything for themselves — not even in San Francisco — but, Hearst feared, their revolutionary excesses might generate a homegrown fascist movement which, in the end, would destroy American democracy. "Fascist movements both in Italy and Germany were born to prevent Communism," he cabled Ed Coblentz from London in September. "Communist movement and Communist atrocities are becoming very disturbing in America. Unless we want Fascist movement there to stop Communism, we must stop it through exposure and by arousing public to its dangers. . . . We must make powerful crusade against Communism and against revolution of all kinds if we want to retain our liberties."[14]

The danger posed by the New Deal was that its policies — especially Section 7a of the National Recovery Act, which recognized and protected labor's right to organize — had provided a cover of legitimacy for radical unionists like Heywood Broun and Harry Bridges and the Communists who worked with them. If Communism was to be stopped before it spawned a Fascist counterrevolution, Hearst concluded, Roosevelt's New Deal, which nourished it, had to be turned back. "The revolution in California against stable government and established order," Hearst argued in a signed editorial published one week after the San Francisco general strike, "would never have occurred except for the sympathy and encouragement which the fomenters of the revolution were receiving or believed they were receiving from those high in the counsel of the Federal Administration. The fires of sedition had been lit by these visionary and voluble politicians."[15]

Although the Chief did not identify Roosevelt directly as one of the politicians who had fomented revolution, he had drawn a direct line from the strikers to the Communists and from the Communists to the Roosevelt administration. The title of his editorial was "Americanism vs. Communism." It was to set the direction and the tone that Hearst and his newspapers would follow for the rest of the decade and the one to come.

Hearst, never one to sit still for long — especially when on holiday — had gathered up his troops from St. Donat's in mid-July, after the dust settled in San Francisco, and set off for the continent. He and his party drove through Belgium and Holland into Germany, then south through Switzerland to Rome and Venice, then north again "through Austria to Germany, stopping at Nuremberg . . . and other marvelous medieval towns." To his surprise — and delight — Hearst found Germany much as he had left it, "picturesque" and orderly. As he wrote in blue pencil to Julia Morgan on a postcard with a Nazi soldier on the front, "Everybody is for Hitler. We think he is a tyrant in America but his own people don't think so. They regard him as a savior. Nine-tenths of the people are for him. Even the Communists — that is the working classes who were Communists — seem to be satisfied with him. His chief opposition is religious. The Catholics registered some objections in the recent elections and of course the Jews hate him. Everything is very quiet and orderly here. There are no evidences of disturbance."[16]

Hearst's observations were not inaccurate. He returned to Germany at a moment when Hitler's popularity — as the "restorer of order" — was greater than it had ever been. While the foreign press, including the Hearst papers, had been horrified by the brutality of the Nazi massacres in late June and early July, within Germany, as Hitler's biographer Ian Kershaw has written, "it was a different matter. . . . What people saw for the most part was the welcome removal of a scourge . . . There was great admiration for what was seen to be Hitler's protection of the 'little man' against the outrageous abuses of power of the overmighty SA [Storm Trooper] leadership."[17]

Hearst was met in Munich by Putzi Hanfstaengl, who asked him for an interview. Though he later claimed that much of the text of the interview, as published on August 23 in the Munich edition of the Nazi party organ, *Völkischer Beobachter,* had been written by Hanfstaengl, the Chief assured Edmond Coblentz in New York that the final two paragraphs were "mine and exact." Responding to a question about the plebiscite that had affirmed Hitler's assumption of the powers of president and chancellor on the death of Field Marshal von Hindenburg, Hearst congratulated the Führer on his victory: "The sweeping majorities with which Hitler at first startled the world and which since we have learned to take for granted, have turned a new leaf in modern history. . . . If Mr. Hitler will give his country peace, order, and opportunity for the civilized development which the Great War largely destroyed everywhere, he will benefit not only his own people but the people of the whole world."[18]

Though Hearst did not object to the republication of the interview, he was furious when he learned that the American papers were reporting that he and his three sons and their families had accepted Hanfstaengl's invitation to attend the upcoming Party Congress in Nuremberg. Either because he had not accepted the invitation or hoped to be able to attend incognito, Hearst warned his American editors not to follow up on the story. "Chief directly . . . telephonically says nobody's business whether not he attends Nazi gathering. Chief hasn't received invitation. Chief says, 'Please say nothing and lay off story.'"[19]

Hearst did not attend the Nuremberg rally. Instead he spent most of September at Bad Nauheim, taking his annual cure at the baths. He was visited there by Dr. Alfred Rosenberg, one of the Nazi party's leading ideologues and most rabid anti-Semites. Hearst surely knew that he was being used by the Nazis to bolster their foreign standing at a time when they were under attack for the brutality of the Night of the Long Knives, but he allowed himself to be interviewed by Rosenberg anyway. The *Völkischer Beobachter* published the interview under the headline, "Confession of the American Newspaper-Baron: Under Adolf Hitler Germany has become a Land of Order." Hearst's own papers printed the interview almost verbatim, though under a very different headline, "W. R. Hearst Discusses a Free Press, Racial Issues, World Peace." In both the German and English texts, Hearst put a positive gloss on Hitler's seizure of power. Given the opportunity to comment on German anti-Semitism in response to Rosenberg's question about American "racial problems," the Chief referred instead to the threat Asia posed to European civilization and argued that since there were no racial differences between European peoples, they might well come together in a "United States of Europe, with all European peoples living in peace, and ready only to defend their Occidental civilization against Oriental invasion."[20]

Hanfstaengl returned to Bad Nauheim after the Nuremberg rally. He had invited Hearst to Nuremberg in the hope that he could arrange a meeting there between the publisher and the Führer. Hitler, Hanfstaengl told Marion, was so anxious to meet Hearst that he had volunteered to come to Bad Nauheim. Hearst was just as anxious to meet with Hitler. A private meeting and interview with the Führer would only enhance the Chief's position as the nation's leading publisher and a world leader of consequence.

Hanfstaengl arranged for a private plane to take Hearst and Harry Crocker to meet the Führer in Berlin. Hanfstaengl went along to translate. Marion, who insisted that she too wanted to meet Hitler, was included. When they arrived in Berlin, Marion was sidetracked by a friend from Hollywood who had run out of money and needed Marion to pay her hotel bill. Marion rode with her friend to her hotel, paid her bill, and helped her pack her things.

While she was still up in her friend's room, the phone rang. It was Hearst: "We're in the lobby, waiting." Marion went downstairs, only to discover that the meeting with Hitler had occurred in her absence. "W. R. was not impressed by him," Marion recalled later. "He wanted to talk about the persecution of the Jews, but Hitler's answer was this: 'There is no persecution of any sort.' Hitler said that the Jews should not have taken over the industries that were supposed to be for Germans. W. R. answered back, 'I should think industries would belong to every nationality.' Then he said goodbye."[21]

Marion's reminiscences, recorded twenty years after the fact, ring true. Hitler's contradictory statements that there was no discrimination against the Jews but that they shouldn't have been taking over German industries were in line with what others reported him as saying at the time.[22] It is also likely that Hearst would have taken exception to what Hitler said. The Chief at this stage of his life was in awe of no one, certainly not a newly elected leader who had only recently been on the Hearst payroll and was mouthing anti-Semitic nonsense.

Hearst's own account of his meeting with Hitler, written in the third person, was published a year after his death in Edmond Coblentz's *William Randolph Hearst: A Portrait in His Own Words*. According to Coblentz, so many questions had been raised about the interview with Hitler that Hearst felt obligated to dictate "the exact facts." In the memorandum published by Coblentz, which unfortunately is undated, Hearst claimed that he had agreed to meet with Hitler only "after consulting his friend Louis B. Mayer as to the advisability of any discussion. . . . Mr. Mayer had advised Hearst to have the interview and had said: 'You may be able to accomplish some good.' . . . After the usual exchange of formal civilities, Hitler speedily came to the point of his inquiries. He asked: 'Why am I so misrepresented, so misunderstood, in America? Why are the people of America so antagonistic to my regime?'" When Hearst responded that Americans were "averse to dictatorship," Hitler interrupted to say that he was "a product of democracy" and had been elected to the offices he held. Hearst then gave Hitler the "second reason" for American antagonism: "There is a very large and influential and respected element in the United States who are very resentful of the treatment of their fellows in Germany." He was referring, of course, to the German Jews. Hitler replied that such treatment was a thing of the past. "All discrimination is disappearing and will soon entirely disappear. That is the policy of my government, and you will soon see ample evidence of it."

Hearst left the interview convinced that he had been "able to accomplish some good," as his friend Louis B. Mayer had hoped.[23]

There is no reason to doubt the essential elements in Hearst's story. He remained close to Louis B. Mayer, who most likely had asked him to use his influence with Hitler. The Chief was now completely convinced of his powers of persuasion, both as an individual confidant and employer of world leaders and as a publisher whose papers reached twenty million Americans daily. He had no reason not to believe that Hitler was going to mend his ways and stop discriminating against the Jews of Germany. If the Davies and Hearst accounts of the meeting with Hitler err in any way, it is probably on the side of omission. It is difficult to believe that the Chief, given an occasion to speak privately with Hitler, would not have congratulated him on his courageous opposition to the League of Nations and his successful destruction of the German Communist party.

When asked by American reporters to "comment on his conversations with Hitler," Hearst claimed diplomatic immunity. "Visiting Hitler," he asserted, "is like calling on the President of the United States — one doesn't talk about it for publication." Only on arriving in London the following week did he begin to report on his visit. In interviews and articles, written in London and in New York, he repeated what he had said on his postcard to Julia Morgan. The German people were fully behind Hitler. "They regard him as a Moses leading them out of their bondage, and their bondage since the war has been utter and bitter." In response to a question about whether Hitler's policies regarding Jews, religion, et cetera, were satisfactory to the German masses, the Chief explained that while Hitler — and his policies — appeared to be popular with the German masses, he was in the process of modifying them "in some respects . . . particularly with regard to the Jews. . . . I think Germany made a great mistake in regard to the Jews. Furthermore I cannot see any reason for any hostility to the Jews in Germany. . . . The whole policy of . . . anti-Semitism is such an obvious mistake that I am sure it must soon be abandoned. In fact, I think it is already well on the way to abandonment."[24]

The Chief's confidence in Hitler was baffling. Though Hjalmar Schacht, who had become minister of the economy in July of 1934, had convinced Hitler that until the economy was in better shape there should be "no major interference with Jewish business," no attempts had been made either before or after Hearst's visit to revoke the 1933 laws that barred Jews from the civil service and most professions and limited their enrollment in German schools and universities. The Chief could not have failed to see the effects of these laws and the informal manifestations of Nazi anti-Semitism everywhere in Germany. Even Marion had been struck by the presence of the "Juden Verboten" signs.[25]

Hearst's public statements about the end of Nazi anti-Semitism were a hybrid mixture of wish fulfillment and press-agentry. In a protean version of "deterrence" theory, he had convinced himself that only the existence of a unified, militarized Germany could guarantee peace in Europe. His need to envision Hitler as the strong man of Europe who would deter aggression was so great that it blinded him — as it did many — to the realities of Nazi rule and Nazi anti-Semitism.

On September 17, near the end of his stay in Germany, Hearst wrote Joe Willicombe in the United States, "The doctor says that I am no worse than I was three years ago. The doctor further reassuringly said that I would last a few years yet if I got thin and took all strain off my heart. So when you see me I will be a slender sapling. No doubt about the 'sap' anyhow. I flew up to Berlin and had a long talk with Hitler yesterday. Hitler certainly is an extraordinary man. We estimate him too lightly in America. He has enormous energy, intense enthusiasm, a marvelous faculty for dramatic oratory, and great organizing ability. Of course all these qualities can be misdirected."[26]

On returning to the United States, the Chief took upon himself the task of making sure that these "qualities" were not misdirected. On November 20, 1934, he wrote Karl von Wiegand of his fears that Hitler, by "becoming involved in religious disputes and antagonism," was squandering the opportunity given him to rebuild Germany, restore the European balance of power, and prevent the outbreak of another world war. Putzi Hanfstaengl and other Nazi "extremists" were, Hearst worried, not giving their "boss the best advice on these religious situations. First the Jews were alienated, then the Catholics, and finally many Protestant sects. The most dangerous things to meddle with are people's religious beliefs. . . . What Germany needs is political unity and that can best be obtained with religious liberty. Religious conflicts can disrupt any nation. . . . If I were dictator I would be firm on essentials and liberal otherwise. I would allow complete freedom of religious belief and I would allow political liberty too, barring only seditious activity to undermine by conspiracy or to overthrow by violence the established government."

Hearst asked von Wiegand not to be "displeased with Hanfstaengl and others in the Government who seem antagonistic. Give them good advice and try to guide them towards a greater liberality which will gain approval both at home and abroad."[27]

This was to be his policy for the next four years, until the events of "Kristallnacht" in November of 1938 convinced him that Hitler was not going to follow his — or anyone else's — advice on Germany's Jews.

In December of 1934, the Chief instructed his chief correspondent in London, William Hillman, to "go to Berlin and deliver personally the following message to Dr. Hanfstaengl; and while there you might incidentally get a little talk with Hitler. QUOTE 'Now that all citizens including Jews given political rights in Saar, why not grant this everywhere and give them representation in proportion to population? That is only one percent and surely the mouse need not terrify the elephant. Such action would strengthen Germany immensely in the United States and I think everywhere. But if you do this, do it strikingly by manifesto in way to compel publication and attention everywhere . . . I think this would be wise, but please pardon me if I am unwarrantably interfering.'"[28]

We do not know where Hearst got his information about the Jews in the Saar, but he was certainly wrong. The Chief, nonetheless, continued to believe that Hitler would, in due course, change his policies toward the Jews. As William Dodd, the American ambassador to Germany, wrote Roosevelt in March of 1935, he had been told by von Wiegand that Hearst correspondents had been instructed to "give only friendly accounts of what happened in Germany." Hearst, it appeared, believed that by staying on the good side of the Nazis he would be able to retain access to Hitler and offer him the kind of advice he was not getting from extremists like Hanfstaengl. This did not mean however that the Chief was going to capitulate entirely to the Nazis. When the German government demanded that he replace von Wiegand as his correspondent in late 1934, he refused to do so.[29]

❦ 32 ❦

The Last Crusade

ALL SUMMER LONG, the Chief's words and actions in Europe had been carefully monitored and analyzed by press, politicians, and the president in Washington. No one, not even Hearst, knew quite where he stood politically. "I do not write as a reactionary — good lord! . . . I am not even a Conservative," he had declared in a front-page editorial cabled to his newspapers from Europe in August of 1934.[1] Two weeks later, in a front-page interview with a *New York Times* correspondent in Germany, he assailed the New Dealers as visionary Pied Pipers who were "wasting the people's money in futile and fantastic experiments. . . . We should end once and for all the NRA and its Nonsensical, Ridiculous, Asinine interference with national and legitimate industrial development."[2]

The president was concerned, as he should have been. "I am told that when Hearst returns he is going to attack the administration," he warned Henry Morgenthau, his secretary of the treasury, the week after Hearst's interview appeared in the *New York Times*. "Can't you look up his income tax and be prepared." Morgenthau did as requested and "found that there was plenty there; also plenty on Marion Davies. I told the President on Tuesday that we thought it would be much better to proceed at once on Hearst and Marion Davies income tax before he attacked because if we started something after he attacked us he would say that we were doing it to revenge and spite. The President agreed."[3]

Though there might indeed have been "plenty" in Hearst's and Marion's tax returns, there is no record that the Roosevelt administration ever took any action against them. With a midterm election on the horizon, the president decided, in the end, that it made more sense to try to placate the Chief than to antagonize him.

In late September, Roy Keehn, Hearst's Chicago editor and a Roosevelt supporter, wrote the president to suggest that a direct appeal from him might succeed in bringing the Chief back into the Democratic camp. "A cable could be sent to him by you expressing your interest in the fact that he had spent the summer studying conditions in Europe . . . and had acquired much information which you would like to share with him. An invitation to visit you at the White House on his return, for this purpose, would lead to discussion of other matters, and I believe would probably adjust the present difficulty." Vincent Astor, a friend, neighbor, distant relative, and yachting partner of the president who was on excellent terms with Hearst, made the same suggestion.[4]

Roosevelt agreed and had Stephen Early, his secretary, issue an invitation to the Chief to visit him. The Chief obliged, probably unaware that the president, who was sending a car to meet him at Union Station and take him directly to the White House "to dine informally at approximately eight o'clock," had only a few weeks earlier initiated a top-level fishing expedition into his and Marion's income tax returns.[5]

By receiving Hearst as he would have one of his own diplomats and engaging him in colloquy on the state of European politics, Roosevelt was able to work his magic again and bring Hearst back into the Democratic fold. On leaving the White House, Hearst declared that a "genuine recovery" was on the way and saluted the president for the encouragement he had given the business community.[6]

The following month, the Hearst papers refrained from attacking the Roosevelt administration or endorsing its Republican opponents in the midterm elections. In California, where the Democratic candidate for governor, Upton Sinclair — novelist, pamphleteer, utopian socialist, vegetarian, and pacifist — was running on the EPIC, "End Poverty in California," program without Roosevelt's support, the Hearst papers endorsed his Republican opponent. Compared with the other publishers in the state — especially Harry Chandler of the *Los Angeles Times* who led the attack on Sinclair — the Hearst papers' coverage was rather muted. Hearst himself waited until October 23, two weeks before Election Day, to announce his rather tepid support for Sinclair's Republican opponent, Frank Merriam. "Do not be too severe," Hearst warned his California editors, "but continue as we have been mildly and logically pointing out that Sinclair is unfit, visionary, and almost foolish." When it became clear that Sinclair was headed for defeat, the Chief urged his editorial writers and columnists to stop criticizing him. "Kill editorial, 'Is Sinclair Honest,'" Hearst had Joe Willicombe telegram his Los Angeles editor the week before the election. "The Chief says it is too abusive. He thinks Sinclair is beaten and does not want to print abuse matter which might create sympathy and votes."[7]

When Sinclair was "handsomely beaten by over 220,000," the Chief proudly telegrammed Arthur Brisbane with praise for the voters of his home state: "People of California do not have to try the smallpox in order to realize that they do not like it. I think an actual experiment with Sinclairism would not merely have been expensive but would have been ruinous. As it is, we are well rid of him, thank heaven."[8]

Though Sinclair had been soundly beaten in California, Democrats elsewhere were almost uniformly victorious. Hearst, still glowing from his visit to the White House, congratulated the president by telegram on his victory:

> There has been no such popular endorsement since the days of Thomas Jefferson and Andrew Jackson. It shows how faithful the American people are to the true spirit of Democracy and how safe American institutions are as long as the American Government is genuinely Democratic and rightfully mindful of the welfare of the plain people. Your equitable Democratic Administration prolongs indefinitely the life of the Republic and I believe your just and judicious measures will soon restore a National prosperity in which all will share with contentment and gratitude. The forgotten man does not forget.[9]

Concealed in this message of congratulations was a thinly disguised threat. Hearst's use of adjectives like "genuine," "true," and "equitable" were intended to remind Roosevelt that he reserved the right to abandon him and the party at a moment's notice should they or their programs cease to be "genuinely democratic."

Although he had refrained from making any statements that might have harmed Roosevelt in these first midterm elections, the Chief was still quite shaken by the events of 1934. Everywhere he looked, including his own newsrooms and Hollywood, Hearst saw threats to the foundations of American democracy, capitalism, and the free press. On November 5, he instructed George Young, the publisher of the *Los Angeles Examiner,* to compose a series of editorials "to this effect . . . If moving pictures are to be used for communistic propaganda, it will not be long before the American government will have to step in either to suppress such propaganda or to take over the film companies responsible for it and see that they are conducted on a patriotic American basis. The Hearst papers will not here specify the objectionable films, but it may be necessary to mention them and arouse the public to the danger of them and possibly stimulate the government to take action."[10]

His implicit threat to campaign for federal censorship of moving pictures was too frightening to be ignored. Fred Beetson of the Hays Office called George Young only days after the first editorial was published to say that he and Mr. Breen, Hays's chief censor, had sent copies of the Hearst editorial on Communism in Motion Pictures to each of the studios with a "warning that no pictures containing red propaganda would be tolerated."[11]

While other newspapers merely complained against Communist subversion, the Hearst papers intended to take an active role in rooting it out wherever it existed. For almost four decades, the Hearst papers had "acted" where others only talked. But this time, instead of going after murderers, kidnappers, corrupt politicians, greedy businessmen, Wall Street tycoons, or international bankers and armament manufacturers, the Chief directed his editors and reporters to target ordinary citizens.

Following the lead of Ralph Easley, who had begun the previous March to report on Communist subversion in the schools and universities, Hearst directed his editors to "support the actions of the universities in throwing out . . . Communists, and say, furthermore, that they ought to be thrown out of the country. Any one who plots to overthrow the government should forfeit his citizenship."[12]

They did what he asked, unleashing in every city with a Hearst paper a witch-hunt for Communists that would continue almost unabated for the next twenty years. In a letter to his editors that he published as an editorial on his front pages Hearst claimed that the Communists, if not stopped in their tracks, were going to unleash a Fascist backlash: "I do not think there is any actual Fascist movement in the United States as YET. . . . The menace of Communism is what developed Fascism in Europe. There was no other cause for it — no other reason for it. . . . Fascism will only come into existence in the United States when such a movement becomes really necessary for the prevention of Communism. We must not let it become necessary. We must not allow the Communists to get control of the machinery of government."[13]

The pressure on his editors to do the Chief's bidding was enormous. From San Simeon, the Chief ruled his empire by telegram and telephone. He delivered the orders and expected them to be followed. Every day, his local editors knew, he read his newspapers cover to cover. Those editors who did not do his bidding were likely to be replaced or moved to a lesser city. Those who did were rewarded. The Chief did not ask questions as to means, he was interested only in the ends achieved.

The editors of Hearst's *Syracuse Journal*, following the Chief's instructions, sent two young reporters, one from Syracuse, the other borrowed from the Hearst paper in Rochester, to Syracuse University to expose the

Communists that were supposedly lurking there. Working undercover, the two contacted Professor John Washburne of the School of Education on November 10, claiming that they were "Communists hoping to go to Russia next summer for study and . . . wanted to take up a special course in Syracuse University along Communist lines." After Washburne encouraged them to enroll at Syracuse, they met with him in his office. On November 22, they published a report of that meeting on the front page of the *Syracuse Journal,* alongside a photograph of the professor. Their story began on the first page and took up the entire second page. On page twelve, the *Journal* published a letter from Washburne denying that he had ever been "connected with any Communistic organization or activities." Two days later, to protect itself from libel charges, the *Syracuse Journal* published a front-page editorial, "Syracuse University and 'Liberalism' — If Communists Do Not Like Our Government, Let Them Go to Russia," in which it made clear that it had not charged any professor with being a Communist or a Socialist, but had only reported that the university had done nothing to root out the Communist professors, students, and clubs on campus.[14]

In the weeks to come, Hearst witch-hunters, sometimes posing as students, sometimes admitting they were reporters, visited professors in Boston, Chicago, Syracuse, Madison, and New York City. On Thanksgiving Day 1934, Professor Sidney Hook of New York University was visited by a former student now working for the *New York American* who "said that he had been sent on this special assignment by the city editor to investigate Professor Hook's radicalism, particularly his connection with the American Workers' Party." In mid-December, Professor George Counts and William H. Kilpatrick of Columbia University's Teachers College were interviewed by Hearst reporters who questioned both men about their positions on Communism, on revolution, student demonstrations on campus, and whether the Soviet experiment was a fit subject to be discussed in college classrooms.[15]

These interviews were then used, selectively of course, as evidence that the universities harbored un-American professors who believed it their right and duty to teach about Communism in their classrooms. Though men like Counts and Hook had little to fear from "exposure" in the Hearst press, many targeted by the Hearst papers feared, rightly, for their futures.

In Chicago, Hearst's *Herald-Examiner* went after an assistant professor of political science at the University of Chicago, Frederick L. Schuman, who had delivered an address on Communism and liberalism before the Cook County League of Women Voters. In an editorial entitled "Schuman of Chicago," the assistant professor was described as one of "these American panderers and trap-baiters for the Moscow mafia," who should be investigated by Congress and "gotten rid of" as a "red."[16]

The *Herald-Examiner* extended its attack against Schuman to the University of Chicago and its president, Robert Maynard Hutchins, who employed him. When Charles Walgreen, the owner of the drugstore chain, wrote Hutchins, with a copy to the *Herald-Examiner*, that he was withdrawing his niece because he was "unwilling to have her exposed to the Communist influences to which she is insidiously exposed," the Illinois state legislature opened an investigation to see if there was cause for rescinding the University of Chicago's state charter. The committee, after investigating, voted four to one against taking any action.[17]

While his editors and reporters were ferreting out Communists in the universities, Hearst took upon himself the task of enlightening his readers on the realities of life under Communist rule in the Soviet Union. On Saturday night, January 5, he arrived at the NBC studios in San Francisco to make his New Year's radio broadcast. This time, instead of focusing on American politics and prosperity, he devoted his entire address to Soviet Communism. His speech was reproduced verbatim on the front pages of his newspapers the next morning, a Sunday, when circulation was at its peak.

Hearst claimed that "five to ten million Russian farmers" were dying of starvation annually, their meager harvests stolen to support the Red Army. He referred to wholesale assassinations of government officials and "so-called conspirators," to people who had been shot in Moscow for stealing bread or sent to Siberia, and to the thousands of peasants who had been slaughtered by the Red Army or forced to flee to Afghanistan.

After assaulting his listeners and readers with facts and figures about assassination, starvation, despotism, and death in Soviet Russia, he brought the discussion back home, directly linking the Soviet Communists — and their campaign of murder and terror — to American leftists by asking "the free citizens of America" if they wanted "the cruel class rule of the proletariat in our country? . . . Do we want to see the violent overthrow of the entire traditional social order? Do any genuinely AMERICAN workers want to see the American working class led toward revolutionary class struggles? . . . Does anybody want the bloody despotism of Communism in our free America except a few incurable malcontents, a few sap-headed college boys and a few unbalanced college professors?"[18]

This was but the first of dozens of similar anti-Communist, anti-left, anti–New Deal editorials. To make sure their message was carried to the entire nation, the Chief directed Ed Coblentz and Tom White to buy space in non-Hearst newspapers and run his editorials as paid advertisements: "If my editorials are really useful, why not give them wide circulation outside of our own papers? . . . We could easily get eight or ten million more circulation for the articles, and perhaps this would help the papers."[19]

The battle was soon joined. The Communist party and its front groups counterattacked with every weapon in their arsenals. Like Hearst, the Communists were not content with simply exposing the sins of their enemies in their newspapers and pamphlets. They organized People's Committees Against Hearst, held rallies, and called for a boycott of all Hearst publications.[20]

Had the Communists been alone, their anti-Hearst activism might not have had much of an effect. But Hearst's simultaneous assaults on New Dealers in general, the American Newspaper Guild, and university professors and students had succeeded in cementing an early Popular Front alliance against him. Non-Communist progressives like John Dewey and George Counts, socialists like Norman Thomas, anti-Communist liberals like Roger Baldwin of the ACLU, and labor leaders like Heywood Broun enthusiastically signed on to the boycotts.

While his opponents did not have access to the millions of readers Hearst spoke to each day, they had media outlets of their own. In leftist journals like *Social Frontier, Common Sense,* the *New Masses,* the *Nation,* and the *New Republic,* in Communist-front pamphlets and publications, and in student newspapers from New York to West Virginia to Texas, Hearst was accused of being an un-American bigot at best and the leading American fascist at worst.[21]

The mainstream press covered the campaign against Hearst with unusual gusto. There were in the *New York Times* alone in the first two months of 1935 no less than twelve different stories about anti-Hearst activities. In late February of 1935, Hearst's opponents enjoyed a publicity breakthrough when they convened an "independent meeting" of educators at Atlantic City, dedicated to the Hearst problem. The keynote address, which was widely covered by the non-Hearst press, was delivered by Charles Beard, the former president of the American Historical Association, who declared Hearst to be an "enemy of everything that is noblest and best in our American tradition." The day after Beard's speech, 15,000 people assembled at a Communist-organized Friends of the Soviet Union rally at Madison Square Garden to attack Hearst again, this time for torpedoing the negotiations in Washington to reduce Soviet war debts.[22]

In mid-March, Coblentz informed the Chief from New York City "that the boycott, which is becoming more intense and widespread every day, is hurting our circulation. . . . Never a day passes that the Radicals do not hold a meeting; not [only] in Union Square, but in school houses, meeting halls, etc., and ask for a boycott of our papers. They are working among the young, the Jews and the parent teachers' organizations. We are countering, of course, with the American Legion organizations in the schools. As I said to you on the phone, it isn't doing us any good at present insofar as circulation figures are concerned, but I think it will eventuate to our advantage."[23]

The boycotts against Hearst's newspapers were soon expanded to include his newsreels. At Williams College, then at Amherst, then elsewhere, students booed the Hearst newsreels — at Amherst, they drowned them out with cries of "We Want Popeye! We Want Popeye!" — and picketed the theaters that carried them, forcing theater owners to protect themselves by removing the name Hearst from the titles. By November of 1936, the boycott became serious enough to compel Hearst to change the name of his newsreel from Hearst Metrotone News to News of the Day.[24]

President Roosevelt, perhaps repaying the Chief for sitting out the 1934 midterm elections, not only refused to join in the attack but went out of his way to do favors for Hearst. On January 22, 1935, Roosevelt issued an administrative order overturning the decision by the National Labor Relations Board that had ordered Hearst's *San Francisco Call-Bulletin* to reinstate Dean Jennings, the Guild delegate who had been forced to resign his position. The move infuriated Roosevelt supporters on the left and in the labor movement. Heywood Broun remarked caustically at a meeting of Guild members in February of 1935 that he now "pictured Roosevelt accompanying every decision with the statement, 'I hope Mr. Hearst is not going to object to this.'"[25]

Hearst also received an unexpected endorsement in *Fortune* magazine, which was owned by his major publishing rival, Henry Luce. In 1935, Ralph Ingersoll, an editor at the magazine, had visited Hearst at Wyntoon to discuss a feature story on Hearst's wealth. The Chief agreed to cooperate, researchers and writers were assigned, photographers dispatched, and the piece was all but ready for publication when Jack Neylan learned that the final version raised questions about the financial stability of the Hearst empire and its stock and bond issues. Neylan contacted Ingersoll, who was now managing editor, and convinced him to start all over again, using figures supplied by the Hearst organization. The rewritten version, Neylan reported to Hearst, was "not the type of article we would write or want at this particular juncture [but] judging it from the standpoint of what has been published and whispered over a long terms of years, by Standard Statistics, Poore's Manual and other [financial] publications, it is infinitely better."[26]

Though Neylan was probably exaggerating his role in the rewriting of the article, *Fortune,* for reasons we do not know, had done Hearst a great service by papering over the extent of his financial problems. In the introduction to the article, *Fortune* announced that it had had no intention of writing about "Hearst the man" or "Hearst the menace." These subjects had already been extensively covered. "Our project is narrower than that and consists simply of adding up Mr. Hearst's assets and his earnings, of estimating the corporate HEARST. And for this apparently arbitrary project we have a reason. All things considered, Mr. Hearst's is *the* most extraordinary fortune in the world."

The article went on to say that the reputation of Hearst as a "big borrower" was untrue. After valuing his assets and liabilities, *Fortune* estimated that Hearst's net worth was in the neighborhood of $140,000,000. Coming from *Fortune,* a well-respected magazine, this "audit" of the Hearst finances went a long way toward calming the fears of the investment community and the public as to the health of the Hearst corporations. That it was largely based on fictional estimates supplied by Hearst and his advisers was not widely known. That it may have been rewritten at the request of Jack Neylan was not known at all. That it presented a highly inaccurate picture of the state of Hearst's finances, especially his debts, would not be known for another two years.[27]

Hearst had for twenty years succeeded in keeping his relationship with Marion out of the newspapers and magazines. As with most Hollywood secrets, however, the story of their relationship had become part of the large body of "pseudo knowledge" movie fans exchanged with one another. In 1932, a New York investigator studying the effects of moving pictures on juvenile behavior interviewed "street boys" who rattled off dozens of rumors that "if publicly stated would be just ground for libel suits." Among them was the allegation that "Marion Davies is the mother of William Randolph Hearst's natural children."[28]

Only in the middle 1930s, as Hearst's opponents reinscribed his public image from rich, eccentric publisher to fascistic press baron, was his relationship to Marion reconfigured into something far more sinister than another item of Hollywood scandal. In November of 1934, Upton Sinclair began serializing what would become his book-length chronicle of his losing campaign for governor, and listed among the outrages that had compelled him to run for office, "our richest newspaper publisher keeping his movie mistress in a private city of palaces and cathedrals, furnished with ship-loads of junk imported from Europe . . . telling it as a jest that he had spent six million dollars to make this lady's reputation, and using his newspapers to celebrate her changes of hats."[29]

Sinclair did not mention Marion by name in 1934. But by the follow-ing year, she was regularly identified in the left-wing press as Hearst's mis-tress. In its devastating August 1935 critique of Louella Parsons as "Hearst's Hollywood Stooge," the popular-front journal *New Theatre* claimed that "Louella's chief function is to ballyhoo Marion Davies, the blond girl friend of her boss." In May of 1936, the *New Republic* claimed that Hearst had di-rected his newspapers to stop mentioning Mae West's new movie because she "had spoken slightingly of Miss Marion Davies." In December, the mainstream magazine *Newsweek* was referring to Marion Davies as Hearst's friend.[30]

Hearst, a pioneer in slash-and-burn journalism, had spent a lifetime rid-iculing public figures in print and editorial cartoons, but he had always drawn a line between the private and the public, if only because with such a complicated private life, he had to. His enemies drew no such lines. The pamphlets, booklets, broadsides, and open letters that were issued with reg-ularity — and circulated widely — by the Communist Party and its front groups indulged in elaborately contrived descriptions of Hearst's sinful pri-vate lives. In "Hearst: Labor's Enemy No. 1," James Casey claimed that the Chief lived with Marion and their twin sons in Santa Monica. His "life re-cord shows him to be, among other things, a liar, a thief, a blackmailer, a re-ceiver of bribes and a swindler. Incidentally, his record as a pervert places him side by side with his companion in fascism, Adolf Hitler."[31]

The centerpiece of the attack on Hearst was not his adulterous relation-ship with Marion, but his political alliance with Hitler and Mussolini. As the *New Masses* explained to its readers in the spring of 1935, "even with today's keen competition from the Huey Longs and Father Coughlins, [Hearst] remains the outstanding demagogue of America." In the final vol-ume of his *U.S.A.* trilogy, *The Big Money,* which he finished in early 1936, John Dos Passos referred to "Handsome Adolf . . . as Hearst's own loved in-vention."[32]

Hearst provided his opponents with continuing evidence of his Nazi sympathies by supporting Hitler's policies, no matter how flagrantly they violated international law and the provisions of the Versailles Treaty. Pub-licly and privately, the Chief did all he could to convince the American public that Hitler was not a madman, but an elected leader who was pursuing the policy he thought best for his nation. When, in March of 1935, the Führer announced that Germany had established an air force and was going to build a half-million-man army in blatant violation of the Versailles Treaty, Hearst dictated the outline of an editorial and asked Ranck to forward it to "Goering or whoever is chief source of articles in Germany in defense of Hitler's military program. . . . The idea is to get an article from Goering or somebody on these lines." The editorial which Hearst wanted Hitler or Goering to publish under their own bylines would explain that Germany, in rearming, was not preparing for war, but "merely doing what the United States would do under similar circumstances, [maintaining] its independence, its equality with other nations and its opportunity for peaceful economic development."[33]

Hearst's visit to Germany and Adolf Hitler in 1934 had quickly taken on major significance for his critics. A photo, purportedly of him leaving his interview with Hitler, flanked by Alfred Rosenberg and a line of storm troopers, became a staple of the Hearst literature. Oliver Carlson and Ernest Sutherland Bates claimed in their Hearst biography published in early 1936 that the Chief had "derived a new political vision from his Nazi contacts" in the summer of 1934. Ferdinand Lundberg, in *Imperial Hearst,* also published in 1936, claimed that Hearst had, on leaving Germany in 1934, "switched to the policy of praising the Hitler regime whenever possible and denouncing the Soviet Union in particular and communism in general" because Hitler had bribed him with a $400,000 contract to the International News Service to provide "news" of the world to the Nazi press offices.[34]

The bribe story had been leaked by Ambassador Dodd to a *New York Times* correspondent, who published it in the early edition of the January 1, 1935, paper. Because the *Times* editors could not verify the story — and feared a libel suit from Hearst — they pulled it from later editions and removed all copies of the issue in which it appeared from their morgue. (The early edition of the *Times* in which the story was carried is also missing from the microfilm collection at the New York Public Library.) The bribe story was picked up by the *Daily Worker* and other Communist party and Popular Front publications and found its way into Ferdinand Lundberg's biography, a 1938 *Saturday Evening Post* article, and a 1940 article in *Liberty.* In 1941, Hearst executives discovered that United Press salesmen were stealing subscribers from Hearst's International News Service by telling them about the Hitler bribe. The story was without foundation and on its face ludicrous, as Hearst needed no financial assistance to support Hitler. But it refused to go away.[35]

Though the Chief had warmly congratulated the president on his electoral victories in the November 1934 elections, he had gone back on the attack in January 1935, when Roosevelt tried to get the Senate to approve American entry into the World Court. With Roosevelt's harshest and most powerful opponents on the right, Senator Huey Long of Louisiana and Father Coughlin, the radio priest, Hearst organized a nationwide campaign against the Court and handed the president a rather humiliating defeat. Through the next few months, his attacks on the New Deal grew increasingly vicious, though he continued to criticize the president's appointees rather than Roosevelt himself. Finally, in April of 1935, he notified Ed Coblentz, his senior editor in New York, that the time had come to "settle down to a consistent policy of opposition to this Administration.... President Roosevelt is responsible for his Administration.... If he is leading the country to disaster, we cannot oppose his policies and support him.... There is no knowing what may occur four years later. We could easily have a permanent dictatorship on this basis. We have practically a dictatorship now."[36]

Though Roosevelt was not privy to this memorandum, he would not have been surprised by it. On April 30, 1935, Harold Ickes, the secretary of the interior, suggested that the president appoint as his undersecretary of the interior a lawyer who had represented John Strachey, the British Marxist the Hearst papers in Chicago had "exposed" as a Communist. Roosevelt was "disturbed. He is anxious just now not to do anything to stir up William Randolph Hearst," Ickes wrote in his diary. "He told me that he had had a talk with Arthur Brisbane [who] told him that Hearst was pretty erratic these days but that he believed that if he kept sending him friendly messages and didn't do anything to disturb him unduly Hearst would support him next year in the campaign. The president remarked that, outside of Hearst and one or two other strings of newspapers, all the balance of the press of the country would be against him and naturally he wants all the support he can get. Therefore, he wants to watch his step on the Hearst matter."[37]

Fearful that he was about to lose the editorial support of the only Democratic press lord in the nation, Roosevelt requested an opportunity to clear the air. The Chief agreed and sent Edmond Coblentz to Washington. Coblentz was received like the emissary of a foreign potentate and invited to spend the night. After being shown to his room to dress for dinner, Coblentz would write later, he was "ushered to the Oval Room where cocktails were served [with] Beluga caviar — plenty of it — supplied by [William] Bullitt, who was then ambassador to Russia. At dinner we drank toasts in California wine . . . Over cordials and highballs the President, in a session that lasted nearly four hours, attempted to explain away the misunderstandings which he said had plagued both our papers and himself."

Present for the discussion were Raymond Moley, one of the few New Dealers whom Hearst had not criticized by name, and Vincent Astor, who remained friendly with both the Chief and the president. The conversation was tense, but cordial. Roosevelt outlined his policy agenda and answered questions on a variety of items. In response to Hearst's concerns about tariffs, the president poured forth facts and figures about Japanese textiles, Swedish matches, French perfume, Brazilian cotton, and Argentine beef and butter. According to the account of the meeting prepared by Coblentz, the discussion proceeded smoothly until the editor asked Roosevelt about his plans for combating Communism. Roosevelt replied that he was fighting not only "Communism," but "Huey Longism, Coughlinism, Townsendism. I want to save our system, the capitalistic system; to save it is to give some heed to world thought of today. To combat [Huey Long's "Share the Wealth" plan] and similar crackpot ideas, it may be necessary to throw the forty-six men who are reported to have incomes in excess of $1,000,000 a year to the wolves. In other words, limit incomes through taxation to $1,000,000. . . . Further, it may be necessary to see to it that vast estates bequeathed to one person are limited in size."

This was not what Hearst would have wanted to hear, as he was one of those forty-six men with incomes over one million dollars a year. Roosevelt, sensing perhaps that he had gone too far, defended his proposals by claiming that such actions were necessary to halt the spread of Communism. "The thinking men, the young men, who are disciples of this new world idea of fairer distribution of wealth, they are demanding that something be done to equalize this distribution. . . . We do not want communism in this country, and the only way to fight communism is by —" As Roosevelt paused, looking for the right word, Coblentz interjected, "Neocommunism." The president laughed. Vincent Astor interjected that the president's tax plan, if enacted, would bankrupt Astor's estate. "The attitude of the President to this remark seemed to be 'well, that's just too bad.'"

Roosevelt had, it appeared, determined before his meeting with Coblentz that he was going to push forward with what historians would call his "second New Deal." As he indicated to Coblentz, he had no other choice. He was threatened on the left by a revived labor movement and the Popular Front and on the right by "business and opposition papers" and crackpots like Long, Coughlin, and Townsend. Of the two, he feared the rightist crackpots much more and was determined to form an alliance on the left to block their advance.

Immediately after the meeting, Roosevelt dispatched an "emissary" to San Simeon to correct what he feared might be Coblentz's negative, if truthful, account. His solicitude had the desired effect. Instead of giving Coblentz the go-ahead to attack the president, Hearst sent his editor a "'hold your fire' admonition." The détente lasted little more than a month. The truth was that there was no way for Roosevelt to build an alliance on the left without alienating Hearst.[38]

In late June, Roosevelt effectively cut Hearst loose when he delivered his new tax message to Congress, "replete," as Kenneth Davis has written, "with phrases which, in the process of 'stealing thunder' from Huey Long, were as lashes of lightning across the back of William Randolph Hearst and of every other scion of enormous wealth." Harold Ickes was meeting with the president at the time his message was being introduced in Congress. Roosevelt read the text of his message out loud to Ickes. "He told me that he thought it was the best thing he had done as President. . . . At one place in the message he looked up at me with a smile and said, 'That is for Hearst.' I can imagine the clamor that will go up from Hearst."[39]

"President's taxation program is essentially Communism," Hearst telegrammed Coblentz and Bainbridge Colby, his chief editorial writer, as soon as he read the tax message. "It is, to be sure, a bastard product of Communism and demagogic democracy, a mongrel creation which might accurately be called demo-communism, evolved by a composite personality which might be labeled Stalin Delano Roosevelt. . . . It divides a harmonious and homogeneous nation into classes, and stimulates class distinction, class discrimination, class division, class resentment, and class antagonism."[40]

Hearst's objections to increased income taxes were motivated as much by self-interest as by his political philosophy. He was already stretched to the limit by outstanding obligations. Worse yet, his corporate and personal finances were so hopelessly intertwined — and had been for half a century — that there was no way to separate his personal income from that of his corporations. He lived rent-free at San Simeon, Wyntoon, St. Donat's, and in hotel suites in New York, Los Angeles, and San Francisco, which were paid for by his corporations. His art was bought by an import-export firm which was a subsidiary of American Newspapers, Inc., his chief holding company. His personal servants were on Hearst company payrolls, as were Millicent, the boys, Marion, and members of Marion's and Millicent's families.

"It is of vital importance to me that nothing shall be charged to me that is not necessary — so that I shall not have to pay any more income taxes than are necessary," he directed the head of his newspaper division, Tom White — by telephone message followed up by written memo — in November of 1935:

> I have got to keep my actual net income under a million dollars. *If it goes over a million dollars, they will practically confiscate the income.* I want $30,000 a week instead of fifty or whatever it is, deposited in my account. Out of that account, which is approximately a million and a half a year, I will be able to charge off, I should say about one-half — such as construction at ranch and similar expenditures that can legitimately be borne by the corporations, and leave me an income on which I will have to pay taxes of from $500,000 to $700,000. That is all the income I can afford to have, and it is all I am going to have.[41]

Following Roosevelt's lead — at a healthy distance — Frank Merriam, the Republican governor of California whom Hearst had helped elect, instituted a steeply graduated state income tax for those who resided in California for at least six months a year. The Chief was outraged. He threatened, in an open letter to *Variety,* that he would leave the state — and encourage the Hollywood studios to do likewise — if the state income tax was not rescinded. "Heaven knows I do not want to leave California. No one does, least of all a native son, whose father was a pioneer; but it is utterly impossible for me to remain here and to occupy a place like San Simeon on account of the Federal and State tax laws." For the next few years, until the residency requirements were changed from six to nine months for the benefit of Hearst and the movie moguls, the Chief evaded the state tax by spending more time in New York than in California.[42]

On July 1, 1935, President Roosevelt sent a personal note to Robert Maynard Hutchins, the president of the University of Chicago, who had just been questioned by the Illinois state senate committee investigating the allegations presented in Hearst's *Chicago Herald-Examiner* that the university was harboring known Communists. "Dear Bob," the president wrote in a note that was marked on top with the notation "Private and Confidential," "You must have had a vile time with that inquisition. I sometimes think that Hearst has done more harm to the cause of Democracy and civilization in America than any three other contemporaries put together."[43]

Roosevelt had good reason to fear Hearst in 1935, as he began to prepare for his reelection campaign. When George Allen, a newspaperman and friend of Mrs. Roosevelt, returned to Washington on August 1, 1935, from five weeks of travel across the country, he wrote her that the only force that was "effectively combating the Administration" was the Hearst papers. A penciled note at the bottom of Allen's letter indicated that Eleanor had forwarded it to her husband: "F.D.R. I'm *sure* this is true. E.R."[44]

Still, the president held his fire. While he continued to complain about Hearst in private, he said nothing in public. Then, in mid-August, he was presented with an opportunity to attack the publisher that was too good to ignore. The White House had intercepted a telegram from Ed Coblentz to Hearst wire service chiefs and editors, informing them that the Chief wanted the words RAW DEAL used instead of NEW DEAL in all editorials and news stories. Roosevelt, on reading the telegram, called in Raymond Moley, his speech writer and adviser, and asked him to draft a response to the telegram. On Thursday morning, the White House released the intercepted telegram with a statement from the president, based on Moley's earlier draft:

"The President believes that it is only fair to the American people to apprise them of certain information which has come to him." After citing an unnamed "public-spirited owner of a great newspaper" who had instructed his staff that "facts must be presented as facts if the value of the news is to be saved" and congratulating the great majority of owners and editors of papers for conducting their papers in this spirit, Roosevelt criticized the minority of editors or owners who engaged "in what is known as the deliberate coloring of so-called news stories, in accordance with orders issued to those responsible for the writing of news." He then reproduced Hearst's telegram and reminded the public that the message referred "not to editorial expression but to news columns."[45]

Roosevelt was, for the first time, returning Hearst's fire with fire of his own. As Harold Ickes noted in his diary on August 27, the breach between Hearst and the administration was now complete.[46]

Hearst responded by delegating Bainbridge Colby, a conservative Democrat who worked for him as an editorial writer, to convene a conference of leading Democrats to discuss the formation of a new "Jeffersonian Democratic" party to replace Roosevelt's "Socialist-Democratic" party. When asked who might lead the new party as its presidential candidate in 1936, Hearst suggested Al Smith, the same man whom he had attacked the year before as the puppet of Wall Street plutocrats.[47]

The Chief's third-party plans were stillborn when the anti-Roosevelt Democrats he had hoped would join him stayed away. The best way to dethrone Roosevelt, he now concluded, was to run a credible Republican against him. Hearst had been checking into the credentials of the governor of Kansas, Alfred Landon, as a possible contender since the summer of 1935, when Richard Berlin, the head of his magazine division, wrote Landon that Damon Runyon and Adela Rogers St. Johns had been assigned to write articles about him and his wife for *Cosmopolitan* and *Good Housekeeping*, respectively. According to Landon's biographer, Donald McCoy, Hearst investigators combed the state over the next few weeks checking through local newspaper files and visiting the governor. On December 10 three private railway cars arrived in Topeka with Hearst, Paul Bloch of the Bloch newspaper chain, and Eleanor Patterson, the publisher of Hearst's *Washington Herald*. Brisbane and Marion Davies were also in the party. The *New York Times* reported the next morning that "after luncheon in the rambling old frame home which serves as the Executive Mansion, Mr. Hearst exclaimed [of Governor Landon]: I think he is marvelous. To say I am favorably impressed puts it very mildly."[48]

By February, the Chief had taken direct control of the Landon campaign. Henceforth, he informed his editors across the country, "all recommendations to the Governor or his managers, regarding general policies or particular acts, shall be sent to me as a clearing house, so that I can prevent confusing and contradictory advices, and also that I can make sure that I agree with the policies recommended."[49]

Hearst's support, as Republican leaders whispered privately and *Fortune* magazine asserted publicly in March, was a decidedly mixed blessing. Landon was committed to running a moderate, progressive campaign; Hearst was only interested in scorched-earth, blame-Roosevelt-for-everything, anti-Communist hysteria. There was little room for compromise. In May of 1936, Hearst embarrassed Landon by running his own pro-Landon slate of delegates in the California primaries. When Landon declined to repudiate Hearst's support, his principal Kansas booster and adviser, William Allen White, made his displeasure public: "Professionally, Hearst is a form of poison. Politically, he has degenerated into a form of suicide. Whoever ties up with him begins to smell lilies and attract the undertaker." By mid-May, according to a report in *Newsweek*, the "Landon lieutenants made little secret of the fact that they had come around to White's way of thinking" and were trying to find a way to "'throw' Hearst off the Landon band-wagon."[50]

Hearst's unpopularity was having a direct impact on his newspapers. Had the Hearst papers spoken with more than one voice, as did, for example, the Scripps-Howard papers which syndicated both Heywood Broun on the left and Westbrook Pegler on the right, they might have been able to weather the storm more easily. Unfortunately, the Chief now allowed no voice but his own. If on other issues he had once permitted alternate viewpoints to be expressed in his pages, he demanded that his newspapers — and all other media outlets — present only his "American" viewpoint. During the 1936 presidential campaign, when the CBS radio network gave fifteen minutes of air time to Earl Browder, the candidate of the Communist party, the Chief was enraged. The next day, his newspapers carried an anti-CBS editorial and published a cartoon in color that showed Bill Paley, the founder and owner of the network, on a soapbox waving a red flag.[51]

The Chief was, his editors feared, becoming so obsessed with his anti-Communist, anti–New Deal crusade that he was damaging his own credibility and that of his newspapers. Arthur Brisbane was, according to Moses Koenigsberg, so worried about the effects of Hearst's anti–New Deal editorials on the readers of the *Mirror,* who voted Democratic and were fans of the president, that he persuaded the Chief "to devote much space to the President's birthday ball . . . whose proceeds were distributed to the welfare of infantile paralysis victims. This sop, it was hoped, would prevent the complete alienation of vast groups of Roosevelt supporters who read Hearst papers."[52]

T. V. Ranck, the editor in charge of the March of Events Sunday section, warned that the Sunday papers had become so "crowded with features" that there was little space left "for active news." He suggested that the Sunday papers devote less space to multipart "communist features" and more to articles on less controversial topics like "reciprocal treaties." Hearst did not agree. Instead of reducing the number of Russian horror-story features, he signed up new series by known anti-Communists like Isaac Don Levine, and unknown ones like an "eye witness" former party member named Andrew Smith.

On more than one occasion, T. V. Ranck and other editors were forced to intervene — gently — to avoid acute embarrassment. In mid-May of 1935, they told Hearst that the photographs of Russian famine victims he wanted to publish — first in his newspapers, then in book form — had been doctored. It was already too late. The Hearst papers had, by this time, published so many faked photographs of purported victims of Soviet violence that a sketch in the left-wing musical revue, *Parade,* featured a Hearst reporter photographing a hungry American family to illustrate a story of Russian famine.[53]

As Tom White, perhaps his most trusted newspaper associate, warned Hearst in January 1936, under the pretext of communicating the sentiments of Jewish leaders, his all-out war against New Dealers and Communist agents was alienating precisely those groups that had steadfastly supported him for a half century. The bitterness of his attacks on Felix Frankfurter as a Communistic New Dealer had, White suggested, created the false impression among some that the Chief was anti-Jewish.[54]

Hearst responded immediately that he would not temper his criticism of Frankfurter or any of Roosevelt's other advisers: "I do not think that any man should be attacked because of his race or religion, or that he should be immune from attack because of race or religion."[55]

Two weeks after White's warning, the issue of anti-Semitism surfaced in a slightly different context. When Hearst indicated an interest in publishing a highly favorable interview with Hitler, his editors in New York telegrammed their reservations. "While the Hitler material will doubtless be interesting," T. V. Ranck wrote the Chief in San Simeon, "both Coblentz and I feel publication of sympathetic interview by us might do very serious harm at this time." Hearst answered that he did not "care whether it does any serious harm or not. If the interview is an important news item we are going to print it. We are running an American newspaper not German paper or a Jewish paper or any other kind of paper. We are printing the news." While his editors in New York dared not contradict the Chief, they were determined not to publish the interview. The next day, Ranck telegrammed from New York that because of questions about the "copyright situation, both the legal department and T. J. White feel we should not take chance on the interview . . . Am greatly distressed." This time Hearst did not object.[56]

In late February 1936, Edmond Coblentz, who had been running the *New York American,* provided the Chief with his progress report:

> The daily *American* has won many new readers and it has lost many readers. Among our new readers are many thousands we call the better class, who approved your policies and were thereby attracted to the paper in the first instance. The loss of circulation is in the districts inhabited by the poorer class of Jews, largely in the Bronx and Brownsville in Brooklyn. A survey of the individual dealers shows that we have lost between twenty and twenty-five thousand copies in these radical Jewish centres. All due, of course, to the vi-

cious campaign that has been carried on by the Communists. This situation can be overcome in time. . . . The survey shows further that the *Times,* and the *Times* only, increased in circulation in the spots where we show losses.

Coblentz concluded that Hearst's "editorial policies appeal, and appeal strongly to intelligent, patriotic Americans," implying that "poor Jews" did not belong to this category. Unfortunately, this was a group that had always supported the Hearst papers and whose loss he could ill afford.[57]

In late April, Hearst, recognizing the negative impact of his editorial policy on circulation among those groups that were joining Roosevelt's New Deal coalition, telegrammed Coblentz from New York that he was "going to cut down on political editorials and try to get a little more variety of topics into the papers. It has gotten so that everybody knows about what they are going to see on the editorial page every day. Besides, I think continual harping along on one string loses effectiveness. I suggest that we have enough variety of editorial to make the occasional exposure of Administration fallacies effective . . . Probably people are tired of attacks. I think I myself am tired of reading them."[58]

Hearst's troubles with the working-class and left-of-center readers that had always been the mainstay of his circulation were exacerbated in February of 1936 when he catalyzed a newspaper strike in Milwaukee by refusing to let the editor of his *Milwaukee News* negotiate a contract with the local chapter of the American Newspaper Guild. The Guild leadership welcomed the strike. As the *Guild Reporter* explained to its readers in March of 1936, Hearst was particularly vulnerable to a newspaper strike because "his papers are based on mass circulation. They must have the confidence of the masses to survive. The workers can make him change his labor policies or destroy him."[59]

Heywood Broun and the Guild seized the opportunity that Hearst gave them to bring attention to their struggle by organizing a Citizens Committee which called for a national boycott of the Hearst papers. John Dewey, Robert Sherwood, Dorothy Thompson, Sinclair Lewis, Edna Ferber, and a variety of other prominent leftists and liberals enlisted as members; Eugene O'Neill contributed to the strike fund; Charles Beard declared his support.[60]

"It must be admitted," Broun wrote in his *Nation* column, "that William Randolph Hearst has done much to unify labor. He has provided in himself the full and perfect symbol for the anti-labor movement." Hearst was indeed the perfect enemy for the developing Popular Front coalition of New Dealers, unionists, and leftists. He even looked the part: immense, jowly, unspeakably rich, a villain as unscrupulous as the ones in Frank Capra's movies, a "robber baron" as avaricious as the ones Matthew Josephson wrote about in his best-selling 1934 book on an earlier generation of American villains.[61]

In mid-August, the Guild called a second strike against a Hearst paper, the *Seattle Post-Intelligencer*. The Seattle Guild had the support of local labor leaders, including the Teamsters Union boss Dave Beck, who dispatched pickets to persuade the mechanical unions to stay off the job in solidarity with the striking guildsmen. Hearst had no choice but to close down publication in Seattle. Two weeks later, he authorized a settlement in Milwaukee. Even the Chief could only afford to fight one strike at a time.[62]

In March of 1936, the president had signaled that it was "open season" on Hearst by ridiculing him, by name, during a press conference. Asked if he had clamped a censorship on his administration, the president, *Newsweek* reported, "snapped back his answer: Preposterous! The correspondent must have read that in a Hearst paper!" Following on the president's comments, congressional Democrats who, with their president, had sat on the sidelines during the first rounds of attacks, joined the battle. Senator Hugo Black of Alabama released a series of telegrams to and from Hearst which he had subpoenaed in an investigation of Western Union lobbying which had nothing to do with the publisher. Though Hearst — and the ACLU — protested that Black had no right to release private communications, the damage had been done. In one of the telegrams, Hearst referred to Representative John J. McSwain of South Carolina as a "Communist" who ought to be impeached. *Newsweek* reported that McSwain, on being informed of Hearst's attack, immediately took to the floor of the House to roar epithets at the "fiend of San Simeon." His blast was seconded by fellow Democrats in the House and Senate. Senator Minton of Indiana, in a slightly veiled attack on Hearst's private life, claimed that not only would Hearst "not know the Goddess of Liberty if she came down off her pedestal and bowed to him, he probably would try to get her telephone number."[63]

Hearst filed suit against Senator Black and the members of his committee for unwarranted seizure of his property — the telegrams. Black responded by asking Congress for an additional $10,000 to continue his investigation. When the vote was called on Black's request for more funding, "not a dissenting voice piped up in the Senate."[64]

By 1936, Hearst had become so immense a figure of controversy that three biographies were published. In March, Ferdinand Lundberg enlarged upon the damning portrait he had written for the leftist journal *Social Frontier* in *Imperial Hearst,* which was first published by the Equinox Cooperative Press, then republished by the Modern Library in 1937. In April 1936, Viking published *Hearst: Lord of San Simeon* by Oliver Carlson and Ernest Sutherland Bates, who had earlier attacked Hearst in a series of articles in *Common Sense.* As an antidote to these portraits, Cora Older, a writer who was married to Fremont Older, Hearst's long-time San Francisco editor, published *William Randolph Hearst: American,* also in 1936.

The most critical of the biographies — and the one that would, in the end, secure the most attention — was Lundberg's. Charles Beard wrote the preface:

> Unless we are to believe in the progressive degradation of the American nation, we are bound to believe that Hearst's fate is ostracism by decency in life, and oblivion in death. Odors of his personality may linger for a time . . . but they will soon evaporate in the sunlight of a purer national life. Even school boys and girls by the thousands now scorn his aged image and cankered heart. . . . The verdict of the American spirit has been rendered in tones which even he cannot mistake. It goes with him to the vale of shadows.[65]

By the late summer of 1936, these demonic representations of Hearst had reached so deeply into the nation's psyche that Roosevelt and his advisers recognized that the worst thing that could be said of Alfred Landon was that he was supported by Hearst. Roosevelt authorized Harold Ickes to tie Landon to Hearst in a series of national radio broadcasts. The response to his broadcasts convinced Ickes, as he wrote in his diary on August 30, that there was "more widespread anti-Hearst feeling among the people than there has been for a great many years, if ever. I am told that when his name appears on the screen in some movie theaters, he is hissed, and there are anti-Hearst clubs being organized in some parts of the country."[66]

Hearst, vacationing in Europe, remained in touch with his editors through the final stages of the 1936 campaign season. He had, in the heat of the election campaign, returned to his editorial attack mode and directed his editors to go after Roosevelt with no holds barred. In mid-September, Ed Coblentz wrote him from New York with a progress report: "I know that you will be pleased to know that our campaign against Communism is bearing fruit. We are carrying stories every day reporting the anti-Communist activities of patriotic organizations, church organizations, and civic and commercial bodies." Coblentz had that day secured a document issued by the Comintern in which Earl Browder, the head of the American Communist Party, had "outlined the official policy of the Communists of America in support of Mr. Roosevelt. It is a damning document. We will print it with facsimiles, and instruct all our papers to display it vigorously."[67]

The charge that Browder and the Comintern were, as H. L. Mencken put it, "rooting for Roosevelt," was, the president believed, so potentially dangerous that he directed his press secretary to rebut it the day before it was scheduled for publication. "My attention," Stephen Early informed the press, "has been called to a planned attempt led by a certain notorious newspaper owner to make it appear that the President passively accepts the support of alien organizations hostile to the American form of Government. Such articles are conceived in malice and born of political spite. . . . The American people will not permit their attention to be diverted from real issues to fake issues which no patriotic, honorable, decent citizen would purposely inject into American affairs."[68]

The effect of Roosevelt's preemptive strike was to publicize the story even more. Hearst answered Early's charges in a cable from Amsterdam that was reprinted on his front pages: "The President has issued a statement through a secretary. He has not had the frankness to say to whom he refers in the statement. . . . Nevertheless, since his conglomerate party of Socialists, Communists, and renegade Democrats has consistently, and rather ridiculously, tried to make me an issue in their muddled campaign, I think I am justified in assuming that I am the object of the statement." Hearst denied that he had ever claimed that the president had "willingly or unwillingly" solicited or received the support of the Communists, only that he deserved it because since his election he had "adopted the platform of the Karl Marx Socialists in almost every word and letter." If further proof were needed of FDR's devotion to Communism and the Soviet Union, it could be found in his recognition of the "bloody dictatorship of Stalin in Moscow," a recognition which, the Chief failed to mention, he had strongly endorsed.[69]

In making his case against the president, Hearst combined two of his favorite political weapons: Red-baiting and guilt by association. His newspapers first identified Roosevelt supporters like Sidney Hillman and David Dubinsky as Communists and then used that identification to prove that Roosevelt was himself a Communist. As Coblentz informed Hearst in his September 25 message, "My slogan for the State campaign is 'remember Dubinsky and vote Landon insky.'"[70]

Spurred on by Coblentz, who insisted that the Chief and his proxy Alfred Landon were winning the battle against Roosevelt, Hearst pounded away. In a front-page editorial on October 1 he wrote:

Mr. Roosevelt declares that he is not a Communist, but the Communists say he is one. The Communists ought to know. Every cow knows its own calf. . . . The Communists may be misguided in many ways, but they are at least sincere. . . . They hail Mr. Roosevelt as a comrade. Stalin hails him, and asks the Communists to support him. . . . Mr. Roosevelt says HE IS NOT a Communist; but what about the marxian professor Frankfurter, Communistic counsellor of the Administration and personal confidant of Mr. Roosevelt? And what about the fiery and flaming labor lawyer, [Donald] Richberg, Communistic spokesman of the Administration, who assures us that the revolution is actually here? And what about the terrible [Rexford Guy] Tugwell, who preaches Bolshevism violently . . . And what about little Miss Pink [Secretary of Labor Frances] Perkins, who wants all the Communists and criminals to be kept in the country and new ones to be invited in? And what about I.W.W. [Secretary of Commerce Henry] Wallace, who is worth a dollar a day or less, and thinks that nobody should have more?[71]

As proof that their anti-Communist onslaught was succeeding, Coblentz reported on his most recent conversation with "our friend [FBI director J. Edgar Hoover], concerning whom I phoned you. He was sent for by the President and asked about the seriousness of the Communist movement. The President was told it was very serious. After some hedging he ordered our friend to start an immediate investigation. . . . He [Hoover] told me of having been sent for by Attorney General Cummings just before we printed that first blast from the Russian document [charging that the Comintern supported Roosevelt for president]. Cummings said to our friend, 'this is a forgery' and was promptly told that it was not a forgery and that if he [Cummings] gave out a statement to that effect he would have his fingers burned."[72]

All through October, the Chief, from Europe, and his editors in New York kept up their barrage against Roosevelt as a Communist dupe. They were so consumed by their campaign that they did not notice that the wind was blowing away from them. It was one thing to "expose" selected professors, college-age "sap-heads," and White House advisers as communistic, but to claim in print that the president was "Moscow's candidate" was to venture a step too far.

Had Hearst kept his name out of his newspaper, as did Adolph Ochs of the *New York Times*, or kept his editorials off his front page, it would have made it easier for those who disagreed with him politically to buy his papers. But the more he paraded his opinions, the more ammunition he provided for the boycott leaders, who argued that to buy a Hearst paper was to endorse his political views. The boycotts organized by the Communists and the American Newspaper Guild were joined by hundreds of informal, quiet protests, as families who had once subscribed to the local Hearst paper abandoned it out of disgust with the Chief's diatribes. Long-time readers, forced to choose between the publisher and the president, banned the Hearst papers from their homes. In the Bronx, New York, the Pelham Parkway Democratic Club responded to Hearst's attack by holding a meeting "attended by a thousand of its members and friends," at which it was resolved "by unanimous accord [to] refrain from purchasing any Hearst publication. . . . It is our thought," the club leaders telegrammed the president, "that this attitude will be followed by all Democratic clubs and communities in this state and the entire country."[73]

By late October, the effect of the anti-Hearst boycotts was such that even the stalwart Cissy Patterson was, according to her friend Harold Ickes, preparing "to resign as publisher of the *Washington Herald*. Her decision was purely a business one. Apparently she cannot sit idly by and see circulation and advertising falling off because of the way Hearst plays politics."[74]

IX

The Fall

❦ 33 ❦

The Fall

THE CHIEF RETURNED FROM EUROPE in early November 1936 on the *Queen Mary*. It was an adventurous trip. Alice Head, who traveled with the party, wrote Jack Neylan that W. R.'s eldest son, George, had become "enamoured of a Polish dancer when we were on the continent and eloped with her. His father managed to get him back just in time to board the *Queen Mary*. We were met by what seemed like a vast army of detectives and Scotland Yard men who warned us that the woman was on the boat. (I saw her — prowling around like a panther.) George was hustled into his cabin and locked in. I said to the Chief, 'Why not let him change cabins with Dick Berlin [the chief of Hearst's magazine division]? Then when the woman goes to find him, she will find Dick.' The Chief said, 'Somebody's going to be shot anyway. Which shall it be?'"[1]

On arriving in New York, with both George and Dick Berlin intact, Hearst gave an impromptu news conference at the pier and expressed his belief that Governor Landon would be elected.[2] The following day, Franklin Delano Roosevelt was reelected by the greatest landslide in U.S. history. Sometime during the evening of Election Day, at Hyde Park, where the Roosevelt family was celebrating its victory, John Boettiger, Roosevelt's son-in-law, was called to the phone. Harold Ickes recounted the incident in his diary. Marion Davies, whom Boettiger knew from Hollywood, was on the line.

"'Hello, John, this is Marion Davies. I just wanted to tell you that I love you. We know that a steam roller has flattened us out, but there are no hard feelings at this end. I just wanted you to know that.' Then, while John was still holding the wire at the request of Marion Davies, Hearst himself took the telephone at the other end and he said something like this: 'Hello, is that you, Boettiger? Well, I just wanted to repeat what Marion said, that we have been run over by a steam roller, but that there are no hard feelings.'"³

Hearst graciously acknowledged his defeat, and, in the weeks that followed his return to the United States, went out of his way to make amends to his former enemies. According to Harold Ickes, he "slobbered all over the president" in a signed congratulatory editorial in his newspapers. He also settled the Seattle strike, and hired John Boettiger to edit the reopened *Post-Intelligencer* with an offer of editorial freedom that was without precedent in the Hearst empire.⁴

Unfortunately, his turnabout was too sudden, his gestures toward Roosevelt too transparent an attempt to curry favor. Instead of mending fences, he made himself into something of a laughing stock.

At Mrs. Roosevelt's fourth annual Gridiron Widows Party, held a month after the election, Washington's newspaperwomen entertained their guests with three different versions of *Romeo and Juliet*. The *New York Times* reported on the second episode the next morning:

> Juliet, in trousers, cap and veil, impersonated John Boettiger, while the Romeo represented William Randolph Hearst. The skit opened with the following dialogue:
>
> ROMEO [Hearst] But, soft, what light through yonder Guild strike breaks? It is the West and John Boettiger is the very man for The Post Intelligencer!
> JULIET [Boettiger] Ah me.
> ROMEO He speaks.
> JULIET Oh, William Randolph, William Randolph, wherefore art thou, William Randolph? Shall I deny my father-in-law and accept thy jack?!
> ROMEO Shall I hear more, or is it too soon after the election?

The skit concluded with Juliet/Boettiger telling Romeo/Hearst that the woods were full of "dangerous radicals and Jim Farley's hatchet men" and that "if my wife's kinsmen [the Roosevelts] see thee they'll make thee pay thy income tax."

Romeo responded, "Alack, there lies more peril in losing circulation than twenty income taxes."⁵

The moral of the tale was not lost on the Roosevelts, the Washington press corps, or Hearst himself. The result of the Chief's anti-Communist, anti-Roosevelt crusade had been a loss of circulation and advertising which no about-face could reverse. Readers forced to choose sides between the president and the publisher had voted twice: at the ballot box for Roosevelt, at their newsstands against Hearst.

* * *

Seven years of depression, combined with the anti-Hearst boycotts and protest movements of the mid-1930s, had had a devastating effect on the Hearst empire. Circulation on the *New York American* had declined 8 percent between 1933 and 1937; circulation on the *Evening Journal* and the *Sunday American* had also fallen. The gap between Hearst's *Mirror* and the *Daily News* had increased in those four years by almost 200,000. It now stood at more than one million. The same trend was at work in Los Angeles, San Francisco, Chicago, and Boston, where the Hearst morning papers had lost about 10 percent of their circulation between 1933 and 1937. The only part of the Hearst newspaper empire that was thriving was the Sunday papers, nearly all of which held their circulation — in large part because of the popularity of their comic supplements.[6]

Had Hearst reduced his spending to compensate for the loss in revenues from circulation and advertising, he might have been able to weather the storm. But, aside from the temporary wage cut that Neylan had forced on him four years earlier, he had taken no effective cost-cutting measures at his publications. Worse yet, he had accelerated his spending on real estate, art, and antiques. "I'm afraid I'm like a dipsomaniac with a bottle," he told Neylan. "They keep sending me these catalogs and I can't resist them."[7]

It was not as if Hearst wasn't kept informed of the bad news. On the contrary, Jack Neylan and his financial advisers pleaded with him to slow down his spending, to institute real economy measures, and to consider selling off some of his assets, particularly those newspapers that continued to lose money. Hearst, hoping that the economy would magically rebound, refused to listen.

On occasion, he would, as he had in the past, call a temporary halt to one or more of his building projects. But such détentes were always partial and never long-lived. In September of 1936, he cabled Miss Morgan from Europe to "bring Wyntoon and San Simeon work to conclusion October first and hold up Arizona until my return which will be soon." (One of Hearst's plans was to build a new mansion on his property near the Grand Canyon.) Only a few weeks later, on a visit to St. Donat's, he spun out a web of new building schemes for the future that so disturbed Alice Head that she wrote a long letter to Jack Neylan. Only after a lengthy heart-to-heart talk with Head had the Chief agreed to postpone his plans for his castle in Wales. Neylan was delighted: "When I think of what a great satisfaction and relief it would be to him if his spasms of virtuous resolution were more extended I cannot understand why he does not see it himself. However, there is no use moaning about it; he is too old to do much reforming."[8]

Neylan was right. Hearst could no longer help himself. From New York, he wrote Morgan in November that he had postponed their building plans because of "taxes, which are becoming confiscatory, and will be worse this coming year. . . . The election was not much help, was it?" He then, incongruously, directed her to "completely finish the beach house [in Santa Monica] now, and proceed with work at San Simeon after the first of the year."[9]

To escape California's state income taxes, he and Marion spent the winter of 1936–37 in New York City in their floor-through suite at the Ritz Tower. Soon after the election, he contacted his old friend Joe Kennedy and asked him to come up with a plan for corporate reorganization that would lighten his tax load and make it possible for his family to inherit his empire without being destroyed by estate taxes. Kennedy was well suited for the job. He was not only friendly with Roosevelt, the New Dealers, and the Washington press corps, but had recently performed miracles as a financial consultant for Paramount Pictures and RCA, and was a former chairman of the Securities and Exchange Commission, which would have to approve any new Hearst stock or bond issues.[10]

According to both Marion and Bill Hearst, Jr., Kennedy offered to buy the Hearst magazines, but the Chief turned him down because the price was too low — and he did not intend to sell any of his publications. While Kennedy and his associates set to work on a long-term reorganization plan, the Chief huddled with his financial advisers, senior editors, and Jack Neylan to find the money he needed to pay his bills in the short term. With debts mounting, revenues shrinking, and income tax obligations looming, the Hearst corporations were stretched beyond the limit. Reluctantly, the Chief agreed to cut his personal expenses, dispose of some of his losing newspapers, and sell off a portion of his overmortgaged real estate.

One of the first properties to go was the Clarendon on Riverside Drive. As Hearst no longer stayed there when he visited New York, it made no sense for the corporation to carry the expense of maintaining the building. The boys had moved out, and Millicent — who wintered in Palm Beach, spent the in-between season at Sands Point, and much of the spring and summer in Europe — did not need the entire apartment for herself. Hearst offered to move her to a property the corporation owned on Park Avenue. The initial negotiations took place through third parties, though when Millicent complained about having to talk to lawyers, W. R. assured her that he would handle the matter himself. Money, he insisted, was not the reason he was abandoning the Clarendon. He was selling it because it was no longer a desirable place to live and Riverside Drive was a deteriorating district. Millicent would be much better off if she relocated across town.[11]

Marion and W. R. celebrated Christmas in New York in 1936. It was not a joyous occasion. "On Christmas morning," Marion Davies recalled in her memoirs, "the phone rang and Cissy Patterson said, 'A. B. [Arthur Brisbane] just died.' I said, 'Good Lord, Cissy, aren't we in enough trouble? I better not say anything to W. R.' But he had heard the phone ringing. He started to cry, because he really liked A. B. . . . The funeral was at St. Thomas's on Fifth Avenue, and it was revolting. The photographers were going up and down taking pictures while the service was on. W. R. and Vincent Astor were pallbearers, and there were hundreds of photographers in the church. I felt I was getting sick."[12]

"I imagine W. R. was rather overcome at Mr. Brisbane's death," Alice Head wrote Jack Neylan in January. "At any rate, he has stopped buying antiques for the time being." Neylan was quite pleased to hear about Hearst's "moratorium on antique buying." The Chief had, Neylan thought, entered a period of reformation. "I would not have you think," he added, "that I have become guileless to the point of believing in the permanency of such a condition. However, every day that it lasts is just that much profit."[13]

Unfortunately for all concerned, Hearst's "reformation" was a chimera. As Joe Kennedy's chief accountant later discovered, during the first five months of 1937, while the Chief was discussing corporate reorganization and downsizing, he was also spending almost $200,000 — about $2.4 million in today's currency — on antiques and another $200,000 on real estate.[14]

As Hearst's advisers at the Ritz Tower and Joe Kennedy's associates in New York and Washington pored over his accounts, they discovered that the situation was far worse than any of them had imagined. By mid-January, Arthur Poole, Kennedy's chief associate, with the help of Tom White, who now served as the chairman of Hearst's newly established executive committee, had calculated that the Chief and his corporations owed $9 million to Canadian paper mills. They also owed $78 million (almost a billion dollars in today's currency) to the banks and the holders of Hearst corporate bonds and preferred stock. Thirty-nine million dollars of that debt was scheduled for repayment within the next twelve months.[15]

Hearst had been on the brink of fiscal catastrophe for decades, but in the past he had always managed to find a way to re-fund his old debts by raising new capital through bond or stock issues. As long as the Hearst newspapers and magazines had churned out sufficient income to pay off the interest on their loans and the dividends on their stock and bonds, no bank officer or broker was going to turn down requests for re-funding.

The Chief had learned early and well the first tenet of the new consumer age: that there was no shame in being in debt. Debt was, on the contrary, the magic ingredient that had made it possible to build his castles and buy his art collections. He didn't believe in the Protestant ethic or trust in Poor Richard's aphorisms. A penny saved might be a penny earned, but a penny borrowed was worth even more.

It had taken almost half a century, but his debts had finally grown to the point where no banker in his right mind would consider re-funding them. By 1936, most of his newspapers were losing money. Worse still, his reputation as a publisher and businessman had turned sour. Potential investors could no longer assume, as they had in the past, that his publications would continue to generate sufficient revenue to pay back the interest on his loans. "WRH is not well thought of by many bankers and investors because of his journalistic policies," Poole concluded in his report to Kennedy in early January, "and his prestige with his readers must have suffered considerably in the course of the last election. There is a steady stream of [unfavorable] articles appearing." In response to Kennedy's suggestion that capital might be raised through a new offering of Hearst stock, Poole cautioned that "the popular reaction to a 50–60 million dollar stock issue would be conditioned to some extent by this unfavorable publicity."[16]

With no ready market for a major stock offering, Joseph Kennedy attempted to raise money for the Chief by floating smaller bond issues, one of them on Hearst's magazines, which were less infected with his politics and, therefore, less suspect for investors. It is possible that Kennedy himself planned to bid on them. Unfortunately, because of regulations passed during Kennedy's tenure at the S.E.C., Hearst was required to draw up "registration statements" for his proposed offering and place them "on exhibition" for public comment. The response was immediate — and entirely negative. In placing the registration statements before the public, Hearst revealed his darkest secret: that he was over his head in debt. *Time* magazine ridiculed the offerings Kennedy had prepared as "two of the most remarkable registration statements ever filed." Buried in the 250 pages of text and tabulations, *Time* reporters claimed to have found "many a Hearst publishing secret, many a Hearst business oddity. . . . One thing is crystal clear: Mr. Hearst needs cash."[17]

Time was not the only critic. Dozens of separate briefs protesting the bond issues were filed with the S.E.C. by individuals, Hearst's political opponents, and even the American Legion, which had up to this point been one of Hearst's staunchest political allies. Kennedy's chief assistant in Washington took note of all the charges, identifying as most serious the claim that the registration statements were fatally flawed because they made "no mention . . . of the nation-wide boycott of Mr. Hearst which is seriously affecting the circulation of his publications."[18]

While Kennedy's lieutenants were convinced that the registration statements would, in amended form, receive S.E.C. approval, they were concerned at the almost total lack of interest among investors in the Hearst offering. They had contacted everyone: Harry Stuart at Bache Halsey Stuart and top executives at Prudential, Kuhn Loeb, and Blythe and Company, but had no commitments as yet. Even with Joseph P. Kennedy, one of Wall Street's shrewdest investors and a former chairman of the S.E.C., behind them, there appeared to be no market for Hearst's issue.[19]

On February 18, Hearst and Marion returned to San Simeon after an absence of almost nine months, still with no resolution of the ongoing financial crisis. "As usual when Mr. Hearst is here he wants a lot of work done," George Loorz, the construction supervisor at San Simeon, wrote Morgan in San Francisco. Recognizing, in the end, that there was no money to start even half the projects he intended, Hearst agreed to scale down his plans. Still, he was quite happy, Loorz reported, when work was renewed on the hillside: "He comes out often and goes around with keen interest in everything."[20]

Relocated in California, Hearst went back to work on Marion's screen career. Since moving to Warner Brothers from MGM, Marion had made three films, each one a critical and commercial flop. Hearst, of course, blamed the failures on the studio, which he claimed had been negligent in finding the right properties and screenwriters for Marion. In February, Marion began shooting her fourth Warner Brothers feature, *Ever Since Eve,* in which she played a stenographer who, tired of men chasing her, disguises herself as an "ugly duckling," only, in the end, to be discovered for her true natural beauty by her co-star, Robert Montgomery. The film failed at the box office.[21]

After four disasters in a row, Hearst was still not ready to give up. There were two more projects on the drawing board. He vetoed the first, a film adaptation of the Broadway play *Boy Meets Girl,* because he thought the project too "outspoken" for Marion, and pursued the second, the film version of George Bernard Shaw's *Pygmalion.* "I would be delighted to do Pygmalion and will break any engagement and go any place to do it," Marion telegrammed Shaw in England. "Please consider me an active candidate for the part." The telegram was in Marion's name, though it had been drafted on Hearst's yellow notepaper and was in his handwriting. There was no response from Shaw. Whatever he might have thought of Marion's acting abilities, she was not seriously considered for the part. When the film was finally cast, Eliza was played by Wendy Hiller, the British stage actress, who was Marion's junior by fifteen years.[22]

Marion's career as an actress, with Hearst as her unofficial producer, was coming to an end. While Hearst's Cosmopolitan Productions continued to be the nominal producer of several Warner Brothers films and a few more at 20th Century-Fox in 1939, Marion was not in the cast of any of them, and there is no evidence that the Chief played any role other than making sure they were praised in his papers. Most were B movies, like *Submarine D-1* with Pat O'Brien, George Brent, and Ronald Reagan; *Gold Is Where You Find It*, a 1938 film about miners in which Senator George Hearst was a minor character; and *Racket Busters*, from 1938, with George Brent and Humphrey Bogart. There were, however, two outstanding 1939 A-list film biographies, *The Story of Alexander Graham Bell*, with Don Ameche, and *Young Mr. Lincoln*, with Henry Fonda.

As he was wont to do in hard times, Hearst tried to ride out the crisis that threatened to strip him of his empire by acting as if nothing were the matter. On April 1, 1937, the day after the Hearst Magazine bond issue was registered, he and Marion attended the annual Warner Brothers dinner dance in Burbank, where photographs show him in his formal dinner clothes, smiling broadly, seemingly without a care in the world. Two days later, in a backhanded acknowledgment that he might need friends in high places in the foreseeable future, he directed Ed Coblentz to make the editorial pages "less contentious and more generally interesting. Let us discuss other questions than politics." Two weeks later, he informed Coblentz that he no longer wanted his papers to be so regularly and bitterly anti-Roosevelt, that the president should be praised when he merited it.[23]

At the end of April, he celebrated another birthday, this one his seventy-fourth, at Marion's Santa Monica beach house with a gigantic masquerade. In a manner befitting the sovereign that he had become, Hearst had directed his personal secretary, Joe Willicombe, to inform Tom White in New York that he expected "all his sons at birthday party." Marion herself invited Joe Kennedy who graciously declined, as he had just accepted Roosevelt's appointment to chair the Maritime Commission.[24] The theme this year was "The Greatest Show on Earth." Under a giant circus tent, with a carousel borrowed from Jack Warner, Marion and W. R. entertained five hundred guests, including Cary Grant, Leslie Howard, Clark Gable, Carole Lombard, Tyrone Power, Sonja Henie, Dolores Del Rio, Maureen O'Sullivan, Pat O'Brien, the producer Hal Wallis, and the directors Mervyn LeRoy and Ernst Lubitsch. W. R. looked dashing in his ringmaster's costume.[25]

W. R. and Marion returned to the ranch after the birthday party. On May 10, the Chief wrote Julia Morgan, "I like LOTS of light. I find almost all of our rooms too dark — sometimes almost gloomy." He had reason to see the world in such terms. Eleven days later, he telegrammed Miss Morgan again: "I have suddenly been called to New York. I am leaving Tuesday in all probability, and may not be back until the first of July."[26]

The inevitable had come to pass. He had learned from his financial advisers, who had converged on San Simeon, that there were no funds to pay out the quarterly dividend on Hearst Consolidated stock due June 4. He had said nothing to Marion, but returned with her to the Santa Monica beach house.

"I was just going to the studio to finish one last scene," Marion recalled in her memoirs, "when Bill Hearst arrived at the house and said, 'Where's the Chief?' It was very early in the morning, but he said, 'I think I'll go up and see Pop.'

"'Look, I don't think it's kind to wake him this early in the morning.'

"'This is a very serious matter. The empire's crashing. . . . We need a million dollars and the Chief has to go east immediately.'"

Marion called the studio to say that she would be late and then got her business manager on the phone. "Get me a million dollars right away," she told him. "I want to sell everything I've got — everything."[27]

Hearst was in more trouble than he had ever been. He cabled Alice Head in London to say that he would not be visiting Europe that summer as planned and to ask her for a loan of 10,000 pounds to pay off a debtor in England. "All I could do was to laugh myself nearly ill," Head reported to Neylan. "The person to whom he owed his 10,000 pounds came in to see me and I only wish I could reproduce the conversation. It was quite unbelievable. However I must in justice add that since then, he [Hearst] has sent me a little bit of money on account, and what with arranging for a more extended credit, we shall no doubt get through."[28]

On May 25, accompanied by Tom White, Bill, Jr., and Marion, who insisted on traveling with him to New York, W. R. boarded the Super Chief in Los Angeles. From the train, he telegrammed Miss Morgan "to stop work entirely at San Simeon." Morgan relayed the Chief's instructions to Randolph Apperson, Hearst's ranch manager and cousin: "Mr. Hearst today instructed me to tell you to close the Hilltop, dispensing with the services of everyone who is not actually required to keep the interior of castle and house in clean condition and prevent unnecessary deterioration."

Half the gardeners, a large part of the orchard crew, two watchmen, and most of the household staff were let go. Hearst instructed Morgan to keep on only a few "mechanical men," a truck driver, and "two or three maids to dust and clean and take care of the inside." W. R. Williams, who managed his San Simeon warehouses, was to be relocated to the castle "to check on the art things and especially the tapestries." The zoo animals were to be sold or given away. The first to go was the elephant — to the Los Angeles Zoo. A Barbary sheep, the black leopards, a java monkey, and most of the bears were sent to the San Francisco Zoo, then known as the Fleishhacker Zoo.[29]

On board the train taking them to New York, Hearst was, Marion remembered, "very worried and after we had dinner in the dining car, he said, 'I guess I'm through.'" When she told him that she had raised $1 million to help him pay off his debts, he refused to accept it. "'Don't give it to me. I'll tear it up. Anyway, what's a million dollars when there's fifty million dollars involved?'"

Marion left the dining car and walked back to the drawing car, where she tried to give her $1 million check to Tom White. He too refused to accept it, but she insisted until he took it from her.

On arriving in New York, W. R. and Marion were driven to their suite at the Ritz Tower on Park and 57th Street. The next morning, Marion awoke to find that "W. R. [had] gathered everybody but me together for a conference in my drawing room." After a lengthy argument, which Marion tried her best to overhear, the decision was made to accept her check — as a loan — with Hearst's Boston newspapers as collateral.[30]

With the markets closed to new bond or stock offerings and the banks and Canadian paper mills unwilling to refinance their outstanding loans, the one way to raise capital was to sell assets, including publications, real estate, and art. The only outstanding questions left were which assets would be sold and who would do the selling.[31]

Everyone agreed that the Chief would have to name some sort of trustee to get him through the current crisis and restore confidence in the investment community. The politicking among his advisers was intense. There were factions within factions, each lining up behind a different candidate. The leading candidates to take over Hearst's financial affairs included Joseph Kennedy, Jack Neylan, Tom White, and Judge Clarence Shearn, who had been Hearst's chief counsel thirty years earlier and now worked for Chase Manhattan. Hearst found it difficult to choose among them.

W. R. and Marion remained at the Ritz Tower for most of June. When

Cissy Patterson wrote that she and President Roosevelt had exchanged "pleasant words" about him, he wrote her back, almost piteously hopeful that the president was prepared to welcome him back to the Democratic camp:

> I am very glad indeed to hear of the President's pleasant words. Of course you know that I have the highest regard and esteem for him personally and that I differed from him merely on certain principles — a difference which he did not have to be concerned about as the result showed. I, however, was concerned about it. I found myself in a Republican camp. I was a fish out of water. I had always been a progressive — a radical. I had nothing in common with reactionaries. . . . After the dust of the campaign has settled, and in view of the great vote of confidence in the President and his POLICIES, I had time for contemplation. I am in heart and soul a democrat. I believe that the people's will should be obeyed. . . . I am naturally pleased that the President feels friendly and I hope you will tell him so. . . . If ever there is anything the President wishes, I hope that he will tell you or me. We will try to comply. If he wants me at any time I am at his command. If he does not, I am going to be a Democrat and not a Republican anyway.[32]

For the first time in his life, the Chief was forced to concentrate his attention on selling rather than acquiring assets. He was, his son Randolph remembered, willing to do "anything else but get rid of papers. He loved his newspapers and the people who worked for them." But the losses were too great and the prospects for recovery minimal. He suspended publication of the morning *New York American*, merging it into the new *Journal-American*, traded newspapers in Albany and Rochester with Frank Gannett so as to eliminate competition, and leased his Washington papers to Cissy Patterson.[33]

In late June, he left New York to attend a newspaper publishers' meeting in Chicago. Though his world was rapidly crumbling, he tried to remain upbeat, writing Joe Kennedy to thank him for his assistance and assure him that he was giving his recommendations "the most thoughtful consideration. . . . There are quite a number of matters encouragingly under way."[34]

From Chicago, Hearst and Marion took the train West as far as Winslow, Arizona, where they boarded a plane for San Simeon. On the first of July, Hearst and Marion's plane touched down on the landing strip at the bottom of the hill. The reduced household staff had been notified in advance to make ready Casa Grande for their return. While waiting for his ritual summons to the hillside to discuss building plans with his Chief, George Loorz received a visit from Randy Apperson, Hearst's cousin, who confided to him that Mr. Hearst had returned from New York "a pathetic, broken man." "I am so sorry for him," Loorz wrote Morgan in San Francisco. "Randy reports Miss Davies to be very considerate of him, to be his only real comfort. They are here on the hilltop alone. She stole him away from New York as he seemed so worried and confined there that she feared he might not stand it."[35]

The unthinkable had come to pass. For fifty years, Hearst had ruled his empire as autocratically as his heroes Julius Caesar and Napoleon Bonaparte had theirs. He had trusted no one, rejected suggestions that he share power or delegate decision-making, and refused to name a successor. At age seventy-four, he was as hearty as ever and convinced that if left alone he could once again pull off a miracle. But no one, with the possible exception of Marion, believed him capable of making the tough decisions that were necessary and cutting back on personal and corporate spending. The Chief was a builder, not a wrecker; an accumulator, not a liquidator. The banks and Canadian paper mills refused to loan the corporation anything as long as the old man was in control. They, too, had read the articles and books about the Lord of San Simeon and his spendthrift habits. They wanted firm guarantees that any funds loaned to the corporation would go to pay off corporate debts, not to buy more art or animals for San Simeon.

To satisfy the demands of his creditors and secure the funding he needed to save his newspapers, Hearst decided in the end to select Judge Clarence Shearn over White, Neylan, and Kennedy as his trustee. On paper, at least, Shearn was an ideal candidate. He was neither an outsider like Joe Kennedy nor one of the Hearst insiders who had gotten him into trouble in the first place. More importantly, he was connected to Chase Manhattan, one of Hearst's principal creditors. Hearst appointed Shearn to an irrevocable ten-year term as trustee and granted him sole voting rights over all stock in Hearst's principal holding company, with the understanding that the Chief would retain editorial control over his publications, subject to the Judge's authority to oversee spending.[36]

Shearn went to work immediately. He finalized the terms for a $1.6 million bridge loan from Chase Manhattan and then, no doubt because it was a requirement for securing the loan, slashed the Chief's salary to $500,000 per year and terminated payment on the $700,000 in preferred stock dividends that were due him. Hearst was directed to deed Wyntoon and much of his art collection to the corporation and informed that if he wished to live at San Simeon he would have to pay rent for it and cover the costs of maintenance, future construction, and noncorporate expenses.[37]

In a series of telegrams, memoranda, and phone calls to associates whom he expected to intervene on his behalf, Hearst pleaded with Shearn to reconsider. Why should he have to pick up all the costs for San Simeon when he lived there only three months a year and it was used more as a "business headquarters" than a private residence? Like a spoiled child, he threatened to close the ranch if he didn't get his way. *"You have got to face some facts along with theories in this matter,"* he wrote the corporation's tax attorney. *"I am talking seriously about this matter. I am not going to be burdened with all these charges. I cannot be."*[38]

Fair or unfair, the decision had been made and Hearst knew it. The problem wasn't Shearn personally, though Jack Neylan, Joseph Kennedy, and later Marion herself would hold the Judge responsible for treating the Chief so harshly. The reality was that Chase Manhattan — and Hearst's other creditors — were now in charge. As Edward Clark, who served as liaison of sorts between Hearst and Shearn, wrote the Chief in December of 1937, corporate money from this point on could be spent only in the "direct interest of the corporation." Though Hearst had insisted — and Clark agreed — that he had assembled "the loveliest Arabians and Morgans in the world" at San Simeon, the corporation would not pay for them because the horse farm was not "a necessary adjunct" to corporate business activities. The same was true of the San Simeon orchards and the gatekeepers and the construction crews and most of the servants, gardeners, and landscapers. The corporation would cover the costs of a "skeleton staff, sufficient to maintain the property" at Wyntoon and San Simeon, but nothing more.[39]

In June, the Hearst corporate treasurer had estimated that the Chief required $803,633.06 (about $9.5 million in today's money) for the remaining six months of the year. Forty percent of this was to be set aside for federal and state taxes, another $120,000 for Mrs. Hearst, and another $167,000 for debt payments, interest, and insurance. This left the Chief with less than $175,000 for personal expenses, out of which he would now have to finance everything the corporation refused to pay.[40]

Construction ceased entirely at San Simeon and Wyntoon. So did much of the partying. Mel Engle, a waiter, recalled in his oral history that after 1937 there were never more than ten to fourteen guests on the hilltop; according to George Loorz, few of them were from the old Hollywood crowd.[41]

Word of Hearst's virtual bankruptcy quickly became public knowledge. On October 11, the *New York Times* confirmed that the anonymous "gentleman" and "well-known collector" whose silver was being auctioned off at Sotheby's in London was none other than William Randolph Hearst. Things had gotten so out of hand that even President Roosevelt, in a mid-October meeting with Edmond Coblentz, felt obligated to offer business advice to the Chief: "Please tell W. R. I advise him to get rid of his poorest papers, to print more news, not to print so many features, keep just the good ones, and to kill his editorial page. Tell him to use it for the good features and to print only an occasional editorial on Page 1."[42]

Judge Shearn, now firmly in control of the Hearst empire, assembled his own team to run the corporations. He selected Chase Manhattan's law firm, Milbank Tweed, as counsel, and tried to raise cash as quickly as possible by, among other measures, selling off the art collections that had been bought and paid for by the Hearst corporations. Rather than spend years trying to sort out what the Chief had paid for out of his own pocket and what had been bought with corporate funds, Shearn and his financial advisers divided his holdings in half, generously allocating $11.5 million worth of art and antiques to Hearst personally and the same amount to International Studio Arts Corporation, the subsidiary of Hearst's holding company through which he had paid for his art. Hearst was advised that he could have any item that belonged to the corporation if he substituted for it an item of equal value of his own.[43]

Before anything could be sold, the contents of San Simeon, Wyntoon, Millicent's Sands Point estate, the Clarendon, St. Donat's, the Ritz Tower, and warehouses in the Bronx, in Manhattan, at San Simeon, in Northern California near Wyntoon, in San Francisco, and in Los Angeles had to be inventoried, catalogued, arranged into lots, and priced for sale. (It was assumed, generously, that none of the contents of Marion's beach house had been paid for with corporate funds.) Teams of experts sorted through Hearst's holdings on two coasts and two continents and segregated them into fifteen discrete collections: Armour; Tapestries; Paintings; Furniture; Gold and Silverware; Art Objects; Pottery, China & Glassware; Buildings and Parts; Autographs, Manuscripts and Original Drawings; Stained Glass; Miscellaneous Hangings; Jewelry and Precious Stones; Flags and Banners; Rugs, Mats, etc.; and Indian Objects.[44]

No one, except for Hearst himself, had had any idea of the magnitude of his holdings until the classification and liquidation process began. The press had visited and written about San Simeon and the Bronx warehouses, but no one knew that there were tapestries, carpets, textiles, and hangings in storage at the Lincoln Warehouse on Third Avenue in Manhattan between 69th and 70th Streets, or that at St. Donat's alone there were major collections of furniture, paintings, sculpture, bronzes, wooden objects, tapestry, needlework, silver, pewter, brass, gold, glass, china, porcelain, stained glass, clocks, ironwork, and arms and armor.

Hearst's advisers and consultants were uncertain as to how to proceed. If they put everything on the market at once, the glut would be such as to depress prices on two continents. They decided to sell the collections in stages. After nine months of sorting, cataloguing, and pricing, it was announced in early March of 1938 that selections from the Hearst collections would be placed on sale and that Macdermid Parish-Watson of East 57th Street had been engaged to oversee the process.[45]

The first sales were arranged privately. John D. Rockefeller, Jr. bought $100,000 of silver to exhibit at the Governor's Palace in colonial Williamsburg; a British shipping millionaire purchased several hundred thousand dollars worth of Gothic tapestries in London. Parish-Watson reported to A. J. Liebling, who visited him for a *New Yorker* article, that he had discovered that there was, indeed, a market for everything. On a recent trip to London, he had been able to sell "two nineteenth-century German paintings of a Tyrolean dance . . . a type of genre painting long out of favor. . . . A London dealer got them . . . for a good price — probably, Parish-Watson thought, for the account of Field Marshal Goering."[46]

When the dealers and private collectors had placed their bids, Parish-Watson opened the Hearst collections to the public. A *New Yorker* cartoon from November 5, 1938, pictured a fat businessman in bowler hat, in front of a San Simeon–like castle, telling his companion, "My wife snapped it up at a Hearst sale." First editions, manuscripts, autographs, historical blue Staffordshire ware, and some early American furniture were consigned to Parke-Bernet for auction in New York. The silver from St. Donat's was auctioned off by Christie's and Sotheby's in London. In mid-November, just in time for the Christmas buying season, M. Parish-Watson opened to the public "a cross-section of the William Randolph Hearst collection, ranging from pre-Christian art to that of the eighteenth century . . . in a five-story building leased for the purpose at 46 East Fifty-seventh Street."[47]

For the next two years, the sales and auctions continued in full force. Some items were sold privately through dealers, others publicly through the auction houses and the 57th Street galleries operated by Parish-Watson. Though only a portion of Hearst's collection was for sale, Parish-Watson estimated that, in the end, the complete catalogue would encompass close to 250 volumes.[48]

None of this was easy on Hearst. He was especially grieved to have to part with his treasures, even those he had seen only in photographs. Though the final decision-making was out of his hands, he was consulted on every sale and asked to verify the authenticity of questionable pieces. In the cartons of correspondence still stored at the Hearst Corporation's Bronx warehouse, there are dozens of letters from Tom White in New York to Hearst at

San Simeon or Wyntoon — White imploring Hearst to accept the price offered for a particular item, the Chief reluctant to let it go. In May of 1938, to cite but one example, Hearst turned down an offer of $4,000 for a pair of fifteenth-century brass candlesticks at Millicent's Sands Point estate and asked that they be shipped west to San Simeon. With dozens of other items of business to transact and railroad cars full of artwork being transported back and forth between California and New York, the candlesticks were soon forgotten by all but the Chief. When he discovered in October that they had been sold, he telephoned White to demand that they be bought back. When the dealer who had sold the candlesticks refused to return them without an additional $1,000 to cover the profit he had made on the sale, Hearst demanded that he be barred from doing further business with the corporation.[49]

❦ 34 ❦

"All Very Sad, But
We Cannot Kick Now"

A S IF NOTHING HAD CHANGED, though everything had, Marion celebrated Hearst's seventy-fifth birthday with a costume party. The theme was American History. Hearst came dressed as President James Madison and smiled broadly for the camera, an Italian countess dressed as an Indian maiden at his side.

Despite the bright lights and the smiles at the beach house that evening in April 1938, his and Marion's world had collapsed and would not easily be put back together again. The Chief had lost control of his empire, the star had retired from moving pictures.

In her memoirs, Marion claims that she left Hollywood not only because she had grown weary of making movies, but because she felt that W. R., now in his middle seventies, "needed companionship. He was having some financial troubles at the time, too, and he was more upset than people realized. I thought that the least I could do for a man who had been so wonderful and great . . . was to be a companion to him."[1]

As Hearst's financial problems mounted, he had begun to look to Marion for solace and counsel. Their roles were neatly reversed. It was she who watched and worried and reassured; she who had found the money to keep "Pops" afloat through bad times. Gretchen Swinnerton, the wife of Hearst's cartoonist and friend Jimmy Swinnerton, recalled that "at Wyntoon, when Mr. Hearst would go out and take a walk alone in the woods . . . Marion would sit there just as nervous as a cat till he showed up again, afraid something had happened to him. He might have fallen or something. Every minute, apprehension — where was he? Was he all right? — unless she was with him. She adored that man."[2]

Hearst worried about Marion, as he always had. Now retired, she had less reason to remain sober and was drinking herself to death. W. R. tried tenderness, anger, offers to send her anywhere in the world to take any cure. "A couple of years ago," he wrote the editor of his *American Weekly* in the summer of 1940, "there was a small article . . . about a doctor who had cured the liquor habit with sugar and yeast. I suggested at the time that you make a page article on this question and on his method, because I thought it was interesting. If you cannot get the page article, will you please at least get a plan and specific prescription for his method to be used on a patient, either directly or through another doctor. If he prefers through a doctor I would advise Dr. Dickinson, of McCloud, California [the town nearest Wyntoon]. At any rate, some way or other, please get the data and oblige."[3]

Hearst tried to restrict Marion's access to liquor, but like all alcoholics, she found new sources to replace the ones he closed off. "She always had me leave her water goblet empty so when I served wine, I filled her water goblet with wine," Mel Engle, who waited table at San Simeon from 1939 to 1940, recalled. "She would dump it down her throat, and back down she'd go for the second time before I got by. She was pretty bad as an alcoholic, and when she'd drink, eventually she would make an ass of herself at the table, start acting up, making noises and things. It wasn't unusual for Mr. Hearst to ask her to be taken from the table."[4]

Fearful that Marion might hurt herself, Hearst hired a succession of nurses to watch over her. But they too succumbed to her requests for liquor. Charles Gates, who became Hearst's chief butler in 1939, admitted that he had supplied Marion with liquor bottles: "Well, we sort of gave them to her. After all you know you're working for the person, you got to treat them, if they ask you for something."[5]

While Hearst commuted back and forth between San Simeon, Los Angeles, and Wyntoon, Judge Shearn in New York continued to sell off his assets to pay off his debts. Had the economy recovered, as Hearst had been expecting since 1929, Shearn's task might have been easier. Unfortunately, Roosevelt's 1937 retreat from his public works projects had resulted in a nationwide recession. In August of 1937, the stock market began to fall again. By March of 1938, unemployment was back at 20 percent. Worse yet for the newspaper industry, newsprint prices were soaring while advertising revenues fell.

On June 1, 1938, Shearn announced that Hearst Consolidated, which through the worst of the Depression had always paid its 7 percent dividend, was deferring payment on the next quarter's dividend because advertising revenues had decreased from $15 million to $12 million and income for the first four months from $2.6 million to between $600,000 and $700,000. With the corporation in desperate need of cash to pay its outstanding obligations, Hearst was called back to New York City to sign off on a new credit agreement with Chase Manhattan and the Canadian paper mills that would have ceded full control of his empire to an executive of Chase Manhattan and a representative of the Canadian mills and tied the publications to a long-term contract with the Canadian mills.[6]

Judge Shearn was in an impossible position. As revenues continued to fall through 1938, he was forced to defer three successive dividends because he could not come up with the cash to pay them. According to the terms of the 1930 offering, if the company missed its fourth consecutive dividend in March of 1939, this would trigger a corporate reorganization with the stockholders gaining the authority to elect a new board of directors. Shearn and his chief advisers flew out to meet with Hearst at San Simeon to apprise him of the situation. Then, at the very last minute, they secured another loan from Chase Manhattan to pay off the March 1939 dividend.[7]

It was now clear that Shearn had failed to stabilize the corporation's finances. Both Hearst and Jack Neylan, whom Hearst had begun to consult again, tried to wrest control from him. Neylan proposed a reorganization plan that would have replaced Shearn with three independent trustees. The Chief, after intimating that he would support Neylan's plan, came up with one of his own, which would have effectively returned all corporate power to him and moved the corporate offices to Los Angeles. Although Shearn appeared to have signed off on Hearst's plan, it was doomed from the start. What the Chief was unable or unwilling to recognize was that until the corporation had paid off its debts, the creditors, not Shearn or Neylan or William Randolph Hearst, would be making the decisions.[8]

"W. R. has blundered again," Neylan wrote Alice Head on March 14, 1939. "By attempting to put himself back in command, he has provoked the newsprint creditors into installing an executive of their choosing, with practically autocratic power. . . . The most disheartening thing of the whole situation is the fact that he has no realization of his own status. . . . The tragic fact is that in these days he can no more understand what is necessary to rehabilitate himself than he could understand in the old days that his extravagance and improvidence could bring him to disaster."[9]

As *Time* magazine reported in its March 13, 1939, cover story on Hearst, Shearn had saved the old man's empire from bankruptcy, but in the process he had reduced it to a shadow of its former self:

> For 17 years millions of U.S. citizens, to whom Hearst has been an institution as well as a legendary figure, have wondered what would happen to the institution when William Randolph Hearst was no more. Of late they have ceased

to wonder, have realized that the institution has already started breaking up before their eyes. . . . Just how far the public thinks the Hearst empire has progressed toward dissolution is neatly summed up in this lyric currently sung on Broadway by Funnyman Jimmy Durante:

> *Mr. Hearst tries to sell me a paper,*
> *But dat don't fit in wid my plan*
> *I said I will buy a paper from you*
> *If you buy a pencil from me —*
> *I'm just a self-made man.*

Though the subject of the article was Shearn's corporate reorganization, the face on the cover was that of a pensive Hearst, his head tilted slightly downward, staring off into the distance. According to *Time*, the old man was finished forever and knew it. The directors of Hearst Consolidated scurried about in New York to raise money. When Tom White flew to Los Angeles to beg Harry Chandler of the *Los Angeles Times* not to call in the $600,000 mortgage he held on San Simeon, Hearst, *Time* reported, was "with Marion Davies, at her Santa Monica beach house. . . . No longer ruler of the empire he built, Hearst has only two desires concerning it: 1) to have some of it survive him; 2) to keep his job. . . . At age 75, the bad boy of U.S. journalism is just a hired editorial writer who has taken a salary cut."[10]

The Hearst mythology was undergoing yet another shift in emphasis. He was no longer looked upon as a menace to the republic, but rather as an eccentric millionaire, struggling to retain some portion of his past glories. Aldous Huxley, who had written for the Hearst papers in the early 1930s, moved to Hollywood in 1937. Though ostensibly employed at MGM, he spent much of his time — and all of his creative energies — on *After Many a Summer Dies the Swan*, a brilliantly satiric novel about Los Angeles. Huxley chose to place a highly eccentric millionaire, modeled on Hearst, at the center of his Hollywood novel. Jo Stoyte lives with his mistress in a castle, as did Hearst, but unlike him is obsessed by the fear of death and has hired Dr. Obispo to find the secret of eternal life for him. The book opens with the visit of an Englishman, Jeremy Pordage, to Stoyte's castle:

About half a mile from the foot of the mountains, like an island off a cliff-bound coast, a rocky hill rose abruptly, in places almost precipitously, from the plain. On the summit of the bluff and as though growing out of it in a kind of stony efflorescence, stood a castle. But what a castle! . . . The thing was Gothic, mediaeval, baronial — double baronial, Gothic with a Gothicity raised, so to speak, to a higher power, more mediaeval than any building of the thirteenth century. . . . He had known, of course, that Mr. Stoyte was rich, collected pictures, owned a show place in California. But no one had ever led him to expect *this*.

Mr. Stoyte, as portrayed by Huxley, was quite as mad as his castle, as was everyone else around him, but his obsessions made him a pathetic rather than a particularly sinister character. There is no evidence — in his public or private papers — that Hearst ever read the book. If he did, he certainly took no action against Aldous Huxley, who continued to live in Hollywood and write for moving pictures. "I heard about Aldous Huxley," Marion recalled in her memoirs. "I don't think I ever met him, nor did I read his book, but I wanted to."[11]

With Shearn, at the behest of the banks and the Canadian paper mills, shedding assets as quickly as he could, there was no way of knowing what would be left behind for Marion, Millicent, and the boys. During the summer or fall of 1938, when it appeared likely that all might be lost — including San Simeon — Hearst flew down from Wyntoon for a family reunion with Millicent and the five boys at the ranch. "He was so happy and content," August Wahlberg, his valet and butler, remembered. "I have never [seen] him that way. . . . That was a very, very nice event for everybody and he enjoyed it immensely. We were there for about three days." Randolph Hearst remembers that, before departing their separate ways, W. R., Millicent, and the five boys posed for a picture in front of the castle.[12]

From England, Joe Kennedy, who was not unaware of the complications incumbent on leading two lives, advised Hearst to protect Marion by putting some of his St. Donat's antiques in her name, before they were all sold off by the corporation. "It strikes me . . . that the 'protectorate' [Shearn and the Chase Manhattan bankers] might not be especially kind to Marion, in the event that they felt they had to move in," Kennedy wrote Hearst. "Therefore it seems to me that her things here should be earmarked for her right away so any disputes might be avoided. Also I am not going to be in this job forever [Kennedy was, at the time, ambassador to Britain] and you might tell her if she needs advice on anything else to call me. I would like nothing better than to see that she had whatever protection I could give her against that hungry horde. I hope I'm not being too forward."[13]

Marion's future should have been provided for — she had been one of Hollywood's wealthiest women — but when she had liquidated more than a million dollars worth of real estate and jewelry to raise cash to lend Hearst, she received, as collateral, only two very shaky Boston newspapers. In February of 1939, perhaps in response to Kennedy's suggestions, W. R. wrote

Heinie MacKay, his Los Angeles attorney, asking him if the $800,000 outstanding on Marion's loan could be repaid by giving her $800,000 worth of art from his collections. MacKay replied that though he would be happy to ask one of his associates in New York to talk to Judge Shearn, he doubted that anything would come of the request. With millions of dollars in debt still outstanding, MacKay did not believe that Hearst's creditors were going to grant Marion any special consideration on her $800,000.[14]

Hearst was concerned not only for Marion's future, but for Millicent and the boys. Millicent's allowance had already been slashed and the Clarendon sold out from under her. Although, as Randolph, their youngest son, remembered, she lived quite well at her Park Avenue apartment, she did so on a much smaller budget than the unlimited one she had been used to.

W. R., who was himself on a strict allowance with no extra cash to provide Millicent, asked Richard Berlin, the head of the magazine division, to give her a "job as editor or sub-editor of one of the magazines. I think she could do a lot with *Town & Country* and would also be useful on *House Beautiful*. She is clever, resourceful, and tasteful. She would like the work and I think should be compensated on about the basis of the children's compensation, — that is, $15,000. She would be satisfied with that I am sure." Berlin rebuffed the request. He was now chairman of the board of the Hearst Corporation, but the real power remained with the creditors who, he wrote Hearst, might very well reduce or remove Millicent's $2,500 monthly allowance if they discovered that she was also on the Hearst payroll.[15]

Hearst worried about his five boys as well. The twins were too young yet to provide entirely for themselves, and Bill, Jr., the second-born, was already well established in New York. His main concerns were George, the oldest, and John, the third-born. While Hearst had demanded that they work for a living and threatened to cut them off if they did not, he had never followed through on any of his threats. Worse yet, as Randolph, one of the twins, remembered, he had "put the older boys in places where they shouldn't have been," given their age and lack of experience, and protected them when they failed to produce. W. R. was now worried that with the organization in the hands of the creditors the boys would be discarded as excess baggage. It was imperative that they learn to take care of themselves while they still had a father to look after them.[16]

George, now thirty-six, was a jovial, overweight man who drank too much, ate even more, and worked not at all. In 1940, after he had failed at a number of newspaper jobs, W. R. moved him to his San Francisco radio station. When George demanded equal authority with the station's manager, his father exploded:

Somebody has got to be in charge of the station. You have not yet demonstrated the ability to run a station. . . . Just remember, George, you have never demonstrated anything in your life yet. You have not even demonstrated a willingness to work. Nobody is going to put you in charge of any important proposition until they know you are going to work, and until they believe you are going to accomplish something. Please be careful, son, not to make yourself unwelcome in San Francisco, because they will not take you back in Los Angeles, and you would have nowhere to go.

Like all his letters to his children, this one was signed "Affectionately, Pop."[17]

The letters that "Pop" wrote John were strikingly similar, if a bit nastier. In early 1939, John was transferred from New York, where he had worked at the magazine division, to Los Angeles. He was almost thirty, though his father still treated him as a child:

Are you carrying out my instructions faithfully to report at the *Examiner* office every morning at nine o'clock, lay out your program for the day, and attend to that program assiduously, and get some results? To the best of my knowledge and belief you are not doing this, and if you do not do it there is only one of two courses open to me — either to have you pack up your bags and baggage and go back East, where nobody wants you or will have anything to do with you, or else put you on a percentage basis.[18]

When Hearst's prophecy was fulfilled and John lost his position at the *Examiner,* he was given ninety days to find a job in New York. Tom White suggested that for his own protection, he should look for a place outside of the organization. John was, in the end, hired at Hearst's *American Weekly,* but at a salary that did not pay what he thought he needed to live. When he asked his father for an additional allowance — as he had in the past — he was refused. "I am sorry, but I am NOT going to allow you any expenses," Hearst wrote him. "You are on your own — sink or swim in New York. If you don't like the job, don't take it. You are not an infant any longer, swinging on a pap bottle."[19]

When John again disappeared from work — he was drinking heavily at the time — and turned up on the West Coast, W. R. instructed his superiors in New York to only "pay John if and when he works." He wrote John again:

I am sorry that you think I am angry with you. I am not. And I do not want to distress you, but I want you to realize that in the compact and economical organization of Hearst Consolidated nobody is going to get paid except for service rendered. In other words, "No tickee no shirtee" is the unvarying motto of the institution. . . . If you are going to stay in our organization, you must work and earn your compensation.

The message was as clear as Hearst could make it. The Chief had lost control of his organization and could protect his boys no longer.[20]

Through late 1939 into 1940, things went from bad to worse for the Chief. In addition to suffering the humiliation of having his art sold out from under him, he was forced to defend himself from shareholder lawsuits that charged him with defrauding Hearst Consolidated by taking a $500,000 salary for part-time work, shifting his personal liabilities to the corporation, and diverting income that rightfully belonged to the shareholders into his private holding companies. By the fall of 1940, he was besieged by so many process servers that his advisers suggested he relocate from San Simeon and Los Angeles, where he was "too open to any legal service," to Wyntoon.[21]

Through the summer and fall of 1940, teams of lawyers arrived at San Simeon to prepare the Chief to be deposed in the stockholder suits. They did their job well. In November of 1941, when the Hearst Consolidated cases finally came to trial, they were dismissed after former executives, including Neylan, offered sufficient testimony to convince the presiding judge that the Chief had indeed been worth his half-million-dollar salary and had not defrauded his shareholders.[22]

By this time, the organization had found its Galahad in the person of John W. Hanes, a former Wall Street banker, adviser to Joe Kennedy at the S.E.C., and undersecretary of the treasury, who in the summer of 1940 had been brought in to restructure the corporation and reduce the debt load. After four years of belt tightening, the Hearst corporations and Hearst himself still carried $30 million in debts, $8 million alone to the Canadian paper mills. In the fall of 1940, the War Department paid $2 million for 154,000 acres of Hearst ranchland adjoining San Simeon, and the Canadian paper mills demanded that every dollar of it be used to pay off corporate debts rather than Hearst's New York real estate obligations. After weeks of threats, bluffs, and recriminations, a deal was struck and Hearst was permitted to apply $1 million of the government funds to reduce his own debts.[23]

While Hanes struggled to reorganize the corporation without shedding its remaining assets, the Hearst empire drifted aimlessly. As Neylan wrote Alice Head in January 1941:

> Shearn sits at one end of the country, scheming and plotting; Hearst sits at the other end of the country, counterscheming and counterplotting . . . My judgement of the situation is that on the one hand, Hearst, in his seventy-seventh year, leads a precarious day-to-day existence, unwilling to look at the facts, incapable of working out a solution and hoping only to hang on. On the other

side of the picture, it looks to me as if the cold-blooded gentlemen who handle money have consulted an actuarial table and having determined the life expectancy of a man of seventy-seven have decided it will not be long before they will revamp the institution without his interference.[24]

Those who had expected Hearst to fade away, either from shame at losing his empire or from simple old age, were mistaken. All one had to do was to read the Hearst papers to see that the old man remained in control. Nothing of importance got into the Hearst papers without his approval. The text of every editorial was sent to him, edited by him, and set in type only when and as approved by him. Major articles and features were cleared through him as well. In late 1939, in response to the publication of John Steinbeck's *Grapes of Wrath*, the editor of his *San Francisco Call-Bulletin* commissioned a series of articles on the menace posed to California by the invasion of migrants. W. R. chastised his editor in a letter written on January 2, 1940:

> To be perfectly frank, I think the migrant articles are disappointing. They do not get anywhere. My contention is this: "The migrants are good Americans who have been subjected to great hardships and privation, partly through natural causes — drought, dust storms, etcetera — partly through the depression and the New Deal perverted economies. These migrants have left the lands where they cannot make a living and where relief is insufficient or dishonest; and have come to California where nature is generous, the State reasonably rich, and the people kind. They are better for California than the Chinese or the Japs or the Filipinos or the Mexicans. We are, and should be, glad to have them — as fast as we can absorb them." . . . Let us accept the migrants and make good citizens out of them.[25]

Although the Chief's editorial voice was quieter now, less that of an angry demagogue than of a wearied prophet, he remained among the nation's most prominent "isolationists." His political stance was the same as it had been before and during the Great War. America, he argued again and again, had no business interfering with or letting itself become entangled in European economic agreements, treaties, or military adventures. No matter how viciously he might attack "lust-crazed Communist mobs in Spain" or "aggressive, belligerent, militaristic, ambitious and impudent" Japan when it invaded China, he insisted that the American government mind its own business and refrain from military or diplomatic entanglements outside the Western Hemisphere.[26]

When Walter Winchell, who was by the middle 1930s the most widely read of all his columnists, began offering his own opinions on the Spanish Civil War in which he supported the Loyalists and opposed Roosevelt's embargo on assistance to them, Hearst was furious and said so. "I must ask all columnists to keep off these highly controversial subjects," he telegrammed his executives at the International News Service, which syndicated Winchell's columns. "There is no occasion to go to Spain to project ourselves into a war between Communists and Fascists. Let us pay attention to our own democracy here in America." He then wrote Winchell directly:

> The above message I sent to the INS, and I mean exactly what the message stated. You were engaged to do a Broadway gossip column. You do a good one. You might be a good war correspondent, but that is not your job. I do not think the sports writer should do society columns . . . or the gossip writers controversial politics. Moreover, any political columns written in my papers will be American in spirit, not alien. They will be democratic in character, not communistic or fascist. Furthermore, Walter, you are not a little youth, although you are acting like one. As a matter of fact, you are old enough to know better.[27]

No matter how threatening the events unfolding on the continent, Hearst continued to believe that peace could be maintained. In March of 1938, when German troops marched into Austria and annexed it to the Third Reich, Hearst used his front pages to lecture the Führer on his duty as strongman of Europe: "Greatness is not made by marching troops nor by howling crowds, but by enduring records of constructive statesmanship." He suggested that Hitler mark his annexation of "liberal" Austria by ceasing "his unjust and unreasonable persecution of the Jews." The tone of his editorial suggests that, although disappointed with Hitler's action, he believed it possible that the Führer might read his editorial and mend his ways.[28]

Through the late 1930s, no matter what actions Hitler took, Hearst refused to demonize him or the Germans. On the contrary, he did all he could to warn readers against English propaganda designed to inveigle Americans into an alliance against Germany. When Judge Clarence Shearn, speaking for his colleagues at Chase Manhattan and in the New York investment community, pleaded with Hearst to mute his criticism of the English, the Chief rebuked him for trying to interfere with the Hearst papers' independence.[29]

Nothing was going to stop the Chief from speaking his mind, not even suggestions from his creditors. In October of 1938, Winston Churchill addressed the American people over the NBC radio network, asking for closer Anglo-American ties. Hearst replied, over the same network, that England had no right to ask the Americans to preserve "the domination which she and France have exercised over Europe since the execution of the Versailles Treaty" or to protect her Asian empire from the Japanese:

> England needs help; and where should she turn for help except to good old Uncle Sam, so sought after when needed — so scoffed at and scorned in all intervening times. . . . Nazis, Communists, Fascists, imperialists are all of the same ilk — all cut from the same cloth — all striving for power and territory — all seeking from time to time a new prize, a new victim . . . They are all ready to go to war, and all eager to get us to go to war, to add to their imperial conquests. . . . Americans should maintain the traditional policy of our great and independent nation, — great largely because it is independent.[30]

In November of 1938, Hitler and his propaganda chief, Joseph Goebbels, seizing on the pretext of the assassination in Paris of Ernst vom Rath, a Nazi official in the German embassy, by Herschel Grynszpan, a Polish Jewish student, unleashed the pogrom of November 9 and 10, the so-called Kristallnacht. As the historian Saul Friedländer has written of the violence that ensued throughout Germany:

> The only immediate aim was to hurt the Jews as badly as the circumstances allowed, by all possible means: to hurt them and to humiliate them. The pogrom and the initiatives that immediately followed have quite rightly been called "a degradation ritual." An explosion of sadism threw a particularly lurid light on the entire action and its sequels; it burst forth at all levels, that of the highest leadership and that of the lowliest party members.[31]

The response of the American press was immediate. Even those papers and those editors and publishers who, like Hearst, had ignored or denied stories of anti-Semitic violence, could no longer look the other way. Hearst responded at once, in an article he claimed had been written in response to a request from the *New York Enquirer* which he republished in his own papers on November 11. Instead of blaming Hitler or the Nazis for the violence they had unleashed, he attributed it to a generalized European madness:

> The shocking outrages perpetrated against harmless and helpless Jews in Germany are not the result of any momentary animal impulse, not the exhibition of any sporadic sentiment or action, not even directly attributable to the mad act of the irresponsible student who attacked the German government representative in Paris. They are the inevitable consequences of the persistent preachments of hate and violence which have characterized European political and social life for a generation, if not for many generations. The creed of

violence and hatred is bearing its foul fruit, and the world is beginning to realize what a destructive and death-dealing fruit it is.[32]

Still, in the days to come, the Hearst papers would join the rest of the nation's newspapers in attributing full responsibility for the crimes of Kristallnacht to Hitler and the Nazis. "The entire civilized world is shocked and shamed by Germany's brutal oppression of the Jewish people," read the editorial on November 12, 1938. Four days later, in an editorial, unsigned though clearly written by him, Hearst revealed the depths of his disappointment that Hitler had failed to learn the lesson he had tried so hard to teach him: "You set out to liberate your country. You are now isolating it . . . You set out to give Germany a deserved place in the sun. You are making it a pariah in the family of civilized nations. You are making the flag of National Socialism a symbol of national savagery."[33]

Two weeks later, in a nationwide radio broadcast from San Simeon, Hearst called for "A Homeland for Dispossessed or Persecuted Jews" to be carved out of the former German colonies in Africa that were being administered by the League of Nations. He had earlier demanded that the British keep their promise to the Jews of a homeland in Palestine, but had become convinced by October of 1938 that British indifference and Arab hostility would render that impossible.[34]

Fearful that his public pronouncements in the fall of 1934 — that he had succeeded in persuading Hitler to stop persecuting the Jews — would come back to haunt him, the Chief, in mid-December of 1938, less than a month after Kristallnacht, asked his London office to locate press clips demonstrating that his visit to Hitler had resulted in an "edict declaring no discrimination between Jews and Aryans in Business or employment." The London office replied the same day by cable. Regrettably, all it could find was a one-paragraph item from Hearst's own news service reporting that the German minister of labor, Franz Seldte, had issued a circular letter stating that "non-Aryan workers enjoy the protection of the German government."[35] There was no mention in any other newspaper, English or American, of the beneficial results of Hearst's 1934 visit.

The Chief had so committed himself by this point to the position that Hitler was not an aggressor but merely righting the wrongs of Versailles that even after the horrors of Kristallnacht in 1938 and the invasion of Poland in the fall of 1939 he continued to argue that peace with Hitler was possible. "Please drive on policy of Grant's 'let us have peace,'" he instructed Ed Coblentz in New York in October of 1939, much as he had instructed his editors a quarter-century before, in the early days of what would from this point on be known as the First World War:

> Germany's terms are not her final terms. The Allies' terms are not their final terms. Both should put forward sincerely their initial terms and should realize that peace can easily be secured by discussion and compromises. . . . Everything will be lost by war. Germany will not win the war. France will not win it. Italy will not win it. England will not win it. . . . Occidental culture and political policies and material advancement will be lost. Only cruel, destructive Asiatic tyranny will triumph. . . . Let the leaders of the nations stop being stupid and obstinate petty politicians and become broad-minded, farseeing world statesmen and let our president light the path and show the way.[36]

The Chief spoke as loudly as ever, but fewer listened. He no longer radiated the personal — and financial — strength that had extended the authority of his editorial voice. Self-exiled from the Democratic party, unwelcomed by Republicans who blamed him for Landon's defeat, he had no political home, organization, or constituency. When the Republicans nominated Wendell Willkie for president in 1940, Hearst supported him, but without enthusiasm. He was not asked to contribute to the campaign.[37]

Still, the old man tried to act as if he mattered. In September of 1940, as England was being bombarded from the air by the Luftwaffe, Hearst telegrammed Lloyd George to propose that the two of them "do something to bring this whole war to a just and reasonable cessation." Lloyd George's reply was courteous but not without a tone of amazement at Hearst's preposterous suggestion that the publisher and former prime minister broker an agreement to end the war: "In complete sympathy with your desire that effort should be made to bring this horrible struggle to a peaceable conclusion, but I am strongly of opinion that this moment inopportune for appeal whilst grim battle now pending has not reached issue. When German plan for invasion definitely checked . . . then appeal for peace conference might succeed. Premature intervention would prejudice chances."[38]

The Chief was becoming more an object of ridicule than of fear. *Time* magazine had already cruelly suggested in its March 1939 cover story that he had been exiled from the corridors of power to Marion's Santa Monica beach house. Worse was yet to come.

On December 29, 1940, newspapers across the country carried on their front pages the news that Armand Hammer, the millionaire petroleum executive and art collector, had agreed to organize an exhibit and sale of Hearst's paintings at a gallery at Saks Fifth Avenue. His other collections would be offered at the Gimbel Brothers department store in Herald

Square; the entire fifth floor of the store was to be dedicated to the Hearst sale.[39]

"I do think the . . . Board ought to have consulted me about the antique sales at Gimbel's and Saks," the Chief wrote Richard Berlin, chairman of Hearst's board of directors, when he heard the news. "It may not have been necessary, as I have already expressed my opinion of such sales; but it would have been desirable and courteous." The Gimbel's sale, Hearst predicted in his six-page letter, was going to prove "a most fatal mistake":

> You will get nothing from the sale of any consequence . . . nothing compared to the injury inflicted upon your remaining art objects by this method of selling them over the bargain counter. In addition, the widespread advertising of these department store sales — advertising which goes through despatches into nearly all the papers of the country — does a very serious injury to the prestige and standing of the institution as a whole, and of those who conspicuously represent it. . . . I have not advised against these sales at department stores because of any personal pride, but because they are bad business — bad for our antique business, bad for our advertising business, bad for our standing.[40]

Hearst was, of course, entirely correct. Unfortunately, the reputation of the old man and his businesses had already been damaged beyond repair. One more embarrassing event was not going to make much difference. For the next few weeks, magazines and newspapers across the country feasted on images of the much touted Hearst collections being sold off in department stores, piece by piece. One *New Yorker* cartoon pictured two matrons before a pile marked "Pillows 79 cents." "Are we still in the Hearst collection?" they asked the saleswoman. In another cartoon, Peter Arno drew an angry gentleman in bowler hat with cane, sternly reminding his shopping wife, "If you're so hell-bent on buying something that belongs to Mr. Hearst, you can get a *Journal-American* for three cents."

Hearst had accepted with relatively good grace his fall from power; he had even learned to live with the front-page humiliations visited upon him during the Gimbel's department store sales. What was hardest to adjust to was the permanent cessation of his building projects. His dream of building a new vacation resort on his land near the Grand Canyon ended when the government bought his property from him in 1941, for considerably less than he thought it was worth. Building at San Simeon was out of the question, though Hearst continued to work with his construction supervisor George Loorz on what Loorz referred to as the Chief's air castles. Hearst was more concerned with Wyntoon, where there was still much to do. "Mr.

Hearst is 'itching' to start something, but to date it is nothing larger than a barbeque oven," Loorz's associate at Wyntoon wrote him during the summer of 1939. With only three carpenters, three stone masons, and two laborers on staff, there was not a great deal that could be accomplished at Wyntoon, but the Chief was delighted that even the smallest building projects were proceeding: "Mr. H. has been jumping around with his program, even more than usual. One day it is one thing and the next day another. I think he tries to get more out of us by heaping on the work."[41]

The Chief had learned to live on a reduced allowance, but he had not become reconciled to it. In September of 1940, he wrote Dick Berlin at his office at 959 Eighth Avenue (where the Hearst Corporation still has its national headquarters) to renew his demand that the corporation pay more for upkeep at San Simeon and Wyntoon: "Will you please relieve me of all electricity charges on the San Simeon ranch when I am not there? . . . I hope you will not demur about this, Dick, but really do it for me and oblige. P.S. Moreover, Dick, I want some more salary. We paid Brisbane $260,000 a year and while I am willing to take a HALF cut from $500,000 I do not think it is a positive reflection not to pay me as much as Brisbane got."[42]

While W. R. was busy asking Berlin to raise his allowance, Millicent was making the same request of him. "I sent you a letter some time ago," Millicent wrote him on May 8, 1941, "asking you if you would increase my allowance by $1,000 a month, but have not yet received an answer. So I am obliged to write you again on this subject — which I assure you I hate having to do. But after trying in every way possible to have this rent [on an apartment in a building owned by a Hearst corporation] reduced, and not being able to do so, I simply must have a larger monthly allowance to live on. . . . I have exhausted my fund at the bank completely, and I am in desperate need as my bills are mounting up too much for me to cope with."[43]

Hearst did not answer Millicent's first letter and asked one of his advisers in New York to answer her second. He disliked having to say "no" and could not admit that not only did he not have the extra $1,000 a month to give her, but also that he too had tried — and failed — to get his allowance increased.

"I feel very bad that you did not answer me direct," Millicent wrote again in June 1941. "I asked you only for what it takes me to live on — and nothing more. I think I am entitled to this as I have always acceded to any request you have ever made of me." With no money to rent even the "lighthouse" at her former Sands Point estate, she informed her husband that she would "be on the move for the summer months."[44]

In February of 1942, Millicent wrote her husband again. She had, she said, by now given up any hope of regaining her old lifestyle. She was worried only for the boys, especially David, one of the twins, who was too frail to take care of himself:

> Now, W. R., you must do something for the boys while Clare [Shearn] is out West. . . . I think the boys should have a contract with the company for five years. This would make them safe until we get our affairs in shape, in case (which God forbid) anything should happen to you. As for myself, I cannot expect anything to be done for me. I shall just have to sit back and take it. I do not care about myself, but I do care about the boys. William is about to take a reduction in his salary . . . I can assure you that without contracts with the company our boys would be put off the payroll faster than you could wink. This is most important, W. R., and only you can save our boys. Clare S. and the banks are just waiting to wreck us. It must not be "after you the deluge" as long as we can face the problem now and get ready and head them off. I feel strongly about this because I get the organization's reaction in so many little ways and I know what is waiting for us at the end. . . . I should like to get your advice about my affairs. . . . I am only looking to the future, because it is so uncertain for us all — young and old alike — and as we are not any longer in the young bracket it is well to face it. As for my own property, most of it had been given over to the banks, and there is nothing left in the trust but a few pieces — and one never can tell when they will go. I shall be able to save a few jewels only (if I can keep them). It is all very sad when you think of it, but as we have lived and seen many happy years, and had a great deal, we cannot kick now. . . . Hoping that you will enjoy good, good health for a long, long while to come. Affectionately, Millicent.[45]

With no more building, no more shopping, nothing to do in Hollywood, and, after the outbreak of hostilities in Europe, no possibility of touring the continent, Hearst had plenty of time on his hands. One full-time job — as editorial director of twenty newspapers — might have been enough for other seventy-seven-year-olds, but not for the Chief. And so, on March 10, 1940, he wrote the first installment of a daily newspaper column and sent it to the editor of the *Los Angeles Examiner*. It appeared, unsigned, on the front page in the space that had been Brisbane's until his death three years before. Within a few days, Hearst's "In the News" column was running in all his papers.[46]

Though he warned his editors that he did "not want to write with the utmost regularity," he published nearly a column a day for the next two years. Each one was researched thoroughly, handwritten and corrected once on yellow paper, then neatly typed, edited again by Hearst, and cabled to Los

Angeles or San Francisco, then relayed to the other newspapers. Hearst's copy was printed as he delivered it; no one dared edit it.

The Chief adopted a different tone in his daily columns than he had employed in his signed editorials. The Old Testament patriarch was replaced by a kindly, wise grandfather who had something to say — at great length — about everything under the sun. With the help of researchers and librarians and full access to his newspaper morgues, he was able to write — fairly knowledgeably — about just about everything.

He had always been fascinated by the uses and abuses of power and now indulged himself in long multipart historical narratives on this theme. He did not study the past for its own sake, but to find clues there that would enable him — and his readers — to understand current events. In September and October of 1941, he published a ten-part series on Russian history, centered on the exploits of Peter the Great and Ivan the Terrible. He began the series with the exhortation that "we Americans ought to have all the information we can glean and gain about Russia, the great political octopus, which has affixed itself to us as OUR ally in ITS plan to control and communize the world." He ended with the thought that would characterize every succeeding piece in the series, that Russia was a "queer land . . . and a queer assortment of people — all basically Asiatic in thought and temperament — in character and conduct. . . . Russian Communism is an Asiatic creed." The moral was clear: the United States had no business allying in any way with the Asiatic nation that, under the reign of Peter the Great, had robbed the Occidental nations of a lot of territory and was trying to repeat that history once again.[47]

In February and March of 1942, after Pearl Harbor, he published a series of columns on Japanese culture, religion, and history, followed a few months later by a series on Roman history, Caesar, Mark Antony, and Cleopatra. Regrettably, considering the time, effort, and resources that went into them, many of these columns were almost unreadable. The major problem was their inordinate length. Newspaper layout and typography — small print in single columns, continued over several pages — do not make for easy reading of history, even when the prose flowed as gently as Hearst's.

When he wasn't immersed in one of his historical series, Hearst displayed the full contents of a mind filled to overflowing with useful tidbits of advice for his readers. It was impossible to know what to expect from day to day: essays on the American navy or the Battle of New Orleans or John Paul Jones; literary criticism comparing California poet Joaquin Miller to Lord Byron and Dante Gabriel Rossetti; autobiographical fragments; calls to build up the nation's armed forces; recipes for Welsh rarebit from Wales; a celebration of "Oh Susannah," the song, and his father's Forty-Niner generation that sang it; articles praising Shirley Temple for being Shirley Temple, Charles Lederer (not identified as Marion's nephew) for singing aloud to himself, Emma Goldman for turning against Communism, and Hollywood stars like Carole Lombard and Clark Gable for honoring their friends at Christmas by sending gifts in their names to "those less fortunate"; advice on how to care for one's heart; a comparison of California and French wines; antivivisection preachments; several lengthy pastoral poems and some humorous verse; an extended meditation on the question, "Do women dress for men or for other women or for themselves?"

Hearst also used his "In the News" column to publish political commentary in the style of Arthur Krock, Walter Lippmann, and Drew Pearson. Even as political commentator, Hearst's voice was unique, his messages entirely unpredictable. When in March of 1940, Martin Dies announced that he was bringing his congressional committee to Hollywood to investigate "un-American affairs" there, Hearst warned him not to expect "a nest of Communists. . . . Genuine Communism [was] dead in Hollywood," he proclaimed, having been killed by Stalin's nonaggression pact with Hitler. All that were left were some publicity-hungry "parlor pinks and society socialists [and] a few thoroughly worthy Jewish people somewhat favorable to Stalin . . . BECAUSE he was a foe of Hitler's."[48]

If Hearst was softer on American Communists than earlier, he was as belligerent as ever on the subject of Franklin Delano Roosevelt who, he was convinced, was doing all he could to provoke war. In the spring of 1940, when the Germans invaded western Europe, Hearst cautioned against any precipitous action and opposed American aid to the Allies. In September of that year, when Roosevelt proposed sending American destroyers to aid the British, the Chief argued that this was tantamount to a declaration of war against the Germans:

> Well folks, as your columnist foretold, we are in the war. We have delivered fifty destroyers from our navy to one of the combatants, and that, of course, is an act of aggression and participation. . . . The first move of the Axis Powers will probably be to make a defensive and offensive alliance with Japan. . . . So the good people on the Pacific Coast would better begin digging bomb-proof cellars because they may have Oriental visitors. Your columnist is thinking of moving his china and glassware from the hilltop at San Simeon over into the Nacimiento Valley and would not feel entirely sure about his more fragile possessions even there. We all have in the neighborhood of three weeks, according to our admirals, in which to prepare to repel boarders . . . The deed is done

— the die is cast — Mr. Roosevelt has his wish at last. His heart's desire had been to get us into war before the election, and apparently he has realized it.[49]

For almost forty years, the Hearst papers had targeted Japan as the major threat to American peace, prosperity, and security in the world. Now, as the war in the Pacific he had predicted came closer to reality, he pleaded with Washington to fortify the nation's Pacific coast. Only enhanced preparedness would derail Japanese global ambitions. The Japanese would not risk an invasion or a war that they knew they would lose.[50]

Hearst was convinced that war with Japan was inevitable, but he placed responsibility for the upcoming conflagration squarely on Roosevelt, who he claimed was pushing the United States into war rather than accepting Japan's claim to an Asian sphere of influence: "We have only to treat Japan in fair and friendly fashion to establish firm peace between Japan and the United States."[51]

Hearst was arguing at cross purposes with himself. The editorial policy he had set and personally articulated for almost fifty years had contributed enormously to the "Yellow Peril" mentality. It supported the fatalistic conclusion that no compromise was possible between a Japan which, in the words of the historian Akira Iriye, sought "to establish an Asian regional bloc under its control" and the United States, which was committed to keeping "Asia open to Western interests and to uphold the rights of . . . the colonial empires."[52]

Up to the very last minute, Hearst counseled against war, but when it came in December of 1941, he enlisted: "Well, fellow Americans, we are in the war and we have got to win it. There may have been some difference of opinion among good Americans about getting into the war, but there is no difference about how we should come out of it. We must come out victorious and with the largest V in the alphabet."[53]

Time magazine, which had since the first sign of fiscal troubles in the middle 1930s taken every opportunity it could to ridicule Hearst, devoted a column to what it called "Hearst's Third War" — his first two having been the Spanish-American and the Great War. The magazine reported that the Chief had left San Simeon for "San Francisco's Fairmont Hotel, whither he summoned his editors and publishers to discuss war policy. Springy of step, looking fitter than he had in years, the old publisher seemed to his admiring Hearstlings well nigh indestructible."[54]

Fearful of invasion, air attack, or sabotage — and compelled by the government to observe the blackout along the coastline and turn off all the lights at night — Hearst decided to close down San Simeon altogether and move to Wyntoon which, deep in the forest and away from the coast, was more secure. Although Hearst would miss his ranch, living at Wyntoon was not a hardship. According to Marion, it was even more beautiful than San Simeon "as far as natural scenery goes. . . . There was a calmness about it that really appealed to me. . . . Our happiest times, I think, were at Wyntoon."[55]

W.R. and Marion spent a good part of the day in Bear House, their residence. For the first time in their lives, they were substantially alone. Marion began sewing more. "She made all his ties. . . . Every tie. . . . All handmade, gorgeous silk ties," recalled Virginia Dragon, whose husband Roland succeeded Joe Willicombe as the Chief's private secretary. Marion also devoted more time to her charities, took first-aid courses, and, with visiting girlfriends, practiced bandaging in the Gables, the big stone lodge. Hearst, though now approaching eighty years of age, worked well into the evening. When he was ready for a late dinner, he called for his chauffeur to drive him and Marion — and their dogs — from Bear House to the Gables. "First the dogs would come out, and you'd get out and you'd open the door," the chauffeur David Christian recalled. "The dogs always got in first. I'm telling you, the dogs were everything. Then they'd get in."[56]

W. R. had always been fond of dogs. His favorites were the dachshunds he bred at San Simeon. As late as 1945, after the zoo and most of the other animals had been sold or given away, there still remained seventy-three dachshunds in his kennels. Hearst and Marion went nowhere without their personal dachshunds. They slept with them, ate with them, drove with them. When guests at San Simeon asked, as they often did, for a dachshund, W. R., according to his son Randolph, would send someone out to buy one, because he didn't want to give away one of his own dogs to someone he was not sure would provide it with the proper love and attention. When one of his dachshunds was injured in a fight with a porcupine, Hearst "got very excited, very excited," David Christian remembered. "He offered a big sum of money for each porcupine killed. . . . Those porcupines were so thick. . . . But you couldn't find a one after they started killing them, those guys killed them all. They killed them, and that's what he wanted."[57]

There are hints that Marion was not having an easy time in retirement at Wyntoon, though she claimed in her autobiography that she loved being there. In 1942, when her special dachshund Gandhi fell ill, she came close to breaking down entirely. "Gandhi was about fifteen, and he promised that he'd live to be fifty," Marion recalled in her memoirs. "He didn't feel well, so I had a nurse take care of him."

When Gandhi continued to deteriorate, W. R. called for the vet. "They had a conference, and then W. R. took me in the bathroom and said, 'Now, this is one time I want you to be brave.'

"'What's the matter?'

"'They have to put him out.'

"'Over my dead body,' I said. I saw Gandhi looking up with those two appealing eyes.

"The nurse gave him a shot and he went.

"I tore the place apart. I broke everything I could lay my hands on. I almost killed everybody, I was so furious."

Gandhi was buried at Wyntoon. "We had the Irish priest from McCloud conduct the services. The whole staff was up there. It sounds silly, but it's so heartbreaking when they go. You feel that not only have you lost your best friend, but a part of your life has gone."[58]

Soon after this incident Marion took ill. The nature of her illness is shrouded in mystery. The only mention of it is in a letter W. R. wrote to Jack Neylan in September of 1942, apologizing for not having seen him during a recent stay in San Francisco: "Marion was very ill and still is. We were in the hands of various doctors in San Francisco. Some advised an immediate operation, and some advised her to get in condition first. . . . I believe we will be back [in San Francisco] soon and Marion will have her operation. It is the second one in a year, and the prospect is not pleasant."[59]

Because Wyntoon was so far away from Los Angeles, fewer of W. R.'s and Marion's Hollywood friends were able to visit them. Still, in the winter of 1943–44, Clark Gable, Louis B. Mayer, Raoul Walsh, and Louella Parsons all made the trip. Among the other guests that winter were Hearst's publishing executives; some old friends, like the Swinnertons; the Lindberghs; Anna Roosevelt and her husband, John Boetigger, who worked for Hearst in Seattle; and Joseph Kennedy and his son Jack, who visited in 1940. Jack, to Randolph Hearst's amazement, went swimming in the freezing waters of the McCloud River during his visit.[60]

Karl von Wiegand, who had been one of Hearst's most valued European correspondents since the 1920s, spent the Christmas and New Year holiday of 1943 at Wyntoon. "Marion had the flu," he wrote Ed Coblentz, and "couldn't participate in Christmas dinner and Mr. Hearst was so worried that he didn't." Though von Wiegand was too polite to say or think it, it was much more likely that Marion, as was often the case now, was too drunk to appear at dinner. By New Year's Eve, she had sobered up enough to return to the dining table. With Marion's reappearance, Hearst was "himself" again, "as lively and full of fun as a boy. . . . The Chief is astoundingly vigorous, keen and alert. It was a delight and an inspiration to see."[61]

❧ 35 ❧

Citizen Kane

I T WAS, IN HINDSIGHT, almost inevitable that Orson Welles should have made his first film about William Randolph Hearst. He had always been fascinated by the power of personality and the personality of power. Before *Citizen Kane*, he had directed for the stage *Doctor Faustus, Julius Caesar, Panic* — Archibald MacLeish's drama about a ruined capitalist — and *Danton's Death*.[1]

Welles had, in the summer of 1939, signed a two-picture contract with RKO. His first project, a screen version of Joseph Conrad's *Heart of Darkness,* was shelved because it was too costly to shoot. While searching for another subject, he visited Herman Mankiewicz, who was bedridden with a broken leg. "They would mainly speak," Welles's biographer Simon Callow has written, "as people in the same business will, of projects. Welles spoke of Dumas, Machiavelli, and the Borgias, but also of an unformed idea for a film about some larger-than-life American figure — who, he wasn't quite sure. . . . Mankiewicz, a keen student of power and its abuses . . . had, for his part, long dreamed of a screenplay about a public figure — a gangster, perhaps." They eventually agreed upon a character nearer at hand, one whom Mankiewicz knew personally and Welles by reputation.[2]

Welles had been associated with the Popular Front cultural community in New York City, the same community that had, in the middle 1930s, identified Hearst as "public enemy number one." The representation of Hearst as fascist menace was, by the late 1930s, being replaced in the popular imagination by that of the millionaire eccentric, like Huxley's fictional character Jo Stoyte. But for Welles and the Popular Front left, Hearst remained, Michael Denning has written, "an emblem of American fascism, a powerful capitalist who was also a visible demagogue."[3]

Here in Southern California was the subject Welles was looking for: a purported American fascist who also happened to be a powerful man in Hollywood. Welles, as much a master of self-promotion and publicity as of the theater, must have seen at once the marketing potential. What reporter or critic could resist covering the battle of the century between the Popular Front's boy genius and the fascist Lord of San Simeon?

Welles commissioned Mankiewicz to write the script and persuaded John Houseman, Welles's on-again-off-again partner, to keep Mankiewicz off the bottle and on the project. In mid-April of 1940, Houseman and Mankiewicz delivered their first draft to Welles. It was too long, unfocused, and so clearly biographical that it almost invited a libel suit. Welles, in condensing, focusing, and reworking the Mankiewicz script, removed a great deal of the overt biographical detail.[4]

When he was finished, there was still no doubt that the film was about Hearst. The *New York Times* Hollywood correspondent reported, tongue in cheek, that "Mr. Welles says the film, which deals with the life of a fictional figure who owns a chain of newspapers, who unsuccessfully runs for Governor of New York, who boasts that he started the Spanish-American War, who marries an obscure singer and attempts to gain recognition for her as an opera star through his publications, and who finally retires to a fabulous castle to die when his newspaper empire crumbles, is in no sense biographical. Representatives of William Randolph Hearst, the publisher, have advised the producer that they believe another interpretation can be put on the story."[5]

The major discrepancy between the life stories of Hearst and Kane was that Hearst's real-life mistress, Marion Davies, was a movie star — and a fairly successful one — and the fictional Susan Alexander had no talent, grace, or charm whatsoever. Mankiewicz and Welles could claim — and did — that Kane was not Hearst because Alexander was not Davies. At the same time, they included in their portrait of Alexander several "insider" details that connected her to Davies. Alexander, like Davies, is blond, does jigsaw puzzles, and has a drinking problem. More than that, Xanadu, where Alexander and Kane retire in defeat and disgrace, was, as movie critic Pauline Kael had observed, "transparently San Simeon; and Susan's fake stardom and the role she played in Kane's life spelled Marion Davies to practically everybody in the Western world."[6]

Mankiewicz had been a visitor at Marion's beach house, the Culver City bungalow, and perhaps San Simeon as well. Details about Marion's drinking habits and jigsaw puzzles came from firsthand observation. He had also done some homework. Mankiewicz denied ever having read Ferdinand

Lundberg's *Imperial Hearst,* but there were three copies in his personal library. The similarities between his script and Lundberg's biography were too striking to have been coincidental. Lundberg later sued Welles for plagiarism. He received as a settlement from RKO $15,000 for damages and several hundred thousand dollars to cover his court costs and attorney's fees.[7]

From the very first frames, Welles and Mankiewicz made clear their intention to tell a story about Hearst. The castle on the hill that we see in the opening shots, the "paintings, pictures, statues, and more statues . . . Enough for ten museums — the loot of the world" that the newsreel announcer describes for us, the unpacked crates, the zoo are unmistakably Hearst's. Welles wisely does not caricature or impersonate W. R. — although as Kane he does dress as Hearst did and gesture from the podium as he had. Simply by playing himself — expressing his own inordinate self-confidence, dominating every scene, looming over every grouping, always having the last word — Welles incarnates the Mankiewicz/Lundberg portrait of the man who, as the newsreel announcer declares in the film's opening shots, was not only the "greatest newspaper tycoon of this or any other generation," but "more newsworthy than the names in his own headlines."[8]

Because so much of Welles went into the portrayal, Kane was not an unsympathetic character. We fall in love with his buoyancy, his joie de vivre; we believe his campaign promises to the "workingman and the slum child," to the "decent, ordinary citizens . . . the unprivileged, the underpaid, and the underfed." We sympathize with him as he grows distant from a wife who parades before him at the dinner table the prejudices of her class and asks him to keep Bernstein, his too visibly Jewish business manager, away from the nursery.

Kane's mother is pathologically cold and unloving; his wife is an anti-Semite and social snob; his mistress is mindless, untalented, a drunk who becomes a shrill harpy, possessed by one of the screen's most gratingly annoying voices. These portraits are infinitely crueler than the portrait of Kane, whose behavior is excused because he had suffered a childhood trauma.

It is possible that Welles was enough of a megalomaniac to believe that Hearst would be so entranced by seeing elements of his own life on the big screen that he would overlook the maliciously false portraits of the three women in his life. As Welles confessed in later years, he had made "Kane . . . better than Hearst [while] Marion was much better than Susan — whom people wrongly equated with her." Marion Davies, he conceded publicly, was a talented actress and a "fine woman" whom he libeled in his film. Of his character assassination of Phoebe and Millicent, he had nothing to say.[9]

While the "Hearst" project was conceived and executed in secrecy, there were leaks, as there always were in Hollywood. In September of 1940, a two-line item in *Newsweek* asserted mistakenly that Welles's script had been "sent to William Randolph Hearst for perusal after columnists had hinted it dealt with his life." When Louella Parsons, who claimed to have known Welles's family in Illinois and "was delighted to give a boost to a local boy who had made good," asked if the rumors were true, Welles denied them, insisting that he was working on a Faustian story about a powerful man. Louella did not question him further. Neither she nor anyone else in Hollywood believed that Welles was mad enough to take on Hearst.[10]

On January 3, Welles and RKO screened a rough cut of *Citizen Kane* for national magazine reviewers with early deadlines. When Hedda Hopper complained that Welles had promised to show her the film before anyone else saw it, he arranged a separate screening for her.

"Only six people sat in a private projection room when the finished product was first unveiled," Hopper recalled in her autobiography. "I was appalled. The film was too well done. An impudent, murderous trick, even for the boy genius, to perpetrate on a newspaper giant . . .

"Early next morning Orson was on the telephone demanding, 'Well, what do you think?'

"'You won't get away with it,' I assured him.

"'Oh, yes I will. You'll see.'

"Cockiness I can take; arrogance I abhor. Deciding that Mr. Hearst should know what was afoot, I passed on the information through channels."[11]

W. R., informed by Bill, Jr., whom Hedda had contacted, asked Louella to investigate. A screening of *Citizen Kane* was arranged for her and the two Hearst Corporation lawyers she brought with her.

"I must say now, so many years later," Louella wrote in her 1961 memoirs, "that I am still horrified by the picture. It was a cruel, dishonest caricature . . . I walked from the projection room without saying a word to Orson. I have not spoken to him since. When the lawyers and I talked with Mr. Hearst, the lawyers told him he had a foolproof libel suit and asked him to take it to court. 'No,' he said, 'I don't believe in lawsuits. Besides, I have no desire to give the picture any more publicity.'" A libel or invasion of privacy suit would have gotten Hearst nowhere. It would, on the contrary, have been an admission that he was indeed Charles Foster Kane and, worse yet, that Marion was Susan Alexander.[12]

Like other long-time, well-paid Hearst editors and columnists, Louella was fiercely loyal to the Chief and to her friend Marion and outraged that Welles, a twenty-five-year-old upstart, braggart, and liar, should have the effrontery to invade Hearst's hometown and baldly caricature him. She also wanted revenge on Welles for lying to her and for granting Hedda a "scoop" on a story involving her boss. Out of loyalty to Hearst, sympathy for Marion, and loathing for Welles, Louella set out to destroy Welles. Hearst did nothing to stop her.

In mid-January, a month before *Citizen Kane* was scheduled to open at Radio City Music Hall, Louella reported to W. R. that she had just received a telegram from Nelson Rockefeller, whose family had a sizable stake in RKO and controlled Radio City Music Hall. Rockefeller wrote Louella that he had had a long talk with George Schaefer, the RKO studio chief, who was "giving the matter serious consideration." Though we don't know precisely what "the matter" was, the implication was that Rockefeller had pressured Schaefer to withdraw *Citizen Kane* or recut it to eliminate the references to Hearst. According to Parsons, "L. B. Mayer, Joseph Schenck [of 20th Century-Fox], Nicholas Schenck and Jack Warner have all refused to book *Citizen Kane*. Joe Schenck told me that if RKO books the picture the companies will book no more RKO movies in their theaters."[13]

If loyalty or sympathy were not reason enough for Hollywood insiders like Mayer, Warner, and the Schencks to decline to exhibit the film, fear of retribution was. On January 19, the *New York Times* reported that Hearst's representatives had contacted Mayer and Warner for help and begun "an investigation of the alien situation in Hollywood, something about which the industry is most sensitive. . . . A rip-snorting newspaper Americanization campaign could prove embarrassing. A Congressional investigation, hinted at by Senator Burton K. Wheeler on Monday, might be disastrous. Those outside RKO are aware of these possibilities, and if they regard them seriously enough they may align themselves with those who think it inadvisable to release 'Citizen Kane.'" The *Times* reported further that Adela Rogers St. Johns was gathering material "for a story of Mr. Welles's romantic adventures in Hollywood." Welles was, at the time, often seen with Dolores Del Rio, who was married. The studios were less worried about his being caught in an adulterous affair than about other Hollywood celebrities whose reputations would not survive a full-scale Hearstian investigation of sexual habits in Hollywood. According to Simon Callow, Louella Parsons, "using every ugly tactic she could think up," had already threatened to print fictional versions of the lives of RKO board members in Hearst papers. "If you boys want private lives," she was saying, "I'll give you private lives." *Variety* reported in early February that a group of Hollywood executives, organized by Louis B. Mayer, had begun to raise funds to buy and destroy the *Citizen Kane* negative to forestall the havoc the Hearst press was prepared to unleash on the industry.[14]

While Parsons and Mayer did W. R.'s dirty work on the Coast, Richard Berlin, the head of his magazine division, joined the battle from New York. In early January he contacted the general manager of Warner Brothers, who told him that *Citizen Kane* would not be shown in their theaters. "I spoke to my friend, Spyros Skouras, about the same thing. Spyros has charge of all Twentieth Century Fox Theaters as well as being the largest independent chain owner in America. Spyros told me that Fox will not play *Citizen Kane* and that none of the Skouras Theaters will play *Citizen Kane,* that he was going to make it his job to talk to every important independent chain theater operator and see that they boycotted the picture."[15]

Berlin had also put his leading subversive-hunter, Howard Rushmore, on the case. Rushmore, Berlin wrote the Chief, had assembled material that proved that "our friend, Welles, is a pretty bad boy and is mixed up with the Leftists. . . . Hollywood is due for a good purging as the picture industry, I am sure, has a healthy representation from the Communist Party. . . . It is an important avenue of propaganda and the Party never neglects such an avenue . . . It might not be a bad idea if Rushmore would come to California incognito, work under cover . . . for a matter of a few weeks in this Communistic activity in the motion picture industry preparatory to an exposé."[16]

Although Hearst asked to see Rushmore's report, he did not give Berlin the go-ahead to release any material or send Rushmore to California to continue his investigation. Two days later, on a Thursday, Berlin called to tell the Chief that George Schaefer, the head of RKO, had asked for a meeting. Hearst had Joe Willicombe call Berlin back to tell him to avoid Schaefer: "Our friends in the business who are handling this matter do not think it wise for you to see that man. They think that everything is going fine and that the man may do some damage by misrepresenting the interview. . . . I think they are right and that we should heed them. Can you not conveniently be out of town? I have studiously avoided meeting anybody in order to leave the whole matter in the hands of our friends."[17]

The message arrived twenty-four hours too late, or so Berlin reported back to the Chief. Anxious to insert himself into the negotiations, Berlin had lunch with Schaefer and informed the studio head that "he had a good Leftist for a partner in Orson Welles."[18]

Through January of 1941, the daily press, trade papers, and news magazines were filled with stories about what *Newsweek* labeled the battle of Hearst vs. Orson Welles. Few in Hollywood or New York had any doubt but that Hearst would prevail. Douglas Churchill in his January 19 *New York Times* article put the odds at two-to-one that the film would not be released.[19]

Though most of the campaign against RKO was fought in private, the Hearst press signaled its intention to retaliate against the studio by refusing to run ads for RKO films in its newspapers or magazines. *Variety* reported in mid-January that an advertisement for RKO's latest picture, *Kitty Foyle,* had been pulled from Hearst's Los Angeles papers. As Richard Berlin explained to the agent who had tried to place an advertisement for *Citizen Kane* in *Cosmopolitan,* he "was refusing the advertisement . . . purely on the grounds that it was an unkind gesture against Mr. Hearst and that he, the agent, could tell Mr. Schaefer that *Cosmopolitan* does not wish to carry advertising on pictures that endeavor to destroy people's character whether it be Mr. Hearst, Mr. Schaefer, Mr. Schenck or anyone else."[20]

In late January, Welles and his press agent flew to New York City, in *Variety*'s words, "to huddle with George Schaefer and other RKO execs on the future of *Citizen Kane,* which is, more or less, stymied by threats of blackouts by the Hearst newspapers." After screening the film for RKO board members and lawyers, Schaefer and Welles agreed to make a number of cuts and in a gesture of conciliation sent a print of the edited film to Hearst. It was returned with the seals unbroken.[21]

Citizen Kane had been rescheduled for a mid-February premiere at Radio City Music Hall, but no one was surprised when the opening was canceled. Louella had threatened the manager of Radio City Music Hall "with a total press blackout if he showed the movie" and, according to Schaefer, had warned Nelson Rockefeller, whose family owned Radio City, that if *Citizen Kane* opened there, Hearst's *American Weekly* would run a "double-page spread on John D. Rockefeller."[22]

As Schaefer had only postponed the opening, not shelved the film, Louella and the Hearst press continued their attack. When a minor European producer was awarded $7,000 after suing RKO for breach of contract, the story was prominently featured in the Hearst papers, with special emphasis on the fact that George Schaefer had been named as co-defendant. While waiting for his picture to be released, Welles agreed to direct an adaptation of *Native Son* by the novelist — and Communist party member — Richard Wright. The Hearst papers attacked Welles as a Communist sympathizer. In April, he wrote and starred in a radio drama produced for CBS by The Free Company, a leftist group of radio writers and directors. The Hearst papers reported on their front pages that the American Legion had discovered that the members of The Free Company included several who were affiliated with groups approved by the *Daily Worker*. In late April, Welles gave the Hearst witch-hunters another opportunity to assail him when he signed on as a "founder" of a defense committee for the union leader Harry Bridges, who was fighting deportation proceedings in San Francisco. From this point on, every reference in the Hearst papers to either Welles or Bridges would prominently mention the former's support for the latter.[23]

The Hearst vs. Welles story was too good to go away. The protagonists were both so "huge" (literally and figuratively) that every rumor got its hearing. In a letter to his friend Alexander Woollcott, Herman Mankiewicz claimed that Hearst had offered Hollywood producers "a hundred examples of unfavorable news — rape by executives, drunkenness, miscegenation and allied sports — which on direct appeal from Hollywood he had kept out of his papers in the last fifteen years," but would no longer keep out if Welles's film were released. Welles claimed that his draft records had been investigated and that he had been harassed by suspicious-looking photographers lurking in bushes. "They were really after me," Welles later told Peter Bogdanovich. "Before *Kane* was released, I was lecturing — I think it was Pittsburgh, some town like that — and a detective came up to me as I was having supper . . . He said, 'Don't go back to your hotel . . . They've got a fourteen-year-old girl in the closet and two cameramen waiting for you to come in.' And of course I would have gone to jail. There would have been no way out of it."[24]

Welles and Schaefer held screenings in Hollywood and New York to demonstrate to the press, the industry, and the RKO board that *Citizen Kane* was a work of art which deserved to be released. So many prominent people were invited to so many screenings that *Variety* joked that RKO had decided not to open the film at premiere prices, because those who might have been able to afford a high-priced ticket had already seen the film for free. (The story was headlined, "So Many Cuffo Gloms at 'Kane' It Kayoes Idea of a $5.50 Preem.") Hearst, asked by *Daily News* film columnist John Chapman to describe the film, telegrammed back that he was "the only other guy in Hollywood who has not seen 'Citizen Kane.' So I cannot discuss the picture."[25]

For more than four months, RKO, fearful that Hearst would sue for libel or invasion of privacy and win, delayed release of the finished film. Finally, on May 1, *Citizen Kane* opened in New York City, and in the weeks to come in Chicago, Los Angeles, Boston, San Francisco, and Washington, D.C.[26]

The reviews of the film were outstanding. *Time* magazine called it Hollywood's "greatest creation." John O'Hara in *Newsweek,* after seeing a screening, reported that it was "the best picture he ever saw." Bosley Crowther, in the *New York Times,* said that it was "far and away the most surprising and cinematically exciting motion picture to be seen here in many a moon."[27]

As good as the reviews were, there was, as Robert Carringer has written, trouble at the box office from the beginning. *Citizen Kane* was not a popular success. While RKO had anticipated being attacked directly in the Hearst papers, that, at least, never happened. "Hearst papers," *Variety* reported on May 7, "apparently now figure they can do Welles and the picture more harm by a campaign of silence. They neither mentioned nor printed reviews of the New York opening and apparently have allowed their campaign against Welles as a 'Communist' to flag."[28]

There are dozens of half-truths about William Randolph Hearst. One of the most fervently held — and widely disseminated — is that *Citizen Kane* was crushed by Hearst's retaliation. As David Thomson reminds us in his biography of Welles, "what is far more instructive about *Kane*'s failure with the first audiences is the number of ways in which Welles had cut himself off from success." Although the decision of the major distributors not to book the film made it difficult, if not impossible, to earn back costs, it is doubtful that the film would have been a box-office hit even had Hearst's associates not interfered with its distribution. "Undoubtedly," Robert Carringer has concluded, "the distribution problems hurt, but it is unlikely that they made a crucial difference; *Citizen Kane* is simply not a film for an ordinary commercial audience." The innovative story-telling techniques that made such an impact on critics and filmmakers may have hurt the film at the box office. "Narrative is steadily denied or evaded by *Kane,* especially in its opening," David Thomson has written. "The convention of giving the audience necessary information is ignored; the moods of the first few sequences are deliberately jarring; there are no characters to identify with." The soundtrack is cluttered with overlapping voices; the lighting and camera angles are bizarre; there are too many flashbacks, and few, if any, close-ups. Audiences, Thomson speculates, must have found the film "obscure, intellectual, overly complex, gloomy or cold." *Citizen Kane,* according to Thomson, may also have failed to attract a mass audience because it violated essential American verities: "It maintains that the pursuit of happiness and the search for meaning are futile."[29]

"In the cities business was good initially," Simon Callow has written, "but quickly slid even in New York, where it closed after fifteen weeks. In the regional theatres, despite a special low-price launch, things were much worse. Among exhibitors, the picture became a byword for disaster. . . . By the end of the year, it had closed everywhere, not to be seen widely again in America till RKO sold its library to television."[30]

RKO retired the film in 1942, having lost more than $150,000 on it.

In her 1951 reminiscences, which were later published as *The Times We Had,* Marion said that neither she nor W. R. ever saw the film:

> My sister Rose did, and she said, "I'll kill him [Welles], it's terrible. You can't even see the picture, because it's all dark."
>
> I said, "Why are you saying it's terrible?"
>
> "It's against you." . . .
>
> I said to her, "Rose, there's one tradition that I have that was taught to me by W. R. Never read criticism about yourself." . . .
>
> His theory was that no matter what anybody said, no matter what they wrote, you didn't read it and you didn't listen. . . .
>
> But plenty of people talked about *Citizen Kane.* They would say that it was terrible and I had to go see it. But we never did.[31]

In the middle 1950s, the film's reputation was enhanced by European filmmakers and critics like François Truffaut, Jean-Luc Godard, and the editors of the British film magazine *Sight and Sound,* who voted it the all-time best film in 1962. *Citizen Kane* resurfaced for American audiences and became a fixture on the college and "art house" circuit. In 1956, when RKO became the first movie studio to sell its films to television, *Citizen Kane* was given a large popular audience.[32]

By the time *Citizen Kane* fully reentered public consciousness, both W. R. and Marion were dead. The film's new viewers, never having seen one of Marion's films or lived through Hearst's heyday as publisher and politician, had no reason to believe that the portrait was not an accurate one. In 1961, when W. A. Swanberg entitled his biography of Hearst *Citizen Hearst,* another strong link was forged between Kane and Hearst.[33]

Although the process by which Hearst became Kane and vice-versa is beyond the scope of this book, the lines between the fictional and the real have become so blurred that today, almost sixty years after the film was made and a half-century since Hearst's death, it is difficult to disentangle the intermingled portraits of Charles Foster Kane and William Randolph

Hearst. Both were powerful; both were enormously wealthy; both had big houses and big egos. But Welles's *Kane* is a cartoon-like caricature of a man who is hollowed out on the inside, forlorn, defeated, solitary because he cannot command the total obedience, loyalty, devotion, and love of those around him. Hearst, to the contrary, never regarded himself as a failure, never recognized defeat, never stopped loving Marion or his wife. He did not, at the end of his life, run away from the world to entomb himself in a vast, gloomy art-choked hermitage.

Orson Welles may have been a great filmmaker, but he was neither a biographer nor a historian. "You know, the real story of Hearst is quite different from Kane's," Welles told Peter Bogdanovich many years later. "And Hearst himself — as a *man,* I mean — was *very* different."[34]

§ 36 €

Old Age

Unlike Aldous Huxley's fictional multimillionaire Jo Stoyte, who was modeled after him, and contrary to the abundant rumors, W. R. was not phobic about old age or death. He greeted the passing of time with untypical insouciance. Aging gave him a license to let down his guard, to compose and publish poetry, to reminisce, to allow elements of playfulness and sentimentality to enter his writing. Old age made everything look and feel a bit different. At his seventy-sixth birthday party, given by Cissy Patterson in Washington, he admitted that he had still not attained the age of discretion, but, having reached the "years of discrimination," had come to "appreciate the fact that there is nothing so valuable in life as friendship and companionship. . . . The only thing of genuine importance is friends."[1]

In old age, Hearst had a number of friends, though they were all either on his payroll or connected to him through some sort of business arrangement. Cissy Patterson and Ed Coblentz edited his newspapers; Tom White, Richard Berlin, Jack Neylan, Martin Huberth, and Alice Head were senior executives in the company; Louella Parsons and Adela Rogers St. Johns were syndicated writers.

Still, while Hearst had any number of men and women he called his friends, he was intimate with none of them. He faced the crises of bankruptcy and liquidation by himself. There is no evidence that he confided in anyone — not Millicent, not his sons, not his oldest friends. Even Marion, in her memoirs, records only one instance in which he confessed that he was in trouble, on the train that carried them to New York in the fall of 1937.

As he aged, W. R. looked more than ever to Marion and to his dachshunds for companionship. When Helen, his favorite dachshund, died at Wyntoon, Hearst was, Marion recalled, inconsolable — as she had been on the death of her dog Gandhi. He recovered only after writing about his loss in his "In the News" column:

A boy and his dog are no more inseparable companions than an old fellow and his dog. An old bozo is a nuisance to almost everybody — except his dog. To his dog he is just as good as he ever was — maybe better . . . Anyhow the dog and the old guy understand each other and get along "just swell." So I do miss Helen, I was very fond of her. She always slept on a big chair in my room and her solicitous gaze followed me to bed at night and was the first thing to greet me when I woke in the morning. . . . Helen died in my bed and in my arms. I have buried her on the hillside overlooking the green lawn — where she used to run — and surrounded by the flowers. I will not need a monument to remember her. But I am placing over her little grave a stone with the inscription — "Here lies dearest Helen — my devoted friend."[2]

Humor remained his best weapon and shield against the losses and infirmities of old age. To the United Press, which congratulated him on his seventy-eighth birthday, he wrote, "Thank you, but I am not having any more birthdays. Or if I do, I will have them in reverse, beginning at seventy-eight and going back to twenty-one. I appreciate your courteous congratulations, but please save them until I get back to twenty-one. Congratulating a man on being seventy-eight is like felicitating him on being in an airplane accident. He may survive, but it is not exactly an enjoyment."[3]

Despite his complaints, the Chief looked remarkably fit. He was a little heavier, his face fuller, his neck thicker. His posture was still perfect, his hair white and a bit thinner. He had begun to wear glasses, but only for reading certain kinds of documents.

He began to write more poetry. Some of it was published in his columns; some printed elsewhere in his paper, unsigned and unacknowledged, like this lullaby:

Father serves his country
Upon the raging main,
Mother's at a night club,
And she's paralyzed again.
Baby's lone and lonely,
There's none to hear its cry,
"Tor-a lor-a lor-a,"
That's a modern lullaby.[4]

In his longer-form verse, he made public display of the pastoral sentimentality that had been hidden away behind the long, stern face and the pompous stentorian prose. Marion thought one of his poems, "Song of the River," in which he compared the course of a human life to a flowing river, "the most beautiful thing ever written." He was quite proud of this poem and had it mounted on special stock and distributed to friends and business associates.[5]

At Wyntoon, he sent Marion a small note or poem every night. "He would shove them under the door and wait until I woke up. . . . I used to answer him back. He used to keep all my little notes in a drawer right next to his bed. But they were stolen from the house. I still have his

> Oh the night is blue and the
>   stars are bright
> Like the eyes of the girl of
>   whom I write. . . .
> And the skies are soft and the
>   clouds are white
> Like the limbs of the girl
>   Of whom I write,
> But no beauty of earth is so
>   fair a sight
> As the girl who lies by my
>   side at night.[6]

Hearst and Marion traveled less than before, though the old man, even in his eighties, was incapable of remaining in one place for very long. In the spring of 1941, he spent a month with Marion in Mexico and returned with praise for the Mexican government, which had recently expropriated some of his land at Babicora. "They were pretty decent about that," he told reporters. "They didn't take any more than was right. After all, it is their country."[7]

Hearst went out of his way now to express his newfound friendship for the Mexicans and their president, Manuel Ávila Camacho, who had protected the bulk of his extensive land holdings from expropriation. In early March, his advertising director sent the president a copy of a recent "In These Times" article: "You can feel the radiation of his friendship. I will send you personally these articles as they appear. I know your country will reap great benefits from these stories which will bring tourists into Mexico and at the same time cement a very wonderful friendship." On his 1941 trip to Mexico, Hearst visited President Ávila Camacho and presented him with a Kerry Blue dog as a present. When the dog ran away, the Chief wrote a long personal note to the president to say how "distressed" he had been "to hear that the foolish animal had wandered away from its lovely home to lose itself in the great city." This time, he was going to send the president a "Dachel" — a dachshund — which was "more of a home dog and less of a wanderer and adventurer. . . . If it once thinks you like it you will find it reciprocates affection most devotedly . . . If you would prefer less of a house dog, please let me know. I want you to have the kind of dog that you really like. You have done so much for me and there is so little I can do in return."[8]

In April of 1943, Hearst quietly celebrated his eightieth birthday at Marion's Santa Monica beach house. On being toasted by his sons, their wives, and a few friends, he rose to respond, "I shall not pretend that I'm happy about being eighty. I would happily exchange that marker for two lifetimes at forty. Just as a woman reaching forty would gladly exchange that milestone for two at twenty. Yet I am thankful and grateful that I find so much in life that is fresh, stimulating, and dear to me."[9]

Time magazine, which still monitored the Chief's activities, reported that he had spent his birthday talking with friends, reading his congratulatory telegrams, and playing "his daily hour of tennis. . . . Despite his age, Tycoon Hearst has not shriveled. Grey, jowled like a coon dog, no longer nimble, he still stands impressively erect [and] is remarkably healthy. He still bubbles with new ideas for his publications, over which he maintains the vigilance of a whimsical despot."[10]

Hearstian journalism, as *Time* reminded its readers, was "still wild-eyed, red-inked, impulsive, dogmatic." It was advocacy journalism at its most extreme. The Hearst papers took positions — and stood by them. There was no commitment to objective, both-sides-of-the-story journalism. In May of 1943, Jack Warner, under attack for having produced *Mission to Moscow* — which his critics claimed was no more than a big-screen paean to Stalin and the Soviet Communists — asked for Hearst's help, "in view of our long friendship." Hearst refused:

> You say our papers "should state the other side of the case" . . . Your film, Mr. Warner, gives "the other side of the case" — the Communist side — quite complete. My contention is that it is entirely essential, not only in the interests of fairness, but in the interests of freedom, for an American newspaper to print the anti-Communist — the Democratic side of the case. . . . I am sorry that we disagree on the proper function of the press — and of the moving picture. But I am sure you will realize that our attitude toward your screen product (an attitude so frequently favorable, but in this case frankly critical) is guided by no personal unfriendliness, but merely by a sense of public duty.[11]

To make sure that his editors across the country knew what he wanted on his front and editorial pages, the Chief wrote them daily from wherever he happened to be. In March 1944, he telegrammed instructions on Irene Castle's campaign for prevention of cruelty to animals: "I am chiefly interested in the protection of dogs." He criticized his editors for "boosting" George Patton — "that brutal 'kick 'em in the pants' General . . . ought to be demoted." He complained about "the lack of size and clearness in the lettering" of the "four column comics" that were being published on Sunday. And he took up the campaign for a Jewish homeland.[12]

Hearst, who had been crusading for a Jewish homeland since 1937, had abandoned his earlier plan to establish it in Africa. He signed on now as a sponsor of the Emergency Conference to Save the Jewish People of Europe, which was organized by Palestinian Jews who were supporters of the rightwing revisionist Zionist, Vladimir Jabotinsky. According to David Wyman, the author of *The Abandonment of the Jews*, Hearst was more active than any other American newspaper publisher in his support for a Jewish homeland in Palestine. He seemed "to have been genuinely concerned about the terrible plight of Europe's Jews. In . . . editorials, he repeatedly pointed out an essential truth that very many of America's religious and secular leaders never grasped: 'Remember, Americans, This Is Not a Jewish Problem. It Is a Human Problem.'"[13]

In his ninth decade, Hearst regained control of his publishing empire. Ironically, it was America's entry into the Second World War, which Hearst had done all he could to prevent, that saved his newspapers. With the coming of war, circulation grew and advertising kept pace with it. Newsprint rationing, at the same time, forced publishers to print fewer pages, which lowered their costs. Simultaneously with the increase in publishing revenues, the Hearst organization began reaping a new windfall by licensing its comics characters, especially Popeye and Blondie, for radio, animated cartoons, ten-cent children's books, and dozens of different novelty items, including pencil sharpeners, molded soap figures, glow lamps, pocket knives, and a wide assortment of foods, candies, and beverages.[14]

Fortified by expanded revenues — and the promise of better times to come — John Hanes, his chief financial adviser, was able to raise enough money to buy back a large portion of the Hearst Consolidated stock and pay off Chase National and the other major creditors. In December of 1943, Judge Shearn retired as trustee. He was replaced by a corporate board of Hearst loyalists. After six very lean years, the Chief was in an expansive mood again. "I am very much interested in the Acapulco gold mining property for several reasons," he wrote Edward Clark in January. "I like gold mines and I like Acapulco. Please do your utmost to press your plans to a successful conclusion. I would like a job in the mine."[15]

By early 1945, after almost eight years in exile, William Randolph Hearst, at eighty-two, was again in control of his finances. The empire that was returned, though reduced in size, remained formidable, with seventeen daily newspapers, four radio stations, nine American and three English magazines, a wire service, a feature service, and a Sunday supplement.

Almost simultaneously with his victory over his creditors, Hearst celebrated the nation's victory over Japan by returning from Wyntoon with Marion to take up residence at San Simeon. As if the previous eight years had never happened, construction began again on the unfinished North or New Wing. The top floor was to be Hearst's and Marion's. Camille Solon, who had painted the murals on the vaulted arches in Hearst's Gothic Study twelve years earlier, returned to paint the arches in one of the sitting rooms; the lamps were sent up from Marion's beach house; Charles Messer from Barker Brothers, the Los Angeles department store, set up his sewing machine on site and created all the draperies.[16]

While construction was in progress in the North Wing, Hearst and Marion lived in House A, or Casa del Mar, which had been the Hearst family's primary residence on the hilltop in the middle 1920s. Marion moved into Millicent's room; Hearst reoccupied his old bedroom with the four-column bed he had bought in 1921. It was to this room that Hearst now returned every evening to work at his Spanish writing table or in his seventeenth-century French tapestry-upholstered chair. "Through the door lattice," Marion remembered, "I could see that his lights were on, all night long. I'd walk in and say, 'Are you going to bed or are you not?' He'd say yes. I'd say, 'Turn the lights off.' Well, half an hour later he would still be writing or playing solitaire or thinking."[17]

As in the old days, family and friends appeared every weekend. Colleen Moore, one of the regulars at San Simeon in the late 1920s and 1930s, had expected that the ranch, once reopened, would be as it had been before the war. To her surprise, she discovered that where there had previously never been "less than thirty-five or forty people, always great crowds, this time there was only Marion, Mr. Hearst, his favorite grandson, Bunky, and Igor Cassini and Bootsie [Mrs. Cassini], who later married Bill [Jr.] . . . and Harry Crocker, who was in bed with the flu." Hearst, Moore noted, was in fine spirits, though she could not help noticing that he had become quite old.[18]

The routine at the castle was much the same as it had been, with cocktails daily in the Assembly Room followed by dinner in the Refectory and a film in the movie theater. The only difference was that, instead of descending by elevator from his Gothic Suite on the third floor, Hearst quietly greeted his guests from the sofa at the north end of the Assembly Room. Although less mobile than he was before the war, he remained involved in every detail of daily life. "He was very particular about the fringes on the rugs," Ann Miller, the new housekeeper, recalled, "and he didn't like spider webs." When he and his guests were served beef that he did not think up to ranch standards, he fired off a note to his ranch manager and cousin, Randy Apperson: "I think beef ought to be hung from eight to twelve weeks. I suggest that you hang it eight weeks at the ranch and then send it up the hill. If you need more cold storage equipment I have no doubt it will be provided."[19]

There was a new generation of servants at the ranch now, all of whom had been instructed "to keep out of Mr. Hearst's way, don't bother him, don't appear and be around when he is." Ann Miller, the housekeeper, did as she was told and altered her route whenever she saw the old man approaching, only to be gently reprimanded for it: "His valet then came to me at a later date and said that Mr. Hearst likes to speak to and encounter and meet up with the employees."[20]

There is a photograph from this period of Hearst, at eighty-three, with his head gardener, Nigel Keep, who was seventy-two. The two stand side by side, Hearst in his three-piece suit, Keep in slacks and a light work shirt. The photograph is inscribed in Hearst's handwriting, "Dear Mr. Keep — This is a good picture of two very handsome *young* men."[21]

Not every employee on the hillside got on as famously with the Chief. He had become more autocratic with age, less tolerant of those who broke his cardinal rules.

Every evening, as the sun set, he and Marion took a long walk along the Esplanade, the pathway that connected the guesthouses to one another and to Casa Grande. "They got back from one of those strolls one night," recalls Roland Dragon, who after Joe Willicombe's retirement served as Hearst's private secretary, "and he called me on the phone. 'Mr. Dragon,' he said, 'somebody has picked a rose.' [Hearst] described where it was on the back part of the Esplanade. . . . He said, 'I want you to find out who did it and see that they're removed from the hilltop.' So I had to call each department head and set up a meeting. . . . It had to be somebody that wasn't familiar with the rules, or something like that. . . . It was about 11:30 at night and I found out who did it. . . . Broke my heart to have to discharge this man."

The culprit was the young fellow who "used to drive the film back and forth every day from Hollywood." He had picked a rose to take back that night to his sweetheart. John Horn, the historian at the San Simeon Historical Monument, speculates that as the young man was probably already on the payroll of one of Hearst's Los Angeles papers, he may not have been fired, but rather reassigned to work in Los Angeles.[22]

In the spring of 1945, Marion was struck ill again with a stomach ailment and was rushed by plane to St. Luke's Hospital in San Francisco. When she was well enough to leave the hospital, she and W. R. moved into Huntington House, as their regular hotel, the Fairmont, was filled with the delegates from the fifty nations who had convened in San Francisco to draft a United Nations charter. According to Marion, Hearst got a chance to meet Molotov, the Soviet representative at the conference, and "though there was a difference of opinion, W. R. thought that . . . he had a sort of amenability towards being sensible." Marion's illness was not as bad as had been feared and two weeks after their emergency flight to San Francisco, she and W. R. were back at San Simeon again. Karl von Wiegand, who was visiting at the time, wrote Bill Curley, one of Hearst's editors and a friend, that the Chief was "in splendid shape, physically and mentally, and just as active as ever. He was full of fun at his [eighty-second] birthday party which all of the boys and their wives, except Jack, attended."[23]

One of the rewards of old age, even for the Chief, is grandchildren. W. R. was blessed with several. His oldest son, George, had two children, the twins Phoebe and George, Jr., born in 1927; John had a son, John, Jr. or Bunky, born in 1933; five more grandchildren would be born in Hearst's lifetime, though he would not get to know them as well as he did the three oldest. He wrote his older grandchildren often, offering gentle advice in a tone quite different from the one he had used with their parents. It was quite all right with Grandpa, he wrote George, Jr. in April 1944, that he was attending a school in the East that "prepares for Harvard if I remember rightly. I suppose you will go to Harvard and come out with a Boston accent like Roosevelt. Well, it has not done him any harm. But don't let your heart be turned away from the West. The West is where the future of our country lies. . . . Be glad you are a westerner. However, I did not mean this letter to be a thesis. I am just interested in your future. What are you studying to be? Do not neglect your English literature. That is useful no matter what you intend to become."[24]

To Phoebe, George, Jr.'s sister, he wrote a charming note at the same time, thanking her and her brother for the birthday presents of ties and pine soap. "The pine soap is . . . going to be very useful as I am digging in the garden right now and will have to have a lot of cleaning up every day to make me look smart and fit in with the ties. . . . I have a picture of you and George and your mother hanging in my room. And when I get cleaned up, and perfumed up, and dressed up in my new ties, I am going to look at it and say, 'Gee! I'm glad I belong to such a nice family.' And I am pretty proud about it."[25]

He was closest to John's son, Bunky, who on his father's divorce from his second wife, Gretchen Wilson, in 1937, was able to spend a great deal of time with his grandfather. "Have a good time on your various vacations," he wrote Bunky in June of 1944 when he was eleven, "but do not forget to spend one of them with your grandpop. By the way, do you know why a duck comes out of the water? The answer is, for sundry reasons. And why does a duck go into the water? The answer is, for divers reasons. I have got another one I will tell you when you come here. But until you do, it is a secret."[26]

Bunky had such a good time with his grandfather that he moved in with him after his visit in the summer of 1946 and was enrolled in the local public school in Cambria. Each morning, he set off with a peanut butter and jelly sandwich specially made by the chef.[27]

To Bunky, the Chief was simply "Grandpop . . . There was nothing austere about him. When he was pleased, he liked to do a little dance, sort of a cross between a time step and a jig. Once a group of his executives came to San Simeon for his birthday and as he walked into the room they all began to sing 'Happy Birthday.' His face lighted up and when they had finished he did an 'Off to Buffalo,' winding up with hand outstretched like an old-time vaudeville hoofer. It broke the place up." As if to signal to the world that he no longer cared a whit what was thought of him, W. R. had given up his dark, three-piece suits for "hand-painted ties and bright suits." Bunky remembered one in particular, "a billiard-table green. Other men who wore clothes like that would have looked as though they were with the circus. But because Grandpop was so dignified, he made the clothes look dignified, too." Bunky remembered also being enormously impressed with his grandpop's whistle: "two fingers in the mouth . . . you could have heard clear to San Luis Obispo, forty-three miles away. It was the shrillest sound I have ever heard any human being make."[28]

There was one thing Bunky did not mention in his 1960 *Reader's Digest* article, "Life with Grandfather." At twelve years of age Bunky was, Bill Hearst, Jr. recalled, enlisted in the battle to keep Marion sober by finding out where she hid her liquor. It didn't much matter by now. Her supplies were endless; her suppliers legion.[29]

In 1945 or 1946, Marion sold her Santa Monica beach house and bought a new home off Benedict Canyon at 1007 North Beverly Drive in Beverly Hills. The "Beverly house," as she referred to it, was a modern-looking version of a Mediterranean villa. Built in 1927, it was shielded from the street by a row of hedges. In the rear were a swimming pool, a fish pond, formal gardens, and a large guesthouse.[30]

Bill Curley, the editor of the *Journal-American*, and his wife, Mary, who had been married at San Simeon in 1937, were among the first of Marion's and W. R.'s friends to visit the Beverly house, in the fall of 1946. Bill had been with the Hearst organization for almost half a century; his wife, Mary, was the daughter of Marion's cook. "A short part of the time," Curley wrote Karl von Wiegand after the visit, "we spent in San Simeon and the rest of it at Miss Davies' new home. The Boss has a new plane — a knock out. It's a DC3 Douglas, appointed with a crew of two and a hostess. The Boss thinks nothing of going to Los Angeles and returning as the plane can make it in an hour."

Curley had been both amazed and delighted at how well the boss was doing at age eighty-three. "You would get a chuckle," he wrote von Wiegand, "out of seeing the Chief busily directing the alterations in the new home. He thinks nothing of putting up a new decorative door and then a few days later taking it down and putting up a different type of door. He is meticulously insistent on getting things done the way he wants them. Besides this he had us all out of breath shopping for furnishings for the new establishments. He raced around the department stores like a youngster. Mary and I were staggering behind him with our tongues hanging out."[31]

In the spring of 1947, after years of avoidance, W. R. finally gave in to the demands of family and business associates and allowed John Hanes, working with teams of accountants and corporation executives, to draft a will for him. His principal objective was to preserve his empire after his death. To minimize the payment of estate taxes, which would have necessitated the sale of assets — there was little cash in the estate — Hanes and the lawyers created three different trusts. The first, for Millicent, contained $6 million of nonvoting Hearst preferred stock. Millicent was also granted a bequest of $1.5 million in cash to pay her tax liabilities. The second trust, the Hearst Family Trust, for his sons, received 30,000 shares of nonvoting preferred stock, enough to provide each of the boys with an annual income of $30,000. The remainder of the estate, and by far the largest portion, was left to two "charitable" trusts. All the trusts established by the will were to be controlled by the same board of directors. To prevent his sons from breaking apart his empire and dividing up its assets, Hearst gave them — and their heirs after them — only five of the seats on the thirteen-member board.[32]

Marion was not mentioned in the body of the will, though a codicil left her the Beverly Drive house and its contents. The codicil was later revoked when Hearst gave her the house as a gift.

In 1938, Joe Kennedy had warned W. R. that as his corporate executives "might not be especially kind to Marion," he should take steps to protect her financial future. Hearst tried in 1938 and 1939 to get Marion's $1 million loan repaid, but failed. Only in the early 1940s, as the war brought with it a circulation boom and increased publishing profits, was the corporation able to repay Marion's debt in full. Through the middle 1940s, as John Hanes reorganized Hearst's corporations, he began to pay closer attention to Marion's finances as well. With the active assistance of Hearst and Hanes, Marion began to invest money in real estate again. By the time she and the Chief moved to their Beverly Drive house in 1947, she had become one of Hollywood's wealthiest women.

The fact that Hearst had permitted a will to be drawn up and signed did not signify that he was ready for retirement. Though he no longer wrote signed editorials, he sent outlines of what he wanted said to his writers, and edited and approved every major editorial that appeared in his papers. After reading parts of *The Memoirs of Hecate County,* Edmund Wilson's sexually charged collection of stories which someone had sent Marion, he picked up the phone and ordered Roland Dragon, his secretary, to call "our editorial writers in New York, San Francisco, and what not" and tell them to compose an editorial condemning the book. "So next day," Dragon recalled, "you . . . pick up his papers and [there was] the editorial commenting about the filthy literature. And it would kick off a campaign on this type of literature."

The Chief's daily routine, at age eighty-four, was much as it had always been. He and Marion arose around nine in the morning. Hearst's valet, according to Dragon, would "alert the switchboard operator who then notified me as secretary, and then the head housekeeper, Joe the butler, and the chief chef, that Mr. Hearst was getting up now. So we're all on alert now. And then this routine was repeated at various stages of his preparation. 'They are now dressing,' we'd get the word, all six of us."

When they had finished their breakfast, somewhere between ten and eleven, Dragon would get a call from the butler and proceed to meet the Chief in the Assembly Room with "the clipboard and the day's business things, and so forth."

Joe Willicombe had years before set up the "clipboard" system, which Dragon maintained. He divided each day's mail from San Luis Obispo into three stacks, "junk mail, quasi-important, and business mail." Dragon took care of the first two stacks by himself and then condensed each business item "to not more than six lines, not six-and-a-half or seven, but six lines." He presented the Chief with these items neatly arranged on his clipboard: "There'd be thirty-five to forty-five items, business things."

Hearst and Dragon spent about an hour and a half each morning on a sofa in the Assembly Room. Hearst went through the items on the clipboard; dictated answers to Dragon who, like Willicombe, knew Gregg shorthand; read and edited the editorials that had been sent by teletype from his newspaper offices; and gave Dragon the art catalogues in which he had marked the items he wanted purchased.

Although his morning meeting with Hearst usually lasted only about an hour and a half, Dragon remained on call twenty-four hours a day, just as Willicombe had. The Chief, Dragon recalled in his oral history, "didn't hire his people, he didn't hire you, he bought you, which he did for me. However, at any time of the day I could use the pools and the tennis courts, and anything, so long as I was within hearing distance of a phone, and my pen and pad with me. Which became routine."

Aside from Hearst's morning meeting with Dragon, he spent most of his day with or close to Marion. "They were like two peas in a pod," Virginia Dragon, the wife of Hearst's secretary, remembered. "They were very close . . . You'd see them walking . . . arm-in-arm."

Dinner was served at 10 P.M. They ate alone now, but always dressed for the occasion, as they had when the Assembly Room was filled with guests. "About 11:00 we'd go to the show," Mrs. Dragon recalled. There was a new movie every evening. The 7:00 show was for the staff. "The 11:00 evening movie was just for the two of them in the first row. He had a telephone right next to him in the movie." Virginia and Roland Dragon stayed in the back row.

After the movie, Dragon would return to his suite of rooms and wait for the phone to ring. Much of his business with Hearst was, he remembered, transacted between 2:00 and 3:00 in the morning. The Chief was a "nocturnal person . . . He seemed to get most of his inspirations in the middle of the night . . . He'd phone me habitually between 1:00, 2:00, 3:00 in the morning in our suite while we were in bed."

One evening, a call was put through at 2 A.M. to Dragon "from Ben McPeake, Mr. Hearst's buyer in London. . . . Obviously upset, he informed me that the Grecian vase item that Mr. Hearst had checked off for him to buy was being contested by another buyer who wanted it too, who happened to be the buyer for Prince Aly Khan (who married Rita Hayworth as you recall)." McPeake was calling directly from the Parke-Bernet gallery. "He said the bid was getting completely out of hand, but he couldn't shake the other bidder . . . I told him to hold the phone . . . I called Mr. Hearst and told him Ben McPeake was on the other line and wanted to know how high he should bid. I returned to McPeake's line with the terse reply, 'Dammit, I said I want that vase.'"

On call twenty-four hours a day, seven days a week, Dragon had little time to himself — and resigned after about a year of service. In his oral history, he remembered fondly one moment of relief which came when Hearst left San Simeon to spend a week in Los Angeles overseeing a restructuring of his newspapers there. With "his entourage carrying his food and supplies and everything else . . . in a convoy of five or six cars," Hearst drove down the winding road from the hilltop. "It looked like Patton was on the move, an army going down there. Anyhow, everybody, I can say, took a deep breath that Mr. Hearst was not on the hill. The phone wouldn't ring. You lived by the phone. . . . Except about 12:00 it did ring — two bells. And it was Joe, the butler, phoning from the beach house, saying that Mr. Hearst forgot his eyeglasses. 'You'll have to drive them down, as fast as you can,' he said . . . So we hopped into changes of clothes and took off." They drove all night to get the Chief's glasses to him in time for his meetings the next day.[33]

In early 1947, the Chief developed a dangerously irregular heartbeat and may have had a mild heart attack as well. His doctors demanded that he cease working and leave San Simeon, which was hundreds of miles away from the specialized care required by an eighty-four-year-old man with a heart condition. Hearst agreed to move to the house Marion had purchased on Beverly Drive. She deeded it to him so that he could spend his final years in his own home.

On May 2, 1947, as Hearst and Marion were driven down the winding, five-mile roadway from San Simeon's hilltop to the landing strip below for the flight to Los Angeles and the house on Beverly Drive, Marion noticed that tears were streaming down the Chief's face. She leaned over to wipe them away. "We'll come back, W. R., you'll see." They never did.[34]

On May 21 and 22, large shipments of beef were sent to Beverly Hills from San Simeon. It was clear that Hearst was not going to return to the ranch any time soon.[35]

In late August, an elevator was installed at Beverly Drive so that Hearst would not have to climb the stairs from the dining room to his second-floor office and bedroom. "I am glad your ticker is OK," he wrote his old friend, Ed Coblentz, who was having heart trouble of his own. "Now mine is acting up something scandalous. But I guess I will come around all right — if I behave myself."[36]

He tried to work in his new home, but was too weak to get much done. "Chief requests that you use your own judgement on editorials and articles about the editorial page. He is not able to take care of them," Richard Stanley, his new secretary, informed his Los Angeles editor on October 5. Four days later, the Chief telegrammed Walt Disney in response to an invitation from Mickey Mouse to celebrate his twentieth birthday party, "I regret that I cannot accept your very kind invitation owing to a slight indisposition."[37]

With the end of the war, and the break-up of the U.S.-Soviet alliance, the Hearst papers picked up where they had left off. In New York, Bill Hearst, Jr. and Richard Berlin, who had become president of the Hearst Corporation in 1943, had, in accordance with the Chief's established policy, put together an impressive list of reporters, columnists, editorial writers, and commentators whose specialty was anti-Communist warnings, diatribes, and rumors. Howard Rushmore had come to the *Journal-American* in 1940; J. B. (Doc) Matthews became Bill Hearst, Jr.'s special assistant for subversive activity in 1944 and brought with him to the Hearst Corporation the files on Communists and Communist sympathizers he had assembled for the House Un-American Activities Committee in 1940; Westbrook Pegler joined the Hearst organization in 1945; George Sokolsky began his Hearst column in 1950. Other Hearst political columnists who specialized in left-wing witch-hunting included Walter Winchell, who had turned sharply anti-Communist after Roosevelt's death, Fulton Lewis, Jr., and George Rothwell Brown.[38]

Though Hearst was not about to temper the crusade he himself had launched in 1934, he worried nonetheless that the reading public might be growing a bit weary of it. When his papers provided what he believed was overly extended coverage of the House Un-American Activities Committee visit to Hollywood in July of 1947, he warned his editors that there was "a little too much political stuff in our papers, and it is sometimes a little too partisan. Try to make political news readable for everybody, and please not only make it reasonably impartial, but take pains to make it clear and understandable."[39]

His own attacks on corrupt politicians and corporate leaders had been vicious, but never, he thought, personal. The new generation of Hearst columnists had crossed that boundary. Westbrook Pegler was by far the most troublesome in this regard. His columns were considered so incendiary that they were sent to the Chief for final approval before publication. In April of 1947, Hearst asked that Pegler moderate a column on Charlie Chaplin that was "too violent." He also tried to get him to cut back on the anti-Roosevelt columns that continued long after the president's death in April of 1945.[40]

Marion recalled in her autobiography that when Pegler attacked Eleanor Roosevelt, W. R. "would wire the editor and say, 'Would you kindly tell this gentleman not to write nasty things about a woman.' . . . They would think they had Pegler under control, and then, the next thing you'd know, there it was again. . . . Mr. Hearst got awfully tired of his attacks. I got tired, and I got mad, too."[41]

As Hearst's anti-Communist crusade entered into its second decade, the Chief pushed his editors to go a step further. The onset of the Cold War, as Richard Berlin wrote Karl von Wiegand, had proved to the American public that Hearst had been right all along about the dangers of Communism at home and abroad. "Indeed the Hearst newspaper can shout 'hurrah.' But then you know how the Boss is. . . . I cannot beat that fellow. He certainly is always thinking about the future and never wants to live in retrospections. Nevertheless, it must be a great satisfaction to him" — to know that the Cold War which he predicted had come to pass.[42]

On October 11, 1947, the Chief, looking ahead to what he believed was going to be the next war, sent his editors an editorial on "universal military service" which he wanted run on the front page:

Almost everybody knows the evils of Communism nowadays. Almost everybody knows the impudence and the insincerity of Russia. We no longer have to give so much space to Russia, to the danger of our free institutions from Communism, to the probable destructive attack upon our nation by Russia. The thing of importance now is the plan for the protection of our country, particularly the plan of universal military service. We must awaken the public and the government to the importance of this plan. Every American must be a soldier ready at a moment's notice to defend his country and to defend it not merely from invasion but from annihilation. There will be no time to make soldiers when war comes.[43]

Two weeks later, his secretary cabled the editor of the *Los Angeles Examiner:* "Chief says, 'Don't you think it very singular that so many explosions of ships at docks and so many other various kinds of explosions have taken place of late at various parts of the country. Make a list of these explosions and let's see if it is anything that would indicate sabotage.'" Only when the editor cabled back that there was no evidence of any such sabotage did Hearst let the matter drop.[44]

Karl von Wiegand was one of the few colleagues permitted to visit the Chief while he lived at Beverly Drive. On arriving in Los Angeles from Europe in mid-October, he contacted Hearst's secretary to arrange an appointment. A few days later, he received a call from Marion, who put the Chief on the phone for a brief talk. After another two days, he received a second call from the *Examiner* office directing him to visit the Chief at six P.M. that evening. He did as instructed, but was turned away at the door by Richard Stanley, who reported that "the Chief was not so well and that the doctor had given both him and Marion some sleeping medicine and that both were sleeping." A few more days passed before von Wiegand received a second invitation to Beverly Drive.

"Marion, looking very lovely and happy that Mr. Hearst was better, took me upstairs," Karl wrote Richard Berlin after his visit:

> The Chief had just opened the door of his rooms and was calling "Marion, Marion." "How are you, Karl," greeted Mr. H. holding out his hand. I had expected to find him in bed. He was up and dressed but without a coat on as it was warm. He sat down and Marion drew a chair for me alongside his and then went into the next room. The Chief looked a little older than when last I saw him eighteen months ago but much better than I had expected. His one sign of being weak was his voice which often fell so low that I had difficulty in hearing what he said and I moved close up to him. . . . He asked questions which revealed that he was giving much thought to foreign and domestic issues and that he was astonishingly vigorous mentally. . . . Everything he said was in short precise terse sentences as if he were conserving his strength.[45]

Hearst was suffering at the time not only from heart disease but from pneumonia. Billy Haines, Marion's old friend from Hollywood and a regular visitor at San Simeon in its glory days, was shocked at how much he had changed. Even after he recovered from the pneumonia, he remained ghastly thin. "It was like looking through the wrong end of a telescope," Billy recalled. "There was this little old man . . . Originally he was a really big man . . . He came towards me and I said, 'Oh, how nice to see you,' and he said, 'Oh, I'm a very old man.' It was rather destroying for me." When Merryle Rukeyser, his financial columnist and long-time friend, asked how he felt, he replied simply that "the process of age and disintegration [was] at work."[46]

Bill, Jr. believed that his father was suffering from depression as well as his other infirmities. He had been moved out of his home into a strange house where he was marooned in a second-floor bedroom. Though handicapped by ill health, the Chief still tried to run his publishing empire from Beverly Hills, as he had from San Simeon and Wyntoon. In March of 1948, he informed his publishers and editors that the Hearst press was going to back General Douglas MacArthur for the Republican nomination for president. "I think we are going to have war with Russia," he wrote Richard Berlin in New York. "I think MacArthur would be the only President who could avert war with Russia and, if it cannot be averted, I think MacArthur would be the only President who could win the war for the United States. You see, therefore, my advocacy for MacArthur for President is not a matter of political expediency. It is a matter upon which the safety of our Country might depend. I am going to advocate MacArthur to the last moment and, if necessary, go down with flags flying."[47]

"He is terribly thin," Richard Berlin wrote Karl von Wiegand after a visit to Beverly Drive in December of 1948, "but he seems to be active in all respects and interested in everything that is going on. . . . His doctor tells me that his physical condition is unchanged although his weight is still too low. He is around 140 pounds, which of course is not enough for W. R. . . . They keep him on digitalis constantly. His doctor feels he could easily live a few more years and then of course like all of us, he could pass away in his sleep at any time."[48]

Bowing to the inevitable, Richard Berlin in July of 1949 asked Bill, Jr. to take "personal charge" of preparing an obituary for his father that would satisfy family members as well as corporate executives: "I agree with you the name is all important, and should be perpetuated. This is exactly what I have been doing and trying to accomplish for the last five years, and have set up the mechanics so that that could be accomplished."[49]

Bill solicited drafts from various writers in the organization and consulted with his brothers. In the end, the obituary in the Hearst papers, as expected, would praise the Chief as the "greatest figure in American journalism," a friend to the people, and a caring employer.[50]

Writers outside the Hearst organization must also have begun to prepare their advance obituaries at about this time. Their task was more difficult, as they were going to have to do more than speak good of the dead. At the very minimum they would have to describe the Chief's political shifts and provide some assessment of his career in publishing.

The political obituary was the most difficult to compose. It had been a full half-century since Hearst, in the spring of 1899, had declared his "internal policy" for the nation. He had, at the time, claimed that he was more in touch with the American people, their likes and dislikes, their fears and dreams, than the nation's politicians. As events were to demonstrate, he had not been entirely wrong. Within two decades of the publication of his "internal policy," every plank in it had been implemented: the federal government was regulating the activity of the trusts; municipal regulation, if not ownership, of public utilities had become widespread; the Constitution had been amended to permit the levying of a federal income tax and mandate direct election to the United States Senate; the nation's public school systems had been improved and expanded; and Congress had established the Federal Reserve Board to oversee the nation's banking and currency.

It would, ironically, have been easier to assess Hearst's influence as a progressive had he retired from politics early. But he did not. After setting the progressive agenda — and promoting it so effectively in the early years of the twentieth century — he turned toward the Republican center and then, in the middle 1930s, veered sharply to the right. Reversing or at least modifying the positions he had taken at the dawn of the century, he proclaimed now that government, having reined in the "criminal trusts," had no right to interfere with the honest businessman's pursuit of profit. Further state intervention in the economy, he argued, was unproductive, undemocratic, un-American, and probably fascistic and/or communistic. Although he was less successful in turning back the New Deal than he had been in promoting the progressive agenda that preceded and prepared the nation for it, he set the terms for the counter-progressive ideological assault that would enter — and, at times, dominate — the nation's political discourse from the mid-1930s onward.

While the ideological positions — and concrete policies — he proposed shifted dramatically in the course of the century, the fervor and frequency with which he espoused his positions did not. In 1932, a former *New York Times* reporter writing for *Vanity Fair* had left open the question as to whether journalism in the years to come would follow the Ochs style of professed objectivity or the Hearst style of outspoken advocacy. By the end of the decade, the question had been decisively answered. While the *New*

York Times had grown steadily in circulation and revenues, the Hearst morning papers had not. Hearst, unlike his colleagues in publishing, had not learned that in mass circulation journalism it was best to disguise one's political opinions. The more a publisher paraded his views, the more likely was he to alienate those who disagreed with him. It was better to hide behind one's editorial writers, to cultivate the appearance of objectivity, to claim to give both sides of every story.

Though his publishing colleagues would, in their obituaries, be generous in assessing his career, few could resist pointing out that his newspapers, once dominant in their markets, were no longer so. The major assets in the Hearst estate were those that were least identified with the Chief — and his politics: his magazines, including the highly profitable *Cosmopolitan* and *Good Housekeeping;* his Sunday supplement, the *American Weekly;* and King Features, his syndicated feature service. His eighteen newspapers were the least valuable part of the estate; most of them would be liquidated in the decade to come.

What then was Hearst's legacy as a publisher? He had, as Mencken had earlier argued, changed the face of American journalism, and nothing that had happened in the next two decades could erase that. "There was scarcely a newspaper in America, in 1900, that did not show his influence," Mencken had written in 1927, "and there is scarcely one today that has quite gotten rid of it. He debauched journalism in the Republic almost as certainly and brilliantly as the movies have debauched the theatre." But that was not, Mencken continued, a bad thing. Hearstian journalism

> shook up old bones, and gave the blush of life to pale cheeks. The American newspapers, for a generation before its advent, had been going down hill steadily. . . . The American mob was rapidly becoming literate, but they were making no rational effort to reach it. Here Hearst showed the way. . . . He did not try to lift up the mob, like Pulitzer; he boldly leaped down to its level. Was the ensuing uproar all evil? I doubt it. Hearst not only vastly augmented the enterprise of the whole American press; he also forced it into some understanding of the rights and aspirations of the common man. A rich man himself, he combated the corruptions of wealth, whether political or social. . . . His papers, publishing exposure after exposure and following them up with denunciations of the utmost vigor and effectiveness, completely broke down the old American respect for mere money, and paved the way for many reforms that are still in being.[51]

In emphasizing the connection between Hearst's journalism and his politics, Mencken located the critical element that distinguished this publisher from his contemporaries. Though the daily press had always played a central role in politics, it had been a dependent one. Hearst was the first publisher to understand that the communications media were potentially more powerful than the parties and their politicians. Through its long history, the daily press had sorted through the positions and candidates offered by the established parties and chosen to boost one or the other. Rarely, if ever, had it set its own political course. Hearst was different. He was not interested in reporting the news, but in making it. And he understood as well as anyone else in the republic how critical a role the messenger played in formulating the message.

In his *New Yorker* obituary for Hearst, "The Man Who Changed the Rules," A. J. Liebling argued that the Chief's primary contribution to journalism had been to "demonstrate that a man without previous newspaper experience could, by using money like a heavy club, do what he wanted in the newspaper world except where comparable wealth opposed him." Liebling was correct. Hearst had changed the rules, in politics as well as in publishing. He had demonstrated decisively, over the course of a half-century, that "by using money like a heavy club," an individual could, with the mass media as a loudspeaker, make his voice heard in every corner of the nation. In the age of the daily newspapers, the radio, and the newsreel, the political party was no longer the most influential political vehicle. With money, anyone could buy access to the public and try, as Hearst had, to influence elections, set the national agenda, and shape political discourse.[52]

The irony in all this was that Hearst, by holding his publishing empire hostage to his politics, lost much of it. Had he been less courageous — or less foolhardy — in branding his newspapers with his views, he might not have lost the confidence of the banking community that he needed to bail him out of the financial crisis of 1937, as it had bailed him out of other crises for more than a quarter century. But he continued to pursue his own path, regardless of the consequences for his newspapers. In the end, as *Life* magazine put it in its obituary, he "managed to antagonize just about every existing segment of informed opinion." And that was not good for business.

"Hearst was the last American journalist who dominated his medium," H. L. Mencken had written in 1927. "His successors . . . are only well-oiled mechanisms. There is little more difference between one and another than there is between two Uneeda biscuits." What Mencken did not fully understand in 1927 was that no one would follow the Chief's path, because it had led him to bankruptcy in 1937. The next generation of publishers and media moguls would learn from Hearst's negative example to keep their politics out of their publications, so as not to offend potential readers, advertisers, or investors.[53]

As W. R. grew frailer, his working hours became increasingly eccentric. He would stay up late into the night, as he always had, but instead of communicating by telegrams — which could be put aside and read in the morning — he phoned his executives, Bill, Jr. recalled, "at ungodly hours . . . long after we had gone home and to bed. Since his voice had weakened, Pop didn't repeat instructions. So editors and publishers had to snap out of their slumber quickly; several kept notebooks beside their phones. We feared missing any instructions because the old man would surely recall them."[54]

When Hearst was too weak to make these calls, Marion made them for him. She had become his gatekeeper, listening post, and liaison with his editors. The more he discussed the papers with her, the greater her interest: "I used to put in my two cents every once in a while. . . . He might ask me what I thought about something, like the antivivisection thing or the Roosevelts. I usually agreed with him."

Inevitably perhaps, Marion began to relay her own opinions to the editors, convinced that because she and the Chief agreed on so much she was speaking for him. In 1949–50, when Marion heard that a women's club was going to ban Ingrid Bergman because she was in love with another man — Roberto Rossellini, with whom she had had a child — and would marry him except that her husband, Dr. Peter Lindstrom, was standing in the way, Marion called the *Los Angeles Examiner* and asked that an article be published defending Bergman. The article appeared in an early edition, but was pulled by the head of the legal department. When Hearst heard what had happened, he called the lawyer directly and, according to Marion, warned him not to overrule Marion. "When she gives an order to the *Examiner*, it has to go through. And don't you dare countermand it."[55]

No one in the organization knew quite what to do with the instructions Marion called in from Beverly Hills. Merryle Rukeyser, who remained close to Marion, recalled in his autobiography that the four years she spent in Beverly Hills with Hearst were difficult "because she had the responsibility of making decisions, but she didn't have any legal authority . . . It was difficult for the organization, too, because when a paragraph of instructions would come signed 'W. R. Hearst,' you wouldn't know whether he was signing them or whether she was."[56]

In October of 1950, the Chief asked Marion's nephew, Charlie Lederer, to find a noncompany lawyer who could draw up a trust agreement for

Marion. That agreement, which was signed in November of 1950, gave Marion 30,000 shares of Hearst preferred stock, the same amount of stock he had willed to the Hearst Family Trust for his five sons and their heirs. Where the boys, however, had to divide the income from their 30,000 shares, five ways, Marion got the undivided income during her life. More important, she was given full voting rights over her stock as well as over all the remaining stock, which, on the Chief's death, was going to be distributed among the trusts set up in his will.[57]

It is impossible to know what was on Hearst's mind when he signed this agreement, the existence of which remained a secret to family members and corporate executives. The agreement gave Marion total control of the Hearst empire. Her power would be equal to his own. She would have the sole right to hire and fire company directors, to set editorial policy, to make all financial decisions. Did Hearst believe that Marion was interested in or capable of running his empire? Was he playing the ultimate dirty trick on his wife, his sons, and his business executives? Or was he simply giving Marion the leverage he thought she might need to survive in the hostile environment that would envelop her once he was gone?

With Hearst no longer able to supervise their work as closely as he once had, his New York editors ignored his advice and extended their already extensive coverage of the House Un-American Activities Committee hearings and the Alger Hiss case. Although W. R. had, in the past, never permitted nonpolitical columnists like Walter Winchell to write about politics, that directive was thrown overboard. Every Hearst columnist was expected to join the witch-hunting. Some, like Victor Riesel, who wrote the "Inside Labor" column, and Igor Cassini, who had taken over the Cholly Knickerbocker society column, did so with glee. As Cassini admitted in his autobiography, he took enormous pleasure in exposing "the rich parlor pinks [who were] traitors to their class." No one dared refrain from the new Hearst party line. Louella used adjectives like "pink" in her gossipy columns about new film projects. Even the Broadway columnist Dorothy Kilgallen joined the campaign, though with some reluctance.

When Senator Joseph McCarthy, in early 1950, charged the Truman administration with harboring Communists in high positions, the Hearst papers not only championed his cause but Bill Hearst, Jr. volunteered the services of his anti-Communist reporters and shared with the senator's staff the Hearst papers' voluminous files on Communists and fellow travelers. On March 16, 1950, the *Daily Mirror,* in an editorial entitled "Go to it, Joe McCarthy," announced that "the Senate investigation of the State Department, forced by Senator Joseph R. McCarthy, fighting young senator from Wisconsin, is one of the most important events of our time." From this point on, scarcely a day passed without Gunner Joe receiving favorable coverage in Hearst's news and editorial pages and from Sokolsky, Pegler, Winchell, Cassini, and Riesel. Every charge, every rumor, every innuendo was dutifully reported with no questions asked. Just as the Hearst papers shared their files with McCarthy, the senator gave his reporters and columnists inside information on his investigations. "Analysis of 3,000 letters to Senator McCarthy," Victor Riesel wrote in the March 21 *Daily Mirror,* "reveals as much concern over infiltration of homosexuals as worry over Stalinists." The following week, Riesel notified his readers that the State Department, pushed by McCarthy, was "directing its security agents to get out into the big cities (especially New York) and discover everything possible about Communist-led white-collar workers' outfits."[58]

The old man, failing now but still able to read his papers, was appalled. On April 23, 1950, he directed Raymond T. Van Ettisch, editor of the *Los Angeles Examiner,* to cable his editors:

> The Chief instructs not, repeat not, to press the campaign against Communism any further. He wishes the campaign held back for a while, particularly in editorials. He feels we have been pressing the fight too hard for too long and might be arousing war hysteria. Chief says, "All papers must be very careful not to use any editorials against Communism unless specifically ordered. Communism is not to be displayed too much in the news. Of course, we must print the news, but henceforth we must not emphasize our general attitude against Communism to the point where it might become irritating to the people. When we stress a point too strongly, it loses its effectiveness. We have been hammering Communism very hard for a considerable time. Now it is time for us to halt the fight for awhile and take a breathing spell until we can more fully determine the international situation. This is a must for all the papers. These instructions must be obeyed to the letter."[59]

Six days after the letter was written, the old man celebrated his eighty-seventh birthday. Two days later, Hearst's editors received a second letter from Van Ettisch, its object to "clarify" the Chief's instructions: "The Chief says that he does not want articles on Communism stopped entirely, but not to go overboard on them. He doesn't want to overdo it. After a conference with his father, W. R. Hearst, Jr. asked that I send you this letter and to say that no fundamental change in our news or editorial policy on Communism is intended or implied."[60]

The letter's implication was clear: written second-hand and invoking the authority of his son, it was a signal that the old man had, voluntarily or not, ceded control of editorial policy. Though Hearst would remain in nominal control of his empire until the day he died, his reign had effectively come to an end.

By late 1950, in his fourth year of illness, Hearst's weight was down to 128 pounds. Although not bedridden, he found it more and more difficult, even with the assistance of an elevator and a wheelchair, to come downstairs to his office or to have dinner with Marion. He still saw friends and business associates, but the meetings never lasted very long. Louis B. Mayer visited once a week; his sons came frequently, as did Louella Parsons and his chief executives, Martin Huberth, William Murray, and Richard Berlin.[61]

On New Year's Eve, Marion hosted a small party at the Beverly Drive house, with Anita Loos, Louella, and Charlie Lederer. Before escorting the group upstairs to see Hearst in his bedroom, Marion warned her guests that W. R. could no longer speak, "so don't ask h-h-how he is," Anita Loos remembered her telling her guests. "Just m-m-make conversation as usual — you know, b-b-be idiotic." "After a few pearls of thought we filed out, vastly shaken."[62] Hearst was dangerously thin, his hands shook badly, his voice so weak he could barely make himself understood.

Four months later, Marion invited five of their closest women friends to celebrate W. R.'s eighty-eighth birthday. Not wanting to receive his guests in his bedroom but unable to get downstairs, Hearst greeted them in a small room on the second floor. A cake was wheeled in and the guests gave Hearst their presents, while Marion sat at his feet. When Marion presented her gift, an oil painting of Phoebe Hearst holding her only son, "his eyes began to fill with tears. Then sobs shook him and he covered his face, while Marion grabbed him behind the knees, pressing his legs to her body and saying, 'It's all right, W. R. It's all right.'"

Hearst was not the only invalid in the Beverly Drive house. According to Fred Guiles, Marion's biographer, her drinking had become incapacitating. Three times a day, she would visit W. R. in his bedroom, "sometimes being given coffee to clear her stumbling tongue before going upstairs." Desperate, W. R. asked Adela Rogers St. Johns to arrange for Alcoholics Anonymous counselors and doctors to come to the house. "I said, 'Mr. Hearst, Marion has to take the first step herself.'"[63]

The old man kept working, up to and beyond his eighty-eighth birthday. In April of 1951, he warned Bill, Jr. "not to let up on front-page publicity for General MacArthur" who had just been recalled from Korea by President Truman. To the general, he wrote a personal note, welcoming him back "to our country. My health has not been good so I have assigned my son, Mr. William Randolph Hearst, Jr., to try to make everything pleasant for you in the United States."[64] In July of 1951, he complained to Bill in New York that the comic strips *Hopalong Cassidy* and *Bringing Up Father* were being run vertically. He wanted them run horizontally. He was concerned that summer about the situation in Iran, where the government was threatening to nationalize oil production. Though he remained as resolutely anti-Soviet and anti-Communist as ever, he was opposed — as he had been all his life — to American military intervention. "The situation in Iran is inflammable enough. We do not want to get in it," he telegrammed his son in mid-July 1951. "Let's revive a sane American policy and keep out of foreign entanglements."[65]

Late in the summer, Warden Woolard, the editor of his Los Angeles newspaper, spoke with him for the last time. Hearst had asked him to write a story about the Pasadena Playhouse, which he did. Thirty-six hours later, Woolard got a call that the Chief was furious and wanted to see him at once. He found Hearst seated in his bedroom, in slippers and his plaid wool bathrobe, with Helena, the dachshund, Helen's successor, at his side. He was shaking visibly and spoke very faintly.

"Mr. Woolard, who owns the *Examiner?*"

"Why, you do, Mr. Hearst."

"Well, if I own it, when I want something in it, why can't I have it?"

"I've tried to please you, Mr. Hearst."

"Didn't I ask you for a story on Pasadena Playhouse?"

"You did."

"Then why couldn't I have it?"

Woolard showed him the story that had been published in the newspaper exactly as he had ordered. The old man stared at it for a long time.

"Mr. Woolard, forgive me. I'm sorry. You know I'm an old man, sick, and I don't notice things as well as I used to."[66]

In August, the Chief's top business executives and Bill, Jr. flew West for the final vigil. Millicent remained on Long Island, where she was spending the summer. According to family members, she had received a call from the Chief, asking her not to go to Europe that summer.[67]

Bill, Jr., his brother David, and Richard Berlin moved into Beverly Drive and took over. They installed their own nurses, conferred with the doctors, made the guesthouse on the property into their headquarters. Marion didn't help matters. For a quarter century, civility had reigned between her and the boys. But now, at the final moment of the old man's life, everything fell to pieces. The boys, according to Bill Hearst, Jr., were furious at her drunkenness and at what they believed to be her meddling in affairs which didn't concern her — like the newspapers. Marion claimed that she had done nothing more than convey the Chief's wishes to his editors.

There was truth to both sides of the argument. Marion was not "running" the newspapers, but she had been taking advantage of the situation to insert items of interest and importance to her. What rankled the boys was that the old man was not only letting her do this, but had come to trust her judgment as much or more than he did theirs.

On August 13, at 2 P.M., the Chief dictated his last letter of the day to his secretary. The Beverly Hills house was now overflowing with doctors, nurses, Hearst executives, children, friends, and family. Marion, frantic that the noise and visitors were making it difficult for W. R. to get the sleep he needed, tried to retain some semblance of order: "There were blazing lights in the hall, and everybody was talking at the top of their lungs. He had no chance to rest. I was furious; I went out and asked them to go downstairs." Another argument broke out. Distraught and out of control, Marion had to be sedated. While Marion slept, Hearst died — at 9:50 in the morning on August 14, 1951.

Dick Berlin and Bill, Jr. had decided earlier that the funeral would be held in San Francisco. Pierce Brothers Undertakers in Beverly Hills arrived to take the body to the Burbank airport and then to San Francisco. It was accompanied on its last flight north by Bill, Jr. and David, who had been joined by George and Randolph.

When Marion awoke, the house was empty. "I asked where he was and the nurse said he was dead. His body was gone, whoosh, like that. Old W. R. was gone, the boys were gone. I was alone. Do you realize what they did? They stole a possession of mine. He belonged to me. I loved him for thirty-two years and now he was gone. I couldn't even say goodbye." Bill, Jr. claimed that there had been no attempt at duplicity, that Marion knew all along about their plans.[68]

That same day, company lawyers filed Hearst's last will and testament. The only mention of Marion was a codicil giving her the Beverly Hills home. Marion said nothing until after the funeral. Then, through Hedda Hopper rather than Louella, who remained too much the corporation loyalist, Marion released news of the secret trust agreement that Hearst had signed in November of 1950, giving her control of the Hearst empire. The boys and company officials were incredulous until they examined the text of the agreement. "In death," as Bill, Jr. put it with considerable understatement, "the old man had left us a dilemma: his concern for Marion, balanced by his responsibility to the company."[69]

There was no way in the world that Millicent, Hearst's five sons, and his corporate executives were going to let Marion become their new "chief." They were prepared to do everything necessary to overturn Marion's trust agreement, including contesting the Chief's "competency" when he signed it. Their most important weapon was California's community property law, which provided that half of everything earned by a husband belonged to his wife. Because the beginnings of the Hearst fortune predated his marriage, it would have been difficult to invoke the community property law, had the Chief himself not thanked Marion in a codicil to his will for loaning him $1 million in 1937 when he was without resources. If Hearst had, in fact, been without resources in 1937, as he had attested in this codicil, then everything in his estate, as of August of 1951, had been earned since then and, under the laws of California, 50 percent belonged to Millicent.

Marion could have stood her ground and might, in the end, have won her case. But in doing so, she risked everything. If the courts accepted the Hearst lawyers' argument about community property, everything that Marion had received from Hearst since 1937 would be placed in jeopardy. And to what end? Neither family nor corporation disputed her claim to the 30,000 shares of preferred stock Hearst had given her or the $150,000 of annual income it generated. The only area of dispute was the voting rights for the corporate stock, which, in themselves, were worth nothing.

Marion chose not to fight. On October 30, she signed an agreement prepared by her lawyers and lawyers representing the family and the corporation. For a token payment of $1, she relinquished her rights "as voting trustee for the stock of the Hearst Corporation." The payment of the dollar was testimony to the fact that she may have had legitimate rights to relinquish. The joint statement announcing the settlement offered no opinion as to the legality of her claim. It said only that the questions required clarification "by long court proceedings which all parties deemed unnecessary and undesirable."

Marion publicly professed her "every faith in the intentions and abilities of Mr. Hearst's sons and the other directors and executives of the Hearst enterprises to ensure the continuity of Mr. Hearst's editorial policies, the furtherance of which would have been Miss Davies' only purpose in serving as a trustee." The statement also announced that Marion had agreed to serve "as official consultant and adviser to the Hearst Corporation," her services to "include advice on motion picture and other amusement activities."[70]

The next day, October 31, 1951, Marion Davies married — for the first time. Though she gave her age as forty-five on the wedding license, she was fifty-four years of age. The marriage, according to the *New York Times*, had caught even the immediate household of Miss Davies by surprise.

Her husband was Horace Gates Brown III, a forty-six-year-old captain in the Merchant Marine. Marion had met Brown the year before when he was courting her sister Rose. When Rose turned him down, Marion, to console him, invited him to dinner at Beverly Drive. He became a frequent visitor there, played cribbage with Hearst, and spent time with Marion. "Horace," according to Marion's biographer, "was a big man with the same long sloping nose that Hearst had, the same narrow-set blue eyes. His resemblance to Hearst was sufficient to make visitors to the Beverly house look twice following Hearst's death."

The wedding took place at the El Rancho Vegas Hotel. Marion and Brown arrived by plane at 2:50 in the morning and got their license at Las Vegas's twenty-four-hour marriage bureau. They were married in the hotel's chapel, celebrated with a wedding breakfast of champagne, turkey sandwiches, coffeecake, and beer, then flew to Palm Springs for their honeymoon. Miss Davies told reporters that her husband was "Mr. Hearst's cousin," though according to the *New York Times*, this was news to both her family and Brown's. "The ceremony was performed by Justice of the Peace James Down, who had to slow down the excited Miss Davies at one point. She got ahead of the Justice at the 'love, honor and obey' stage."[71]

The funeral for William Randolph Hearst had been held in San Francisco on August 16, 1951, presided over by Hearst's sons, who had accompanied his body from Beverly Hills, and their mother, who had flown in from New York, with her son John. Davies remained in Beverly Hills. "I thought I might go to church," she told a *Time* magazine reporter, "but I'll just stay here. He knew how I felt about him, and I know how he felt about me. There's no need for dramatics."[72]

Hearst's sons and his executives made sure he was afforded the respects due a chief of state or Hollywood celebrity. His body lay in state for a day and a half at the Grace Episcopal Cathedral on Nob Hill. The funeral was ornate, overproduced, and spectacular, as it should have been. Some 1,500 people attended with many more gathered on the street outside. Among the honorary pallbearers were figures from politics, business, and journalism: former President Hoover, former Vice President John Nance Garner, Governor Earl Warren of California, Mayor Elmer Robinson of San Francisco, Mrs. Ogden Reid and Arthur Hays Sulzberger from New York, Colonel Robert McCormick from Chicago, and Roy Howard of the Scripps-Howard chain. Others in attendance included Louis B. Mayer,

A. O. Giannini of the Bank of America, and Robert G. Sproul, chancellor of the University of California. The service closed with a reading from Hearst's poem "Song of the River," composed ten years before at Wyntoon.[73]

> The snow melts on the mountain
> And the water runs down to the spring,
> And the spring in a turbulent fountain,
> With a song of youth to sing,
> Runs down to the riotous river,
> And the river flows to the sea,
> And the water again
> Goes back in rain
> To the hills where it used to be.
> And I wonder if life's deep mystery
> Isn't much like the rain and the snow
> Returning through all eternity
> To the place it used to know.[74]

The Chief might have deserved a better sendoff, but these verses were fitting nonetheless. He was entombed with his parents at Cypress Lawn Cemetery outside San Francisco — the city where he was born and published his first newspaper, the place he used to know.

EPILOGUE

THE CHIEF, recognizing that San Simeon was too expensive for any individual to maintain, had hoped that the University of California would accept the castle, guesthouses, pools, and gardens as a gift. When the university's regents declined the properties, the Hearst Corporation deeded them to the State of California, which placed them under the direction of the California Parks System. The Hearst Corporation retained control of the surrounding land, which it continues to operate as a cattle ranch. The Hearst San Simeon State Historical Monument was opened to the public in 1958.

Wyntoon remains the property of the Hearst Corporation. St. Donat's was requisitioned by the British government as a military training facility in 1938 and is today the campus of Atlantic College.[1]

Millicent Hearst was seventy years old when her husband died in 1951. As she grew older, she traveled less, but continued to devote time to her charities and to her family, which had grown to include fifteen grandchildren, thirteen great-grandchildren, and two great-great-grandchildren. She died on December 4, 1974, at her home on East 66th Street in New York City. She was ninety-three years of age and had outlived two of her sons, John, who died in 1958, and George, who died in 1972.

Eight months after her marriage to Horace Brown, Marion Davies filed for a divorce. Horace was devoted to her, but he didn't get along with her friends or family, was ill-tempered, and, she feared, a bit too eccentric. When he ripped out all thirteen phone lines in their home because he thought Marion was spending too much time on the phone, she decided to leave him. Days later she changed her mind and agreed to a reconciliation. Though their marriage would never be a particularly stable one, Marion would remain with Horace for the rest of her life.

In the years following the Chief's death, Marion expanded her already considerable real estate holdings in New York and Los Angeles. In 1954, she erected a twenty-two-story office building in New York City, on Park Avenue at 57th Street. In 1955, she put up a second building, at Madison and 55th, and bought the Desert Inn in Palm Springs, which she sold in 1960 for a considerable profit.

Marion did not entertain or go out much after Hearst died. Too many of her old friends from Hollywood were dead or dying. She was quite distressed when, in June of 1956, her former Santa Monica beach house — the scene of so many glorious parties — was torn down to make way for a motel. In October of 1957, Louis B. Mayer died of leukemia; in December, Norma Talmadge died after suffering a stroke; six months later, Harry Crocker died after a long illness. "There aren't many of us left," Marion confided to Mary Pickford at Crocker's funeral.

She stayed in touch with her nephew Charlie Lederer, and her sister Rose, with Louella Parsons and Hedda Hopper, and with a few old friends like Billy Haines, Frances Goldwyn, and Mary Pickford. Hollywood celebrities, among them Frank Sinatra and Clark Gable, occasionally stopped by to pay their respects. Part of the void in her social life was filled by Joseph Kennedy, who made sure that Marion and Horace were invited to the weddings of Eunice Kennedy to Sargent Shriver, John Kennedy to Jacqueline Bouvier, and Pat Kennedy to Peter Lawford.

As she approached her sixtieth birthday, Marion's health, after decades of heavy drinking, continued to deteriorate. She had increasing trouble with her balance, and had to be accompanied everywhere she went by Horace or one of her nurse/companions. In 1956, she suffered a minor stroke. In 1959, doctors discovered a growth in her jaw which was diagnosed as cancer. She refused to have surgery and was given cobalt treatments that discolored her jaw, but did little to retard the spread of the cancer or stop her pain.

In January 1961, Marion flew to Washington to attend John F. Kennedy's inauguration, as an honored guest of the Kennedy family. In May, she was admitted to Cedars of Lebanon Hospital in Los Angeles for treatment of her cancer. Joe Kennedy arranged for three cancer specialists to be flown out from the East Coast to examine Marion. On their recommendation, she underwent jaw surgery for malignant osteomyelitis on June 7. Ten days later, recovering from what she thought had been a successful operation, she fell and broke her leg. Her condition continued to worsen through the summer months. She died in the hospital at 7 P.M. on September 22, 1961. At her bedside were her husband, her sister Rose, her nephew Charlie Lederer, and her niece, Rose's daughter Pat Lake. She was sixty-four years of age.

Though Marion had had no contact with the Hearst family or corporate executives since the settlement of Hearst's estate in 1951, Richard Berlin, the chief executive officer of the corporation, joined Bing Crosby and Joseph Kennedy as an honorary pallbearer.[2]

When the Chief died in August of 1951, the Hearst Corporation's first-half net income was $1.3 million, which is the equivalent of an annual net income of $16.8 million in today's currency. In 1998, the annual net income of the Hearst Corporation is estimated by reliable sources to be in the vicinity of $450 million. With revenues of about $5 billion, the Hearst Corporation was among the nation's largest privately held companies in 1999.[3]

The corporation is today wholly owned by the Hearst Family Trust, run by a thirteen-member board of trustees, five of whom are family members and the other eight members of management. In 1975, the Family Trust purchased the remaining nonvoting common stock of the Hearst Corporation, which, on Hearst's death, had been left to the two charitable trusts he had established in his will. According to the terms of that will, the Family Trust will expire with the death of the last family member alive in August of 1951, when the Chief died. Actuarial tables indicate that this should occur around the year 2042 or 2043.

Richard Berlin, who was appointed president of the corporation in 1943, became its chief executive officer in 1951 and remained in that position through the early 1970s. While each of Hearst's five sons was given a seat on the corporation's board in 1951, only Bill and Randolph took active leadership roles. Bill, who had been publisher of the *Journal-American,* was named editor in chief of the Hearst newspapers in 1955 and served as chairman of the board of directors from 1960 until 1973. Randolph, who was president of the *San Francisco Examiner* in 1974 when his daughter Patty was kidnapped, succeeded Bill as chairman of the board and remained in that position until 1996.

Under Richard Berlin's tenure, the Hearst Corporation closed down, merged, or sold Hearst newspapers in Chicago, San Francisco, Pittsburgh, Detroit, Boston, Los Angeles, Milwaukee, and New York, while expanding its magazine division. The corporation today owns a total of twelve daily papers, only three of them — the *San Francisco Examiner,* the *Seattle Post-Intelligencer,* and the *Albany Times Union* — holdovers from the Chief's regime. It is the largest publisher of monthly magazines in the world, with distribution in more than one hundred countries. Hearst magazines include *Esquire, Smart Money, Redbook, Country Living, Marie Claire, Popular Mechanics,* and *Sports Afield,* all of which were acquired after the Chief's death — and *Cosmopolitan, Good Housekeeping, Harper's Bazaar, House Beautiful, Motor Boating & Sailing,* and *Town and Country,* which the Chief bought and developed. The corporation is currently a 50 percent owner of *Talk* magazine, edited by Tina Brown, and is developing a new magazine with Oprah Winfrey.

Berlin was succeeded by two chief executives, Frank Massi (1973–75) and John R. Miller (1975–78), who served relatively short tenures but oversaw several critical events, including the recapitalization that moved ownership of the company from the foundations to the Family Trust. Under the leadership of Frank A. Bennack, Jr., who became president and chief executive officer in 1979, the corporation acquired nine newspapers, including the *Houston Chronicle* and the *San Antonio Express-News,* and extended its communications and entertainment holdings into broadcast and cable television and new media. In 1997, the corporation created Hearst-Argyle Television, a publicly traded company in which the Hearst Corporation holds the majority stake. Hearst-Argyle Television today has twenty-six television stations broadcasting in twenty states. The Hearst Corporation also owns 20 percent of ESPN, Inc., and is a founding partner of the A&E Television Networks, the History and Biography Channels, and Lifetime Entertainment Services. Among the traditional media companies, it holds perhaps the strongest position in Internet businesses and services.

In the nineteenth century, William Randolph Hearst's major rivals were Michel H. De Young, publisher of the *San Francisco Chronicle,* and Joseph Pulitzer, publisher of the *New York World.*

In March of 1999, the Hearst Corporation closed out the twentieth century with the purchase by Hearst-Argyle Television of the Pulitzer Publishing Company's nine television and five radio stations. Five months later, in August of 1999, the corporation announced that it had bought the *San Francisco Chronicle* from the De Young family.

NOTES

In the notes that follow, I reference primary source materials and direct citations. I have used abbreviations wherever possible to refer to manuscript collections, newspapers and periodicals, and individuals.

Some of the letters in the Hearst family collections in the Bancroft Library have had dates appended. When these dates were not part of the original letter, I have put them within brackets. They are supplied for identification purposes only; many are inaccurate.

Selections from the Writings and Speeches of William Randolph Hearst, privately published by the *San Francisco Examiner* in 1948, contains several of his newspaper editorials and "In the News" columns, abbreviated as ITN. Those editorials and columns not collected in *Selections* can be found in the *New York American*, the *San Francisco Examiner*, the *Los Angeles Examiner*, or Hearst's other newspapers.

Abbreviations for Manuscript Collections and Repositories

ABp	Brisbane Family Papers, Special Collections, Syracuse University.
ASOp	Adolph Ochs Papers, *New York Times* Archives, New York City.
AZp	Adolph Zukor Collection, Margaret Herrick Library, Academy of Motion Picture Arts and Sciences, Beverly Hills, California.
Barry	Diary of Thomas F. Barry, transcript, 1879 May-Aug., Bancroft Library, University of California at Berkeley.
BH	Bunkhouse papers (William Randolph Hearst, correspondence and business papers), San Simeon, California.
BI	Bureau of Investigation, Justice Department, National Archives, Washington, D.C.
Boettiger	John Boettiger Papers, Franklin Roosevelt Library, Hyde Park, New York.
Brewing	United States Senate, 66th Congress, 1st Session, Document No. 61, *Brewing and Liquor Interests and German and Bolshevik Propaganda: Report and Hearings of the Subcommittee on the Judiciary*, vol. 2 (Washington, D.C.: Government Printing Office, 1919).
BRTC	Billy Rose Theatre Collection, New York Public Library at Lincoln Center.
BW	Bronx warehouse papers (William Randolph Hearst, correspondence and business papers), Hearst Corporation, New York City.
CHS	Chicago Historical Society, Chicago, Illinois.
DWG	D. W. Griffith Papers, Museum of Modern Art, New York City.
Early	Stephen Early Papers, Franklin Roosevelt Library, Hyde Park, New York.
EDCp	E. D. Coblentz Papers, Bancroft Library, University of California at Berkeley.

EMPp	Eleanor Medill Patterson Papers, Special Collections, Syracuse University.
Fall	Albert Fall Papers, Department of Manuscripts, Huntington Library, San Marino, California.
FDRp	Franklin D. Roosevelt Library, Hyde Park, New York.
GHauto	George Hearst Autobiography, Bancroft Library, University of California at Berkeley.
HSSSHM	Hearst San Simeon State Historical Monument, San Simeon, California.
HUA	Harvard University Archives, Nathan Marsh Pusey Library, Harvard University.
JAMp	Joseph A. Moore Papers, Manuscripts Division, Library of Congress.
JCp	James Creelman Papers, Rare Books and Manuscripts, Ohio State University Libraries, Columbus, Ohio.
JFNp	John F. Neylan Papers, Bancroft Library, University of California at Berkeley.
JM-oh	Julia Morgan Architectural History Project Interviews, Bancroft Library, University of California at Berkeley.
JMp	Julia Morgan Collection, Special Collections, California Polytechnic State University, San Luis Obispo, California.
JPp	Joseph Pulitzer Papers, Manuscripts Division, Library of Congress.
JPKp	Joseph P. Kennedy Papers, John F. Kennedy Library, Boston, Massachusetts.
JSp	James G. Phelps Stokes Papers, Rare Books and Manuscripts Library, Columbia University.
JUp	Joseph Urban collection, Rare Books and Manuscripts Library, Columbia University.
Kilroe	Kilroe Collection, Rare Books and Manuscripts Library, Columbia University.
KVW	Karl von Wiegand Papers, Hoover Institution Archives, Hoover Institution on War, Revolution and Peace, Stanford University.
LAE	*Los Angeles Examiner* archives, Regional History Collection, University of Southern California, Los Angeles, California.
Mannix	Eddie Mannix ledger, Howard Strickland Papers, Margaret Herrick Library, Academy of Motion Picture Arts and Sciences, Beverly Hills, California.
MID	Military Intelligence Division Correspondence, National Archives, Washington, D.C.
Morgenthau	Morgenthau diaries, Franklin D. Roosevelt Library, Hyde Park, New York.
MPAA	MPAA papers, Margaret Herrick Library, Academy of Motion Picture Arts and Sciences, Beverly Hills, California.
NCF	National Civic Federation, Special Collections, New York Public Library.
Oh-CU	Oral History Research Office, Columbia University, New York City.
Oh-DN	Oral histories in author's possession.
Oh-SS	Oral History Project, Hearst San Simeon State Historical Monument, San Simeon, California.
PAHdiary	In author's possession.
PAHp	Phoebe A. Hearst Papers, Bancroft Library, University of California at Berkeley.
Peck	Orrin M. Peck Collection, Department of Manuscripts, Huntington Library, San Marino, California.
PeckFamily	Peck Family Collection, Bancroft Library, University of California at Berkeley.
Pershing	General John Joseph Pershing Papers, Manuscripts Division, Library of Congress.
Presidentes	Presidentes Series, Archivo General de la Nación, Mexico City, Mexico.
Stimson	Henry Lewis Stimson Papers, Manuscripts and Archives, Sterling Memorial Library, Yale University.
TRp	Theodore Roosevelt Papers, Manuscripts Division, Library of Congress.
TVRp	Than Vanneman Ranck Papers, Manuscripts and Archives, Sterling Memorial Library, Yale University.

Warner   Jack Warner Collection, USC Cinema-Television Library, University of Southern California, Los Angeles, California.

WAS   William A. Swanberg Papers, Special Collections, Columbia University.

WB   USC Warner Bros. Archives, School of Cinema-Television, University of Southern California, Los Angeles, California.

Wheeler   Charles Stetson Wheeler, "In the matter of the estate of Phebe Hearst, deceased, re estate tax. Brief in support . . ." Bancroft Library, University of California at Berkeley.

WJBp   William Jennings Bryan Papers, Manuscripts Division, Library of Congress.

WHTp   William Howard Taft Papers, Manuscripts Division, Library of Congress.

WMp   William McKinley Papers, Manuscripts Division, Library of Congress.

World   *New York World* Papers, Rare Books and Manuscripts Library, Columbia University.

WRHp   W. R. Hearst correspondence (1977), Bancroft Library, University of California at Berkeley.

WRH82   William Randolph Hearst papers (1982), Bancroft Library, University of California at Berkeley.

WRH85   Hearst Family Papers (1985), Bancroft Library, University of California at Berkeley.

WRH87   William Randolph Hearst letters: to Phoebe Apperson Hearst (1987), Bancroft Library, University of California at Berkeley.

WRH, Jr.91   William Randolph Hearst, Jr. Papers (1991), Bancroft Library, University of California at Berkeley.

Abbreviations for newspapers and magazines

BA	Boston American	NYHT	New York Herald Tribune
CDT	Chicago Daily Tribune	NYJ	New York Journal
CR-H	Congressional Record-House	NYS	New York Sun
EP	Editor and Publisher	NYT	New York Times
LAE	Los Angeles Examiner	NYTr	New York Tribune
MPN	Motion Picture News	NYW	New York World
MPW	Motion Picture World	SAL	San Antonio Light
NYA	New York American	SFE	San Francisco Examiner
NYDN	New York Daily News	SFNL	San Francisco News-Letter
NYDT	New York Daily Tribune	SFS	The [San Francisco] Star
NYEJ	New York Evening Journal	SJ	Syracuse Journal
NYEP	New York Evening Post	TT	Town Topics
NYEW	New York Evening World	V	Variety
NYH	New York Herald	WP	Washington Post

Abbreviations of individual names

AB	Arthur Brisbane	EC	Edward Clark
AH	Alice Head	EDC	Edmond D. Coblentz
AP	Arthur Poole	EH	Eddie B. Hatrick
ASO	Adolph Simon Ochs	EMP	Eleanor Medill (Cissy) Patterson
AZ	Adolph Zukor	EP	Elizabeth Pike
CEH	Charles Evans Hughes	FK	Frank Knox
CMG	Christy MacGregor	FZ	Florenz Ziegfeld
CS	Judge Clarence Shearn	GBS	George Bernard Shaw
DLG	David Lloyd George	GH	George Hearst

HCL	Henry Cabot Lodge	MU	Mary Urban
IS	Irwin Stump	OP	Orrin Peck
IT	Irving Thalberg	PAH	Phoebe Apperson Hearst
JAM	Joseph A. Moore	PP	Phil Payne
JC	James Creelman	RB	Richard Berlin
JFN	John Francis Neylan	RH	Randolph Hearst
JM	Julia Morgan	SC	Simon Carvalho
JP	Joseph Pulitzer	TJW	Thomas J. White
JPK	Joseph Patrick Kennedy	TR	Theodore Roosevelt
JU	Joseph Urban	TVR	Than Vanneman Ranck
JW	Joseph Willicombe	VW	Victor Watson
KVW	Karl von Wiegand	WC	William Curley
LBM	Louis B. Mayer	WJB	William Jennings Bryan
LOR	Lawrence O'Reilly	WRH	William Randolph Hearst
LP	Louella Parsons	WRH, Jr.	William Randolph Hearst, Jr.
MH	Millicent Hearst	WW	Woodrow Wilson
MHu	Martin Huberth		

Preface

1. Winston Churchill–Clementine Churchill, September 29, 1929, in *Winston and Clementine: The Personal Letters of the Churchills,* ed. Mary Soames (Boston: Houghton Mifflin, 1998), 347.

1. A Son of the West

1. WRH, "In the News" [hereafter abbreviated as ITN], March 27, 1940.
2. Philip Ethington, *The Public City* (New York: Cambridge U.P., 1994), 425; William Issel and Robert Cherny, *San Francisco, 1865–1932* (Berkeley, University of California Press, 1986), 13–18, 24–30.
3. GHauto.
4. J. S. Holliday, *The World Rushed In: The California Gold Rush Experience* (New York: Simon & Schuster, 1981), 45–49.
5. GHauto.
6. Holliday, 304–5.
7. Ralph Mann, *After the Gold Rush: Society in Grass Valley and Nevada City, California: 1849–1870* (Stanford: Stanford U.P., 1982), 224.
8. Robert Silverberg, *Ghost Towns of the American West* (Athens: Ohio University Press, 1968), 99–102.
9. GHauto, 15–16; W. W. Allen and R. B. Avery, *California Gold Book* (SF and Chicago: Donohue and Henneberry, 1893), 332–33.
10. Judith Robinson, *The Hearsts* (New York: Avon, 1992), 49–51, 55.
11. Mark Twain, *Roughing It* (New York: Penguin, 1981), 314.
12. Robinson, 58.
13. Cora Older, *William Randolph Hearst, American* (New York: Appleton-Century, 1936), 9.
14. PAH-EP, June 16, 1864, PAHp.
15. PAH-EP, July 2, 1865, PAHp.
16. PAH-EP, July 7, 1865, November 18, 1866, PAHp; Older, 12.
17. January, 1, 1866, PAHdiary.
18. January 4, 10, February 11, 15, 16, 1866, PAHdiary.

19. William Randolph Hearst, Jr., *The Hearsts: Father and Son* (Niwot, Col.: Roberts Rinehart, 1991), 9.
20. WRH, ITN, in Edmond D. Coblentz, ed., *William Randolph Hearst: A Portrait in His Own Words* (New York: Simon & Schuster, 1952), 7–19.
21. January 18, 21, February 1, 1866, PAHdiary.
22. February 4, 1866, PAHdiary.
23. February 7, 1866, PAHdiary.
24. PAH-EP, September 18, 1866, PAHp.
25. PAH-EP, November 18, 1866, PAHp.
26. PAH-EP, December 9, 1866, PAHp.
27. PAH-EP, February 20, 1867, PAHp.
28. PAH-EP, September 19, November 18, 1866, June 19, 1867, July 21, 1867, PAHp.
29. PAH-GH, July 14, 1868, PAHp.
30. PAH-EP, June 7, 1868, June 10, 1868, PAHp.
31. PAH-EP, January 8, 1869, PAHp.
32. PAH-EP, November 13, 1870, PAHp.
33. Older, 22–23.
34. PAH-EP, May 22, 1871, PAHp.
35. PAH-GH, August 16, 1873, PAHp.
36. GH-PAH, January 10, January 31, 1874; PAH-GH, April 20, 1874, PAHp.
37. PAH-EP, December 10, 1873, PAHp.
38. GH-PAH, February 26, 1874, PAHp.
39. PAH-GH, April 20, 1874, PAHp.
40. PAH-GH, August 3, December 3, 1873, PAHp; John Winkler, *William Randolph Hearst: A New Appraisal* (New York: Hastings House, 1955), 4.
41. Werner Muensterberger, *Collecting: An Unruly Passion* (Princeton: Princeton U.P., 1994), 27.

2. To Europe Again and on to Harvard

1. Rodman Paul, *The Far West and the Great Plains in Transition: 1859–1900* (New York: Harper & Row), 270–71; GHauto.
2. August 11, 1879, Barry.
3. WRH, ITN, in Edmond Coblentz, ed., *William Randolph Hearst: A Portrait in His Own Words* (New York: Simon & Schuster, 1952), 20.
4. WRH-PAH, n.d., box 1, WRH82.
5. GH-WRH, November 4, 1879, PAHp.
6. WRH-PAH, n.d., box 1, WRH82.
7. WRH-PAH, September 19, 1879, box 1, WRH82.
8. WRH-PAH, n.d., box 1, WRH82.
9. WRH-PAH, September 21, 1879, box 1, WRH82.
10. WRH, ITN, in Coblentz, 20–21.
11. WRH-PAH, September 27, 1879, PAHp.
12. Letters in author's possession, collected by George S. Grove, Executive Director, Alumni Association of St. Paul's School.
13. See photographs, c. 1884, labeled Morse's Palace of Art, San Francisco, in California Historical Society.
14. WRH, ITN, May 27, 1940.
15. PAH diary, January 18, 19, 1882, PAHp.

16. *Annual Reports of the President and Treasurer of Harvard College,* 1883–84, 53; Harvard University Catalogue, 1881–82, 64–72; Faculty Records, Vol. III, 1880–84, September 27, 1882, 196, HUA.

17. John Dizikes, *Opera in America* (New Haven: Yale U.P., 1993), 327.

18. Cora Older, *William Randolph Hearst, American* (New York: Appleton-Century, 1936), 46.

19. Samuel Eliot Morison, *Three Centuries of Harvard, 1636–1936* (Cambridge: Harvard U.P., 1936), 419; Older, 48.

20. *Annual Reports,* 1882–3, 10–11, HUA; Harvard University Catalogue, 1882–83, 58–64, HUA.

21. Flint interview, WAS; WRH-PAH, n.d. [1883], box 1, WRH82; WRH-GH, April 19, 1883, box 1, WRH82.

22. WRH-PAH, n.d. [from Harvard, possibly 1884], box 1, WRH82.

23. WRH-PAH, n.d. [1883], box 1, WRH82; WRH-PAH, n.d. [erroneously labeled "from Harvard, possibly 1884"], box 1, WRH82.

24. "Harvard letter," November 29, 1882, box 1, WRHp; Hugh Hawkins, *Between Harvard and America: The Educational Leadership of Charles W. Eliot* (New York: Oxford U.P., 1972), 111; WRH-GH, December 30, 1882, box 1, WRH82.

25. George Santayana, *Character and Opinion in the United States* (New York: George Braziller, 1955), 33.

26. WRH-GH, December 30, 1882, box 1, WRH82.

27. WRH-PAH, n.d. [Harvard, 1885], box 1, WRH82.

28. R. L. Duffus, *The American Renaissance* (New York: Knopf, 1928), 17–36.

29. WRH-PAH, n.d. [Harvard, 1885], box 1, WRH82.

30. George Santayana, "The Lampoon from 1883 to 1886," in *Reminiscences and a List of Editors of the Harvard Lampoon, 1876–1901* (Cambridge, 1901), reprinted in *George Santayana's America,* ed. James Ballowe (Urbana: University of Illinois, 1967), 42–43; George Santayana, *Persons and Places: The Background of My Life* (New York: Charles Scribner's Sons, 1944), 198–99.

31. WRH-PAH, n.d. [Harvard, 1885], box 2, WRH82.

32. On Porcellian, see Dixon Wechter, *The Saga of American Society: A Record of Social Aspiration, 1607–1937* (New York: Charles Scribner's Sons, 1937), 276–78; Jack Follansbee-GH, February 14, 1884, PAHp; Med. Facs., general, HUA.

33. WRH-PAH, April 27, 1884; n.d. [Harvard, 1883?], box 1, WRH82.

34. WRH-PAH, n.d. [Harvard, 1885], box 2, WRH82.

35. Santayana, *Persons and Places,* 198.

36. Flint interview, WAS.

37. Jack Follensbee-PAH, January 14, May 10, 1884, PAHp.

38. OP-PAH, n.d., Orrin Peck Papers, California Historical Society, in Judith Robinson, *The Hearsts* (New York: Avon, 1992), 191.

39. 1871 usage, cited in *Dictionary of American English* III (1976), 1580.

40. WRH-PAH, n.d. [marked 1883 from Harvard], box 1, WRH82.

41. Faculty Records, Vol. III, 1880–1884, 379, HUA; WRH-PAH, n.d. [marked Harvard, 1885], box 1, WRH82.

42. WRH-PAH, n.d. [from Harvard, possibly 1884], box 1, WRH82.

43. WRH-PAH, n.d. [Harvard, 1885], box 1, WRH82.

44. WRH-PAH, n.d. [May-the don't know], box 1, WRH82.

45. PAH-WRH, May 5, 1884, PAHp.

46. WRH-PAH, April 27, 1884, box 1, WRH82.

3. "Something Where I Could Make a Name"

1. WRH-GH, December 30, 1882, box 1, WRH82; WRH-PAH, n.d., box 1, WRH82; WRH-PAH [Harvard, 1885], box 1, WRH82.
2. GH-PAH, September 16, 1882, PAHp.
3. James Creelman, "The Real Mr. Hearst," *Pearson's*, September 1906, 256–57.
4. WRH-PAH, n.d. [Cambridge, May — the don't know], box 1, WRH82.
5. WRH-PAH, n.d. [1884, from Harvard], box 1, WRH82.
6. WRH-PAH, n.d. [1884], PAHp.
7. WRH-PAH, n.d. [fall, 1884], PAHp.
8. WRH-PAH, n.d. [November, 1884], box 1, WRH82.
9. WRH, 6th sophomore theme, box 1, WRHp.
10. WRH, ITN, June 13, 1940; Older, 54, 61; William A. Swanberg, *Citizen Hearst* (New York: Scribner's, 1961), 33.
11. Eliot correspondence, 662; "William Randolph Hearst," course listings, HUA.
12. WRH-PAH, n.d. [fall, 1883, from Harvard], box 1, WRH82.
13. PAH-WRH, November 10, 1884, PAHp.
14. PAH-WRH, November 15, 1884, PAIIp.
15. WRH-PAH, n.d. [fall, 1883], box 2, WRH82.
16. GH-PAH, September 21, 1884, PAHp.
17. WRH-PAH, n.d. [November, 1884], box 1, WRH82.
18. PAH-GH, January 4, 1885, PAHp.
19. WRH-GH, January 4, 1885, PAHp.
20. WRH-GH, January 29, 1885, PAHp.
21. "Minutes," faculty meeting, February 3, 1885, HUA. The playbill for the Hasty Pudding Club production is found in the Harvard University Theater Collection, Pusey Library.
22. Wheeler-WRH, March 15, 1885, box 1, WRHp.
23. "Minutes," faculty meeting, March 31, 1885, HUA.
24. PAH-WRH, April 11, 1885, PAHp.
25. PAH-Janet Peck, April 15, 1885, Peck.
26. WRH-PAH, April 29, 1885, PAHp.
27. Handwritten transcript marked "W. R. Hearst," in Eliot correspondence, 662, HUA.
28. J. Rathbone-WRH, August 23, 1885, box 1, WRHp.
29. WRH-PAH, October 4, 1885, box 2, WRH82.
30. PAH-WRH, October 4, 1885, box 2, WRH82.
31. O. Huntington-GH, November 11, 1885; J. Oliver-PAH, October 21, 1885, PAHp.
32. PAH-GH, October 22, 1885, PAHp.
33. PAH-GH, October 28, 1885, PAHp.
34. PAH-GH, November 12, 1885, PAHp.
35. WRH-GH, November 23, 1885, box 2, WRH82.
36. Julian Rammelkamp, *Pulitzer's Post-Dispatch, 1878–1883* (Princeton: Princeton U.P., 1967), 284–98.
37. George Juergens, *Joseph Pulitzer and the New York World* (Princeton: Princeton U.P., 1966), 348–49; Don C. Seitz, *Joseph Pulitzer: His Life & Letters* (New York: Simon & Schuster, 1924), 153–54.
38. Juergens, 331, 339.
39. William A. Swanberg, *Pulitzer* (New York: Scribner's, 1967), 125.

40. WRH, ITN, June 13, 1940.
41. WRH-GH, n.d. [1885], box 2, WRH82.
42. WRH-GH, January 26, 1886, PAHp.
43. J. P. Oliver-GH, February 6, 1886, PAHp.
44. See receipts and playbills in box 1, WRHp.
45. Cora Older, *William Randolph Hearst, American* (New York: Appleton-Century, 1936), 56, 58.
46. "Minutes," faculty meeting, May 4, 1886, HUA; WRH-PAH, n.d. [1885, from Boston], PAHp.
47. WRH-PAH, July 25, 1886, box 2, WRH82.
48. PAH-OP, December 22, 1886, Peck.
49. On Babicora, see EC-John Bramhall, n.d., PAHp; WRH-PAH, n.d., in Judith Robinson, *The Hearsts* (New York: Avon, 1992), 202–3.
50. WRH-PAH, September 28, 30, 1886, box 2, WRH82.
51. WRH-PAH, n.d. [Mexico-1886?], box 2, WRH82; Gray Brechin, "Imperial San Francisco: The Environmental Impact of Urban Elites upon the Pacific Basin" (Ph.D. diss., University of California at Berkeley, 1998), 327.
52. Ramón Ruiz, *Triumphs and Tragedy: A History of the Mexican People* (New York: W. W. Norton, 1993), 277–78; T. R. Fehrenbach, *Fire and Blood: A History of Mexico* (New York: Macmillan, 1973), 460–64.
53. WRH-PAH, n.d. [Mexico-1886?], box 2, WRH82.
54. PAH-OP, December 22, 1886, Peck.
55. WRH-GH, n.d. [marked 1887?], box 2, WRH82.
56. PAH-Mrs. Peck, n.d., Peck.
57. PAH-GH, cited in Robinson, 204–6.
58. WRH-PAH, n.d., WRH82; WRH-GH, in Older, 68–69.

4. At the *Examiner*

1. *Journalist,* March 17, 1894, 2.
2. William Randolph Hearst, Jr., with Jack Casserly, *The Hearsts: Father and Son* (Niwot, Col.: Roberts Rinehart, 1991), 13.
3. Florence Finch Kelly, *Flowing Stream* (New York: Dutton, 1939), 239.
4. John Winkler, *William Randolph Hearst: A New Appraisal* (New York: Avon, 1955), 63–64; *Journalist,* February 11, 1888. On Winkler's relationship with Bill Hearst, Jr., see John Winkler-WRH, Jr., January 28, 1952, incoming box 9, EDCp.
5. PAH-OP, December 22, 1886, Peck.
6. Swinnerton interview, Flint interview, WAS.
7. Gray Brechin, "Imperial San Francisco: The Environmental Impact of Urban Elites upon the Pacific Basin" (Ph.D. diss., University of California at Berkeley, 1998), 249–56.
8. Works Project Administration of Northern California [hereafter abbreviated as WPA], "History of San Francisco Journalism," vol. 4 (1940), 32; WRH, "Pacific Coast Journalism," *Overland Monthly,* April, 1888, 403.
9. *Journalist,* February 19, 1887, 7.
10. *Journalist,* March 12, 1887, 7; March 19, 1887, 4.
11. WRH-GH, n.d. [1888?], box 2, WRH82; Leonard Dinnerstein, *Anti-Semitism in America* (New York: Oxford U.P., 1994), 35, 42.
12. WRH-GH, n.d., box 2, WRH82.

13. WRH-GH, n.d. [1887?], box 2, WRH82.
14. WRH-Edward Townsend, n.d., box 1, WRHp.
15. WRH-GH, n.d. [SF, 1889?], box 2, WRH82.
16. WRH-PAH, n.d., box 2, WRH82.
17. WRH-GH, n.d. [1885?], box 2, WRH82.
18. Ambrose Bierce, *The Collected Works of Ambrose Bierce* (1912: republished 1966, New York: Gordian Press), vol. 12, 5; *Journalist,* April 9, 1887, 5.
19. Winifred Black, "Rambles Through My Memories," chapter 4, *Good Housekeeping,* February 1936, 217.
20. Black, 214.
21. WRH-GH, n.d. [March, 1887], March 19, 1887, box 1, WRHp; WRH-E. Townsend, March 25, March 27, April 7, 1887, box 1, WRHp.
22. SFE, May 23, 1887, 1.
23. *Journalist,* June 11, 1887, 4; October 15, 1887, 4.
24. WRH-GH, n.d. [1885], box 2, WRH82.
25. *Journalist,* April 2, 1887, 4; WRH-GH, n.d. [1885?], box 2, WRH82.
26. SFE, April 3, 1887, 1.
27. WRH, *Overland Monthly,* 404; *Journalist,* December 29, 1888, 2.
28. WRH, *Overland Monthly,* 403.
29. WRH-Townsend, n.d., box 1, WRHp.
30. Arthur McEwen, *Arthur McEwen's Letter,* March 30, 1895, 2; SFE, April 24, 1887, 12; June 12, 1887, 9
31. WPA, *History of San Francisco Journalism,* vol. 4, 32.
32. John D. Stevens, *Sensationalism and the New York Press* (New York: Columbia U. P., 1991), 43.
33. SFE, May 19, May 20, 1887, 1.
34. SFE, July 21, 23, 27, August 2, 4, 1887.
35. SFE, October 30, 1887, 4.
36. Michael Robertson, *Stephen Crane, Journalism, and the Making of Modern American Literature* (New York: Columbia U. P., 1997), 57–58.
37. SFE, May 29, 1887, 9.
38. SFE, March 4, 1888, 4.
39. SFE, March 17, 1888, 4; March 20, 1891, 6; Roger Daniels, *The Politics of Prejudice* (Berkeley: University of California Press, 1977), 16–17; SFE, March 7, 1890, 4; March 1, 1888, 1.
40. Ben Procter, *William Randolph Hearst: The Early Years, 1863–1910* (New York: Oxford U. P., 1998), 53–54.
41. SFE, March 24, 1892, 1.
42. WRH-GH, n.d. [1888], box 2, WRH82; WPA, vol. 4, chart 3.
43. WPA, vol. 4, 109, 111.
44. A. J. Liebling, "The Man Who Changed the Rules," *New Yorker,* September 8, 1951.
45. GHauto, 35–36.

5. "I Can't Do San Francisco Alone"

1. WRH-GH, n.d. [1889?], box 2, WRH82.
2. WRH-GH, n.d. [1889], box 2, WRH82.
3. OP-PAH, March 24, 1888, PAHp.
4. PAH-GH, July 21, 1888, PAHp.

5. PAH-GH, August 7, 1888, PAHp.

6. PAH-GH, August 11, 1888, PAHp.

7. Alexandra Marie Nickliss, "Phoebe Apperson Hearst: The Most Powerful Woman in California" (Ph.D. diss., U. C. Davis, 1994), 98–140.

8. Judith Robinson, *The Hearsts* (New York: Avon, 1992), 223–28.

9. WRH-PAH, January, 1889, box 2, WRH82.

10. WRH-PAH, n.d., PAHp.

11. PAH-GH, August 17, September 28, October 16, 1889, PAHp.

12. WRH-PAH, n.d. [Hoffman House], PAHp.

13. NYT, March 17, 1891, 1.

14. IS-GH, March 22, 1890, PAHp.

15. OP-PAH, April 29, 1891, PAHp.

16. WRH-PAH, July 28, 1891, PAHp; Don C. Seitz, *Joseph Pulitzer: His Life & Letters* (New York: Simon & Schuster, 1924), 183–84.

17. PAH-Mrs. Hester Holden, September 7, 1892, in Robinson, 241.

18. WRH-PAH, n.d. [1893?], box 2, WRH82.

19. WRH-PAH, n.d., box 2, WRH82.

20. WRH-PAH, n.d. [November, 1894], box 2, WRH82.

21. Flint interview, WAS; EC-PAH, July 20, 1895, PAHp.

6. Hearst in New York: "Staging a Spectacle"

1. EC-PAH, July 20, August 1, 1895, PAHp.

2. PAH-OP, September 29, 1895, PAHp.

3. NYT, October 21, 1895, 5; Isaac Marcosson, *Anaconda* (New York: Dodd, Mead, 1957), 90–92.

4. Frank Luther Mott, *American Journalism,* third edition (New York: Macmillan, 1962), 529; *Fourth Estate,* September 5, October 3, 1895.

5. IS-PAH, September 18, 22, 1895, PAHp.

6. IS-PAH, September 29, 1895, PAHp.

7. IS-PAH, October 8, 1895, PAHp.

8. Mott, 418–29.

9. *Fourth Estate,* October 10, 1895, 1.

10. Winifred Black, "Rambles Through My Memories," chapter 4, *Good Housekeeping,* February 1936, 218.

11. Walt McDougall, *This Is the Life!* (New York: Knopf, 1926), 253.

12. *Fourth Estate,* December 26, 1895, 3.

13. Arthur Lubow, *The Reporter Who Would Be King: A Biography of Richard Harding Davis* (New York: Scribner's, 1992), 130.

14. Don Seitz, *Joseph Pulitzer* (New York: Rinehart, 1958), 71–72; Mott, 524–25.

15. Seitz, 212–13; James Wyman Barrett, *Joseph Pulitzer and His World* (New York: Vanguard, 1941), 172–73.

16. *Fourth Estate,* February 13, 1896, 1.

17. Wheeler.

18. Seitz, 216–17; Moses Koenigsberg, *King News* (Freeport: Books for Libraries, 1941), 324.

19. TT, April 2, 1896, 12–13; April 16, 1896, 10.

20. *Fourth Estate,* October 17, 1895, 1.

21. NYJ, January 11, February 12, April 24, 1896.

22. NYJ, February 26, November 1, 1896.

23. Ian Gordon, *Comic Strips and Consumer Culture, 1890–1945* (Washington: Smithsonian, 1998), 24–33.

24. Stephen Becker, *Comic Art in America* (New York: Simon & Schuster, 1959), 14–15.

25. Peter Conolly-Smith, "Reading the Funnies: Yellow Journalism, Comic Strips and the Immigrant Connection," in author's possession; *R. F. Outcault's The Yellow Kid* (Northhampton, Mass.: Kitchen Sink Press, 1995).

26. Koenigsberg, 448–52; "Image," SFE, March 17, 1987; *Smithsonian Collection of Newspaper Comics,* ed. Bill Blackbeard and Martin Williams (Washington: Smithsonian and Harry Abrams, 1977).

27. Koenigsberg, 384, 452; Blackbeard and Williams, 80–81.

28. Richard A. Schwarzlose, *The Nation's Newsbrokers,* vol. 2 (Evanston: Northwestern U.P., 1990), 176–78.

29. Oliver Carlson, *Brisbane: A Candid Biography* (New York: Stackpole Sons, 1937), 18; David Gray, "The Early Arthur Brisbane," typescript ms., box 2, 18–19, ABp; John T. Hettrick, oh-CU.

30. Samuel Crowther, "A Talk with Arthur Brisbane," typescript ms., box 2, 16, ABp.

31. "My dear old man," letter, n.d., 1896 folder, *World;* "Memorandum from Joseph Pulitzer," May 28, 1897; "Memorandum," n.d. [March–April, 1896]; JP-Seitz, August 25, December 3, 1897, box 1, JPp.

32. JP-Norris, December 7, 8, 1897, box 2, JPp.

33. Cora Older, *William Randolph Hearst, American* (New York: Appleton-Century, 1936), 201–2.

34. WRH, ITN, June 3, 1940.

35. Willis Abbott, *Watching the World Go By* (Boston: Little, Brown, 1933), 145–46.

36. *The Girl from Paris,* clipping and programme files; *The Telephone Girl,* clipping file, BRTC.

37. Flint, 2nd interview, WAS; Henry H. Klein, *My Last Fifty Years* (New York: n.p., 1935), 14.

38. Adela Rogers St. Johns, *The Honeycomb* (Garden City: Doubleday, 1969), 131–32.

39. Flint, 2nd interview, WAS; Flint interview, WAS; Frederick Palmer, "Hearst and Hearstism," part 1, *Collier's,* September 22, 1906, n.p.

40. *Journalist,* August 14, 1897, 133; October 9, 1897, 197.

41. James Ford, *Forty-Odd Years in the Literary Shop* (New York: Dutton, 1921), 259–60.

42. Upton Sinclair, *The Industrial Republic* (New York: Doubleday, Page, 1907), 203.

43. *Congressional Record,* 54th Congress, 2nd sess., January 8, 1897, 592–93.

44. *World's Work,* October 1922.

45. Abbott, 181–82.

46. Richard L. McCormick, "A Reappraisal of the Origins of Progressivism," in *The Party Period and Public Policy* (New York: Oxford U. P., 1986), 327.

47. Kevin Starr, *Inventing the Dream* (New York: Oxford U.P., 1985), 199–200; R. Hal Williams, *The Democratic Party and California Politics, 1880–1896* (Stanford: Stanford U.P., 1973), 206.

48. William Deverell, *Railroad Crossing* (Berkeley: University of California Press, 1994), 132.

49. Mark D. Hirsch, "Richard Croker," in *Essays in the History of New York City,* ed.

Irwin Yellowitz (Port Washington: Kennikat, 1978), 101–27; David C. Hammack, *Power and Society* (New York: Columbia U.P., 1987), 159–72.

50. WRH-JC, n.d., JCp.
51. WRH-JC, May 10, 1898, JCp.

7. "How Do You Like the *Journal's* War?"

1. SFE, August 13, September 20, 1895, March 1, 1896, in Ian Mugridge, *The View from Xanadu* (Montreal: McGill-Queen's U.P., 1995), 8–9.
2. NYJ, December 7, 1896.
3. WRH, ITN, July 1, 1940; Joyce Milton, *The Yellow Kids: Foreign Correspondents in the Heyday of Yellow Journalism* (New York: Harper & Row, 1989), 140; Arthur Lubow, *The Reporter Who Would Be King: A Biography of Richard Harding Davis* (New York: Scribner's, 1992), 137–38.
4. Lubow, 142.
5. James Creelman, *On the Great Highway: The Wanderings and Adventures of a Special Correspondent* (Boston: Lothrop, 1901), 177–78.
6. *London Times,* November 4, 1907, 5.
7. Milton, 160.
8. Creelman, 179–81; Willis Abbott, *Watching the World Go By* (Boston: Little, Brown, 1933), 215; WRH-Mrs. McKinley, August 22, 1897, WMp.
9. TT, August 26, 1897, 13.
10. NYJ, October 12, 1897, 1; Cora Older, *William Randolph Hearst, American* (New York: Appleton-Century, 1936), 164–80; Wilbur Cross, "The Perils of Evangelina," *American Heritage* 19 (1968), 36–39, 104–7; Creelman, 258–59.
11. John Offner, *An Unwanted War: The Diplomacy of the United States and Spain over Cuba, 1895–1898* (Chapel Hill: The University of North Carolina Press, 1992), 117; Abbott, 217–18; Walter LaFeber, *The New Empire* (Ithaca: Cornell U.P., 1963), 347.
12. WRH, ITN, July 1, 1940, 1.
13. G. J. A. O'Toole, *The Spanish War* (New York: Norton, 1984), 127.
14. WRH-JC, February 19, 23, 1898, JCp; William A. Swanberg, *Citizen Hearst* (New York: Scribner's, 1961), 137–45.
15. TT, April 7, 1898, 12.
16. John Stevens, *Sensationalism and the New York Press* (New York: Columbia U.P., 1991), 97.
17. Offner, 229–30; Walter LaFeber, *The Cambridge History of American Foreign Relations.* Vol II: *The American Search for Opportunity* (New York: Cambridge U.P., 1993), 140.
18. Charles Musser, *The Emergence of Cinema: The American Screen to 1907* (New York: Scribner's, 1990), 241.
19. Musser, 247; *New York Clipper,* April 30, 1898, 153.
20. Milton, 164–65; Charles Michelson, *The Ghost Talks* (New York: G. O. Putnam's, 1944), 90.
21. Abbott, 141.
22. TT, April 28, 1898, 13; May 19, 1898, 9; May 26, 1898, 1.
23. Gail Bederman, *Manliness and Civilization: A Cultural History of Gender and Race in the United States, 1880–1917* (Chicago: University of Chicago Press, 1995), 191.

24. NYJ, June 10, 1898, 2, 3.
25. EC-PAH, June 9, 1898, PAHp.
26. WRH-JC, May 26, 1898, JCp; Creelman, 188–91.
27. NYW, June 8, 1898; NYT, June 10, 1898; NYJ, June 10, 1.
28. M. F. Tighe-Creelman, n.d. [1898], JC; John C. Hemment, *Cannon and Camera* (New York: n.p., 1898), 171–72; WRH, ITN, July 1, 1940, 1–2.
29. G. W. Bitzer, *Billy Bitzer: His Story* (New York: Farrar, Straus, and Giroux, 1973), 36.
30. TT, June 23, 1898, 8; Charles Johnson Post, *The Little War of Private Post* (Boston: Little, Brown, 1960), 162.
31. WRH-PAH, [1898], PAHp.
32. Post, 162–63.
33. Milton, 332–33; Creelman, 211–12; Hemment, 148–50, 171–72.
34. WRH, ITN, July 2, 1940, 1; Hemment, 224–25.
35. NYT, July 7, 1898, 6.
36. JC-WRH, July 5, 1898, JCp.
37. WRH-n.p., n.d. [1898], JCp.
38. WRH-PAH, July 19, 1898, PAHp.

8. Representing the People

1. WRH-JC, July 25, JCp.
2. WRH-PAH, n.d. [1898 or 1899], box 2, WRH82.
3. TT, October 6, 1898, 9; November 3, 1898, 12; William A. Swanberg, *Pulitzer* (New York: Scribner's, 1967), 223–24, 253; "Memorandum for Pulitzer," October 20, 1898, box 2, JPp.
4. JP-Merrill, August 29, 1898, box 2, JPp.
5. Ben Procter, *William Randolph Hearst: The Early Years* (New York: Oxford U.P., 1998), 132–34.
6. OP-PAH, n.d. [circa 1898], PAHp.
7. John Milton Cooper, Jr., *The Warrior and the Priest* (Cambridge: Harvard U.P., 1983), 13–14; NYJ, January 1, 1897, in Swanberg, 102.
8. WRH-PAH, n.d. [1898 or 1899], box 2, WRH82.
9. NYJ, September 22, October 12, 13, 15, 28, 1898.
10. WRH-PAH, August 29, 1899, box 2, WRH82.
11. "Memo for Mr. Pulitzer on a 'Journal' Threat Conveyed by Los," December 19, 1898, box 2, JPp.
12. David Nasaw, *Children of the City* (New York: Oxford U.P., 1985), 167–77.
13. Procter, 144–46.
14. NYJ, February 5, March 19, June 25, 1899.
15. Procter, 148.
16. TT, June 7, 1900, 12.
17. PAH-OP, May 3, 1899, Peck.
18. OP-PAH, [1899], in Judith Robinson, *The Hearsts* (New York: Avon, 1992), 326.
19. George Willson, clipping film, BRTC; WRH-PAH, March 17, 1900, in Procter, 152.
20. WRH-WJB, May 19, 1900, box 24, WJBp.
21. John Cooney, *The Annenbergs* (New York: Simon & Schuster, 1982), 32–33; Frank Luther Mott, *American Journalism*, third edition (New York: Macmillan, 1962), 540.

22. M. R. Werner, *Bryan* (New York: Harcourt, Brace, 1929), 126–29; Abbot to WJB, May 29, 1900; JC-WJB, June 2, 1900, box 24, WJBp.
23. WRH-JC, June 30, 1900, JCp.
24. WRH-WJB, July 5–6, box 24, WJBp.
25. Frederick Opper, *Willie and His Papa and the Rest of the Family* (New York: Grosset and Dunlap, 1901), Kilroe.
26. JC-WJB, June 2, 1900, box 24, WJBp; Louis W. Koenig, *Bryan: A Political Biography of William Jennings Bryan* (New York: G. P. Putnam's Sons, 1971), 335–36; Werner, 128–29; Ihmsen-WJB, July 24, 1900, box 24, WJBp.
27. NYT, August 10, 1900, 3; WRH-R. E. Burke, September 12, 1900, Hearst file, CHS.
28. WRH-BS, Philadelphia, September 26, 1900, JCp.
29. WRH-JC, October 8, 1900, JCp.
30. Paolo E. Coletta, *William Jennings Bryan.* Vol. 1: *Political Evangelist, 1860–1908* (Lincoln: University of Nebraska Press, 1964), 316–18.
31. EP, June 29, 1901, 1–2.
32. Ambrose Bierce, "A Thumbnail Sketch," in *Collected Works* (1912: republished 1966, Gordian Press), vol. 12, 305; NYJ, April 10, 1901; Oliver Carlson, *Brisbane* (New York: Stackpole Sons, 1937), 128–29.
33. Bierce, 308–10; James Creelman, "The Real Mr. Hearst," *Pearson's*, September 1906, 264.
34. Cora Older, *William Randolph Hearst, American* (New York: Appleton-Century, 1936), 238.
35. *New-Yorker*, September 26, 1901, 5.
36. TR-HCL, September 9, 1901, Series 2, TRp.
37. WRH-PAH, September 10, 1901, PAHp.
38. Ian Gordon, *Comic Strips and Consumer Culture, 1890–1945* (Washington: Smithsonian, 1998), 93; Victor Rosewater, *History of Cooperative News-Gathering in the United States* (New York: D. Appleton and Co., 1930), 256–58, 357; Richard Schwarzlose, *The Nation's Newsworkers*, vol. 2 (Evanston, Ill.: Northwestern University Press, 1990), 229–30.
39. Wheeler, 19, 22.
40. ASO-WRH, March 25, 1902, ASOp.
41. Michael Schudson, *Discovering the News* (New York: Basic, 1978), 106–20.
42. WRH-PAH, n.d. [1902], PAHp.
43. *New-Yorker*, October 8, 1902, 3–4; EP, October 11, 1902, 4.
44. *New-Yorker*, October 8, 1902, 3–4.
45. Anthony-PAH, June 20, 1898, PAHp.
46. *New-Yorker*, October 29, 1902, 7.
47. NYEJ, October 27, 5; October 28, 3; NYS, October 28, 1902, 3; NYT, October 28, 1902, 1.
48. NYEJ, November 3, 1902.
49. Moses Rischin, *The Promised City: New York's Jews, 1870–1914* (New York: Harper & Row, 1970), 229.
50. NYEJ, November 6, 1902, 16.
51. NYT, November 5, 1902, 1.
52. Adela Rogers St. Johns, *The Honeycomb* (Garden City: Doubleday, 1969), 131–32.
53. *New-Yorker*, May 6, 1903, 5.
54. WRH-PAH, April 20 [1903], box 1, WRH87.
55. WRH-PAH, April 28, 1903, box 1, WRH87.

56. WRH-PAH, May, 1903, PAHp.
57. WRH-PAH, n.d., box 1, WRH87.
58. WRH-PAH, May 5, 1903; MH-PAH, May 5, 1903, box 1, WRH87.
59. WRH-PAH, n.d., box 1, WRH87.
60. PAH-Janet Peck, March, 1904, in Robinson, 344–45.

9. "Candidate of a Class"

1. Frederick Palmer, "Hearst and Hearstism," part 3, *Collier's,* October 6, 1902, n.p.
2. James Murray Allison, "The Men Who Make Presidents," *Leslie's,* June 1904, 126.
3. TT, February 19, 1903, 12.
4. TT, July 16, 1903, 15; TR-Henry Clay Payne, July 16, 1903, in *The Letters of Theodore Roosevelt,* vol. 3, ed. Elting E. Morrison (Cambridge: Harvard U.P., 1951), 518.
5. EP, August 29, 1903, 8.
6. EP, August 29, 8; September 5, 1903, 7; NYEJ, September 12, 5; September 16, 7; September 18, 7; September 23, 6; September 24, 1903, 4.
7. H. S. Barnard, "Congressional Trip by Special Train Through the South-Western Territories in the Interest of Statehood . . . ," Huntington Library, San Marino, California.
8. NYEJ, October 20, 1903, 4.
9. CDT, January 19, 1904, 1,6; NYH, January 19, 1904, 5.
10. Cora Older, *William Randolph Hearst, American* (New York: Appleton-Century, 1936), 5.
11. Ambrose Bierce, "A Thumbnail Sketch," in *Collected Works* (1912: republished 1966, Gordian Press), vol. 12, 310–11; TT, August 22, 1901, 11.
12. *Harper's Weekly,* March 5, 1904, 344; Anne W. Lane and Louise H. Wall, eds., *The Letters of Franklin K. Lane* (Boston: Houghton Mifflin, 1922), 45; CDT, February 8, 1904.
13. SFS, February 27, 1904, 2.
14. Regsford Jangsby, "The Message from Bill," SFS, March 27, 1904, 5.
15. SFNL, April 2, 1904, 33; April 9, 1904, 1; May 14, 1904, 1.
16. SFEP, March 1, 1904, 5.
17. Moses Koenigsberg, *King News: An Autobiography* (Freeport, N.Y.: Books for Libraries Press, 1941), 277; Oswald Garrison Villard, *Fighting Years: Memoirs of a Liberal Editor* (New York: Harcourt, Brace, 1939), 166.
18. *Forum,* April, 1904, 292–93.
19. Lincoln Steffens, "Hearst, the Man of Mystery," *American Magazine,* November 1906, 14–15.
20. Walter Wellman, cited in "Mr. Hearst No Longer a Joke," *Current Literature,* May 1904, 495; NYT, April 8, 1904, 9.
21. NYT, April 8, 1904, 9; Louis Brownlow, *A Passion for Politics* (Chicago: University of Chicago Press, 1955), 395.
22. NYT, April 8, 1904, 9.
23. NYT, April 1, 1904, 8.
24. NYE, April 7, 1904; Susan E. Tifft and Alex S. Jones, *The Trust* (New York: Little, Brown, 1999), 71–72; NYT, April 8, 1904.
25. CDT, April 18, 1904, 4.
26. CDT, April 24, 1904, 1; *Harper's Weekly,* May 21, 1904, 780.
27. NYT, NYA, July 9, 1904.

28. WRH-PAH, n.d. [1904?], box 1, WRH87.
29. MH-PAH, [summer of 1904], PAHp.
30. MH-PAH, August 16, 1904, PAHp.
31. WRH-PAH, n.d., carton 1, WRH87.
32. "The Talk about a New Party," *Current Literature,* January 1905, 10–11.

10. "A Force to Be Reckoned With"

1. WRH-PAH, n.d. [Mexico City, 1905?], box 1, WRH87.
2. Roy Everett Littlefield, *William Randolph Hearst: His Role in American Progressivism* (Lanham, Md.: University Press of America, 1980), 128; *Congressional Record Index,* 58th Congress, Sessions 1–3, 1903–5, xxxvii–xxxviii.
3. Frederick Palmer, "Hearst and Hearstism," *Collier's,* September 22, 1906, n.p.
4. NYA, February 9, 1905.
5. *Congressional Record-House,* February 10, 1905, 2479–81.
6. Kevin Starr, *Material Dreams* (New York: Oxford U.P., 1990), 53–54; Lloyd Wendt and Herman Kogan, *Bosses in Lusty Chicago* (Bloomington: Indiana U.P., 1967), 243–51; Walton Bean, *Boss Ruef's San Francisco* (Berkeley: University of California Press, 1967), 132–35.
7. Nat Ferber, *I Found Out* (New York: Dial, 1939), 40–42, 62–63.
8. NYEJ, February 6, 1905.
9. WRH-Utassy, n.d., in Cora Older, *William Randolph Hearst, American* (New York: Appleton-Century, 1936), 257–58.
10. Matthew Schneirov, *The Dream of a New Social Order* (New York: Columbia U.P., 1994), 230–31, John Tebbel and Mary Ellen Zuckerman, *The Magazine in America* (New York: Oxford U.P., 1991), 117.
11. David Hammack, *Power and Society* (New York: Columbia U.P., 1987), 65.
12. WRH-PAH, [early 1905], box 1, WRH87.
13. TT, June 11, 1904, 18; WRH-PAH, [early 1905], box 1, WRH87.
14. PAH-OP, February 9, 1905, April 16, 1905; PAH-Janet Peck, April 16, 1905, May 23, 1905, n.d. [Sunday], August 7, 1905; PAH-Mrs. Peck, n.d., box 15; ephemera box, Peck.
15. Elizabeth Hawes, *New York, New York* (New York: Knopf, 1993), 159–61.
16. *Apartment Houses of the Metropolis* (New York: G. C. Hesselgren, 1908), 40–41.
17. William Randolph Hearst, Jr., with Jack Casserly, *The Hearsts: Father and Son* (Niwot, Col.: Roberts Rinehart, 1991), 237; MH-PAH, September 22, 1905, PAHp.
18. NYT, October 13, 1905, 1–2.
19. NYW, October 31, 1905, 3.
20. Socialist Party, "What Are You Going to Do with Your Vote?"; "An Appeal to the Workingmen!"; n.a., "The Hearst Ticket," in Socialist Party (US) NYC 1905 folder, Tamiment Library, New York University.
21. NYDT, November 2, 1905, 6; *Literary Digest,* November 18, 1905, 729–30.
22. NYT, November 2, 1905, 1; NYW, November 2, 1905, 3.
23. NYW, October 31, 1905, 1.
24. NYT, October 12, 1905, 8; November 3, 1905, 8; TT, October 19, 1905, 11; November 2, 1905, 12–13.
25. NYH, November 5, 1905, 2.
26. NYW, November 6, 1905, 6; NYT, November 6, 1905, 1.
27. *Independent,* November 16, 1905, 1177.

28. *Literary Digest,* November 18, 1905, 729.

29. NYT, November 8, 1905, 8.

30. Irwin Yellowitz, *Labor and the Progressive Movement in New York State* (Ithaca: Cornell U.P., 1965), 198–201; Thomas M. Henderson, *Tammany and the New Immigrants* (New York: Arno, 1976), 100, 106–7, 111; NYT, November 8, 1905, 2; NYW, November 9, 1905, 2; George B. McClellan, Jr., *The Gentleman and the Tiger: The Autobiography of George B. McClellan, Jr.,* ed. Harold Syrett (Philadelphia: Lippincott, 1956), 226.

31. *Current Literature,* December, 1905, 581; *Harper's Weekly,* November 18, 1905, 1656.

32. William Riordan, *Plunkitt of Tammany Hall* (New York: E. P. Dutton, 1963), 17; Moses Rischin, *The Promised City: New York's Jews, 1870–1914* (New York: Harper & Row, 1970), 229.

33. *Independent,* November 16, 1905, 1178; Nancy Joan Weiss, *Charles Francis Murphy, 1858–1924: Respectability and Responsibility in Tammany Politics* (Northampton, Mass.: Smith College, 1968), 41–42; John D. Buenker, *Urban Liberalism and Progressive Reform* (New York: Norton, 1973), 37.

11. Man of Mystery

1. WRH-AB, December 1, 1905; Roy Everett Littlefield, *William Randolph Hearst: His Role in American Progressivism* (Lanham, Md.: University Press of America, 1980), 197–98.

2. Ben Procter, *William Randolph Hearst: The Early Years, 1863–1910* (New York: Oxford U.P., 1998), 211–13; Ihmsen-Stokes, December 7, 1905, February 9, 1906, box 19, JSp; EC-PAH, February 19, 1906, PAHp.

3. MH-PAH, March 10, 1906, PAHp.

4. Cora Older, *William Randolph Hearst, American* (New York: Appleton-Century, 1936), 292.

5. Memorandum for the Secretary, April 20, 1906; WRH-Taft, April 20, 1906, Series 3, WHTp.

6. *Congressional Record Index,* 59th Congress, 448; Older, 292–94.

7. EC-PAH, two letters, April 28, 1906, PAHp.

8. WRH-PAH, n.d., box 1, WRH87.

9. PAH-Mrs. Peck, n.d., Peck.

10. MH-PAH, July 30, 1906, PAHp.

11. MH-PAH, October 10, 1906, PAHp.

12. *Reader's Guide to Periodical Literature* for 1906, 1014; Lincoln Steffens, *The Autobiography of Lincoln Steffens* (New York: Harcourt, Brace & World, 1931), 536, 539; Lincoln Steffens, "William Randolph Hearst: The Man of Mystery," *American Magazine,* November 1906, 3.

13. Steffens, *American Magazine,* 20.

14. James Creelman, "The Real Mr. Hearst," *Pearson's,* September 1906, 263.

15. Upton Sinclair, *The Industrial Republic* (New York: Doubleday, Page, 1907), 199–200.

16. TR-HCL, September 27, 1905, series 2, vol. 67, TRp; Robert F. Wesser, *Charles Evans Hughes, Politics and Reform in New York, 1905–1910* (Ithaca: Cornell U.P., 1967), 61, 64–69.

17. TR-HCL, September 27, 1905, series 2, vol. 67, TRp.

18. TR-HCL, October 2, 1906, series 2, vol. 67, TRp.
19. TR-Sherman, TR-Charles Sprague Smith, October 3, 1906, series 2, vol. 67, TRp.
20. TR-CEH, October 4, 1906; TR-Woodruff, October 5, 1906; TR-Straus, October 9, 1906; Straus-TR, October 25, 1906, Series 1, TRp; *Independent,* November 1, 1906, 1062–63.
21. NYT, October 18, 1906, 3.
22. NYT, October 10, 1906, 1.
23. NYT, October 16, 5; October 30, 3; November 16, 1906, 5.
24. *Outlook,* October 20, 1906, 383–84.
25. Steffens, *Autobiography,* 539.
26. TR-Strachey, October 25, 1906, series 2, vol. 68, TRp.
27. TR-CEH, October 5, 1906, series 2, vol. 67, TRp.
28. *Outlook,* October 20, 1906, 400; *Bookman* 24, December 1906, 315.
29. WRH-PAH, n.d., in Older, 302.
30. Merlo J. Pusey, *Charles Evans Hughes,* vol. 1 (New York: Columbia U.P., 1963), 178–80; NYS, November 2, 1906, 2.
31. Older, 313–14.
32. *Current Literature,* December 1906, 594.

12. Party Leader

1. WRH-PAH, n.d. [1906, but marked 1905?], box 1, WRH87.
2. WRH-PAH, n.d., box 2, WRH87.
3. WRH-PAH, n.d., box 1, WRH87.
4. PAH-OP, January 14, 1907, Peck; NYT, November 16, 1906, 1.
5. Herbert Mitgang, *The Man Who Rode the Tiger* (Philadelphia: Lippincott, 1963), 93–94.
6. MH-PAH, October 29, 1907, PAHp.
7. NYT, November 6, 1907.
8. WRH-PAH, n.d. [*New York American* stationery], box 1, WRH87.
9. William Randolph Hearst, Jr., with Jack Casserly, *The Hearsts: Father and Son* (Niwot, Col.: Roberts Rinehart, 1991), 49; WRH-PAH, n.d., box 1, WRH87; Ben Procter, *William Randolph Hearst: The Early Years, 1863–1910* (New York: Oxford U.P., 1998), 241.
10. Cora Older, *William Randolph Hearst, American* (New York: Appleton-Century, 1936), 336–37; WRH, Jr., 26–28; Sara Holmes Boutelle, *Julia Morgan, Architect* (New York: Abbeville, 1988), 171–73, 217.
11. Judith Robinson, *The Hearsts* (New York: Avon, 1992), 333–34; Boutelle, 217.
12. WRH-PAH, November 10, 16th, 1908, box 1, WRH87.
13. WRH-PAH, April 28, 1915, in Robinson, 352.
14. WRH-PAH, n.d., in Robinson, 353.
15. WRH, Jr., 64.
16. WRH-PAH, n.d. [April 1908], box 1, WRH87; WRH, Jr., 17.
17. MH-PAH, 1908 [on Cunard RMS *Lusitania*], PAHp.
18. NYDT, July 28, 1908, 2; NYA, July 27, 28, 1.
19. U.S. Congress. Senate, *Campaign Contributions: Testimony before a Subcommittee of the Committee on Privileges and Elections,* vol. II, 62nd Congress, Third Session, 1912–13, 1371–1465.
20. NYT, NYDT, September 19, 1908.

21. NYDT, September 21, 1908, 1; September 22, 1908, 6; Josephus Daniels, *Editor in Politics* (Chapel Hill: University of North Carolina Press, 1941), 543–47.
22. Michael McGerr, *The Decline of Popular Politics* (New York: Oxford U.P., 1986), 185.
23. NYA, November 3, 1908.
24. WRH-PAH, November 16, 1908, box 1, WRH87.
25. Mortimer Smith, *William Jay Gaynor* (Chicago: Henry Regnery, 1951), 66–72.
26. *The Life of William R. Hearst,* 43–46, Collection of Tammaniana, Kilroe.
27. NYDT, November 3, 1909, 1, December 15, 1909, 1; NYT, December 15, 1909, 1–2; MH-PAH, assorted letters from 1910–11, PAHp.
28. Older, 358–59.
29. WRH-PAH, March 14, 1910, box 1, WRH87.
30. WRH-PAH, n.d., box 1, WRH87.
31. NYDT, October 21, 1910, 3.
32. James Allen Myatt, "William Randolph Hearst and the Progressive Era, 1900–1912" (Ph.D. diss., University of Florida, 1960), 108, 140–43.
33. NYDT, November 9, 1910, 5.

13. Hearst at Fifty: Some Calm Before the Storms

1. Cordell Hull, *Memoirs of Cordell Hull,* vol. 1 (New York: Macmillan, 1948), 67; James Allen Myatt, "William Randolph Hearst and the Progressive Era, 1900–1912" (Ph.D. diss., University of Florida, 1960), 148–49.
2. CDT, August 6, 1912, in *Papers of Woodrow Wilson,* vol. 25, ed. Arthur Link (Princeton: Princeton U.P., 1977), 299.
3. SFE, April 14, 1913.
4. William Kent-Joseph P. Tumulty, August 12, 1913, case file 95A, series 4, WWp.
5. Henry Lane Wilson-Pedro Lascurain, July 6, 1912, July 17, 1912, September 30, 1912; J. C. Hayes-Marion Letcher, October 5, 1912, Letcher-WJB, October 11, 1912, case file 3885, series 6, WHTp; SFE, November 13, 1913.
6. Parker H. Sercombe-WJB, August 11, 1913, case file 95a, series 4, WWp.
7. NYEJ, April 28, 1914; Isaac Russell, "Hearst-Made War News," *Harper's Weekly,* July 25, 1914, 76–78; Russell-Tumulty, July 30, 1914, case file 399, series 4, WWp; NYA, June 11, 1914, 1.
8. OP-Janet Peck, n.d., box 1, Peck Family.
9. Irene Castle, as told to Bob and Wanda Duncan, *Castles in the Air* (Garden City: Doubleday, 1958), 89.
10. Cora Older, *William Randolph Hearst, American* (New York: Appleton-Century, 1936), 345; NYT, July 26, 1913.
11. Andrew Alpern, *Historic Manhattan Apartment Houses* (New York: Dover, 1996), 31–32.
12. William Randolph Hearst, Jr., with Jack Casserly, *The Hearsts: Father and Son* (Niwot, Col.: Roberts Rinehart, 1991), 24–25.
13. NYT, March 25, 1914, 8; July 11, 1914, 5.
14. Wesley Towner, *The Elegant Auctioneers* (New York: Hill & Wang, 1970), 182–83.
15. OP-Janet Peck, September 29, 1914, box 1, Peck Family; Wheeler.
16. George M. Payne to William H. Taft, July 18, August 8, October 8, 1907, series 3, WHTp; the Hearst News Service is listed in the 1909 *Boyd's Directory of D.C.* (R. Polk and Co., 1909), 660; Ian Gordon, *Comic Strips and Consumer Cul-*

ture (Washington, D.C.: Smithsonian, 1998), 37; Moses Koenigsberg, *King News* (Freeport: Books for Libraries, 1941), 404–5.

17. Terry Ramsaye, *A Million and One Nights: A History of the Motion Picture Through 1925* (New York: Simon & Schuster, 1926), 654–61; Earl Theisen, "Story of the Newsreel," *International Photographer,* September 1933, 24; Raymond Fielding, *The American Newsreel 1911–1967* (Norman: University of Oklahoma Press, 1972), 70–85.

18. *Motography,* March 7, 1914, 23; MPW, March 14, 1914, 1351.

19. Gene Fernett, *American Film Studios: An Historical Encyclopedia* (Jefferson, N.C.: McFarland, 1988), 254–68.

20. John Winkler, *William Randolph Hearst: A New Appraisal* (New York: Hastings House, 1955), 268–70; *New York Dramatic Mirror,* April 15, 1914, 31.

21. Raymond Stedman, *The Serials,* 2nd ed. (Norman: University of Oklahoma Press, 1977), 16; *New York Dramatic Mirror,* April 1, 1914, April 8, 1914.

22. Craig Campbell, *Reel America and World War I: A Comprehensive Filmography and History of Motion Pictures in the United States, 1914–1920* (Jefferson, N.C.: McFarland, 1985), 37; Stedman, 18.

23. Donald Crofton, *Before Mickey: The Animated Film 1898–1928* (Cambridge: MIT Press, 1982), 98–111, 178–184; Joe Adamson, "Animation Studio Auteur: Gregory La Cava and William Randolph Hearst," *Griffithiana,* September 1996, 73–105.

14. "A War of Kings"

1. WRH, September 10, 1914, in *Selections,* 570.

2. Cora Older, *William Randolph Hearst, American* (New York: Appleton-Century, 1936), 369; NYT, September 28, 1914, 4.

3. Roger Daniels, *The Politics of Prejudice* (Berkeley: University of California Press, 1977), 70–71.

4. WRH, SFE, February 2, 1915, in Ian Mugridge, *The View from Xanadu* (Montreal: McGill-Queen's U.P., 1995), 112.

5. A. J. P. Taylor, *The First World War* (New York: Perigree, 1980), 22.

6. Walter LaFeber, *The American Age* (New York: Norton, 1989), 270–71; Akira Iriye, *The Globalizing of America, 1913–1945* (New York: Cambridge U.P., 1993), 21–25.

7. Nat Ferber, *I Found Out* (New York: Dial, 1939), 63.

8. Older, 362–63; Shari Benstock, *No Gifts from Chance: A Biography of Edith Wharton* (New York: Scribner's, 1994), 326.

9. Cited in Edmond D. Coblentz, ed., *William Randolph Hearst: A Portrait in His Own Words* (New York: Simon & Schuster, 1952), 83–84.

10. *Brewing,* 1433; Craig Campbell, *Reel America and World War I* (Jefferson, N.C.: McFarland, 1985), 32.

11. Translated transcript of letter from Fuehr to Herr Doctor Schumacher, Berlin, October 15, 1915, case file 9140–4561, record group 165, MID.

12. Ralph Martin, *Cissy: The Extraordinary Life of Eleanor Medill Patterson* (New York: Simon & Schuster, 1979), 136–37.

13. "Memorandum for Mr. Hoover," June 18, 1920, case file 2290, record group 65, BI; EH-A. F. Beach, December 18, 1915, case file 9140–4561, record group 165, MID; *Brewing,* 1590, 1951–60; NYA, October 8, 1916.

14. Count von Bernstorff, *My Three Years in America* (New York: Scribner's, 1920), 336.

15. Bradford Merrill-Lee S. Overman, December 14, 1918, *Brewing,* 1910.

16. John Womack, in *Mexico Since Independence,* ed. Leslie Bethel (Cambridge: Cambridge U.P., 1991), 157–66; NYT, December 25, 1915, 3; January 11, 1916, 9, 11; WRH-TVR, January 2, 1916, carton I, WRHp.

17. NYA, March 10, 1916; *Film and Propaganda in America: A Documentary History.* vol. 1, *World War I,* ed. Richard Wood (New York: Greenwood, 1990), 94–102.

18. "Old German" case file 2290, Mex. case file 877, record group 65, BI.

19. TR-WRH, April 15, 1916, series 4A, TRp.

20. WRH-TR, April 17, 1916, series 1, TRp.

21. TR-WRH, May 13, 1916, Series 2, vol. 104, p. 253; WRH-TR, May 17, 1916, May 26, 1916, Series 1, TRp.

22. WRH-JAM, July 1, 1916, box 1, JAMp.

23. Flint interview, January 18, 1960, WAS.

24. OP-Janet Peck, n.d. [summer, 1910], Peck.

25. WRH-PAH, August 30, 1917, box 2, WRH87.

26. WRH-PAH, n.d., box 2, WRH87.

27. WRH-PAH, December 2, 1915, in Judith Robinson, *The Hearsts* (New York: Avon, 1992), 354.

28. WRH-Randolph Hearst or [Elbert] Willson Hearst, November 30, 1916, in Robinson, 354.

29. WRH, Jr., oh-SS, 30–31; Ethel Whitmire-PAH, October 2 [1914?], in Robinson, 349.

30. WRH, Jr., oh-SS, 30–31.

31. Lewis Erenberg, *Steppin' Out: New York Nightlife and the Transformation of American Culture, 1890–1930* (Chicago: University of Chicago Press, 1981), 215, 219.

32. Marion Davies, *The Times We Had* (Indianapolis: Bobbs-Merrill, 1975), 8; Erenberg, 222–24.

33. Laurence Bergreen, *As Thousands Cheer: The Life of Irving Berlin* (New York: Viking, 1990), 130–31.

34. Fred Lawrence Guiles, *Marion Davies* (New York: McGraw-Hill, 1972), 45.

35. Davies, 9–10.

36. Anita Loos, *Kiss Hollywood Good-by* (New York: Viking, 1974), 142.

37. NYA, February 7, 13, May 4, 1916.

38. WRH-JAM, November 17, 1917, box 1, JAMp; WRH-H. Robert [editor of *San Francisco Examiner*], January 15, 1915, carton 1, WRHp.

39. P. G. Wodehouse and Guy Bolton, *Bring On the Girls* (New York: Simon & Schuster, 1953), 65–72.

40. WRH-JAM, December 17, 1916, October 5, 1916, JAMp.

41. WRH-DWG, October 21, 1916, DWGp.

42. Davies, 18.

43. SFE, December 21, 1916; NYA, January 12, 1917.

44. WRH-Carvalho, February 25, 16, 1917, *Brewing,* 1608, 1610.

45. Van Hamm-WRH, February 26, 1917, in *Brewing,* 1609.

15. "Hearst, Hylan, the Hohenzollerns, and the Habsburgs"

1. Case file 10497–253, record group 165, MID; "Old German" case file 26588, record group 65, BI; Case file PF 15962, record group 165, MID; Case file 2290, record group 65, BI.

2. J. A. Berst-WW, June 8, 1917, case file 4020, series 4; Frank Polk-WW, June 12, 1917, case file 4020, series 4, WWp.

3. William Redfield-WW, June 1, 1917; WW-J. A. Berst, June 4, 1917, Frank Polk-WW, June 12, 1917, case file 4020, series 4, WWp.

4. J. A. Berst-WW, June 8, 1917; WW-J. A. Berst, August 11, 1917, case file 4020, series 4, WWp.

5. MacFarland-WW, August 23, 1917, case file 4020, series 4, WWp.

6. Lansing-MacFarland, October 4, 1917, case file 4020, series 4, WWp.

7. MacFarland-WW, September 21, 1917, case file 4020, series 4; Tumulty-WW, November 8, 1917, WW-Tumulty, n.d., case file 399, series 4, WWp.

8. Memorandum for Colonel Marten, October 7, 1918, case file 3528, record group 165, MID.

9. NYA, June 16, November 2, 1917; NYT, March 5, August 25, 1917.

10. NYT, October 2, 1917, 1; October 3, 1917, 1; October 31, 1917, 12; November 3, 1917, 1, 6.

11. Bradford Merrill-Lee S. Overman, December 14, 1918, in *Brewing*, 1914–15; NYTr, October 4, 5, 6, 1917; "Old German" case file 117993, record group 65, BI.

12. *Brewing*, 1978, 2452; case file 9140–4561, record group 165, MID; on interviews with Hearst's neighbors, see report from Frank Stone, October 17, 1917, and W. H. Vander Pool, November 3, 1917, record group 165, MID.

13. Churchill-Bielaski, July 27, 1918, case file 9140–4561, item 33, record group 165, MID.

14. Moses Koenigsberg, *King News* (Freeport: Books for Libraries, 1941), 427–29.

15. WRH-JAM, January 2, 3, 1918, JAMp.

16. WRH-MD [marked Bernard Douras-Marion Douras], May 15, box 7, WRH, Jr.91.

17. TT, June 3, 1918, 13.

18. Marion Davies, *The Times We Had* (Indianapolis: Bobbs-Merrill, 1975), 10–15; WRH-JAM, August 31, 1918, JAMp.

19. Peter J. D. Conolly-Smith, "The Translated Community: New York City's German-Language Press as an Agent of Cultural Resistance and Integration, 1910–1918" (Ph.D. diss., Yale University, 1996), 191, 524–25.

20. WRH, May 31, 1918, in *Selections*, 587–90.

21. Case file 9140–4561, item 72, record group 165, MID.

22. Kenneth Macgowan, *Coiled in the Flag: Hears-s-s-s-t,* reprinted from the *New York Tribune* of Sunday April 28, Sunday May 5, Sunday May 12, Sunday May 19, Sunday May 26, and Sunday June 2, 1918.

23. NYTr, July 1, 2, 17, 22, 31, 1918.

24. John R. Dunlap-WW, January 10, 1918, case file 350, Series 4, WWp; NYTr, July 3, 1918; Herbert Mitgang, *The Man Who Rode the Tiger* (Philadelphia: Lippincott, 1963), 151; NYTr, July 24, 1918.

25. Garrett-Gregory, October 7, 1918, case file 9140–4561, item 72, record group 165, MID.

26. WRH, December 13, 1918, in *Selections*, 599–600.

27. WRH, January 26, 1920, in *Selections*, 607–8.

28. NYT, May 24, 1919; WRH, May 24, 1919, in *Selections*, 602–3.

29. WRH-HH Tammen, March 29, 1919, incoming box 3, EDCp.

30. WRH, NYA, August 2, 1919.

31. Cora Older, *William Randolph Hearst, American* (New York: Appleton-Century, 1936), 415; SFE, November 21, 1919.

32. NYT, January 10, 7; January 15, 4, January 24, 7, January 29, 1919, 12; Robert W. Owens-Mayor Hylan, n.d., PF 47918, record group 165, MID.

33. NYTr, December 13, 1919, 9; "Hearst and His Enemies," compiled for The Committee of Relatives of American Soldiers, Sailors and Marines of Greater New York by Edward T. O'Loughlin ([New York], 1919).

34. Nat Ferber, *I Found Out* (New York: Dial, 1939), 81–82.

35. NYT, March 26, 1919, 4.

36. WRH, December 20, 1919, in *Selections*, 108–9.

37. Peter Filene, *Americans and the Soviet Experiment, 1917–1933* (Cambridge: Harvard U.P., 1967), 39–46; Gerald MacFarland, BA, December 26, 1918, in folder marked PF 15962, record group 165, MID.

38. Chief of Staff, G-2, American Expeditionary Forces to MID, Washington, June 8, 1919, item 10058–383, record group 165, MID.

39. NYA, October 27, 31, November 1, 2, 1920.

16. Building a Studio

1. Judith Robinson, *The Hearsts* (New York: Avon, 1992), 376–77.

2. Wheeler, 49.

3. PAH-WRH, February 27, 1919, in Wheeler, 47.

4. Robinson, 378–80.

5. William Randolph Hearst, Jr., with Jack Casserly, *The Hearsts: Father and Son* (Niwot, Col.: Roberts Rinehart, 1991), 22; Cora Older, *William Randolph Hearst, American* (New York: Appleton-Century, 1936), 529.

6. NYT, April 14, 17, 1919.

7. Last Will and Testament of Phoebe A. Hearst, HSSSHM; NYT, November 18, 1919, 3.

8. WRH-Ihmsen, February 7, 1919, DWGp.

9. MPW, March 22, June 18, 1919.

10. MPW, August 9, 23, 1919.

11. WRH-JAM, April 26, 1919, JAMp.

12. WRH-LeBaron, June 21, 1919, JAMp.

13. Peter Bogdanovich, *Allan Dwan, The Last Pioneer* (New York: Praeger, 1971), 49.

14. Frances Marion, *Off with Their Heads!* (New York: Macmillan, 1972), 70–71.

15. WRH-JAM, September 5, 1919, JAMp.

16. JAM-WRH, September 13, 1919, JAMp.

17. AZ-WRH, August 9, 1919, AZp.

18. WRH-Zittel, August 14, 1919, AZp.

19. WRH-AZ, December 17, 1920, AZp.

20. Randolph Carter and Robert Reed Cole, *Joseph Urban: Architecture, Theatre, Opera, Film* (New York: Abbeville Press, 1992); John Dizikes, *Opera in America: A Cultural History* (New Haven: Yale U.P., 1993), 364–68.

21. Contract between Joseph Urban and International Film Service Co., Inc., dated February 19, 1920, JUp.

22. Notes from Gretl's autobiography, box 45, JUp.

23. WRH-JAM, June 23, 1920, JAMp.

24. Notes from Gretl's autobiography, box 45; Mary's diary, Mary Urban box, JUp.
25. Notes from Gretl's autobiography, box 45, JUp.

17. Builder and Collector

1. Steilberg, 57, JM-oh; Cora Older, *William Randolph Hearst, American* (New York: Appleton-Century, 1936), 528–29.
2. Sara Holmes Boutelle, *Julia Morgan, Architect* (New York: Abbeville, 1988), 7.
3. Boutelle, 249–58.
4. Steilberg, 57–58, JM-oh.
5. WRH-JM, August 11, 1919; WRH-JM, n.d. [marked 1919, c. September 12 or a few days earlier], JMp.
6. William Randolph Hearst, Jr., with Jack Casserly, *The Hearsts: Father and Son* (Niwot, Col.: Roberts Rinehart, 1991), 67.
7. JM-WRH, September 13, 1919; WRH-JM, September 20, 1919; WRH-Bogart, September 21, 1919; WRH-JM, September 21, 1919, JMp.
8. JAM-WRH, September 13, 1919; Henry Bicknell-WRH, October 23, 1919, JAMp.
9. WRH-JM, October 25, 1919, JMp.
10. JM-WRH, November 7, October 18, 1919, JMp.
11. Boutelle, 178–79.
12. JM-WRH, April 6, 1920; May 19, 1920, JMp.
13. WRH-JM, June 2, 1921, JMp.
14. Thomas A. Aidala, *Hearst Castle* (New York: Harrison House, 1981), 101–2; Boutelle, 181–82.
15. WRH-JM, December 31, 1919, JMp; Kevin Starr, *Americans and the California Dream: 1850–1915* (New York: Oxford U.P., 1973), 401–410; Robert Pavlik, "Something a Little Different," *California History*, Winter 1992/3, 470–72.
16. Starr, 413–14.
17. WRH-JM, December 19, 1919; WRH-Fairchild, February 20, 1920, JMp.
18. WRH-JM, January 19, 1921; JM-WRH, February 4, 1921; WRH-JM, February 10, 1921, JMp.
19. JM-WRH, May 19, 1920; WRH-JM, May 23, 1920, JMp.
20. Jean Strouse, *Morgan* (New York: Random House, 1999), 381, 384; WRH-AH, June 2, 1926; JW-Gallandt, January 9, 1920, BW.
21. WRH-KVW, March 27, 1921, BW.
22. KVW-WRH, October 21, November 14, 1921, BW.
23. KVW-WRH, October 28, 1922, BW; A. Byne-JM, September 14, 1925, JMp.
24. WRH-LOR, June 25, 1921, BW.
25. Rémy Saisselin, *The Bourgeois and the Bibelot* (New Brunswick: Rutgers U.P., 1984), 133–68.
26. Joseph Duveen-WRH, May 24, 1926, BW.
27. Emile Gauvreau, *My Last Million Readers* (New York: Dutton, 1941), 141.
28. H. J. Kelekian-WRH, May 28, 1924, BW.
29. S. N. Behrman, *Duveen* (New York: Random House, 1952), 97; JW-CMG, October 31, 1923, BW.
30. WRH-Joseph Duveen, June 2, 1927, BW.
31. A. Byne-JM, June 5, 1924, JMp.
32. WRH-Kobler, February 29, 1927; George Buckingham-Kobler, enclosed with

Kobler-WRH, March 8, 1927; WRH-Kobler, March 21, 1927, carton 2, WRHp; Wesley Towner, *The Elegant Auctioneers* (New York: Hill & Wang, 1970), 414–15.

33. W. G. Constable, *Art Collecting in the United States of America* (London: Thomas Nelson and Sons, Ltd., 1964), 139–40; Marion Davies, *The Times We Had* (Indianapolis: Bobbs-Merrill, 1975), 132.

34. S. N. Behrman, *Duveen* (New York: Random House, 1952), 117.

35. Towner, 182–83, 241, 308, 314, 452–53.

36. WRH-MH, February 26, 1927, carton 2, WRHp; WRH, Jr., 25.

37. Assorted warehouse bills and statements, BW; *Fortune*, May 1931, 60.

38. WRH-LOR, July 3 [1921], BW.

39. JW-LOR, June 17, 1921, BW.

18. Marion, Millicent, and the Movies

1. JAM-WRH, June 29, 1920, 4, JAMp; *New York Star*, July 5, 1920.

2. WRH, Jr., oh-SS, 3, 6–7.

3. WRH, Jr., oh-SS, 6–8; I viewed "The Lighthouse Keeper's Daughter" at San Simeon. I am indebted to John Horn and the staff at the castle for dating the film for me.

4. Cari Beauchamp, *Without Lying Down* (New York: Scribner, 1997), 133; Fred Lawrence Guiles, *Marion Davies* (New York: McGraw-Hill, 1972), 98–100; WRH-JAM, August 17, 26, 1920; WRH-JAM, August 22, 1920, JAMp.

5. M. R. Werner, "Yellow Movies," *New Yorker*, September 14, 1940, 61, 65.

6. Kevin Brownlow, *Behind the Mask of Innocence* (Berkeley: University of California Press, 1990), 285–92; Frances Marion, *Off with Their Heads!* (New York: Macmillan, 1972), 71–75; *Photoplay*, December, 1921.

7. JAM-WRH, August 30, 31, 1920; WRH-JAM, August 27, 30, September 1, 3, October 14, 1920, JAMp; W. R. Benson, "Boudoir Politics in the Movies," *Screenland*, March, 1923, 38.

8. WRH-LeBaron, May 5, 1921, carton 1, WRHp; WRH-JU, May 3, 1921, folder marked "Hearst International Film: Cosmopolitan Pictures 1921," JUp.

9. Notes from Gretl's autobiography, box 45; JU-Mary Urban, May 30, [1921] and Mary's diary, in Mary Urban box, JUp.

10. WRH-JAM, October 14, 1921, JAMp.

11. JAM-WRH, October 19, 1921; WRH-JAM, October 21, 1921, JAMp.

12. WRH-JAM, November 7, 1921; JAM-WRH, November 10, 1921, JAMp.

13. WRH-JAM, November 12, 1921, JAMp.

14. MH-Pershing, June 8, 1918, June 14, 1919; Colonel Carl Boyd-Major J. H. Perkins, June 8, 1918; Ralph J. Preston-Colonel Carl Boyd, June 14, 1918, box 91, Pershing; NYT, July 3, 1921, 18; July 27, 1923, 1.

15. William Randolph Hearst, Jr., with Jack Casserly, *The Hearsts: Father and Son* (Niwot, Col.: Roberts Rinehart, 1991), 239.

16. WRH-JM, March 15, 1922; WRH-JM, August 28, 1922; WRH-JM, September 20, 1922, JMp.

17. Birge-JW, November 29, 1922, BW.

18. Edwin Emery, *The Press and America,* third edition (New York: Prentice-Hall, 1972), 448; WRH-JAM, April 12, 1920, JAMp.

19. JAM-WRH, May 5, 1920, JAMp; Gene Fowler, *Skyline: A Reporter's Reminiscence of the 1920s* (New York: Viking, 1961), 91.

20. JW-LOR, May 16, 1921; JW-KVW, May 1, 1922, BW.

21. WRH, March 28, 1918, in *Selections,* 153.

22. Swinnerton interview, WAS.

23. JW-LOR, June 6, 1921; February 7, 1921, BW.

24. JAM-WRH, May 5, June 10, June 29, July 19, 1920; WRH-JAM, July 12, 1920, JAMp.

25. WRH-JAM, October 7, 8, 1920, JAMp.

26. WRH-JAM, June 30, July 21, August 24, 26, 1921, JAMp; WRH-AZ, July 2, 1921, folder 4, AZp.

27. WRH-JAM, August 28, 1921, JAMp.

28. JAM-WRH, September 7, 1921, JAMp; Giuliana Muscio, *Hollywood's New Deal* (Philadelphia: Temple U.P., 1997), 115.

19. A Return to Normalcy

1. John Witte, *The Politics and Development of the Federal Income Tax* (Madison: University of Wisconsin Press, 1985), 88; Select Senate Committee of the Internal Revenue Bureau (Couzens Committee), Senate Report *27*, 69th Congress, 1st Session, 1926, 206–11, 284–89.

2. JAM-WRH, December 29, 1922, JAMp.

3. WRH-JAM, December 29, 1922, JAMp.

4. Minutes of Finance Committee, March 22, 1923, JAMp; NYT, March 31, 1923, 8; JAM-WRH, July 22, 1924; WRH-JAM, August 9, 1924, JAMp.

5. JAM-WRH, July 20, 1923, JAMp.

6. JAM-WRH, July 25, 1923, JAMp; JAM-JFN, July 30, 1923, box 63, JFNp.

7. Kevin Starr, *Inventing the Dream: California Through the Progressive Era* (New York: Oxford U.P., 1985), 273–75; Roger Lotchin, "John Francis Neylan: San Francisco Irish Progressive," in *The San Francisco Irish: 1850–1976,* ed. James D. Walsh (San Francisco: Irish Literary and Historical Society, 1978), 96–101.

8. WRH-JFN, October 8, 1923, box 63, JFNp.

9. WRH-JFN, February 7, 1924, box 64, JFNp.

10. JFN-WRH, March 5, June 13, 1924, box 64, JFNp.

11. B. C. Forbes, NYA, April 24, 1924, 26.

12. NYA, April 26, 1924, 18; NYHT, April 29, 1924, 23; NYA, April 29, 1924, 1, 19, 20.

13. NYT, May 6, 1924, 30.

14. AB-Marks, May 15, 1922; August 19, 1922; Fall-WRH, August 19, 1922; WRH-Fall, August 28, 1922, Fall.

15. Norman Hapgood, *The Changing Years* (New York: Farrar & Rinehart, 1930), 263, 268; WRH-JAM, February 17, 21, 1924, JAMp.

16. WRH-AB, January 29, 1928, box 6, ABp.

17. Richard Norton Smith, *The Colonel: The Life and Legend of Robert R. McCormick* (New York: Houghton Mifflin, 1997), 220, 246; WRH-JAM, December 28, 1921, JAMp.

18. Emile Gauvreau, *My Last Million Readers* (New York: Dutton, 1941), 109–112.

19. EP, June 14, 1924, 1.

20. Oswald Villard, *Some Newspapers and Newspaper-Men* (New York: Knopf, 1923), 20, 15; Moses Koenigsberg, *King News* (Freeport: Books for Libraries, 1941), 441.

21. "Serials Published in the *Examiner* (1923–1927)," in folder marked Serials, 1935, LAE; Koenigsberg, 447–49.

22. WRH-DWG, October 21, 1921, DWGp; Randolph Carter and Robert Reed Cole, *Joseph Urban* (New York: Abbeville, 1992), 153–54; MPW, March 4, 1922, 53; April 15, 1922, 730; September 2, 1922, 33.
23. Marion Davies, *The Times We Had* (Indianapolis: Bobbs-Merrill, 1975), 24.
24. V, September 22, 1922.
25. MPW, November 25, 1922, 334; December 23, 1922, 749; MPN, September 16, 1922.
26. *Screenland,* January 1924, 38.
27. Davies, 26; MPW, March 24, 1923, 455.
28. MPW, January 6, 1923, 68; January 27, 1923, 383; February 10, 1923, 591; Richard Koszarski, *An Evening's Entertainment* (New York: Scribner's, 1990), 128.
29. V, August 9, 1923.
30. NYT, January 19, 1923, 3; MPW, May 25, 323.
31. Davies, 28.
32. *Screenland,* March 1924, 17; MPW, November 10, 1923, 216.
33. NYT, April 29, 1923.
34. WRH-JW, [1923], BW.
35. WRH-JAM, February 13, 24, 1924, JAMp.
36. WRH-JAM, February 17, 23, 1924, JAMp; Thomas Schatz, *The Genius of the System* (New York: Pantheon, 1988), 30–32.

20. Another Last Hurrah

1. NYT, May 4, 1922, 5.
2. NYT, June 23, 1922, 1, 8; June 25, 1922, Section II, 1; ECL-WRH, June 2, 1922, JAMp.
3. NYT, May 23, 1922.
4. Fred Lawrence Guiles, *Marion Davies* (New York: McGraw-Hill, 1972), 107; WRH-JAM, June 2, 1922, JAMp; NYT, June 2, 1922, 17.
5. Guiles, 107–8; NYT, June 22, 1922, 19.
6. NYH, June 28, 1922.
7. NYH, June 26, 27, 28, July 7, 1922; NYDN, June 26, 27, 28, 1922.
8. NYT, June 22, 27, July 15, 1922.
9. NYT, July 8, 1922.
10. NYT, June 25, 1922.
11. NYT, July 8, 1922, 1.
12. NYT, September 28, 29, 1922; Al Smith, *Up to Now* (Garden City: Garden City Publishing Co., 1929), 195–96.
13. NYT, September 30, 1922.
14. NYT, November 7, 8, 1923, 1, 2.
15. NYT, June 26, 1924, 9.
16. AB-WJB, July 3, 1924, box 40, WJBp.
17. WRH-Publishers and Managing Editors, July 10, 1924, box 64, JFNp.
18. WRH-SC, August 7, 1925, JAMp.
19. NYA, September 3, 1925, 1.
20. WRH-JAM, September 18, 1925, JAMp.

21. "Do You Know Miss Marion Davies, the Movie Actress?"

1. Nat Ferber, *I Found Out* (New York: Dial, 1939), 219–20.
2. NYDN, July 23, 1924, 1; NYT, July 23, 1924, 17; NYEW, July 23, 1924, 6.

3. NYT, August 7, 1924, 1; NYDN, August 7, 8, 9, 10, 1924, 1; NYHT, August 7, 1924, 1; WP, August 7, 1924, 3.

4. Wells interview, September 23, 1959, WAS.

5. Alice Marble, oh-SS, 11; Fred Lawrence Guiles, *Marion Davies* (New York: McGraw-Hill, 1972), 137.

6. Guiles, 134–35; JU-MU, n.d., erroneously catalogued in 1919 folder, JUp.

7. Marion Davies, *The Times We Had* (Indianapolis: Bobbs-Merrill, 1975), 34; Charles Higham, *Merchant of Dreams: Louis B. Mayer, M.G.M., and the Secret Hollywood* (New York: Dell, 1993), 101–2; JU-MU, n.d., in Mary Urban box, 1919 folder, JUp.

8. Louella Parsons, *The Gay Illiterate* (Garden City: Doubleday, Doran, 1944), 89; Charles Chaplin, *My Autobiography* (New York: Simon and Schuster, 1964), 309.

9. Chaplin, 316.

10. JAM-WRH, July 5, 1924, JAMp.

11. Higham, 88; JU-MU, September 21, 1924 folder, JUp.

12. Vera Burnett, oh-SS, 4–5; Mary's diary, Mary Urban box, JUp; Davies, 30.

13. NYDN, November 9, 1924, 24; November 16, 1924, 22.

14. Notes from Gretl's autobiography, box 45; Mary's diary, Mary Urban box, JUp.

15. Notes from Gretl's autobiography, box 45, JUp.

16. NYT, November 21, 1924, 22; Notes from Gretl's autobiography, box 45, JUp.

17. NYDN, November 20, 1924, 3; December 11, 1924, 4; Davies, 66–68.

18. For the latest story, ostensibly given the author by "one of Hollywood's most senior and best-informed insiders," see Amy Fine Collins, "Idol Gossips," *Vanity Fair,* April 1997, 368.

19. WRH-JAM, January 28, 1925; March 1, 1925; JAM-WRH, March 18, 1925, JAMp; WRH-Hatrick, August 23, 1927, carton 4, WRHp.

20. Irene Mayer Selznick, *A Private View* (New York: Knopf, 1983), 84.

21. Bosley Crowther, *Hollywood Rajah* (New York: Holt, 1960), 126; Selznick, 84.

22. Davies, 37–40; [entries] May 29, June 8, June 9, July 7, Notes of Mr. Urban Secretary 1925, Folder marked notes. JUp.

23. Cari Beauchamp, *Without Lying Down* (New York: Scribner, 1997), 165–66.

24. LP, NYA, May 3, 1925.

25. NYT, May 23, 1925, 18.

26. Alice Head, *It Could Never Have Happened* (London: Heinemann, 1939), 79, 81.

27. Head, 86; AH-WRH, assorted telegrams cited in Clive Aslet, *The Last Country Houses* (New Haven: Yale U.P., 1982), 199; NYT, August 16, 1925, 1.

28. NYT, May 21, 1925, 3.

22. Family Man

1. William Randolph Hearst, Jr., with Jack Casserly, *The Hearsts: Father and Son* (Niwot, Col.: Roberts Rinehart, 1991), 239.

2. Charles Chaplin, *My Autobiography* (New York: Simon and Schuster, 1964), 313.

3. WRH, Jr., 239.

4. WRH, Jr., oh-SS, 49.

5. WRH, Jr., 183, 240.

6. WRH, Jr., 77.

7. WRH, Jr., 240; Cora Older, *William Randolph Hearst, American* (New York: Appleton-Century, 1936), 406–8.

8. Elsa Maxwell, *R.S.V.P.* (Boston: Little, Brown, 1954), 128–29.
9. WRH-JAM, April 16, 1926, JAMp; WRH-JM, October 18, 25, 1926, JM-WRH, December 28, 1926, JMp.
10. Chaplin, 313.
11. WRH-JAM, January 17, 1926; JAM-WRH, January 28, 1926, JAMp.
12. WRH-MH, July 16, 1926, box 1, WRH, Jr.91.
13. JW-CMG, September 9, 1926, BW; MH-WRH, February 24, 1927, carton 2, WRHp; Jones-WRH, February 24, 1927, carton 3, WRHp.
14. Hunter-Schrader, August 1, 1927, carton 4, WRHp.
15. WRH-MH, September 23, 1926, box 1, WRH, Jr.91.
16. WRH-MH, May 7, 1927, box 1, WRH, Jr.91.; WRH-JM, July 18, 1927, JMp.
17. WRH-MH, June 22, 1926; October 29, 1930, box 1, WRH, Jr.91.
18. JW-CM, November 30, 1928, BW; WRH, Jr., 64.
19. WRH-GH, September 16, 1927, in WRH, Jr., 92; WRH-WRH, Jr., October 2, 1927, box 1, WRH, Jr.91.
20. RH, oh-DN; WRH, Jr., 89–90.
21. WRH, Jr., 90–91.
22. WRH-MH, in Edmond D. Coblentz, ed., *William Randolph Hearst: A Portrait in His Own Words* (New York: Simon & Schuster, 1952), 78–79; Older, 501–2.
23. WRH, Jr., 90.
24. WRH, Jr., 91.
25. WRH-JAM, Nov. 2, 1923, JAMp.
26. WRH-JFN, May 9, 1924, box 65, JFNp; EP, October 23, 1926, 5.
27. WRH-GH, October 7, 1927, box 1, WRH, Jr.91.
28. WRH-WRH, Jr., July 24, 1927, box 1, WRH, Jr.91.
29. WRH-WRH, Jr., December 7, 14, 1933, box 1, WRH, Jr.91.
30. WRH-JM, February 28, 1927, carton 2, WRHp.
31. JH-WRH, September 13, 1927, in WRH, Jr., 94.
32. WRH-JH, September 20, 24, 1927, in WRH, Jr., 95; WRH-Edwards, September 26, 1927, carton 2, WRHp.
33. Sally Bedell Smith, *In All His Glory* (New York: Simon & Schuster, 1990), 96; *Time*, May 1, 1933, 19; WRH-JH, September 25, 1929, box 1, WRHp.
34. MH-WRH, February 21, 24, 1927, carton 1, WRHp; WRH-MH, October 29, 1930, box 1, WRH, Jr.91.

23. Dream Houses

1. Marion Davies, *The Times We Had* (Indianapolis: Bobbs-Merrill, 1975), 101.
2. Fred Lawrence Guiles, *Marion Davies* (New York: McGraw-Hill, 1972), 175–76.
3. Jesse Lasky, Jr., *Whatever Happened to Hollywood?* (New York: Funk & Wagnalls, 1975), 29–30.
4. Irene Mayer Selznick, *A Private View* (New York: Knopf, 1983), 85–86.
5. Davies, 101.
6. WRH-JM, June 15, 1926, JMp.
7. Anne Edwards, "Marion Davies' Ocean House," *Architectural Digest*, April 1994, 175, 277.
8. Louise Brooks, "Marion Davies' Niece," *Film Culture*, 1974, 249; David Niven, *Bring On the Empty Horses* (London: Hamish Hamilton, 1975), 241–42.
9. Memorandum: "International Magazine Company," December 1924, JAMp.

10. WRH-JFN, November 24, 1927, box 65, JFNp.
11. Robert B. King with Charles O. McLean, *The Vanderbilt Homes* (New York: Rizzoli, 1989), 164–67; Clarice Stasz, *The Vanderbilt Women: Dynasty of Wealth, Glamour, and Tragedy* (New York: St. Martin's, 1991), 234; NYT, August 7, October 30, 1927.
12. King, 167.
13. NYT, October 30, 1927; MH-WRH, October 5, 1927, box 7, WRH, Jr.91.
14. Emile Gauvreau, *My Last Million Readers* (New York: Dutton, 1941), 137–39.
15. Steilberg, 62, JM-oh.
16. Basic Training Manual Tour 1, February 16, 1997 revision, 13, HSSSHM.
17. WRH-JM, April 24, 1927, JMp.
18. WRH-JM, February 19, 1927, JMp.
19. WRH-Schrader, June 15, 1929, July 27, 1929, August 11, 1929, carton 9, WRHp.
20. Davies, 45.
21. WRH-JM, April 12, July 4, August 7, 14, 1926; C. C. Rossi-JM, February 7, 1927, JMp.
22. WRH-JM, October 2, 1927, JMp.
23. Davies, 143.
24. NYT, December 20, 1924, 27; JM-WRH, October 20, 1925, JMp.
25. WRH-I. S. Horne, April 23, 1927, carton 2, WRHp; NYT, July 21, 1927, 8; JM-WRH, July 27, 1927, JMp.
26. WRH-JM, October 18, 1927, JMp.
27. "Check list of animals," June 15, 1928, record group VI, Baldwin Collection, HSSSHM.
28. Davies, 144.
29. WRH-Slattery, June 13, 1929, carton 7, WRHp.
30. Vidor, oh-SS, 6; Frances Marion, oh-SS, 3.
31. St. Johns, oh-SS, 3.
32. Moore, oh-SS, 22.
33. St. Johns, *The Honeycomb* (Garden City: Doubleday, 1969), 123–31.
34. WRH-JM, June 2, 1926, JMp.
35. St. Johns, 129.
36. Alice Head, *It Could Never Have Happened* (London: Heinemann, 1939), 101.
37. Rotanzi, "The Ranch Dairy, Orchard, and Grounds," oh-SS.
38. Rotanzi, "Fifty-Four Years at San Simeon," oh-SS.
39. C. C. Rossi-JM, with WRH-Rossi letter attached, February 7, 1926, JMp; I have rearranged the quotation.
40. WRH-C. C. Rossi, February 16, 1927, JMp.
41. WRH-JM, February 21, 1927; JM-WRH, February 25, 1927, JMp.

24. Businesses as Usual

1. H. L. Mencken, *American Mercury,* May, 1927, 28–30.
2. Melvyn Leffler, "Political Isolationism, Economic Expansionism, or Diplomatic Realism: American Policy Toward Western Europe 1921–33," in *Perspectives in American History* VIII (1974), 419.
3. Richard Coke Lower, *A Bloc of One: The Political Career of Hiram W. Johnson* (Stanford: Stanford U.P., 1993), 191–93.

4. Wayne S. Cole, *Roosevelt & the Isolationists,* 1932–45 (Lincoln: University of Nebraska Press, 1983), 6–7.
5. WRH, NYA, February 12, 1922, in *Selections,* 193.
6. WRH-publishers, October, 1928, in *Selections,* 307–8.
7. WRH-editors, February 10, 1929, in *Selections,* 316–17; WRH-PP, September 16, 1926, carton 2, WRHp.
8. Philip V. Cannistraro and Brian R. Sullivan, *Il Duce's Other Woman* (New York: Morrow, 1993), 360.
9. PP-WRH, n.d.; WRH-PP, Feb. 24, 1927, carton 3, WRHp; WRH-Ettelson, January 19, 1927, carton 2, WRHp.
10. MH-WRH, August 19, 1927, carton 4, WRHp.
11. WRH-EDC, copy to PP, September 2, 1927, in NYA, September 8, 1927, 1; WRH-Shiber, September 3, 1927, carton 4, WRHp.
12. WRH-Obregón, October 4, 1924; Obregón-WRH, November 1, 1924, file 802-H-34, Obregón-Calles, Presidentes.
13. U.S. Congress. Senate. Special Committee to Investigate Propaganda Or Money Alleged To Have Been Used By Foreign Governments To Influence United States Senators, *Alleged Payments by the Mexican Government to United States Senators: Hearings,* 70th Cong., 1st sess., testimony by Hearst, Coblentz, Clark, Avila, and Page, December 15, 16, 17, 1927, Part One; December 27, 1927 and January 4 and 7, 1928, Part Three.
14. SAL, November 14, 1927, 1.
15. BA, November 15-December 9, 1927.
16. NYHT, December 16, 1927.
17. NYT, December 20, 1927.
18. NYA, December 20, 1927.
19. U.S. Congress. Senate. Special Committee, *Alleged Payments,* Part Three, 219–220; NYA, NYT, NYDT, January 12, 1928.
20. NYHT, January 12, 1928.
21. Field report from Headquarters 8th Corps Area, Fort Sam Houston, Texas, March 10, 1928, item 2064–521–1, record group 165, MID.
22. WRH-C. S. Stanton, July 7, 1929, carton 9, WRHp.
23. WRH-EDC, December 2, 1929, incoming box 3, EDCp.
24. Silas Bent, "What Explains Hearst," *Outlook,* January 1928, 86.
25. Ayer and Sons, *American Newspaper Annual & Directory,* 1925, 1928.
26. WRH-AB, January 18, 29, April 12, 13, 14, 1928, box 6, ABp.
27. A. J. Liebling, *The Press* (New York: Pantheon, 1975), 450. These articles appeared in March 1933.
28. WRH-TVR, May 6, 1928, box 4, TVRp.
29. NYA, "March of Events" section, September 23, 1928; September 1, 15, 1929.
30. Dan H. Laurence, *Bernard Shaw: A Bibliography,* vol. II (Oxford: Clarendon Press, 1983).
31. GBS-WRH, March 11, 1927, carton 4, WRHp.
32. WRH-GBS, March 17, 1927, carton 4, WRHp.
33. GBS-WRH, March 28, 1927, carton 4, WRHp.
34. WRH-GBS, March 30, 1927, carton 4, WRHp.
35. WRH-AB, January 20, 1925, box 6, ABp.
36. WRH-W. E. Miller, June 2, 1926, carton 1, WRHp.
37. WRH-Young, November 23, 1926, carton 1, WRHp.

38. WRH-SC and Executive Council, September 27, 1927, carton 3, WRHp.
39. WRH-all Hearst evening newspapers, September 30, 1927, carton 4, WRHp.
40. LAE, September 14, 1928.
41. JW-publishers, January 17, 1930, carton 10a, WRHp.
42. Town-WRH, June 13, 1929; WRH-Town, June 16, 1929, carton 9, WRHp; Circulation figures from Ayer and Sons, *American Newspapers Annual and Directory,* 1920, 1928.
43. WRH-Long, August 23, 1929, carton 9, WRHp.
44. WRH-Long, August 24, 1929, carton 9, WRHp.
45. IT-WRH, June 24, 1926, carton 4, WRHp.
46. Gloria Swanson, *Swanson on Swanson* (New York: Random House, 1980), 182; WRH-Mayer, July 14, 1927, carton 3, WRHp.
47. IT-WRH, July 15, 1927, carton 4, WRHp.
48. LBM-WRH, September 28, 1927; WRH-LBM, September 28, 1927, carton 3, WRHp.
49. WRH-Koenigsberg, February 9, 1927; WRH-Publishers, September 19, 1927, carton 4, WRHp.
50. EH-WRH, July 19, 1927; WRH-EH, December 30, 1927, carton 2, WRHp.
51. EH-WRH, June 27, 1927; WRH-EH, August 23, 1927, carton 2, WRHp.
52. WRH-EH, July 23, 1927, September 19, 1927, carton 2, WRHp.
53. WRH-EH, October 17, 1927, carton 4, WRHp.
54. Mannix; King Vidor, *A Tree Is a Tree: An Autobiography* (Hollywood: Samuel French, 1953), 159.
55. Vidor, 159; Charles Higham, *Merchant of Dreams* (New York: Dell, 1993), 125–26.
56. Fred Lawrence Guiles, *Marion Davies* (New York: McGraw-Hill, 1972), 108–9.
57. Boardman, oh-SS, 3–4.
58. Vidor, 165–71.
59. Mannix.

25. A New Crusade: Europe

1. WRH-MH, September 13, 1926, box 1, WRH, Jr.91.
2. Ronald Brownstein, *The Power and the Glitter* (New York: Vintage, 1992), 31; WRH-EDC, August 12, 1927, carton 5, WRHp.
3. John Winkler, *William Randolph Hearst: A New Appraisal* (New York: Avon, 1955), 262.
4. WRH-AB, June 29, July 4, 1928, box 6, ABp.
5. WRH-FK, July 13, 1928, carton 6, WRHp.
6. WRH-publishers, July 10, 1928, box 6, ABp; NYT, October 6, 1928, 2.
7. NYT, July 21, 1928, 29; JW-CMG, July 19, 1928, BW.
8. Fred Lawrence Guiles, *Marion Davies* (New York: McGraw-Hill, 1972), 214.
9. Alice Head, *It Could Never Have Happened* (London: Heinemann, 1939), 114; Marion Davies, *The Times We Had* (Indianapolis: Bobbs-Merrill, 1975), 115.
10. Davies, 116.
11. Davies, 118, 116.
12. Head 117–18; I have slightly changed Head's punctuation.
13. Davies, 118.
14. Arnold Wolfers, *Britain and France Between Two Wars* (New York: Norton, 1966), 76–84; G. M. Gathorne-Hardy, *A Short History of International Affairs: 1920–1939* (London: Oxford U.P., 1942), 173–76.

15. Head, 87.
16. Head, 118–24; Clive Aslet, *The Last Country Houses* (New Haven: Yale U.P., 1982), 207–10. I thank John Horn, the historian at the Hearst San Simeon State Historical Monument, for the information on the final disposition of the Bradenstoke Priory.
17. NYT, October 6, 1928.
18. AB-WRH, September 13, 1929, carton 10, WRHp.
19. WRH-publishers, December 29, 1929, in *Selections*, 197–98.
20. WRH-John A. Kennedy, January 28, 1930, carton 11, WRHp.
21. Joan Hoff Wilson, *Herbert Hoover: Forgotten Progressive* (Boston: Little, Brown, 1975), 195–96; Diary of Henry Stimson, December 11, 1930, 214–15, Stimson.
22. Head, 139–44; Cora Older, *William Randolph Hearst, American* (New York: Appleton-Century, 1936), 505–6.
23. Edmond D. Coblentz, *William Randolph Hearst, A Portrait in His Own Words* (New York: Simon & Schuster, 1952), 96.
24. Davies, 121–22; WRH, September 2, 1930, in *Selections*, 264.
25. Coblentz, 99; NYT, September 16, 1930, 29.
26. LAE, October 10, 1930; NYT, September 29, 23; October 6, 32; October 10, 4; October 17, 9; October 23, 1930, 11.
27. WRH, September 29, 1930, in *Selections*, 273.
28. Diary of Henry Stimson, October 4, 1930, 51–52, Stimson.
29. Older, 514; NYT, December 1, 1930, 6.

26. The Talkies and Marion

1. Marion Davies, *The Times We Had* (Indianapolis: Bobbs-Merrill, 1975), 72.
2. St. Johns, oh-SS, 3–4.
3. Davies, 74.
4. WRH-FZ, February 12, March 4, November 10, 13, 1928; MH-FZ, March 30, 1928; FZ-WRH, November 13, December 22, 1928, BW.
5. Ilka Chase, *Past Imperfect* (Garden City: Doubleday, Doran, 1942), 120; V, January 16, 1929, 4; January 17, 1929, 5; "The Marion Davies Fan Club, Family Chapter Newsletter," April 30, 1997; Richard Barrios, *A Song in the Dark: The Birth of the Musical Film* (New York: Oxford U.P., 1995), 225.
6. WRH-IT, July 24, 1929, August 13, 1929, carton 7, WRHp; Mannix.
7. WRH-IT, October 6, 9, 1929; IT-WRH, October 8, 1929, carton 7, WRHp.
8. *King Vidor,* interviewed by Nancy Dowd and David Shepard (Metuchen, N.J.: Scarecrow Press, 1988), 110; WRH-IT, IT-WRH, October 14, 1929, carton 7, WRHp; Mannix.
9. Chase, 120.
10. Fred Lawrence Guiles, *Marion Davies* (New York: McGraw-Hill, 1972), 135.
11. [MD]-WRH, May 31, 1929, carton 9, WRHp.
12. Boardman, oh-SS, 4.
13. Moore, oh-SS, 24. I have reversed the order of the sentences.
14. St. Johns, oh-SS, 16.
15. Guiles, 174–75, 232–35; Martha Sherrill, "San Simeon's Child," *Vanity Fair* 58, April 1995, 304–13, 319–21, 326–27.
16. V, May 8, 1929, 5; May 15, 1929, 5; contracts, in Cosmopolitan Studios legal file, WB; WRH-EH, June 12, 1929, carton 6, WRHp.

17. WRH-EH, June 2, 4, 1929, carton 6, WRHp.
18. WEH-EH, June 2, 4, 1929, carton 6, WRHp.
19. LAE, September 22, October 2, 1929.
20. WRH-EH, October 9, 1929, carton 13, WRHp; LAE, October 28, 1929.
21. WRH-AB, March 16, 1929, carton 8, WRHp.
22. WRH-IT, July 22, 24, 1929, carton 7, WRHp; Samuel Marx, *Mayer and Thalberg* (New York: Random House, 1975), 123.
23. Davies, 77; Guiles, 255.
24. WRH-ASO, January, 1929; ASO-WRH, February 18, 1929, ASOp.
25. Duncan Aikman, "A Renaissance Palace in Our West," NYT, July 21, 1929, Section V, 10–11.
26. "Hearst at Home," *Fortune*, May 1931, 130.
27. Randolph Churchill, *Twenty-One Years* (Boston: Houghton Mifflin, 1965), 86–87.
28. William Manchester, *The Last Lion* (Boston: Little, Brown, 1983), 826.
29. John Spencer Churchill, *A Churchill Canvas* (Boston: Little, Brown, 1961), 89–91.
30. Winston Churchill–Clementine Churchill, September 29, 1929, in *Winston and Clementine: The Personal Letters of the Churchills,* ed. Mary Soames (Boston: Houghton Mifflin, 1998), 346.
31. NYT, October 19, 1929, 12; MH-WRH, October 19, 1929, box 7, WRH, Jr. 91.

27. "Pretty Much Flattened Out"

1. WRH-AB, April 10, 1929, carton 10, WRHp.
2. NYA, November 15, 1929; WRH-Young, November 14, 1929, carton 10, WRHp.
3. "Hearst," *Fortune*, October, 1935, 51–52; "Real estate Folder," carton 49, WRHp. NYT, June 10, 1929, 27; July 10, 1929, 49; July 24, 1929, 45; November 8, 1929, 46; December 9, 1929, Section XIII, 1.
4. WRH-AH, November 15, 1929, carton 9, WRHp.
5. WRH-JM, February 26, March 1, 1930 JMp; WRH-EH, February 7, 1930, carton 11, WRHp; NYT, June 19, 1931, 47; WRH-Jypeakelm, March 2, 1930, carton 11, WRHp.
6. Judith Robinson, *The Hearsts* (New York: Avon, 1992), 381.
7. On Wyntoon, see Sara Holmes Boutelle, *Julia Morgan, Architect* (New York: Abbeville, 1988), 216–32; Sally Woodbridge, "Historic Architecture: Wyntoon," *Architectural Digest,* January, 1988, 98–103, 156; *Fortune*, 43–54.
8. Frank Luther Mott, *American Journalism,* third edition (New York: Macmillan, 1962), 675.
9. WRH-Eleanor Patterson, March 20, July 7, 1931, box 1, EMPp; Ralph Martin, *Cissy* (New York: Simon & Schuster, 1979), 266, 297, 330.
10. E. J. Kahn, Jr., *The World of Swope* (New York: Simon & Schuster, 1965), 343–49.
11. WRH-EDC, February 26, 1931, incoming box 3, EDCp.
12. WRH-EDC, March 1, 1933, incoming box 4, EDCp.
13. Alva Johnson, "Twilight of the Ink-stained Gods," *Vanity Fair,* February, 1932, 36, 70.
14. WRH-EDC, March 10, 1931, incoming box 3, EDCp.
15. "Introduction," *Aldous Huxley's Hearst Essays,* ed. James Sexton (New York: Garland, 1994), xxii–xxiii.
16. NYA, September 9, 12, 1931.
17. A. J. Liebling, "The Man Who Changed the Rules," *New Yorker,* September 8,

1951, in *The Press* (New York: Pantheon, 1981), 492; A. J. Liebling, *Chicago: The Second City,* in *Liebling at Home* (n.p.: Wideview Books, 1982), 185; WRH-editors and publishers, January 30, 1930, in *Selections,* 335.

18. John Winkler, *William Randolph Hearst: A New Appraisal* (New York: Avon, 1955), 96; Mott, 582; Liebling, "The Man," 449–50.

19. WRH-Gough, April 22, 1930, carton 11, WRHp.

20. NYA, July 12, October 17, 1931; *Fortune,* 126; LAE, February 5, 1932.

21. *Fortune,* 128.

22. NYA, July 12, 1931, 10; Ferdinand Lundberg, *Imperial Hearst* (New York: Modern Library, 1936), 320.

23. WRH, January 4, 1925, in *Selections,* 466–69; JW-CMG, February 15, 1927, BW.

24. WRH, January 16, 1930, in *Selections,* 480–82.

25. Edward Robb Ellis, *A Nation in Torment* (New York: Putnam's, 1971), 129–30.

26. Studs Terkel, *Hard Times* (New York: Pantheon, 1986), 2.

27. NYA, June 3, 1931.

28. NYA, June 6, 1931.

29. NYA, July 14, 1931.

30. WRH EDC, October 9, 1931, incoming box 3, EDCp; WRH, NYA, October 28, 1931.

28. "An Incorrigible Optimist"

1. JFN interview, WAS; JW-all papers, December 23, 1931, incoming box 3, EDCp.

2. WRH-JM, April 26, 1932, JMp.

3. Kenneth Anger, *Hollywood Babylon* (New York: Dell, 1975), 140.

4. Apperson, oh-SS; Dragon, oh-SS, 43–4.

5. Marion, oh-SS, 3.

6. Vidor, oh-SS, 21.

7. LP, NYA, January 3, 1932.

8. David Niven, *Bring On the Empty Horses* (London: Hamish Hamilton, 1975), 283–84; Ouida Rathbone, "Happy Birthday, W. R.," *Esquire,* December 1972, 165–77.

9. WRH, Jr., oh-SS, 20.

10. Moore, oh-SS, 23.

11. Moore, oh-SS, 9.

12. Kastner, oh-DN.

13. McCrea, oh-SS, 47.

14. Apperson, oh-SS; William J. Mann, *Wisecracker* (New York: Viking, 1998), 131.

15. Ilka Chase, *Past Imperfect* (Garden City: Doubleday, Doran, 1942), 119.

16. Vidor, oh-SS, 16; Boardman, oh-SS, 4–5.

17. Fairbanks, Jr., oh-SS, 4.

18. St. Johns, oh-SS, 10.

19. Rukeyser, oh-SS, 8.

20. Swinnerton, oh-SS, 59.

21. St. Johns, oh-SS, 12–13.

22. David King Dunaway, *Huxley in Hollywood* (New York: Harper & Row, 1989), 81.

23. St. Johns, oh-SS, 12.

24. Joan Drake, "San Simeon Suppers," *Los Angeles Times,* July 29, 1998; JW-Layne, December 20, 1939, Record group IB, HSSSHM.

25. Drake; St. Johns, oh-SS, 10.
26. Marble, oh-SS, 8.
27. Niven, 276–77.
28. St. Johns, oh-SS, 6.
29. WRH, Jr., oh-SS, 22.
30. Anita Loos, *Kiss Hollywood Good-by* (New York: Viking, 1974), 139.
31. Niven, 282.
32. St. Johns, oh-SS, 5.
33. WRH, October 14, 1927, in *Selections*, 471; WRH-Will Hays, February 20, 1929, carton 6, WRHp; WRH, June 3, 1933, in *Selections*, 487; NYA, July 22, 1934.
34. Colin Shindler, *Hollywood in Crisis* (New York: Routledge, 1996), 25–26; V, November 10, 1931, 1, 6; November 17, 1931, 4, 6; WRH-Jack Warner, November 6, 1931, carton 12, WRHp.
35. Moore, oh-SS, 22.
36. McCrea, oh-SS, 18–21.
37. Wahlberg, oh-SS, 42; JW-W. Woolard, February 4, 1940, carton 31, WRHp.
38. Shindler, 21–22; Molly Haskell, *From Reverence to Rape* (New York: Holt, Rinehart, and Winston, 1974), 91.
39. WRH-IT, March 9, 1931, carton 11, WRHp.
40. Marion Davies, *The Times We Had* (Indianapolis: Bobbs-Merrill, 1975), 91.
41. Mannix.
42. WRH-LBM, April 22, 1932, carton 14, WRHp.
43. Cari Beauchamp, *Without Lying Down* (New York: Scribner, 1997), 280–81, 187; WRH-Vidor, January 23, 1932, box 1, BH.
44. Beauchamp, 287–90; Loos, 134–35; Richard Barrios, *A Song in the Dark* (New York: Oxford U.P., 1995), 362; Mannix.
45. Bing Crosby, *Call Me Lucky* (New York: Simon & Schuster, 1953), 118–21; Davies, 86.
46. Mannix.
47. LP, LAE, November 1, 1934; Douglas W. Churchill, "Out of the Golden West," NYT, November 4, 1934, section IX, 5.
48. Excerpt of Cosmopolitan Corporation Contract, December 3, 1934, Cosmopolitan Pictures Legal File, box WB1, WB; JW-G. G. Young, November 2, 1934, carton 19, WRHp.

29. The Chief Chooses a President

1. WRH-EDC, January 21, 1931, incoming box 3, EDCp.
2. NYA, January 3, 1932.
3. WRH-EDC, Jan 5, [1932], incoming box 3, EDC; EDC-WRH, January 5, 1932, outgoing box 1, EDCp; WRH, NYA, January 8, 10, 17, 1932.
4. WRH-all publishers, transcript of phone message, January 23, 1932, carton 15, WRHp; WRH-various editors, January, 1932, box 1, BH.
5. Howe-FDR, January 30, 1932, PPF 2095, FDRp.
6. NYT, February 3, 1932; Cordell Hull, *The Memoirs of Cordell Hull,* vol. I (New York: Macmillan, 1948), 150.
7. WRH-Homer Guck, February 21, 1932, box 1, BH.
8. WRH-KVW, February 28, 1932, box 1, BH.
9. WRH-F.J. McCarthy, March 21, 1932, box 2, BH.

10. JPK-Godsol, June 17, 1921; JPK-Grenville MacFarland, June 18, 1921; WRH-JPK, April 19, 1932, JPKp.
11. Arthur Krock, oh-CU; WRH-MH, July 3, 1932, box 12, WRHp.
12. WRH-W. A. Curley, November 21, 1942, carton 38, WRHp; MH-WRH, July 2, 1932, box 7, WRH, Jr.91.
13. WRH-MH, July 3, 1932, carton 12, WRHp.
14. WRH-EDC, July [2]9, 1932, incoming box 3, EDCp.
15. Stimson diaries XXIII, July 27, 1932, 2, Stimson.
16. AB-FDR, September 5, 1932, PPF 1405, FDRp; Jane Collings, "Streamlining the National Body: Newsreel Spectatorship in the New Era" (Ph.D. diss., UCLA, 1995), 192.
17. JW-JPK, October 14, 1932, carton 13, WRHp.
18. JFN-WRH, November 8, 1932, box 65, JFNp; MH-WRH, November 9, 1932, box 7, WRH, Jr.91.
19. JW-JFN, November 19, 1932, box 65, JFNp.
20. WRH-JPK, November 14, 1932, JPKp.
21. WRH-JPK, November 24, 30, December 22, 1932, JPK-WRH, December 23, 1932, JPKp.
22. WRH-JPK, November 24, 30, December 28, 1932, JPKp.
23. Edmond D. Coblentz, ed., *William Randolph Hearst: A Portrait in His Own Words* (New York: Simon & Schuster, 1952), 143–45.
24. Dana Frank, *Buy American* (Boston: Beacon Press, 1999), 59.
25. I thank Dana Frank for sharing information about this newsreel with me.
26. EDC-WRH, January 11, 1933, carton 17, WRHp.
27. WRH-EDC, January 20, 1933, carton 17, WRHp; WRH-FDR, February 7, 1933, PPF62, FDRp.
28. Neylan interview, WAS.
29. TJW-JPN, January 21, 1933, carton 17, WRHp.
30. TJW-WRH, January 27, 1933, carton 16, WRHp.
31. JFN-WRH, March 23, 1933, carton 17, WRHp.
32. Wingate-Hays, January 23, 1933, GOWH file, MPAA.
33. Wingate-Hays, January 30, 1933; Wingate-IT, February 8, 1933, GOWH file, MPAA.
34. Wingate-Hays, February 11, 1933, GOWH file, MPAA.
35. Hays-Early, no date but marked at top, Ack[nowledg]ed 3/11," OF 73, FDRp.
36. Schenck-Hays, March 11, 1933, OF 73, FDRp.
37. WRH-LBM, March 25, 1933, carton 17, WRHp.
38. FDR-WRH, April 1, 1933, PPF 62, FDRp.
39. MPH, April 8, 1933; Walter Lippmann, "Politics Over Hollywood," NYHT, April 4, 1933, 15.
40. Mannix.

30. Hearst at Seventy

1. "Hearst at Home," *Fortune*, May, 1931, 56–57; *Time*, May 1, 1933, 19, 20, 22.
2. WRH-FDR, March 6, 1933, FDR-WRH, March 9, 1933, PPF 62, FDRp.
3. NYA, March 19, 1933.
4. SFE, April 12, 1933.
5. MH-WRH, March 29, 1930, box 10a, WRHp.

6. MH, "Millicent Hearst Describes Her Chat with Mussolini," NYA, May 11, 1930.
7. Philip Cannistraro and Brian Sullivan, *Il Duce's Other Woman* (New York: Morrow, 1993), 361.
8. Cannistraro and Sullivan, 364–65; NYA, March 27, September 11, 1932.
9. WRH-TVR, December 16, 1932; TVR-WRH, December 17, 1932, box 4, TVRp; Cannistraro and Sullivan, 367–68.
10. WRH-TVR, February 19, 20, 1933; TVR-WRH, February 23, 1933, box 5, TVRp.
11. TVR-WRH, October 9, 1933, box 5, TVRp.
12. WRH-TVR, October 21, 1933, box 5, TVRp.
13. WRH-TVR, May 21, 1936, carton 20, WRHp; Cannistraro and Sullivan, 492–93.
14. TJR-WRH, September 25, 1930, box 4, TVRp; Ian Kershaw, *Hitler, 1889–1936: Hubris* (New York: Norton, 1999), 338.
15. TVR-WRH, December 13, 1931; WRH-TVR, December 14, 15, 1931, box 4, TVRp.
16. TVR-WRH, December 30, 1931, box 4, TVRp.
17. TVR-WRH, January 28, 1932, February 19, 1932; WRH-TVR, January 29, 1932, February 14, 1932, box 4, TVRp.
18. Laemmle-WRH, January 18, 1932, carton 13, WRHp.
19. Kershaw, 288.
20. TVR-WRH, September 10, 1932, box 4, TVRp.
21. Kershaw, 186.
22. WRH-TVR, June 17, 1933, BW.
23. WRH-TVR, June 19, 1933, BH.
24. WRH-TVR, June 19, 1933, BW.
25. WRH-EDC, n.d., incoming box 4, EDCp.
26. Edmond D. Coblentz, ed., *William Randolph Hearst: A Portrait in His Own Words* (New York: Simon & Schuster, 1952), 159–60; EP, August 12, 1933, 1; HM Bitner-editors, August 16, 1933; JW-publishers, August 16, 1933, BW.
27. WRH-EC, September 9, 1933, BW.
28. WRH, NYA, October 31, 1933.
29. AB-FDR, December 2, 1933, PPF 1405, FDRp.
30. JW-James T. William, Jr., March 17, 1934, OF 846, FDRp.
31. WRH, NYA, February 2, 1934, 1; Benito Mussolini, NYA, March 11, 1934.
32. Warren L. Bassett, "President's Remarks Draw Press Fire," EP, February 24, 1934, 5.
33. Arthur M. Schlesinger, Jr., *Coming of the New Deal* (Boston: Houghton Mifflin, 1958), 137.
34. WRH-TVR, December 19, 1933, box 5, TVRp.
35. WRH-J. V. Connolly, December 23, 1933, BW; see also correspondence in December between WRH and TVR, box 5, TVRp.
36. WRH-George Young, n.d. [summer, 1933], BH.
37. NYA, November 22, 1933.
38. NYA, May 11, October 31, 1933.
39. Confirmation of telephone message, WRH-T. J. White, April 4, 1934, carton 19, WRHp.
40. Rodney Carlisle, *Hearst and the New Deal* (New York: Garland, 1979), 113, 118; Daniel Leab, *A Union of Individuals* (New York: Columbia U.P., 1970), 124–25.
41. Leab, 132.
42. Carlisle, 121.
43. Richard Powers, *Not Without Honor* (New York: Free Press, 1995), 81–91.

44. Ralph Easley-TVR, March 2, 1934, box 39, NCF.
45. Ralph Easley-Milton Hershey, March 16, 1934, box 39, NCF.
46. WRH-TVR, March 24, 1934, box 5, TVRp; Easley-Gifford, March 6, 1934, box 39, NCF.
47. LAE, April 21, 1934; JW-EDC, May 7, 1934, carton 18, WRHp.
48. WRH-FDR, n.d., PPF 62, FDRp.
49. Stimson diaries XXVIII, May 18, 1934, 38, Stimson.
50. NYT, May 27, 1934, 3.

31. Hearst and Hitler

1. NYT, May 27, 1934, 3.
2. Deborah Lipstadt, *Beyond Belief: The American Press and the Coming of the Holocaust 1933–45* (New York: Free Press, 1986), 20–21, 43–44.
3. WRH-JVC, August 15, 1933, BW.
4. LAE, October 17, 1933.
5. TVR-WRH, December 19, 1933, box 5, TVRp.
6. William Shirer, *20th Century Journey* (Boston: Little, Brown, 1984), 193.
7. JW-KVW, May 16, 19, 1934, carton 18, WRHp; NYT, June 11, 1934, 13; William Randolph Hearst, Jr., with Jack Casserly, *The Hearsts: Father and Son* (Niwot, Col.: Roberts Rinehart, 1991), 53–54; Fred Lawrence Guiles, *Marion Davies* (New York: McGraw-Hill, 1972), 173–75.
8. Ian Kershaw, *Hitler, 1889–1936: Hubris* (New York: Norton, 1999), 519.
9. WRH-EDC, July 2, 1934, incoming box 4, EDCp; LAE, July 4, 1934.
10. LAE, August 29, 1934.
11. Michael Denning, *The Cultural Front* (New York: Verson, 1996), xiii.
12. Kevin Starr, *Endangered Dreams* (New York: Oxford U.P., 1996), 115–16.
13. WRH-JFN, July 20, 1934, box 65, JFNp.
14. WRH-EDC, September 13, 1934, incoming box 4, EDCp.
15. WRH, NYA, July 23, 1934, 1.
16. WRH, NYA, September 24, 1934, 1; WRH-JM, n.d., box 2, JMp.
17. Kershaw, 519–20.
18. *Völkischer Beobachter,* August 23, 1934, trans. by S. Naftzger; WRH-EDC, August 24, 1934, incoming box 4, EDCp.
19. NYT, August 23, 1934; Hillman-TJW, August 25, 1934, EDCp.
20. *Völkischer Beobachter,* Munich edition, September 15, 1934, trans. by S. Naftzger; NYA, September 17, 1934, 1–2.
21. Marion Davies, *The Times We Had* (Indianapolis: Bobbs-Merrill, 1975), 147–49.
22. Saul Friedländer, *Nazi Germany and the Jews,* vol. I (New York: Harper Collins, 1997), 102–12.
23. Edmond D. Coblentz, ed., *William Randolph Hearst: A Portrait in His Own Words* (New York: Simon & Schuster, 1952), 103–5.
24. NYA, NYHT, September 17, 1934; WRH, NYA, September 25, 28, 1934.
25. Friedländer, 26–33, 69; Davies, 149.
26. Coblentz, 106.
27. WRH-KVW, November 20, 1934, carton 18, WRHp.
28. WRH-William Hillman, December 4, 1934, box 6, BH.
29. Dodd-FDR, March 20, 1935, PSF Dodd, FDRp. I thank Blanche Wiesen Cook for bringing this letter to my attention.

32. The Last Crusade

1. NYA, August 15, 1934.
2. NYT, September 2, 1934, 1–2.
3. Morgenthau Diaries, September 11, 1934, Morgenthau.
4. Keehn-FDR, September 24, 1934; Hand-Astor, October 4, 1934, PPF62, FDRp.
5. Early-WRH, October 6, 1934, OF846, FDRp.
6. WRH, NYA, October 9, 1934.
7. Greg Mitchell, *The Campaign of the Century* (New York: Random House, 1992), 32, 402; JW-George Young, November 1, 1934, box 5, BH.
8. WRH-AB, November 7, 1934, carton 18, WRHp.
9. WRH-FDR, November 8, 1934, OF 846, FDRp.
10. WRH-George Young, November 5, 1934, box 5, BH.
11. George Young-JW, November 30, 1934, carton 19, WRHp.
12. WRH-publishers, November 2, 1934, box 6, BH.
13. WRH-managing editors, November 16, 1934, carton 19, WRHp.
14. SJ, November 22, 24, 1934; *Nation,* April 24, 1935, 480–81.
15. *Social Frontier,* February, 1935, 28–31.
16. Frederick L. Schuman, letter to editor, *Nation,* April 24, 1935, 481.
17. Harry S. Ashmore, *Unseasonable Truths: The Life of Robert Maynard Hutchins* (Boston: Little, Brown, 1989), 128–32.
18. WRH, NYA, December 9, 1934, in *Selections,* 110–11; WRH, NYA, January 5, 1935, in *Selections,* 112–20.
19. WRH-EDC and TJW, April 2, 1935, incoming box 4, EDCp.
20. Ann Weedon, "Hearst Counterfeit American" (New York: American League Against War and Fascism, 1936), 22.
21. William F. Dunne, "An Open Letter to William Randolph Hearst" [1935]; James Casey, "Hearst: Labor's Enemy No. 1" (New York: Workers Library Publishers, Inc., 1935); Robert Cohen, *When the Old Left Was Young* (New York: Oxford U.P., 1993), 130, 374 n118.
22. NYT, February 25, 1935, 18; February 26, 1935, 8.
23. EDC-WRH, March 14, 1935, outgoing box 1, EDCp.
24. *Nation,* January 15, 1936; *Newsweek,* May 18, 1935, 22; *Time,* November 23, 1936.
25. Rodney Carlisle, *Hearst and the New Deal* (New York: Garland, 1979), 118, 126–29.
26. JFN-WRH, September 9, 1935, box 66, JFNp.
27. *Fortune,* October, 1935.
28. Paul Cressy, "A Social Setting for the Motion Picture" [c. 1932], in *Children and the Movies,* ed. Garth S. Jowett, et al. (New York: Cambridge U.P., 1996), 180–81.
29. Upton Sinclair, *I, Candidate for Governor, and How I Got Licked* [c. 1934] (Berkeley: University of California Press, 1994), 4–5.
30. Joel Faith, "Louella Parsons: Hearst's Hollywood Stooge," *New Theatre,* August, 1935, 8; "Keeping Tabs on Hearst," *New Republic,* May 27, 1936, 41; *Newsweek,* December 5, 1936.
31. Casey, 3, 5, 15.
32. William Randorf, "Heil Hearst," *New Masses,* April 9, 1935, 9; Virginia Spencer Carr, *Dos Passos: A Life* (New York: Doubleday, 1984), 346; John Dos Passos, *U.S.A.* (New York: Library of America, 1996), 1169.
33. "Received from San Simeon," March, 1935, box 5, TVRp.
34. Peoples Committee Against Hearst of the American League Against War and

Fascism, NYC Division, "Capone, Karpis, Luciano . . . Convicted! How much longer will this vilest racketeer of all get away with it?" (New York: American League against War and Fascism, 1936); Oliver Carlson and Ernest Sutherland Bates, *Hearst: Lord of San Simeon* (New York: Viking, 1936), 249; Ferdinand Lundberg, *Imperial Hearst* (New York: Modern Library, 1937), 352–53.

35. Lundberg, 352; *Saturday Evening Post,* August 27, 1938, 66; Connolly-CS, January 28, 1941, BW; John Winkler, *William Randolph Hearst: A New Appraisal* (New York: Avon, 1955), 323–24.

36. WRH-EDC, April 9, 1935, incoming box 4, EDCp.

37. Harold Ickes, *The Secret Diary of Harold L. Ickes* (New York: Simon & Schuster, 1953), 354–55.

38. EDC-WRH, May 9, 1935, outgoing box 1, EDCp; WRH-EDC, May 15, 1935, incoming box 4, EDCp; Edmond D. Coblentz, ed., *William Randolph Hearst: A Portrait in His Own Words* (New York: Simon & Schuster, 1952), 175–78.

39. Kenneth Davis, *FDR: The New Deal Years* (New York: Random House, 1986), 544; Ickes, 383–84.

40. Coblentz, 179–80.

41. JW-TJW, November 13, 1935, box 2, WRH, Jr.91.

42. NYT, October 23, 1935, 1, 4; *Time,* November 4, 1935, 21.

43. FDR-Hutchins, July 1, 1935, PPF 1834, FDRp.

44. Summary of George Allen letter, August 1, 1935, OF 846, FDRp.

45. Statement, August 15, 1935, PPF 62, FDRp; Moley-Early, August 14, 1935, with attachment, box 7, Early.

46. Ickes, 428.

47. NYT, August 29, 30, 1935.

48. Donald R. McCoy, *Landon of Kansas* (Lincoln: University of Nebraska Press, 1966), 230–32; NYT, December 10, 1935, 6.

49. WRH-publishers and editors, February 7, 1936, carton 20, WRHp.

50. *Newsweek,* May 16, 1936, 13.

51. Sally Bedell Smith, *In All His Glory: The Life of William S. Paley* (New York: Simon & Schuster, 1990), 168.

52. Emile Gauvreau, *My Last Million Readers* (New York: Dutton, 1941), 242, 252.

53. TVR-WRH, May 11, 1935, box 5; July 1, 9, 1935, box 6, TVRp; JW-TVR, May 21, 1935, box 5, TVRp; Michael Denning, *The Cultural Front* (New York: Verso, 1996), 299.

54. TJW-WRH, January 3, 1936, carton 20, WRHp.

55. WRH-TJW, January 11, 1936, carton 20, WRHp.

56. WRH-TVR, January 24, 1936; TVR-WRH, January 24, 25, 1936, box 6, TVRp.

57. EDC-WRH, February 21, 1936, outgoing box 1, EDCp.

58. WRH-EDC, April 29, 1936, incoming box 4, EDCp.

59. On strike, see Daniel Leab, *A Union of Individuals* (New York: Columbia U.P., 1970), 248–90; Rodney Carlisle, *Hearst and the New Deal* (New York: Garland, 1979), 132–33.

60. Leab, 256.

61. Heywood Broun, *Nation,* May 6, 1936, 584.

62. *Time,* August 31, 1936, 25.

63. *Newsweek,* March 28, 1936, 11; April 11, 1936, 14.

64. *Newsweek,* April 11, 1936, 14.

65. Charles Beard, in Lundberg, ix–x.

66. Ickes, 670–71.

67. EDC-WRH, September 11, 1936, outgoing box 1, EDCp.
68. H. L. Mencken, September 29, 1936, in *On Politics* (Baltimore: Johns Hopkins U.P., 1956), 324; Early, "For the press," September 19, 1936, OF 263, FDR.
69. WRH, NYA, September 27, 1936, in *Selections*, 129–33.
70. James Ryan, *Earl Browder: The Failure of American Communism* (Tuscaloosa: University of Alabama Press, 1997), 108–9; EDC-WRH, September 23, 25, October 9, 1936, outgoing box 1, EDCp.
71. EDC-WRH, October 9, 1936, outgoing box 1, EDCp; WRH, NYA, October 1, 1936.
72. EDC-WRH, October 9, 1936, outgoing box 1, EDCp.
73. Pelham Parkway Democratic Club-FDR, September 21, 1936, OF263, FDRp.
74. Ickes, 696.

33. The Fall

1. AH-JFN, November 26, 1936, box 39, JFNp.
2. NYT, November 3, 1936.
3. Harold Ickes, *The Secret Diary of Harold L. Ickes* (New York: Simon & Schuster, 1953), 704.
4. Ickes, 704; NYT, November 6, 1936; John Boettiger-Will Hays, September 2, 1941, box 20, Boettiger.
5. NYT, December 22, 1936. I thank Blanche Wiesen Cook for bringing this to my attention.
6. Ayer & Sons, *American Newspapers Annual and Directory*, 1933, 1936, 1937; Ian Gordon, *Comic Strips and Consumer Culture* (Washington: Smithsonian, 1998), 87–89.
7. Neylan interview, WAS.
8. WRH-JM, September 15, 1936, JMp; AH-JFN, November 26, 1936; JFN-AH, December 16, 1936, box 39, JFNp.
9. WRH-JM, November 13, 1936, JMp.
10. Doris Kearns Goodwin, *The Fitzgeralds and the Kennedys* (New York: Simon & Schuster, 1987), 573.
11. WRH-MH, December 9, 10, 1936, box 1, WRH, Jr.91.
12. Marion Davies, *The Times We Had* (Indianapolis: Bobbs-Merrill, 1975), 198–99.
13. AH-JFN, January 18, 1937; JFN-AH, Feb 20, 1937, box 39, JFNp.
14. AP-JPK, May 27, 1937, JPKp.
15. TJW-JPK, December 21, 1936; AP-JPK, January 13, 24, 1937, JPKp.
16. AP-JPK, January 2, 1937; "Properties of W. R. Hearst," in AP-JPK, April 3, 1937; AP, "Proposed Hearst Financing," in AP-JPK, January 2, 1937, JPKp.
17. *Time*, April 26, 1937, 49–51.
18. WRH-AP, April 1, 1937, JPKp; John Tebbel, *The Life and Good Times of William Randolph Hearst* (New York: E. P. Dutton, 1952), 317.
19. Hickey-JPK, February 5, February 17, 1937; AP-JPK, April 1, May 27, 1937, JPKp.
20. George Loorz-JM, February 24, March 9, 1937, cited in Taylor Coffman, *The Builders Behind the Castle* (San Luis Obispo: San Luis Obispo County Historical Society, 1990), 165, 168.
21. Warner Bros. Pictures, Inc., "Comparison of Negative Costs and Gross Income," William Schaefer Collection, WB.
22. Fred Lawrence Guiles, *Marion Davies* (New York: McGraw-Hill, 1972), 287; MD-GBS, March 18, [1937], box 2, WRH, Jr.91.

23. WRH-EDC, April 3, 27, 1937, incoming box 4, EDCp.

24. JW-TJW, April 16, 1937, carton 23, WRHp; JPK-MD, April 23, 1937, JPKp.

25. Ouida Rathbone, "Happy Birthday, W. R.," *Esquire*, December, 1972, 165–77.

26. WRH-JM, May 10, 21, 1937, JMp.

27. Davies, 200.

28. AH-JFN, May 25, 1937, box 39, JFNp.

29. WRH-JM, May 21, 1937; WRH-JM, May 25, 1937; JM-RA, May 25, 1937, JMp, Coffman, 172–3, 177, 179; Richard A. Addison Collection, HSSSHM.

30. Davies, 200; AP-JPK, June 16, 1937, JPKp.

31. JFN-AH, July 19, 1937, box 39, JFNp.

32. WRH-EMP, June 14, 1937, carton 23, WRHp.

33. RH, oh-DN, *Time*, July 5, 1937, 41–42; July 12, 1937, 26.

34. WRH-JPK, June 27, 1937, JPKp.

35. Coffman, 185.

36. AP-JPK, September 24, 1937, JPKp.

37. AP-JPK, Oct. 12, 1937, JPKp.

38. JW-Konta, transcript of telephone message, December 3, 4, 1937, carton 23, WRHp.

39. WRH-EC, December 16, 1937; EC-WRH, December 23, 1937, carton 23, WRHp.

40. Hagelberg-JW, June 18, 1937, box 2, WHR, JR.91.

41. Engle, oh-SS, 4–5; Coffman, 186.

42. NYT, October 11, 1937, 19; EDC-WRH, October 22, 1937, carton 22, WRHp.

43. "A Partial Inventory of Antiques," June 4, 1937, carton 22, WRHp; WRH-[Konta or Williams], March 8, 1938, BW.

44. "Classification of Inventory at International Studio Art Corporation," BW.

45. *Time*, March 29, 1938, 42.

46. NYT, April 29, 1938, 23; A. J. Liebling, "A Reporter at Large — Hearst with His Own Petard," *New Yorker*, November 19, 1938, 40.

47. *NYT*, November 15, 1938, 20.

48. Liebling, 41; NYT, December 19, 1939, 30.

49. Uncatalogued correspondence, 1938–39, collected by Konta, BW.

34. "All Very Sad, But We Cannot Kick Now"

1. Marion Davies, *The Times We Had* (Indianapolis: Bobbs-Merrill, 1975), 170, 195.

2. Swinnerton, oh-SS, 36.

3. WRH-A. Merritt, August 7, 1940, carton 30, WRHp.

4. Engle, oh-SS, 7–8.

5. Gates, oh-SS.

6. NYT, June 1, 1938, 38; Ferdinand Lundberg, "Mr. Hearst in Eclipse," *Nation*, November 12, 1938, 501; JFN-Board of Directors, February 28, 1939, carton 27, WRHp; JFN-AH, March 14, 1939, box 39, JFNp.

7. MHu-MacKay, Jr., February 24, 1939, carton 27, WRHp; MacKay-WRH, February 23, 1939, box 4, WRH, Jr.91.

8. JFN-WRH, April 4, 1945, box 66, JFNp; JFN-Board of Directors, March 10, 1939, carton 27, WRHp; WRH-WRH, Jr., March 11, 1939, box 16, BH.

9. JFN-AH, April 11, 1939, box 39, JFNp.

10. *Time*, March 13, 1939, 49–50, 56.

11. Aldous Huxley, *After Many a Summer Dies the Swan* (New York: Harper & Row, 1965), 13; Davies, 265.

12. Wahlberg, oh-SS, 18–19; RH, oh-DN.
13. JPK-WRH, August 3, 1938, box 4, WRH, Jr.91.
14. WRH-MacKay, February 14, 1939, box 4, WRH, Jr.91.
15. WRH-RB, October 4, 1940, carton 29; RB-WRH, October 6, 1942, carton 37, WRHp.
16. RH, oh-DN.
17. WRH-GH, October 25, 1940, box 1, WRH, Jr.91.
18. WRH-JH, January 19, 1939, box 1, WRH, Jr.91.
19. TJW-JH, June 13, 1939, box 4; WRH-JH, November 6, 1941, box 1, WRH, Jr.91.
20. WRH-Gortatowsky, June 13, 1942, in William Randolph Hearst, Jr., with Jack Casserly, *The Hearsts: Father and Son* (Niwot, Col.: Roberts Rinehart, 1991), 97; WRH-JH, June 23, 1942, box 1, WRH, Jr.91.
21. MHu-MacKay, September 13, 1940, carton 30, WRHp.
22. JFN-AH, May 21, 1941, box 39, JFNp; *Time*, November 3, 1941, 82.
23. RB-WRH, July 9, 1940, box 15, BH; MacKay-WRH, December 21, 1940, RB-MacKay, December 21, 23, 1940, Wm. Howard-RB, December 21, 1940, carton 30, WRHp; December 12, 1940, v. 699, 12, Monterey County Records, in author's possession, courtesy of John Horn, HSSSHM.
24. JFN-AH, January 13, 1941, box 39, JFNp.
25. WRH-Ettelson, January 2, 1940, carton 29a, WRHp.
26. WRH, December 30, 1937, in *Selections*, 282–83; Evelyn Seeley, "Hearst Fights the Spanish Republic," *New Republic*, September 30, 1936, 217; LAE, June 1, 1937; WRH-EDC, June 2, 1938, box 15, BH.
27. WRH-Winchell, February 6, 1938, incoming box 5, EDCp.
28. NYJA, March 16, 1938, 1.
29. WRH-CS, September 24, 1938; WRH-WRH, Jr. and EDC, September 25, 1938, BH.
30. WRH-EDC, October 20, 1938, BH.
31. Saul Friedländer, *Nazi Germany and the Jews*, vol. 1 (New York: Harper, 1997), 270, 277.
32. WRH, November 11, 1938, in *Selections*, 31.
33. LAE, November 12, 16, 1939.
34. WRH-W. A. Curley, July 17, 1938, box 12, BH; WRH-EDC, October 12, 1938, BH; WRH-EDC, December 21, 1938; draft of "A Homeland for a Great Jewish Nation," carton 26, WRHp; excerpts from radio address, May 28, 1939, in *Selections*, 36–39.
35. JW-Univalser; Woolard-JW, December 18, 1938, BH.
36. WRH-EDC, October 9, 1939, incoming box 5, EDCp.
37. WRH-EDC, July 1, 1940, carton 29, WRHp.
38. WRH-DLG, September 22, 1940; DLG-WRH, September 25, 1940, carton 28, WRHp.
39. NYT, December 29, 1940.
40. WRH-RB, December 29, 1940, carton 29, WRHp.
41. Neylan interview, WAS; WRH-MHu, December 5, 1941, carton 34, WRHp; Taylor Coffman, *Building for Hearst and Morgan* (Summerfield, Calif.: Coastal Heritage Press, 1999), 303–304.
42. WRH-RB, September 6, 1940, carton 29, WRHp.
43. MH-WRH, May 8, 1941, box 7, WRH, Jr.91.
44. MH-WRH, June 9, 1941, box 7, WRH, Jr.91.

45. MH-WRH, February 16, 1942, box 7, WRH, Jr.91.
46. Curley-WRH, March 4, 1940, outgoing box 2, EDCp.
47. WRH, ITN, September 8, October 2, 1941; see also, WRH, ITN, September 9, 10, 18, 19, 22, 23, 26, October 6, 1941.
48. WRH, ITN, March 11, 1940.
49. WRH, ITN, September 5, 1940.
50. WRH, ITN, October 31, 1940.
51. WRH, ITN, April 17, 1941.
52. Akira Iriye, *The Globalizing of America* (New York: Cambridge U.P., 1993), 189.
53. WRH, ITN, December 8, 1941.
54. *Time*, March 23, 1942, 40.
55. Davies, 214; Apperson, oh-SSp.
56. Dragon, oh-SS, 4; Davies, 220; Christian, oh-SS.
57. RH, oh-DN; Christian, oh-SS, 30.
58. Davies, 225–27.
59. WRH-JFN, September 26, 1942, box 66, JFNp.
60. 1943–44 Wyntoon guest list, carton 40, WRHp; RH, oh-DN.
61. KVW-EDC, January 1, 1944, box 7, KVWp.

35. *Citizen Kane*

1. Michael Denning, *Cultural Front* (New York: Verso, 1996), 275–381; Simon Callow, *Orson Welles* (New York: Penguin, 1995), 483–84.
2. Callow, 483–85.
3. Denning, 385.
4. Robert L. Carringer, *The Making of Citizen Kane* (Berkeley: University of California, 1996), 23; Callow, 493–94.
5. Douglas Churchill, "Orson Welles Scares Hollywood," NYT, January 19, 1941, section 9, 5.
6. Pauline Kael, *Citizen Kane Book* (New York: Limelight, 1984), 68.
7. Carringer, 21–23; Kael, 82,
8. "The Shooting Script," in Kael, 100, 114.
9. Orson Welles and Peter Bogdanovich, *This Is Orson Welles* (New York: HarperCollins, 1992), 49.
10. *Newsweek*, September 16, 1940, 12; Louella Parsons, *Tell It to Louella* (New York: Putnam's, 1961), 131.
11. Hedda Hopper, *From Under My Hat* (Garden City: Doubleday, 1952), 290.
12. Parsons, 131–32.
13. LP-JW, January 14, 1941, oversized box, WRHp.
14. NYT, January 19, 1941, section 9, 5; Callow, 532, citation rearranged; V, February 5, 1941, 18; Kael, 5–6.
15. RB-JW, January 2, 1941, carton 34, WRHp.
16. RB-JW, January 21, 1941, carton 34, WRHp.
17. JW-RB, telephone message, January 25, 1941, carton 34, WRHp.
18. RB-JW, January 28, 1941, carton 34, WRHp.
19. *Newsweek*, January 20, 1941, 62–63; NYT, January 19, 5; *Time*, January 27, 1941, 69.
20. V, January 10, 1941, 1; RB-JW, January 2, 1941, carton 34, WRHp.
21. V, January 22, 1941, 63; January 29, 1941, 2; February 5, 1941, 4, 18; Carringer, 111, 113, 115.

22. NR-LP, January 14, 1941, oversized box, WRHp; Kael, 6; V, February 5, 18.

23. V, February 19, 1941, 2, 18; April 16, 3; David Thomson, *Rosebud: The Story of Orson Welles* (New York: Vintage, 1997), 190–92; NYJA, April 21–May 6, 1941; Callow, 555–58.

24. Callow, 532–33; V, April 16, 1941, 62; April 23, 1941, 7; Welles and Bogdanovich, 85–86.

25. Thomson, 180–81, 188; V, April 2, 1941, 2; WRH-John Chapman, April 12, 1941, carton 32, WRHp.

26. Welles and Bogdanovich, 86; Michael Sage, "Hearst Over Hollywood," *New Republic,* February 24, 1941, 270; Carringer, 115.

27. Kael, 42–44.

28. V, May 7, 1941, 6.

29. Thomson, 182–84, 187.

30. Callow, 575.

31. Marion Davies, *The Times We Had* (Indianapolis: Bobbs-Merrill, 1975), 264–65.

32. Carringer, 117–21.

33. John Tebbel, *The Life and Good Times of William Randolph Hearst* (New York: Dutton, 1952), 287–88.

34. Welles and Bogdanovich, 49.

36. Old Age

1. Edmond D. Coblentz, ed., *William Randolph Hearst: A Portrait in His Own Words* (New York: Simon & Schuster, 1952), 285–86.

2. WRH, ITN, April 29, 1942.

3. Coblentz, 286–77.

4. WRH-Von Ettisch, July 26, 1947, carton 42, WRHp.

5. Marion Davies, *The Times We Had* (Indianapolis: Bobbs-Merrill, 1975), 214; WRH-EDC, May-September, 1941, BW.

6. Davies, 241.

7. NYJA, April 1, 1941, 6.

8. Arthur Holliday-Manuel Ávila Camacho, March 3, 1941; WRH-Ávila Camacho, July 12, 1942, Ávila Camacho, Presidentes.

9. William Randolph Hearst, Jr., with Jack Casserly, *The Hearsts: Father and Son* (Niwot, Col.: Roberts Rinehart, 1991), 168.

10. *Time,* May 10, 1943, 50.

11. JW-WRH, May 17, 1943; WRH-JW, May 20, 1943, WB.

12. WRH-Howey, March 8, 1944; JW-Howey, March 16, 1944, BW; WRH-Connolly, March 10, 1944, BW; WRH-C. S. Ryckman, March 28, 1944, carton 41, WRHp.

13. David Wyman, *The Abandonment of the Jews* (New York: Pantheon, 1984), 147–48.

14. W. L. Brennan-E. M. Gundy, May 7, 1943; WRH-Connolly, May 8, 1943, carton 39, WRHp.

15. WRH-EDC, January 10, 1944, carton 40, WRHp.

16. "Basic Training Manual, Tour 3," March 11, 1997 revision, 40–41, HSSSHM.

17. Davies, 252.

18. Moore, oh-SS, 10

19. WRH-RWA, November 28, 1945, BW.

20. Miller, oh-SS.

21. Photograph archives, HSSSHM.
22. Dragon, oh-SS, 18; communication with John Horn.
23. Davies, 244–45; John Boettiger-WRH, May 13, 1945, carton 41, WRHp; WC-KVW, May 16, 1945, box 8, KVWp.
24. WRH-George Hearst, Jr., April 18, 1944, box 1, WRH, Jr.91.
25. WRH-Phoebe Hearst, April 18, 1944, box 1, WRH, Jr.91.
26. WRH-John Hearst, Jr., June 24, 1944, box 1, WRH, Jr.91.
27. John Hearst, Jr., oh-DN.
28. John Hearst, Jr., "Life with Grandfather," *Reader's Digest*, May 1960, 154.
29. WRH, Jr., 189–90; John Hearst, Jr., oh-DN.
30. Fred Lawrence Guiles, *Marion Davies* (New York: McGraw-Hill, 1972), 329–30.
31. Guiles, 199, 241; JFN-AH, March 22, 1937, box 39, JFNp; WC-KVW, December 11, 1946, box 8, KVWp.
32. On will, which was sealed in 1975 for security reasons, after Patty Hearst kidnapping, see WRH, Jr., 254–56; Lindsay Chaney and Michael Cieply, *The Hearsts* (New York: Simon & Schuster, 1981), 65–69, 87–92, 275–79; NYT, August 14, 1951, 21, 25; August 28, 1951, 25.
33. Dragon, oh-SS.
34. May 1 entry, 1947 Datebook, record group V., Wahlberg Collection, HSSSHM; WRH, Jr., 191; Guiles, 329.
35. May 21, 22 entries, 1947 datebook, HSSSHM.
36. WRH-EDC, August 22, 1947, box 5, EDCp.
37. WRH-Van Ettisch, October 5, 1947; WRH-Walt Disney, October 9, 1947, carton 42, WRHp.
38. Jim Tuck, *McCarthyism and New York's Hearst Press* (Lanham: University Press of America, 1995), 7–14, 45–48; WRH, ITN, April 7, 1942, in *Selections*, 135–37; Murray Kempton, *Part of Our Time* (New York: Dell, 1967), 172–75.
39. WRH-editors, July 26, 1947, carton 42, WRHp.
40. WRH-Seymour Berkson, April 29, 1947; WRH-Ward Greene, October 20, 1948, carton 42, WRHp.
41. Davies, 173.
42. RB-KVW, April 4, 1947, box 5, KVWp.
43. WRH-Van Ettisch, October 11, 1947, carton 42, WRHp.
44. WRH-Van Ettisch, October 24, 1947, carton 42, WRHp.
45. KVW-RB, October 24, 1947, box 5, KVWp.
46. William J. Mann, *Wisecracker* (New York: Viking, 1998), 331; Rukeyser, oh-SS, 17–18; RB-KVW, March 8, 1948, box 5, KVWp.
47. WRH-RB, May 8, 1948, incoming box 5, EDCp.
48. RB-KVW, December 14, 1948, box 5, KVWp.
49. RB-WRH, Jr., July 6, 1949, carton 49, WRHp.
50. John Tebbel, *The Life and Good Times of William Randolph Hearst* (New York: Dutton, 1952), 370–72.
51. H. L. Mencken, "editorial," *American Mercury*, May 1927, 28–30.
52. A. J. Liebling, in *The Press* (New York: Pantheon, 1981), 487–501.
53. Mencken, 28–30.
54. WRH, Jr., 233.
55. Davies, 173, 258.
56. Rukeyser, oh-SS, 16.
57. WRH, Jr., 255.

58. Tuck, 32–33, 46–49, 79–80.
59. Van Ettisch-editors, April 23, 1950, box 23, KVWp.
60. Van Ettisch-editors, May 1, 1950, box 23, KVWp.
61. WRH, Jr., 233–34; Stanley interview, WAS.
62. Anita Loos, *Cast of Thousands* (New York: Grosset & Dunlap, 1977), 140; *Kiss Hollywood Good-by* (New York: Viking, 1974), 145.
63. Guiles, 333; St. Johns interview, WAS.
64. WRH-WRH, Jr., April 18, 1951; WRH-Douglas MacArthur, April 16, 1951, carton 32, WRHp.
65. WRH-WRH, Jr., July 7, 15, 1941, box 1, WRH, Jr.91.
66. Woolard interview, WAS.
67. Mrs. John Hearst, Jr., oh-DN.
68. Stanley interview, WAS; Davies, 252; *Life*, August 27, 1951.
69. WRH, Jr., 256.
70. NYT, October 31, 1951.
71. NYT, November 1, 1951; Guiles, 338–39.
72. *Life*, August 27, 1951.
73. NYT, August 18, 1951, 11.
74. "Song of the River," in Coblentz, 308–9.

Epilogue

1. William Randolph Hearst, Jr., with Jack Casserly, *The Hearsts* (Niwot, Col.: Roberts Rineheart, 1991), 5.
2. Fred Lawrence Guiles, *Marion Davies* (New York: McGraw-Hill, 1972), 349–73; NYT, September 23, 1961.
3. NYT, August 15, 1951, 21.

INDEX

David Nasaw is the author of *Going Out: The Rise and Fall of Public Amusements* and two previous books. His work on Hearst has appeared in *The New Yorker* and *Condé Nast Traveler*. For *The Chief* he was awarded the Bancroft Prize, the Ambassador Book Award, the J. Anthony Lukas Prize, and was a finalist for the National Book Critics Circle Award. Currently Distinguished Professor of History and director of the Center for the Humanities at the Graduate Center of the City University of New York, he lives in Manhattan.